The University of Law

14 Store Street
London
WC1E 7DE

International Humanitarian Law
Cases, Materials and Commentary

Drawing together key documents, case law, reports and other essential materials, *International Humanitarian Law* offers students, lecturers and practitioners an accessible and critically informed account of the theory, law and practice of international

humanit
Providin
cases an
to help r
jurispruc
book als
challeng

- Cyber
- Detent
- Direct
- Huma
- Terror

Suitable
*Internati
the subjε

Nicholas
also on
member

Alasdair
Colonel
operatioι
instructiι

Bloomsbury Library
T: 01483 216387
library-bloomsbury@law.ac.uk

Moorgate Library
T: 01483 216371
library-moorgate@law.ac.uk

International Humanitarian Law

Cases, Materials and Commentary

NICHOLAS TSAGOURIAS

University of Sheffield

LT COL (RETD) ALASDAIR MORRISON

Land Warfare Centre

CAMBRIDGE
UNIVERSITY PRESS

CAMBRIDGE
UNIVERSITY PRESS

University Printing House, Cambridge CB2 8BS, United Kingdom

One Liberty Plaza, 20th Floor, New York, NY 10006, USA

477 Williamstown Road, Port Melbourne, VIC 3207, Australia

314–321, 3rd Floor, Plot 3, Splendor Forum, Jasola District Centre, New Delhi – 110025, India

79 Anson Road, #06–04/06, Singapore 079906

Cambridge University Press is part of the University of Cambridge.

It furthers the University's mission by disseminating knowledge in the pursuit of education, learning, and research at the highest international levels of excellence.

www.cambridge.org
Information on this title: www.cambridge.org/9781107090590
DOI: 10.1017/9781316107010

© Nicholas Tsagourias and Alasdair Morrison 2018

First published 2018

Printed in the United Kingdom by Clays, St Ives plc, 2018

A catalogue record for this publication is available from the British Library.

ISBN 978-1-107-09059-0 Hardback

ISBN 978-1-107-46274-8 Paperback

Cambridge University Press has no responsibility for the persistence or accuracy of URLs for external or third-party internet websites referred to in this publication and does not guarantee that any content on such websites is, or will remain, accurate or appropriate.

Brief Contents

Contents

Preface and Acknowledgements

There has been increased academic and professional interest in international humanitarian law (IHL) generated by certain defining events such as '9/11', the so-called 'war on terror', the protracted armed conflicts in Afghanistan and Iraq, and the manifest upsurge in violent armed conflicts in the post–cold war era. According to the 2016 Conflict Barometer published by the Heidelberg Institute for International Conflict Research, there were thirty-eight highly violent conflicts in 2016 alone.[1] Contemporary armed conflicts are often very complex, involving diverse parties, and are fought on different levels: military, political, economic, social, individual, intra-state, inter-state or trans-state. They are also characterised by extensive human and physical destruction, to which the armed conflicts currently raging in the Middle East and Africa attest. The use of new-technology weapons such as cyber weapons or automated and autonomous weapons adds another dimension to modern armed conflicts.

Against this background, there is renewed emphasis on IHL as a tool for managing armed conflicts and for alleviating human suffering. One could even say that we are currently witnessing a process of legalisation and judicialisation of armed conflicts. More specifically, in the last three decades, international courts and tribunals have been established for the prosecution and punishment of individuals for violations of IHL while the case load of national or regional courts on matters concerning the law of armed conflict has increased. Courts have been called upon to adjudicate on issues concerning the legality of the use of lethal force, the treatment of detainees during an armed conflict, the obligations of occupying powers, the application of human rights law in situations of armed conflict or the classification of armed conflicts. It is not only judicial bodies, but also non-judicial bodies such as the Human Rights Council, Human Rights Committees, Commissions of Enquiry, NGOs and organs of international organisations that have dealt with armed conflicts and with matters pertaining to IHL. States have also been active in developing and clarifying IHL through the publication of Law of War manuals, through legislative and regulatory acts and, in general, through their practice prior to, during and after an armed conflict. To this, the role of the International Committee of the Red Cross (ICRC) in

---

[1] http://hiik.de/en/konfliktbarometer/pdf/ConflictBarometer_2016.pdf. According to other surveys there were forty-nine armed conflicts in 2016. See Peace Research Institute Ohio, *Conflict Trends 02/2017: Trends in Armed Conflict, 1946–2016*, (ISBN 978-82-7288-794-9 (online)) accessed at: www.prio.org/utility/Download File.ashx?id=1373&type=publicationfile.

promulgating new norms, in monitoring compliance and in disseminating IHL should be mentioned. As a result, the content, scope, application and enforcement of IHL has been debated, examined, adjudicated and contested in many different fora.

The growing and somewhat fragmented IHL jurisprudence, coupled with the challenges that new situations and developments such as new-technology weapons pose to IHL present a challenge to students, academics and legal practitioners as to how to navigate their way through the vast array of materials for the purposes of instruction, research, information and application.

The aim of this book is to present in a systematic manner this body of law and offer students and teachers as well as practitioners an accessible and instructive, but also critically informed account of the relevant law and practice. Having been compiled by a former army legal officer and an academic international lawyer, the book tries to maintain the right balance between doctrine, practice and critical analysis.

The book has certain distinct features. First, it offers a comprehensive exposition of IHL covering all its substantive areas. The topics covered include the classification of armed conflicts, the fundamental IHL principles, the application of human rights law, the distinction between combatants and civilians, the protection of civilians, the treatment of prisoners of war (POW), the rights and duties of occupying powers and of the civilian population in occupied territories, the regulation of the means and methods of warfare and in particular the regulation of targeting, the regulation of non-international armed conflicts (NIACs) and the rights and duties of armed groups, the rights and duties of neutrals, the available mechanisms for the enforcement of IHL and their effectiveness, the accountability of armed groups for violations of IHL, and the responsibility of commanders for violations of IHL committed by their subordinates.

Secondly, the book examines contemporary phenomena and the challenges they pose to IHL. They include new-technology weapons (for example, cyber, automatic or automated weapons), detention and transfer of detainees, detention by armed groups, the enforcement of IHL by armed groups, the accountability of armed groups for violations of IHL, reparations, transformative occupations, the participation of the United Nations or of other international organisations in armed conflicts, the civilianisation of modern armed conflict, the humanisation of IHL and the involvement of human rights institutions in the interpretation, application and enforcement of IHL. The examination of how these phenomena impact on IHL is weaved efficiently into the different chapters.

Thirdly, in addition to leading jurisprudence, the book includes contemporary reports, policy documents or directives on diverse IHL topics such as detention, weapons review or targeting, which explain current legal thinking and policy on such matters.

Fourthly, the navigation layout of each chapter fulfils the book's aim of providing knowledge and critical understanding of IHL in a systematic and accessible manner. The introduction maps out the area and highlights the important issues dealt with in the cases and materials and in the commentary. The resources highlight important legal provisions mentioned in the cases and materials. They are, however, indicative and their role is to assist the reader in locating pertinent legal provisions. The cases and materials section provides a wealth of primary and secondary source material on diverse IHL issues. The authors have endeavoured, where feasible, to include materials from a broader spectrum of national and international jurisprudence, thus offering the end user a panorama of relevant legal issues. Moreover, all the national and international cases are preceded by a short description of facts to assist the reader in understanding the background and the IHL issues raised by the case as well as how the particular court interpreted and applied the IHL rules. The cases and materials are also organised in thematic subsections which assist the reader to indentify the most critical issues and to navigate easily through the materials. Finally, the commentary offers analytical and critical insights on the jurisprudence and on the issues and themes dealt with in each chapter by also engaging with academic and policy arguments and opinions.

We believe that the juxtaposition of materials and commentary will help readers to gain a firm grasp of IHL, appreciate its practical implications and understand the challenges it faces. It is therefore hoped that the book should prove useful not only as a source of knowledge, information and critical analysis, but also as a source for further research.

The authors would like to thank the anonymous reviewers for their helpful and constructive comments and suggestions. Also, they want to thank Maj. B. Gray, Col. J. Johnston, Lt. Col. CP Larkin, and Lt. Col. E-P Grant for their comments on aspects of the book. They are also grateful to Adam Keenaghan for his excellent research assistance. Finally, both authors would like to thank Cambridge University Press and in particular Caitlin Lisle for their support and assistance.

Nicholas Tsagourias and Alasdair Morrison

November 2017

Abbreviations

ACtHPR	African Court on Human and Peoples' Rights
ALC	Armée de Libération du Congo
API	Additional Protocol I, Protocol Additional to the Geneva Conventions of 12 August 1949, and Relating to the Protection of Victims of International Armed Conflicts, 8 June 1977
APII	Additional Protocol II, Protocol Additional to the Geneva Conventions of 12 August 1949, and Relating to the Protection of Victims of Non-International Armed Conflicts, 8 June 1977
AU	African Union
BH	Bosnia-Herzegovina
CAR	Central African Republic
CCW	Convention on Prohibitions or Restrictions on the Use of Certain Conventional Weapons which May Be Deemed to Be Excessively Injurious or to Have Indiscriminate Effects (1980)
CEDAW	Committee on the Elimination of Discrimination Against Women
CPERS	Captured persons
DARIO	Draft Articles on the Responsibility of International Organizations
DPH	Direct Participation in Hostilities
DRC	Democratic Republic of the Congo
ECCC	Extraordinary Chambers in the Courts of Cambodia
ECHR	European Convention on Human Rights
ECtHR	European Court of Human Rights
EECC	Eritrea–Ethiopia Claims Commission
EoL	Exchange of Letters
EU	European Union
EWCA	England and Wales Court of Appeal
FARC	Fuerzas Armadas Revolucionarias de Colombia
FARDC	Forces Armées de la République Démocratique du Congo
FDLR	Forces Démocratiques pour la Liberation du Rwanda
FPLC	Forces Patriotiques pour la Libération du Congo
FRY	Federal Republic of Yugoslavia
GA	General Assembly

GCs	Geneva Conventions
GCI	Geneva Convention (I) for the Amelioration of the Condition of the Wounded and Sick in Armed Forces in the Field, of 12 August 1949
GCII	Geneva Convention (II) for the Amelioration of the Condition of the Wounded, Sick and Shipwrecked Members of Armed Forces at Sea, of 12 August 1949
GCIII	Geneva Convention (III) Relative to the Treatment of Prisoners of War, of 12 August 1949
GCIV	Geneva Convention (IV) Relative to the Protection of Civilian Persons in Time of War, of 12 August 1949
HC	Hague Convention
HL	House of Lords (United Kingdom)
HRC	Human Rights Committee
HRDDP	Human Rights Due Diligence Policy
HVO	Croatian Defence Council
IAC	International Armed Conflict
IACHR	Inter-American Commission on Human Rights
IACtHR	Inter-American Court of Human Rights
ICC	International Criminal Court
ICCPR	International Covenant on Civil and Political Rights
ICC St	Rome Statute of the International Criminal Court
ICESCR	International Covenant on Economic, Social and Cultural Rights
ICJ	International Court of Justice
I.C.J. Rep.	International Court of Justice Reports of Judgments, Advisory Opinions and Orders
ICRC	International Committee of the Red Cross and Red Crescent
ICTR	International Criminal Tribunal for Rwanda
ICTY	International Criminal Tribunal for the former Yugoslavia
IDF	Israel Defense Forces
IDP	Internally displaced person
IHL	International humanitarian law
IHRL	International human rights law
ILA	International Law Association
ILC	International Law Commission
ILM	International Legal Materials
ILR	International Law Reports
IMT	International Military Tribunal
Inter Am. CHR	Inter-American Commission on Human Rights
Inter-Am. Ct. H.R.	Inter-American Court of Human Rights
IO	International Organisation
ISAF	International Security Assistance Force
ISIS	Islamic State of Iraq and Syria
JNA	Yugoslav National Army

KFOR	Kosovo Force
KLA	Kosovo Liberation Army
LOAC	Law of armed conflict
LRTWC	Law Reports of Trials of War Criminals
MIF	Maritime Interception Force
MLC	Mouvement de Libération du Congo
MONUSCO	United Nations Organisation Stabilization Mission in the Democratic Republic of Congo
MoU	Memorandum of understanding
NATO	North Atlantic Treaty Organization
NDS	National Directorate of Security
NIAC	Non-International Armed Conflict
OAS	Organization of American States
OHCHR	Office of the High Commissioner for Human Rights
OSCE	Organization for Security and Cooperation in Europe
PCIJ	Permanent Court of International Justice
PKK	Kurdistan Workers' Party
PMSC	Private military and security company
POW	Prisoner of war
PSO	Peace support operations
RDF	Rwanda Defence Force
RUF	Revolutionary United Front
SC	Security Council
SEA	Sexual exploitation and abuse
SFOR	Stabilisation Force in Bosnia and Herzegovina
SKA	Sarajevo Romanija Corps
SOFA	Status of Forces Agreement
SRK	Serbian Republic of Krajina
SVK	Serbian Army of Krajina
SWAPO	South West African People's Organisation
TCC	Troop-contributing countries
UAV	Unmanned aerial vehicle
UKSC	UK Supreme Court
UN	United Nations
UNCC	United Nations Compensation Commission
UNHCR	United Nations High Commissioner for Refugees
UNMIK	UN Interim Administration for Kosovo
UNPROFOR	United Nations Protection Force
UNSC	United Nations Security Council
UNSCR	United Nations Security Council Resolution
UPDF	Uganda People's Defence Force

Table of Cases

Arbitral Tribunals and Claims Commissions

European Court of Human Rights

Inter-American Commission on Human Rights

Inter-American Court of Human Rights

International Criminal Tribunal for the Former Yugoslavia

Table of Other Documents

Africa

African Union, *Guidelines on Detention and DDR* (2014)

General Comment No. 3 on the African Charter on Human and Peoples' Rights: The Right to Life (Article 4) (Adopted during the 57th Ordinary Session of the African Commission on Human and Peoples' Rights, held from 4 to 18 November 2015, Banjul, The Gambia)

Protocol Relating to the Establishment of the Peace and Security Council of the African Union (adopted 9 July 2002, entered into force 26 December 2003)

Resolution 185 on the Safety of Journalists and Media Practitioners in Africa (African Commission on Human and Peoples' Rights, Banjul, The Gambia, 12 May 2011)

Standing Orders of the Central African Multinational Force (FOMAC) (2002)

Amnesty International

Iraq: Looting, Lawlessness and Humanitarian Consequences (11 April 2003, MDE14/085/2003)

Australia

Law of Armed Conflict (Australian Defence Force, Executive Series, Australian Defence Doctrine Publication 06.4, 11 May 2006)

Canada

Arrangement for the transfer of detainees between the Government of Canada and the Government of the Islamic Republic of Afghanistan (3 May 2007)

Law of Armed Conflict at the Operational and Tactical Levels (Office of the Judge Advocate General, Joint Doctrine Manual, 13 August 2001)

Denmark

Copenhagen Process on the Handling of Detainees in International Military Operations (19 October 2012)

El Salvador

Human Rights Agreement between El Salvador and the Frente Farabundo Marti para la Liberación Nacional (FMLN) (26 July 1990)

European Union

Agreement between the European Union and the Central African Republic Concerning Detailed Arrangements for the Transfer to the Central African Republic of Persons Detained by the European Union Military Operation (EUFOR RCA) in the Course of Carrying out its Mandate, and Concerning the Guarantees Applicable to Such Persons

Updated European Union Guidelines on Promoting Compliance with International Humanitarian Law (IHL) (Official Journal of the European Union, 2009/C303/06, 15.12.2009)

Germany

Law of Armed Conflict – Manual – Joint Service Regulation (ZDv) 15/2 (Federal Ministry of Defence, May 2013)

HPRC

Manual on International Law Applicable to Air and Missile Warfare (Bern, 15 May 2009)

Human Rights Watch

Up in Flames: Humanitarian Law Violations and Civilian Victims in the Conflict Over South Ossetia (2009)

ICTY

Final Report to the Prosecutor by the Committee Established to Review the NATO Bombing Campaign Against the Federal Republic of Yugoslavia (1999)

Independent International Fact-Finding Mission on the Conflict in Georgia

Report of the Independent International Fact-Finding Mission on the Conflict in Georgia, Volume II (September 2009)

India

Deed of Commitment under Geneva Call for the Protection of Children from the Effects of Armed Conflict (2 March 2016, Appel de Genève/Geneva Call)

Inter-American Commission on Human Rights

Report on Terrorism and Human Rights (22 October 2002, OEA/Ser.L/V/II.116 Doc.5 rev. 1 corr.)

Third Report on the Human Rights Situation in Colombia (26 February 1999, OEA/Ser.L/V/II.102, Doc. 9 rev. 1)

International Commission of Jurists

Legal Commentary on Elements of the Basic Principles and Guidelines Pertaining to Detention in Armed Conflict (September 2015)

Siracusa Principles on the Limitation and Derogation Provisions in the International Covenant on Civil and Political Rights, American Association for the International Commission of Jurists (1984)

International Criminal Court

Situation in Mali Article 53(1) Report (The Office of the Prosecutor, 16 January 2013)

International Humanitarian Fact-Finding Commission

What is the International Humanitarian Fact Finding Commission and What is its Role in Armed Conflict Situations?

International Institute of Humanitarian Law

San Remo Manual on International Law Applicable to Armed Conflicts at Sea (12 June 1994)

The Manual on the Law of Non-International Armed Conflict with Commentary (San Remo, 2006)

International Law Association

Final Report on the Meaning of Armed Conflict in International Law (Use of Force Committee, The Hague, 2010)

Reparation for Victims of Armed Conflict, Declaration of International Law Principles on Reparation for Victims of Armed Conflict (Substantive Issues) (Resolution No. 2/2010, 74th Conference, The Hague, 2010)

International Law Commission

Statement by Ms Patricia O'Brien, Under-Secretary-General for Legal Affairs, The Legal Counsel (Geneva, 23 May 2013)

Iraq

CPA Order No 39 (As Amended) (20 December 2003)

Islamic Emirate of Afghanistan

The Layha [Code of Conduct] For Mujahideen: An Analysis of the Code of Conduct for the Taliban Fighters Under Islamic Law 93 (881) IRRC (March 2011) 81

Israel

The Operation in Gaza 27 December 2008–18 January 2009: Factual and Legal Aspects (July 2009)

Kurdistan Workers Party

Statement to the United Nations (Geneva, 24 January 1995)

Libya

Codes of Conduct National Transitional Council 2011, 93 (882) IRRC (June 2011) 483

Myanmar

Deed of Commitment under Geneva Call for the Protection of Children from the Effects of Armed Conflict (17 November 2014, Appel de Genève/Geneva Call)

Philippines

Agreement on the Civilian Protection Component of the International Monitoring Team Bangerter Internal Control (IMT) [Government of the Republic of the Philippines and Moro Islamic Liberation Front] (27 October 2009)
Comprehensive Agreement on Respect for Human Rights and International Humanitarian Law between the Government of the Republic of the Philippines and the National Democratic Front of the Philippines (16 March 1998)

Polisario Front

Unilateral Declaration of 21 June 2015 (Appel de Genève/Geneva Call)

Sudan

Agreement between the Government of the Republic of Sudan and the Sudan People's Liberation Movement to Protect Non-Combatant Civilians and Civilian Facilities from Military Attack (31 March 2002)

Agreement Between the Government of Sudan and the United Nations Concerning the Status of the United Nations Mission in Sudan (2005)

Syria

Code of Conduct of the Free Syrian Army (2014)

Uganda

Juba Peace Agreement on Accountability and Reconciliation (29 June 2007)

United Kingdom

Government Strategy on the Protection of Civilians in Armed Conflict (Foreign and Commonwealth Office, 7 December 2011)

Joint Doctrine Publication 1-10 Captured Persons (British Ministry of Defence, January 2015, Third Edition)

Joint Service Manual of the Law of Armed Conflict (British Ministry of Defence, Joint Service Publication 383, 2004 Edition)

Letter from the Clerk of the Committee to Philip Spoerri, Legal Adviser, International Committee of the Red Cross and Reply (Select Committee on International Development, Appendices to the Minutes of Evidence, 28 November 2002)

Memorandum of Understanding between the Government of the United Kingdom of Great Britain and Northern Ireland and the Government of the Islamic Republic of Afghanistan Concerning Transfer by the United Kingdom Armed Forces to Afghan Authorities of Persons Detained in Afghanistan (Select Committee on Foreign Affairs, 23 April 2005)

UK Weapon Reviews (Ministry of Defence, Development, Concepts and Doctrine Centre, 2016)

United States

Air Force Instruction 51-402, Legal Reviews of Weapons and Cyber Capabilities (27 July 2011)

Directive 3000.09, Autonomy in Weapons Systems (US Department of Defense, 21 November 2012)

Final Report to Congress: Conduct of the Persian Gulf War – The Role of the Law of War (US Department of Defense, (1992) 31 ILM 615)

General Orders No. 100: Instructions for the Government of Armies of the United States in the Field (Lieber Code) (adopted 24 April 1863)

Joint Publication 3-60, Joint Targeting (31 January 2013)

Law of War Manual (Office of General Counsel, United States Department of Defense, June 2015, Updated 2016)

Memorandum Opinion on the Geographic Scope of the International Covenant on Civil and Political Rights (Office of the Legal Adviser, United States Department of State, Washington, D.C, 19 October 2010)

Military Commissions Act of 2009, 10 U.S.C. § 948a

Report on the Legal and Policy Frameworks Guiding the United States' Use of Military Force and Related National Security Operations (The White House, December 2016)

Report on Process for Determining Targets of Lethal or Capture Operations (U) An explanation of the legal and policy considerations and approval processes used in determining whether an individual or group of individuals could be the target of a lethal or capture operation conducted by the Armed Forces of the United States outside the United States and outside of Afghanistan (U), Submitted in response to the reporting requirement contained in section 1043 of the National Defense Authorization Act for Fiscal Year 2014 (Public Law 113-66)

UN Documents

General Assembly

Basic Principles and Guidelines on the Right to a Remedy and Reparation for Victims of Gross Violations of International Human Rights Law and Serious Violations of International Humanitarian Law (16 December 2005, UN Doc. A/RES/60/147)

Comprehensive Review of the Whole Question of Peacekeeping Operations in All Their Aspects, Model Status-of-Forces Agreement for Peacekeeping Operations, Report of the Secretary-General (9 October 1990, UN Doc. A/45/594)

Comprehensive Strategy to Eliminate Future Sexual Exploitation and Abuse in United Nations Peacekeeping Operations, Report of the Secretary-General's Special Advisor, Prince Zeid Ra'ad Zeid al-Hussain (24 March 2005, 59th Session, UN Doc. A/59/710)

Financing of the United Nations Protection Force, the United Nations Confidence Restoration Operation in Croatia, the United Nations Preventive Deployment Force and the United Nations Peace Forces headquarters; Administrative and Budgetary Aspects of the Financing of the United Nations Peacekeeping Operations: Financing of the United Nations Peacekeeping Operations, Report of the Secretary-General, (20 September 1996, UN Doc. A/51/389)

Impact of Armed Conflict on Children, Report of the Expert of the Secretary-General, Ms Graça Machel, Submitted Pursuant to General Assembly Resolution 48/157 (26 August 1996, 51st Session, UN Doc. A/51/306)

Report of the Group of Legal Experts on Ensuring the Accountability of United Nations Staff and Experts on Mission with Respect to Criminal Acts Committed in Peacekeeping Operations (16 August 2006, UN Doc. A/60/980, Annex III)

Third-Party Liability: Temporal and Financial Limitations (17 July 1998, UN Doc. A/RES/52/247)

High Commissioner for Refugees

'Under What Circumstances Can a Person Who Has Taken an Active Part in the Hostilities of an International or a Non-International Armed Conflict Become an Asylum Seeker?', Stéphane Jaquemet (June 2004, PPLA/2004/01)

Human Rights Commission

Report on the Situation of Human Rights in Occupied Kuwait, prepared by Mr. Walter Kälin, Special Rapporteur of the United Nations Human Rights Commission (16 January 1992, E/CN/1992/26)

Human Rights Committee

Consideration of Reports submitted by States Parties under Article 40 of the Covenant, Concluding Observations of the Human Rights Committee (12 August 2004, 81st Session, UN Doc. CCPR/CO/81/BEL)

General Comment 29: Article 4: Derogation During a State of Emergency (31 August 2001, 72nd Session, UN Doc. CCPR/C/21/Rev.1/Add.11)

General Comment No. 31 on the Nature of the General Legal Obligation Imposed on States Parties to the Covenant (26 May 2004, 18th Session, UN Doc. CCPR/C/21/Rev.1/ Add.13)

General Comment No. 32, Article 14: Right to Equality Before Courts and Tribunals and to a Fair Trial (23 August 2007, 19th Session, UN Doc. CCPR/C/GC/32)

General Comment No. 35, Article 9: Liberty and Security of Person (16 December 2014, 112th Session, UN Doc. CCPR/C/GC/35)

Draft General Comment No. 36, Article 6: Right to Life (2 September 2015, 115th Session, UN Doc. CCPR/C/GC/R.36/Rev.2)

Statement of U.S. State Department Legal Adviser, Conrad Harper, Summary of the 1405th Meeting, Held at Headquarters, NY on 31 March 1995 (24 April 1995, 53rd Session, UN Doc. CCPR/C/SR 1405)

Human Rights Council

Human Rights in Palestine and Other Occupied Arab Territories, Report of the United Nations Fact-Finding Mission on the Gaza Conflict ('The Goldstone Report') (25 September 2009, 12th Session, UN Doc. A/HRC/12/48)

Investigation by the Office of the United Nations High Commissioner for Human Rights on Libya: Detailed Findings (15 February 2016, 31st Session, UN Doc. A/HRC/31/ CRP.3)

Report of the International Commission of Inquiry to Investigate all Alleged Violations of International Human Rights Law in the Libyan Arab Jamahiriya (1 June 2011, 17th Session, UN Doc. A/HRC/17/44)

Report of the International Commission of Inquiry on Libya (8 March 2012, 19th Session, UN Doc. A/HRC/19/68)

Human Rights Office of the High Commissioner

Secretariat

Security Council

Other

Report of the Secretary-General's Panel of Experts on Accountability in Sri Lanka (31 March 2011)

Report of the Secretary-General's Panel of Inquiry on the 31 May 2010 Flotilla Incident (September 2011)

Schmitt, M.N. (ed.), *Tallinn Manual on the International Law Applicable to Cyber Warfare* (CUP, 2013)

The Status of Forces Agreement Between the United Nations and the Government of the Republic of South Sudan Concerning the United Nations Mission in South Sudan ('SOFA') (2011)

Conventions

African Charter on Human and Peoples' Rights (adopted 27 June 1981, entered into force 21 October 1986) 1520 UNTS 363

Agreement for the Prosecution and Punishment of the Major War Criminals of the European Axis, and Charter of the International Military Tribunal (adopted 8 August 1945, entered into force 8 August 1945) 82 UNTS 280

American Convention on Human Rights (adopted 22 November 1969, entered into force 18 July 1978) OAS Treaty Series No. 36

American Declaration of the Rights and Duties of Man (adopted 1948)

Charter of the United Nations (adopted 26 June 1945, entered into force 24 October 1945) 892 UNTS 119

Convention on the Privileges and Immunities of the United Nations (adopted 13 February 1946, entered into force 17 September 1946) 1 UNTS 15

Convention on the Safety of United Nations and Associated Personnel (adopted 9 December 1994, entered into force 15 January 1999) 2051 UNTS 363

Hague Convention (II) with Respect to the Laws and Customs of War on Land and its annex: Regulations Concerning the Laws and Customs of War on Land (adopted 29 July 1899, entered into force 4 September 1900)

Hague Convention (IV) respecting the Laws and Customs of War on Land and its annex: Regulations Concerning the Laws and Customs of War on Land (adopted 18 October 1907, entered into force 26 January 1910)

Hague Convention (V) respecting the Rights and Duties of Neutral Powers and Persons in Case of War on Land (adopted 18 October 1907, entered into force 26 January 1910)

Hague Convention (XIII) concerning the Rights and Duties of Neutral Powers in Naval War (adopted 18 October 1907, entered into force 26 January 1910)

Declaration Renouncing the Use, in Time of War, of Explosive Projectiles Under 400 Grammes Weight (St Petersburg Declaration) (adopted on 29 November 1868, entered into force 11 December 1868)

Declaration Respecting Maritime Law ('Paris Declaration') (16 April 1856, entered into force 16 April 1856) 46 BFSP (1855–1856) 26

European Convention for the Protection of Human Rights and Fundamental Freedoms (ECHR) (adopted 4 November 1950, entered into force 3 September 1953) (as amended: 1 June 2010) ETS No. 5 (Protocol 14: ETS No. 194)

1

Definition and Classification of Armed Conflicts

INTRODUCTION

International humanitarian law (IHL) is the body of rules that applies to armed conflicts.[1] An armed conflict is triggered when there is recourse to armed force. When the opposing parties are States, the armed conflict is international (IAC) whereas when the opposing parties are States and organised armed groups or only armed groups, the armed conflict is non-international (NIAC).[2] The classification of armed conflicts as either IACs or NIACs is critical for legal, political and operational purposes because of the different rules that apply to them. The existence of an IAC or a NIAC is a question of fact; it is not determined by the views of the parties nor is it determined by the legality or morality of the initial use of force.[3] That said, the required degree of violence, the degree of organisation of the parties, and the geographic and temporal scope of an armed conflict are not easily determined, which complicates the process of classification of armed conflicts and of determining the applicable law. Furthermore, the multiplicity of actors (States, international organisations, individuals and groups) participating in armed conflicts, the diverse aims they pursue and the use of new technologies pose serious challenges to the definition and categorisation of armed conflicts as, for example, in cases of external intervention by States, the use of proxies, terrorism or the use of cyber weapons. International and national jurisprudence has grappled with these issues but, as the materials show, their conclusions have not always been consistent.

Resources: Common Articles 2 and 3, Geneva Conventions (GCs); Article 1, Additional Protocol I (API); Article 1, Additional Protocol II (APII)

---

[1]   The term 'armed conflict' is used in this context as a generic term to describe a situation of armed violence.
[2]   Common Articles 2 and 3, GCs and Art. 1, API and APII. For NIACs, see Chapter 10.
[3]   The distinction between *jus ad bellum* and *jus in bello* is well established and underpins the IHL principle of equality between belligerents.

1.1 DEFINITION OF ARMED CONFLICT

1.1.1 ICTY, *Prosecutor* v. *Tadić*, (Decision on the Defence Motion for Interlocutory Appeal on Jurisdiction), Case No. IT-94-1-A, Appeals Chamber (2 October 1995)

Note: *The ICTY considered an indictment of Dusko Tadić for crimes against humanity and violations of the laws or customs of war following his involvement in the conflict in Bosnia-Herzegovina between 23 May 1992 and 3 December 1992. On the issue of the definition of 'armed conflict', the Tribunal said:*

70. . . . an armed conflict exists whenever there is a resort to armed force between States or protracted armed violence between governmental authorities and organized armed groups or between such groups within a State.

1.1.2 ICTR, *The Prosecutor* v. *Akayesu*, (Judgment), Case No. ICTR-96-4-T, Trial Chamber I (2 September 1998)

Note: *Following the deaths of Presidents Juvénal Habyarimana of Rwanda and Cyprien Ntaryamira of Burundi, widespread violence erupted in Kigali and other parts of Rwanda. Jean Paul*

Akayesu was indicted for genocide, crimes against humanity and war crimes. On the issue of whether an armed conflict existed at the time, the Tribunal said as follows:

603. It should be stressed that the ascertainment of the intensity of a non-international conflict does not depend on the subjective judgment of the parties to the conflict. . . . If the application of international humanitarian law depended solely on the discretionary judgment of the parties to the conflict, in most cases there would be a tendency for the conflict to be minimized by the parties thereto.

1.1.3 ICTR, *The Prosecutor* v. *Rutaganda*, (Judgment and Sentence), Case No. ICTR-96-3-T, Trial Chamber I (6 December 1999)

Note: *Georges Rutaganda was indicted for genocide, crimes against humanity and violations of Common Article 3 GCs for his involvement in the widespread killings of Tutsis in the prefectures of Kigali and Gitarama territory of Rwanda between 1 January 1994 and 31 December 1994. On the issue of the definition of armed conflict, the Tribunal confirmed:*

93. . . . the definition of an armed conflict *per se* is termed in the abstract, and whether or not a situation can be described as an 'armed conflict', meeting the criteria of common Article 3, is to be decided upon on a case-by-case basis.

1.1.4 ICTR, *The Prosecutor* v. *Alfred Musema*, (Judgment and Sentence), Case No. ICTR-96-13-A, Trial Chamber I (27 January 2000)

Note: *Alfred Musema in concert with others brought armed individuals to the area of Bisesero and directed them to attack the Tutsis seeking refuge there. In addition, Alfred Musema personally attacked and killed Tutsis seeking refuge in Bisesero. In determining the existence of an armed conflict, the Trial Chamber reinforced the approach of the Tribunal in the earlier cases of Akayesu and Rutaganda in the following terms:*

248. The expression "armed conflicts" introduces a material criterion: the existence of open hostilities between armed forces which are organized to a greater or lesser degree. Internal disturbances and tensions, characterized by isolated or sporadic acts of violence, do not therefore constitute armed conflicts in a legal sense, even if the government is forced to resort to police forces or even armed units for the purpose of restoring law and order.

1.1.5 UK, British Ministry of Defence, *The Joint Service Manual of the Law of Armed Conflict* (Joint Service Publication 383, 2004 Edition)

3.3. Neither the Geneva Conventions nor Additional Protocol I contain any definition of the expression 'armed conflict' but the following guidance has been given:

a. 'any difference arising between States and leading to the intervention of members of the armed forces is an armed conflict';

b. 'an armed conflict exists whenever there is a resort to armed force between States or protracted armed violence between governmental authorities and organised armed groups within a State'.

3.3.1. These definitions do not deal with the threshold for an armed conflict. Whether any particular intervention crosses the threshold so as to become an armed conflict will depend on all the surrounding circumstances. For example, the replacing of border police with soldiers or an accidental border incursion by members of the armed forces would not, in itself, amount to an armed conflict, nor would the accidental bombing of another country. At the extreme, a full-scale invasion would amount to an armed conflict. ...

3.12. One of the most important characteristics of the law of armed conflict is its universal application. It applies with equal force to all parties engaged in an armed conflict, whether or not any party is considered to be 'an aggressor' or 'a victim of aggression'.

1.1.6 Australia, Australian Defence Force, *Law of Armed Conflict,* (Executive Series, Australian Defence Doctrine Publication 06.4,11 May 2006)

3.5. Whether any particular factual situation meets the threshold so as to become an armed conflict will depend on all circumstances surrounding a particular event.

1.1.7 ICTY, *Prosecutor* v. *Boškoski and Tarčulovski,* (Judgment), Case No. IT-04-82-T, Trial Chamber II (10 July 2008)

Note: *The case of Boškoski and Tarčulovski concerns crimes committed between 12 and 15 August 2001 against the ethnic Albanians from Ljuboten village near Skopje in the former Yugoslav Republic of Macedonia. Both Defendants challenged the jurisdiction of the Tribunal on the basis there was no armed conflict at the relevant time. The Tribunal held:*

174. . . . the question of whether there was an armed conflict at the relevant time is a factual determination to be made by the Trial Chamber upon hearing and reviewing the evidence admitted at trial.

1.1.8 ILA, Use of Force Committee, *Final Report on the Meaning of Armed Conflict in International Law,* (The Hague, 2010), p. 28

The discussion above supports the position that armed conflict is to be distinguished from "incidents"; "border clashes"; "internal disturbances and tensions such as riots, isolated and sporadic acts of violence"; "banditry, unorganised and short lived insurrections or terrorist activities" and "civil unrest, [and] single acts of terrorism". The distinction between these situations and armed conflict is achieved by reliance on the criteria of organisation and intensity.

1.1.9 US, Department of Defense, *Law of War Manual*, Office of General Counsel (June 2015, Updated 2016)

3.3.1 <u>International Armed Conflict and Non-International Armed Conflict</u>. The law of war treats situations of "war," "hostilities," or "armed conflict" differently based on the legal status of parties to the conflict. If two or more States oppose one another, then this type of armed conflict is known as an "international armed conflict" because it takes place between States. However, a state of war can exist when States are not on opposite sides of the conflict.

These other types of conflict are described as "not of an international character" or "non-international armed conflict." For example, two non-State armed groups warring against one another or States warring against non-State armed groups may be described as "non-international armed conflict," even if international borders are crossed in the fighting. . . .

3.4.1 <u>Intent-Based Test for Applying *Jus in Bello* Rules</u>. *Jus in bello* rules apply when a party intends to conduct hostilities. . . .

3.4.1.2 *<u>Non-State Armed Groups With the Intention of Conducting Hostilities</u>*. A non-State armed group, such as a rebel group, might also intend to conduct hostilities. . . .

3.5.1 *<u>General Distinction Between Jus in Bello and Jus ad Bellum</u>*. As a general matter, jus in bello and jus ad bellum address different legal issues and should not be conflated . . .

3.5.2.1 *<u>Compliance With Jus in Bello Is Required Regardless of Compliance With Jus ad Bellum</u>*.

1.2 DEFINITION OF INTERNATIONAL AND NON-INTERNATIONAL ARMED CONFLICT

1.2.1 Definition of International Armed Conflict

1.2.1.1 **ICC**, *The Prosecutor* v. *Thomas Lubanga Dyilo*, (Decision on the Confirmation of Charges), Case No. ICC-01/04-01/06 (29 January 2007)

Note: *Thomas Lubanga was charged with war crimes arising out of his involvement in the conflict in the Congo between September 2002 and 2 June 2003, when he enlisted and conscripted children under the age of fifteen into the Forces Patriotiques pour la Libération du Congo (FPLC) to actively participate in hostilities in the Congo. Defining IAC, the ICC said:*

209. The Chamber considers an armed conflict to be international in character if it takes place between two or more States; this extends to the partial or total occupation of the territory of another State, whether or not the said occupation meets with armed resistance. In addition, an internal armed conflict that breaks out on the territory of a State may become international – or, depending upon the circumstances, be international in character alongside an internal armed conflict – if (i) another State intervenes in that conflict through its troops (direct intervention), or if (ii) some of the participants in the internal armed conflict act on behalf of that other State (indirect intervention).

1.2.1.2 **Cambodia**, *Kaing Guek Eav alias Duch*, (Judgment), Case File/Dossier No. 001/18-07-2007/ECCC/TC, Extraordinary Chambers in the Courts of Cambodia (26 July 2010)

Note: *Case 001 was the first case before the Extraordinary Chambers in the Courts of Cambodia. The Defendant, Kaing Guek Eav alias Duch, was the former Chairman of the Khmer Rouge S-21 Security Center in Phnom Penh. He was indicted for crimes against humanity and war crimes. In relation to the clashes between Cambodia and Vietnam in 1975, it was held:*

423. The Chamber finds that armed hostilities existed between Cambodia and Vietnam from 17 April 1975 through 6 January 1979. Continuous clashes, whether border skirmishes or more serious incursions into both Cambodian and Vietnamese territory, continued throughout this period, despite DK and Vietnam's desire to keep them covert at the outset. The Chamber concludes that an international armed conflict accordingly existed at all times.

1.2.1.3 **Germany**, Federal Ministry of Defence, *Law of Armed Conflict – Manual – Joint Service Regulation (ZDv) 15/2* (May 2013)

203. An international armed conflict triggering the applicability of LOAC exists if one State Party to a conflict uses armed force against another State. It is irrelevant, however, whether the Parties to the conflict consider themselves to be at war with each other, and how they denote this conflict.

1.2.2 Direct State Intervention

1.2.2.1 **ICTY**, *Prosecutor* v. *Blaškić*, (Judgment), Case No. IT-95-14-T, Trial Chamber (3 March 2000)

Note: *Tihomir Blaškić was indicted for grave breaches of the GCs, violations of the laws and customs of war and crimes against humanity committed by the Croatian Defence Council (HVO) between May 1992 and January 1994 against Bosnian Muslims. Blaškić was commander of the HVO. The Tribunal concluded as follows as to Croatia's involvement in Bosnia-Herzegovina (BH):*

94. . . . Based on Croatia's direct intervention in BH, the Trial Chamber finds ample proof to characterise the conflict as international.

1.2.2.2 **ICTY**, *Prosecutor* v. *Kordić and Čerkez*, (Judgment), Case No. IT-95-14/2-T, Trial Chamber (26 February 2001)

Note: *This case concerned attacks on Vitez and the Muslim villages of Lašva Valley in April 1993. The Tribunal found the attacks were the product of a well-organised and planned attack by the HVO. The Tribunal concluded:*

109. . . . the Chamber finds that the conflict between the Bosnian Croats and the Bosnian Muslims in Bosnia and Herzegovina was internationalised by the intervention of Croatia in that conflict through its troops.

1.2.2.3 ICC, *The Prosecutor* v. *Mbarushimana*, (Decision on the Confirmation of Charges), Case No. ICC-01/04-01/10-465-Red, Pre-Trial Chamber I (16 December 2011)

Note: *Callixte Mbarushimana was a member of the Comité Directeur of the Forces Démocratiques pour la Liberation du Rwanda (FDLR). The ICC concluded as follows in relation to the intervention of Rwandan forces in DRC (Democratic Republic of the Congo) territory:*

101. The Chamber finds substantial grounds to believe that the presence and involvement of Rwandan troops in DRC territory during Umoja Wetu was aimed at assisting and supporting the FARDC in its efforts aimed at neutralising the FDLR. It was a joint military operation, whereby the presence of the Rwandan forces was, at all times, with the consent of the authorities of the DRC. The participation of Rwanda in operation Umoja Wetu cannot therefore be characterised as arising from a "difference arising between two states" since the two governmental forces (FARDC and Rwanda Defence Force (RDF)) fought side by side against a common enemy, the FDLR.

102. Accordingly, the Chamber finds that the armed conflict waged in the Kivus during operation Umoja Wetu does not satisfy the conditions that would establish the existence of an international armed conflict within the meaning of international humanitarian law.

1.2.3 State Control Over an Armed Group

1.2.3.1 ICJ, *Case Concerning Military and Paramilitary Activities in and Against Nicaragua (Nicaragua* v. *United States of America)* (Merits, Judgment) [1986] I.C.J. Rep. 14

Note: *The case was brought by Nicaragua, which accused the United States of planning and undertaking armed activities against Nicaragua by using paramilitaries, the contras, with the intention of overthrowing the new Sandinista government. Nicaragua alleged the United States was 'in control' of the contras and that consequently it was responsible for violations of international law. In assessing whether the acts of the contras could be attributed to the United States and thus whether it could be held responsible for violations of IHL, the ICJ said:*

115 The Court has taken the view . . . that United States participation, even if preponderant or decisive, in the financing, organizing, training, supplying and equipping of the contras, the selection of its military or paramilitary targets, and the planning of the whole of its operation, is still insufficient in itself, on the basis of the evidence in the possession of the Court, for the purpose of attributing to the United States the acts committed by the contras in the course of their military or paramilitary operations in Nicaragua. All the forms of United States participation mentioned above, and even the general control by the respondent State over a force with a high degree of dependency on it, would not in themselves mean, without further evidence, that the United States directed or enforced the perpetration of the acts contrary to human rights and humanitarian law alleged by the applicant State. Such acts could well be committed by members of the contras without the control of the United States. For this conduct to give rise to legal responsibility of the United States, it would in principle have to be proved that that State had effective control of the military or paramilitary operations in the course of which the alleged violations were committed.

1.2.3.2 ICTY, *Prosecutor* v. *Tadić*, (Judgment), Case No. IT-94-1-A, Appeals Chamber (15 July 1999)

Note: *The facts of this case are set out in Section 1.1.1. The ICTY also addressed the question of what level of control by a State over an organised armed group or individuals can internationalise an armed conflict.*

115. The "effective control" test enunciated by the International Court of Justice was regarded as correct and upheld by Trial Chamber II in the Judgment. The Appeals Chamber, with respect, does not hold the Nicaragua test to be persuasive. . . .

137. In sum, the Appeals Chamber holds the view that international rules do not always require the same degree of control over armed groups or private individuals for the purpose of determining whether an individual not having the status of a State official under internal legislation can be regarded as a *de facto* organ of the State. The extent of the requisite State control varies. Where the question at issue is whether a *single* private individual or a *group that is not militarily organised* has acted as a *de facto* State organ when performing a specific act, it is necessary to ascertain whether specific instructions concerning the commission of that particular act had been issued by that State to the individual or group in question; alternatively, it must be established whether the unlawful act had been publicly endorsed or approved *ex post facto* by the State at issue. By contrast, control by a State over subordinate *armed forces or militias or paramilitary units* may be of an overall character (and must comprise more than the mere provision of financial assistance or military equipment or training). This requirement, however, does not go so far as to include the issuing of specific orders by the State, or its direction of each individual operation. Under international law it is by no means necessary that the controlling authorities should plan all the operations of the units dependent on them, choose their targets, or give specific instructions concerning the conduct of military operations and any alleged violations of international humanitarian law. The control required by international law may be deemed to exist when a State (or, in the context of an armed conflict, the Party to the conflict) *has a role in organising, coordinating or planning the military actions* of the military group, in addition to financing, training and equipping or providing operational support to that group. Acts performed by the group or members thereof may be regarded as acts of *de facto* State organs regardless of any specific instruction by the controlling State concerning the commission of each of those acts. . . .

145. In the light of the above discussion, the following conclusion may be safely reached. In the case at issue, given that the Bosnian Serb armed forces constituted a "military organization", the control of the FRY authorities over these armed forces required by international law for considering the armed conflict to be international was overall control going beyond the mere financing and equipping of such forces and involving also participation in the planning and supervision of military operations. By contrast, international rules do not require that such control should extend to the issuance of specific orders or instructions relating to single military actions, whether or not such actions were contrary to international humanitarian law.

1.2.3.3 ICJ, *Case Concerning Application of the Convention on the Prevention and Punishment of the Crime of Genocide (Bosnia and Herzegovina v. Serbia and Montenegro)* (Judgment) [2007] I.C.J. Rep. 43

Note: The ICJ was asked to declare that the Federal Republic of Yugoslavia had directly or through the use of 'surrogates' violated the Convention on the Prevention and Punishment of the Crime of Genocide. Addressing the requisite degree of State control over an armed group, the ICJ stated:

404. ... Insofar as the "overall control" test is employed to determine whether or not an armed conflict is international, which was the sole question which the Appeals Chamber was called upon to decide, it may well be that the test is applicable and suitable; ... On the other hand, the ICTY presented the "overall control" test as equally applicable under the law of State responsibility for the purpose of determining — as the Court is required to do in the present case — when a State is responsible for acts committed by paramilitary units, armed forces which are not among its official organs. In this context, the argument in favour of that test is unpersuasive.

1.2.3.4 ICC, *The Prosecutor* v. *Thomas Lubanga Dyilo*, (Decision on the Confirmation of Charges), Case No. ICC-01/04-01/06 (29 January 2007)

Note: The facts are set out in Section 1.2.1.1. In addition to defining IAC, the ICC considered the circumstances in which a non-State armed group can be considered to be acting on behalf of a foreign State, rendering the armed conflict international in character. The ICC said as follows:

211. The Chamber holds the view that when a State does not *intervene directly* on the territory of another State through its own troops, the overall control test will be used to determine whether armed forces are acting on behalf of the first State. The test will be met where the first State has a role in organising, co-ordinating or planning the military actions of the military group, in addition to financing, training and equipping the group or providing operational support to it.

1.2.3.5 ICC, *The Prosecutor* v. *Jean-Pierre Bemba Gombo*, (Judgment Pursuant to Article 74 of the Statute), Case No. ICC-01/05-01/08 66/364, Trial Chamber III (21 March 2016)

Note: Jean-Pierre Bemba was the President of the Mouvement de Libération du Congo (MLC) and Commander-in-Chief of its military branch, the Armée de Libération du Congo (ALC), charged with crimes against humanity and war crimes within the territory of the neighbouring Central African Republic (CAR). The armed conflict in CAR involved its government supported by the MLC and the organised armed group of General Bozizé's rebels. The ICC opined on the character of the armed conflict in CAR as follows:

130. The Chamber considers that an armed conflict not of an international character, but involving the governmental authorities of one state, may become internationalised owing to a second state's participation on an opposing side of the conflict. In this regard, the Chamber notes that Trial Chambers I and II found that an armed conflict may be considered

internationalised when it is established that armed groups are acting *on behalf of* a foreign government. . . .

302. For determining whether an armed group is acting on behalf of a state, Trial Chambers I and II endorsed the "overall control" test, as set out by the ICTY Appeals Chamber in the *Tadić* case . . .

654. Recalling that a conflict will only be transformed to an international armed conflict where a second state is involved, directly or indirectly, on an *opposing* side of the conflict, the Chamber focuses its analysis on whether General Bozizé's rebels, or any aligned forces, were acting on behalf of a foreign government.

655. . . . there is no evidence that the Chadian government had any role in organizing, coordinating, or planning the military actions of General Bozizé's rebels. Accordingly, the Chamber finds that General Bozizé's rebels were not acting on behalf, i.e. under the "overall control", of any foreign government.

656. In light of the above, the armed conflict, which was confined to the territory of the CAR, cannot be viewed as one in which two or more states opposed each other, or one in which territory was occupied by a hostile, foreign state. The Chamber thus finds beyond reasonable doubt that the armed conflict in the context of the 2002–2003 CAR Operation was not of an international character.

1.2.4 Definition of Non-International Armed Conflict[4]

1.2.4.1 IACHR, *Juan Carlos Abella* v. *Argentina*, Case 11.137, Report No. 55/97, Inter-Am. C.H.R., OEA/Ser.L/V/II.95, Doc 7 rev. (18 November 1997)

Note: *The case concerned events that occurred on 23 and 24 January 1989 at the barracks of the General Belgrano Mechanized Infantry Regiment No. 3, located at La Tablada, Buenos Aires province, when a group of forty-two persons launched an armed attack on the barracks. The attack and the ensuing conflict lasted for some thirty hours and resulted in the deaths of twenty-nine of the attackers and several State agents. As to what constitutes a NIAC, the Commission said:*

152. . . . Common Article 3 is generally understood to apply to low intensity and open armed confrontations between relatively organized armed forces or groups that take place within the territory of a particular State. Thus, Common Article 3 does not apply to riots, mere acts of banditry or an <u>unorganized</u> and short-lived rebellion. Article 3 armed conflicts typically involve armed strife between governmental armed forces and organized armed insurgents. It also governs situations where two or more armed factions confront one another without the intervention of governmental forces where, for example, the established government has dissolved or is too weak to intervene. It is important to understand that application of Common Article 3 does <u>not</u> require the existence of large-scale and generalized hostilities or a situation comparable to a civil war in which dissident armed groups exercise control over parts of national territory.

---

[4]   For NIACs, see Chapter 10.

1.2.4.2 **ICTR,** *The Prosecutor* v. *Alfred Musema,* (Judgment and Sentence), Case
No. ICTR-96-13-A, Trial Chamber I (27 January 2000)

Note: *The facts are set out in Section 1.1.4. Addressing the criteria required to engage APII and the interpretation thereof, the ICTR said as follows:*

254. Thus the conditions to be met to fulfil the material requirements of applicability of Additional Protocol II at the time of the events alleged in the Indictment would entail showing that:

- an armed conflict took place in Rwanda, between its armed forces and dissenting armed forces or other organized armed groups;
- the dissident armed forces or other organized armed groups were:
  - under responsible command;
  - able to exercise such control over a part of their territory as to enable them to carry out sustained and concerted military operations; and
  - able to implement Additional Protocol II

256. ... It is sufficient to recall that an armed conflict is distinguished from internal disturbances by the level of intensity of the conflict and the degree of organization of the parties to the conflict. Under Additional Protocol II, the parties to the conflict will usually either be the government confronting dissident armed forces, or the government fighting insurgent organized armed groups. The term "armed forces" of the High Contracting Party should be understood in the broadest sense, so as to cover all armed forces as described within national legislation.

257. Furthermore, the armed forces opposing the government must be under responsible command. This requirement implies some degree of organization within the armed groups or dissident armed forces, but this does not necessarily mean that there is a hierarchical system of military organization similar to that of regular armed forces. It means an organization capable of, on the one hand, planning and carrying out sustained and concerted military operations - operations that are kept up continuously and that are done in agreement according to a plan, and on the other, of imposing discipline in the name of the de facto authorities

258. In addition to this, these dissident armed forces must be able to dominate a sufficient part of the territory so as to maintain these sustained and concerted military operations and the insurgents must be in a position to implement this Protocol.

1.2.4.3 **UK,** Select Committee on International Development (Appendices to the
Minutes of Evidence), *Letter from the Clerk of the Committee to Philip
Spoerri, Legal Adviser, International Committee of the Red Cross and Reply*
(28 November 2002)[5]

Note: *The Letter explains why the conflict in Afghanistan became non-international after the overthrow of the Taliban regime following the 2001 US action.*

---

[5]   www.publications.parliament.uk/pa/cm200203/cmselect/cmintdev/84/84ap09.htm.

... Following the convening of the Loya Jirga in Kabul in June 2002 and the subsequent establishment of an Afghan transitional government on 19 June 2002 which not only received unanimous recognition by the entire community of States but could also claim broad-based recognition within Afghanistan through the Loya Jirga process the ICRC has changed its initial qualification as follows: The ICRC no longer views the ongoing military operations in Afghanistan directed against suspected Taliban or other armed groups as an international armed conflict.

Hostilities conducted by United States and allied forces against groups such as the Taliban and al-Qaeda in Afghanistan after 19 June 2002 are therefore governed by the rules applicable to situations of non-international armed conflict, since the military operations in question are being carried out with the consent of the government of a recognized sovereign State, the Islamic State of Afghanistan.

1.2.4.4 Syria, UN General Assembly, Human Rights Council, *Report of the Independent International Commission of Inquiry on the Syrian Arab Republic* (16 August 2012) 21st Session, UN Doc. A/HRC/21/50

Note: *In its August 2012 Report, the Commission re-characterised the conflict in Syria as NIAC. The Commission concluded as follows*:

12. In its previous reports, the Commission did not apply international humanitarian law. During the present reporting period, the commission determined that the intensity and duration of the conflict, combined with the increased organizational capabilities of anti-Government armed groups, had met the legal threshold for a non-international armed conflict. With this determination, the commission applied international humanitarian law in its assessment of the actions of the parties during hostilities.

1.2.4.5 Germany, *Aerial Drone Deployment on 4 October 2010 in Mir/Ali Pakistan (Targeted Killing in Pakistan Case)*, Decision to Terminate Proceedings, Federal Prosecutor General, Case No 3 BJs 7/12-4 (23 July 2013), 157 ILR 722, pp. 744–6

Note: *The case concerned the killing of a German national by a drone in the border region between Pakistan and Afghanistan where cross-border attacks were taking place.*

(c) Non-international conflict

Both the internal Pakistani conflict as well as the military clashes in Afghanistan each represent a non-international conflict, since they are not being carried out between national states but rather between government forces on the one hand and armed, organised groups on the other. This classification holds true regardless of the fact that both the Afghan and Pakistani government troops are receiving support from the military units of other nations acting as co-participants in the conflict. Both the ISAF deployment in Afghanistan as well as the aerial drone missions in Pakistan) have occurred with the official and/or unofficial consent of the affected territorial state, meaning that none of these states has had its sovereignty breached by another. By the same token, the fact that ISAF forces mount crossborder operations or that combat drones may potentially be launched from

Afghani territory does not entail an "internationalisation" of the conflict. As long as a deployment of government troops in the territory of another state is directed against non-state actors, and as long as the latter state has consented to this deployment, even these types of hostilities will in principle qualify as "non-international armed conflicts", despite their cross-border dimension.

1.2.5 Intensity of Armed Violence and Protracted Violence

1.2.5.1 IACHR, *Juan Carlos Abella* v. *Argentina*, Case 11.137, Report No. 55/97, Inter-Am. C.H.R., OEA/Ser.L/V/II.95, Doc 7 rev. (18 November 1997)

Note: *The facts of this case are set out in Section 1.2.4.1. On the question of the requisite intensity of violence capable of giving rise to an armed conflict, the Commission commented as follows:*

149. The notion of internal disturbances and tensions has been studied and elaborated on most particularly by the International Committee of the Red Cross ("ICRC"). In its 1973 Commentary on the Draft Additional Protocols to the Geneva Conventions, the ICRC defined, albeit not exhaustively, such situations by way of the following three examples:

– riots, that is to say, all disturbances which from the start are not directed by a leader and have no concerted intent [emphasis in the original];
– isolated and sporadic acts of violence, as distinct from military operations carried out by armed forces or organized armed groups [emphasis in the original];
– other acts of a similar nature which incur, in particular, mass arrests of persons because of their behavior or political opinion

151. Situations of internal disturbances and tensions are expressly excluded from the scope of international humanitarian law as not being armed conflicts. Instead, they are governed by domestic law and relevant rules of international human rights law.

153. The most difficult problem regarding the application of Common Article 3 is not at the upper end of the spectrum of domestic violence, but rather at the lower end. The line separating an especially violent situation of internal disturbances from the "lowest" level Article 3 armed conflict may sometimes be blurred and, thus, not easily determined. When faced with making such a determination, what is required in the final analysis is a good faith and objective analysis of the facts in each particular case.

154. Based on a careful appreciation of the facts, the Commission does not believe that the violent acts at the La Tablada military base on January 23 and 24, 1989 can be properly characterized as a situation of internal disturbances. . . .

155. What differentiates the events at the La Tablada base from these situations are the concerted nature of the hostile acts undertaken by the attackers, the direct involvement of governmental armed forces, and the nature and level of the violence attending the events in question. More particularly, the attackers involved carefully planned, coordinated and executed an armed attack, i.e., a military operation, against a quintessential military objective - a military base. The officer in charge of the La Tablada base sought, as was his duty, to repulse the attackers, and President Alfonsín, exercising his constitutional

authority as Commander-in-Chief of the armed forces, ordered that military action be taken to recapture the base and subdue the attackers.

156. The Commission concludes therefore that, despite its brief duration, the violent clash between the attackers and members of the Argentine armed forces triggered application of the provisions of Common Article 3, as well as other rules relevant to the conduct of internal hostilities.

1.2.5.2 ICTY, *Prosecutor* v. *Ramush Haradinaj*, (Judgment), Case No. IT-04-84-T, Trial Chamber I (3 April 2008)

Note: *In this case, the ICTY was concerned with events between 1 March and 30 September 1998 in the Dukagjin area of Kosovo when the Kosovo Liberation Army persecuted and murdered Serb and Kosovar Roma civilians. The Tribunal set down factors to be taken into account when considering the notion of 'protracted armed violence' and whether it is sufficiently 'intense' for the purposes of establishing an armed conflict:*

49. The criterion of protracted armed violence has therefore been interpreted in practice, including by the *Tadić* Trial Chamber itself, as referring more to the intensity of the armed violence than its duration. Trial Chambers have relied on indicative factors relevant for assessing the 'intensity' criterion. ... These ... include the number, duration and intensity of individual confrontations; the type of weapons and other military equipment used; the number and calibre of munitions fired; the number of persons and type of forces partaking in the fighting; the number of casualties; the extent of material destruction; and the number of civilians fleeing from combat zones. The involvement of the UN Security Council may also be a reflection of the intensity of a conflict.

1.2.5.3 ICTY, *Prosecutor* v. *Boškoski and Tarčulovski*, (Judgment), Case No. IT-04-82-T, Trial Chamber II (10 July 2008)

Note: *The factual background to this case is set out in Section 1.1.7. The Tribunal offered some further guidance on the 'intensity' criterion. The Tribunal said as follows:*

177. Various indicative factors have been taken into account by Trial Chambers to assess the 'intensity' of the conflict. These include the seriousness of attacks and whether there has been an increase in armed clashes, the spread of clashes over territory and over a period of time, any increase in the number of government forces and mobilisation and the distribution of weapons among both parties to the conflict, as well as whether the conflict has attracted the attention of the United Nations Security Council, and whether any resolutions on the matter have been passed. Trial Chambers have also taken into account in this respect the number of civilians forced to flee from the combat zones; the type of weapons used, in particular the use of heavy weapons, and other military equipment, such as tanks and other heavy vehicles; the blocking or besieging of towns and the heavy shelling of these towns; the extent of destruction and the number of casualties caused by shelling or fighting; the quantity of troops and units deployed; existence and change of front lines between the parties; the occupation of territory, and towns and villages; the deployment of government forces to the crisis area; the closure of roads; cease fire orders and agreements,

and the attempt of representatives from international organisations to broker and enforce cease fire agreements.

1.2.5.4 ICC, *The Prosecutor* v. *Jean-Pierre Bemba Gombo*, (Judgment Pursuant to Article 74 of the Statute), Case No. ICC-01/05-01/08 66/364, Trial Chamber III (21 March 2016)

Note: *The background to this case is detailed in Section 1.2.3.5. In addition to approving of the approach taken by the ICTY in assessing the intensity criterion in relation to a NIAC, the ICC offered guidance as to the concept of 'protracted conflict' as follows:*

137. ... In order to assess the intensity of a conflict, Trial Chambers I and II endorsed the ICTY's finding that relevant factors include "the seriousness of attacks and potential increase in armed clashes, their spread over territory and over a period of time, the increase in the number of government forces, the mobilisation and the distribution of weapons among both parties to the conflict, as well as whether the conflict has attracted the attention of the United Nations ("UN") Security Council, and, if so, whether any resolutions on the matter have been passed". The Chamber follows the approach of Trial Chambers I and II in this respect. ...

139. The Chamber notes that the concept of "protracted conflict" has not been explicitly defined in the jurisprudence of this Court, but has generally been addressed within the framework of assessing the intensity of the conflict. When assessing whether an armed conflict not of an international character was protracted, however, different chambers of this Court emphasised the duration of the violence as a relevant factor. This corresponds to the approach taken by chambers of the ICTY. The Chamber follows this jurisprudence.

140. The Chamber notes the Defence's submission that "if the conflict devolves to the level of riots, internal disturbances or tensions, or isolated or sporadic acts of violence, or if the conflict ceases to be between organized armed groups", the threshold for the existence of a "protracted armed conflict" would cease to be met. The Chamber considers that the intensity and "protracted armed conflict" criteria do not require the violence to be continuous and uninterrupted. Rather, ... the essential criterion is that it go beyond "isolated or sporadic acts of violence".

1.2.6 Organisation

1.2.6.1 ICTY, *Prosecutor* v. *Fatmir Limaj, Haradin Bala and Isak Musliu*, (Judgment), Case No IT-03-66-T, Trial Chamber II (30 November 2005)

Note: *In this case, the ICTY was concerned with the abduction, detention, inhumane treatment and murder of some thirty-five Serbian civilians by the accused who were members of the Kosovo Liberation Army. The Defence submitted that the Kosovo Liberation Army did not meet the level of organisation required to establish the existence of an armed conflict. Disagreeing, the Tribunal said as follows:*

90. ... With respect to the organisation of the parties to the conflict Chambers of the Tribunal have taken into account factors including the existence of headquarters, designated zones of operation, and the ability to procure, transport, and distribute arms.

1.2.6.2 ICTY, *Prosecutor* v. *Ramush Haradinaj*, (Judgment), Case No. IT-04-84-T, Trial Chamber I (3 April 2008)

Note: *The facts of this case are set out in Section 1.2.5.2. In addition to considering the level of intensity required to establish an armed conflict, the Tribunal also addressed the 'organisation' criterion in the following terms*:

60 . . . As for armed groups, Trial Chambers have relied on several indicative factors none of which are, in themselves, essential to establish whether the "organization" criterion is fulfilled. Such indicative factors include the existence of a command structure and disciplinary rules and mechanisms within the group; the existence of a headquarters; the fact that the group controls a certain territory; the ability of the group to gain access to weapons, other military equipment, recruits and military training; its ability to plan, coordinate and carry out military operations, including troop movement and logistics; its ability to define a unified military strategy and use military tactics; and its ability to speak with one voice and negotiate and conclude agreements such as cease-fire and peace accords.

1.2.6.3 ICTY, *Prosecutor* v. *Boškoski and Tarčulovski*, (Judgment), Case No. IT-04-82-T, Trial Chamber II (10 July 2008)

Note: *The facts are set out in Section 1.1.7. As to the level of organisation required of a non-State armed group, the ICTY offered the following guidance*:

197. While the jurisprudence of the Tribunal requires an armed group to have "some degree of organisation", the warring parties do not necessarily need to be as organised as the armed forces of a State. Neither does the degree of organisation for an armed group to a conflict to which Common Article 3 applies need be at the level of organisation required for parties to Additional Protocol II armed conflicts, . . .

199. Trial Chambers have taken into account a number of factors when assessing the organisation of an armed group. These fall into five broad groups. In the first group are those factors signalling the presence of a command structure, such as the establishment of a general staff or high command, which appoints and gives directions to commanders, disseminates internal regulations, organises the weapons supply, authorises military action, assigns tasks to individuals in the organisation, and issues political statements and communiqués, and which is informed by the operational units of all developments within the unit's area of responsibility. Also included in this group are factors such as the existence of internal regulations setting out the organisation and structure of the armed group; the assignment of an official spokesperson; the communication through communiqués reporting military actions and operations undertaken by the armed group; the existence of headquarters; internal regulations establishing ranks of servicemen and defining duties of commanders and deputy commanders of a unit, company, platoon or squad, creating a chain of military hierarchy between the various levels of commanders; and the dissemination of internal regulations to the soldiers and operational units.

200. Secondly, factors indicating that the group could carry out operations in an organised manner have been considered, such as the group's ability to determine a unified military strategy and to conduct large scale military operations, the capacity to control territory,

whether there is territorial division into zones of responsibility in which the respective commanders are responsible for the establishment of Brigades and other units and appoint commanding officers for such units; the capacity of operational units to coordinate their actions, and the effective dissemination of written and oral orders and decisions.

201. In the third group are factors indicating a level of logistics have been taken into account, such as the ability to recruit new members; the providing of military training; the organised supply of military weapons; the supply and use of uniforms; and the existence of communications equipment for linking headquarters with units or between units.

202. In a fourth group, factors relevant to determining whether an armed group possessed a level of discipline and the ability to implement the basic obligations of Common Article 3 have been considered, such as the establishment of disciplinary rules and mechanisms; proper training; and the existence of internal regulations and whether these are effectively disseminated to members.

203. A fifth group includes those factors indicating that the armed group was able to speak with one voice, such as its capacity to act on behalf of its members in political negotiations with representatives of international organisations and foreign countries; and its ability to negotiate and conclude agreements such as cease fire or peace accords.

1.2.6.4 ICC, *The Prosecutor* v. *Thomas Lubanga Dyilo*, (Judgment Pursuant to Article 74 of the Statute), Case No. ICC-01/04-01/06, Trial Chamber I (14 March 2012)

Note: *The facts are set out in Section 1.2.1.1. On the level of organisation required of a non-State armed group in the context of a NIAC, the ICC said as follows:*

537. When deciding if a body was an organised armed group (for the purpose of determining whether an armed conflict was not of an international character), the following non-exhaustive list of factors is potentially relevant: the force or group's internal hierarchy; the command structure and rules; the extent to which military equipment, including firearms, are available; the force or group's ability to plan military operations and put them into effect; and the extent, seriousness, and intensity of any military involvement. None of these factors are individually determinative. The test, along with these criteria, should be applied flexibly when the Chamber is deciding whether a body was an organised armed group, given the limited requirement in Article 8(2)(f) of the Statute that the armed group was "organized".

1.3 MIXED CONFLICTS

1.3.1 ICJ, *Case Concerning Military and Paramilitary Activities in and Against Nicaragua (Nicaragua v. United States of America)* (Merits, Judgment) [1986] I.C.J. Rep. 14

Note: *The facts of this case are set out in Section 1.2.3.1. In addition to considering the law applicable in circumstances where a foreign State exercises control over an armed group, the ICJ* *considered the legal framework applicable to mixed conflicts, that is a conflict combining both IAC and NIAC. The ICJ said as follows:*

219. The conflict between the contras' forces and those of the Government of Nicaragua is an armed conflict which is "not of an international character". The acts of the contras towards the Nicaraguan Government are therefore governed by the law applicable to conflicts of that character; whereas the actions of the United States in and against Nicaragua fall under the legal rules relating to international conflicts. . . .

1.3.2 ICTY, *Prosecutor* v. *Tadić*, (Decision on the Defence Motion for Interlocutory Appeal on Jurisdiction), Case No. IT-94-1-A, Appeals Chamber (2 October 1995)

Note: *The facts of this case are set out in Section 1.1.1. On the issue whether the conflict in the former Yugoslavia could rightly be characterised as a 'mixed conflict', the ICTY commented in the following terms:*

72. As the members of the Security Council well knew, in 1993, when the Statute was drafted, the conflicts in the former Yugoslavia could have been characterized as both internal and international, or alternatively, as an internal conflict alongside an international one, or as an internal conflict that had become internationalized because of external support, or as an international conflict that had subsequently been replaced by one or more internal conflicts, or some combination thereof. The conflict in the former Yugoslavia had been rendered international by the involvement of the Croatian Army in Bosnia-Herzegovina and by the involvement of the Yugoslav People's Army ("JNA") in hostilities in Croatia, as well as in Bosnia-Herzegovina at least until its formal withdrawal on 19 May 1992. To the extent that the conflicts had been limited to clashes between Bosnian Government forces and Bosnian Serb rebel forces in Bosnia-Herzegovina, as well as between the Croatian Government and Croatian Serb rebel forces in Krajina (Croatia), they had been internal (unless direct involvement of the Federal Republic of Yugoslavia (Serbia-Montenegro) could be proven).

1.3.3 Georgia, *Independent International Fact-Finding Mission on the Conflict in Georgia* Report Volume II, (September 2009), pp. 300–4

Note: *In 2008, tensions between Georgia and Russia escalated into a military conflict after Georgia attempted to forcibly retake South Ossetia and Abkhazia. Russia subsequently launched a counter-attack and expelled Georgian troops from South Ossetia and Abkhazia. With regard to the classification of the conflict, the Fact-Finding Commission opined as follows:*

The hostilities between Georgia and the Russian Federation constitute an international armed conflict between two states as defined by Common Article 2 of the 1949 Geneva Conventions. . . . This was asserted by both the Russian Federation and Georgia. . . .

The hostilities between South Ossetia and Abkhazia on the one hand, and Georgia on the other, are governed by the IHL applicable to non-international armed conflict, since both are recognised internationally as being part of Georgia and, at the time of the 2008 conflicts, this was undisputed. The Russian Federation also reached this conclusion. However Georgia seems to classify it overall as an international armed conflict. … This could be the case if one considers that Russia exercises sufficient control over the Abkhaz/South Ossetian forces, as will be discussed later. …

An armed conflict between a State and an armed group may be qualified as international if this group, under certain conditions, is under the control of another State, i.e., a second State. Georgia and the Russian Federation hold opposing views on whether the latter exercised control over the Abkhaz and Ossetian forces. …

In factual terms, one may have to draw a distinction with regard to the nature of the relationship between Russia and South Ossetia on the one hand, and between Russia and Abkhazia on the other. In the former, ties seem to be stronger. …

At this point it is appropriate to underline that although the classification of an armed conflict as international or non-international is important in terms of the responsibilities of the various parties involved, when it comes to the effective protection by IHL of the persons and objects affected by the conflict it does not make much difference. Indeed, it is generally recognized that the same IHL customary law rules generally apply to all types of armed conflicts.

1.3.4 ICC, *The Prosecutor* v. *Thomas Lubanga Dyilo*, (Judgment Pursuant to Article 74 of the Statute), Case No. ICC-01/04-01/06, Trial Chamber I (14 March 2012)

Note: *The facts of this case are set out in Section 1.2.1.1. In terms of classifying the conflict in the DRC as 'mixed', the ICC said the following:*

543. The evidence in the case demonstrates beyond reasonable doubt that during the entirety of the period covered by the charges there were a number of simultaneous armed conflicts in Ituri and in surrounding areas within the DRC, involving various different groups. …

565. Focusing solely on the parties and the conflict relevant to the charges in this case, the Ugandan military occupation of Bunia airport does not change the legal nature of the conflict between the UPC/FPLC, RCD-ML/APC and FRPI rebel groups since this conflict, as analysed above, did not result in two states opposing each other, whether directly or indirectly, during the time period relevant to the charges. In any event, the existence of a possible conflict that was "international in character" between the DRC and Uganda does not affect the legal characterisation of the UPC/FPLC's concurrent non-international armed conflict with the APC and FRPI militias, which formed part of the internal armed conflict between the rebel groups.

1.3.5 Libya, UN General Assembly, Human Rights Council, *Report of the International Commission of Inquiry to Investigate all Alleged Violations of International Human Rights Law in the Libyan Arab Jamahiriya* (1 June 2011) 17th Session, UN Doc. A/HRC/17/44

Note: *The report of the Human Rights Council was prompted by the popular uprising in Libya in 2011. As to the categorisation of the conflict in Libya, it reported as follows:*

60. The escalation of the situation in Libya has particular consequences in terms of the application of international law. In legal terms, the periods can be demarked as (i) "peacetime," (ii) "non-international armed conflict" and (iii) "co-existing international armed conflict."

61. **Peace-time Libya:** When the demonstrations began in mid-February, Libya could be classified as being in a normal state of peace.

62. **Non-International Armed Conflict:** The precise date for determining when this change from peace to non-international armed conflict occurred is somewhat difficult in the current circumstances. . . .

64. In determining whether a non-international armed conflict exists, the Commission has thus had to consider the intensity of the conflict, the extent of relevant control of territory and the nature of the armed group in opposition to the Government. . . .

65. Information is more readily available concerning the intensity of the conflict and how the opposition forces have gained territorial control than many aspects of the organisation of the armed opposition forces. . . . Whilst the Commission lacks full information concerning several aspects of the opposition forces organization, it has reached the preliminary view that by or around 24 February, a non-international armed conflict had developed sufficient to trigger the application of AP II and Common Article 3 of the Geneva Conventions.

66. **Co-existing International Armed Conflict:** The airstrikes to enforce the no-fly zone imposed by the Security Council through Resolution 1973 which began on 19 March brought into being an international armed conflict between the States participating in this military action and the Libyan state. . . . It is also satisfied that the actions of NATO and other foreign States involved are not exercising control over the military actions of either of the parties to the non-international armed conflict. As such, it concludes that the international armed conflict is legally separate to the continuing non-international armed conflict, and is thus a "co-existing international armed conflict."

1.3.6 US, Department of Defense, *Law of War Manual*, Office of General Counsel (June 2015, Updated 2016)

3.3.1.2 Mixed Conflicts Between Opposing States and Non-State Armed Groups.

Rather than viewing a situation as either an international armed conflict or a non-international armed conflict, it may be possible to characterize parts of a conflict as international in character, while other parts of that armed conflict may be regarded as non-international in character. For example, under this view, during a situation involving conflict between a variety of States and non-State armed groups, as between the States, the rules of international armed conflict would apply, while as between the States and non-State armed groups, the rules of non-international armed conflicts would apply.

1.4 GEOGRAPHIC AND TEMPORAL SCOPE OF AN ARMED CONFLICT[6]

1.4.1 ICTY, *Prosecutor* v. *Tadić*, (Decision on Defence Motion for Interlocutory Appeal on Jurisdiction), Case No. IT-94-1-A, Appeals Chamber (2 October 1995)

Note: *The background to this case is outlined in Section 1.1.1. As to the geographical and temporal application of IHL, the ICTY commented in the following terms:*

68. Although the Geneva Conventions are silent as to the geographical scope of international "armed conflicts," the provisions suggest that at least some of the provisions of the Conventions apply to the entire territory of the Parties to the conflict, not just to the vicinity of actual hostilities. Certainly, some of the provisions are clearly bound up with the hostilities and the geographical scope of those provisions should be so limited. Others, particularly those relating to the protection of prisoners of war and civilians, are not so limited. . . .

69. The geographical and temporal frame of reference for internal armed conflicts is similarly broad. . . . This indicates that the rules contained in Article 3 also apply outside the narrow geographical context of the actual theatre of combat operations. Similarly, certain language in Protocol II to the Geneva Conventions . . . also suggests a broad scope. . . .

Under [Art. 2, para. 2 APII], the temporal scope of the applicable rules clearly reaches beyond the actual hostilities. Moreover, the relatively loose nature of the language "for reasons related to such conflict", suggests a broad geographical scope as well. The nexus required is only a relationship between the conflict and the deprivation of liberty, not that the deprivation occurred in the midst of battle.

70. . . . International humanitarian law applies from the initiation of such armed conflicts and extends beyond the cessation of hostilities until a general conclusion of peace is reached; or, in the case of internal conflict, a peaceful settlement is achieved. Until that moment, international humanitarian law continues to apply in the whole territory of the warring States or, in the case of internal armed conflicts, the whole territory under the control of a party, whether or not actual combat takes place there.

1.4.2 ICTY, *Prosecutor* v. *Dragoljub Kunarac, Radomir Kovač and Zoran Vuković*, (Judgment), Case No. IT-96-23 & IT-96-23/1-A, Appeals Chamber (12 June 2002)

Note: *The Defendants were accused of committing crimes against humanity and war crimes between April 1992 and February 1993 against Bosnian Muslims. As to the geographical reach of the rules of IHL, the ICTY said as follows:*

---

[6] For the geographic and temporal scope of NIACs, see also Chapter 10.

57. .... The laws of war apply in the whole territory of the warring states or, in the case of internal armed conflicts, the whole territory under the control of a party to the conflict, whether or not actual combat takes place there, and continue to apply until a general conclusion of peace or, in the case of internal armed conflicts, until a peaceful settlement is achieved. A violation of the laws or customs of war may therefore occur at a time when and in a place where no fighting is actually taking place. As indicated by the Trial Chamber, the requirement that the acts of the accused must be closely related to the armed conflict would not be negated if the crimes were temporally and geographically remote from the actual fighting. It would be sufficient, for instance, for the purpose of this requirement, that the alleged crimes were closely related to hostilities occurring in other parts of the territories controlled by the parties to the conflict.

1.4.3 ICTR, *The Prosecutor* v. *Semanza*, (Judgment and Sentence), Case No. ICTR-97-20-T, Trial Chamber III (15 May 2003)

Note: *The Defendant was charged with genocide, crimes against humanity, violations of Common Article 3 GCs and APII following his involvement in the conflict in Rwanda between April and July 1994. As to the scope of application of Common Article 3, the Tribunal said as follows:*

367. Once the conditions for applicability of Common Article 3 and Additional Protocol II are satisfied, their scope extends throughout the territory of the State where the hostilities are taking place without limitation to the "war front" or to the "narrow geographical context of the actual theatre of combat operation.

1.4.4 Special Court for Sierra Leone, *Prosecutor* v. *Brima, Kamara and Kanu*, (Judgment), Case No. SCSL 04-16-T, Trial Chamber II (20 June 2007)

Note: *The Defendants were senior officers in the Armed Forces Revolutionary Council participating in the armed conflict in Sierra Leone and were charged with crimes against humanity and violations of IHL. Defining the geo-temporal reach of IHL, the Special Court said:*

245. International humanitarian law applies from the initiation of such armed conflicts and extends beyond the cessation of hostilities until a general conclusion of peace is reached; or, in the case of internal conflicts, until a peaceful settlement is achieved. Until that moment, international humanitarian law continues to apply on the whole territory of the warring States or, in the case of internal conflicts, the whole territory under the control of a party, whether or not actual combat takes place there.

1.4.5 ICTY, *Prosecutor* v. *Gotovina et al.*, (Judgment), Case No. T-06-90-T, Trial Chamber I (15 April 2011)

Note: *This case concerned war crimes committed between July 1995 and September 1995 against the Serbian population and property in the Krajina region of Croatia during what was termed 'Operation Storm'. On the issue when IHL ceases to apply to an armed conflict, the ICTY said:*

1694. ... Once the law of armed conflict has become applicable, one should not lightly conclude that its applicability ceases. Otherwise, the participants in an armed conflict may find themselves in a revolving door between applicability and non-applicability, leading to a considerable degree of legal uncertainty and confusion. The Trial Chamber will therefore consider whether at any point during the indictment period the international armed conflict had found a sufficiently general, definitive and effective termination so as to end the applicability of the law of armed conflict. It will consider in particular whether there was a general close of military operations and a general conclusion of peace.

1.4.6 Germany, Federal Ministry of Defence, *Law of Armed Conflict – Manual – Joint Service Regulation (ZDv) 15/2* (May 2013)

221. The **end of active hostilities** by itself does not terminate an international armed conflict. **Hostilities can be stopped temporarily** or permanently, conditionally or unconditionally, in general or locally, unilaterally or multilaterally. Even in case of an ongoing military occupation, the law of international armed conflict is applicable

1.4.7 US, Department of Defense, *Law of War Manual*, Office of General Counsel (June 2015, Updated 2016)

3.8.1 *General Cessation of the Application of the Law of War at the End of Hostilities.*

Hostilities end when opposing parties decide to end hostilities and actually do so, *i.e.*, when neither the intent-based nor act-based tests for when hostilities exist are met. Of course, if the test for the existence of hostilities continues to be met, then hostilities cannot be deemed to have ceased. For example, hostilities may be terminated by:

- an agreement to end hostilities, normally in the form of a treaty of peace;
- unilateral declaration of one of the parties to end the war, provided the other party does not continue hostilities or otherwise decline to recognize the act of its enemy;
- the complete subjugation of an enemy State and its allies; or
- a simple cessation of hostilities.

1.4.8 ICC, *The Prosecutor* v. *Jean-Pierre Bemba Gombo,* (Judgment Pursuant to Article 74 of the Statute), Case No. ICC-01/05-01/08 66/364, Trial Chamber III (21 March 2016)

Note: *The background of this case is outlined in Section 1.2.3.5. Addressing the issue of when the rules of IHL may cease to apply to an armed conflict, the ICC said as follows:*

141. The Chamber additionally recalls that following the initiation of an armed conflict, international humanitarian law continues to apply to the whole territory under the control of a party, until a "peaceful settlement" is achieved. The Chamber finds that, contrary to the

Defence's allegation, the meaning of a "peaceful settlement" does not reflect only the mere existence of an agreement to withdraw or a declaration of an intention to cease fire.

1.4.9 US, *Hamid Al Razak* v. *Barack H. Obama, et al.*, United States District Court, District of Columbia, 174 F. Supp. 3d 300, 306 (D.D.C. 2016)

Note: *Mr Hamdullah was an Afghan citizen detained by the United States in Guantanamo Bay. A petition for a Writ of Habeas Corpus was filed in 2005 challenging the legality of Mr Hamdullah's detention. The issue under consideration was whether detention was authorised for the duration of 'active combat' or 'active hostilities'. The Court concluded in the following terms:*

For the foregoing reasons, the Court concludes that the appropriate standard is cessation of active hostilities and that active hostilities can continue after combat operations have ceased. But, cessation of active hostilities is not so demanding a standard that it requires total peace, signed peace agreements, or an end to all fighting.

1.4.10 US, The White House, *Report on the Legal and Policy Frameworks Guiding the United States' Use of Military Force and Related National Security Operations* (December 2016),[7] pp. 11–12

As the President has also said, however, "this war, like all wars, must end." At a certain point, the United States will degrade and dismantle the operational capacity and supporting networks of terrorist organizations like al-Qa'ida to such an extent that they will have been effectively destroyed and will no longer be able to attempt or launch a strategic attack against the United States. At that point, there will no longer be an ongoing armed conflict between the United States and those forces.

1.5 WARS OF SELF-DETERMINATION

1.5.1 Gaza, UN General Assembly, Human Rights Council, *Report of the United Nations Fact-Finding Mission on the Gaza Conflict* (25 September 2009) 12th Session, UN Doc. A/HRC/12/48

Note: *The UN Fact Finding Commission on the Gaza Conflict was established to investigate violations of international human rights law (IHRL) and IHL in the context of military operations in Gaza between December 2008 and January 2009. Considering the right to self-determination and its relevance to the classification of an armed conflict, the Commission reported as follows:*

308. ... Armed conflicts opposing national liberation movements and/or resistance movements against colonialism and occupation are regarded as international armed conflicts by Additional Protocol I, article 1 (4). Under international law, notably Additional

---

[7] https://fas.org/man/eprint/frameworks.pdf.

Protocol I to the Geneva Conventions, any action of resistance pursuant to the right to self-determination should be exercised with full respect of other human rights and IHL.

1.5.2 UK, British Ministry of Defence, *The Joint Service Manual of the Law of Armed Conflict* (Joint Service Publication 383, 2004 Edition)

3.4. Article 1(4) of Additional Protocol I applies the Protocol, and by extension the 1949 Conventions, to armed conflicts in which 'peoples are fighting against colonial domination and alien occupation and against racist regimes in the exercise of their right of self-determination'.

. . .

3.4.2 Three conditions must be complied with before this provision comes into effect:

a. First, there must be an 'armed conflict'. The threshold of violence required to render the situation an armed conflict is the same as that required for internal armed conflicts.
b. Secondly, the people concerned must genuinely be 'fighting against colonial domination and alien occupation and against racist regimes in the exercise of their right of self-determination'. It is not sufficient for the authority representing the people simply to claim that this is happening. This condition has to be assessed objectively. A substantial degree of international recognition of the legitimacy of the 'liberation movement' is necessary, as a minimum recognition by the appropriate regional inter-governmental organization.
c. Thirdly, the authority representing the people must undertake to apply Additional Protocol I and the Geneva Conventions. This undertaking is given by means of a unilateral declaration addressed to the Swiss government. The effect of the undertaking is to impose upon both the state and the authority all the rights and obligations created by Additional Protocol I and the Geneva Conventions, so that they become responsible for ensuring the due observance of those rights and obligations. Authorities cannot become parties to the Protocol or the Conventions since this status is reserved for states.

1.5.3 US, Department of Defense, *Law of War Manual*, Office of General Counsel (June 2015, Updated 2016)

3.3.4 AP I Provision on National Liberation Movements. AP I treats as international armed conflicts "armed conflicts in which peoples are fighting against colonial domination and alien occupation and against racist regimes in the exercise of their right of self-determination."

The United States has strongly objected to this provision as making the applicability of the rules of international armed conflict turn on subjective and politicized criteria that would eliminate the distinction between international and non-international conflicts. The United States has understood these types of conflicts to be non-international armed conflicts.

1.5.4 Appel de Genève (Geneva Call), Polisario Front, Unilateral Declaration of 21 June 2015

Note: *On behalf of the people of Western Sahara, the Polisario Front unilaterally declared it was to apply the GCs and API to the conflict between the people of Western Sahara and the Kingdom of Morocco. In making the Declaration, the Polisario Front relied upon Article 96(3) API, which permits a party to a conflict in which the right to self-determination is engaged to apply the GCs and API aforesaid. The Declaration was as follows:*

Conformément à l'article 96.3 du Protocole additionnel aux Conventions de Genève du 12 août 1949 relatif à la protection des victimes des conflits armés internationaux (Protocole I) du 8 juin 1977, le Front POLISARIO, en tant qu'autorité représentant le peuple du Sahara Occidental luttant pour son droit à disposer de lui-même, déclare s'engager à appliquer les Conventions de Genève de 1949 et le Protocole I dans le conflit l'opposant au Royaume du Maroc.

1.6 TERRORISM[8]

1.6.1 Israel, *The Public Committee against Torture in Israel et al.* v. *The Government of Israel et al. ('Targeted Killing Case'),* (Judgment), Case No. HCJ 769/02, Israeli Supreme Court Sitting as the High Court of Justice (11 December 2005)

Note: *The case arose in response to the Israeli policy of preventive and targeted killings of terrorists in Judea, Samaria and the Gaza Strip. Petitioners in the case argued the policy contravened IHRL as well as Israeli law. The High Court commented as follows:*

21. Our starting point is that the law that applies to the armed conflict between Israel and the terrorist organizations in the *area* is the international law dealing with armed conflicts. ... According to that view, the fact that the terrorist organizations and their members do not act in the name of a state does not turn the struggle against them into a purely internal state conflict. Indeed, in today's reality, a terrorist organization is likely to have considerable military capabilities. At times they have military capabilities that exceed those of states. Confrontation with those dangers cannot be restricted within the state and its penal law. Confronting the dangers of terrorism constitutes a part of the international law dealing with armed conflicts of international character. ... As stated, for years the starting point of the Supreme Court – and also of the State's counsel before the Supreme Court – is that the armed conflict is of an international character. In this judgment we continue to rule on the basis of that view. It should be noted that even those who are of the opinion that the armed conflict between Israel and the terrorist organizations is not of international character, think that international humanitarian or international human rights law applies to it.

---

[8]   See also Chapter 3 Section 3.8 on terrorism and IHL and IHRL.

1.6.2 US, *Hamdan* v. *Rumsfeld Secretary of Defense et al.*, Supreme Court of the United States, 548 U.S. 557, 65–7, 69 (2006)

Note: *During the 2001 hostilities in Afghanistan, Hamdan, a Yemeni national, was captured and detained by the United States at Guantanamo Bay. Hamdan filed petitions for writs of Habeas Corpus and Mandamus on the grounds (i) the offences with which he was charged were not violations of IHL and (ii) the procedures of the military commission trying him violated international law. On the issue of the applicable law, the Court held as follows:*

The Court of Appeals thought, and the Government asserts, that Common Article 3 does not apply to Hamdan because the conflict with al Qaeda, being "'international in scope,'" does not qualify as a "'conflict not of an international character.'" That reasoning is erroneous. The term "conflict not of an international character" is used here in contradistinction to a conflict between nations. ... Common Article 3, by contrast, affords some minimal protection, falling short of full protection under the Conventions, to individuals associated with neither a signatory nor even a nonsignatory who are involved in a conflict "in the territory of" a signatory. The latter kind of conflict does not involve a clash between nations (whether signatories or not). ...

Common Article 3, then, is applicable here and, as indicated above, requires that Hamdan be tried by a "regularly constituted court affording all the judicial guarantees which are recognized as indispensable by civilized peoples."

1.6.3 ICTY, *Prosecutor* v. *Boškoski and Tarčulovski*, (Judgment), Case No. IT-04-82-T, Trial Chamber II, (10 July 2008)

Note: *The facts of this case are outlined in Section 1.1.7. As to the question whether terrorist acts fall within the ambit of IHL, the ICTY commented as follows:*

190. ... national courts and UN bodies have not discounted acts of a terrorist nature in their consideration of acts amounting to armed conflict. Nothing in the jurisprudence of the Tribunal suggests a different approach should be taken to the issue provided that terrorist acts amount to "protracted violence". In view of the above considerations, the Chamber considers that while isolated acts of terrorism may not reach the threshold of armed conflict, when there is protracted violence of this type, especially where they require the engagement of the armed forces in hostilities, such acts are relevant to assessing the level of intensity with regard to the existence of an armed conflict.

1.6.4 Human Rights Council, *Report of the Special Rapporteur on the Promotion and Protection of Human Rights and Fundamental Freedoms While Countering Terrorism*, Ben Emmerson (11 March 2014) 25th Session, UN Doc. A/HRC/25/59

71. There is thus an urgent and imperative need to reach a consensus between States on, inter alia, the following issues:

... .

(c) Does the international humanitarian law test of intensity of hostilities (which is one of the criteria determining whether a non-international armed conflict exists) require an assessment of the severity and frequency of armed attacks occurring within defined geographical boundaries? In applying the intensity test to a non-State armed group operating transnationally, is it legitimate to aggregate armed attacks occurring in geographically diverse locations in order to determine whether, taken as a whole, they cross the intensity threshold so as to amount to a non-international armed conflict? If it is possible for a State to be engaged in a non-international armed conflict with a non-State armed group operating transnationally, does this imply that a non-international armed conflict can exist which has no finite territorial boundaries?

. . .

(e) Do the pattern and frequency of the armed attacks currently being perpetrated by Al-Qaida, and the various affiliate organizations in different parts of the world that claim allegiance to Al-Qaida, satisfy (or continue to satisfy) the criteria of organization and intensity required under international humanitarian law to qualify as a state of armed conflict?

1.7 OCCUPATION[9]

1.7.1 ICTY, *Prosecutor* v. *M. Naletilić and V. Martinović* (Judgment), Case No. IT-98-34-T, Trial Chamber (31 March 2003)

Note: *The case concerns events between April 1993 and January 1994 during the course of the conflict between the army of Bosnia-Herzegovina and the Croat Defence Council in the area of Mostar in the south-western part of Bosnia-Herzegovina. On the application of IHL to occupation, the ICTY said as follows:*

216. Article 42 of the Hague Regulations provides the following definition of occupation:

> territory is considered occupied when it is actually placed under the authority of the hostile army. The occupation extends only to the territory where such authority has been established and can be exercised.

The Chamber endorses this definition.

1.7.2 ICJ, Case Concerning Armed Activities on the Territory of the Congo (*Democratic Republic of the Congo* v. *Uganda*) (Judgment) [2005] I.C.J. Rep. 168

Note: *In this case, the DRC filed an application instituting proceedings against Uganda alleging acts of armed aggression by Uganda on the territory of the DRC. As to the requirements of occupation, the ICJ commented in the following terms:*

---

[9] See also, Chapter 9.

173. In order to reach a conclusion as to whether a State, the military forces of which are present on the territory of another State as a result of an intervention, is an "occupying Power" in the meaning of the term as understood in the *jus in bello*, the Court must examine whether there is sufficient evidence to demonstrate that the said authority was in fact established and exercised by the intervening State in the areas in question. In the present case the Court will need to satisfy itself that the Ugandan armed forces in the DRC were not only stationed in particular locations but also that they had substituted their own authority for that of the Congolese Government. In that event, any justification given by Uganda for its occupation would be of no relevance; nor would it be relevant whether or not Uganda had established a structured military administration of the territory occupied.

1.8 INTERNATIONAL FORCES AND ARMED CONFLICT

1.8.1 United Nations Forces[10]

1.8.1.1 UN, Secretary-General's Bulletin, *Observance by United Nations Forces of International Humanitarian Law* (6 August 1999) UN Doc. ST/SGB/1999/13
Note: *For the purpose of setting out the principles of IHL applicable to UN forces, the UN Secretary-General issued the following guidance:*

Section 1 – Field of application
1.1 The fundamental principles and rules of international humanitarian law set out in the present bulletin are applicable to United Nations forces when in situations of armed conflict they are actively engaged therein as combatants, to the extent and for the duration of their engagement. They are accordingly applicable in enforcement actions, or in peacekeeping operations when the use of force is permitted in self-defence.

1.8.1.2 UK, British Ministry of Defence, *The Joint Service Manual of the Law of Armed Conflict* (Joint Service Publication 383, 2004 Edition)
14. 3. The extent to which PSO (peace support operations) forces are subject to the law of armed conflict depends upon whether they are party to an armed conflict with the armed forces of a state or an entity which, for these purposes, is treated as a state. . . .

14.5. A PSO force can become party to an armed conflict, and thus subject to the law of armed conflict:

a. where it was mandated from the outset to engage in hostilities with opposing armed forces as part of its mission . . .;
b. where its personnel, though not originally charged with such a task, become involved in hostilities as combatants . . . to such a degree that an armed conflict comes into being between the PSO force and the opposing forces. The latter situation may arise in any type of PSO . . .

---

[10]   As to the status of UN forces, see also Chapter 4 Section 4.4.

14.7 It is not always easy to determine whether a PSO force has become a party to an armed conflict or to fix the precise moment at which that event has occurred . . ..

14.9 A PSO force which has not become a party to an armed conflict is not subject to the law of armed conflict as such.

1.8.1.3 Sudan, *Agreement Between the Government of Sudan and the United Nations Concerning the Status of the United Nations Mission in Sudan* (2005)[11]

6. Without prejudice to the mandate of UNMIS and its international status:

(a) The United Nations shall ensure that UNMIS shall conduct its operations in the territory with full respect for the principles and rules of the general conventions applicable to the conduct of military personnel. These international conventions include the Four Geneva Conventions of 12 August 1949 and their Additional Protocols of 8 June 1977 and the UNESCO Convention of 14 May 1954 on the Protection of Cultural Property in the event of armed conflict;

(b) The Government undertakes to treat at all times the military personnel of UNMIS with full respect for the principles and rules of the general international conventions applicable to the treatment of military personnel. These international conventions include the Four Geneva Conventions of 12 April 1949 and their additional Protocols of 8 June 1977.

(c) UNMIS and the Government shall ensure accordingly that members of the respective military personnel are fully acquainted with the principles and rules of the above-mentioned international instruments.

1.8.1.4 SC, Security Council Resolution 2098 (28 March 2013) UN Doc. S/RES/2098/2013 [MONUSCO-Intervention Brigade]

Note: *Security Council Resolution 2098 created and approved an 'offensive' combat force to undertake targeted operations to 'neutralize and disarm' the 23 March Movement, Congolese rebels and foreign armed groups in eastern Democratic Republic of Congo.*

12 . . . (b) In support of the authorities of the DRC, . . . carry out targeted offensive operations through the Intervention Brigade referred to in paragraph 9 and paragraph 10 above, either unilaterally or jointly with the FARDC, in a robust, highly mobile and versatile manner and in strict compliance with international law, including international humanitarian law and with the human rights due diligence policy on UN-support to non-UN forces (HRDDP)

1.8.1.5 International Law Commission, *Statement by Ms Patricia O'Brien, Under-Secretary-General for Legal Affairs, The Legal Counsel* (Geneva, 23 May 2013)[12] p. 18

By virtue of the tasks foreseen for the Intervention Brigade, it would appear that MONUSCO may end up becoming a party to armed hostilities in the DRC, thus triggering the application of international humanitarian law. This would mean that MONUSCO would be required

---

[11]   www.un.org/en/peacekeeping/missions/unmiss/documents/unmiss_sofa_08082011.pdf.
[12]   http://legal.un.org/ola/media/info_from_lc/ILC%20Legal%20Counsel%20statementrev3may20.pdf.

to conduct its operations in compliance with IHL . . .. In addition, MONUSCO itself would also become subject to the application of IHL. While the law remains somewhat unclear in this area, this may mean that military members of MONUSCO, and any persons taking a direct part in hostilities, may lose their protected status under the Convention on the Safety of United Nations and Associated Personnel.

1.8.1.6 ICTY, *Prosecutor* v. *Radovan Karadžić*, (Judgment), Case No. IT-95-5/18-T, Trial Chamber (24 March 2016)

Note: *Between 26 May and 19 June 1995, the Defendant participated in a joint criminal enterprise which involved taking over 200 UN peacekeepers and military observers hostage in order to compel NATO to cease conducting airstrikes against Bosnian Serb military targets. As to the status of UN peacekeepers, the ICTY said as follows:*

5942. The Accused has argued throughout the case, that the status of the UN personnel at the time of the alleged hostage taking was determinative for a finding on the existence of the crime. He argued that due to the NATO air strikes, the UN personnel were transformed into persons taking active part in the hostilities and thus not entitled to the protections of Common Article 3.

5943. The Chamber finds the Accused's argument in this regard to be unconvincing. As a preliminary matter, the Chamber recalls that the UN and its associated peacekeeping forces were not a party to the conflict. . . . . Accordingly, at the time the UN personnel were detained on 25 and 26 May 1995, they were persons taking no active part in the hostilities and, as such, were afforded the protection of Common Article 3. The NATO air strikes of 25 and 26 May 1995 did not transform the status of all of the UN personnel in BiH into that of persons taking active part in the hostilities. However, even if the UN personnel had been combatants prior to their detention, as the Accused argues, they were in any event rendered *hors de combat* by virtue of their detention and thus were also entitled to the minimum protections guaranteed by Common Article 3. As confirmed by the Appeals Chamber in this case, Common Article 3 applies to the detained UN personnel irrespective of their status prior to detention. Therefore, the Chamber finds that all UN personnel who were detained by the Bosnian Serb Forces were entitled to the protections under Common Article 3, including the prohibition against hostage-taking.

1.8.2 Forces of Other International Organisations

1.8.2.1 AU, *Protocol Relating to the Establishment of the Peace and Security Council of the African Union* (adopted 9 July 2002, entered into force 26 December 2003)

ARTICLE 13 AFRICAN STANDBY FORCE

Training

13. The Commission shall provide guidelines for the training of the civilian and military personnel of national standby contingents at both operational and tactical levels. Training on International Humanitarian Law and International Human Rights Law,

with particular emphasis on the rights of women and children, shall be an integral part of the training of such personnel.

1.8.2.2 Economic Community of Central African States, *Standing Orders of the Central African Multinational Force (FOMAC)* 2002
ARTICLE 11:

The FOMAC shall be deployed in conformity with the basic rules and principles contained in the conventions which codify the International Humanitarian Law including the Conventions of Vienna of 12 August 1949 and their additional Protocols.

1.8.2.3 EU, *Updated European Union Guidelines on Promoting Compliance with International Humanitarian Law (IHL)*, Official Journal of the European Union, 2009/C 303/06, 15.12.2009

2. These Guidelines are in line with the commitment of the EU and its Member States to IHL, and aim to address compliance with IHL by third States, and, as appropriate, non-State actors operating in third States. Whilst the same commitment extends to measures taken by the EU and its Member States to ensure compliance with IHL in their own conduct, including by their own forces, such measures are not covered by these Guidelines ...

5. States are obliged to comply with the rules of IHL to which they are bound by treaty or which form part of customary international law. They may also apply to non-State actors. Such compliance is a matter of international concern.

1.8.2.4 ICTY, *Prosecutor* v. *Đorđević*, (Judgment), Case No. IT-05-87/1-T, Trial Chamber II (23 February 2011)
Note: *Vlastimir Đorđević was indicted for his involvement in war crimes committed by Serbian forces against Kosovo Albanians between March and June 1999. On 24 March 1999 NATO commenced military operations in the Federal Republic of Yugoslavia (FRY) against Serbian forces. As to the existence of an armed conflict between NATO and Serbian forces, the ICTY concluded:*

1580. On 24 March 1999 NATO commenced its military operations in the FRY. On the same day the government of the FRY declared a state of war. On this basis the Chamber is satisfied that from 24 March 1999, until the end of hostilities in June 1999, an international armed conflict existed in Kosovo between Serbian forces and the forces of NATO

1.8.2.5 NATO, *Letter of 23 January 2012 from the NATO Legal Adviser to the Chair of the International Commission of Inquiry on Libya* in Human Rights Council, *Report of the International Commission of Inquiry on Libya* (8 March 2012) 19th Session, UN Doc. A/HRC/19/68, Annex II

... NATO believes that its attentiveness during the course of OUP (Operation United Protector) to a rigorous implementation of the rules of that body of law (IHL) – and, indeed, to a standard exceeding what was required by international humanitarian law – contributed significantly to an extraordinary low incidence of harm to civilians and civilian property.

1.9 CYBER WAR

1.9.1 M.N. Schmitt (ed.), *Tallinn Manual on the International Law Applicable to Cyber Warfare* (CUP, 2013), pp. 79, 84

RULE 22 – Characterization as International Armed Conflict

An international armed conflict exists whenever there are hostilities, which may include or be limited to cyber operations, occurring between two or more States.

RULE 23 – Characterization as Non-International Armed Conflict

A non-international armed conflict exists when there is protracted armed violence, which may include or be limited to cyber operations, occurring between governmental armed forces and the forces of one or more armed groups, or between such groups. The confrontation must reach a minimum level of intensity and the parties involved in the conflict must show a minimum degree of organization.

COMMENTARY

1. The classification of armed conflicts is important for legal, political and operational purposes because of the different body of rules that apply to each category. As the ICTY held in *Tadić*, an armed conflict exists when there is a resort to armed force. Armed force is the use of means and methods of warfare which cause or are intended to cause loss of life, injury, damage or destruction. Whether an armed conflict is an IAC or a NIAC depends on the status of the parties to the conflict. It should be noted, however, that armed conflicts can be mixed, implicating both regimes, or they may occupy a continuum. For this reason, the classification of an armed conflict cannot be a one-off event, but must be a continuous one.

2. The existence of an armed conflict is a factual determination but, inevitably, facts need to be identified and assessed, such as, for instance, the intensity of violence or the level of organisation of an armed group. As a result, subjectivity and political considerations may creep in, with States and armed groups disputing the existence or the construction of facts. Although recognition of States or governments does not in principle play a role in the classification of an armed conflict, it often becomes relevant in situations of turmoil where different factions claim to represent the government of a State, as the cases of Libya or Syria show. Uncertainty in the determination and classification of armed conflicts is exacerbated by the lack of a central authority to make such determinations, with the ICRC[13] or the UN often playing such a role.

3. The question of whether a minimum degree of intensity and/or belligerent intent are required in order for an IAC to arise is contentious.[14] According to the prevalent view, any

---

[13] See ICRC Operational Update, 17 July 2012, which states: 'the ICRC concludes that there is currently a non-international (internal) armed conflict occurring in Syria opposing Government Forces and a number of organised armed opposition groups operating in several parts of the country (including, but not limited to, Homs, Idlib and Hama)', www.icrc.org/eng/resources/documents/update/2012/syria-update-2012-07-17.htm.
[14] See, for example, the US Law of War Manual (Department of Defense, Office of General Counsel (June 2015, updated 2016)).

resort to armed force irrespective of intensity or intent triggers an IAC. In this way, the determination of the existence of an IAC becomes relatively objective but the risk of mischaracterizing incidents and of applying IHL too quickly arises. Requiring a minimum degree of intensity as well as belligerent intent can prevent such risks. Often these criteria can be deduced from the same facts; for example, grave uses of armed force can demonstrate both intensity and belligerent intent but, otherwise, intent can be inferred from the nature of the action and all the surrounding circumstances. That said, deciphering intent is not an easy exercise and there is no clarity as to what the required threshold of intensity should be. If intensity and intent are, however, accepted as elements in determining the existence of an armed conflict, unilateral uses of armed force can initiate an IAC if they satisfy these criteria.

4. For a NIAC to exist, two main conditions need to be fulfilled: intensity of violence and organisation of the armed groups.[15] International jurisprudence has identified a number of qualitative and quantitative factors that can be taken into account when determining the required threshold of intensity. It has also identified four main factors in assessing the level of organisation of armed groups: command structure; ability to conduct coordinated military operations; logistics; and ability to respect and ensure respect for IHL. Yet, the question that can be asked is whether intensity and organisation should be demonstrated from the outset in order for a NIAC to arise or whether this is something that can only be determined retrospectively. Another question is whether a unilateral use of armed force can initiate a NIAC. If intensity refers to the gravity of violence per se and not to the gravity of the exchanges between parties, then recourse by a State *or* an armed group to grave armed force would satisfy this criterion. It should be noted, however, that current definitions of NIAC require exchanges between and among States and armed groups. Whether belligerent intent is required seems to be critical in order to distinguish an armed conflict from violent criminal acts perpetrated by armed groups or from law enforcement action against armed groups.

5. Under what circumstances the use of proxies by States transforms a NIAC into an IAC is a fraught issue. The *ad hoc* tribunals and the ICC employ the 'overall control' criterion introduced by the ICTY in the *Tadić* case,[16] but other standards may also be employed such as that of effective control.[17] The question is whether IHL should develop its own standards or rely on standards developed in other areas of the law such as the law of State responsibility. On our view, the 'overall control' standard describes in a more holistic manner the relationship between a State and armed groups and for this reason it is the most appropriate test.

6. The classification of armed conflict when a State conducts operations against armed groups on the territory of another State is complex. The Syrian conflict is such an example where States such as the United States or Russia fight ISIS, an armed group, on Syrian territory. According to one line of reasoning, the conflict between intervening States and

---

[15] See also the 2016 ICRC Commentary on Common Article 3, https://ihl-databases.icrc.org/applic/ihl/ihl.nsf/Comment.xsp?action=openDocument&documentId=59F6CDFA490736C1C1257F7D004BA0EC. APII has some additional conditions such as territorial control.
[16] See, for example: *The Prosecutor* v. *Lubanga*, ICC, Case No. ICC-01/04-01/06 and *The Prosecutor* v. *Bemba*, ICC, Case No. ICC-01/05/01/08 66/364.
[17] See: *Case Concerning Military and Paramilitary Activities in and Against Nicaragua (Nicaragua* v. *United States of America)* (Merits, Judgment) [1986] I.C.J. Rep. 14.

armed groups is a NIAC, but if the territorial State has not consented to the operation, an IAC also arises between the intervening States and the territorial State, even if the latter's assets or people are not directly targeted. According to another line of reasoning, there is no separate IAC to the extent that the territorial State's assets are not involved. According to the 2016 ICRC's Commentary on Common Article 2 GCs, non-consensual as well as unilateral uses of force by a State on the territory of another State initiate an IAC.[18] There are some difficulties with this line of reasoning because it introduces *jus ad bellum* criteria into the determination of armed conflicts. It also classifies armed conflicts according to what triggers them and not according to the status of the parties. Furthermore, it should be recalled that territory and people in such cases are controlled by armed groups and not by the territorial State.[19] For these reasons, in our opinion, it is only when the territorial and intervening State are engaged in hostilities or the former's assets are deliberately targeted that a parallel IAC arises.

7. When an armed conflict has come to an end is important for the temporal application of IHL,[20] but it is particularly challenging in situations of occupation and in NIACs.[21] The end of conflict depends on whether military operations have been brought to a close on a stable and permanent basis regardless of whether a peace treaty has been concluded. Thus, a long-lasting ceasefire will end an armed conflict if hostilities do not resume whereas a peace treaty may not end an armed conflict if hostilities continue. It thus transpires that it is often the passage of time that will determine this question. For example, was the armed conflict between the United States and Iraq terminated following the 1991 ceasefire resolution?[22] If intensity is a requirement for NIACs and possibly for IACs, does decreased intensity bring the armed conflict to an end and what is the time span for such a determination to the extent that violence may flare up? With regard to cyber conflicts, does the presence of viruses or logic bombs in a State's critical national infrastructure indicate the continuation of a cyber conflict? The existence of parallel conflicts can complicate the determination of the end of an armed conflict even further. Be that as it may, it should be noted that the end of an armed conflict does not necessarily mean the complete disapplication of IHL because certain of its provisions continue to operate.

8. Defining the territorial scope of armed conflict is also critical for the application of IHL. It is broadly held that IHL applies to the whole territory of the parties involved in an IAC or a NIAC. Yet, in light of the concurrent application of IHRL, the question of which IHL rules apply and how they apply outside the 'battlefield' has been posed.[23] This question is particularly important in cases of extraterritorial NIACs.[24]

---

[18] https://ihl-databases.icrc.org/applic/ihl/ihl.nsf/Comment.xsp?action=openDocument&documentId=BE2D518CF5DE54EAC1257F7D0036B518.
[19] See T.D. Gill, 'Classifying the Conflict in Syria' (2016) 92 *Int'l L. Stud.* 353.
[20] For example, in relation to POWs or detainees.
[21] See Chapter 9 in relation to occupation and Chapter 10 in relation to NIACs.
[22] See SC Resolution 687 (8 April 1991) UN Doc. S/RES/687, but also SC Resolution 686 (2 March 1991) UN Doc. S/RES/686, Preamble.
[23] See Chapter 3. Also see ICRC, Nils Melzer, Legal Adviser (ICRC), *Interpretive Guidance on the Notion of Direct Participation in Hostilities under International Humanitarian Law*, Recommendation IX (Geneva, May 2009).
[24] See Chapter 10 for NIACs.

9. It is now broadly accepted that IHL applies to UN peacekeeping operations but when it applies and what are the modalities of its application are not always clear. Is, for example, the threshold for the application of IHL to UN peacekeeping forces higher than the one provided in Common Articles 2 and 3 GCs? Should UN forces be deployed in the course of an armed conflict in order for IHL to apply as the Secretary-General's Bulletin of 1999 seems to require? Should they act beyond self-defence by engaging other parties in order for IHL to apply? Does IHL apply when UN forces provide support to a government engaged in a NIAC? Does IHL apply to the whole mission or only to its military component and is this for the entire duration of the operation? Is it the UN or the troop-contributing countries that become parties to the armed conflict? In response to these questions, it is submitted that IHL applies to UN forces as soon as the conditions of Common Articles 2 or 3 are met.[25] It has been contended in this respect that the involvement of UN forces automatically transforms the armed conflict into an IAC, mainly because of the latter's comprehensive system of protections. The better view, however, is to maintain the differentiated classification of armed conflicts depending on whether the UN forces engage States or armed groups. Furthermore, the view that logistical, intelligence or other support provided by the UN mission to a State that is party to a pre-existing NIAC transforms the UN into a party to the armed conflict to the extent that such assistance impacts on the opponent's ability to carry out military operations lowers dangerously the criteria for the application of IHL.[26] When the application of IHL is triggered, it is the UN force that becomes party to the armed conflict and not the troop-contributing countries provided that the force remains under UN command and control. This means that military members of the UN force become combatants and remain combatants for the entire duration of the UN mission whereas civilian members of the force are protected from attacks unless they directly participate in hostilities.[27] The status of forces of other international organisations may differ depending on the level and degree of command and control that the organisation and/or the troop-contributing countries exercise over the troops.

10. Wars of self-determination are classified as IAC, but there are questions as to whether Article 1(4) API represents customary law since many States have expressed opposition to this rule. Moreover, the scope of this article is limited to situations that nowadays are not very common such as colonial domination or alien occupation. There are also questions as to whether the national liberation group needs to be recognised as

---

[25]   UN, Department of Peacekeeping Operations and Department of Field Support, Authority, Command and Control in UN Peacekeeping Operations, 15 February 2008, Ref. 2008.4, p. 24 and Art. 7, Articles on the Responsibility of International Organizations. Responsibility of International Organizations: Comments and Observations Received from International Organizations, UN Doc. A/CN.4/637/Add.1, 17 February 2011, p. 10. NATO, Allied Joint Doctrine, AJP-01 (D), December 2010, available at: www.gov.uk/government/uploads/system/uploads/attachment_data/file/33694/AJP01D.pdf. See also, NATO Allied Joint Doctrine for the Conduct of Operations, AJP-3 (B), March 2011, available at: www.cicde.defense.gouv.fr/IMG/pdf/20110316_np_otan_ajp-3b.pdf. In cases where the international organization (IO) has no legal personality or command and control is shared between States and the IO, it can be said that the troop-contributing country (TCC) become parties or that both the IO and the TCC become parties as in the case of NATO.

[26]   See T. Ferraro, 'The Applicability and Application of International Humanitarian Law to Multinational Forces' (2013) 95 *IRRC*, 561–612.

[27]   See also Chapter 4 Sections 4.2 and 4.4 and Chapter 5 Section 5.11.

such and whether it should be able to implement its API obligations in order for the conflict to be categorised as IAC.

11. The classification of conflicts involving terrorist groups is complicated. In the first place it should be noted that the political designation of a group as 'terrorist' does not remove it from the purview of IHL if its conditions are satisfied. Thus, if the terrorist group belongs to a State which is party to an IAC in the sense of Article 4(A)(2) GCIII, the conflict is international, but, evidently, such groups will not satisfy all the conditions laid down in Article 4(A)(2) GCIII.[28] For a NIAC to arise, there needs to be violence of certain intensity and the terrorist group needs to have some level of organisation. Neither criterion is easily satisfied by terrorist groups, which are often amorphous; their leadership or organisation is hazy or decentralized; and terrorist attacks may be sporadic or less intense. In this respect, the question can be asked as to whether a series of terrorist attacks can reach the level of intensity needed for a NIAC. A related question is how such attacks can be linked to each other, in particular when they are perpetrated by associated, affiliated or splinter groups. Furthermore, APII requires control over territory,[29] which is not what terrorist groups do. The *Hamdan* decision categorised the conflict with Al-Qaida as NIAC, but the Court did not specifically address the criteria for the existence of a NIAC in Common Article 3, neither did it consider whether said terrorist group is able to comply with Common Article 3 obligations. In the *Targeted Killing Case*, instead, the Israeli Supreme Court characterised the conflict with a terrorist group as international when it involves crossing a frontier. This view is not, however, convincing.

12. The classification of cyber conflicts is fraught with difficulties. Are cyber-attacks equivalent to armed force? Do they trigger IHL only if they produce physical consequences and should these be directly caused by the attack? Does loss of functionality constitute resort to armed force? What should the relationship between a State and individuals or cyber groups be in order to trigger an IAC and how can it be proven? Can 'online' cyber groups satisfy the organisation criteria laid down in jurisprudence? Can there be command and control if members are not known or visible? Can there be enforcement of IHL having legal and factual consequences in the absence of physical control? Can cyber groups control territory in order for APII to apply? Answers to these questions are not always conclusive and there is no relevant State practice to provide direction and clarification. In our opinion, it is not only physical consequences, but also severe loss of functionality that can trigger a cyber armed conflict. It is also our view that purely virtual groups cannot satisfy the requirements of organisation.

13. Uncertainty in the classification of conflicts due to their complexity can cause many legal, political and operational difficulties. Questions have been asked as to whether the dual classification of armed conflicts is adequate to achieve the aims of IHL or whether a single regime is more appropriate. The current dual classification has been challenged by the development of customary rules that apply to both types of conflicts as demonstrated by

---

[28]   See Chapter 6, Section 6.1.
[29]   Art. 1, APII.

the 2005 ICRC *Study on Customary International Humanitarian Law*[30] as well as by the jurisprudence of *ad hoc* tribunals exemplified in the *Tadić* judgment.[31] Convergence between the two regimes is also evident in certain treaties that apply to both types of conflict.[32] At a more conceptual level, the dichotomy of armed conflicts has been challenged by the development of IHRL and its application to armed conflicts.[33] However, attempts at convergence need to be viewed against persistent State opposition expressed, for example, during the debates surrounding the 1977 Additional Protocols or treaties such as the Rome Statute of the International Criminal Court. Questions may also be asked as to whether such convergence is actually feasible vis-à-vis armed groups, which may not have the resources or capacity to comply with obligations (in particular positive ones) transposed from IACs. The law of occupation and the law of neutrality also pose challenges to any convergence since they apply in relation to a particular type of conflict. Finally, it should be noted that the effectiveness of IHL protections is based on clear distinctions between peace and war, and combatants and civilians, which are not always apparent (at least in NIACs).

14. The legal difficulties in classification are often overcome by political fiat. Certain States such as the United States apply IHL to all armed conflicts as a matter of policy; however, they do this without specifying which rules and principles apply.[34] The policy fills legal gaps and provides flexibility on the one hand, but, on the other, it can still cause legal uncertainty as far as the application of specific rules is concerned.

---

[30]   ICRC, *Customary International Humanitarian Law, Vol. I: Rules*, Jean-Marie Henckaerts and Louise Doswald-Beck (eds) (Cambridge University Press, 2005).
[31]   See *Tadić* judgment, Chapter 1, Section 1.1.1.
[32]   Convention on Prohibitions or Restrictions on the Use of Certain Conventional Weapons Which May be Deemed to be Excessively Injurious or to Have Indiscriminate Effects (2001), Art. 1; Arts 3, 18, 22 Second Protocol to The Hague Convention of 1954 for the Protection of Cultural Property in the Event of Armed Conflict of 26 March 1999.
[33]   See Chapter 3.
[34]   See DoD Directive 2311.01E (19 August 2014).

2

Fundamental Principles of International Humanitarian Law

INTRODUCTION

International humanitarian law is based on two foundational principles: the principle of humanity and the principle of military necessity. The principle of humanity attempts to 'humanise' the conduct of war by imposing limits on the means and methods of warfare, by according protection to certain categories of persons, by requiring humane treatment of captured persons and, in general, by limiting or mitigating unnecessary suffering. The principle of humanity was first proclaimed in the context of armed conflicts by Professor de Martens, the Russian Delegate to the Hague Peace Conferences of 1899, and for this reason it is often referred to as the Martens Principle or the Martens Clause. The principle of military necessity allows a belligerent to use lawful means and methods of war in order to overpower an enemy. The principles of humanity and military necessity inform all the rules of humanitarian law and, in cases of doubt, they assist in the interpretation of IHL rules. Two other principles that derive from the principles of humanity and military necessity are the principle of distinction and the principle of proportionality. According to the principle of distinction, parties to the conflict should at all times distinguish civilians and civilian objects from combatants and military objectives and afford protection to the former. According to the principle of proportionality, any harm caused by military action to civilians and civilian objects should not exceed the anticipated military advantage expected from the operation. The content and scope of these principles, and how they interact with each other in general or in particular situations, are important issues to be examined in this chapter but also in subsequent chapters.[1]

Resources: Preamble and Art. 6, Hague Convention II (HCII); Art. 5, Hague Convention V (HCV); Common Article 3, GCs; Arts 12 and 63, Geneva Convention I (GCI); Arts 12 and 62, Geneva Convention II (GCII); Arts 4, 13, 55 and 142, Geneva Convention III (GCIII); Arts 27 and 158, Geneva Convention IV (GCIV); Arts 1, 35, 43, 48–51 and 57, API; Arts 4 and 17, APII

---

[1] For a more detailed analysis of these principles see Chapters 4 to 7.

Cases and Materials

2.1 THE PRINCIPLE OF HUMANITY

2.1.1 HC II, *Convention (II) with Respect to the Laws and Customs of War on Land and Its Annex: Regulations Concerning the Laws and Customs of War on Land* (adopted 29 July 1899, entered into force 4 September 1900)

Preamble . . .

Until a more complete code of the laws of war is issued, the High Contracting Parties think it right to declare that in cases not included in the Regulations adopted by them, populations and belligerents remain under the protection and empire of the principles of international law, as they result from the usages established between civilized nations, from the laws of humanity and the requirements of the public conscience.

2.1.2 API, *Protocol Additional to the Geneva Conventions of 12 August 1949, and relating to the Protection of Victims of International Armed Conflicts (Protocol I)* (adopted 8 June 1977, entered into force 7 December 1978)

1(2) In cases not covered by this Protocol or by other international agreements, civilians and combatants remain under the protection and authority of the principles of international law derived from established custom, from the principles of humanity and from the dictates of public conscience.

2.1.3 ICTY, *Prosecutor* v. *Kupreškić et al.*, (Judgment), Case No. IT–95–16–T, Trial Chamber (14 January 2000)

Note: *The accused were indicted for grave breaches of the GCs as well as violations of the laws and customs of war when in October 1992 and April 1993 they directly participated in attacks of mainly Muslim villages including the village of Ahmici in the Lašva River Valley in Bosnia-Herzegovina. The attacks on Ahmici were particularly ferocious and involved HVO soldiers shelling the villages from a distance before moving from house to house attacking civilians* *using tracer rounds and explosives. Every Muslim house was burned down and unarmed Muslim civilians were systematically shot. On the issue of humanity and how it assists in the interpretation of IHL, the Chamber held as follows:*

525. More specifically, recourse might be had to the celebrated Martens Clause which, ..., has by now become part of customary international law. True, this Clause may not be taken to mean that the "principles of humanity" and the "dictates of public conscience" have been elevated to the rank of independent sources of international law, for this conclusion is belied by international practice. However, this Clause enjoins, as a minimum, reference to those principles and dictates any time a rule of international humanitarian law is not sufficiently rigorous or precise: in those instances the scope and purport of the rule must be defined with reference to those principles and dictates.

2.2 THE PRINCIPLE OF MILITARY NECESSITY

2.2.1 *Declaration Renouncing the Use, in Time of War, of Explosive Projectiles Under 400 Grammes Weight* (St Petersburg Declaration) (adopted on 29 November 1868, entered into force 11 December 1868)

... Undersigned are authorized by the orders of their Governments to declare as follows: Considering:

That the progress of civilization should have the effect of alleviating as much as possible the calamities of war;

That the only legitimate object which States should endeavour to accomplish during war is to weaken the military forces of the enemy;

That for this purpose it is sufficient to disable the greatest possible number of men;

That this object would be exceeded by the employment of arms which uselessly aggravate the sufferings of disabled men, or render their death inevitable;

That the employment of such arms would, therefore, be contrary to the laws of humanity...

2.2.2 US, *General Orders No. 100: Instructions for the Government of Armies of the United States in the Field* (Lieber Code) (adopted 24 April 1863)

Art 14

Military necessity, as understood by modern civilized nations, consists in the necessity of those measures which are indispensable for securing the ends of the war, and which are lawful according to the modern law and usages of war.

2.2.3 US Military Tribunal, *United States* v. *Wilhelm List et al.*, Case No. 47 (Nuremberg, 19 February 1948) Law Reports of Trials of War Criminals, Vol. VIII (1949), p. 66

Note: *The accused were charged with war crimes and crimes against humanity during the occupation of Greece, Yugoslavia, Albania and Norway. On the issue of military necessity, the Tribunal found:*

Military necessity permits a belligerent, subject to the laws of war, to apply any amount and kind of force to compel the complete submission of the enemy with the least possible expenditure of time, life, and money. .... It permits the destruction of life of armed enemies and other persons whose destruction is incidentally unavoidable by the armed conflicts of the war; it allows the capturing of armed enemies and others of peculiar danger, but it does not permit the killing of innocent inhabitants for purposes of revenge or the satisfaction of a lust to kill. The destruction of property to be lawful must be imperatively demanded by the necessities of war. Destruction as an end in itself is a violation of international law. There must be some reasonable connection between the destruction of property and the overcoming of the enemy forces. It is lawful to destroy railways, lines of communication, or any other property that might be utilized by the enemy. Private homes and churches even may be destroyed if necessary for military operations. It does not admit the wanton devastation of a district or the wilful infliction of suffering upon its inhabitants for the sake of suffering alone.

It is apparent from the evidence of these defendants that they considered military necessity, a matter to be determined by them, a complete justification of their acts. We do not concur in the view that the rules of warfare are anything less than they purport to be. Military necessity or expediency do not justify a violation of positive rules. International law is prohibitive law. Articles 46, 47, and 50 of the Hague Regulations of 1907 make no such exceptions to its enforcement. The rights of the innocent population therein set forth must be respected even if military necessity or expediency decree otherwise.

2.2.4 US Military Tribunal, *US* v. *Wilhelm Von Leeb et al.*, Case No. 72 (Nuremberg, 27–28 October 1948) Law Reports of Trials of War Criminals, Vol. XII (1949), pp. 93–4

Note: *The Tribunal considered the criminal responsibility of the accused for crimes against peace, war crimes, crimes against humanity and conspiracy to commit such crimes. On the issue of compulsory use of civilian labour in occupied territories and seizure of property, the Tribunal said as follows:*

It was pointed out, however, by the Tribunal that "the doctrine of military necessity has been widely urged. In the various treatises on International Law there has been much discussion on this question. It has been the viewpoint of many German writers and to a certain extent has been contended in this case that military necessity includes the right to do anything that contributes to the winning of a war."

The Tribunal expressed itself as follows:

"We content ourselves on this subject with stating that such a view would eliminate all humanity and decency and all law from the conduct of war and it is a contention which this Tribunal repudiates as contrary to the accepted usages of civilized nations. Nor does military necessity justify the compulsory recruitment of labour from an occupied territory either for use in military operations or for transfer to the Reich, nor does it justify the seizure of property or goods beyond that which is necessary for the use of the army of occupation. Looting and spoliation are none the less criminal in that they were conducted, not by individuals, but by the army and the State."

"The devastation prohibited by the Hague Rules and the usages of war is that not warranted by military necessity. This rule is clear enough but the factual determination as to what constitutes military necessity is difficult. Defendants in this case were in many instances in retreat under arduous conditions wherein their commands were in serious danger of being cut off. Under such circumstances, a commander must necessarily make quick decisions to meet the particular situation of his command. A great deal of latitude must be accorded to him under such circumstances. What constitutes devastation beyond military necessity in these situations requires detailed proof of an operational and tactical nature. We do not feel that in this case the proof is ample to establish the guilt of any defendant herein on this charge."

2.2.5 Israel, *Beit Sourik Village Council* v. *The Government of Israel and Commander of the IDF Forces in the West Bank,* (Judgment) Case No. HCJ 2056/04, Israeli Supreme Court Sitting as the High Court of Justice (2 May 2004)

Note: *The petition in this case challenged the legality of the seizure orders issued by the Commander of the Israel Defense Forces (IDF) to facilitate the erection of a separation fence on private land. The Court said as follows:*

32. ... Regarding the central question raised before us, our opinion is that the military commander is authorized – by the international law applicable to an area under belligerent occupation – to take possession of land, if this is necessary for the needs of the army. ... The construction of the separation fence falls within this framework. The infringement of property rights is insufficient, in and of itself, to take away the authority to build it. It is permitted, by the international law applicable to an area under belligerent occupation, to take possession of an individual's land in order to erect the separation fence upon it, on the condition that this is necessitated by military needs. To the extent that construction of the fence is a military necessity, it is permitted, therefore, by international law.

2.2.6 ICJ, *Legal Consequences of the Construction of a Wall in the Occupied Palestinian Territory* (Advisory Opinion) [2004] I.C.J. Rep. 136

Note: *Among other issues, it appeared on the evidence that the construction of the wall by Israel had led to the destruction and requisitioning of properties in the Palestinian occupied territories.*

The ICJ considered whether such actions could be justified on the ground of military necessity. The Court said as follows:

135. The Court would observe, however, that the applicable international humanitarian law contains provisions enabling account to be taken of military exigencies in certain circumstances.

... As to Article 53 [GCIV] concerning the destruction of personal property, it provides for an exception "where such destruction is rendered absolutely necessary by military operations".

... However, on the material before it, the Court is not convinced that the destructions carried out contrary to the prohibition in Article 53 of the Fourth Geneva Convention were rendered absolutely necessary by military operations.

2.2.7 ICTY, *Prosecutor* v. *Milan Martić*, (Judgment), Case No. IT-95-11-T, Trial Chamber I (12 June 2007)

Note: *During the course of the conflict between Serb and Croat forces in Krajina, public and private property was intentionally destroyed and plundered. In assessing whether the destruction of property can be justified on grounds of military necessity, the Trial Chamber said as follows:*

93. ... military necessity may justify the infliction of collateral damage to civilian objects and as such constitutes an exception to the principles of the protection of civilian objects. The protection of civilian objects may cease entirely or be reduced or suspended when belligerents cannot avoid causing collateral damage to civilian property even though the object of a military attack is comprised of military objectives. ... An assertion of military necessity or the absence thereof will be assessed on a case-by-case basis. In principle, destruction carried out before fighting begins or after fighting has ceased cannot be justified by claiming military necessity.

2.2.8 UK, British Ministry of Defence, *The Joint Service Manual of the Law of Armed Conflict* (Joint Service Publication 383, 2004 Edition)

2.2. Military necessity permits a state engaged in an armed conflict to use only that degree and kind of force, not otherwise prohibited by the law of armed conflict, that is required in order to achieve the legitimate purpose of the conflict, the complete or partial submission of the enemy at the earliest possible moment with the minimum expenditure of life and resources.

2.2.1 The principle of military necessity contains four basic elements:

a. the force used can be and is being controlled;

b. since military necessity permits the use of force only if it is 'not otherwise prohibited by the law of armed conflict', necessity cannot excuse a departure from that law;

c. the use of force in ways which are not otherwise prohibited is legitimate if it is necessary to achieve, as quickly as possible, the complete or partial submission of the enemy;

d. conversely, the use of force which is not necessary is unlawful, since it involves wanton killing or destruction.

2.2.9 Germany, Federal Ministry of Defence, *Law of Armed Conflict – Manual – Joint Service Regulation (ZDv) 15/2* (May 2013)

142. LOAC is a compromise between military and humanitarian requirements. Its rules take account of both military necessity and the dictates of humanity. Considerations of military necessity can therefore not justify a departure from the rules of humanitarian law; to seek a military advantage using forbidden means is not permissible.

2.2.10 ICC, *The Prosecutor* v. *Germain Katanga*, (Judgment Pursuant to Article 74 of the Statute), Case No. ICC-01/04-01/07, Trial Chamber II (7 March 2014)

Note: *Germain Katanga was the former leader of the Patriotic Resistance Force (FRPI), an armed opposition group in the Democratic Republic of Congo. Katanga was accused of war crimes and crimes against humanity in relation to an attack on the village of Bogoro in the Ituri district of DRC, which included destruction of enemy property and pillaging. On the question whether destruction of enemy property was justified by reasons of military necessity, the ICC said:*

894. The destruction of property therefore does not constitute a crime under article 8(2)(e) (xii) of the Statute where such destruction is justified by military necessity. . . . The Chamber observes that only "imperative" reasons of military necessity, where the perpetrator has no other option in this regard, could justify acts of destruction which would otherwise be proscribed by this provision. To determine whether the destruction of property fell within military necessity, the Chamber will conduct a case-by-case assessment by considering, for example, whether the destroyed property was defended or whether specific property was destroyed.

2.2.11 US, Department of Defense, *Law of War Manual*, Office of General Counsel (June 2015, Updated 2016)

2.2 MILITARY NECESSITY

Military necessity may be defined as the principle that justifies the use of all measures needed to defeat the enemy as quickly and efficiently as possible that are not prohibited by the law of war. . . .

    2.2.2.1 *Military Necessity Does Not Justify Actions Prohibited by the Law of War.*

    Military necessity does not justify actions that are prohibited by the law of war. . . .

    Military necessity cannot justify departures from the law of war because States have crafted the law of war specifically with war's exigencies in mind. In devising law of war rules, States considered military requirements. Thus, prohibitions on conduct in the law of war may be understood to reflect States' determinations that such conduct is militarily unnecessary *per se*.

2.3 INTERACTION BETWEEN THE PRINCIPLE OF HUMANITY AND THE PRINCIPLE OF MILITARY NECESSITY

2.3.1 Japan, *Ryuichi Shimoda et al.* v. *The State*, District Court of Tokyo (7 December 1963) 32 ILR 626, pp. 627–630

Note: *Residents of Hiroshima and Nagasaki brought a joint action against the Japanese government for damages suffered as a consequence of the use of atomic bombs by the United States in August 1945. It was alleged the use of such bombs was an unlawful act and the waiver by the Japanese government of claims, in domestic and international law, against the United States for damages, imposed on Japan an obligation to meet the claims.*

It can naturally be assumed that the use of a new weapon is legal as long as international law does not prohibit it. However, the prohibition in this context is to be understood to include not only the case where there is an express rule of direct prohibition, but also the case where the prohibition can be implied *de plano* from the interpretation and application by analogy of existing rules of international law. ...

Any weapon the use of which is contrary to the customs of civilized countries and to the principles of international law should *ipso facto* be deemed to be prohibited even if there is no express provision in the law; the new weapon may be used as a legal means of hostilities only if is not contrary to the legal principles of international law. ...

For the international law of war is not formulated simply on the basis of humanitarian feelings. It has at its basis both consideration of military necessity and effectiveness and humanitarian considerations, and is formulated on a balance of these two factors. ... It is doubtful whether the atomic bomb with its tremendous destructive power was appropriate from the viewpoint of military effect and was really necessary at that time. ... Indeed, the act of dropping this bomb may be regarded as contrary to the fundamental principle of the law of war which prohibits the causing of unnecessary suffering.

2.3.2 Israel, *The Public Committee against Torture in Israel et al.* v. *The Government of Israel et al.* ('Targeted Killing Case'), (Judgment) Case No. HCJ 769/02, Israeli Supreme Court Sitting as the High Court of Justice (11 December 2005)

Note: *The facts of this case are set out in Chapter 1, Section 1.6.1. As to the interaction of the principles of humanity and military necessity, the High Court commented as follows:*

22. The international law dealing with armed conflicts is based upon a delicate balance between two contradictory considerations. ... One consists of the humanitarian considerations regarding those harmed as a result of an armed conflict. These considerations are based upon the rights of the individual, and his dignity. The other consists of military need and success. ... The balance between these considerations is the basis of international law of armed conflict.

2.3.3 US, Department of Defense, *Law of War Manual*, Office of General Counsel (June 2015, Updated 2016)

2.1.2.3 *Law of War Principles as a Coherent System.* Law of war principles work as interdependent and reinforcing parts of a coherent system.

Military necessity justifies certain actions necessary to defeat the enemy as quickly and efficiently as possible. Conversely, *humanity* forbids actions unnecessary to achieve that object. *Proportionality* requires that even when actions may be justified by *military necessity*, such actions not be unreasonable or excessive. *Distinction* underpins the parties' responsibility to comport their behavior with *military necessity, humanity*, and *proportionality* by requiring parties to a conflict to apply certain legal categories, principally the distinction between the armed forces and the civilian population. Lastly, *honor* supports the entire system and gives parties confidence in it.

2.4 THE PRINCIPLE OF DISTINCTION[2]

2.4.1 Colombia, *Constitutional Conformity of Protocol II, The Principle of Distinction Between Combatants and Non-Combatants*, Ruling No. C-225/95, Re: File No. L.A.T.-040, Colombian Constitutional Court (18 May 1995)[3]

28. One of the basic rules of international humanitarian law is the principle of distinction according to which the parties in conflict must differentiate between combatants and non-combatants, since the latter may never be the targets of acts of war. There is an elementary reason for this: although war seeks to weaken the enemy's military capacity, it may not target those who do not actively participate in the hostilities – either because they have never taken up arms (civilian population), or because they have ceased to be combatants (disarmed enemy troops) – since they are not military personnel. The law of armed conflicts therefore considers that military attacks against such persons are unlawful, as stated in Article 48 of Protocol I, . . .

Article 4 of the treaty [APII] under review takes up this rule, which is essential in introducing an effective measure of humanity in any armed conflict, . . .

30. The distinction between combatants and non-combatants has fundamental consequences. Firstly, as stated in the rule regarding immunity of the civilian population (Art. 13 APII), the parties have the general obligation to protect civilians from the dangers arising from military operations. From this follows, as stated in paragraph 2 of this same article, that the civilian population as such may not be the object of attack, and acts or threats of violence the primary purpose of which is to spread terror are prohibited. General protection of the civilian population from the dangers of war also implies that it is not in keeping with international humanitarian law for one of the parties to involve

---

[2] See also Chapters 4 and 5.
[3] https://casebook.icrc.org/case-study/colombia-constitutional-conformity-protocol-ii.

the population in the armed conflict, as in so doing it would turn civilians into participants in the conflict and would thus expose them to military attacks by the adverse party.

31. This general protection of the civilian population also covers objects indispensable to the latter's survival, which are not military objectives (Art. 14 APII). Cultural objects and places of worship (Art. 16 APII) may not be used for military purposes or be the object of attack, and it is prohibited to attack works and installations containing dangerous forces, if such attack may cause severe losses among the civilian population (Art. 15 APII). Finally, Protocol II also prohibits ordering the displacement of the civilian population for reasons related to the conflict, unless the security of civilians or imperative military reasons so demand. In the latter case, the Protocol states that "all possible measures shall be taken in order that the civilian population may be received under satisfactory conditions of shelter, health, hygiene, safety and nutrition" (Art. 17 APII).

32. Humanitarian protection extends, without discrimination, to the wounded, the sick and the shipwrecked, whether or not they have taken part in hostilities. . . .

These rules providing for humanitarian assistance to the wounded, the sick and the shipwrecked obviously imply that guarantees and immunities must be granted to persons entrusted with giving such aid; Protocol II thus protects medical and religious personnel (Art. 9), medical duties (Art. 10) and medical units and transports (Arts 11 and 12), which must be respected at all times by the parties in conflict.

34. The Court does not share the rather confused argument put forward by one of the speakers that the protection of the civilian population is unconstitutional since combatants could use the population as a shield, thereby exposing it "to suffer the consequences of the conflict". On the contrary, the Court considers that, pursuant to the principle of distinction, the parties to the conflict may not use and endanger the civilian population in order to gain a military advantage, as that contradicts their obligations to afford general protection to the civilian population and to direct their military operations exclusively against military objectives.

2.4.2 ICJ, *Legality of the Threat or Use of Nuclear Weapons* (Advisory Opinion) [1996] I.C.J. Rep. 226

Note: *The ICJ responded to a request from the General Assembly of the United Nations (Resolution 49/75K of 15 December 1994) that it provide its opinion on the question whether 'the threat or use of nuclear weapons in any circumstance [was] permitted under international law'. In rendering its advisory opinion, the ICJ considered the following IHL principles:*

78. The cardinal principles contained in the texts constituting the fabric of humanitarian law are the following. The first is aimed at the protection of the civilian population and civilian objects and establishes the distinction between combatants and non-combatants; States must never make civilians the object of attack and must consequently never use weapons that are incapable of distinguishing between civilian and military targets.

2.4.3 ICTY, *Prosecutor* v. *Galić*, (Judgment), Case No. IT-98-29-A, Appeals Chamber (30 November 2006)

Note: *The Galić case arises out of the events that occurred in Sarajevo, Bosnia and Herzegovina between September 1992 and August 1994. Stanislaw Galić was the de jure Sarajevo Romanija Corps (SKA) Commander. Galić directly targeted civilians in Sarajevo by conducting a campaign of shelling and sniping against civilian areas of Sarajevo. Reinforcing the principle of distinction, the Tribunal held:*

130. The Appeals Chamber has previously emphasized that "there is an absolute prohibition on the targeting of civilians in customary international law" and that "the prohibition against attacking civilians and civilian objects may not be derogated from because of military necessity". The Trial Chamber was therefore correct to hold that the prohibition of attacks against the civilians and the civilian population "does not mention any exceptions [and] does not contemplate derogating from this rule by invoking military necessity".

2.4.4 ICTY, *Prosecutor* v. *Radovan Karadžić*, (Judgment), Case No. IT-95-5/18-T, Trial Chamber (24 March 2016)

Note: *The facts of this case are outlined in Chapter 1, Section 1.8.1.7. Affirming the principle of distinction in armed conflicts, the Tribunal said:*

449. . . . Thus, the targeting of civilians has been deemed by this Tribunal to be absolutely prohibited at all times and, as such, cannot be justified by military necessity or by the actions of the opposing side.

2.5 THE PRINCIPLE OF PROPORTIONALITY[4]

2.5.1 ICTY, *Final Report to the Prosecutor by the Committee Established to Review the NATO Bombing Campaign Against the Federal Republic of Yugoslavia* (1999)[5]

48. The main problem with the principle of proportionality is not whether or not it exists but what it means and how it is to be applied. It is relatively simple to state that there must be an acceptable relation between the legitimate destructive effect and undesirable collateral effects. . . . One cannot easily assess the value of innocent human lives as opposed to capturing a particular military objective.

49. The questions which remain unresolved once one decides to apply the principle of proportionality include the following:

a) What are the relative values to be assigned to the military advantage gained and the injury to non-combatants and or the damage to civilian objects?

b) What do you include or exclude in totaling your sums?

---

[4] See also Chapter 7 Section 7.5.3 in relation to targeting.
[5] www.icty.org/x/file/Press/nato061300.pdf.

c) What is the standard of measurement in time or space? and

d) To what extent is a military commander obligated to expose his own forces to danger in order to limit civilian casualties or damage to civilian objects?

50. The answers to these questions are not simple. It may be necessary to resolve them on a case by case basis, and the answers may differ depending on the background and values of the decision maker. It is unlikely that a human rights lawyer and an experienced combat commander would assign the same relative values to military advantage and to injury to noncombatants. Further, it is unlikely that military commanders with different doctrinal backgrounds and differing degrees of combat experience or national military histories would always agree in close cases. It is suggested that the determination of relative values must be that of the "reasonable military commander". Although there will be room for argument in close cases, there will be many cases where reasonable military commanders will agree that the injury to noncombatants or the damage to civilian objects was clearly disproportionate to the military advantage gained.

2.5.2 Israel, *The Public Committee against Torture in Israel et al.* v. *The Government of Israel et al.*, *('Targeted Killing Case')*, Case No. HCJ 769/02, Israeli Supreme Court Sitting as the High Court of Justice (11 December 2005)

Note: *The facts of this case are set out in Chapter 1, Section 1.6.1. On the issue of proportionality, the High Court said as follows:*

42. The principle of proportionality is a substantial part of international law regarding armed conflict. .... That law is of customary character. .... The principle of proportionality arises when the military operation is directed toward combatants and military objectives, or against civilians at such time as they are taking a direct part in hostilities, yet civilians are also harmed. The rule is that the harm to innocent civilians caused by collateral damage during combat operations must be proportionate. .... Civilians might be harmed due to their presence inside of a military target, such as civilians working in an army base; civilians might be harmed when they live or work in, or pass by, military targets; at times, due to a mistake, civilians are harmed even if they are far from military targets; at times civilians are forced to serve as "human shields" from attack upon a military target, and they are harmed as a result. In all those situations, and in other similar ones, the rule is that the harm to the innocent civilians must fulfil, inter alia, the requirements of the principle of proportionality.

45. The proportionality test determines that attack upon innocent civilians is not permitted if the collateral damage caused to them is not proportionate to the military advantage (in protecting combatants and civilians). In other words, attack is proportionate if the benefit stemming from the attainment of the proper military objective is proportionate to the damage caused to innocent civilians harmed by it. That is a values based test. It is based upon a balancing between conflicting values and interests. ....

46. That aspect of proportionality is not required regarding harm to a combatant, or to a civilian taking a direct part in the hostilities at such time as the harm is caused. Indeed, a civilian taking part in hostilities is endangering his life, and he might – like a

combatant – be the objective of a fatal attack. That killing is permitted. However, that proportionality is required in any case in which an innocent civilian is harmed. Thus, the requirements of proportionality *stricto senso* must be fulfilled in a case in which the harm to the terrorist carries with it collateral damage caused to nearby innocent civilians. ... Indeed, in international law, as in internal law, the ends do not justify the means. The state's power is not unlimited. Not all of the means are permitted.

2.5.3 UK, British Ministry of Defence, *The Joint Service Manual of the Law of Armed Conflict*, (Joint Service Publication 383, 2004 Edition)

2.7.1 The application of the proportionality principle is not always straightforward. Sometimes a method of attack that would minimize the risk to civilians may involve increased risk to the attacking forces. The law is not clear as to the degree of risk that the attacker must accept. The proportionality principle does not itself require the attacker to accept increased risk. Rather, it requires him to refrain from attacks that may be expected to cause excessive collateral damage. It will be a question of fact whether alternative, practically possible methods of attack would reduce the collateral risks. If they would, the attacker may have to accept the increased risk as being the only way of pursuing an attack in a proportionate way.

2.5.4 ICTY, *Prosecutor* v. *Galić*, (Judgment), Case No. IT-98-29-A, Appeals Chamber (30 November 2006)

Note: *The facts of this case are outlined in Section 2.4.3. In addition to considering the principle of distinction, the Tribunal also considered the issue of proportionality. The Tribunal was of the view*:

58. ... Once the military character of a target has been ascertained, commanders must consider whether striking this target is "expected to cause incidental loss of life, injury to civilians, damage to civilian objectives or a combination thereof, which would be excessive in relation to the concrete and direct military advantage anticipated." If such casualties are expected to result, the attack should not be pursued. The basic obligation to spare civilians and civilian objects as much as possible must guide the attacking party when considering the proportionality of an attack.

2.5.5 ICTY, *Prosecutor* v. *Boškoski and Tarčulovski*, (Judgment), Case No. IT-04-82-T Trial Chamber II (10 July 2008)

Note: *The facts of this case are outlined in Chapter 1, Section 1.1.7. In reaching its judgment, the Tribunal reflected on the principles of proportionality, as follows*:

357. When assessing whether the destruction of property was "justified by military necessity", the principle of proportionality enshrined in Article 51 of Additional Protocol I must also be taken into account. The principle of proportionality is inherent to military necessity

and was already reflected in early definitions of military necessity. Damage to property must not be disproportionate to the concrete and direct military advantage anticipated before the attack. In other words, unnecessary or wanton use of force against persons and property is prohibited. In determining whether an attack on military objectives was proportionate, it is necessary to adopt the perspective of a person in the circumstances of the actual perpetrator contemplating the attack and making reasonable use of the information available to him.

2.5.6 Gaza, UN General Assembly, Human Rights Council, *Report of the United Nations Fact Finding Commission on the Gaza Conflict* (25 September 2009) 12th Session, UN Doc. A/HRC/12/48

435. . . . the Mission examined whether the attacks on the police stations could be justified on the basis that there were, allegedly, members of Palestinian armed groups among the policemen. The question would thus be one of proportionality. . . .

436. The Mission has earlier accepted that there may be individual members of the Gaza police that were at the same time members of al-Qassam Brigades or other Palestinian armed groups and thus combatants. Even if the Israeli armed forces had reliable information that some individual members of the police were also members of armed groups, this did not deprive the whole police force of its status as a civilian law-enforcement agency.

437. From the facts available to it, the Mission finds that the deliberate killing of 99 members of the police at the police headquarters and three police stations during the first minutes of the military operations, while they were engaged in civilian tasks inside civilian police facilities, constitutes an attack which failed to strike an acceptable balance between the direct military advantage anticipated (i.e. the killing of those policemen who may have been members of Palestinian armed groups) and the loss of civilian life (i.e. the other policemen killed and members of the public who would inevitably have been present or in the vicinity). The attacks on the Arafat City police headquarters and the Abbas Street police station, al-Tuffah police station and the Deir al-Balah investigative police station constituted disproportionate attacks in violation of customary international humanitarian law.

2.5.7 UN, *Report of the Secretary-General's Panel of Inquiry on the 31 May 2010 Flotilla Incident* (September 2011)

162. At the same time, the manner in which a blockade is enforced requires particular attention if similar incidents are to be avoided in the future. The basic norms of international humanitarian law, including precaution and proportionality must be respected. When the direct use of force is contemplated against a non-military vessel carrying large numbers of passengers, military commanders and planners must consider their legal obligations, and also act with prudence and caution in light of those facts. . . . Force once used must be kept to the minimum necessary, proportional and carefully weighed against

the risk of collateral casualties. In such circumstances where the magnitude of the risk is great, it is important that the level of force is not escalated too quickly.

COMMENTARY

1. The principles of humanity and military necessity and the associated principles of distinction and proportionality are widely regarded as providing the foundations of IHL. The US *Law of War Manual* (2015, updated 2016) contains six principles: military necessity, humanity, distinction, proportionality, unnecessary suffering and chivalry.[6] The UK *Joint Service Manual* (2004) contains four principles: humanity, necessity, distinction and proportionality. The UK Manual subsumes the principle of unnecessary suffering under humanity and omits chivalry.

2. Humanity, necessity and proportionality are also general principles of international law that apply in other areas of international law, for instance, in the *jus ad bellum*. It is by now well established that the *jus ad bellum* and the *jus in bello* are distinct regimes, but sometimes the distinction is blurred. According to the ICJ Advisory Opinion on the *Threat or Use of Nuclear Weapons*,[7] the *jus ad bellum* regime seemed to override the *jus in bello* regime at least in extreme circumstances of 'state survival'. In any case, overlaps between these two regimes cannot be avoided. For example, the proportionality of a self-defence action will inevitably affect the assessment of the *jus in bello* proportionality regarding the caused harm because the former will delimit the overall advantage sought by the operation.[8] To that, one should add current strategic thinking concerning limited wars, effects-based operations, or humanitarian wars.

3. The principle of humanity counter-balances the principle of military necessity and reminds parties of the inherent humanity of those participating in an armed conflict. However, questions have been asked as to whether it constitutes an independent legal principle.[9] If it is an independent legal principle, a number of further questions arise: can it be the source of new rules? Can it fill gaps in existing law? Does it facilitate the interpretation of specific IHL rules? What are the legal consequences of violating this principle? Is the principle of humanity more important in certain types of operations such as peacekeeping operations or in certain fields such as the use of weapons? Even more critically, are we currently moving towards the 'humanisation' of IHL?[10] These issues need to be considered against the diversification of the mandates of military

---

[6]   US Department of Defense, *Law of War Manual*, Office of General Counsel (June 2015, updated 2016), chapter II.

[7]   ICJ, *Legality of the Threat or Use of Nuclear Weapons* (Advisory Opinion) [1996] I.C.J. Rep. 226, paras 2E and 42. See also Separate Opinion of Judge Fleischhauer, (ibid) para. 4 and Dissenting Opinion of Judge Higgins, (ibid) paras 25–9.

[8]   Dissenting Opinion of Judge Higgins, (ibid) paras 18–21.

[9]   Kjetil Mujezinović Larsen, Camilla Guldahl Cooper and Gro Nystuen (eds), *Searching for a 'Principle of Humanity' in International Humanitarian Law* (Cambridge University Press, 2013).

[10]   Theodor Meron, *The Humanization of International Law* (Martinus Nijhoff Publishers, 2000).

operations and the diversification of the legal regimes that apply thereto, in particular the application of IHRL.[11]

4. Military necessity should be distinguished from the general international law principle of 'state of necessity', which describes a situation of emergency that can excuse breaches of international law.[12] Military necessity in the *jus in bello* context acts as a limitation, not as an excuse. This also means that military necessity, being embedded in IHL rules, cannot be invoked *de novo* to justify departure from existing rules unless the rule itself explicitly allows the invocation of military necessity, as, for example, in Art. 42 GCIV.[13]

5. The assessment of the proportionality of any incidental injuries or collateral damage is a difficult exercise.[14] It involves strategic, operational, tactical, legal, ethical and political enquiries. It is also information dependent, which gives rise to questions about the level and probity of intelligence and information needed to assess proportionality. Any assessment should also be flexible and adapt to the changing operational environment. Proportionality assessments are particularly complicated in the case of modern weaponry such as in relation to automated and autonomous systems or cyber weapons. Whether existing methodologies for assessing collateral damage are suited to such weapons can be questioned.[15] For example, should non-physical effects be included in the proportionality assessment? When all has been said and done, proportionality assessments rely on sound judgements by decision makers at the time decisions are made.

6. New typologies of warfare such as asymmetric wars where participants differ in terms of power, organisation, tactics and values; hybrid wars where parties pursue their military aims by integrating military and non-military means and methods and by exploiting legal thresholds and gaps; or modern military doctrines such as the effects-based operations doctrine where strategic objectives are prioritised, pose challenges to the IHL principles and, consequently, to IHL rules, because they blur the normative and physical boundaries, which are necessary in order for these principles to apply and undermine the notion of comparable belligerents, which underpins the effectiveness of IHL norms. To give some examples of how these principles may be affected by such developments, if a party to an armed conflict blurs the distinction between combatants and civilians this may lead to more lax proportionality assessments by the other. Also, blurring military objectives with political or other objectives may expand the notion of military necessity to the detriment of the principle of humanity. Questions then are raised as to whether these principles should be adapted to the new environment and, if that is necessary, to what extent.[16]

---

[11] See Chapter 3.
[12] Art. 25, ARSIWA, UNGA Res A/RES/56/83 (Taken Note 12 December 2001).
[13] See also Arts 12, 42 and 33 GCI; Art. 23 GCIII; Arts 16, 18, 49 and 53 GCIV; Arts 54 and 62 API.
[14] See also Chapter 7 in relation to targeting.
[15] See Chapter 7. Also see Terry D. Gill, 'International Humanitarian Law Applied to Cyber-Warfare: Precautions, Proportionality and the Notion of "Armed" under the Humanitarian Law of Armed Conflict' in Nicholas Tsagourias and Russell Buchan (eds), *Research Handbook on International Law and Cyberspace* (Edward Elgar, 2015), p. 366.
[16] See also Chapter 7.

3

The Relationship Between International Humanitarian Law and Human Rights Law

INTRODUCTION

IHL and IHRL apply concurrently during armed conflicts. However, how these two regimes apply to specific situations or how any normative conflict that may arise due to their different scope and content is settled are critical questions to which national and international jurisprudence offer different responses. Sometimes, the *lex specialis* principle, according to which IHL takes precedence over IHRL, is applied; whereas, other times, IHRL is viewed as complementing IHL by filling its gaps or by assisting in the interpretation of its rules. The issue of the relationship between these two regimes can be explained better by looking into specific rights such as the right to life, the right to a fair trial and the prohibition of arbitrary detention as well as in the context of military responses to terrorism. Critical to the application of IHRL to situations of armed conflict is the question of whether human rights apply extraterritorially and, if so, what the scope of their application is, and what the effects of any limitations or derogations are. Whether armed groups have IHRL obligations and, if they do, what the scope of their obligations is are also critical questions, particularly in the context of NIACs. Similar questions are raised in relation to international organisations, as, for example, in the context of peacekeeping operations. Related to this is the issue of the effects of UN Security Council resolutions on IHL and IHRL.

Resources: Arts 2, 4, 6, 7, 8, 10, 11 International Covenant on Civil and Political Rights (ICCPR); Arts 1, 2, 3, 5, 6, 15 European Convention on Human Rights (ECHR); Arts I, II, IV, XVIII, XXV American Declaration of the Rights and Duties of Man; Arts 1, 4, 7, 27 American Convention on Human Rights; Arts 4, 5, 7 African Charter on Human and Peoples' Rights; Common Article 3 GCs, Arts 27, 41–43, 78 GCIV; Art. 75 API; Arts 4–6 APII; Arts 25, 103 UN Charter

Cases and Materials

3.1 Interrelationship between IHL and IHRL
3.2 Derogations from IHRL in Situations of Armed Conflict
3.3 Extraterritorial Application of IHRL
3.4 The Right to Life
3.5 The Right to a Fair Trial
3.6 Detention in Armed Conflict
3.7 Transfer of Detainees
3.8 Terrorism
3.9 The Effects of UN Mandates
3.10 UN Peacekeeping Operations and Human Rights
Commentary

3.1 INTERRELATIONSHIP BETWEEN IHL AND IHRL

3.1.1 ICJ, *Legality of the Use or Threat of Nuclear Weapons* (Advisory Opinion) [1996] I.C.J. Rep. 226

Note: *The facts of this case are set out in Chapter 2, Section 2.4.2. In this case, the ICJ also opined on the relationship between IHL and IHRL and on those rights from which States may derogate in an armed conflict. The ICJ balanced the relationship between IHL and IHRL in the following terms:*

24. The Court observes that the protection of the International Covenant on Civil and Political Rights does not cease in times of war, except by operation of Article 4 of the Covenant whereby certain provisions may be derogated from in a time of national emergency. Respect for the right to life is not, however, such a provision. In principle, the right not arbitrarily to be deprived of one's life applies also in hostilities. The test of what is an arbitrary deprivation of life, however, then falls to be determined by the applicable lex specialis, namely, the law applicable in armed conflict which is designed to regulate the conduct of hostilities. Thus whether a particular loss of life, through the use of a certain weapon in warfare, is to be considered an arbitrary deprivation of life contrary to Article 6 of the Covenant, can only be decided by reference to the law applicable in armed conflict and not deduced from the terms of the Covenant itself.

3.1.2 IACHR, *Juan Carlos Abella* v. *Argentina*, Case No. 11.137, Report No. 55/97, Inter-Am. C.H.R., OEA/Ser.L/V/II.95, Doc 7 rev. (18 November 1997)[1]

Note: *The background to this case is dealt with in Chapter 1, Section 1.2.4.1. In the context of IHL and IHRL, the Commission offered guidance on how the two legal frameworks interact in*

---

[1]   See also Chapter 10 Section 10.3.

circumstances amounting to an armed conflict. The Commission made the following comments:

158. The American Convention, as well as other universal and regional human rights instruments, and the 1949 Geneva Conventions share a common nucleus of non-derogable rights and a common purpose of protecting human life and dignity. These human rights treaties apply both in peacetime, and during situations of armed conflict. . . .

160. It is, moreover, during situations of internal armed conflict that these two branches of international law most converge and reinforce each other. . . .

161. For example, both Common Article 3 and Article 4 of the American Convention protect the right to life and, thus, prohibit, *inter alia*, summary executions in all circumstances. Claims alleging arbitrary deprivations of the right to life attributable to State agents are clearly within the Commission's jurisdiction. But the Commission's ability to resolve claimed violations of this non-derogable right arising out of an armed conflict may not be possible in many cases by reference to Article 4 of the American Convention alone. This is because the American Convention contains no rules that either define or distinguish civilians from combatants and other military targets, much less, specify when a civilian can be lawfully attacked or when civilian casualties are a lawful consequence of military operations. Therefore, the Commission must necessarily look to and apply definitional standards and relevant rules of humanitarian law as sources of authoritative guidance in its resolution of this and other kinds of claims alleging violations of the American Convention in combat situations.

3.1.3 IACHR, *Coard et al.* v. *United States*, Case No. 10.951, Report No. 109/99, Inter–Am. C.H.R. (29 September 1999)

Note: *The case relates to events that took place during the US invasion of Grenada. A number of individuals, including the Petitioners in this case, were arrested and detained. The legality of the US actions was challenged. The Commission evaluated the relationship between IHL and IHRL in relation to detention:*

42. . . ., in a situation of armed conflict, the test for assessing the observance of a particular right, such as the right to liberty, may, under given circumstances, be distinct from that applicable in a time of peace. For that reason, the standard to be applied must be deduced by reference to the applicable *lex specialis*. The American Declaration is drawn in general terms, and does not include specific provisions relating to its applicability in conflict situations. . . . In the present case, the standards of humanitarian law help to define whether the detention of the petitioners was "arbitrary" or not under the terms of Articles I and XXV of the American Declaration. As a general matter, while the Commission may find it necessary to look to the applicable rules of international humanitarian law when interpreting and applying the norms of the inter-American human rights system, where those bodies of law provide levels of protection which are distinct, the Commission is bound by its Charter-based mandate to give effect to the normative standard which best safeguards the rights of the individual.

3.1.4 ICTY, *Prosecutor* v. *Kunarac et al.*, (Judgment), Case No. IT-96-23-T and IT-96-23/1-T, Trial Chamber (22 February 2001)

Note: *The facts of this case are dealt with in Chapter 1, Section 1.4.2. In the context of IHL and IHRL, the Trial Chamber considered the role IHRL might play in assisting the development of IHL and said as follows:*

467. Because of the paucity of precedent in the field of international humanitarian law, the Tribunal has, on many occasions, had recourse to instruments and practices developed in the field of human rights law. Because of their resemblance, in terms of goals, values and terminology, such recourse is generally a welcome and needed assistance to determine the content of customary international law in the field of humanitarian law. With regard to certain of its aspects, international humanitarian law can be said to have fused with human rights law

471. The Trial Chamber is therefore wary not to embrace too quickly and too easily concepts and notions developed in a different legal context. The Trial Chamber is of the view that notions developed in the field of human rights can be transposed in international humanitarian law only if they take into consideration the specificities of the latter body of law. The Trial Chamber now turns more specifically to the definition of the crime of torture.

3.1.5 IACHR, *Report on Terrorism and Human Rights*, OEA/Ser.L/V/II.116 Doc.5 rev. 1 corr. (22 October 2002)

61. In situations of armed conflict, both international human rights law and international humanitarian law apply. Nevertheless, the American Convention and other universal and regional human rights instruments were not designed specifically to regulate armed conflict situations and do not contain specific rules governing the use of force and the means and methods of warfare in that context. Accordingly, in situations of armed conflict, international humanitarian law may serve as *lex specialis* in interpreting and applying international human rights instruments.

3.1.6 ICJ, *Legal Consequences of the Construction of a Wall in the Occupied Palestinian Territory* (Advisory Opinion) [2004] I.C.J. Rep. 136

Note: *The facts of this case are dealt with in Chapter 2, Section 2.2.6. Considering the relationship between IHL and IHRL and in what circumstances one may supersede the other, the ICJ said as follows:*

106. More generally, the Court considers that the protection offered by human rights conventions does not cease in case of armed conflict, save through the effect of provisions for derogation of the kind to be found in Article 4 of the International Covenant on Civil and Political Rights. As regards the relationship between international humanitarian law and human rights law, there are thus three possible situations: some rights may be exclusively matters of international humanitarian law; others may be exclusively matters of human rights law; yet others may be matters of both these branches of international law. In order to answer the question put to it, the Court will have to take into consideration both

these branches of international law, namely human rights law and, as *lex specialis*, international humanitarian law.

3.1.7 Human Rights Committee, *General Comment No. 31 on the Nature of the General Legal Obligation Imposed on States Parties to the Covenant* (26 May 2004), 18th Session, UN Doc. CCPR/C/21/Rev.1/ Add.13

Note: *In its General Comment No. 31, the UN Human Rights Committee confirmed the complementary nexus of IHL and IHRL in the following terms:*

11. ... the Covenant applies also in situations of armed conflict to which the rules of international humanitarian law are applicable. While, in respect of certain Covenant rights, more specific rules of international humanitarian law may be specially relevant for the purposes of the interpretation of Covenant rights, both spheres of law are complementary, not mutually exclusive.

3.1.8 Germany, Federal Ministry of Defence, *Law of Armed Conflict – Manual – Joint Service Regulation (ZDv) 15/2* (May 2013)

105. ... Human rights and LOAC thus complement each other in many ways. The rules of LOAC are more specific, however, and for soldiers take priority in armed conflicts (*lex specialis* principle).

3.1.9 US, Department of Defense, *Law of War Manual*, Office of General Counsel (June 2015, Updated 2016)

1.6.3.1 *Relationship Between Human Rights Treaties and the Law of War.*
In some circumstances, the rules in the law of war and the rules in human rights treaties may appear to conflict; these apparent conflicts may be resolved by the principle that the law of war is the *lex specialis* during situations of armed conflict, and, as such, is the controlling body of law with regard to the conduct of hostilities and the protection of war victims.

3.2 DEROGATIONS FROM IHRL IN SITUATIONS OF ARMED CONFLICT

3.2.1 *Siracusa Principles on the Limitation and Derogation Provisions in the International Covenant on Civil and Political Rights*, American Association for the International Commission of Jurists (1984)[2]

Note: *At the 1984 Siracusa Conference, the participants closely examined the circumstances in which States might limit and derogate from certain rights under IHRL in order to try and reduce abuse of the applicable provisions. To this end:*

---

[2] http://icj.wpengine.netdna-cdn.com/wp-content/uploads/1984/07/Siracusa-principles-ICCPR-legal-submission-1985-eng.pdf.

39. A state party may take measures derogating from its obligations under the International Covenant on Civil and Political Rights pursuant to Article 4 (hereinafter called "derogation measures") only when faced with a situation of exceptional and actual or imminent danger which threatens the life of the nation. A threat to the life of the nation is one that:

> (a) affects the whole of the population and either the whole or part of the territory of the state; and (b) threatens the physical integrity of the population, the political independence or the territorial integrity of the state or the existence or basic functioning of institutions indispensable to ensure and protect the rights recognized in the Covenant.

40. Internal conflict and unrest that do not constitute a grave and imminent threat to the life of the nation cannot justify derogations under Article 4.

41. Economic difficulties per se cannot justify derogation measures.

3.2.2 ECtHR, *Brannigan and McBride* v. *United Kingdom* (App Nos 14553/89 and 14554/89) (Judgment, 26 May 1993)

Note: *The European Court of Human Rights (ECtHR) was asked to determine an application by Brannigan and McBride, who had been detained in Northern Ireland under the Prevention of Terrorism (Temporary Provisions) Act 1984, claiming that the UK's derogation from Article 15 of the ECHR was invalid because the Applicants' detention was without judicial control. In assessing the legality of the UK's derogation, the ECtHR said as follows:*

43. The Court recalls that it falls to each Contracting State, with its responsibility for "the life of [its] nation", to determine whether that life is threatened by a "public emergency" and, if so, how far it is necessary to go in attempting to overcome the emergency. By reason of their direct and continuous contact with the pressing needs of the moment, the national authorities are in principle in a better position than the international judge to decide both on the presence of such an emergency and on the nature and scope of derogations necessary to avert it. Accordingly, in this matter a wide margin of appreciation should be left to the national authorities ...

Nevertheless, Contracting Parties do not enjoy an unlimited power of appreciation. It is for the Court to rule on whether inter alia the States have gone beyond the "extent strictly required by the exigencies" of the crisis. The domestic margin of appreciation is thus accompanied by a European supervision. At the same time, in exercising its supervision the Court must give appropriate weight to such relevant factors as the nature of the rights affected by the derogation, the circumstances leading to, and the duration of, the emergency situation.

3.2.3 ICTY, *Prosecutor* v. *Anto Furundžija*, (Judgment), Case No. IT-95-17/1-T, Trial Chamber (10 December 1998)

Note: *The Defendant was charged with serious violations of IHL, namely torture and outrages upon personal dignity, including rape. The Tribunal reinforced the position that States could not derogate from certain rights and prohibitions under IHRL, including the prohibition on torture:*

144. It should be noted that the prohibition of torture laid down in human rights treaties enshrines an absolute right, which can never be derogated from, not even in time of

emergency (on this ground the prohibition also applies to situations of armed conflicts). This is linked to the fact, discussed below, that the prohibition on torture is a peremptory norm or *jus cogens.*

3.2.4 Human Rights Committee, *General Comment 29: Article 4: Derogation During a State of Emergency* (31 August 2001), 72nd Session, UN Doc. CCPR/C/21/Rev.1/Add.11

Note: *In its General Comment 29, the UN Human Rights Committee examined the right of States to derogate from IHRL in states of emergency:*

2. Measures derogating from the provisions of the Covenant must be of an exceptional and temporary nature. Before a State moves to invoke article 4, two fundamental conditions must be met: the situation must amount to a public emergency which threatens the life of the nation, and the State party must have officially proclaimed a state of emergency. The latter requirement is essential for the maintenance of the principles of legality and rule of law at times when they are most needed. . . .

3. Not every disturbance or catastrophe qualifies as a public emergency which threatens the life of the nation, as required by article 4, paragraph 1. . . . The Covenant requires that even during an armed conflict measures derogating from the Covenant are allowed only if and to the extent that the situation constitutes a threat to the life of the nation. . . .

7. Article 4, paragraph 2, of the Covenant explicitly prescribes that no derogation from the following articles may be made: article 6 (right to life), article 7 (prohibition of torture or cruel, inhuman or degrading punishment, or of medical or scientific experimentation without consent), article 8, paragraphs 1 and 2 (prohibition of slavery, slave-trade and servitude), article 11 (prohibition of imprisonment because of inability to fulfil a contractual obligation), article 15 (the principle of legality in the field of criminal law, i.e. the requirement of both criminal liability and punishment being limited to clear and precise provisions in the law that was in place and applicable at the time the act or omission took place, except in cases where a later law imposes a lighter penalty), article 16 (the recognition of everyone as a person before the law), and article 18 (freedom of thought, conscience and religion).

9. Furthermore, article 4, paragraph 1, requires that no measure derogating from the provisions of the Covenant may be inconsistent with the State party's other obligations under international law, particularly the rules of international humanitarian law.

3.3 EXTRATERRITORIAL APPLICATION OF IHRL

3.3.1 Human Rights Committee, *Statement of US State Department Legal Adviser, Conrad Harper,* (Summary of the 1405th Meeting, Held at Headquarters, NY on 31 March 1995) (24 April 1995), 53rd Session, UN Doc. CCPR/C/SR 1405

20. Mr. Klein had asked whether the United States took the view that the Covenant did not apply to government actions outside the United States. The Covenant was not regarded as

having extraterritorial application. In general, where the scope of application of a treaty was not specified, it was presumed to apply only within a party's territory. Article 2 of the Covenant expressly stated that each State party undertook to respect and ensure the rights recognized "to all individuals within its territory and subject to its jurisdiction". That dual requirement restricted the scope of the Covenant to persons under United States jurisdiction and within United States territory. During the negotiating history, the words "within its territory" had been debated and were added by vote, with the clear understanding that such wording would limit the obligations to within a Party's territory.

3.3.2 IACHR, *Alejandro Jimenez Blanco* v. *Cuba*, Case No. 11.589, Report No. 86/99, Inter-Am. C.H.R. (29 September 1999)

Note: *On 24 February 1996, two unarmed, civilian light aeroplanes belonging to the 'Brothers of the Rescue', flying in international airspace, were downed by two MiG-29 military aircraft belonging to Cuba. It was found that agents of the Cuban State, although outside Cuban territory, had placed the civilian pilots of the 'Brothers of the Rescue' under their control and, therefore, the obligation to respect human rights continued:*

23. . . . Because individual rights are inherent to the human being, all the American states are obligated to respect the protected rights of any person subject to their jurisdiction. Although this usually refers to persons who are within the territory of a state, in certain instances it can refer to extraterritorial actions, when the person is present in the territory of a state but subject to the control of another state, generally through the actions of that state's agents abroad. In principle, the investigation refers not to the nationality of the alleged victim or his presence in a particular geographic area, but to whether, in those specific circumstances, the state observed the rights of a person subject to its authority and control.

3.3.3 ECtHR, *Banković and Others* v. *Belgium and Others (Decision on Admissibility)* [GC], (App No. 52207/99) (ECHR, 12 December 2001)

Note: *The case was brought by citizens of the FRY and concerned events in April 1999 when NATO bombed the building of the Radio Televizija Srbije (RTS) during the Kosovo crisis. The question for the ECtHR was whether the Applicants, being the subjects of the extra-territorial act of bombing, fell within the jurisdiction of the Respondent States; the ECtHR assessed the legal position as follows:*

71. In sum, the case-law of the Court demonstrates that its recognition of the exercise of extra-territorial jurisdiction by a Contracting State is exceptional: it has done so when the respondent State, through the effective control of the relevant territory and its inhabitants abroad as a consequence of military occupation or through the consent, invitation or acquiescence of the Government of that territory, exercises all or some of the public powers normally to be exercised by that Government. . . .

73. Additionally, the Court notes that other recognised instances of the extra-territorial exercise of jurisdiction by a State include cases involving the activities of its diplomatic or consular agents abroad and on board craft and vessels registered in, or flying the flag of, that State. In these specific situations, customary international law and treaty provisions have recognised the extra-territorial exercise of jurisdiction by the relevant State. . . .

75. . . . However, the Court is of the view that the wording of Article 1 does not provide any support for the applicants' suggestion that the positive obligation in Article 1 to secure "the rights and freedoms defined in Section I of this Convention" can be divided and tailored in accordance with the particular circumstances of the extra-territorial act in question . . .

80. . . . In short, the Convention is a multi-lateral treaty operating, . . ., in an essentially regional context and notably in the legal space (espace juridique) of the Contracting States.

3.3.4 Human Rights Committee, *General Comment No. 3: The Nature of the General Legal Obligation Imposed on States Parties to the Covenant* (26 May 2004), 18th Session, UN Doc. CCPR/C/21/Rev.1/Add.13

10 States Parties are required by article 2, paragraph 1, to respect and to ensure the Covenant rights to all persons who may be within their territory and to all persons subject to their jurisdiction. This means that a State party must respect and ensure the rights laid down in the Covenant to *anyone within the power or effective control of that State Party, even if not situated within the territory of the State Party.* . . . the enjoyment of Covenant rights is not limited to citizens of States Parties but must also be available to all individuals, regardless of nationality or statelessness, such as asylum seekers, refugees, migrant workers and other persons, who may find themselves in the territory or subject to the jurisdiction of the State Party. This principle also applies to those within the power or effective control of the forces of a State Party acting outside its territory, regardless of the circumstances in which such power or effective control was obtained, such as forces constituting a national contingent of a State Party assigned to an international peacekeeping or peace-enforcement operation.

3.3.5 US, *Memorandum Opinion on the Geographic Scope of the International Covenant on Civil and Political Rights*, Office of the Legal Adviser, United States Department of State (Washington, DC, 19 October 2010)[3] pp. 55–56

. . . Based on all of the foregoing, I conclude that:

An interpretation of Article 2(1) . . . would provide:

(I) *that in fact, the Covenant does impose obligations on a State Party's extraterritorial conduct in certain exceptional circumstances - specifically, that a state is obligated to respect rights under its control in circumstances in which the State exercises*

---

[3] www.justsecurity.org/wp-content/uploads/2014/03/state-department-iccpr-memo.pdf.

authority or effective control over a particular person or context without regard to territory; but

(2) *that the Covenant only imposes positive obligations on a state to rights – whether by legislating extraterritorially or otherwise affirmatively protecting its nationals or other individuals abroad from the acts of third parties or entities - for individuals who are both within the territory and subject to the jurisdiction of the State Party. Because attempting to protect persons under the primary jurisdiction of another sovereign otherwise could produce conflicting legal authorities.*

3.3.6 ECtHR, *Al-Skeini and Others* v. *The United Kingdom* [GC], (App No. 55721/07) Judgment (7 July 2011)

Note: *The case concerned the deaths of six Iraqi civilians at the hands of British soldiers in Southern Iraq, including the death of one man while he was detained in a British army base. On the issue of the territorial limits of the UK's human rights obligations, the ECtHR said as follows:*

130. .... "Jurisdiction" under Article 1 is a threshold criterion. The exercise of jurisdiction is a necessary condition for a Contracting State to be able to be held responsible for acts or omissions imputable to it which give rise to an allegation of the infringement of rights and freedoms set forth in the Convention .....

(α) The territorial principle

(β) State agent authority and control

. . .

134. Firstly, it is clear that the acts of diplomatic and consular agents, who are present on foreign territory in accordance with provisions of international law, may amount to an exercise of jurisdiction when these agents exert authority and control over others .....

135. Secondly, the Court has recognised the exercise of extraterritorial jurisdiction by a Contracting State when, through the consent, invitation or acquiescence of the Government of that territory, it exercises all or some of the public powers normally to be exercised by that Government .....

136. In addition, the Court's case-law demonstrates that, in certain circumstances, the use of force by a State's agents operating outside its territory may bring the individual thereby brought under the control of the State's authorities into the State's Article 1 jurisdiction. This principle has been applied where an individual is taken into the custody of State agents abroad. .... What is decisive in such cases is the exercise of physical power and control over the person in question.

137. It is clear that, whenever the State, through its agents, exercises control and authority over an individual, and thus jurisdiction, the State is under an obligation under Article 1 to secure to that individual the rights and freedoms under Section I of the Convention that are relevant to the situation of that individual. In this sense, therefore, the Convention rights can be "divided and tailored" .....

(γ) Effective control over an area

138. Another exception to the principle that jurisdiction under Article 1 is limited to a State's own territory occurs when, as a consequence of lawful or unlawful military action, a Contracting State exercises effective control of an area outside that national territory. The obligation to secure, in such an area, the rights and freedoms set out in the Convention, derives from the fact of such control, whether it be exercised directly, through the Contracting State's own armed forces, or through a subordinate local administration . . . .

139. It is a question of fact whether a Contracting State exercises effective control over an area outside its own territory. In determining whether effective control exists, the Court will primarily have reference to the strength of the State's military presence in the area. Other indicators may also be relevant, such as the extent to which its military, economic and political support for the local subordinate administration provides it with influence and control over the region . . . .

(δ) The legal space ("espace juridique") of the Convention

141. The Convention is a constitutional instrument of European public order. . . . It does not govern the actions of States not Parties to it, nor does it purport to be a means of requiring the Contracting States to impose Convention standards on other States . . . .

142. . . . However, the importance of establishing the occupying State's jurisdiction in such cases does not imply, a contrario, that jurisdiction under Article 1 of the Convention can never exist outside the territory covered by the Council of Europe member States. The Court has not in its case-law applied any such restriction.

3.3.7 US, Department of Defense, *Law of War Manual*, Office of General Counsel (June 2015, Updated 2016)

1.6.3.3 *International Covenant on Civil and Political Rights (ICCPR)*.

The United States is a Party to the International Covenant on Civil and Political Rights (ICCPR). The ICCPR creates obligations for a State with respect to persons within its territory and subject to its jurisdiction. The United States has long interpreted the ICCPR not to apply abroad.

3.4 THE RIGHT TO LIFE[4]

3.4.1 ECtHR, *Isayeva* v. *Russia*, (App No. 57950/00), Judgment (24 February 2005)

Note: *The Applicant alleged she had been the victim of the indiscriminate bombing by the Russian military of her village of Katyr-Yurt in February 2000 in violation of her Article 2 and 13 rights under ECHR. As to the Article 2 protection, the ECtHR said as follows:*

173. Article 2 covers not only intentional killing but also the situations in which it is permitted to "use force" which may result, as an unintended outcome, in the deprivation of

---

[4] See also Chapter 7 for targeting.

life. However, the deliberate or intended use of lethal force is only one factor to be taken into account in assessing its necessity. Any use of force must be no more than "absolutely necessary" for the achievement of one or more of the purposes set out in sub-paragraphs (a) to (c). . . .

174. In the light of the importance of the protection afforded by Article 2, the Court must subject deprivations of life to the most careful scrutiny, taking into consideration not only the actions of State agents but also all the surrounding circumstances.

175. In particular, it is necessary to examine whether the operation was planned and controlled by the authorities so as to minimise, to the greatest extent possible, recourse to lethal force. The authorities must take appropriate care to ensure that any risk to life is minimised. The Court must also examine whether the authorities were not negligent in their choice of action . . ..

176. Similarly, the State's responsibility is not confined to circumstances where there is significant evidence that misdirected fire from agents of the state has killed a civilian. It may also be engaged where they fail to take all feasible precautions in the choice of means and methods of a security operation mounted against an opposing group with a view to avoiding and, in any event, minimising, incidental loss of civilian life. . . .

180. The Court accepts that the situation that existed in Chechnya at the relevant time called for exceptional measures by the State in order to regain control over the Republic and to suppress the illegal armed insurgency. . . .

181. Accepting that the use of force may have been justified in the present case, it goes without saying that a balance must be achieved between the aim pursued and the means employed to achieve it. The Court will now consider whether the actions in the present case were no more than absolutely necessary for achieving the declared purpose. In order to do so the Court will examine, on the basis of the information submitted by the parties and in view of the above enumerated principles, whether the planning and conduct of the operation were consistent with Article 2 of the Convention. . . .

191. The Court considers that using this kind of weapon [bombs and missiles] in a populated area, outside wartime and without prior evacuation of the civilians, is impossible to reconcile with the degree of caution expected from a law-enforcement body in a democratic society. No martial law and no state of emergency has been declared in Chechnya, and no derogation has been made under Article 15 of the Convention. The operation in question therefore has to be judged against a normal legal background. Even when faced with a situation where, as the Government submit, the population of the village had been held hostage by a large group of well-equipped and well-trained fighters, the primary aim of the operation should be to protect lives from unlawful violence. The massive use of indiscriminate weapons stands in flagrant contrast with this aim and cannot be considered compatible with the standard of care prerequisite to an operation of this kind involving the use of lethal force by State agents. . . .

193. The documents reviewed by the Court confirm that a measure of information about a safe passage had indeed been conveyed to the villagers. . . .

195. Once the information about the corridor had spread, the villagers started to leave, taking advantage of a lull in the bombardments. The presence of civilians and civilian cars

on the road leading to Achkhoy-Martan in the afternoon of 4 February 2000 must have been fairly substantial. . . . This must have been known to the commanders of the operation and should have led them to ensure the safety of the passage.

196. However, no document or statement by the military refers to an order to stop the attack or to reduce its intensity. While there are numerous references in the servicemen's statements to the declaration of a humanitarian corridor, there is not a single statement which refers to the observance of any such corridor. . . .

200. To sum up, accepting that the operation in Katyr-Yurt on 4–7 February 2000 was pursuing a legitimate aim, the Court does not accept that it was planned and executed with the requisite care for the lives of the civilian population.

3.4.2 ECtHR, *Al-Skeini and Others v. The United Kingdom* [GC], (App No. 55721/07), Judgment (7 July 2011)

Note: The facts of this case are set out in Section 3.3.6. Reviewing the procedural obligations attendant to violations of Article 2 ECHR, the ECtHR commented:

163. The general legal prohibition of arbitrary killing by agents of the State would be ineffective in practice if there existed no procedure for reviewing the lawfulness of the use of lethal force by State authorities. The obligation to protect the right to life under this provision, . . . requires by implication that there should be some form of effective official investigation when individuals have been killed as a result of the use of force by, inter alios, agents of the State. The essential purpose of such an investigation is to secure the effective implementation of the domestic laws safeguarding the right to life and, in those cases involving State agents or bodies, to ensure their accountability for deaths occurring under their responsibility . . . .

164. The Court has held that the procedural obligation under Article 2 continues to apply in difficult security conditions, including in a context of armed conflict . . . .

. . .

166. As stated above, the investigation must be effective in the sense that it is capable of leading to a determination of whether the force used was or was not justified in the circumstances and to the identification and punishment of those responsible. This is not an obligation of result, but of means. The authorities must take the reasonable steps available to them to secure the evidence concerning the incident, including, inter alia, eyewitness testimony, forensic evidence and, where appropriate, an autopsy which provides a complete and accurate record of injury and an objective analysis of clinical findings, including the cause of death. Any deficiency in the investigation which undermines its ability to establish the cause of death or the person or persons responsible will risk falling foul of this standard . . . .

167. For an investigation into alleged unlawful killing by State agents to be effective, it is necessary for the persons responsible for and carrying out the investigation to be independent from those implicated in the events. . . . For the same reasons, there must be a sufficient element of public scrutiny of the investigation or its results to secure accountability in practice as well as in theory. The degree of public scrutiny required may well vary from case

to case. In all cases, however, the victim's next of kin must be involved in the procedure to the extent necessary to safeguard his or her legitimate interests.'

3.4.3 Human Rights Council, *Report of the International Commission of Inquiry on Libya* (8 March 2012), 19th Session, UN Doc. A/HRC/19/68

145. The noted international human rights law standards differ to a degree from those applicable to fighters/combatants during an armed conflict under international humanitarian law. For example, one would not expect soldiers to warn their enemies before an attack. Still, international human rights law obligations remain in effect and operate to limit the circumstances when a state actor – even a soldier during internal armed conflict – can employ lethal force. This is particularly the case where the circumstances on the ground are more akin to policing than combat. For example, in encountering a member of the opposing forces in an area far removed from combat, or in situations where that enemy can be arrested easily and without risk to one's own forces, it may well be that the international humanitarian law regime is not determinative. In such situations, combatants/fighters should ensure their use of lethal force conforms to the parameters of international human rights law.

3.4.4 IACtHR, *Case of the Santo Domingo Massacre* v. *Colombia*, (Judgment: Preliminary Objections, Merits and Reparations), Inter-Am. Ct. H.R., Series C No. 259 (30 November 2012)

Note: *The case arose out of events on 13 December 1998 when the Colombian Air Force dropped six fragmentation bombs on the village of Santo Domingo. The bombardment resulted in the deaths of seventeen and the injury of twenty-seven civilians. Discussing the relationship between IHRL and IHL in a NIAC, the IACtHR said the following:*

211. Having established how the incident occurred, the Court will now examine the State's responsibility in the effects on the life and integrity of the victims of the bombardment. To this end, . . ., it will analyze the facts of the case interpreting the provisions of the American Convention in light of the pertinent norms and principles of international humanitarian law, namely: (a) the principle of distinction between civilians and combatants; (b) the principle of proportionality, and (c) the principle of precaution in attack.

212. As established in international humanitarian law, the principle of distinction refers to a customary rule for both international and non-international armed conflicts . . .

213. In the instant case, the Court has found proved that, in the context of confrontations with the FARC guerrilla, on December 13, 1998, the Colombian Air Force launched an AN-M1A2 cluster bomb on the village of Santo Domingo, causing the death and injury of civilians. The Court takes note that the domestic judicial and administrative organs have considered that the State failed to comply with the principle of distinction when conducting the said airborne operation.

214. As established by international humanitarian law, the principle of proportionality refers to a customary rule for both international and non-international armed conflicts . . .

Thus the said principle establishes a limitation to the purpose of the war, stipulating that the use of force must not be disproportionate, limiting it to what is essential to obtain the military advantage pursued.

215. In this regard, as already indicated, although the launch of the cluster bomb directly affected the population of the village of Santo Domingo, the more general military objective of the airborne operation was the members of the guerrilla who were presumably located in a wooded area near Santo Domingo. In this hypothesis, the military advantage that the Colombian Air Force hoped to obtain was to undermine the military capability of the guerrilla located in a place where, presumably, there was no civilian population that could be incidentally affected by the cluster bomb. Consequently, the Court considers that it is not appropriate to analyze the launch of the said device in light of the principle of proportionality, because an analysis of this type would involve determining whether the deceased and injured among the civilian population could be considered an "excessive" result in relation to the specific and direct military advantage expected if it had hit a military objective, which did not occur in the circumstances of the case.

216. According to international humanitarian law, the principle of precaution in attack refers to a customary rule for both international and non-international armed conflicts . . .

229. . . . given the lethal capacity and limited precision of the device used, its launch in the urban center of the village of Santo Domingo or nearby, was contrary to the principle of precaution in attack.

230. Based on all the above, this Court finds that the State is responsible for the violation of the right to life recognized in Article 4(1) of the Convention,

3.4.5 African Commission on Human and Peoples' Rights, *General Comment No. 3 on the African Charter on Human and Peoples' Rights: The Right to Life (Article 4)*, 57th Ordinary Session (4 to 18 November 2015)

32. In armed conflict, what constitutes an 'arbitrary' deprivation of life during the conduct of hostilities is to be determined by reference to international humanitarian law. This law does not prohibit the use of force in hostilities against lawful targets (for example combatants or civilians directly participating in hostilities) if necessary from a military perspective, provided that, in all circumstances, the rules of distinction, proportionality and precaution in attack are observed. Any violation of international humanitarian law resulting in death, including war crimes, will be an arbitrary deprivation of life.

3.4.6 Human Rights Committee, *Draft General Comment No. 36, Article 6: Right to Life* (2 September 2015), 115th Session, UN Doc. CCPR/C/GC/R.36/Rev.2

63. . . ., article 6 [right to life] continues to apply also in situations of armed conflict to which the rules of international humanitarian law are applicable. While rules of international humanitarian law may be relevant for the interpretation and application of

article 6, both spheres of law are complementary, not mutually exclusive. Uses of lethal force authorized and regulated by and complying with international humanitarian law are, in principle, not arbitrary. By contrast, practices inconsistent with international humanitarian law, entailing a real risk to the lives of civilians and persons hors de combat, including the targeting of civilians and civilian objects, failure to apply adequate measures of precaution to prevent collateral death of civilians, and the use of human shields, violate article 6 of the Covenant. Furthermore, State parties should, subject to compelling security considerations, disclose the criteria for attacking with lethal force individuals or objects whose targeting is excepted to result in deprivation of life, including the legal basis for specific attacks, the process of identification of military targets and combatants or persons taking a direct part in hostilities, the circumstances in which relevant means and methods of warfare have been used, and whether less lethal alternatives for attaining the same military objective were considered.

3.5 THE RIGHT TO A FAIR TRIAL

3.5.1 IACtHR, *Case of Castillo Petruzzi et al.* v. *Peru,* (Judgment: Merits, Reparations and Costs) Series C No. 52 (30 May 1999)

Note: *During counter-insurgency operations, the Applicants, arrested for terrorism, were tried by a 'faceless' military tribunal for treason and sentenced to life imprisonment. It was alleged that when the Applicants were brought before the tribunal they were, inter alia, hooded or blind-folded, shackled, unaware of the charges against them and prevented from liaising with counsel acting in their defence, therefore being unable to put forward a defence to the tribunal. On the issue of whether the Applicants' rights to a fair trial were violated, the IACtHR commented in the following terms*:

128. ... Transferring jurisdiction from civilian courts to military courts, thus allowing military courts to try civilians accused of treason means that the competent, independent and impartial tribunal previously established by law is precluded from hearing these cases. ... When a military court takes jurisdiction over a matter that regular courts should hear, the individual's right to a hearing by a competent, independent and impartial tribunal previously established by law and, a fortiori, his right to due process are violated. That right to due process, in turn, is intimately linked to the very right of access to the courts. ...

130. Under Article 8(1) of the American Convention, a presiding judge must be competent, independent and impartial. In the case under study, the armed forces, fully engaged in the counter-insurgency struggle, are also prosecuting persons associated with insurgency groups. This considerably weakens the impartiality that every judge must have. Moreover, under the Statute of Military Justice, members of the Supreme Court of Military Justice, the highest body in the military judiciary, are appointed by the minister of the pertinent sector. Members of the Supreme Court of Military Justice also decide who among their subordinates will be promoted and what incentives will be offered to whom; they also assign functions. This alone is enough to call the independence of the military judges into serious question.

3.5.2 Human Rights Committee, *General Comment No. 32, Article 14: Right to Equality Before Courts and Tribunals and to a Fair Trial* (23 August 2007), 19th Session, UN Doc. CCPR/C/GC/32

22. The provisions of article 14 apply to all courts and tribunals within the scope of that article whether ordinary or specialized, civilian or military. The Committee notes the existence, in many countries, of military or special courts which try civilians. While the Covenant does not prohibit the trial of civilians in military or special courts, it requires that such trials are in full conformity with the requirements of article 14 and that its guarantees cannot be limited or modified because of the military or special character of the court concerned. The Committee also notes that the trial of civilians in military or special courts may raise serious problems as far as the equitable, impartial and independent administration of justice is concerned. Therefore, it is important to take all necessary measures to ensure that such trials take place under conditions which genuinely afford the full guarantees stipulated in article 14. Trials of civilians by military or special courts should be exceptional, i.e. limited to cases where the State party can show that resorting to such trials is necessary and justified by objective and serious reasons, and where with regard to the specific class of individuals and offences at issue the regular civilian courts are unable to undertake the trials.

3.6 DETENTION IN ARMED CONFLICT[5]

3.6.1 IACHR, *Coard et al.* v. *United States*, Case 10.951, Report No. 109/99, Inter. Am. C.H.R. (29 September 1999)

Note: *The facts of this case are set out in Section 3.1.3. As to the issue of safeguards against arbitrary detention, the Commission said as follows:*

52. Under exceptional circumstances, international humanitarian law provides for the internment of civilians as a protective measure. It may only be undertaken pursuant to specific provisions, and may be authorized when: security concerns require it; less restrictive measure could not accomplish the objective sought; and the action is taken in compliance with the grounds and procedures established in pre-existing law. . . .

55. The requirement that detention not be left to the sole discretion of the state agent(s) responsible for carrying it out is so fundamental that it cannot be overlooked in any context. The terms of the American Declaration and of applicable humanitarian law are largely in accord in this regard. Article 78 of the Fourth Geneva Convention provides a recourse which, implemented according to its object and purpose, is generally consistent with the supervisory control required under Article XXV of the American Declaration. Supervisory control over detention is an essential safeguard, because it provides effective assurance that the detainee is not exclusively at the mercy of the detaining authority. This is

---

[5]   For detention see also Chapter 5 Section 5.4. For detention in occupation see Chapter 9 Section 9.9 and for detention in NIACs see Chapter 10 Section 10.6. The detention of prisoners of war is considered in Chapter 6.

an essential rationale of the right to *habeas corpus*, a protection which is not susceptible to abrogation. . . .

57. Under normal circumstances, review of the legality of detention must be carried out without delay, which generally means as soon as practicable. Article 78 of the Fourth Geneva Convention indicates that review is to be carried out "with the least possible delay." . . .

60. . . ., the same rules which authorize [detention] as an exceptional security measure require that it be implemented pursuant to a regular procedure which enables the detainee to be heard and to appeal the decision "with the least possible delay." . . . This is a fundamental safeguard against arbitrary or abusive detention, and the relevant provisions of the American Declaration and Fourth Geneva Convention analyzed above establish that this protection is to be afforded with the least possible delay.

3.6.2 IACHR, *Report on Terrorism and Human Rights*, OEA/Ser.L/V/II.116 Doc.5 rev. 1 corr. (22 October 2002)

143. . . ., international humanitarian law generally permits the administrative detention or internment of civilians and others who have not taken any active part in hostilities only under exceptional circumstances. In particular, such detention may only be undertaken pursuant to specific provisions, and may be authorized only when imperative concerns of security require it, when less restrictive measure could not accomplish the objective sought, and when the action is taken in compliance with the grounds and procedures established in pre-existing law. The applicable rules of international humanitarian law relative to the detention of civilians also require that any detention be made pursuant to a "regular procedure," which shall include the right of the detainee to be heard and to appeal the decision, and any continuation of the detention must be subject to regular review. The particular requirements of the review process may vary depending upon the circumstances of a particular case, including, for example the capabilities of the detainee. In all instances, however, minimum standards of human rights law require that detention review proceedings comply with the rules of procedural fairness. These rules include the requirements that the decision-maker meets prevailing standards of impartiality, that the detainee is given an opportunity to present evidence and to know and meet the claims of the opposing party, and that the detainee be given an opportunity to be represented by counsel or other representative. It should be emphasized that even where armed hostilities may occur over a prolonged period, this factor alone cannot justify the extended detention or internment of civilians; their detention is only justified as long as security concerns strictly require it.

146. Notwithstanding these specific rules and mechanisms governing the detention of persons in situations of armed conflict, there may be circumstances in which the continued existence of active hostilities becomes uncertain, or where a belligerent occupation continues over a prolonged period of time. . . . Accordingly, where detainees find themselves in uncertain or protracted situations of armed conflict or occupation, the Commission considers that the supervisory mechanisms as well as judicial guarantees under international human rights law and domestic law, including *habeas corpus* and *amparo* remedies, may necessarily supercede international humanitarian law where this is necessary to safeguard the fundamental rights of those detainees.

3.6.3 US, *In re Guantanamo Detainee Cases*, United States District Court, District of Columbia, F.Supp.2d 443, 464–5 and 480 (D.D.C. 2005)

Note: *The case concerned eleven coordinated habeas corpus petitions from detainees at Guantanamo Bay. The petitions asserted the detainees' classification as 'enemy combatants' subject to indefinite detention violated their right to due process of law under Article 5 of the US Constitution. The District Court of Columbia found as follows:*

In sum, there can be no question that the Fifth Amendment right asserted by the Guantanamo detainees in this litigation—the right not to be deprived of liberty without due process of law—is one of the most fundamental rights recognized by the U.S. Constitution. In light of the Supreme Court's decision in Rasul, it is clear that Guantanamo Bay must be considered the equivalent of a U.S. territory in which fundamental constitutional rights apply. Accordingly, . . . the respondents' contention that the Guantanamo detainees have no constitutional rights is rejected, and the Court recognizes the detainees' rights under the Due Process Clause of the Fifth Amendment. . . .

Although the detainees in the cases before this Court are aliens and are therefore not being detained by their own governments, that fact does not lessen the significance of their interests in freedom from incarceration and from being held virtually incommunicado from the outside world. There is no practical difference between incarceration at the hands of one's own government and incarceration at the hands of a foreign government; significant liberty is deprived in both situations regardless of the jailer's nationality.

3.6.4 Israel, *A and B* v. *State of Israel*, (Judgment), Case Nos CrimA, 6659/06, CrimA 1757/07, CrimA 8228/07, CrimA 3261/08, Israeli Supreme Court Sitting as the Court of Criminal Appeals (11 June 2008)

Note: *The case concerned the internment of two inhabitants of Gaza on the grounds they were 'unlawful combatants', had associations with Hezbollah and had committed hostile acts against Israel. The Applicants had been detained since 2002 and 2003 respectively and claimed their detentions violated their right to liberty and dignity under Israel's Basic Law and further that it violated IHL. As to whether an 'unlawful combatant' can be detained, the Supreme Court of Israel said as follows:*

18. It is one of the first principles of our legal system that administrative detention is conditional upon the existence of a ground for detention that derives from the individual threat of the detainee to the security of the state. . . . The requirement of an individual threat for the purposes of placing someone in administrative detention is an essential part of the protection of the constitutional right to dignity and personal liberty. This court has held in the past that administrative detention is basically a preventative measure; administrative detention was not intended to punish someone for acts that have already been committed or to deter others from committing them, but its purpose is to prevent the tangible risk presented by the acts of the detainee to the security of the state. It is this risk that justifies the use of the unusual measure of administrative detention that violates human liberty

19. It should be noted that the individual threat to the security of the state represented by the detainee is also required by the principles of international humanitarian law. . . .

22. . . . The question that arises in this regard is: what evidence is required in order to persuade the court that the detainee satisfies the conditions of the definition of an 'unlawful combatant' with the aforesaid meaning. This court has held in the past that since administrative detention is an unusual and extreme measure, and in view of its violation of the constitutional right to personal liberty, clear and convincing evidence is required in order to prove a security threat that establishes a basis for administrative detention

3.6.5 ECtHR, *Hassan* v. *United Kingdom* [GC], (App No. 29750/09) Judgment (16 September 2014)

Note: *Following British occupation of Basrah the Applicant went into hiding. In April 2003, British forces attended at his home in order to detain him. The Applicant was not there but his brother Tarek Hassan was. Tarek was arrested and subsequently detained at Camp Bucca, south of Basrah. Tarek was purportedly released from Camp Bucca in May 2003. In September 2003, Tarek's body was found in nearby countryside. The Applicant subsequently brought a claim alleging his brother's detention was arbitrary and unlawful and lacking in procedural safeguards. The Applicant claimed violations of Articles 2, 3 and 5 ECHR. The ECtHR found as follows:*

104. . . . By reason of the co-existence of the safeguards provided by international humanitarian law and by the Convention in time of armed conflict, the grounds of permitted deprivation of liberty set out in subparagraphs (a) to (f) of that provision should be accommodated, as far as possible, with the taking of prisoners of war and the detention of civilians who pose a risk to security under the Third and Fourth Geneva Conventions. The Court is mindful of the fact that internment in peacetime does not fall within the scheme of deprivation of liberty governed by Article 5 of the Convention without the exercise of the power of derogation under Article 15. It can only be in cases of international armed conflict, where the taking of prisoners of war and the detention of civilians who pose a threat to security are accepted features of international humanitarian law, that Article 5 could be interpreted as permitting the exercise of such broad powers.

105. As with the grounds of permitted detention . . ., deprivation of liberty pursuant to powers under international humanitarian law must be "lawful" to preclude a violation of Article 5 § 1. This means that the detention must comply with the rules of international humanitarian law and, most importantly, that it should be in keeping with the fundamental purpose of Article 5 § 1, which is to protect the individual from arbitrariness . . ..

106. As regards procedural safeguards, the Court considers that, in relation to detention taking place during an international armed conflict, Article 5 §§ 2 and 4 must also be interpreted in a manner which takes into account the context and the applicable rules of international humanitarian law. . . . Articles 43 and 78 of the Fourth Geneva Convention provide that internment "shall be subject to periodical review, if possible every six months, by a competent body". Whilst it might not be practicable, in the course of an international armed conflict, for the legality of detention to be determined by an independent "court" in the sense generally required by Article 5 § 4, nonetheless, if the Contracting State is to comply with its obligations under Article 5 § 4 in this context, the "competent body" should

provide sufficient guarantees of impartiality and fair procedure to protect against arbitrariness. Moreover, the first review should take place shortly after the person is taken into detention, with subsequent reviews at frequent intervals, to ensure that any person who does not fall into one of the categories subject to internment under international humanitarian law is released without undue delay. While the applicant in addition relies on Article 5 § 3, the Court considers that this provision has no application in the present case since Tarek Hassan was not detained in accordance with the provisions of paragraph 1(c) of Article 5.

107. Finally, although, for the reasons explained above, the Court does not consider it necessary for a formal derogation to be lodged, the provisions of Article 5 will be interpreted and applied in the light of the relevant provisions of international humanitarian law only where this is specifically pleaded by the respondent State. It is not for the Court to assume that a State intends to modify the commitments which it has undertaken by ratifying the Convention in the absence of a clear indication to that effect.

3.6.6 Human Rights Committee, *General Comment No. 35, Article 9: Liberty and Security of Person* (16 December 2014), 112th Session, UN Doc. CCPR/C/GC/35

65. Article 9 is not included in the list of non-derogable rights of article 4, paragraph 2, of the Covenant, but there are limits on States parties' power to derogate. States parties derogating from normal procedures required under article 9 in circumstances of armed conflict or other public emergency must ensure that such derogations do not exceed those strictly required by the exigencies of the actual situation. Derogating measures must also be consistent with a State party's other obligations under international law, including provisions of international humanitarian law relating to deprivation of liberty, and nondiscriminatory. The prohibitions against taking of hostages, abductions or unacknowledged detention are therefore not subject to derogation.

3.7 TRANSFER OF DETAINEES[6]

3.7.1 UK, Select Committee on Foreign Affairs, *Memorandum of Understanding between the Government of the United Kingdom of Great Britain and Northern Ireland and the Government of the Islamic Republic of Afghanistan concerning transfer by the United Kingdom armed forces to Afghan authorities of persons detained in Afghanistan, 23 April 2005*[7]

PARA 3 – RESPONSIBILITIES OF PARTICIPANTS

3.1 The UK AF will only arrest and detain personnel where permitted under ISAF Rules of Engagement. All detainees will be treated by UK AF in accordance with applicable

---

[6] For transfer of POW see Chapter 6 Section 6.2.2; for transfer in NIAC see Chapter 10 Section 10.6.3.
[7] www.publications.parliament.uk/pa/cm200607/cmselect/cmfaff/44/4412.htm.

provisions of international human rights law. Detainees will be transferred to the authorities of Afghanistan at the earliest opportunity where suitable facilities exist. Where such facilities are not in existence, the detainee will either be released or transferred to an ISAF approved holding facility.

3.2 The Afghan authorities will accept the transfer of persons arrested and detained by the UK AF for investigation and possible criminal proceedings. The Afghan authorities will be responsible for treating such individuals in accordance with Afghanistan's international human rights obligations including prohibiting torture and cruel, inhumane and degrading treatment, protection against torture and using only such force as is reasonable to guard against escape. The Afghan authorities will ensure that any detainee transferred to them by the UK AF will not be transferred to the authority of another state, including detention in another country, without the prior written agreement of the UK.

PARA 4 – ACCESS TO DETAINEES

4.1 Representatives of the Afghan Independent Human Rights Commission, and UK personnel including representatives of the British Embassy, members of the UK AF and others as accepted between the Participants, will have full access to any persons transferred by the UK AF to Afghan authorities whilst such persons are in custody. The International Committee of the Red Cross and Red Crescent (ICRC) and relevant human rights institutions with the UN system will be allowed to visit such persons.

4.2 UK personnel, including members of the UK AF will have full access to question any persons they transfer to the Afghan authorities whilst such persons are in custody.

3.7.2 Canada, *Arrangement for the Transfer of Detainees Between the Government of Canada and the Government of the Islamic Republic of Afghanistan*, 3 May 2007[8]

. . .

4. The Afghan authorities will be responsible for treating such individuals in accordance with Afghanistan's international human rights including prohibiting torture and cruel, inhuman or degrading treatment, protection against torture and using only such force as is reasonable to guard against escape. . . .

10. In the event that allegations come to the attention of the Government of Afghanistan that a detainee transferred by the Canadian Forces to Afghan authorities has been mistreated, the following corrective action will be undertaken: the Government of Afghanistan will investigate allegations of abuse and mistreatment and prosecute in accordance with national law and internationally applicable legal standards; the Government of Afghanistan will inform the Government of Canada, the AIHRC and the ICRC of the steps it is taking to investigate such allegations and any corrective action taken.

---

[8]   www.unodc.org/tldb/pdf/AFG-CANagreement2007.pdf. This agreement supplemented *the Arrangement for the transfer of detainees between the Canadian Forces and the Ministry of Defence of the Islamic Republic of Afghanistan*, 18 December 2005.

3.7.3 US, *Munaf v. Geren*, 553 U.S. 674, 128 S. Ct. 2207, 2218 (2008)

Note: *The Petitioners travelled to Iraq where they allegedly committed crimes. The Petitioners were subsequently captured and detained by the international coalition force MNF-I. Habeas corpus petitions were filed on the Petitioners' behalf alleging their transfer to Iraqi custody would result in torture. The Supreme Court held:*

Petitioners contend that these general principles are trumped in their cases because their transfer to Iraqi custody is likely to result in torture. ... Such allegations are of course a matter of serious concern, but in the present context that concern is to be addressed by the political branches, not the judiciary.

3.7.4 ECtHR, *Al-Saadoon and Mufdhi* v. *The United Kingdom*, (App No. 61498/08) Judgment (2 March 2010)

Note: *In March 2003, two British servicemen were ambushed and killed in Iraq. The Applicants were part of the group who slapped, rifle-butted and shot the soldiers at a time when they were POW. Such acts constituted war crimes. The Applicants were arrested and detained by British forces. In 2007, the Iraqi High Tribunal (IHT) requested the Applicants be transferred into its custody to stand trial for crimes, which carried the death penalty. The Applicants alleged their transfer to the IHT would violate their rights under Articles 2, 3, 6, 13 and 34 of the ECHR. The ECtHR held:*

143. In summary, therefore, the Court considers that, in the absence of any such binding assurance, the referral of the applicants' cases to the Iraqi courts and their physical transfer to the custody of the Iraqi authorities failed to take proper account of the United Kingdom's obligations under Articles 2 and 3 of the Convention and Article 1 of Protocol No. 13 since, throughout the period in question, there were substantial grounds for believing that the applicants would face a real risk of being sentenced to death and executed.

144. ..., it is the case that through the actions and inaction of the United Kingdom authorities the applicants have been subjected, since at least May 2006, to the fear of execution by the Iraqi authorities. The Court has held above that causing the applicants psychological suffering of this nature and degree constituted inhuman treatment. It follows that there has been a violation of Article 3 of the Convention.

3.7.5 EU, *Agreement Between the European Union and the Central African Republic Concerning Detailed Arrangements for the Transfer to the Central African Republic of Persons Detained by the European Union Military Operation (EUFOR RCA) in the Course of Carrying Out Its Mandate, and Concerning the Guarantees Applicable to Such Persons*[9]

Article 3

1. EUFOR RCA may transfer to the CAR the persons it detains under the conditions hereinafter laid down. 2. EUFOR RCA shall not transfer any person to the CAR if there is

---

[9]   Official Journal of the European Union L251/3 (23 August 2014).

reason to believe that the guarantees laid down in this Agreement will not be respected. . . .

Article 4

1. The CAR shall treat all transferred persons humanely at all times, without making any adverse distinction, and in accordance with the applicable rules of international law. . . . 4. In the event that a transferred person risks the death penalty or a penalty constituting cruel, inhumane or degrading treatment, such a penalty shall neither be sought, imposed nor carried out by the CAR with respect to that person. 5. No person transferred pursuant to this Article may subsequently be transferred to a third party without the prior written agreement of the EU. In the event of subsequent transfer to a third party, the CAR shall ensure that the third party complies with the guarantees laid down in paragraphs 1, 2 and 3 and shall ensure that in the event that a transferred person risks the death penalty or a penalty constituting cruel, inhumane or degrading treatment, such a penalty shall not be sought, imposed or carried out with respect to that person. In the event of subsequent transfer to any third party, the CAR shall guarantee the EU a right of unrestricted access to the persons so transferred.

Article 5

1. Transferred persons may present requests or complaints to the CAR regarding the way they are treated. The CAR shall undertake to examine any such request or complaint without delay and to communicate it immediately to EUFOR RCA. . . .

Article 7

EUFOR RCA may transfer to the International Criminal Court persons detained by EUFOR RCA.

3.7.6 African Union, *Guidelines on Detention and DDR* (2014)[10]

1.2.3 . . .

To be effective however, such an [transfer] agreement must contain at the very least – but not be limited to – the following commitments:

- to treat transferred detainees in accordance with international law and internationally recognised standards,
- where there are doubts as to the likely lack of a fair trial, not to execute them,
- to detain them at specified sites where treatment and conditions have been ascertained to respect international law and internationally recognised standards, and
- to establish a strong monitoring mechanism by the mission, that include notably allowing members of the mission to visit the detainees on a regular basis to ensure that those commitments are respected, and a corresponding commitments by the receiving State to address any concerns that might arise; and
- to allow other appropriate organisations, such as the International Committee of the Red Cross (ICRC), to visit transferred detainees.

---

[10]   www.peaceau.org/uploads/au-operational-guidance-note-on-detention-and-ddr.pdf.

3.8 TERRORISM

3.8.1 IACHR, *Report on Terrorism and Human Rights*, OEA/Ser.L/V/II.116 Doc.5 rev. 1 corr. (22 October 2002)

57. To the extent that terrorist or counter-terrorist actions may give rise to or occur in the context of the use of armed force between states or armed violence between governmental authorities and organized armed groups or between such groups within a state, as described in further detail below, they may implicate the possible application of rules of international humanitarian law in evaluating states' human rights obligations.

3.8.2 Israel, *The Public Committee Against Torture in Israel et al. v. The Government of Israel et al. ('Targeted Killing Case')*, Case No. HCJ 769/02, Israeli Supreme Court Sitting as the High Court of Justice (11 December 2005)

Note: *The facts of this case are outlined in Chapter 1, Section 1.6.1. Discussing the rights enjoyed by terrorists directly participating in hostilities, the Supreme Court of Israel commented as follows:*

40. .... Thus, if a terrorist taking a direct part in hostilities can be arrested, interrogated, and tried, those are the means which should be employed. Trial is preferable to use of force. .... Arrest, investigation, and trial are not means which can always be used. At times the possibility does not exist whatsoever; at times it involves a risk so great to the lives of the soldiers, that it is not required. However, it is a possibility which should always be considered. It might actually be particularly practical under the conditions of belligerent occupation, in which the army controls the area in which the operation takes place, and in which arrest, investigation, and trial are at times realizable possibilities. Of course, given the circumstances of a certain case, that possibility might not exist. At times, its harm to nearby innocent civilians might be greater than that caused by refraining from it. In that state of affairs, it should not be used. Third, after an attack on a civilian suspected of taking an active part, at such time, in hostilities, a thorough investigation regarding the precision of the identification of the target and the circumstances of the attack upon him is to be performed (retro actively). That investigation must be independent.

3.9 THE EFFECTS OF UN MANDATES

3.9.1 UK, *R (On the Application of Al-Jedda) (FC) v. Secretary of State for Defence* [2007] UKHL 58

Note: *On 10 October 2004, US soldiers, acting on UK intelligence, arrested the Applicant and conveyed him to Basra where he was detained by British forces at the Sha'aibah Divisional Temporary Detention Facility. The Applicant was interned until December 2007. The Applicant subsequently claimed his internment violated his rights under Article 5 ECHR (right to liberty and security). Assessing the way in which the UN Charter and UN Security*

Council Resolutions interact with ECHR rights, the House of Lords of the United Kingdom said as follows:

30. [...] For while the Secretary of State contends that the Charter [of the United Nations], and UNSCRs [United Nations Security Council Resolutions] 1511 (2003), 1546 (2004), 1637 (2005) and 1723 (2006), impose an obligation on the UK to detain the appellant which prevails over the appellant's conflicting right under Article 5 § 1 of the European Convention, the appellant insists that the UNSCRs referred to, read in the light of the Charter, at most authorise the UK to take action to detain him but do not oblige it to do so, with the result that no conflict arises and Article 103 is not engaged. . . .

33. . . . There is, however, a strong and to my mind persuasive body of academic opinion which would treat article 103 as applicable where conduct is authorised by the Security Council as where it is required . . .

34. I am further of the opinion, thirdly, that in a situation such as the present "obligations" in article 103 should not in any event be given a narrow, contract-based, meaning. . . .

35. Emphasis has often been laid on the special character of the European Convention as a human rights instrument. But the reference in article 103 to "any other international agreement" leaves no room for any excepted category, and such appears to be the consensus of learned opinion. . . .

39. Thus there is a clash between on the one hand a power or duty to detain exercisable on the express authority of the Security Council and, on the other, a fundamental human right which the UK has undertaken to secure to those (like the appellant) within its jurisdiction. How are these to be reconciled? There is in my opinion only one way in which they can be reconciled: by ruling that the UK may lawfully, where it is necessary for imperative reasons of security, exercise the power to detain authorised by UNSCR 1546 and successive resolutions, but must ensure that the detainee's rights under article 5 are not infringed to any greater extent than is inherent in such detention.

3.9.2 ECtHR, *Al-Jedda* v. *The United Kingdom* [GC], (App No. 27021/08) Judgment (7 July 2011)

Note: *On appeal to the ECtHR, the issue of the interaction of the UN Charter, UNSCRs and ECHR rights was considered again. The ECtHR reinforced the obligation on States to respect IHRL and rights under the ECHR in the following terms:*

102. . . ., the Court considers that, in interpreting its resolutions, there must be a presumption that the Security Council does not intend to impose any obligation on Member States to breach fundamental principles of human rights. In the event of any ambiguity in the terms of a Security Council Resolution, the Court must therefore choose the interpretation which is most in harmony with the requirements of the Convention and which avoids any conflict of obligations. In the light of the United Nations' important role in promoting and encouraging respect for human rights, it is to be expected that clear and explicit language would be used were the Security Council to intend States to take particular measures which would conflict with their obligations under international human rights law. . . .

105. The Court does not consider that the language used in this Resolution [1546] indicates unambiguously that the Security Council intended to place member States within the Multinational Force under an obligation to use measures of indefinite internment without charge and without judicial guarantees, in breach of their undertakings under international human rights instruments including the Convention. . . . In the absence of clear provision to the contrary, the presumption must be that the Security Council intended States within the Multinational Force to contribute towards the maintenance of security in Iraq while complying with their obligations under international human rights law.

3.10 UN PEACEKEEPING OPERATIONS AND HUMAN RIGHTS

3.10.1 Human Rights Committee, *Consideration of Reports submitted by States Parties under Article 40 of the Covenant,* Concluding Observations of the Human Rights Committee (12 August 2004), 81st Session, UN Doc. CCPR/CO/81/BEL

6. The State party should respect the safeguards established by the Covenant, not only in its territory but also when it exercises its jurisdiction abroad, as for example in the case of peacekeeping missions or NATO military missions, and should train the members of such missions appropriately.

3.10.2 ECtHR, *Agim Behrami and Bekir Behrami* v. *France* [GC] (App No. 71412/01) and *Ruzhdi Saramati* v. *France, Germany and Norway* [GC] (App No. 78166/01), (Decision as to Admissibility) (2 May 2007)

Note: Behrami v. France: *On 11 March 2000, the Applicant's sons, Gadaf and Bekim, were killed or injured when they stepped in a cluster bomb that had been dropped during the 1999 NATO bombardment of Yugoslavia. The UN Interim Administration for Kosovo (UNMIK) investigated the incident: in relation to Gadaf's death they declared it an unintentional homicide caused by imprudence and in relation to Bekim no prosecution was brought as the bomb did not explode in the bombardment;* Saramati v. France: *In April 2001, Mr Saramati was arrested by UNMIK police on suspicion of attempted murder and illegal possession of a weapon. From April 2001 to January 2002, Mr Saramati's detention was extended on numerous occasions, which he claimed violated his Article 5 rights under the ECHR. Addressing the nexus between UN peacekeeping missions, the UN Charter and IHRL, the ECtHR said:*

141. . . ., the Court observes that KFOR was exercising lawfully delegated Chapter VII powers of the UNSC so that the impugned action was, in principle, "attributable" to the UN within the meaning of the word outlined at paragraphs 29 and 121 above. . . .

143. . . ., the Court notes that UNMIK was a subsidiary organ of the UN created under Chapter VII of the Charter so that the impugned inaction was, in principle, "attributable" to the UN in the same sense.

144. It is therefore the case that the impugned action and inaction are, in principle, attributable to the UN. It is, moreover, clear that the UN has a legal personality separate from that of its member states ...

149. ... Since operations established by UNSC Resolutions under Chapter VII of the UN Charter are fundamental to the mission of the UN to secure international peace and security and since they rely for their effectiveness on support from member states, the Convention cannot be interpreted in a manner which would subject the acts and omissions of Contracting Parties which are covered by UNSC Resolutions and occur prior to or in the course of such missions, to the scrutiny of the Court. To do so would be to interfere with the fulfilment of the UN's key mission in this field including, as argued by certain parties, with the effective conduct of its operations. It would also be tantamount to imposing conditions on the implementation of a UNSC Resolution which were not provided for in the text of the Resolution itself. ...

152. In these circumstances, the Court concludes that the applicants' complaints must be declared incompatible *ratione personae* with the provisions of the Convention.

3.10.3 ECtHR, *Stichting Mothers of Srebrenica and Others against the Netherlands (Decision)*, (App No. 65542/12) (27 June 2013)

Note: *The Applicants in this case were the relatives of the victims of the 1995 Srebrenica genocide and an NGO representing the victims' relatives. The basis of the claim was a complaint against the decisions of the Netherlands courts to declare their case against the UN inadmissible on the grounds the UN possessed immunity from national courts' jurisdiction. The ECtHR said as follows:*

154. The Court finds that since operations established by United Nations Security Council resolutions under Chapter VII of the United Nations Charter are fundamental to the mission of the United Nations to secure international peace and security, the Convention cannot be interpreted in a manner which would subject the acts and omissions of the Security Council to domestic jurisdiction without the accord of the United Nations. To bring such operations within the scope of domestic jurisdiction would be to allow individual States, through their courts, to interfere with the fulfilment of the key mission of the United Nations in this field, including with the effective conduct of its operations. ...

158. ... International law does not support the position that a civil claim should override immunity from suit for the sole reason that it is based on an allegation of a particularly grave violation of a norm of international law, even a norm of *ius cogens*. ...

164. It does not follow, however, that in the absence of an alternative remedy the recognition of immunity is *ipso facto* constitutive of a violation of the right of access to a court. ...

169. The above findings lead the Court to find that in the present case the grant of immunity to the United Nations served a legitimate purpose and was not disproportionate.

COMMENTARY

1. IHRL and IHL may share common purposes but they differ in many respects. IHRL creates obligations incumbent on States whereas IHL imposes obligations on all parties to an armed conflict, including individuals and non-State actors. Certain human rights are subject to limitations or derogations whereas no derogations are permitted in IHL. Violations of IHRL give rise to State (civil) responsibility whereas violations of IHL give rise to both State (civil) and individual (criminal) responsibility, the latter for grave breaches of IHL. IHRL contains permanent monitoring and adjudication mechanisms where States and individuals have *locus standi*; however, IHL does not contain permanent enforcement mechanisms.[11]

2. There is no uniform approach to the relationship between IHRL and IHL. In certain instances, Courts follow the *lex specialis* principle according to which specific IHL rules trump IHRL whereas in other instances they follow variations of the complementary theory. The ECtHR traditionally applies the complementary approach, with the *Hassan* case being such an example.

3. Applying the *lex specialis* principle is not free from difficulties because the scope of IHL is limited, as in the case of NIACs.[12] Furthermore, it is not always evident whether a norm is general or specific. The complementary approach itself gives rise to questions concerning the 'correct' interpretation of IHL and IHRL.[13] Also, it often ignores the fact that IHL may apply exclusively to certain situations. Another question regarding the complementary approach is whether a breach of IHL, for instance a breach of the rules on the use of lethal force, would revive IHRL to the extent that such use of force would also be arbitrary under IHRL.[14] If IHRL revives in such situations, individuals will be able to seek reparations before national or international courts dealing with human rights violations, as will be discussed later and in Chapter 11.

4. Most IHRL covenants permit derogations from certain human rights in time of war or other public emergency threatening the life of the nation.[15] The question is whether the phrase 'in time of war' includes both IACs and NIACs and whether derogations 'in time of war' are automatic or require instead proof of a threat to the life of the nation. In *Hassan* the ECtHR indicated that specific derogation is required in situations amounting to a NIAC. Concerning the second basis of derogation – public emergency – there is debate as to whether it should affect the whole State or just parts of a State. In our opinion, even threats to parts of the State can justify derogations. Another critical question is whether derogations can be filed when the threat is not directed against the nation. Can, for instance, a

---

[11]   See Chapter 11 on enforcement and Chapter 12 on command responsibility.
[12]   See Chapter 10.
[13]   Compare, for example, the *Al-Jedda* (App No. 27021/08) (ECHR, 7 July 2011) and *Hassan* (App No. 29750/09) (ECHR, 16 September 2014) judgments of the ECtHR.
[14]   See, in this respect, the *Santo Domingo Massacre Case* (Judgment: Preliminary Objections, Merits and Reparations), Inter-Am. Ct. H.R., Series No. 259 and General Comment No. 3 of the African Commission on Human and Peoples' Rights.
[15]   See, for example, Art. 4 ICCPR and Art. 15 ECHR. Certain rights are, however, non-derogable, although such rights may vary between IHRL treaties.

State derogate from its human rights obligations when it is involved in an extraterritorial armed conflict as part of a UN force or as part of a coalition of States? In our view, to the extent that jurisdiction extends extraterritorially according to relevant jurisprudence,[16] the possibility of extraterritorial derogations should also be admitted. Although States have not as of yet filed derogations in relation to their extraterritorial operations, derogations may be an effective mechanism of setting the relationship between IHL and IHRL on the correct footing. It should finally be noted that, to the extent that derogations should not violate IHL, their effects are limited when there are overlaps between IHRL and IHL.

5. The use of lethal force is an area where IHL and IHRL often clash. Although both regimes include the requirements of necessity, precautions and proportionality, the scope and interpretation of these variables differ. According to the conduct of hostilities paradigm, the use of force is employed as a first resort whereas, according to the law enforcement paradigm, it is employed as a last resort, only if it is absolutely necessary to attain the legitimate purpose of protecting people against death, injury or serious crime and only if it is proportionate to the risk posed by the targeted individual. The law enforcement mantra is to capture rather than to kill. Determining which paradigm is applicable is crucial in NIACs[17] as well as in situations where no active hostilities take place. Whether in such situations the conduct of hostilities paradigm applies to all lawful targets or whether, depending on the circumstances, something more akin to the law enforcement paradigm should apply[18] is debated, with the former approach being the most credible in our view. In cases where lawful targets and protected persons intermingle and force is to be used against them, the two paradigms can apply in parallel, regulating the respective uses of force; however, in practical terms, this is extremely difficult.

6. The right to a fair trial is protected by both IHRL and IHL.[19] It has been contended that fair trial guarantees in IHRL and IHL form an integral whole. If they are thus integrated, the immediate question is whether the *lex specialis* formula is at all applicable. Related to this is the question of whether fair trial guarantees in IHL can be restricted in view of the IHRL restrictions on this right and, conversely, whether fair trial guarantees in IHRL can be derogated from in situations of an armed conflict.[20] If IHRL derogations should be compliant with IHL, no derogation should be permitted under the integrated approach. Another question is whether the use of military courts to try civilians in situations of armed conflict is permitted in view of the fact that IHRL does not prohibit such trials.[21]

---

[16] See *Al-Skeini and Others* v. *The United Kingdom* [GC], (App No. 55721/07) (ECtHR, Judgment, 7 July 2011), paras 130–142.

[17] See Chapter 10.

[18] See, for example, *The Targeted Killings* Case (Judgment), Case No. HCJ 769/02, Israeli Supreme Court Sitting as the High Court of Justice (11 December 2005). Also ICRC, Nils Melzer, Legal Adviser (ICRA), *Interpretive Guidance on the Notion of Direct Participation in Hostilities Under International Humanitarian Law*, Recommendation IX (Geneva, May 2009). The Interpretive Guidance is discussed in Chapters 4 and 10.

[19] See Common Article 3, GCs; Arts 96–98 GCIII; Arts 54, 64–74, 117–126 GCIV; Art. 75 API; Art. 6 APII.

[20] See Report of UN Working Group on Arbitrary Detention, *United Nations Basic Principles and Guidelines on Remedies and Procedures on the Right of Anyone Deprived of Their Liberty to Bring Proceedings before a Court* (6 July 2015), 30th Session, UN Doc. A/HRC/30/37, B. Principles, Principle 4.

[21] See *Case of Castillo Petruzzi et al.* v. *Peru* (Judgment: Merits, Reparations and Costs) Series C No. 52 (30 May 1999).

7. Detention in armed conflict implicates IHRL, particularly in NIACs where there are fewer rules regarding detention.[22] IHRL can thus complement the existing IHL rules, in particular with regard to the grounds for detention, the process of detention and the treatment of detainees. The transfer of detainees also brings into play IHRL, in particular the principle of *non-refoulement*, which prohibits the transfer of persons if there is a risk of their human rights being violated. Although IHL regulates transfers in certain situations, such as in the case of POW, its rules are limited,[23] particularly in NIACs. Thus, IHRL is considered to provide a complementary regulatory framework.[24] More specifically, IHRL can inform the grounds for *non-refoulement* and the procedural obligations of States before, during and after transfer. It can also prohibit secondary transfers or transfers when the risk arises from the activities of non-State actors. States often require diplomatic assurances in cases of transfer, but monitoring compliance with such assurances as well as enforcing their conditions in cases of non-compliance are critical issues. As the agreements and case law included in this chapter and further discussed in Chapter 10 show, certain types of conditions imposed on transfers are viewed favourably, such as requiring access to detainees, regular visits or suspension of transfers when individuals claim maltreatment. Yet, assurances can only be case specific. Other issues that may affect transfers include the lack of a functioning transferee State and intelligence challenges when reviewing detention.

8. Concerning armed groups, even if it is accepted that they are bound by IHRL,[25] questions remain as to the scope of their obligations and of their ability to implement them. Such questions are also pertinent in relation to detention by armed groups as discussed in more detail in Chapter 10. If armed groups are bound by certain customary human rights and indeed by non-derogable ones, the extent to which they can realise their obligations in cases of detention depends on whether they have a functioning legal and judicial system.[26]

9. The basis upon which a State's human rights jurisdiction extends to extraterritorial armed conflicts or occupation and which obligations apply in such cases have generated debates and disagreements. The two main bases of extraterritorial human rights jurisdiction as pronounced by the ECtHR in the *Al-Skeini* case are territorial and personal jurisdiction. The former arises when a State exercises control over territory and the latter when a State agent exercises control over a person outside a State's territory. In cases of occupation, the application of IHRL is complicated by differences in the degree of control required for

---

[22] See also Chapter 10 Section 10.6.
[23] Arts 12 and 118 GCIII; Art. 45 GCIV; Art. 5(4) APII. See Chapter 6 Section 6.2.2.
[24] Human Rights Committee, General Comment No. 20, Prohibition of Torture and Cruel Treatment or Punishment, UN Doc. CCPR/C/21/Rev.1/Add 13, 26 May 2004, para. 12 and General Comment No. 31, Nature of the General Legal Obligation Imposed on States Parties to the Covenant, UN Doc. HRI/GEN/1/Rev.1, 28 July 1994, p. 31, para. 9. European Court of Human Rights (ECtHR): *Soering* v. *The United Kingdom*, Judgment of 7 July 1989, Series A No. 161, para. 91; *Chahal* v. *United Kingdom* (App No. 70/1995/576/662) Judgment of 11 November 1996, para. 74.
[25] See Chapter 10 Section 10.2.
[26] See Chapter 10 and Chapter 11 Section 11.10.

occupation and for human rights jurisdiction, by the character and purpose of occupation, and by the occasional eruption of hostilities.[27]

10. Concerning the effects of Article 103 of the UN Charter on IHRL, it is broadly accepted that it applies to Security Council (SC) decisions as well as to SC authorisations. It is equally accepted that Article 103 does not invalidate contrary obligations, but jurisprudence and academic opinion are not in agreement as to its exact legal effects. Certain commentators hold the view Article 103 qualifies a State's IHRL obligations unless a contrary obligation is explicitly imposed by the SC. It is claimed, for example, that when the SC authorises States to 'use all necessary means', human rights continue to apply, albeit in a qualified form.[28] Others hold the view that Article 103 displaces derogable human rights obligations. The *Al-Jedda* jurisprudence provides evidence of these two approaches. The latter approach is, in our view, in sync with the function of Article 103 and of the UN as a whole. The only limitations to Article 103 seem to be non-derogable rights and *jus cogens* norms.

11. Whether international organisations, such as the UN, that are parties to an armed conflict have IHRL obligations and, if they do, what the scope of their obligations is has given rise to many debates. In our opinion, international organisations are bound by customary IHRL and, if they possess international personality, they can also be held responsible for violations of IHRL as well as of IHL. They can be held responsible for violations of IHRL committed by their troops if they exercise command and control over them although the International Law Commission (ILC) Draft Articles on the Responsibility of International Organisations require effective control by the international organisation over the impugned act.[29] It should be conceded, however, that realising their responsibility is difficult because the UN as well as other organisations enjoy immunity from legal process.[30]

12. Human rights bodies are often called upon to interpret or apply IHL. This is because IHL does not provide individuals with means of redress[31] and for this reason they often petition human rights bodies for related violations of IHRL. Human rights bodies do not, however, have competence to adjudicate on the basis of IHL. They instead adjudicate on the basis of IHRL, particularly when no derogation has been filed, and take into account IHL in the interpretation of IHRL. Sometimes they directly interpret IHL rules, but their interpretation is often contested.[32] This becomes apparent in cases involving the use of lethal force where, as was noted above, the human rights 'law enforcement' model is applied, often

---

[27]   See Chapter 9 on occupation.
[28]   In cases where forces are party to an armed conflict, the issue is about the relationship between IHL and IHRL.
[29]   ILC, Draft Articles on the Responsibility of International Organisations, 2011.
[30]   See Chapter 11 Section 11.8.
[31]   See Chapter 11 Section 11.3.
[32]   The IACHR has declared itself competent to address IHL in light of the common objectives and purposes of IHL and IHRL treaties (see *Abella* v. *Argentina* Case 11.137, Report No. 55/97, Inter-Am. C.H.R., OEA/Ser.L/V/ II.95, Doc 7 rev. (18 November 1997), para. 161) whereas the IACtHR addressed IHL because 'certain acts or omissions that violate human rights, pursuant to the treaties that they do have competence to apply, also violate other international instruments for the protection of the individual, such as the 1949 Geneva Conventions and, in particular, common Article 3'. See *Case of Bámaca Velásquez* v. *Guatemala* (Merits Judgment) Inter. Am. Ct. H.R. Series C, No. 70 (25 November 2000), para. 209.

interspersed with IHL considerations.[33] This approach also becomes apparent in relation to the procedural requirement of investigation attached to the right to life.[34] Although IHL imposes an obligation to investigate in an IAC, which can also be extended to NIAC,[35] deaths of lawful targets do not require investigation. However, according to IHRL, every death resulting from the use of force should be investigated. Moreover, IHL does not lay down any specific criteria according to which such investigations should be performed. Human rights courts often apply human rights standards of investigation in situations of armed conflict, as the *Al-Skeini* judgment shows, but one should recall the differences regarding the purpose and nature of investigation under IHL and IHRL. Another area where IHRL and IHL interpretations seem to diverge is with regard to the IHRL positive obligation to secure the right to life, with human rights courts often finding the planning and execution of lethal operations as falling below the required standards and thus violating the right to life. Another area of divergence concerns the proportionality assessment in cases where deaths occur, where human rights courts often assess military operations against the IHRL purposes of legitimate force.

13. In addition to the issues mentioned above, the relationship between IHRL and IHL is complicated further by the fact that the boundaries between war and peace are not clearly defined but there is often a spectrum of violence, sometimes rising to the level of an armed conflict, whereas other times falling below that threshold.

14. Lack of clarity as to what legal regime (IHRL or IHL) applies and how it applies creates uncertainty among service personnel that may affect their operational effectiveness.[36] Without denying the importance of IHRL and the importance of legal scrutiny of military operations, points of contention need to be addressed, perhaps within the IHL context, and not by IHRL institutions. In the meantime, however, high-quality training, updating military manuals and providing better legal advice may assist armed forces in fulfilling their IHRL and IHL obligations.

---

[33] See *Isayeva* v. *Russia*, (App No. 57950/00) (ECtHR, Former First Section Judgment, 24 February 2005), paras 170–200 or *Ergi* v. *Turkey* (App No. 23818/94) (ECHR, 28 July 1998), para. 79.

[34] See, for example, the *Al-Skeini* case (App No. 55721/07) (ECHR, 7 July 2011) from the ECtHR.

[35] CA1; Arts 49, 50, GCI; Arts 50, 51, GCII; Arts 129–130, GCIII; Arts 146–147, GCIV; Arts 11 and 85–87, API.

[36] For a rather dramatic approach to the effects of IHRL see T Tugendhat and L Croft, 'The Fog of Law: An Introduction to the Legal Erosion of British Fighting Power', *Policy Exchange* (2013) and Richard Ekins, Jonathan Morgan and Tom Tugendhat, 'Clearing the Fog of War', *Policy Exchange* (2015).

4

Principle of Distinction

INTRODUCTION

According to the principle of distinction, one of the foundational principles of IHL,[1] civilians and civilian objects should be distinguished from combatants and military objectives and they should be afforded protection against direct attack. The operation of the principle of distinction was relatively straightforward in the days of conventional warfare, although there have always been instances where the question arose as to whether an individual who participated in an armed conflict was a combatant or whether a civilian object was a military objective. Changes in the nature of armed conflict have posed challenges to this principle, ranging from the civilianisation of the functions of armed forces, the urbanisation of armed conflict, asymmetric wars, the increasing participation of civilians in armed conflicts, the outsourcing of war, to the development of new means and methods of warfare. The application of the principle of distinction has important legal and factual consequences concerning the treatment of those caught in an armed conflict. The most important consequence is that whereas combatants are legitimate targets, but enjoy combatant privilege (that is, immunity from prosecution for lawful acts of war), civilians enjoy protection from direct attacks unless they directly take part in hostilities. This chapter will focus on the personal scope of application of the principle of distinction by examining the question of who are combatants and who are civilians and when the latter are protected from direct attacks. The chapter will also consider the status of peacekeepers and the application of the principle of distinction to cyber war. Chapter 5 expands on the protections afforded to civilians and Chapter 7 examines the application of the principle in relation to targeting.

Resources: Art. 1, Hague Convention IV (HCIV); Common Article 3, GCs; Art. 4, GCIII; Arts 43, 44, 48, 51–54, 56–58 and 67, API; Art. 13, APII

---

[1]   See Chapter 2 Section 2.4 and also ICJ, *Legality of the Threat or Use of Nuclear Weapons* (Advisory Opinion) [1996] ICJ Rep. 226, para. 78.

Cases and Materials

4.1 PRINCIPLE OF DISTINCTION

4.1.1 Principle of Distinction

4.1.1.1 UK, British Ministry of Defence, *The Joint Service Manual of the Law of Armed Conflict* (Joint Service Publication 383, 2004 Edition)

2.5.1 The principle of distinction, sometimes referred to as the principle of discrimination or identification, separates combatants from non-combatants and legitimate military targets from civilian objects. This principle, and its application to warfare, is given expression in Additional Protocol I 1977.

2.5.2 Only combatants are permitted to take a direct part in hostilities. It follows that they may be attacked. Civilians may not take a direct part in hostilities and, for so long as they refrain from doing so, are protected from attack. . . .

4.4.3 The general obligation for a combatant to distinguish himself from the civilian population now applies only when the former is engaged in an attack or in a military operation preparatory to an attack. In order that the civilian population should be adequately protected, the expression 'military operation preparatory to an attack' must be given a wide meaning. Members of the armed forces who do not wear uniform, combat gear, or an adequate distinctive sign and whose sole arm is a concealed weapon, or who hide their arms on the approach of the enemy, will be considered to have lost their combatant status. . . .

4.5 'There are situations in armed conflicts where, owing to the nature of the hostilities, an armed combatant cannot so distinguish himself'. In such situations, a special rule applies and the individual will retain his status as a combatant provided that he 'carries his arms openly: (a) during each military engagement, and (b) during such time as he is visible to the adversary while he is engaged in a military deployment preceding the launching of an attack in which he is to participate'. In these exceptional situations, there is no obligation for a combatant to distinguish himself from the civilian population at any other time. The combatant is permitted, in effect, to disguise himself as a member of the civilian population and thereby seek to obtain the protection from attack given to the latter, except during the period of the attack and deployment.

4.5.1 Wide application of this special rule would reduce the protection of civilians to vanishing point. Members of the opposing armed forces would come to regard every civilian as likely to be a combatant in disguise and, for their own protection, would see them as proper targets for attack. The special rule is thus limited to those exceptional situations where a combatant is truly unable to operate effectively whilst distinguishing himself in accordance with the normal requirements. The United Kingdom, together with other states, made a formal statement on ratifying Additional Protocol I that this exception could only apply in occupied territory or in conflicts to which Additional Protocol I, Article 1(4) apply. Even in those cases, there are many occasions on which combatants can still comply with the general rule of distinction, which remains in force, when the special rule would not apply.

4.5.3 Even when the special rule applies, it requires, as a condition of retaining combatant status, that arms be carried openly in two cases. The first is during a military engagement, that is, when the combatant is in contact with the enemy. The second is during such time as he is visible to the adversary while engaged in a military deployment preceding the launching of an attack in which he is to participate. The term 'deployment' includes individual as well as group deployments. On ratifying Additional Protocol I, the United Kingdom, together with other states, made a formal declaration that the expression 'military deployment' means any movement towards a place from which an attack is to be launched. The requirement to carry arms openly during any such movement is limited to such time as the combatant is visible to the adversary. In the light of modern technical developments, 'visible' cannot be construed as meaning only 'visible to the naked eye'. A combatant is accordingly required to carry his arms openly if he is visible through binoculars or, during the night, visible by the use of infra-red or image intensification devices. The test is whether the adversary is able, using such devices, to distinguish a civilian from a combatant carrying a weapon. If such distinction can be made, the combatant is 'visible to the adversary'. The wide availability of these devices means that combatants who are seeking to take advantage of the special rule should carry their arms openly well before they are actually in contact with the enemy.

4.1.1.2 Germany, Federal Ministry of Defence, *Law of Armed Conflict – Manual – Joint Service Regulation (ZDv) 15/2* (May 2013)

301. In international armed conflicts, the law of armed conflict (LOAC) distinguishes first and foremost between combatants and civilians. Only combatants are entitled by LOAC to participate directly in hostilities.

302. According to LOAC the combatant status only exists in **international armed conflicts**.

303. While combatants are permissible military objectives, and thus may be attacked, it is not allowed to attack civilians. Civilians must to the maximum extent feasible be protected against the effects of hostilities, unless and for such time as they take a direct part in hostilities. If the latter is the case, they lose their protection.

304. Therefore, combatants must always be **distinguishable** from the civilian population by their uniform or another permanent distinctive emblem recognisable at a distance. Combatant and civilian status are also referred to as primary status.

4.1.1.3 M.N. Schmitt (ed.), *Tallinn Manual on the International Law Applicable to Cyber Warfare* (CUP, 2013), p. 112
Rule 31 – Distinction

The principle of distinction applies to cyber attacks.
. . .

5. Certain operations directed against the civilian population are lawful. For instance, psychological operations such as dropping leaflets or making propaganda broadcasts are not prohibited even if civilians are the intended audience. In the context of cyber warfare, transmitting email messages to the enemy population urging capitulation would likewise comply with the law of armed conflict. Only when a cyber operation against civilians or civilian objects (or other protected persons and objects) rises to the level of an attack is it prohibited by the principle of distinction and those rules of the law of armed conflict that derive from the principle.

4.1.1.4 UK, *Serdar Mohammed* v. *Ministry of Defence* [2014] EWHC 1369 (QB)
Note: On 7 April 2010, while participating in the International Security Assistance Force (ISAF) in Afghanistan, UK forces captured the Claimant who was a suspected Taliban commander. ISAF policy authorised detention for up to ninety-six hours, after which time the Claimant was to be released. However, UK ministers authorised his further detention for the purpose of gathering intelligence. The Claimant was questioned over a period of a further twenty-five days, following which, due to overcrowding in Afghan prisons, he was detained for a further eighty-one days. The Claimant was never given the opportunity to challenge the legality of his detention. Emphasising the difficulty one may encounter in distinguishing combatants from civilians, the UK High Court said:

247. In the context of non-international armed conflicts, defining these matters poses intractable problems. The rules applicable to international armed conflicts are based on the assumption that there is a reasonably clear distinction between combatants and civilians. . . . In non-international armed conflicts such as that taking place in Afghanistan the distinction between combatants and civilians may often be elusive. UNSCR 1890 (2009), for example, refers to "violent and terrorist activities by the Taliban, Al-Qaida, illegally armed groups, criminals and those involved in the narcotics trade" – descriptions which themselves indicate that there are no clear distinctions between those who can be said to be parties to an armed conflict and ordinary criminals.

4.1.1.5 US, Department of Defense, *Law of War Manual*, Office of General Counsel (June 2015, Updated 2016)
4.2 THE ARMED FORCES AND THE CIVILIAN POPULATION
The law of war has recognized that the population of an enemy State is generally divided into two classes: the armed forces and the civilian population, also sometimes called,

respectively, "combatants" and "civilians." This division results from the principle of distinction.

4.2.1 *Development of the Distinction Between the Armed Forces and the Civilian Population.* A citizen or national of a State that is a party to a conflict, as one of the constituents of a State that is engaged in hostilities, may be subjected to the hardships of war by an enemy State. However, because the ordinary members of the civilian population make no resistance, it has long been recognized that there is no right to make them the object of attack. . . .

4.2.2 *No Person May Claim the Distinct Rights Afforded to Both Combatants and Civilians at the Same Time.* The classes of combatants and civilians have distinct rights, duties, and liabilities; no person may claim the distinct rights afforded both classes at the same time. For example, a person may not claim the combatant's right to attack enemy forces while also claiming the civilian's right not to be made the object of attack

4.1.2 Combatants and Civilians

4.1.2.1 ICRC, *The Montreux Document on Pertinent International Legal Obligations and Good Practices for States Related to Operations of Private Military and Security Companies During Armed Conflict* (17 September 2008)

26. The personnel of PMSCs: . . .

b) are protected as civilians under international humanitarian law, unless they are incorporated into the regular armed forces of a State or are members of organized armed forces, groups or units under a command responsible to the State; or otherwise lose their protection as determined by international humanitarian law;

4.1.2.2 Germany, *Federal Ministry of Defence, Law of Armed Conflict – Manual – Joint Service Regulation (ZDv) 15/2* (May 2013)

1. Regular Armed Forces

307. The members of the armed forces of a Party to a conflict (with the exception of medical and religious personnel) are combatants, which means they have the right to participate directly in hostilities. . . .

2. Other Members of the Armed Forces

. . .

314. Members of **militias and volunteer corps** that **form part of** the armed forces are combatants, too. They must wear a permanent **distinctive sign** recognisable at a distance and carry their arms openly.

315. Moreover, combatants are members of **militias and volunteer corps,** including **organised resistance movements,** that do not form part of the (regular) armed forces but **belong to a Party to the conflict,** provided these militias and volunteer corps

– are commanded by a person responsible for his or her subordinates,
– have a fixed distinctive sign recognisable at a distance,
– carry their arms openly and
– are fighting in accordance with the laws and customs of war.

316. Situations in which the law of international armed conflict is applicable include armed conflicts which peoples are fighting against colonial domination and alien occupation as well as against racist regimes in the exercise of their right of **self-determination**. It thus follows that such peoples as Parties to a conflict also possess armed forces which are awarded the status of combatants in their struggle for the right of self-determination, provided they observe the following minimum rules: in such **struggles for liberation** and in **occupied territories** situations may occur in which, owing to the nature of the hostilities, combatants (especially guerrilla fighters) cannot distinguish themselves from the civilian population; they retain their status as combatants, however, provided that

– they carry their arms openly during all military operations and
– they carry their arms openly during such time as they are visible to the adversary while they are engaged in a military deployment preceding the launching of an attack in which they are to participate.

According to the German understanding, the term 'military deployment' in this context refers to any movement towards the point from which an attack is to be launched.

These criteria are, as a rule, only applicable in **occupied territories** and in **struggles for liberation**. . . .

317. Combatants are usually part of the armed forces, but in the case of a *levée en masse* they can also be found **outside** the armed forces. . . .

323. Violations of LOAC, however, do not deprive combatants of their right to be considered combatants.

4.1.2.3 US, Department of Defense, *Law of War Manual*, Office of General Counsel (June 2015, Updated 2016)

4.3.3 <u>Types of Lawful Combatants</u>. Three classes of persons qualify as "lawful" or "privileged" combatants:

- members of the armed forces of a State that is a party to a conflict, aside from certain categories of medical and religious personnel;
- under certain conditions, members of militia or volunteer corps that are not part of the armed forces of a State, but belong to a State; and
- inhabitants of an area who participate in a kind of popular uprising to defend against foreign invaders, known as a *levée en masse*.

5.8.2 <u>Categories of Persons Who Are Combatants for the Purpose of Assessing Their Liability to Attack</u>. The following categories of persons are combatants who may be made the object of attack because they are sufficiently associated with armed forces or armed groups:

- members of the armed forces of a State;
- members of militia and volunteer corps;
- participants in a *levée en masse*;
- persons belonging to non-State armed groups; and
- leaders whose responsibilities include the operational command and control of the armed forces or of a non-State armed group.

5.8.3 <u>Persons Belonging to Non-State Armed Groups</u>. Like members of an enemy State's armed forces, individuals who are formally or functionally part of a non-State armed group that is engaged in hostilities may be made the object of attack because they likewise share in their group's hostile intent.

4.1.3 Consequences of the Distinction

4.1.3.1 M.N. Schmitt (ed.), *Tallinn Manual on the International Law Applicable to Cyber Warfare* (CUP, 2013), pp. 113, 115–16

Rule 32 – Prohibition on attacking civilians

The civilian population as such, as well as individual civilians, shall not be the object of cyber attack.

. . .

Rule 34 – Persons as lawful objects of attack

The following persons may be made the object of cyber attacks:

(a) members of the armed forces;
(b) members of organized armed groups;
(c) civilians taking a direct part in hostilities; and
(d) in an international armed conflict, participants in a levée en masse.

. . .

2. Status or conduct may render an individual liable to attack. The targetability of the first two categories of persons is based on their status, whereas the targetability of the latter two depends on the conduct in which they engage.

4.1.3.2 US, Department of Defense, *Law of War Manual*, Office of General Counsel (June 2015, Updated 2016)

5.6 DISCRIMINATION IN CONDUCTING ATTACKS

Under the principle of distinction, combatants may make enemy combatants and other military objectives the object of attack, but may not make the civilian population and other protected persons and objects the object of attack.

4.2 DIRECT PARTICIPATION IN HOSTILITIES

4.2.1 Definition

4.2.1.1 Israel, *The Public Committee against Torture in Israel et al.* v. *The Government of Israel et al. ('Targeted Killing Case')*, (Judgment), Case No. HCJ 769/02, Israeli Supreme Court sitting as the High Court of Justice (11 December 2005)

Note: *The facts of this case are set out in Chapter 1, Section 1.6.1. As to the interpretation and limits of 'direct participation', the Israeli High Court said:*

34. Civilians lose the protection against military attack, granted to them by customary international law dealing with international armed conflict if "they take a direct part in hostilities". ... It seems accepted in the international literature that an agreed upon definition of the term "direct" in the context under discussion does not exist. ...

In that state of affairs, and without a comprehensive and agreed upon customary standard, there is no escaping going case by case, while narrowing the area of disagreement. ...

Indeed, a civilian bearing arms (openly or concealed) who is on his way to the place where he will use them against the army, at such place, or on his way back from it, is a civilian taking "an active part" in the hostilities. ... However, a civilian who generally supports the hostilities against the army is not taking a direct part in the hostilities ....

Similarly, a civilian who sells food or medicine to unlawful combatants is also taking an indirect part in the hostilities. ...

... And what is the law in the space between these two extremes? On the one hand, the desire to protect innocent civilians leads, in the hard cases, to a narrow interpretation of the term "direct" part in hostilities. ... On the other hand, it can be said that the desire to protect combatants and the desire to protect innocent civilians leads, in the hard cases, to a wide interpretation of the "direct" character of the hostilities, as thus civilians are encouraged to stay away from the hostilities to the extent possible. ...

35. Against the background of these considerations, the following cases should also be included in the definition of taking a "direct part" in hostilities: a person who collects intelligence on the army, whether on issues regarding the hostilities ..., or beyond those issues ...; a person who transports unlawful combatants to or from the place where the hostilities are taking place; a person who operates weapons which unlawful combatants use, or supervises their operation, or provides service to them, be the distance from the battlefield as it may. All those persons are performing the function of combatants. The function determines the directness of the part taken in the hostilities. ... However, a person who sells food or medicine to an unlawful combatant is not taking a direct part, rather an indirect part in the hostilities. The same is the case regarding a person who aids the unlawful combatants by general strategic analysis, and grants them logistical, general support, including monetary aid. The same is the case regarding a person who distributes propaganda supporting those unlawful combatants. If such persons are injured, the State is likely not to be liable for it, if it falls into the framework of collateral or incidental damage. ...

In the international literature there is a debate surrounding the following case: a person driving a truck carrying ammunition ... Some are of the opinion that such a person is taking a direct part in the hostilities (and thus he can be attacked), and some are of the opinion that he is not taking a direct part (and thus he cannot be attacked). Both opinions are in agreement that the ammunition in the truck can be attacked. The disagreement regards the attack upon the civilian driver. Those who think that he is taking a direct part in the hostilities are of the opinion that he can be attacked. Those who think that he is not taking a direct part in the hostilities believe that he cannot be attacked, but that if he is wounded, that is collateral damage caused to civilians proximate to the attackable military objective. In our opinion, if the civilian is driving the ammunition to the place from which it will be used for the purposes of hostilities, he should be seen as taking a direct part in the hostilities ...

36. What is the law regarding civilians serving as a "human shield" for terrorists taking a direct part in the hostilities? Certainly, if they are doing so because they were forced to do so by terrorists, those innocent civilians are not to be seen as taking a direct part in the hostilities. They themselves are victims of terrorism. However, if they do so of their own free will, out of support for the terrorist organization, they should be seen as persons taking a direct part in the hostilities ...

37. We have seen that a civilian causing harm to the army is taking "a direct part" in hostilities. What says the law about those who enlist him to take a direct part in the hostilities, and those who send him to commit hostilities? Is there a difference between his direct commanders and those responsible for them? Is the "direct" part taken only by the last terrorist in the chain of command, or by the entire chain? In our opinion, the "direct" character of the part taken should not be narrowed merely to the person committing the physical act of attack. Those who have sent him, as well, take "a direct part". The same goes for the person who decided upon the act, and the person who planned it. It is not to be said about them that they are taking an indirect part in the hostilities. Their contribution is direct (and active). ...

38. ... The provisions of article 51(3) of *The First Protocol* present a time requirement. A civilian taking a part in hostilities loses the protection from attack "for such time" as he is taking part in those hostilities. If "such time" has passed – the protection granted to the civilian returns. ...

39. ... With no consensus regarding the interpretation of the wording "for such time", there is no choice but to proceed from case to case. Again, it is helpful to examine the extreme cases. On the one hand, a civilian taking a direct part in hostilities one single time, or sporadically, who later detaches himself from that activity, is a civilian who, starting from the time he detached himself from that activity, is entitled to protection from attack. He is not to be attacked for the hostilities which he committed in the past. On the other hand, a civilian who has joined a terrorist organization which has become his "home", and in the framework of his role in that organization he commits a chain of hostilities, with short periods of rest between them, loses his immunity from attack "for such time" as he is committing the chain of acts. Indeed, regarding such a civilian, the rest between hostilities is nothing other than preparation for the next hostility.

4.2.1.2 ICTY, *Prosecutor* v. *Pavle Strugar et al.*, (Judgment), Case No. IT-01-42-A, Appeals Chamber (17 July 2008)

Note: *The events giving rise to this claim occurred during combat operations undertaken by the Yugoslav People's Army (JNA) in Dubrovnik (Croatia) between October and December 1991. The accused ordered the shelling of Dubrovnik, which resulted in death and injury to civilians whom the ICTY found were not actively taking part in hostilities. As to what conduct might amount to 'direct participation' and the distinction between 'direct' and 'indirect' participation, the ICTY Appeals Chamber said:*

176. Conduct amounting to direct or active participation in hostilities is not, however, limited to combat activities as such. ... The notion of direct participation in hostilities must

therefore refer to something different than involvement in violent or harmful acts against the adverse party. At the same time, direct participation in hostilities cannot be held to embrace all activities in support of one party's military operations or war effort. This is made clear by Article 15 of Geneva Convention IV, which draws a distinction between taking part in hostilities and performing "work of a military character". Moreover, to hold all activities in support of military operations as amounting to direct participation in hostilities would in practice render the principle of distinction meaningless.

177. ... Examples of active or direct participation in hostilities include: bearing, using or taking up arms, taking part in military or hostile acts, activities, conduct or operations, armed fighting or combat, participating in attacks against enemy personnel, property or equipment, transmitting military information for the immediate use of a belligerent, transporting weapons in proximity to combat operations, and serving as guards, intelligence agents, lookouts, or observers on behalf of military forces. Examples of indirect participation in hostilities include: participating in activities in support of the war or military effort of one of the parties to the conflict, selling goods to one of the parties to the conflict, expressing sympathy for the cause of one of the parties to the conflict, failing to act to prevent an incursion by one of the parties to the conflict, accompanying and supplying food to one of the parties to the conflict, gathering and transmitting military information, transporting arms and munitions, and providing supplies, and providing specialist advice regarding the selection of military personnel, their training or the correct maintenance of the weapons.

4.2.1.3 ICRC, *Interpretive Guidance on the Notion of Direct Participation in Hostilities Under International Law* (Geneva, May 2009),[2] pp. 32–4

Dissident armed forces: Although members of dissident armed forces are no longer members of State armed forces, they do not become civilians merely because they have turned against their government. At least to the extent, and for as long as, they remain organized under the structures of the State armed forces to which they formerly belonged, these structures should continue to determine individual membership in dissident armed forces as well.

Other organized armed groups: ... As has been shown above, in governing non-international armed conflict, the concept of organized armed group refers to non-State armed forces in a strictly functional sense. For the practical purposes of the principle of distinction, therefore, membership in such groups cannot depend on abstract affiliation, family ties, or other criteria prone to error, arbitrariness or abuse. Instead, membership must depend on whether the continuous function assumed by an individual corresponds to that collectively exercised by the group as a whole, namely the conduct of hostilities on behalf of a non-State party to the conflict. Consequently, under IHL, the decisive criterion for individual membership in an organized armed group is whether a person assumes a continuous function for the group involving his or her direct participation in hostilities (hereafter: "continuous combat function"). Continuous combat function does not imply de jure entitlement to combatant privilege. Rather, it distinguishes members of the organized fighting forces of a non-State party from civilians who directly participate in hostilities on a

---

[2]   See also Chapter 10.

merely spontaneous, sporadic, or unorganized basis, or who assume exclusively political, administrative or other non-combat functions.

Continuous combat function requires lasting integration into an organized armed group acting as the armed forces of a non-State party to an armed conflict. Thus, individuals whose continuous function involves the preparation, execution, or command of acts or operations amounting to direct participation in hostilities are assuming a continuous combat function. An individual recruited, trained and equipped by such a group to continuously and directly participate in hostilities on its behalf can be considered to assume a continuous combat function even before he or she first carries out a hostile act. This case must be distinguished from persons comparable to reservists who, after a period of basic training or active membership, leave the armed group and re-integrate into civilian life. Such "reservists" are civilians until and for such time as they are called back to active duty. Individuals who continuously accompany or support an organized armed group, but whose function does not involve direct participation in hostilities, are not members of that group within the meaning of IHL. Instead, they remain civilians assuming support functions, similar to private contractors and civilian employees accompanying State armed forces. Thus, recruiters, trainers, financiers and propagandists may continuously contribute to the general war effort of a non-State party, but they are not members of an organized armed group belonging to that party unless their function additionally includes activities amounting to direct participation in hostilities. The same applies to individuals whose function is limited to the purchasing, smuggling, manufacturing and maintaining of weapons and other equipment outside specific military operations or to the collection of intelligence other than of a tactical nature. Although such persons may accompany organized armed groups and provide substantial support to a party to the conflict, they do not assume continuous combat function and, for the purposes of the principle of distinction, cannot be regarded as members of an organized armed group. As civilians, they benefit from protection against direct attack unless and for such time as they directly participate in hostilities, even though their activities or location may increase their exposure to incidental death or injury.

4.2.1.4 US, Department of Defense, *Law of War Manual*, Office of General Counsel (June 2015, Updated 2016)

5.9.1 *Civilians Taking a Direct Part in Hostilities – Notes on Terminology*. This manual uses the phrase "direct part in hostilities" to indicate what activities cause a civilian to forfeit his or her protection from being made the object of attack. This usage does not mean that the United States has adopted the direct participation in hostilities rule that is expressed in Article 51 of AP I.

. . .

5.9.1.2. *AP I, Article 51(3) Provision on Direct Participation in Hostilities*. Although, as drafted, Article 51(3) of AP I does not reflect customary international law, the United States supports the customary principle on which Article 51(3) is based. Similarly, although parts of the ICRC's interpretive guidance on the meaning of direct participation in hostilities are consistent with customary international law, the United States has not accepted significant parts of the ICRC's interpretive guidance as accurately reflecting customary international law. But some States that are Parties to AP I may interpret and apply Article 51(3) of AP I consistent with the customary international law standard.

5.9.2 *Persons to Whom This Rule Applies*. For the purpose of applying the rule discussed in this section, "civilians" are persons who do not fall within the categories of combatants. ... Accordingly, for the purposes of this section, "civilians" include:

- members of the civilian population;
- persons authorized to accompany the armed forces; and
- members of the merchant marine and civil aircraft of parties to a conflict.

4.2.2 Consequences of Direct Participation in Hostilities

4.2.2.1 IACHR, *Juan Carlos Abella* v. *Argentina*, Case No. 11.137, Report No. 55/97, Inter-Am. C.H.R., OEA/Ser.L/V/II.95, Doc 7 rev. (18 November 1997)

Note: *The background to this case is dealt with at page 10. On the nexus between the right to life under IHRL and the effects, under IHL, of civilians directly participating in hostilities, the Commission said as follows:*

178. ... Specifically, when civilians, such as those who attacked the Tablada base, assume the role of combatants by directly taking part in fighting, whether singly or as a member of a group, they thereby become legitimate military targets. As such, they are subject to direct individualized attack to the same extent as combatants. Thus, by virtue of their hostile acts, the Tablada attackers lost the benefits of the above mentioned precautions in attack and against the effects of indiscriminate or disproportionate attacks pertaining to peaceable civilians. In contrast, these humanitarian law rules continued to apply in full force with respect to those peaceable civilians present or living in the vicinity of the La Tablada base at the time of the hostilities. ...

179. When they attacked the La Tablada base, those persons involved clearly assumed the risk of a military response by the State. The fact that the Argentine military had superior numbers and fire power and brought them to bear against the attackers cannot be regarded in and of itself as a violation of any rule of humanitarian law. This does not mean, however, that either the Argentine military or the MTP attackers had unlimited discretion in their choice of means of injuring the other. Rather, both parties were required to conduct their military operations within the restraints and prohibitions imposed by applicable humanitarian law rules.

4.2.3 Direct Participation in Hostilities in Cyber Warfare

4.2.3.1 M.N. Schmitt (ed.), *Tallinn Manual on the International Law Applicable to Cyber Warfare* (CUP, 2013), pp. 120–2

Rule 35–Civilian Direct Participants in Hostilities

Civilians enjoy protection against attack unless and for such time as they directly participate in hostilities.

. . .

5. Clearly, conducting cyber attacks related to an armed conflict qualifies as an act of direct participation, as do any actions that make possible specific attacks, such as identifying vulnerabilities in a targeted system or designing malware in order to take advantage of particular vulnerabilities. Other unambiguous examples include gathering information on enemy operations by cyber means and passing it to one's own armed forces and conducting DDoS operations against enemy military systems. On the other hand, designing malware and making it openly available online, even if it may be used by someone involved in the conflict to conduct an attack, does not constitute direct participation. Neither would maintaining computer equipment generally, even if such equipment is subsequently used in the hostilities. A more difficult situation arises when malware is developed and provided to individuals in circumstance where it is clear that it will be used to conduct attacks, but where the precise intended target is unknown to the supplier. The International Group of Experts was divided as to whether the causal connection between the act of providing the malware and the subsequent attack is, in such a situation, sufficiently direct to qualify as direct participation.

. . .

7. Any act of direct participation in hostilities by a civilian renders that person targetable for such time as he or she is engaged in the qualifying act of direct participation. All of the Experts agreed that this would include actions immediately preceding or subsequent to the qualifying act. For instance, travelling to and from the location where a computer used to mount an operation is based would be encompassed in the notion. Some of the Experts took the position that the period of participation extended as far 'upstream' and 'downstream' as a causal link existed. In a cyber operation this period might begin once an individual began probing the target system for vulnerabilities, extend throughout the duration of activities against that system, and include the period during which damage is assessed to determine whether re-attack is required.

8. A particularly important issue in the cyber context is that of 'delayed effects'. An example is emplacement of a logic bomb designed to activate at some future point. . . . The majority of the International Group of Experts took the view that the duration of an individual's direct participation extends from the beginning of his involvement in mission planning to the point when he or she terminates an active role in the operation. In the example the duration of the direct participation would run from the commencement of planning how to emplace the logic bomb through activation upon command by that individual. Note that the end of the period of direct participation may not necessarily correspond with the point at which the damage occurs. This would be so in the case emplacement of the logic bomb by one individual and later activation by another. . . .

9. A minority of the International Group of Experts would characterize emplacement and activation by the same individual as separate acts of direct participation. . . .

10. A further issue regarding the period of direct participation and this susceptibility to attack, involves a situation in which an individual launches repeated cyber operations that qualify as direct participation. Such circumstances are highly likely to arise in the context of cyber operations, for an individual may mount repeated separate operations over time,

either against the same cyber target or different ones. ... Some of the Experts took the position ... that each act must be treated separately in terms of direct participation analysis. Other Experts argued that this position makes little operational sense ... For these Experts, direct participation begins with the first such cyber operation and continues throughout the period of intermittent activity.

4.3 LOSS OF COMBATANT PROTECTION – 'UNLAWFUL COMBATANTS'

4.3.1 US, *Ex Parte Quirin*, 317 U.S. 1, 30–1 (1942)

Note: *The Petitioners in this case were all born in Germany, but lived in the United States. The Petitioners returned to Germany between 1933 and 1941. After the declaration of war between the US and the German Reich, the Petitioners received military training at a sabotage school near Berlin. The Petitioners subsequently boarded a German submarine at a seaport in occupied France and returned to the United States with instructions to destroy war industries and facilities in the United States. The Petitioners were subsequently captured and brought before a military commission for offences against the law of war. As to the distinction between lawful and unlawful combatants, the US Supreme Court said:*

By universal agreement and practice, the law of war draws a distinction between the armed forces and the peaceful populations of belligerent nations, and also between those who are lawful and unlawful combatants. Lawful combatants are subject to capture and detention as prisoners of war by opposing military forces. Unlawful combatants are likewise subject to capture and detention, but, in addition, they are subject to trial and punishment by military tribunals for acts which render their belligerency unlawful. The spy who secretly and without uniform passes the military lines of a belligerent in time of war, seeking to gather military information and communicate it to the enemy, or an enemy combatant who without uniform comes secretly through the lines for the purpose of waging war by destruction of life or property, are familiar examples of belligerents who are generally deemed not to be entitled to the status of prisoners of war, but to be offenders against the law of war subject to trial and punishment by military tribunals.

4.3.2 Privy Council (Malaysia), *Osman Bin Haji Mohamed Ali and Another v. Public Prosecutor* [1969] 1 AC 430, pp. 452–3

Note: *In March 1965, during the armed conflict between Malaysia and Indonesia, two Indonesian soldiers dressed in civilian clothing planted explosives in a civilian building in Singapore. The explosion killed civilians. As to the limits of the civilian protection, the Privy Council said:*

In this appeal it is not necessary to attempt to define all the circumstances in which a person coming within the terms of Article I of the Regulations and of Article 4 of the Convention as a member of an army or armed force ceases to enjoy the right to be treated as a prisoner of war. The question to be decided is whether members of such a force who engage in sabotage while in civilian clothes and who are captured so dressed are entitled to be treated as protected by the Convention.

..., their lordships are of the opinion that under international law it is clear that the appellants, if they were members of the Indonesian armed forces, were not entitled to be treated on capture as prisoners of war under the Geneva Convention when they had landed to commit sabotage and had been dressed in civilian clothes both when they had placed the explosives and lit them and when they were arrested. In their opinion Chua J. and the Federal Court were right in rejecting the appellants' plea on this ground.

4.3.3 US, *United States of America* v. *Buck*, 690 F. Supp. 1291 (S.D.N.Y., 1988)

Note: The Defendants were African Americans who sought protection under international law on the grounds they were a colonised people, 'New Afrikans', engaged in a struggle for self-determination and as such they were entitled to judicial recognition of the 'war-like nature of their struggle' and their status as POWs. As to the criteria organised resistance groups must satisfy to benefit from POW status, the District Court for the Southern District of New York said:

Article 4(A) (2) [GCIII] requires that to qualify as prisoners of war, members of "organized resistance movements" must fulfil the conditions of command by a person responsible for his subordinates; having a fixed distinctive sign recognizable at a distance; carrying arms openly; and conducting their operations in accordance with the laws and customs of war. The defendants at bar and their associates cannot pretend to have fulfilled those conditions.

4.3.4 US, **Military Commissions Act of 2009, 10 U.S.C. §948a**

...

(7) UNPRIVILEGED ENEMY BELLIGERENT- The term 'unprivileged enemy belligerent' means an individual (other than a privileged belligerent) who –

(A) has engaged in hostilities against the United States or its coalition partners;
(B) has purposefully and materially supported hostilities against the United States or its coalition partners; or
(C) was a part of al Qaeda at the time of the alleged offense under this chapter.

4.3.5 US, *United States of America* v. *Omar Ahmed Khadr*, **Stipulation of** Fact (31 October 2010)[3]

Note: Khadr was a fifteen-year-old Canadian citizen captured in a firefight in Afghanistan in July 2002. Khadr was accused of throwing a grenade that killed a US army sergeant. As to the loss of Khadr's civilian protection, the US Military Commission said:

...

---

[3] https://graphics8.nytimes.com/packages/pdf/politics/20101026-gitmo/Signed-Stipulation-of-Fact-ICO-Omar-Khadr.pdf.

1. Omar Khadr is an alien unprivileged enemy belligerent, as defined by the Military Commissions Act of 2009 (MCA). . . . Omar Khadr is an enemy belligerent because he has purposefully and materially supported hostilities against the United States and its coalition partners. Omar Khadr is an unprivileged belligerent because he does not fall within one of the eight categories enumerated under Article 4 of the Geneva Convention Relative to the Treatment of Prisoners of War.

4.3.6 Germany, Federal Ministry of Defence, *Law of Armed Conflict – Manual – Joint Service Regulation (ZDv) 15/2* (May 2013)

344. Occasionally, the terms 'unlawful, illegal, illegitimate or unprivileged combatants' are used. These terms are frequently used for civilians that take a direct part in hostilities without being entitled to do so, or mercenaries. A special category such as this is not, however, recognised by LOAC. In international law, the term combatant refers only to persons who are **entitled and authorised** as agents of the State to take a direct part in hostilities as part of international armed conflicts. If, after capture by the adversary, the status of a person is unclear, his or her status must be determined by a competent authority of the Detaining Power ('competent tribunal') such as a court.

4.3.7 US, Department of Defense, *Law of War Manual*, Office of General Counsel (June 2015, Updated 2016)

4.3 LAWFUL COMBATANTS AND UNPRIVILEGED BELLIGERENTS

In addition to distinguishing between the armed forces and the civilian population, the law of war also distinguishes between "privileged" and "unprivileged," or "lawful" and "unlawful" combatants. . . .

"Unlawful combatants" or "unprivileged belligerents" are persons who, by engaging in hostilities, have incurred one or more of the corresponding liabilities of combatant status (*e.g.*, being made the object of attack and subject to detention), but who are not entitled to any of the distinct privileges of combatant status (*e.g.*, combatant immunity and POW status).

4.3.1 *"Unprivileged Belligerents" as a Category in Treaty Law.* States have, in a few cases, explicitly recognized in treaties certain categories of unprivileged belligerents, such as spies and saboteurs. However, States have generally refrained from explicitly recognizing unprivileged belligerents as a class in treaties in the way that classes of lawful combatants have been defined. . . .

Although seldom explicitly recognized as a class in law of war treaties, the category of unprivileged belligerent may be understood as an implicit consequence of creating the classes of lawful combatants and peaceful civilians. The concept of unprivileged belligerency, *i.e.*, the set of legal liabilities associated with unprivileged belligerents, may be understood in opposition to the rights, duties, and liabilities of lawful combatants and peaceful civilians. Unprivileged belligerents include lawful combatants who have forfeited the privileges of combatant status by engaging in spying or sabotage, and private persons who have forfeited one or more of the protections of civilian status by engaging in hostilities.

4.4 UN PEACEKEEPERS

4.4.1 UN, Secretary-General's Bulletin, *Observance by the United Nations Forces of International Humanitarian Law* (6 August 1999), UN Doc. ST/SGB/1999/13

Note: *For the purpose of setting out the principles of IHL applicable to UN forces, the UN Secretary-General issued the following guidance:*

Section 1 – Field of application

1.1 The fundamental principles and rules of international humanitarian law set out in the present bulletin are applicable to United Nations forces when in situations of armed conflict they are actively engaged therein as combatants, to the extent and for the duration of their engagement. They are accordingly applicable in enforcement actions, or in peacekeeping operations when the use of force is permitted in self-defence.

1.2 The promulgation of this bulletin does not affect the protected status of members of peacekeeping operations under the 1994 Convention on the Safety of United Nations and Associated Personnel or their status as non-combatants, as long as they are entitled to the protection given to civilians under the international law of armed conflict.

4.4.2 SCSL, *Prosecutor v. Issa Hassan Sesay, Morris Kallon and Augustine Gbao ('the RUF Trial')*, (Judgment), Case No. SCSL-04-15-T Trial Chamber I (2 March 2009)

Note: *The Defendants were members of the Revolutionary United Front charged, inter alia, with killing members of the United Nations Mission in Sierra Leone (UNAMSIL). On the issue of the status of UN forces in armed conflicts, the Special Court commented as follows:*

233. In the Chamber's view, common sense dictates that peacekeepers are considered to be civilians only insofar as they fall within the definition of civilians laid down for non-combatants in customary international law and under Additional Protocol II as discussed above – namely, that they do not take a direct part in hostilities. It is also the Chamber's view that by force of logic, personnel of peacekeeping missions are entitled to protection as long as they are not taking a direct part in the hostilities – and thus have become combatants – at the time of the alleged offence. Where peacekeepers become combatants, they can be legitimate targets for the extent of their participation in accordance with international humanitarian law. As with all civilians, their protection would not cease if the personnel use armed force only in exercising their right to individual self-defence. Likewise, the Chamber opines that the use of force by peacekeepers in self-defence in the discharge of their mandate, provided that it is limited to such use, would not alter or diminish the protection afforded to peacekeepers.

234. In determining whether the peacekeeping personnel or objects of a peacekeeping mission are entitled to civilian protection, the Chamber must consider the totality of the circumstances existing at the time of the alleged offence, including, *inter alia*, the relevant Security Council resolutions for the operation, the specific operational mandates, the role and practices actually adopted by the peacekeeping mission during the particular conflict,

their rules of engagement and operational orders, the nature of the arms and equipment used by the peacekeeping force, the interaction between the peacekeeping force and the parties involved in the conflict, any use of force between the peacekeeping force and the parties in the conflict, the nature and frequency of such force and the conduct of the alleged victim(s) and their fellow personnel.

4.4.3 ICC, *The Prosecutor* v. *Bahar Idriss Abu Garda*, (Decision on the Confirmation of Charges), Case No. ICC-02/05-02/09, Pre-Trial Chamber I (8 February 2010)

Note: *Mr Abu Garda was charged with intentionally directing attacks against 'personnel, installations, material, units and vehicles involved in peacekeeping missions' during the conflict in Darfur. On the protection afforded to UN forces, the ICC commented:*

78. Article 13 (3) of APII provides that "civilians shall enjoy the protection afforded by [Part IV of the Protocol], *unless and for such time* as they take a direct part in hostilities" [emphasis added]. The same exclusion applies, under article 2(2) of the Convention on the Safety of United Nations and Associated Personnel, to personnel engaged as combatants....

80. On the other hand, neither treaty law nor customary law expressly define what constitutes direct participation in hostilities. However, the Commentary to article 13 of APII provides guidance as to its meaning. According to the Commentary, "[h]ostilities have been defined as 'acts of war' that by their nature or purpose struck at the personnel and 'matériel' of enemy armed forces." The Commentary further indicates that taking direct part in hostilities "implies that there is a sufficient causal relationship between the act of participation and its immediate consequences." ...

83. In light of the foregoing considerations, the Majority concludes that, under the Statute, personnel involved in peacekeeping missions enjoy protection from attacks unless and for such time as they take a direct part in hostilities or in combat-related activities. The Majority also finds that such protection does not cease if such persons only use armed force in exercise of their right to self-defence. ...

89. ... the Majority concludes that installations, material, units or vehicles involved in a peacekeeping mission in the context of an armed conflict not of an international character shall not be considered military objectives, and thus shall be entitled to the protection given to civilian objects, unless and for such time as their nature, location, purpose or use make an effective contribution to the military action of a party to a conflict and insofar as their total or partial destruction, capture or neutralization, in the circumstances ruling at the time, offers a definite military advantage.

4.4.4 Germany, Federal Ministry of Defence, *Law of Armed Conflict – Manual – Joint Service Regulation (ZDv) 15/2* (May 2013)

Armed Forces on UN Missions

332. The combatant status of members of armed forces will not be affected by their employment in international armed conflicts as part of **United Nations** missions.

COMMENTARY

1. The principle of distinction is juxtaposed between the principle of humanity and the principle of military necessity and holds that civilians and civilian objects should be protected from direct attacks whereas combatants and military objectives can be made the object of direct attacks. This is because civilians and civilian objects, by status or function, do not make a direct contribution to the armed conflict. In addition to this, the professionalisation of armed conflict – fought by a class of professionals – and the rejection of total wars can be mentioned as reasons that also underpin the principle of distinction.

2. Determining who is a combatant is critical for the application of the principle of distinction because civilians are defined negatively as those persons who are not combatants. There are three categories of persons entitled to combatant status according to Article 4 GCIII:[4] (i) members of the armed forces of a State including incorporated militia and volunteer corps;[5] (ii) members of militias, armed groups and organised resistance movements belonging to a party to the conflict that are under responsible command, possess a fixed distinctive sign, carry arms openly and respect IHL;[6] and (iii) members of a *levée en masse*.[7] Whether members of armed groups need to satisfy the criteria mentioned above individually as well as collectively has led to controversy. Certain commentators maintain that, if a member of such a group or the group itself does not fulfil all four criteria, combatancy is denied. This of course creates disparity in the treatment of such groups compared to the regular army. Others have even claimed that these criteria apply to the regular army. The controversy surrounding the treatment of Taliban and Al-Qaeda fighters captured in Afghanistan during the 2001 armed conflict is indicative.[8] That said, the definition of combatancy in Art. 4, GCIII needs to be viewed in light of Art. 43, API, which provides an integrated and streamlined definition of 'armed forces' and, consequently, of combatancy; it encompasses armed forces, groups and militias who are under responsible command.[9] Art. 44, API reduces even further the conditions for combatancy in the case of wars of self-determination or in occupation.[10] It should be noted, however, that States differ in their approach to the conditions applicable under API and contest its customary law status.

---

[4] See also Art. 1, Hague Convention IV. The GCs do not define who is 'combatant', but a definition is usually drawn from Art. 4, GCIII, which determines who is entitled to POW status. As will be discussed in Chapter 5, whereas combatants are entitled to POW status, not all POW need to be combatants. See also Art. 50(1), API.

[5] Art. 4(A)(1), GCIII.

[6] Art. 4(A)(2), GCIII.

[7] Art. 4(A)(6), GCIII.

[8] *White House Press Secretary announcement of President Bush's determination re. legal status of Taliban and Al Qaeda detainees* (White House, 7 February 2002) www.state.gov/s/l/38727.htm. UN Commission on Human Rights, Situation of Detainees at Guantánamo Bay (27 February 2006), 62nd Session, UN Doc. E/CN.4/2006/120. Also see sections on terrorism in Chapter 1 Section 1.6 and in Chapter 3 Section 3.8.

[9] Art. 44(1) and (2), API.

[10] Art. 44(3) and (4), API.

3. The principle of distinction applies to both IACs and NIACs,[11] but, with the increasing participation of civilians in armed conflict, its application became more problematic as was noted in the *Serdar Mohammed* case, particularly in NIACs.[12] The ICRC *Interpretive Guidance* builds on Art. 51(3), API and Art. 13, APII by defining which acts amount to direct participation in hostilities (DPH) rendering civilians undertaking such acts direct targets of attack. For DPH three conditions need to be satisfied: (i) threshold of harm; (ii) direct causation and (iii) belligerent nexus.[13] The first condition broadens the type of acts beyond attacks[14] by including acts that adversely affect the military operations of a party to the conflict. In this regard, even acts that cause no physical harm can be included but it does not include war-sustaining activities. Direct causation requires that the harm is caused in one causal step but it has been criticised as being too restrictive. According to the *Interpretive Guidance*, direct causation extends also to acts integral to a concrete and coordinated tactical operation[15] but, even in this case, it is limited to acts integral to the execution of the operation. The condition of belligerent nexus raises questions about the objective or subjective nature of the nexus. Finally, the temporal scope of DPH is equally questioned. Civilians who directly participate in hostilities can be attacked for such time as their participation lasts, which also includes preparatory measures as well as return from the action. With regard to preparatory measures, only those aimed at carrying out the specific hostile act are included.

4. The ICRC *Interpretive Guidance* makes a distinction between civilians sporadically participating in hostilities and those participating regularly as members of an organised armed group. The latter have 'continuous combatant function'. The consequences of such distinction is that civilians who sporadically take part in hostilities are targetable in limited circumstances, regaining civilian status when not taking a direct part in hostilities, whereas those having continuous combatant function are targetable at any time until they cease to have such function. This issue is particularly important in NIACs and is discussed in Chapter 10. As will be explained there, it is membership of the military wing of an armed group rather than function that should remove the civilian protection. In this way, parity between members of a State's armed forces and members of armed groups will be restored.

5. Applying the concept of DPH to cyber war is fraught with difficulties. If DPH includes acts that directly relate or are integral to the execution of a specific attack and not acts that relate to building the capacity to attack, which civilians – those that develop malware, those that install malware to a system or those that execute the command – directly participate in hostilities? In what sense does an act become integral to the execution of a cyber attack? Is, for instance, a general mapping of the adversary's cyber systems integral to the attack that follows or should such mapping be specific? Is loading data to a machine integral to the attack? Is technical or scientific support integral to an attack due to the technical

---

[11]   ICRC, J. Henckaerts and L. Doswald-Beck, *Customary International Humanitarian Law*, Vol. 1: Rules (CUP, 2009), Rule 1.

[12]   For NIACs, see Chapter 10.

[13]   For a general discussion and critique see Forum: The ICRC Interpretive Guidance on the Notion of Direct Participation in Hostilities Under International Humanitarian Law (2009–2010) 42 *N.Y.U. J. Int'l L. & Pol.* 637f.

[14]   Art. 49(1), API.

[15]   *Interpretive Guidance on the Notion of Direct Participation in Hostilities Under International Law* (Geneva, May 2009), pp. 54–5.

knowledge needed to operate cyber systems? How can the time frame for DPH be applied to cyber operations that have delayed effects or involve repeated attacks? In the latter case, should they be treated as separate acts of DPH or viewed as a whole? In our opinion, the latter approach is more appropriate, but where is the line between sporadic and regular acts of DPH drawn? Do individuals whose identities have been spoofed directly participate in hostilities? It is claimed that they are protected from direct attack,[16] but being able to correctly attribute the attack is critical in this case. Regarding the concept of 'continuous combatant function', in Chapter 1 we expressed our reservations as to whether cyber groups can satisfy the criterion of organisation; therefore, individual DPH is critical in cyber war.

6. The status of members of private military security companies may differ depending on their formal status or on their function. If they are incorporated into the armed forces of a State, they become combatants by status. Otherwise, they are civilians who accompany the armed forces[17] and are not entitled to participate in the armed conflict. In this case, they can be protected from direct attack and be granted POW status if captured. If they directly participate in hostilities, they can, as proposed in Chapter 6, be targeted and be denied POW status.

7. 'Unlawful combatants' or 'unprivileged belligerents' is not a third category of persons in IHL. As was said, IHL recognises only two categories of persons: combatants and civilians. These terms describe persons who participate in hostilities without being entitled to do so. Such persons are civilians who lose their immunity from direct attack and, if captured, are not entitled to POW status. They can also be prosecuted for their participation in the armed conflict.

8. The status of peacekeepers has given rise to debate. A UN peacekeeping force deployed during an armed conflict usually has a civilian and a military component and operates under UN command and control. The 1999 Secretary-General's Bulletin implies that when peacekeepers are 'actively engaged' in an armed conflict they are combatants for the duration of their engagement; otherwise they are protected as civilians. If this does not create a new category of temporarily limited combatancy, it is equivalent to the notion of DPH. The *RUF* and *Abu Garda* cases treat peacekeepers as civilians who directly participate in hostilities. Both approaches seem to overlook the fact that the military component of the UN force consists of military personnel lent by member States who are by definition combatants. They also seem to indicate that even if the UN force becomes party to an armed conflict, its military personnel remain civilians who may occasionally directly participate in hostilities or that they become 'combatants' when actively engaged in hostilities. This of course does not accord with the principle of equality of belligerents. As we said in Chapter 1, members of the military component of a UN peacekeeping force are combatants and remain combatants for the duration of the mission whereas members of the civilian component are protected as civilians, unless they directly participate in hostilities.

---

[16] Nils Melzer, Legal Adviser (ICRC), *Interpretive Guidance on the Notion of Direct Participation in Hostilities Under International Law* (Geneva, May 2009), p. 66.
[17] Art. 4(A)(4), GCIII.

9. As was said in the introduction to the chapter, the application of the principle of distinction to objects and to new means and methods of warfare such as cyber war[18] will be examined in Chapter 7. What can be said though, at this juncture, is that changes in the nature of armed conflict pose significant challenges to its application because no bright lines can be drawn between participants. Extending the rules on targeting to civilians who directly participate in hostilities and the interpretive penumbra that surrounds the DPH criteria provide evidence of the degree of normative erosion of this principle.

[18]   K. Bannelier-Christakis, 'Is the Principle of Distinction Still Relevant in Cyberwarfare?' in N. Tsagourias and R. Buchan (eds), *Research Handbook on International Law and Cyberspace* (Edward Elgar Publishing, 2015) pp. 353ff.

5

Protection of Civilians

INTRODUCTION

The protection of civilians in armed conflict derives from and is moulded by the principles of humanity and distinction.[1] More specifically, civilians should be protected against direct attacks and against the effects of military operations; civilians should also be afforded protection when they fall into the hands of the enemy, particularly civilians in occupied territory.[2] In NIACs civilians receive comparable protection, although the more rudimentary nature of the protective regime reflects the less-developed nature of IHL governing such conflicts.[3] IHRL plays an important role in supplementing the provisions of IHL, particularly in the case of low-intensity NIAC.[4] Modern armed conflict poses a range of challenges to the protection of civilians arising primarily from the failure on the part of both States and armed groups to observe their obligations under IHL. Asymmetric warfare, the urbanisation of conflict and the use of new technologies such as cyber technologies in warfare also put pressure on the protective regime.

The scope and range of protections afforded to civilians will be reviewed in this chapter by focusing on the protections afforded to civilians against the conduct of military operations and on their protection against the misuse of power. While IHL is concerned with the protection of all civilians during armed conflict, certain groups, including women, children, journalists and peacekeepers, are particularly vulnerable and the protections afforded to them are also discussed in this chapter. Chapter 7 will examine the protection of civilians from attacks by focusing on the law of targeting.[5]

Resources: Art. 43, HCIV, Common Article 3, GCs, Arts 4, 14, 17, 23, 24, 27–34, 35–46, 47–48, 49, 50, 76, 78 82, 89, 94 and 132 GCIV, Arts 72–79 API, Art. 4, APII

---

[1] See Chapter 2 Sections 2.4 and 2.5; Chapter 4 for the principle of distinction.
[2] See Art. 4 GCIV and Chapter 9 for occupation.
[3] See Chapter 10.
[4] See Chapter 3.
[5] See Chapter 7 Sections 7.5.3 and 7.5.4.

Cases and Materials

5.1 PROTECTION AGAINST ATTACKS AND AGAINST THE EFFECTS OF MILITARY OPERATIONS

5.1.1 Prohibition of Attacks on Civilians

5.1.1.1 **ICTY**, *Prosecutor* v. *Kupreškić et al.*, (Judgment), Case No. IT-95-16T, Trial Chamber (14 January 2000)

Note: *The facts of this case are outlined in Chapter 2, Section 2.1.3. Affirming the fundamental importance of the principle of distinction and outlining the circumstances in which the protection might be breached, the ICTY said:*

521. The protection of civilians in time of armed conflict, whether international or internal, is the bedrock of modern humanitarian law. ... Indeed, it is now a universally recognised principle, recently restated by the International Court of Justice, that deliberate attacks on civilians or civilian objects are absolutely prohibited by international humanitarian law.

522. The protection of civilians and civilian objects provided by modern international law may cease entirely or be reduced or suspended in three exceptional circumstances: (i) when civilians abuse their rights; (ii) when, although the object of a military attack is comprised of military objectives, belligerents cannot avoid causing so-called collateral damage to civilians; and (iii) at least according to some authorities, when civilians may legitimately be the object of reprisals.

5.1.1.2 UK, Foreign and Commonwealth Office, *Government Strategy on the Protection of Civilians in Armed Conflict* (7 December 2011)[6]

What is Protection of Civilians?

In the context of armed conflict, the concept of protection encompasses "all activities aimed at ensuring full respect for the rights of the individual in accordance with the letter and spirit of the relevant bodies of law, i.e. human rights law, international humanitarian law and refugee law." ...

The character of armed conflict now sees an increased blurring of the distinctions between adversaries and the way they use force to achieve political goals. Future conflict will blend the lethality traditionally associated with state conflict and the fanatical and protracted fervour of irregular warfare. This confused, messy and uncontrollable aspect of conflict complicates the practicalities of how you protect civilians. Separating "the people" from the conflict is often impossible and their protection relies on a comprehensive approach to conflict resolution.

5.1.1.3 US, Department of Defense, *Law of War Manual*, Office of General Counsel (June 2015, Updated 2016)

5.3 OVERVIEW OF RULES FOR THE PROTECTION OF CIVILIANS

The protection of civilians against the harmful effects of hostilities is one of the main purposes of the law of war. Many of the rules for the protection of civilians are derived from the principles of distinction and proportionality. Specific rules for the protection of civilians may be grouped into two categories: (1) essentially negative duties to respect civilians and to refrain from directing military operations against them; (2) affirmative duties to take feasible precautions to protect civilians and other protected persons and objects.

5.1.2 Prohibition of Indiscriminate Attacks on Civilian Population[7]

5.1.2.1 International Institute of Humanitarian Law, *The Manual on the Law of Non-International Armed Conflict With Commentary* (San Remo, 2006)

3. There are two types of indiscriminate methods of combat. The first is the carrying out of attacks where no attempt is made to identify specific military objectives. The classic modern example is the Iraqi use of SCUD missiles against Israel during the 1991 Gulf War. Although their guidance systems were unsophisticated, they were capable of being used discriminately against military objectives, for instance troop concentrations in desert areas. However, in this case, they were fired blindly into Israeli population centres with no attempt to identify and target specific military targets therein.

The second method is an attack that treats a number of clearly separate and distinct military objectives collocated with civilians or civilian objects as a single entity, such as carpet-bombing an entire urban area containing dispersed legitimate targets. This

---

[6]   www.gov.uk/government/publications/uk-government-strategy-on-the-protection-of-civilians-in-armed-conflict.

[7]   See Chapter 7 Section 7.1.3 for the use of indiscriminate weapons.

prohibition only applies where it is militarily feasible to conduct separate attacks on each of the objectives. If it is not, then the issue is proportionality, not discrimination

5.1.2.2 UN, *Human Rights in Palestine and Other Occupied Arab Territories: Report of the United Nations Fact-Finding Mission on the Gaza Conflict ('The Goldstone Report')* (25 September 2009), 12th Session, UN Doc. A/HRC/12/48

108. The Mission has determined that the rockets and, to a lesser extent, the mortars fired by the Palestinian armed groups are incapable of being directed towards specific military objectives and have been fired into areas where civilian populations are based. The Mission has further determined that these attacks constitute indiscriminate attacks upon the civilian population of southern Israel and that, where there is no intended military target and the rockets and mortars are launched into a civilian population, they constitute a deliberate attack against a civilian population.

5.1.2.3 IACtHR, *Case of the Santo Domingo Massacre v. Colombia* (Judgment: Preliminary Objections, Merits and Reparations), Inter-Am. Ct. H.R., Series No. 259 (30 November 2012)

Note: *The facts of this case are dealt with in Chapter 3, Section 3.4.4. Confirming that indiscriminate attacks may constitute direct attacks on civilians, the IACtHR said as follows:*

213. In the instant case, the Court has found proved that, in the context of confrontations with the FARC guerrilla, on December 13, 1998, the Colombian Air Force launched an AN–M1A2 cluster bomb on the village of Santo Domingo, causing the death and injury of civilians. . . .

. . .

234. Regarding the principle of distinction between civilians and combatants, the Court recalls that, according to the norms of international humanitarian law . . ., conducts that constitute indiscriminate attacks are also prohibited "which employ a method or means of combat which cannot be limited as required by international humanitarian law . . . and, consequently, . . . are of a nature to strike military objectives and civilians or civilian objects without distinction." Similarly, the case law of the International Criminal Tribunal for the Former Yugoslavia . . . has indicated that "indiscriminate attacks, that is to say, attacks which strike civilians or civilian objects and military objectives without distinction, may qualify as direct attacks against civilians," and that these "are expressly prohibited by Additional Protocol I [and this] prohibition reflects a well-established rule of customary law applicable in all armed conflicts."

5.1.2.4 Syria, *Report of the Independent International Commission of Inquiry on the Syrian Arab Republic* (13 August 2015), 13th Session, UN Doc. A/HRC/30/48

26. Warring parties conduct hostilities with little, if any, regard for the laws of war and, in particular, its foundational principle of distinction. Regardless of the belligerent involved, the majority of attacks are not directed at a specific military objective or fail to employ a

method or means of combat that can be directed at a specific military objective. Indiscriminate attacks on residential areas have led to massive casualties among Syrian civilians.

5.2 PROTECTION OF PERSONS IN THE HANDS OF A PARTY TO AN IAC[8]

5.2.1 ICTY, *Prosecutor* v. *Kordić and Čerkez*, (Judgment), Case No IT-95-14/2-T, Trial Chamber (26 February 2001)

Note: *The facts of this case are set out in Chapter 1, Section 1.2.2.2. As to the interpretation of Article 4, GCIV, the ICTY said:*

149. As to the contention ..., that, since the Bosnian Muslims victims were of the same nationality as their Bosnian Croat captors, the requirement under Article 4 of Geneva Convention IV is not met, the Appeals Chamber's judgements in Tadić, Aleksovski and Celebici provide two responses.[9]

150. In the first place, the Aleksovski Appeal Judgement, following the reasoning in Tadić, concludes that the finding that the conflict was international by reason of Croatia's participation necessarily means that the Bosnian Muslim victims were in the hands of a party to the conflict, namely Croatia, of which they were not nationals. Therefore, Article 4 of Geneva Convention IV is applicable. ...

152. Secondly, on the basis of a teleological interpretation of Article 4 of Geneva Convention IV, the Appeals Chamber in Tadić concluded that "allegiance to a Party to the conflict and, correspondingly, control by this Party over persons in a given territory, may be regarded as the crucial test." In such a case, nationality is not as crucial as allegiance to a party. In accordance with this interpretation, which the Appeals Chamber in Aleksovski found to be "particularly apposite in the context of present day inter-ethnic conflicts", the Bosnian Muslim victims are protected persons since they owe no allegiance to the Bosnian Croats under whose effective control they were. This interpretation accords with the general purpose of Geneva Convention IV, which is to provide protection for civilians in an armed conflict.

153. If Tadić might have been equivocal as to the application of the allegiance test in determining the status of protected persons under Article 4 of Geneva Convention IV, the Appeals Chamber in Celebici put this matter beyond doubt. In the first place, the Chamber stressed that the meaning to be given to nationality under Article 4 must be determined on the basis of international, not national, law. Then, emphasising the need for a purposive construction of Article 4, the Appeals Chamber held, first, that:

> "[d]epriving victims, who arguably are of the same nationality under domestic law as their captors,
>
> of the protection of the Geneva Conventions solely based on that national law would not be

---

[8] See Chapter 9 for occupation.
[9] ICTY *Prosecutor* v. *Tadić*, (Judgment), Case No IT-94-1-A, Appeals Chamber (15 July 1999); ICTY *Prosecutor* v. *Aleksovski*, (Judgment on Appeal by Anto Nobilo Against Finding of Contempt), Case No IT-95-14/1-AR77, Appeals Chamber (30 May 2001); ICTY *Prosecutor* v. *Delalić et al*, (Judgment), Case No IT-96-21-A, Appeals Chamber (20 February 2001).

consistent with the object and purpose of the Conventions. Their very object could indeed be defeated if undue emphasis were placed on formal legal bonds, which could also be altered by governments to shield their nationals from prosecution based on the grave breaches provisions of the Geneva Conventions."

and

"The nationality of the victims for the purpose of the application of Geneva Convention IV should not be determined on the basis of formal national characterisations, but rather upon an analysis of the substantial relations, taking into consideration the different ethnicity of the victims and the perpetrators, and their bonds with the foreign intervening State."

5.2.2 Ethiopia-Eritrea Claims Commission, *Partial Award: Civilian's Claims – Eritrea's Claims 15,16, 23 & 27–32* (2004) 26 (6) RIAA 195

Note: *The Eritrea government asked the Commission to find the Federal Democratic Republic of Ethiopia liable for loss, damage and injury suffered by Eritrean nationals and other persons resulting from infractions of international law in the treatment of civilians during the 1998–2000 IAC between the two parties. As to the protection afforded by Article 75, API, the Commission said:*

30. ... Article 75 [API] articulates fundamental guarantees applicable to all "persons who are in the power of a Party to the conflict who do not benefit from more favorable treatment under the Conventions or under this Protocol." It thus applies even to a Party's treatment of its own nationals. These guarantees distil basic human rights most important in wartime. Given their fundamental humanitarian nature and their correspondence with generally accepted human rights principles, the Commission views these rules as part of customary international humanitarian law.

5.2.3 ICJ, *Case Concerning Armed Activities on the Territory of the Congo (Democratic Republic of the Congo v. Uganda)* (Judgment) [2005] I.C.J. Rep. 168

Note: *The facts of this case are set out in Chapter 1, Section 1.7.2. As to the liability of Occupying Powers towards inhabitants of occupied territories, the ICJ said:*

178. The Court thus concludes that Uganda was the Occupying Power in Ituri at the relevant time. As such it was under an obligation, according to Article 43 of the Hague Regulations of 1907, to take all the measures in its power to restore, and ensure, as far as possible, public order and safety in the occupied area, while respecting, unless absolutely prevented, the laws in force in the DRC. This obligation comprised the duty to secure respect for the applicable rules of international human rights law and international humanitarian law, to protect the inhabitants of the occupied territory against acts of violence, and not to tolerate such violence by any third party.

5.3 PROTECTION OF PERSONS IN THE HANDS OF A PARTY TO A NIAC[10]

5.3.1 UK, British Ministry of Defence, *The Joint Service Manual of the Law of Armed Conflict* (Joint Service Publication 383, 2004 Edition)

15.30 Humane treatment

Persons in the hands of a party to the conflict, whether the government side, dissident armed forces, or other armed groups, are entitled to humane treatment at all times. They must not be discriminated against on grounds of race, colour, religion or faith, sex, birth, or wealth, or similar criteria. The following acts are always prohibited with respect to these persons: a. violence to life and person, in particular murder of all kinds, mutilation, cruel treatment, and torture; b. taking of hostages; c. 'rape, sexual slavery, enforced prostitution, forced pregnancy, forced sterilization, and any other form of sexual violence also constituting a serious violation of' Common Article 3; d. other outrages upon personal dignity, in particular humiliating and degrading treatment; e. 'physical mutilation or... medical or scientific experiments of a kind which are neither justified by medical, dental or hospital treatment of the person concerned nor carried out in his or her interest, and which causes death to or seriously endangers the health of' that person; f. the passing of sentences and the carrying out of executions without previous judgment pronounced by a regularly constituted court, affording all the judicial guarantees which are recognized as indispensable by civilized peoples.

5.3.2 ICC, *The Prosecutor* v. *Jean-Pierre Bemba Gombo*, (Judgment Pursuant to Article 74 of the Statute), Case No ICC-01/05-01/08, Trial Chamber III (21 March 2016)[11]

Note: *The facts of this case are detailed in Chapter 1, Section 1.2.3.5. As to the measures that might be taken to prevent abuse and injury to civilians during armed conflicts, the ICC said*:

739. Further clear training, orders, and hierarchical examples indicating that the soldiers should respect and not mistreat the civilian population would have reduced, if not eliminated, crimes motivated by a distrust of the civilian population, as enemies or enemy sympathisers. Recalling Mr Bemba's position of high authority as President of the MLC and Commander-in-Chief of the ALC, as well as of his effective authority and control, the Chamber finds that Mr Bemba's position obligated him to take such measures, both personally and through the hierarchical chain of command. Likewise, if the soldiers had received adequate payment and rations, the risk that they would pillage or rape for self-compensation, and murder those who resisted, would have been reduced, if not eliminated.

---

[10]   See Chapter 10.
[11]   See Chapter 12 for command responsibility.

5.4 DETENTION

5.4.1 Detention in IAC[12]

5.4.1.1 ICTY, *Prosecutor* v. *Delalić et al.*, (Judgment), Case No IT-96-21-T, Trial Chamber (16 November 1998)

Note: *The case concerned events that occurred at a detention facility in the village of Čelebići located in the Konjic municipality in Bosnia-Herzegovina. On the issue of detention in armed conflict, the ICTY said as follows:*

572. The drafters of the Fourth Geneva Convention, . . ., only permitted internment and assigned residence as a last resort, and makes them subject to strict rules (articles 41 to 43 and article 78). . . .

576. Clearly, internment is only permitted when absolutely necessary. Subversive activity carried on inside the territory of a party to the conflict, or actions which are of direct assistance to an opposing party, may threaten the security of the former, which may, therefore, intern people or place them in assigned residence if it has *serious and legitimate reasons* to think that they may seriously prejudice its security by means such as sabotage or espionage.

577. On the other hand, the mere fact that a person is a national of, or aligned with, an enemy party cannot be considered as threatening the security of the opposing party where he is living and is not, therefore, a valid reason for interning him or placing him in assigned residence. To justify recourse to such measures, the party must have good reason to think that the person concerned, by his activities, knowledge or qualifications, represents a real threat to its present or future security. The fact that an individual is male and of military age should not necessarily be considered as justifying the application of these measures.

583. For the reasons set out above, it is the opinion of this Trial Chamber that the confinement of civilians during armed conflict may be permissible in limited cases, but has in any event to be in compliance with the provisions of articles 42 and 43 of Geneva Convention IV. The security of the State concerned might require the internment of civilians and, furthermore, the decision of whether a civilian constitutes a threat to the security of the State is largely left to its discretion. However, it must be borne in mind that the measure of internment for reasons of security is an exceptional one and can never be taken on a collective basis. An initially lawful internment clearly becomes unlawful if the detaining party does not respect the basic procedural rights of the detained persons and does not establish an appropriate court or administrative board as prescribed in article 43 of Geneva Convention IV.

5.4.2 Detention in NIAC[13]

5.4.2.1 UK, British Ministry of Defence, *Joint Service Manual of the Law of Armed Conflict* (Joint Service Publication, 2004 Edition)

15.6.4 . . . the law of non-international armed conflict clearly requires that any person (whether a combatant or a civilian) detained by either dissident or government forces must be treated humanely. . . .

---

[12] See Chapter 3 Sections 3.6 and 3.7; Chapter 6 for POW and Chapter 9 Section 9.9.
[13] See also Chapter 10 Section 10.6 and commentary.

15.10.2 Detainees should be provided with sufficient food and drinking water, facilities for health and hygiene, and shelter from the weather and the dangers of armed conflict.

5.4.2.2 UK, *Abd Ali Hameed Al-Waheed* v. *Ministry of Defence; Serdar Mohammed* v. *Ministry of Defence* [2017] UKSC 2

Note: *The UK Supreme Court heard appeals arising out of actions brought against the UK government by individuals claiming they had been unlawfully detained. The Supreme Court, by a majority of seven to two, held the UK government did have a legal power to detain individuals for periods in excess of ninety-six hours. The Supreme Court held the power to detain in NIAC was conferred by the relevant UNSCR:*

64. The relevance of the Geneva Conventions in Hassan[14] was that in the context of an international armed conflict, they provided an appropriate alternative legal standard to the literal application of article 5 [ECHR]. But it does not follow that in a conflict to which the relevant provisions of the Geneva Conventions do not directly apply, anyone detained by the peacekeeping forces must necessarily be treated as being detained arbitrarily. The present question is whether there is an appropriate legal standard in a non-international armed conflict, notwithstanding that the relevant provisions of the Geneva Conventions do not directly apply.

65. As far as the right of detention itself is concerned, the answer is reasonably straightforward. There is, for the reasons which I have explained, a sufficient legal basis for detention in the Security Council Resolutions. The implicit limitation to occasions where detention is necessary for imperative reasons of security, provides a clear legal standard which is no wider than the purpose of the UN mandate requires. Indeed, it is the same standard as that which applies under articles 42 and 78 of the Fourth Geneva Convention, which the Grand Chamber endorsed in the context of an international armed conflict.

66. The claimants argue that the Grand Chamber could not have envisaged that its reasoning would be applied to non-international armed conflicts because the procedural safeguards derived from international humanitarian law, which they regarded as an acceptable substitute for the protection of article 5, were available only to those detained in the course of an international armed conflict. I recognise the force of this argument, but I think that it is mistaken. ... It is in my opinion clear that they regarded the duty of review imposed by articles 43 and 78 of the Fourth Convention as representing a model minimum standard of review required to prevent the detention from being treated as arbitrary. They were adopting that standard not just for cases to which those articles directly applied, but generally.

67. Given that the Security Council Resolutions themselves contain no procedural safeguards, it is incumbent on Convention states, if they are to comply with article 5, to specify the conditions on which their armed forces may detain people in the course of an armed conflict and to make adequate means available to detainees to challenge the lawfulness of their detention under their own law. There is no reason why a Convention state should not

---

[14]   See Chapter 3 Section 3.6 and commentary; ECtHR, *Hassan* v. *United Kingdom* [GC], (App No. 29750/09), (ECtHR, 16 September 2014).

comply with its Convention obligations by adopting a standard at least equivalent to articles 43 and 78 of the Fourth Geneva Convention, as those participating in armed conflicts under the auspices of the United Nations commonly do. Provided that the standard thus adopted is prescribed by law and not simply a matter of discretion, I cannot think that it matters to which category the armed conflict in question belongs as a matter of international humanitarian law. The essential purpose of article 5, as the court observed at para 105 of Hassan, is to protect the individual from arbitrariness. This may be achieved even in a state of armed conflict if there are regular reviews providing "sufficient guarantees of impartiality and fair procedure to protect against arbitrariness" (para 106).

5.4.3 Detention by UN and UN-authorised Peacekeeping Forces[15]

5.4.3.1 UN, Secretary-General's Bulletin, *Observance by United Nations Forces of International Humanitarian Law* (6 August 1999) UN Doc. ST/SGB/1999/13

. . .

Section 8 Treatment of detained persons

The United Nations force shall treat with humanity and respect for their dignity detained members of the armed forces and other persons who no longer take part in military operations by reason of detention. Without prejudice to their legal status, they shall be treated in accordance with the relevant provisions of the Third Geneva Convention of 1949, as may be applicable to them mutatis mutandis.

5.4.3.2 ICTY, *Prosecutor* v. *Dragan Nikolić*, (Defence Motion Challenging the Exercise of Jurisdiction by the Tribunal), Case No. IT-94-2-PT, Trial Chamber II (9 October 2002)

Note: *The accused was indicted for crimes against humanity, grave breaches of the GCs and violations of the laws and customs of war in relation to acts committed while commander of the Sušica detention camp established by Serb forces in 1992. Addressing a challenge to the legality of Nikolić's arrest and detention by the Stabilisation Force in Bosnia and Herzegovina (SFOR), a multinational peacekeeping force, the ICTY said as follows:*

52. The legal basis for the authority of SFOR to arrest, detain and transfer persons indicted by this Tribunal is, in the view of this Chamber, firmly established. . . . The Rule of Engagement adopted by the NAC on 16 December 1995 forms the core provision for the authority of SFOR in this respect. This Rule should of course be considered against the entire legal framework as it forms part of a number of resolutions of the Security Council, obligations for the Parties to the Dayton Agreement and the Statute and Rules of this Tribunal. . . . It has regularly been argued that SFOR is merely *authorised* to arrest, detain and transfer persons indicted by the Tribunal and, sometimes even, that SFOR is *obliged* to arrest, detain and transfer those persons.

53. That IFOR and SFOR have the authority to arrest, detain and transfer persons indicted by the Tribunal has been repeatedly reiterated by SFOR officials. In such statements, it has

---

[15] See Chapter 3 Section 3.6 and Chapter 10 Section 10.6.5.

consistently been made clear that if IFOR or SFOR come into contact with war criminals, it is their responsibility to turn them over to the Tribunal. . . . From the practice of SFOR under the ROE, the Chamber deduces that SFOR does have a clear mandate to arrest and detain a person indicted by the Tribunal and to have that person transferred to the Tribunal whenever, in the execution of tasks assigned to it, SFOR comes into contact with such a person. These are the modalities which are defined by the NAC and which fall within the mandate given by the Security Council.

5.4.3.3 ECtHR, *Agim Behrami and Bekir Behrami* v. *France* [GC] (App No. 71412/01) and *Ruzhdi Saramati* v. *France, Germany and Norway* [GC] (App No. 78166/ 01), (Decision as to Admissibility) (2 May 2007)

Note: *The facts of this decision are outlined in Chapter 3, Section 3.10.2. Affirming the ambit of the security mandate of the Kosovo Force (KFOR), the ECtHR said:*

124. Having regard to the MTA (notably paragraph 2 of Article 1), UNSC Resolution 1244 (paragraph 9 as well as paragraph 4 of Annex 2 to the Resolution) as confirmed by FRAGO997 and later COMKFOR Detention Directive 42 (see paragraph 51 above), the Court considers it evident that KFOR's security mandate included issuing detention orders.

5.4.3.4 African Union, *Guidelines on Detention and DDR* (2014)[16]

1.2.1 Authority and grounds to detain

There are various possible sources ("legal bases") for a peace support mission's authority to detain. These can include:

- a binding mandate from the UN Security Council under Chapter VII of the UN Charter and/or the AU Peace and Security Council, in conformity with international law, authorising the use of "all necessary means" to achieve certain objectives;
- where the mission is party to an armed conflict, the inherent authority, under international humanitarian law, to intern persons for imperative reasons of security;
- the Status of Forces / Status of Mission Agreement between the AU and the host State, which may permit the Mission to apprehend and detain persons committing, or attempting to commit, a crime, and / or persons suspected of having committed a crime; and / or
- an ad hoc request by the competent authorities of the host State

5.5 PROHIBITION OF ARBITRARY PUNISHMENTS

5.5.1 ICC, The Office of the Prosecutor, *Situation in Mali Article 53(1) Report* (16 January 2013)

Note: *In or about January 2012, a NIAC broke out in the territory of Mali between government forces and non-State organised armed groups, as well as between the non-State armed groups.*

---

[16]   www.peaceau.org/uploads/au-operational-guidance-note-on-detention-and-ddr.pdf.

In July 2012 the government referred the situation to the ICC. On the issue of use of arbitrary punishments, the ICC said:

103. The actus reus of the war crime of sentencing or execution without due process pursuant to Article 8(2)(c)(iv) requires that the perpetrator pass a sentence or carry out an execution of one or more persons who were either combatants hors de combat, civilians, medical personnel or religious personnel taking no active part in hostilities; and that the passing of the sentence or execution is carried out without previous judgement pronounced by a "regularly constituted" court, that is, a court which affords the essential guarantees of independence and impartiality, and the other judicial guarantees generally recognized as indispensable under international law.

104. Based on the information available, there seem to exist two categories of cases of imposing sentences on the civilian population and hors de combat in detention by the armed groups in Mali in the North, particularly in the regions of Kidal, Timbuktu and Gao. The first includes cases where the accused are brought before a panel of judges for a trial. Following the conclusion of the trial, sentences are imposed by judges and subsequently enforced by members of armed groups. The second includes cases where persons are punished by members of armed groups for an alleged conduct without previous trial.

5.6 INTERNAL DISPLACEMENT, EXPULSION AND DEPORTATION[17]

5.6.1 ICTY, *Prosecutor* v. *Simić et al.*, (Judgment), Case No IT-95-9-T, Trial Chamber II (17 October 2003)

Note: *The accused were indicted for crimes against humanity and grave breaches of GCs following their involvement in events in the municipalities of Bosanski Šamac and Odžak between April 1992 and December 1993, which involved unlawful deportation and transfer constituting a systematic attack on the civilian population. On the issue of displacement of persons during conflict, the ICTY said:*

125. The displacement of persons is only illegal where it is forced, i.e. not voluntary, and "when it occurs without grounds permitted under international law". . . . The requirement that the displacement be forced or forcible has been interpreted broadly by Trial Chambers. The term "forced" is not limited to physical force; it may also include the "threat of force or coercion, such as that caused by fear of violence, duress, detention, psychological oppression or abuse of power against such person or persons or another person, or by taking advantage of a coercive environment". The essential element is that the displacement be involuntary in nature, that "the relevant persons had no real choice". . . .

127. Whether the adoption and implementation of agreements for "exchanges" supervised by the ICRC, and the presence of members of international organisations

---

[17]   See also Chapter 9 Sections 9.7 and 9.8.

(ICRC, UNPROFOR), may have an impact on the voluntary nature and the lawfulness of a person's displacement arises in the present case. The jurisprudence of the Tribunal indicates that agreements concluded by military commanders or other representatives of parties in a conflict cannot make a displacement lawful. ... The Trial Chamber agrees that the adoption of similar agreements, such as those concluded under the auspices of the ICRC in the present case, as well as the presence of ICRC or UNPROFOR members, has no impact on whether the persons' displacement was voluntary. Article 49 of Geneva Convention IV only mentions the security of the population and imperative military reasons as grounds permitting the displacement of civilian population.

5.6.2 Eritrea–Ethiopia Claims Commission, *Partial Award: Civilians' Claims – Eritrea's Claims 15, 16, 23 & 27–32* (2004) 26 (6) RIAA 195[18]

Note: *The facts of this case are outlined in Section 5.2.2. On Ethiopia's expulsion of Eritrean nationals, the Commission found as follows:*

81. International humanitarian law gives belligerents broad powers to expel nationals of the enemy State from their territory during a conflict. ...

82. The Commission concluded above that Ethiopia lawfully deprived a substantial number of dual nationals of their Ethiopian nationality following identification through Ethiopia's security committee process. Ethiopia could lawfully expel these persons as nationals of an enemy belligerent, although it was bound to ensure them the protections required by Geneva Convention IV and other applicable international humanitarian law. ...

5.7 SEXUAL VIOLENCE IN ARMED CONFLICT[19]

5.7.1 UN, Committee on the Elimination of Discrimination Against Women (CEDAW), *CEDAW General Recommendation No. 19: Violence Against Women* (11th Session, 1992)

6. The Convention in article 1 defines discrimination against women. The definition of discrimination includes gender-based violence, that is, violence that is directed against a woman because she is a woman or that affects women disproportionately. It includes acts that inflict physical, mental or sexual harm or suffering, threats of such acts, coercion and other deprivations of liberty. Gender-based violence may breach specific provisions of the Convention, regardless of whether those provisions expressly mention violence.

---

[18] See Chapter 9 Section 9.8.
[19] See Chapter 3 Section 3.1.

5.7.2 ICTY, *Prosecutor* v. *Anto Furundžija*, (Judgment), Case No IT-95-17/ 1-T, Trial Chamber (10 December 1998)

Note: *The facts of this case are detailed in Chapter 3, Section 3.2.3. Reinforcing the prohibition on rape and serious sexual assault in treaty and customary international law, the ICTY said:*

165. Rape in time of war is specifically prohibited by treaty law: the Geneva Conventions of 1949, Additional Protocol I of 1977 and Additional Protocol II of 1977. Other serious sexual assaults are expressly or implicitly prohibited in various provisions of the same treaties. . . .

168. The prohibition of rape and serious sexual assault in armed conflict has also evolved in customary international law. It has gradually crystallised out of the express prohibition of rape in article 44 of the Lieber Code and the general provisions contained in article 46 of the regulations annexed to Hague Convention IV, read in conjunction with the 'Martens clause' laid down in the preamble to that Convention.

5.8 SEXUAL EXPLOITATION AND ABUSE (SEA) BY UN PEACEKEEPERS

5.8.1 UN, Secretary-General's Bulletin, *Special Measures for Protection from Sexual Exploitation and Sexual Abuse* (9 October 2003), UN Doc. ST/SGB/2003/13

3.1 Sexual exploitation and sexual abuse violate universally recognized international legal norms and standards and have always been unacceptable behaviour and prohibited conduct for United Nations staff. Such conduct is prohibited by the United Nations Staff Regulations and Rules.

3.2 In order to further protect the most vulnerable populations, especially women and children, the following specific standards which reiterate existing general obligations under the United Nations Staff Regulations and Rules, are promulgated: (a) Sexual exploitation and sexual abuse constitute acts of serious misconduct and are therefore grounds for disciplinary measures, including summary dismissal; (b) Sexual activity with children (persons under the age of 18) is prohibited regardless of the age of majority or age of consent locally. Mistaken belief in the age of a child is not a defence; (c) Exchange of money, employment, goods or services for sex, including sexual favours or other forms of humiliating, degrading or exploitative behaviour, is prohibited. This includes any exchange of assistance that is due to beneficiaries of assistance; (d) Sexual relationships between United Nations staff and beneficiaries of assistance, since they are based on inherently unequal power dynamics, undermine the credibility and integrity of the work of the United Nations and are strongly discouraged; (e) Where a United Nations staff member develops concerns or suspicions regarding sexual exploitation or sexual abuse by a fellow worker, whether in the same agency or not and whether or not within the United Nations system, he or she must report such concerns via established reporting mechanisms; (f) United Nations staff are obliged to create and maintain an environment that prevents sexual exploitation and sexual abuse. Managers at all levels have a particular responsibility to support and develop systems that maintain this environment.

3.3 The standards set out above are not intended to be an exhaustive list.

5.8.2 UN, Report of the Secretary-General's Special Advisor, Prince Zeid Ra'ad Zeid al-Hussain, *'A Comprehensive Strategy to Eliminate Future Sexual Exploitation and Abuse in United Nations Peacekeeping Operations'* (24 March 2005), 59th Session, UN Doc. A/59/710

Recommendations

94. Recommendations for action on four broad fronts are set out in the present report. Rules against sexual exploitation and abuse must be unified for all categories of peacekeeping personnel. A professional investigative process must be established and modern scientific methods of identification must be utilized. A series of organizational, managerial and command measures must be instituted to address sexual exploitation and abuse. A number of recommendations are made to ensure that peacekeeping personnel who commit acts of sexual exploitation and abuse are held individually accountable through appropriate disciplinary action, that they are held financially accountable for the harm they have done to victims and that they are held criminally accountable if the acts constitute crimes under applicable law.

95. There will always be those who do not meet the established standards of conduct, however. Adoption of these recommendations will go a long way towards eliminating sexual exploitation and abuse in peacekeeping missions.

5.8.3 SC, *Security Council Resolution 2272 on Sexual Exploitation and Abuse by United Nations Peacekeepers* (11 March 2016), 7643rd Meeting, UN Doc. S/RES/2272(2016)

. . .

Reaffirming that proper conduct by, and discipline over, all personnel deployed in United Nations peace operations are crucial to their effectiveness,

Stressing that sexual exploitation and abuse by United Nations peacekeepers undermines the implementation of peacekeeping mandates, as well as the credibility of United Nations peacekeeping, and reaffirming its support for the United Nations zero tolerance policy on all forms of sexual exploitation and abuse,

Expressing deep concern about the serious and continuous allegations and under-reporting of sexual exploitation and abuse by United Nations peacekeepers and non-United Nations forces, including military, civilian and police personnel, and underscoring that sexual exploitation and abuse, among other crimes and forms of serious misconduct, by any such personnel is unacceptable,

Recalling the primary responsibility of troop-contributing countries to investigate allegations of sexual exploitation and abuse by their personnel and of troop- and police-contributing countries to hold accountable, including through prosecution, where appropriate, their personnel for acts of sexual exploitation and abuse, taking into account due process,

...

Welcoming the Secretary-General's continued efforts to implement and reinforce the United Nations zero tolerance policy on sexual exploitation and abuse, in particular to strengthen the Organisation's prevention, reporting, enforcement and remedial action in order to promote greater accountability.

5.9 PROTECTION OF CHILDREN

5.9.1 UN, Report of the Expert of the Secretary–General, Ms Graça Machel Submitted Pursuant to General Assembly Resolution 48/157, *Impact of Armed Conflict on Children* (26 August 1996), 51st Session, UN Doc. A/51/306

226. The most comprehensive and specific protection for children is provided by the Convention on the Rights of the Child, adopted by the General Assembly in resolution 44/25 in November 1989. The Convention establishes a legal framework that greatly extends the previous recognition of children as the direct holders of rights and acknowledges their distinct legal personality. . . .

227. The Convention recognizes a comprehensive list of rights that apply during both peacetime and war. As stressed by the Committee on the Rights on the Child (A/49/41) these include protection of the family environment; essential care and assistance; access to health, food and education; the prohibition of torture, abuse or neglect; the prohibition of the death penalty; the protection of the child's cultural environment; the right to a name and nationality; and the need for protection in situations of deprivation of liberty. States must also ensure access to, and the provision of, humanitarian assistance and relief to children during armed conflict.

228. In addition, the Convention on the Rights of the Child contains, in articles 38 and 39, provisions specifically related to armed conflict. The former article is of major significance because it brings together humanitarian law and human rights law, showing their complementarity. Its provisions require that States Parties undertake to respect and to ensure respect for rules of international humanitarian law applicable to children in armed conflicts, and paragraph 4 states that: "In accordance with their obligations under international humanitarian law to protect the civilian population in armed conflicts, States Parties shall take all feasible measures to ensure protection and care of children who are affected by an armed conflict."

229. If the Convention on the Rights of the Child were to be fully implemented during armed conflicts, this would go a long way towards protecting children. Children's right to special protection in these situations has long been recognized.

5.9.2 SCSL, *Prosecutor* v. *Sam Hinga Norman*, (Decision on Preliminary Motion Based on Lack of Jurisdiction (Child Recruitment)), Case No. SCSL-2004-14-AR72(E), Appeals Chamber (31 May 2004)

Note: *The case concerned the recruitment of children under the age of fifteen into the armed forces during the Sierra Leone Civil War. The SCSL said as follows:*

51. The overwhelming majority of states, . . ., did not practice recruitment of children under 15 according to their national laws and many had, whether through criminal or administrative law, criminalised such behaviour prior to 1996. . . . It cannot be said that there is a contrary practice with the corresponding opinio iuris as states clearly consider themselves to be under a legal obligation not to practice child recruitment.

52. The rejection of the use of child soldiers by the international community was widespread by 1994. In addition, by the time of the 1996 Graca Michel Report, it was no longer possible to claim to be acting in good faith while recruiting child soldiers . . .. Specifically concerning Sierra Leone, the Government acknowledged in its 1996 Report to the Committee of the Rights of the Child that there was no minimum age for conscripting into armed forces "except the provision in the Geneva Convention that children below the age of 15 years should not be conscripted into the army." This shows that the Government of Sierra Leone was well aware already in 1996 that children below the age of 15 should not be recruited. Citizens of Sierra Leone, and even less, persons in leadership roles, cannot possibly argue that they did not know that recruiting children was a criminal act in violation of international humanitarian law.

5.9.3 SC, *Security Council Resolution 1612 on Children in Armed Conflict* (26 July 2005), 5235th Meeting, UN Doc. S/RES/1612 (2005)

2. Takes note of the action plan presented by the Secretary-General relating to the establishment of a monitoring and reporting mechanism on children and armed conflict as called for in paragraph 2 of its resolution 1539 (2004) and, in this regard: (a) Underlines that the mechanism is to collect and provide timely, objective, accurate and reliable information on the recruitment and use of child soldiers in violation of applicable international law and on other violations and abuses committed against children affected by armed conflict, and the mechanism will report to the working group to be created in accordance with paragraph 8 of this resolution; (b) Underlines further that this mechanism must operate with the participation of and in cooperation with national Governments and relevant United Nations and civil society actors, including at the country level; (c) Stresses that all actions undertaken by United Nations entities within the framework of the monitoring and reporting mechanism must be designed to support and supplement, as appropriate, the protection and rehabilitation roles of national Governments; (d) Also stresses that any dialogue established under the framework of the monitoring and reporting mechanism by United Nations entities with non-State armed groups in order to ensure protection for and access to children must be conducted in the context of peace processes where they exist and the cooperation framework between the United Nations and the concerned Government;

3. Requests the Secretary-General to implement without delay, the abovementioned monitoring and reporting mechanism,...

8. Decides to establish a working group of the Security Council consisting of all members of the Council to review the reports of the mechanism referred to in paragraph 3 ...

9. Recalls paragraph 5 (c) of its resolution 1539 (2004), and reaffirms its intention to consider imposing, through country-specific resolutions, targeted and graduated measures, such as, inter alia, a ban on the export and supply of small arms and light weapons and of other military equipment and on military assistance, against parties to situations of armed conflict which are on the Security Council's agenda and are in violation of applicable international law relating to the rights and protection of children in armed conflict;

10. Stresses the responsibility of United Nations peacekeeping missions and United Nations country teams, consistent with their respective mandates, to ensure effective follow-up to Security Council resolutions, ensure a coordinated response to CAAC concerns and to monitor and report to the Secretary-General; ...

19. Reiterates its request to the Secretary-General to ensure that, in all his reports on country-specific situations, the protection of children is included as a specific aspect of the report, and expresses its intention to give its full attention to the information provided therein when dealing with those situations on its agenda;

5.9.4 SCSL, *Prosecutor* v. *Fofana and Kondewa*, (Judgment), Case No SCSL-04-14-A, Appeals Chamber (28 May 2008)

Note: *Like Sam Hinga Norman in the earlier case of 31 May 2004, the accused were charged with enlisting children under the age of fifteen into the armed forces and/or using them to actively participate in hostilities. The SCSL confirmed such acts entail individual responsibility in the following terms:*

139. The Appeals Chamber affirms that the crime of recruitment by way of conscripting or enlisting children under the age of 15 years into an armed force or group and/or using them to participate actively in hostilities constitutes a crime under customary international law entailing individual criminal responsibility. Pursuant to Article 4.c. of the Statute, the crime of conscripting or enlisting children or using them to participate actively in hostilities, constitutes another serious violation of international humanitarian law. ... These modes of recruiting children are distinct from each other and liability in one form does not necessarily preclude liability for the other.

5.9.5 ICC, *Prosecutor* v. *Thomas Lubanga Dyilo*, (Judgment), Case No. ICC-01/04-01/06-2842, Trial Chamber (4 April 2012)

Note: *The facts of this case are outlined in Chapter 1, Section 1.2.1.1. As to the interpretation of Article 8 of the Statute of the ICC, the Court held:*

607. The Chamber accepts the approach adopted by the Pre-Trial Chamber that "conscription" and "enlistment" are both forms of recruitment, in that they refer to the incorporation of a boy or a girl under the age of 15 into an armed group, whether coercively (conscription)

or voluntarily (enlistment). The word "recruiting", which is used in the Additional Protocols and in the Convention on the Rights of the Child, was replaced by "conscripting" and "enlisting" in the Statute. Whether a prohibition against voluntary enrolment is included in the concept of "recruitment" is irrelevant to this case, because it is proscribed by Article 8.

608. This interpretation gives the relevant provisions of the Statute their plain and ordinary meaning. It is to be noted that "enlisting" is defined as "to enrol on the list of a military body" and "conscripting" is defined as "to enlist compulsorily". Therefore, the distinguishing element is that for conscription there is the added element of compulsion. Whether this distinction is of relevance in this case is considered below.

609. Bearing in mind the use of the word "or" in Article 8(2)(e)(vii), in the Chamber's view the three alternatives (viz. conscription, enlistment and use) are separate offences. It follows that the status of a child under 15 who has been enlisted or conscripted is independent of any later period when he or she may have been "used" to participate actively in hostilities, particularly given the variety of tasks that he or she may subsequently be required to undertake. Although it may often be the case that the purpose behind conscription and enlistment is to use children in hostilities, this is not a requirement of the Rome Statute. If Article 8(2)(e)(vii) is taken on its own, the position is potentially ambiguous, given it reads "[c]onscripting or enlisting children under the age of fifteen years into armed forces or groups or using them to participate actively in hostilities" (emphasis added). However, the Elements of Crimes clarify the issue by requiring "1. The perpetrator conscripted or enlisted one or more persons into an armed force or group or used one or more persons to participate actively in hostilities" (emphasis added). The Chamber therefore rejects the defence contention that "the act of enlistment consists in the integration of a person as a soldier, within the context of an armed conflict, for the purposes of participating actively in hostilities on behalf of the group." ...

617. In all the circumstances, the Chamber is persuaded that the Statute in this regard is aimed at protecting vulnerable children, including when they lack information or alternatives. The manner in which a child was recruited, and whether it involved compulsion or was "voluntary", are circumstances which may be taken into consideration by the Chamber at the sentencing or reparations phase, as appropriate. However, the consent of a child to his or her recruitment does not provide an accused with a valid defence.

618. Therefore, the Chamber agrees with the Pre-Trial Chamber that under the provisions set out above, the offences of conscripting and enlisting are committed at the moment a child under the age of 15 is enrolled into or joins an armed force or group, with or without compulsion. ... These offences are continuous in nature. They end only when the child reaches 15 years of age or leaves the force or group.

5.9.6 Geneva Call, *Deed of Commitment under Geneva Call for the Protection of Children from the Effects of Armed Conflict* (2 March 2016)

WE, the ZOMI RE-UNIFICATION ORGANIZATION, through our duly authorized representative(s), ...

HEREBY solemnly commit ourselves to the following terms:

1. TO ADHERE to a total ban on the use of children in hostilities.
2. TO ENSURE that children are not recruited into our armed forces, whether voluntarily or non voluntarily. Children will not be allowed to join or remain in our armed forces.
3. TO NEVER COMPEL children to associate with, or remain associated with, our armed forces. By associate, we mean any type of direct or supporting activity whether combat related or otherwise. In the event that children have been compelled to do so, they will be released at the earliest possible opportunity in accordance with Article 6 of this Deed of Commitment.
4. TO ENSURE that children do not accompany our armed forces during our military operations and to take all feasible measures so that children in areas where we exercise control are not present during military operations. . . .
6. The release or disassociation of children from our armed forces must be done in safety and security, and whenever possible, in cooperation with specialized child protection actors. . . .
8. TO ISSUE the necessary orders and directives to our political and military organs, commanders and fighters for the implementation and enforcement of our commitment, including measures for information dissemination and training. Commanders and superiors are responsible for their subordinates. In case of non-compliance, we will take all necessary measures to cease violations immediately, initiate appropriate investigations and impose sanctions in accordance with international standards.

5.10 PROTECTION OF JOURNALISTS[20]

5.10.1 ICTY, *Prosecutor* v. *Brdjanin and Talic*, (Decision on Interlocutory Appeal), Case No. IT-99-36-AR 73.9, Appeals Chamber (11 December 2002)

Note: *The case concerned a subpoena issued by the Trial Chamber to compel a war correspondent to testify before the Tribunal. On the issue whether the Tribunal should recognise qualified testimonial privilege for such correspondents, the ICTY Appeals Chamber said:*

42. The Appeals Chamber considers reasonable the claims of both the Appellant and the *Amici Curiae* that, in order to do their jobs effectively, war correspondents must be perceived as independent observers rather than as potential witnesses for the Prosecution. Otherwise, they may face more frequent and grievous threats to their safety and to the safety of their sources. . . .

43. What really matters is the perception that war correspondents can be forced to become witnesses against their interviewees. . . . If war correspondents were to be perceived as potential witnesses for the Prosecution, two consequences may follow. First, they may have difficulties in gathering significant information because the interviewed persons,

---

[20]   See also Chapter 4 and related commentary.

particularly those committing human rights violations, may talk less freely with them and may deny access to conflict zones. Second, war correspondents may shift from being observers of those committing human rights violations to being their targets, thereby putting their own lives at risk.

44. In view of the foregoing, the Appeals Chamber is of the view that compelling war correspondents to testify before the International Tribunal on a routine basis may have a significant impact upon their ability to obtain information and thus their ability to inform the public on issues of general concern. The Appeals Chamber will not unnecessarily hamper the work of professions that perform a public interest.

5.10.2 SC, *Security Council Resolution 1738 on Protection of Civilians in Armed Conflict* (23 December 2006), 5613th Meeting, UN Doc. S/RES/1738 (2006)

. . . Deeply concerned at the frequency of acts of violence in many parts of the world against journalists, media professionals and associated personnel in armed conflict, in particular deliberate attacks in violation of international humanitarian law,

Recognizing that the consideration of the issue of protection of journalists in armed conflict by the Security Council is based on the urgency and importance of this issue, and recognizing the valuable role that the Secretary-General can play in providing more information on this issue,

1. Condemns intentional attacks against journalists, media professionals and associated personnel, as such, in situations of armed conflict, and calls upon all parties to put an end to such practices;
2. Recalls in this regard that journalists, media professionals and associated personnel engaged in dangerous professional missions in areas of armed conflict shall be considered as civilians and shall be respected and protected as such, provided that they take no action adversely affecting their status as civilians. This is without prejudice to the right of war correspondents accredited to the armed forces to the status of prisoners of war provided for in article 4.A.4 of the Third Geneva Convention;
3. Recalls also that media equipment and installations constitute civilian objects, and in this respect shall not be the object of attack or of reprisals, unless they are military objectives;

5.10.3 UN Human Rights Council, *Report of the Special Rapporteur on the Promotion and Protection of the Right to Freedom of Opinion and Expression* (20 April 2010), 14th Session, UN Doc. A/HRC/14/23

97. The Special Rapporteur must also draw attention to the serious risk that exercising freedom of the press in a professional, objective and pluralistic manner constitutes in areas of conflict, where journalists have come to be seen by the parties to the conflict as just another target. . . .

100. The Special Rapporteur considers it necessary to remind States of their obligation to ensure that both the national and the international press have access to all the facts and to all conflict zones and to provide members of the press with the protection due them in accordance with the aforementioned resolution.

5.10.4 African Commission on Human and Peoples' Rights, *Resolution 185 on the Safety of Journalists and Media Practitioners in Africa* (Banjul, The Gambia, 12 May 2011)

... **Recalling** the United Nations Security Council's Resolution 1738 (2006), which condemns attacks against journalists in conflict situations, and UNESCO Resolution 29(1997) on "Condemnation of Violence Against Journalists" adopted by the UNESCO General Conference;

Noting that freedom of expression, press freedom and access to information can only be enjoyed when journalists and media practitioners are free from intimidation, pressure and coercion;

Concerned by the declining safety and security situation of journalists and media practitioners in some African countries;

Noting that killings, attacks and kidnapping of journalists, which are contrary to international humanitarian and human rights law, are often committed in an environment of impunity;

Deeply concerned about the frequency of allegations of the violations of killings and injury against journalists and media practitioners;

Calls on States Parties to the African Charter, to take all necessary measures to uphold their obligations under the African Charter and other international and regional instruments, providing for the right to freedom of expression and access to information;

Urges States Parties to the African Charter, to implement the principles enshrined in the Declaration of Principles on Freedom of Expression in Africa;

Calls on States Parties to the African Charter and concerned authorities to fulfil their obligation on preventing and investigating all crimes allegedly committed against journalists and media practitioners and also to bring the perpetrators to justice;

Urges all parties involved in situations of armed conflicts to respect the independence and freedom of journalists and media practitioners to exercise their profession and guarantee their safety and security in accordance with international humanitarian law;

Finally urges States Parties to African Charter, to cooperate with the Special Rapporteur on Freedom of Expression and Access to Information in Africa of the African Commission, in the execution of its mandate.

5.10.5 UN Security Council, *Report of the Secretary-General on the Protection of Civilians in Armed Conflict* (22 May 2012), UN Doc. S/2012/376

14. The violence in the Syrian Arab Republic and last year's conflict in Libya also highlighted the dangers for journalists and other media professionals working in such

situations. Six journalists were killed in Libya in March and April 2011, while at least 11 have been killed in the Syrian Arab Republic since November 2011. Journalists play a crucial role by reporting on the treatment and suffering endured by civilians in situations of conflict and on violations of humanitarian law and human rights. In some situations, journalists were killed by parties to conflict, abducted, subject to arbitrary arrest and detention, subjected to forcible disappearance or harassed. Impunity for such violations remains widespread.

15. I remind the Security Council of the need, as expressed in its resolution 1738 (2006), for States and other parties to conflict to prevent attacks against journalists and to prosecute those responsible for such attacks.

5.10.6 SC, *Security Council Resolution 2222 on Protection of Journalists* (27 May 2015), 7450th Meeting, UN Doc. S/RES/2222 (2015)

. . .

5. Emphasizes the responsibility of States to comply with the relevant obligations under international law to end impunity and to prosecute those responsible for serious violations of international humanitarian law;

6. Urges Member States to take appropriate steps to ensure accountability for crimes committed against journalists, media professionals and associated personnel in situations of armed conflict and through the conduct of impartial, independent and effective investigations within their jurisdiction and to bring perpetrators of such crimes to justice;

7. Recalls its demand that all parties to an armed conflict comply fully with the obligations applicable to them under international law related to the protection of civilians in armed conflict, including journalists, media professionals and associated personnel;

8. Urges the immediate and unconditional release of journalists, media professionals and associated personnel who have been kidnapped or taken as hostages, in situations of armed conflict;

9. Urges all parties involved in situations of armed conflict to respect the professional independence and rights of journalists, media professionals and associated personnel as civilians;

10. Recalls also that media equipment and installations constitute civilian objects, and in this respect shall not be the object of attack or of reprisals, unless they are military objectives;

11. Recognizes the important role that education and training in international humanitarian law can play in supporting efforts to halt and prevent attacks against civilians affected by armed conflict, including journalists, media professionals and associated personnel;

12. Affirms that United Nations peacekeeping and special political missions, where appropriate should include in their mandated reporting information on specific acts of violence against journalists, media professionals and associated personnel in situation of armed conflict;

13. Urges all parties to armed conflict to do their utmost to prevent violations of international humanitarian law against civilians, including journalists, media professionals and associated personnel;

14. Calls upon Member States to create and maintain, in law and in practice, a safe and enabling environment for journalists, media professionals and associated personnel to perform their work independently and without undue interference in situations of armed conflict; . . .

15. Stresses the need to ensure better cooperation and coordination at the international level, including among the United Nations and relevant international regional and sub-regional organizations, including through technical assistance and capacity-building, with regard to promoting and ensuring the safety of journalists, media professionals and associated personnel in armed conflicts;

16. Encourages the United Nations and regional and sub-regional organizations to share expertise on good practices and lessons learned on protection of journalists, media professionals and associated personnel in armed conflict and, in close co-operation, to enhance the coherent and effective implementation of applicable international humanitarian law and relevant Security Council resolutions including those on protection of journalist, media professionals and associated personnel in situations of the armed conflict

5.11 PROTECTION OF PEACEKEEPERS[21]

5.11.1 ICC, *Prosecutor* v. *Bahar Idriss Abu Garda*, (Decision on the Confirmation of Charges), Case No. ICC-02/05-02/09, Pre-Trial Chamber I (8 February 2010)

Note: *The facts of this case are set out in Chapter 4, Section 4.4.3. As to the extent of the protection offered to peacekeeping missions during an armed conflict, the ICC said as follows:*

77. The Majority notes that an attack against a peacekeeping mission constitutes a crime under the Statute as long as its personnel, installations, material, units or vehicles are entitled to the protection given to civilians or civilian objects under the international law of armed conflict.

78. Article 13 (3) of APII provides that civilians shall enjoy the protection afforded by [Part IV of the Protocol], *unless and for such time* as they take a direct part in hostilities" [emphasis added]. The same exclusion applies, under article 2(2) of the Convention on the Safety of United Nations and Associated Personnel, to personnel engaged as combatants. . . .

83. In light of the foregoing considerations, the Majority concludes that, under the Statute, personnel involved in peacekeeping missions enjoy protection from attacks unless and for such time as they take a direct part in hostilities or in combat-related activities. The Majority also finds that such protection does not cease if such persons only use armed

---

[21]   See Chapter 1 Section 1.8.1, Chapter 4 Section 4.4, Chapter 6 Section 6.1.2.3 and Chapter 10 Section 10.6.5.

force in exercise of their right to self-defence. Finally, and adopting the precedent of the ICTY, the Majority finds that any determination as to whether a person is directly participating in hostilities must be carried out on a case-by-case basis.

5.11.2 SC, *Press Statement on Democratic Republic of Congo,* SC/11108-AFR/2688-PKO/370, 29 August 2013

... The members of the Security Council expressed their condolences to the family of the peacekeeper killed in the attack, as well as to the Government of the United Republic of Tanzania and to MONUSCO. They called on the Government of the Democratic Republic of the Congo to swiftly investigate the incident and bring the perpetrators to justice.

They recalled that intentionally directing attacks against personnel, installations, material, units or vehicles involved in a peacekeeping mission in accordance with the Charter of the United Nations, as long as they are entitled to the protection given to civilians or civilian objects under the international law of armed conflict, constitutes a crime under international law.

5.12 PROTECTION OF PRIVATE MILITARY AND SECURITY CONTRACTOR (PMSC) PERSONNEL[22]

5.12.1 ICRC, *The Montreux Document on Pertinent International Legal Obligations and Good Practices for States Related to Operations of Private Military and Security Companies During Armed Conflict* (17 September 2008)

26. The personnel of PMSCs:...b) are protected as civilians under international humanitarian law, unless they are incorporated into the regular armed forces of a State or are members of organized armed forces, groups or units under a command responsible to the State; or otherwise lose their protection as determined by international humanitarian law;

5.12.2 US, **Department of Defense**, *Law of War Manual*, **Office of General Counsel (June 2015, Updated 2016)**

4.15 PERSONS AUTHORIZED TO ACCOMPANY THE ARMED FORCES

4.15.2.1 *Liability to Being Made the Object of Attack.* For the purposes of determining whether they may be made the object of attack, persons authorized to accompany the armed forces are treated as civilians. They may not be made the object of attack unless they take direct part in hostilities.

...

4.15.2.6 *Provision of Security Services.* Persons authorized to accompany the armed forces who provide security against criminal elements generally would not be viewed as

---

[22] See also Chapter 4 Section 4.1.2.

taking a direct part in hostilities (and do not forfeit their protection from being made the object of attack). However, providing such services to defend against enemy armed forces of a State would be regarded as taking a direct part in hostilities (and would forfeit their protection from being made the object of attack). DoD policies have addressed the use of non-military personnel to provide security services for DoD components. Where there has been a significant risk of attack by enemy armed forces of a State, DoD practice generally has been to use military personnel to provide security.

COMMENTARY

1. The IHL rules on the protection of civilians have a long pedigree. Although the current comprehensive regime of protection is a post–World War II phenomenon that is in sync with the 'humanisation' of war, there have always been protections afforded to certain civilians. Civilians are protected against the dangers resulting from military operations in the course of an IAC.[23] Accordingly, civilians are protected against direct attacks and against indiscriminate attacks unless they directly participate in hostilities.[24] Civilians defined as protected persons under Article 4 GCIV, in particular those in territory under enemy occupation, enjoy the protections contained in said Convention. Other civilians in the hands of a party to the conflict who do not benefit from more favourable protection under the GCs are afforded a minimum standard of protection under Article 75 API, which is generally regarded as representing customary international law, whereas Common Article 3 offers minimum protections applied in all circumstances. Despite the rudimentary structure of IHL regulating NIACs, fundamentally similar protections to those afforded in IAC are applicable to civilians who find themselves in the hands of a party to the conflict. Again, Additional Protocol II offers more detailed protections than under Common Article 3.

2. Detention is an 'accepted feature' in armed conflict. IHL contains rules on the authority and grounds for detention; the conditions of detention; the protection of detainees and their procedural rights. The IHL rules differ depending on whether detention takes place in an IAC or a NIAC. In an IAC, two forms of detention can be identified. First, combatants are detained as POW. This is status-based detention and is examined in Chapter 6. Second, civilians can be detained if they pose a security threat to the detaining power. This is non-criminal and non-status-based administrative detention based on individual threat assessment. According to GCIV, civilians in the territory of a party to a conflict can be detained 'if the security of the Detaining Power makes it absolutely necessary' whereas in occupied territories such internment can only occur 'for imperative reasons of security'.[25] The question that arises is when civilians pose a security threat and whether it includes direct as well as indirect participation in hostilities. With slight differences, IHL provides for a periodic review process and appeals against decisions to detain[26] but does not specify the

---

[23] Art. 51, API.
[24] See Chapter 4, Section 4.2.
[25] Arts 42(1) and 78(1), GCIV.
[26] Arts 42, 43, 78, GCIV and Art. 75, API.

character of the reviewing bodies, the applicable guarantees as well as the powers of the reviewing bodies. IHRL can thus fill the gaps as the *Hassan* judgment indicates.[27] Review bodies need to be independent and impartial, respect fair trial guarantees and release detainees if they do not pose a security threat anymore. Yet questions remain as to the level of information and assistance detainees should be provided with, particularly when information is classified, and how the security threat is interpreted by the reviewing bodies. Detainees should be released when the justification for detention ends and, in any case, as soon as possible after the close of hostilities.[28] However, what are the upper limits of detention during an armed conflict or after the close of hostilities?

3. Detention in NIAC is examined in Chapter 10.[29] As will be explained in more detail there, Common Article 3 and Article 5 of APII provide a basis for the regulation of detention in NIAC but the authority and grounds for detention in NIACs have been debated. It has been argued, for example, that there is an inherent right to detain under customary IHL but the English courts and the European Court of Human Rights do not support this position. Detention by armed groups is also discussed in Chapter 10. Again questions about the authority, grounds, procedures and guarantees of detention are raised. Nonetheless, detentions by armed groups occur, hence the need for their regulation. This is reinforced by international jurisprudence which makes it clear that senior commanders are expected under the doctrine of command responsibility to ensure the proper observance of IHL by their subordinates in cases of detention.[30]

4. Closely associated with detention is the question of transfer of detainees.[31] In the context of IACs the transfer of protected persons is regulated under Art. 49 GCIV, with transfer restricted to within the occupied territory. In recent NIACs, issues were raised with respect to the transfer of captured insurgents to the host nation. On the basis of the transfer arrangements established between certain States and Afghanistan, the basis for such transfer appears to be a combination of the host nation domestic law, IHL and IHRL obligations of the host State and of the troop-contributing nation whose troops carried out the detention. Clearly Common Article 3 and if applicable APII are relevant in view of their requirement for humane treatment.

5. In the case of armed groups, the transfer of detainees would appear to be limited to those occasions when justified on the basis of the security of the detainees or on imperative military necessity. In the event that detainees were transferred between armed groups, the question arises as to the responsibilities of those concerned. Adopting the position in the ICTY jurisprudence regarding the existence of individual responsibility on the part of those concerned in the transfer of prisoners from one unit to another, a continuing liability would arguably arise on their part to ensure the safety of those transferred.

---

[27]   ECtHR, *Hassan v. United Kingdom* [GC], (App No. 29750/09), (ECtHR, 16 September 2014), para. 104. See also Chapter 3 Section 3.6.
[28]   Arts 132 and 133 GCIV; Art. 75(3), API.
[29]   See Chapter 10, Section 10.6.
[30]   See Chapter 12.
[31]   See Chapter 3 Section 3.7 and Chapter 10 Section 10.6.3.

6. The basic approach under IHL is that men and women are treated equally and without discrimination as far as detention is concerned.[32] It is accepted, however, that in certain circumstances the needs of women require to be specifically addressed, as for example in Article 84 GCIV and Article 75 API, concerning gender-separated accommodation in internment.[33]

7. Sexual violence against women is a continuing and unacceptable feature of armed conflict, being particularly prevalent in the context of NIACs. The lack of adequate protection has led to widespread and justifiable criticism. Should this criticism be targeted at the available legal structure? GCIV does provide that women are to be protected against sexual violence although the language of the Convention has been criticised for its outdated nature. In NIACs protection is afforded through the application of Common Article 3. Building upon these foundations, the two Additional Protocols have more explicitly prohibited sexual violence. The development of international criminal law in the *ad hoc* international criminal tribunals and with the establishment of the ICC has seen rape and other serious forms of sexual violence prosecuted in both IACs and NIACs.

8. The question arises as to how the reality on the ground concerning sexual violence should be addressed. The answer appears to lie both in changes in societal attitudes and also in the effective enforcement of the applicable law by State and non-State armed groups as proposed in Committee on the Elimination of Discrimination Against Women (CEDAW) General Recommendation No. 19. The issue is particularly complex in the case of armed groups and relates to cultural attitudes, legal gaps and lack of enforcement. Whereas prosecution and holding to account of culprits can be a step in the right direction, achieving change in the underlying culture of the armed group is a prerequisite as well as the armed group's engagement with IHL and IHRL.

9. Linked to the foregoing issue is the question of sexual exploitation and abuse of the local civilian population committed by UN peacekeepers. Such conduct has long been recognised by the UN as having seriously detrimental effects on the peacekeeping operation and undermining the guiding principles of UN peacekeeping operations.[34] The 2005 *Zeid* Report clearly specified the impact that such conduct was having and the measures which required to be adopted in order to address it effectively. The question then arises as to how to address the gap that continues to exist between that recognition by the UN and the situation on the ground.

10. The 2017 Report by the UN Secretary-General on the issue identified that exploitation and abuse have been most prevalent in circumstances where the local population is particularly vulnerable, as in failed and failing States.[35] Systemic weaknesses have been identified among both the military and civilian components linked to selection, training, leadership, a lack of understanding of UN values and standards, a sense of impunity and

---

[32] Art. 27, GCIV.

[33] See also UN Secretary-General's Bulletin, Observance by United Nations Forces of International Humanitarian Law (6 August 1999), UN Doc. ST/SGB/1999/13, section 8 (e) regarding this issue in the case of UN-operated detention facilities.

[34] See UN Secretary-General's Bulletin: Special Measures for Protection from Sexual Exploitation and Sexual Abuse (9 October 2003), UN Doc. ST/SGB/2003/13, section 3.

[35] See UN Report of the Secretary-General: Special Measures for Protection from Sexual Exploitation and Abuse: A New Approach (28 February 2017), UN Doc. A/71/818.

lack of interest both at a senior level within the organisation and on the part of troop-contributing States. The proposed four-strand strategy to deal with the issue seeks to establish a sustained and coherent approach, putting the rights and dignity of victims first, ending impunity, engaging external partners, and improving strategic communication and sustainment.[36]

11. In order to effectively address the issue of SEA, it will be necessary for preventive action to be taken with pre-deployment training of personnel concerning SEA awareness and greater representation of women in the peacekeeping operations' gender advisory roles. Monitoring of prior training and of performance while on mission requires the establishment of an oversight process by the Office of Internal Oversight Services. In the event of incidents occurring, effective disciplinary action is required in the case of military personnel, with court martials being held in territory to demonstrate the UN's commitment to eradicate such behaviour. In the case of civilian UN personnel, similar arrangements require to be put in place for the effective prosecution of offenders. If necessary, the extension of the host State's national criminal jurisdiction should be pursued in order to enable effective prosecution of those personnel who would otherwise escape prosecution.

12. Children are particularly vulnerable to the effects of conflict and, as with women, are also the subjects of additional protection, with particular emphasis placed on the prevention of their participation in armed conflict. As with the protection of women from sexual violence, IHL, IHRL and international criminal law provide a structure of protection. The former two bodies of law establish prohibitions on recruitment and employment of child soldiers in armed conflict with the criminalisation of such recruitment and employment under ICL. Difficulties exist, however, in view of the differences in the age thresholds under the various applicable international instruments and the position of States and of armed groups.[37]

13. While encouraging States to assume their responsibilities with regard to children, the more difficult question relates to how armed groups can best be encouraged to assume obligations in this regard. One possible solution involves engagement with such groups with the aim of their adopting these obligations and signing up to soft law agreements, as with the Geneva Call Deed of Commitment for the Protection of Children from the Effects of Armed Conflict.[38] This provides not only for the prohibition of their recruitment into the military wing as child soldiers, but also association in the sense of direct or supporting activity.

14. While most approaches seek to address the recruitment of children as child soldiers, the question remains as to the approach to be adopted with respect to safeguarding children directly participating in armed conflict. Should children directly participating in hostilities be regarded as a legitimate military target or should they be regarded as enjoying the protection afforded to civilians? As discussed in Chapter 11, children would lose protection in such cases.

---

[36] See ibid, Annex I, Summary of Actions and Recommendations.
[37] Art. 77(2), API; Art. 4 (3(c), APII; Art. 38, Convention on the Rights of the Child (adopted 20 November 1989, entered into force 2 September 1990); First Optional Protocol to the Convention on the Rights of the Child (adopted 25 May 2000, entered into force 12 February 2002) 2173 UNTS 222.
[38] See Deed of Commitment executed by the Zomi Re-Unification Organization (2 March 2016).

15. The risks facing journalists during war are not only murder, but also include arrest, kidnapping, threats, harassment and restrictions on their work. The special status of journalists has been recognised in IAC in Article 79 API, which grew out of a UN initiative to protect journalists on dangerous missions. The term journalist is not defined in the provision. It has been described as including those working as 'correspondent, reporter, photographer and their technical film, radio and television assistants'. This definition, however, excludes many part-time fixers, stringers, bloggers or citizen journalists who are also exposed to the dangers of armed conflict. Article 79 API confirms the status of both war correspondents and independent journalists as civilians. They are thus protected as civilians, irrespective of whether they are war correspondents or 'embedded journalists',[39] unless of course they directly participate in hostilities. War correspondents, that is, journalists authorised by armed forces, are entitled to POW status whereas 'embedded journalists' accompany the armed forces without being so authorised; consequently, they are not entitled to POW status. Embedded journalists may have access to information but such information may be controlled. Because of their closeness to the army, they are often collateral victims of attacks.[40] In the event that independent journalists fall into the hands of a party to the conflict, they enjoy the protection afforded by GCIV if the nationality criteria of Art. 4 GCIV are satisfied, and otherwise are entitled to the protections afforded under Article 75 API or the minimum protections of Common Article 3. It should be noted that these protections only apply in IACs whereas in NIACs journalists are protected by IHRL. Moreover, even when IHL applies, it does not address every issue that may arise, which is thus regulated by IHRL or domestic law.

16. One major difficulty in situations of armed conflict is determining when a journalist directly participates in hostilities. Whereas ordinary reporting does not amount to DPH, reporting certain information such as the capabilities of an adversary may affect military operations but the immediate question is whether there is direct causation or belligerent nexus. Propaganda does not constitute DPH, being a war-sustaining activity, but incitement to violence could amount to DPH. Spying as the gathering and passing of information may constitute DPH and expose the journalist to attacks or criminal trial whereas war correspondents who spy forfeit POW status.

17. Under the functional approach adopted until recently by the United States *Law of War Manual*, a broad view was taken of what amounted to direct participation by journalists reporting on armed conflict.[41] The approach was controversial and differed from the approach adopted in other military manuals, which adopted a narrower approach to the definition. A 2016 amendment to the *Manual* has removed the controversial text.[42]

---

[39]   Art. 4(4), GCIII; Art. 79, API.
[40]   For proportionality, see Chapter 7.
[41]   US Department of Defense, *Law of War Manual* (2015, updated 2016), para. 4.24.3 '. . . in some cases, the relaying of information (such as providing information of immediate use in combat operations) could constitute taking a direct part in hostilities.' See also para. 4.24.4: 'Reporting on military operations can be very similar to collecting intelligence or even spying.' See DJ Moore, 'Twenty First Century Embedded Journalists: Lawful Targets?' [2009] *Army Lawyer* 1 and in particular the discussion on direct participation in hostilities at pp. 19–21.
[42]   See US Department of Defense, *Law of War Manual* (2015, updated 2016), section 4.24 'Journalists', which emphasises the vital role of journalists in reporting armed conflict.

18. Given the continuing issue of violence towards journalists, another approach has been urged under which journalists would, as with the earlier proposals from the UN, be the subject of a specific convention governing their protection in armed conflict. This, it has been proposed, would avoid the current fractured approach under IHL's meagre regulation. The question then is whether further fracturing the general protection afforded to civilians in both IACs and NIACs can provide practical benefits justifying this step. Against this it has been contended that the problem is not with the legal structure but with its implementation in practice.[43] Rather than creating further law, it is arguable that what is required is countering the culture of impunity that drives many of the attacks upon journalists.

19. Private military and security companies (PMSCs) play an increasingly important part in modern armed conflict through the provision of a broad range of services from logistical support, to catering, to maintenance of facilities, security for military facilities, convoy security, the provision of close protection to embassies, NGOs and commercial operations, communications support, intelligence analysis, and advice and training to local security forces. Clearly, PMSC employees providing support services to military forces in armed conflict, even if the adverse party in the conflict does not make them the direct object of attack, are at risk of suffering incidental loss of life or injury in the event of attack when working in a military facility or using military transportation.

20. As civilians, PMSC employees may not directly participate in hostilities without losing their protection. This is problematic regarding PMSCs employed in a security function, particularly in respect of facilities or equipment which are military objectives under IHL. If a civilian security guard uses force to protect a military objective from criminal activity, this does not amount to DPH. If, however, the military objective is subject to attack by the adverse party in the conflict, then the PMSC security guard who uses force for the purpose of protecting it will be directly participating in hostilities. If a PMSC employee uses force to protect a civilian or a civilian object against a direct attack, this would not amount to DPH, with the employee here being regarded as acting in lawful self-defence. Particular difficulties may arise in circumstances where the same PMSC is providing security and logistic services. While seemingly straightforward, the situation on the ground poses significant difficulties for such employees who may well be unaware of whether the facility they are guarding is indeed classed as a military objective or whether the individuals seeking, for example, to breach a perimeter fence are engaged in criminal activity or are combatants.

21. Changes in the character and mandates of peacekeeping operations, their deployment in hostile environments, and the extension of the right to use force in self-defence to the defence of the mission have challenged the traditional assumptions surrounding peace-keeping and marked increasing levels of attacks against peacekeepers.[44] Their protection from direct attacks is necessary in view of the functions they perform on behalf of the

---

[43] See UNSCR 2222 on Protection of Journalists (27 May 2015) 7450th Meeting, UN Doc. S/RES/2222 (2015), para. 7: 'Recalls its demand that all parties to an armed conflict comply fully with the obligations applicable to them under international law related to the protection of civilians in armed conflict, including journalists, media professionals and associated personnel.'
[44] See Convention on the Safety of United Nations and Associated Personnel (adopted 9 December 1994, entered into force 15 January 1999) 2051 UNTS 363, Preamble. Also see Chapters 1 and 4.

international community. Furthermore, if UN peacekeeping forces are subjected to increasing levels of attacks, this is likely to impact on the willingness of States to provide the troops necessary in order to carry out these operations.

22. In an attempt to deal with the perceived culture of impunity among those who were responsible for attacks on peacekeepers, the UN introduced the 1994 Convention on the Safety of United Nations and Associated Personnel. The Convention prohibits attacks on peacekeepers and associated personnel, their equipment and premises, and requires that States criminalise such attacks and prosecute or extradite suspects.[45] It does not, however, apply directly to armed groups, and the obligations accordingly require national implementation. Article 2(2) of the Convention appears to have been intended to limit the application of the Convention to situations where peacekeepers are not engaged as combatants and the law of international armed conflict is applicable.[46] The circumstances covered by this exclusion have been questioned as the language is not entirely clear, and arguably, it also extends to NIACs. The Convention has since been supplemented by the 2005 Optional Protocol, which, reflecting concerns over the continuing attacks on UN personnel, sought to expand the application of the Convention through reference to its terms in Status of Forces Agreements (SOFAs) with the host State and the widening of the definition of missions covered by the Convention. The limited level of ratifications of both the Convention and its associated Protocol has affected the impact of these measures. A potentially more effective provision is Article 8 of the Rome Statute of the International Criminal Court (ICC St), which criminalises attacks on peacekeepers, provided they are entitled to the protection afforded civilians.

23. Critical to the issue of protection of peacekeepers is to determine when IHL applies and when peacekeepers become combatants. The issue has been discussed in Chapters 1 and 4 in light of the *Secretary-General's Bulletin on Observance by United Nations Forces of International Humanitarian Law.*[47] As was said there, when the UN force becomes party to an armed conflict, members of the military component are combatants whereas members of the civilian component are protected as civilians unless they directly participate in hostilities. In the case of MONUSCO (United Nations Organisation Stabilization Mission in the Democratic Republic of Congo) a controversial issue was whether it was the Intervention Brigade or the whole UN force that was a party to the conflict. The UN Secretariat has subsequently confirmed that the whole of the force has become a party to the conflict and, accordingly, all its troops are regarded as having combatant status.

24. The issue of engaging armed groups with respect to the issue of the protection afforded to UN peacekeepers under the Safety Convention raises questions. The Convention and its Optional Protocol do not directly bind such groups and, while action to reduce the culture of impunity through the prosecution of offenders has some validity, positive action to seek to achieve their observance of the prohibition of attack on peacekeepers and their release following capture and detention is clearly required.

---

[45] See Arts 7, 9–19 of the Convention.

[46] See also UN *Secretary-General's Bulletin on Observance by United Nations Forces of International Humanitarian Law* (6 August 1999) UN Doc. ST/SGB/1999/13, Art. 1.1.

[47] Chapter 1 Section 1.8.1 and Chapter 4 Section 4.4. See UN *Secretary-General's Bulletin on Observance by United Nations Forces of International Humanitarian Law* (6 August 1999) UN Doc. ST/SGB/1999/13, Art. 1.1.

25. In conclusion, although the legal framework concerning the protection of civilians is quite developed, particularly in IACs, there are problems of implementation and compliance as the tremendous suffering of civilians in contemporary conflicts attests to. Lack of implementation and compliance are due to certain features of modern armed conflicts such as the inequality between parties, the political-ideological nature of certain conflicts, the increased urbanisation of conflicts and, of course, the prevalence of NIACs. As was noted in Chapter 4, these features often blur the distinction between civilians and combatants with detrimental effects on the former. Violations of the protective regime on civilians are often deliberate but, other times, they are incidental. Measures that can prevent violations should involve all parties and may include training, clear operational rules, internal oversight, and repressive mechanisms. They should also involve third parties through assistance or sanctions. The most critical factor is, however, ownership of the rules and decoupling the conduct of hostilities from the overall political aims pursued by the parties.

6

Protection of Prisoners of War

INTRODUCTION

It is only in the context of IAC that the status of POW exists. In essence, members of the armed forces of a State, party to an IAC, are combatants and are entitled to POW status on capture by the hostile State. However, Art. 4 GCIII, which defines those who are entitled to POW status, widens the category to also include specified categories of civilians who are entitled to POW status. Under Art. 33 GCIII captured medical and religious personnel are not POW but may be retained to assist POW and are treated on the same basis. The deficiencies of the pre-1945 regime concerning captured combatants were exposed by the Second World War and in response GCIII established a comprehensive and detailed protection regime designed to protect the interests of the hostile State, the POW's State of origin and those of the prisoner. Despite the increasing levels of protection afforded to other categories of individuals in IAC, only POW are afforded combatant immunity with respect to their DPH. There is, however, no requirement that detention as a POW is subjected to initial or periodic review similar to that afforded to civilian internees under GCIV.[1] This position is linked to the status of POW as former combatants. They represent accordingly a continuing threat to the hostile State in whose hands they are held and may therefore be detained until the cessation of active hostilities. Despite the existence of a comprehensive regime of protections, significant challenges remain ranging from the determination of POW status, the treatment of 'unlawful combatants', the range of protections afforded to POW and to children or women, the transfer and repatriation of POW, the status of captured UN personnel as well as the possible application of the POW regime to NIACs.

Resources: Arts 4–20, 33(1), GCIII; Arts 4, 5, GCIV; Articles 41, 43–47, 67(2), 75, API

---

[1]   See Chapters 5 and 10.

Cases and Materials

6.1 POW STATUS

6.1.1 Entitlement to POW Status

6.1.1.1 UK, British Ministry of Defence, *The Joint Service Manual of the Law of Armed Conflict*, (Joint Service Publication 383, 2004 Edition)

8.3 The basic rule is that members of the armed forces of a party to the conflict have prisoner of war status on capture. They enjoy this status from the moment that they fall into the hands of the enemy, irrespective of whether they have been formally registered as prisoners of war or whether their capture has been acknowledged by their own government. In addition, there are certain non-combatants who are entitled to this status. A person does not normally forfeit prisoner of war status because of violations of the law of armed conflict.

8.3.1 A consolidated list of those entitled to prisoner of war status is as follows:

a. All members (except medical and religious personnel) of the organized armed forces of a party to the conflict, even if that party is represented by a government or authority not recognized by the adversary, provided that those forces: (1) are under a command responsible to a party to the conflict for the conduct of its subordinates; and (2) are subject to an internal disciplinary system which enforces compliance with the law of armed conflict.

b. Members of any other militias, volunteer corps, or organized resistance movements, belonging to a party to the conflict and operating in or (3) carry their arms openly; and (4) conduct their operations in accordance with the law of armed conflict.

c. Those who accompany the armed forces without actually being members thereof (for example, civilian members of military aircraft crews, war correspondents, supply contractors, members of labour units or of services responsible for the welfare of the armed forces) if duly authorized by the armed forces which they accompany. That armed force must issue these personnel with an appropriate identity card.

d. Members of crews, including masters, pilots, and apprentices, of the merchant marine and crews of civil aircraft of the parties to the conflict, who do not benefit by more favourable treatment under any other provisions of international law.

e. Inhabitants of non-occupied territory who, on the approach of the enemy, spontaneously take up arms to resist the invading forces without having had time to form themselves into regular armed units, provided they carry their arms openly and respect the laws of armed conflict (levée en masse).

6.1.2 Special Cases

6.1.2.1 Retained Personnel
6.1.2.1.1 **UK**, British Ministry of Defence, *The Joint Service Manual of the Law of Armed Conflict*, (Joint Service Publication 383, 2004 Edition)
10.8 Status of captured medical and religious personnel.

Medical personnel and chaplains who fall into enemy hands do not become PW but, until they are returned, are to be treated in accordance with the provisions of the GCIII. They must be treated as PW and be provided with all necessary medical facilities to care for their own PW. PW who are medically qualified but not attached to the medical branch of their own forces may be required by the detaining power to exercise their medical functions on behalf of PW. Although prisoners, they are to be treated as other medical personnel and are exempt from any other work.

6.1.2.2 Civilians Authorised to Accompany the Armed Forces
6.1.2.2.1 **US**, Department of Defense, *Law of War Manual*, Office of General Counsel (June 2015, Updated 2016)
. . . 4.15.2.2 Employment in Hostilities. The law of war does not prohibit persons authorized to accompany the armed forces from providing authorized support that constitutes taking direct part in hostilities. Even if the authorized support that they provide constitutes taking

a direct part in hostilities, such persons retain their entitlement to POW status under Article 4A(4) of the GPW. . . .

4.15.3 Persons Authorized to Accompany the Armed Forces – Detention.

For the purposes of detention, persons authorized to accompany the armed forces are treated like combatants. These persons may be detained by the enemy and are entitled to POW status during international armed conflict. . . .

4.24.1.1 War Correspondents and Other Journalists Authorized to Accompany the Armed Forces.

Journalists authorized to accompany the armed forces have the status of such persons. For example, if they fall into the power of the enemy during international armed conflict, they are entitled to POW status. Such journalists are sometimes called "war correspondents," which is a term used in Geneva Conventions of 1949. Since journalists authorized to accompany the armed forces are liable to become POWs, they must be issued identification cards so that they may establish their entitlement to POW status upon falling into the power of the enemy during international armed conflict.

6.1.2.3 Captured Peacekeepers
6.1.2.3.1 **UN, General Assembly,** *Convention on the Safety of United Nations and Associated Personnel* (Adopted 9 December 1994, Entered into Force 15 January 1999) 2051 UNTS 363

Art 8. Except as otherwise provided in an applicable status-of-forces agreement, if United Nations or associated personnel are captured or detained in the course of the performance of their duties and their identification has been established, they shall not be subjected to interrogation and they shall be promptly released and returned to United Nations or other appropriate authorities. Pending their release such personnel shall be treated in accordance with universally recognized standards of human rights and the principles and spirit of the Geneva Conventions of 1949.

6.1.2.3.2 **UN, Secretary General's Bulletin,** *Observance by United Nations Forces of International Humanitarian Law* (6 August 1999) UN Doc. ST/SGB/1999/13

1.2 The promulgation of this bulletin does not affect the protected status of members of peacekeeping operations under the 1994 Convention on the Safety of United Nations and Associated Personnel or their status as non-combatants, as long as they are entitled to the protection given to civilians under the international law of armed conflict

6.1.3 'Unlawful Combatants'

6.1.3.1 General
6.1.3.1.1 **US Supreme Court,** *Ex Parte Quirin,* 317 U.S. 1, 30–31 (1942)
Note: *The facts of this case are discussed in Chapter 4, Section 4.3.1. As to the distinction between lawful and unlawful combatants, the US Supreme Court said:*

By universal agreement and practice, the law of war draws a distinction between the armed forces and the peaceful populations of belligerent nations, and also between those who are lawful and unlawful combatants. Lawful combatants are subject to capture and detention as prisoners of war by opposing military forces. Unlawful combatants are likewise subject to capture and detention, but, in addition, they are subject to trial and punishment by military tribunals for acts which render their belligerency unlawful.

6.1.3.1.2 Privy Council (Malaysia), *Osman Bin Haji Mohamed Ali and Another* v. *Public Prosecutor* [1969] 1 AC 430, p. 449

Note: *The facts of this case are set out in Chapter 4, Section 4.3.2. As to the protections afforded to unlawful combatants, the Privy Council said:*

In this appeal it is not necessary to attempt to define all the circumstances in which a person coming within the terms of Article I of the Regulations and of Article 4 of the Convention as a member of an army or armed force ceases to enjoy the right to be treated as a prisoner of war. The question to be decided is whether members of such a force who engage in sabotage while in civilian clothes and who are captured so dressed are entitled to be treated as protected by the Convention.

..., their lordships are of the opinion that under international law it is clear that the appellants, if they were members of the Indonesian armed forces, were not entitled to be treated on capture as prisoners of war under the Geneva Convention when they had landed to commit sabotage and had been dressed in civilian clothes both when they had placed the explosives and lit them and when they were arrested.

6.1.3.1.3 US, *United States of America* v. *Buck* 690 F. Supp. 1291 (S.D.N.Y. 1988)

Note: *The facts of this case are detailed in Chapter 4, Section 4.3.3. As to the criteria organised resistance groups must satisfy to benefit from POW status, the District Court for the Southern District of New York said:*

Article 4(A) (2) requires that to qualify as prisoners of war, members of "organized resistance movements" must fulfil the conditions of command by a person responsible for his subordinates; having a fixed distinctive sign recognizable at a distance; carrying arms openly; and conducting their operations in accordance with the laws and customs of war. The defendants at bar and their associates cannot pretend to have fulfilled those conditions.

6.1.3.1.4 Israel, *The Public Committee Against Torture in Israel and Others* v. *The Government of Israel and Others* ('Targeted Killing Case'), Case No. HCJ 769/02, Israeli Supreme Court Sitting as the High Court of Justice (11 December 2005)

Note: *The facts of this case are dealt with in Chapter 1, Section 1.6.1. As to whether terrorists can enjoy the status of POW, the Israeli HCJ said:*

25. The terrorists and their organizations, with which the State of Israel has an armed conflict of international character, do not fall into the category of combatants. They do not belong to the armed forces, and they do not belong to units to which international law

grants status similar to that of combatants. Indeed, the terrorists and the organizations which send them to carry out attacks are unlawful combatants. They do not enjoy the status of prisoners of war. They can be tried for their participation in hostilities, judged, and punished.

6.1.3.1.5 Human Rights Watch, *Up in Flames: Humanitarian Law Violations and Civilian Victims in the Conflict over South Ossetia* (2009)

2.8 Georgian Detentions and Ill-Treatment of Ossetians

Under international humanitarian law Ossetians who were not members of any regular forces, but members of militias or otherwise took up arms against the Georgian military, are not entitled to POW status, but are detained as non-privileged combatants, and should be treated in accordance with the protections guaranteed to civilians under the Fourth Geneva Convention.

6.1.3.2 Mercenaries

6.1.3.2.1 UN, General Assembly, International Convention against the Recruitment, Use, Financing and Training of Mercenaries (Adopted 4 December 1989, Entered into Force 20 October 2001) 2163 UNTS 75

Article 3

1. A mercenary, as defined in article 1 of the present Convention, who participates directly in hostilities or in a concerted act of violence, as the case may be, commits an offence for the purposes of the Convention.

Article 10

1. Upon being satisfied that the circumstances so warrant, any State Party in whose territory the alleged offender is present shall, in accordance with its laws, take him into custody or take such other measures to ensure his presence for such time as is necessary to enable any criminal or extradition proceedings to be instituted. The State Party shall immediately make a preliminary inquiry into the facts.

6.1.3.2.2 UK, British Ministry of Defence, *The Joint Service Manual of the Law of Armed Conflict*, (Joint Service Publication 383, 2004 Edition)

8.12 Mercenaries are not entitled to be prisoners of war unless their captors so decide. Even if not treated as prisoners of war, captured mercenaries remain entitled to the basic humanitarian guarantees provided by Additional Protocol I.

6.1.4 Relationship Between IHL and IHRL

6.1.4.1 ECtHR, *Hassan* v. *UK* [GC], (App No. 27950/09) (ECtHR, 16 September 2014)
Note: *The facts of this case are set out in Chapter 3, Section 3.6.5. As to the nexus between IHL and IHRL, the ECtHR said:*

97. . . . As regards combatants detained as prisoners of war, since this category of person enjoys combatant privilege, allowing them to participate in hostilities without incurring

criminal sanctions, it would not be appropriate for the Court to hold that this form of detention falls within the scope of Article 5 § 1(c). ...

103. ... the Court accepts the Government's argument that the lack of a formal derogation under Article 15 does not prevent the Court from taking account of the context and the provisions of international humanitarian law when interpreting and applying Article 5 in this case.

104. Nonetheless, and consistently with the case-law of the International Court of Justice, the Court considers that, even in situations of international armed conflict, the safeguards under the Convention continue to apply, albeit interpreted against the background of the provisions of international humanitarian law. By reason of the co-existence of the safe-guards provided by international humanitarian law and by the Convention in time of armed conflict, the grounds of permitted deprivation of liberty set out in subparagraphs (a) to (f) of that provision should be accommodated, as far as possible, with the taking of prisoners of war ... who pose a risk to security under the Third ... Geneva Convention ... It can only be in cases of international armed conflict, where the taking of prisoners of war ... [is an accepted feature of] international humanitarian law, that Article 5 could be interpreted as permitting the exercise of such broad powers.

105. ... deprivation of liberty pursuant to powers under international humanitarian law must be "lawful" to preclude a violation of Article 5 § 1. This means that the detention must comply with the rules of international humanitarian law and, most importantly, that it should be in keeping with the fundamental purpose of Article 5 § 1, which is to protect the individual from arbitrariness.

106. As regards procedural safeguards, the Court considers that, in relation to detention taking place during an international armed conflict, Article 5 §§ 2 and 4 must also be interpreted in a manner which takes into account the context and the applicable rules of international humanitarian law.

6.1.5 Determination of POW Status

6.1.5.1 Privy Council (Malaysia), *Public Prosecutor* v. *Koi [and Associated Appeals]* [1968] AC 829

Note: *Twelve Chinese Malays, under Indonesian command and armed with military weapons, were parachuted into Malaysia at a time when Indonesia and Malaysia were in armed conflict. All twelve were subsequently captured by Malaysian forces and charged pursuant to the Internal Security Act 1960. All were convicted and sentenced to death. On the issue whether the twelve prisoners were entitled to POW status, the Privy Council said:*

In these associated appeals the main question is whether the accused were entitled to be treated as protected prisoners of war by virtue of the Geneva Conventions Act, 1962, to which the Geneva Conventions of 1949 are scheduled. ...

All the accused were convicted of offences under the Internal Security Act, 1960 of the Federation of Malaya and sentenced to death. ...

All the accused appealed against their convictions ... and their appeals were dismissed by the Federal Court of Malaysia save in two cases namely that of Oie Hee Koi (Appeal No 16 of 1967) and that of Ooi Wan Yui (Appeal No 17 of 1967) in both of which the appeals were allowed on the ground that the accused were prisoners of war within the meaning of the Geneva Conventions Act, 1962, of the Federation of Malaya (herein referred to as "the Act of 1962") and as such were entitled to protection under the Geneva Convention relative to the treatment of prisoners of war (Sch 3 to the Act of 1962). . . .

Article 5 of the Convention [GCIII] is directed to a person of the kind described in art 4 about whom "a doubt arises" whether he belongs to any of the categories enumerated in art 4 [GCIII]. By virtue of art 5 such a person is given the protection of the Convention for the time being, ie, until such time as his "status has been determined by a competent tribunal". The question then arises whether the description "protected prisoner of war" in s 2 of the Act of 1962 includes persons entitled to provisional protection under art 5 of the Convention, as well as persons falling within art 4 of the Convention.

Their lordships are of opinion that this is the case. Thus a person to whom art 5 applies is a protected prisoner of war within s 2 of the Act of 1962 so long as that protection lasts. If the determination is positive, then he is protected because he falls within one of the categories in art 4, and the provision for notice in s 4 of the Act of 1962 must be complied with. If the determination is negative, the protection of the Convention ceases so far as the individual is concerned, and his trial can proceed free from any further restriction arising under s 4 of the Act of 1962.

. . .

In the two cases in which the public prosecutor is appellant, that is to say that of Oie Hee Koi and that of Ooi Wan Yui, already mentioned, the Federal Court, on the point being taken on appeal from the trial judge, held that the accused were entitled to protection. By decisions of the Federal Court in the other cases where the convictions were upheld, the contention that the accused were entitled to the protection of the Convention was rejected. In these cases with the single exception referred to above no point had been raised at the trial, and therefore no "doubt arose" so as to bring s 4 into operation.

Their lordships are of opinion that on the hearing of their appeals by the Federal Court no burden lay on the prosecution to prove that those of the accused who had raised no doubt at their trials as to the correctness of the procedure followed were not entitled to be treated as protected prisoners of war. Although the burden of proof of guilt is always on the prosecution, this does not mean that a further burden is laid on it to prove that an accused person has no right to apply for postponement of his trial until certain procedural steps have been taken. Until "a doubt arises" art 5 does not operate, and the court is not required to be satisfied whether or not this safeguard should be applied. Accordingly where the accused did not raise a doubt no question of mistrial arises.

The only authority to which their lordships' attention was drawn which supports the view that the Geneva Convention, or rather its predecessor which used similar language, applied so to speak automatically without the question of protection or no protection being raised is the case of *R v Guiseppe*. Twelve Italian prisoners of war were tried by a magistrate and convicted on a charge of theft, no notice having been given to the representative of the protecting power as required by the Convention. It was held on an application for review at the special request of the Crown that the conviction and sentences should be set aside. Thus it appears that the Crown asked for review in a case where the prisoners of war were nationals of the opposing forces and plainly entitled to the protection of the Convention. Their lordships do not regard this decision as good authority for the proposition that there was a mistrial in the cases under review.

... Except in the one case where the accused claimed the protection of the Convention at the trial there was no mistrial in proceedings without the notices required by s 4 having been given. There was nothing to show that the accused were protected prisoners of war or to raise a doubt whether they were or were not. The mere fact that they landed as part of the Indonesian armed force did not raise a doubt and no claim was made to provide any basis for the court, before whom the accused were brought for trial, to apply s 4 of the Act except in the one case.

... The claim, having been made to the court before whom the accused was brought up for trial in the circumstances already stated, was in their lordships' opinion sufficient to raise a doubt whether he was a prisoner of war protected by the Convention. The court should have treated him as a prisoner of war for the time being and either proceeded with the determination whether he was or was not protected, or refrained from continuing the trial in the absence of notices. In this case only their lordships consider that there was a mistrial and that justice requires that the appeal be allowed and the convictions quashed and the case remitted for retrial.

6.1.5.2 UK, British Ministry of Defence, *The Joint Service Manual of the Law of Armed Conflict*, (Joint Service Publication 383, 2004 Edition)

Presumption of prisoner of war status

8.20 There is a presumption in favour of entitlement to prisoner of war status if: a. the person concerned claims, or appears to be entitled to, that status; or b. the party to the conflict to which he belongs claims that status on his behalf by notification to either the detaining power or the protecting power.

8.20.1 In view of the difficulties ... of distinguishing combatants from non-combatants, it may not be easy to decide whether to give prisoner of war status to a person who has taken part in hostilities and has subsequently been captured, so the law makes this presumption in favour of prisoner of war status.

Cases of doubt

8.21 In cases of doubt as to entitlement, the person concerned continues to have the protection of the Convention and Protocol until his status has been determined by a competent tribunal. ...

Claiming prisoner of war status

8.22. Where a person in the power of an adverse party is not held as a prisoner of war and is to be tried by that party for an offence arising out of the hostilities, he has the right to claim prisoner of war status and to have that question adjudicated by a judicial tribunal. Whenever procedurally possible, this adjudication should occur before the trial for the offence. Representatives of the protecting power are entitled to attend the adjudication proceedings unless, exceptionally, in the interests of state security, they are to be held *in camera* in which event the protecting power is to be advised accordingly by the detaining power.

6.1.5.3 US, *In re Guantanamo Detainee Cases*, 355 F.Supp.2d 443, 480 (D.D.C. 2005)

Note: *The case concerned eleven coordinated habeas corpus petitions from detainees at Guantanamo Bay. The petitions asserted the detainees' classification as 'enemy combatants' subject to indefinite detention violated their right to due process of law under Article 5 of the US Constitution. The District Court of Columbia found as follows:*

Nothing in the Convention itself or in Army Regulation 190-8 authorizes the President of the United States to rule by fiat that an entire group of fighters covered by the Third Geneva Convention falls outside of the Article 4 definitions of "prisoners of war." To the contrary, ..., the President's broad characterization of how the Taliban generally fought the war in Afghanistan cannot substitute for an Article 5 tribunal's determination on an individualized basis of whether a particular fighter complied with the laws of war or otherwise falls within an exception denying him prisoner of war status. ... But although numerous petitioners in the above-captioned cases were found ... to have been Taliban fighters, nowhere do the ... records for any of those petitioners reveal specific findings that they committed some particular act or failed to satisfy some defined prerequisite entitling the respondents to deprive them of prisoner of war status. Accordingly, the Court denies that portion of the respondents' motion to dismiss addressing the Geneva Convention claims of those petitioners who were found to be Taliban fighters but who were not specifically determined to be excluded from prisoner of war status by a competent Article 5 tribunal.

6.2 RESPONSIBILITY FOR POW

6.2.1 Basic Rules

6.2.1.1 Germany, Federal Ministry of Defence, *Law of Armed Conflict – Manual – Joint Service Regulation (ZDv) 15/2* (May 2013)

802. The Detaining Power is responsible for the treatment of prisoners of war (3 12 para.1). Prisoners of war may in no circumstances renounce in part or in entirety the rights secured to them by the Third Geneva Convention (3 7).

6.2.2 Transfer of POW

6.2.2.1 ICTY, *Prosecutor* v. *Mrkšić and Šljvančanin*, (Judgment), Case No IT-95-13/1-A, Appeals Chamber (5 May 2009)

Note: *The accused were a colonel and major, respectively, in the Yugoslav National Army (JNA) indicted for the mistreatment and execution of Croat and other non-Serb persons taken from Vukovar hospital on 20 and 21 November 1991. As to the protection afforded to POW, the ICTY affirmed as follows:*

71. The fundamental principle enshrined in Geneva Convention III, which is non-derogable, that prisoners of war must be treated humanely and protected from physical and mental

harm, applies from the time they fall into the power of the enemy until their final release and repatriation. It thus entails the obligation of each agent in charge of the protection or custody of the prisoners of war to ensure that their transfer to another agent will not diminish the protection the prisoners are entitled to. ...

74. The Appeals Chamber therefore considers that Šljivančanin was under a duty to protect the prisoners of war held at Ovčara and that his responsibility included the obligation not to allow the transfer of custody of the prisoners of a war to anyone without first assuring himself that they would not be harmed. Mrkšić's order to withdraw the JNA troops did not relieve him of his position as an officer of the JNA. As such, Šljivančanin remained an agent of the Detaining Power and thus continued to be bound by Geneva Convention III not to transfer the prisoners of war to another agent who would not guarantee their safety.

6.2.2.2 **Germany**, Federal Ministry of Defence, *Law of Armed Conflict – Manual – Joint Service Regulation (ZDv) 15/2* (May 2013)

803. A Detaining Power may only transfer prisoners of war to another power if

– the other power is a Party to the Third Geneva Convention and
– the Detaining Power has satisfied itself of the willingness and ability of such transferee power to apply the Convention.

6.3 TREATMENT OF POW

6.3.1 Entitlement to Humane Treatment

6.3.1.1 **US Military Commission**, *Trial of Lieutenant General Kurt Maelzer*, Case No. 63 (Florence, Italy, 9th–14th September 1946) Law Reports of Trials of War Criminals, Vol. XI (1949), p. 53

Note: *The case concerned the parade of hundreds of British and American POW through the streets of Rome. As to the treatment of POW, the Commission said as follows:*

OUTLINE OF THE PROCEEDINGS

(1) THE CHARGE The accused was charged with "... exposing prisoners of war ... in his custody ... to acts of violence, insults and public curiosity."

(2) THE EVIDENCE Sometime in January 1944, Field Marshal Kesselring, commander-in-chief of the German forces in Italy, ordered the accused who was commander of Rome garrison to hold a parade of several hundreds of British and American prisoners of war in the streets of the Italian capital. ... The accused ordered the parade which took place on 2nd February, 1944. 200 American prisoners of war were marched from the Coliseum, through the main streets of Rome under armed German escort. The streets were lined by forces under the control of the accused. The accused and his staff officers attended the parade. According to the Prosecution witnesses ..., the population threw stones and sticks at the prisoners, but, according to the defence witnesses, they threw cigarettes and flowers. The prosecution also alleged that when some of the prisoners were giving the "victory sign" with their

fingers the accused ordered the guards to fire. This order, however, was not carried out. A film was made of the parade and a great number of photographs taken which appeared in the Italian press under the caption "Anglo Americans enter Rome after all ... flanked by German bayonettes." The accused pleaded in the main that the march was planned and ordered by his superiors and that his only function as commander of Rome garrison was to guarantee the safe conduct and security of the prisoners during the march, which he did. He stated that the march was to quell rumours of the German defeat and to quieten the population of Rome, not to scorn or ridicule the prisoners.

(3) FINDINGS AND SENTENCE The accused was found guilty and sentenced to 10 years' imprisonment. The sentence was reduced to three years' imprisonment by higher military authority.

6.3.1.2 US, US Department of Defense, *Final Report to Congress: Conduct of the Persian Gulf War – The Role of the Law of War* (1992) 31 ILM 615, 629–30

Photographs and videotapes of the first Iraqi EPWs [Enemy Prisoners of War] captured were taken and shown by the public media. The capture or detention of EPWs is recognized as newsworthy events and, as such, photography of such events is not prohibited by the GPW. However, Article 13, GPW does prohibit photography that might humiliate or degrade any EPW. Media use of photographs of EPWs raised some apprehension in light of formal US condemnation of the forced videotapes of US and Coalition POWs being made and shown by Iraq. CENTCOM and other DOD officials also expressed concern for the safety of the family of any Iraqi defector who might be identified from media photographs by Iraqi officials. Because of these sensitivities, and consistent with Article 13, GPW, DOD developed guidelines for photographing EPWs. These guidelines limited both the opportunities for photography and the display of EPW photographs taken, while protecting Iraqi EPWs and their families from retribution by the Government of Iraq. . . .

US and Coalition personnel captured by Iraq were POWs protected by the GWS (if wounded, injured, or sick) and GPW. All US POWs captured during the Persian Gulf War were moved to Baghdad by land after their capture. . . . Although some were physically abused during their transit to Baghdad, most were treated reasonably well.

On arrival in Baghdad, most Air Force, Navy, and Marine POWs were taken immediately to what the POWs referred to as "The Bunker" (most probably at the Directorate of Military Intelligence) for initial interrogation. They then were taken to what appeared to be the main long-term incarceration site, located in the Iraqi Intelligence Service Regional Headquarters (dubbed "The Biltmore" by the POWs). Since this building was a legitimate military target, the detention of POWs in it was a violation of Article 23, GPW; POWs thus were unnecessarily placed at risk when the facility was bombed on 23 February.

In contravention of Article 26, GPW, all US POWs incarcerated at the "Biltmore" experienced food deprivation. US POWs also were provided inadequate protection from the cold, in violation of Article 25, GPW.

After the 23 February bombing of the "Biltmore" by Coalition aircraft, the POWs were relocated to either Abu Abu [sic] Ghurayb Prison (dubbed "Joliet Prison") or Al-Rashid

Military Prison ("The Half-Way House"), both near Baghdad. . . . The detention of prisoners of war in a prison generally is prohibited by Article 22, GPW.

All US POWs suffered physical abuse at the hands of their Iraqi captors, in violation of Articles 13, 14, and 17, GPW. Most POWs were tortured, a grave breach, in violation of Article 130, GPW. Some POWs were forced to make public propaganda statements, in violation of Article 13. In addition, none was permitted the rights otherwise afforded them by the GPW, such as the right of correspondence authorized by Article 70. Although the ICRC had access to Iraqi EPWs captured by the Coalition, ICRC members did not see Coalition POWs until the day of their repatriation.

6.3.1.3 UN, Secretary-General's Bulletin, *Observance by United Nations Forces of International Humanitarian Law* (6 August 1999) UN Doc. ST/SGB/1999/13

Section 8

Treatment of detained persons

The United Nations force shall treat with humanity and respect for their dignity detained members of the armed forces and other persons who no longer take part in military operations by reason of detention. Without prejudice to their legal status, they shall be treated in accordance with the relevant provisions of the Third Geneva Convention of 1949, as may be applicable to them mutatis mutandis.

6.3.1.4 Eritrea–Ethiopia Claims Commission, *Partial Award: Prisoners of War – Ethiopia's Claim 4* (2003) 26 (3) RIAA 73

Note: *The claim was brought by the Federal Democratic Republic of Ethiopia seeking a finding of liability on the part of the State of Eritrea for loss and damage suffered by Ethiopia as a result of Eritrea's unlawful treatment of POW during the Eritrea–Ethiopian War. The Commission found:*

12. Based on the extensive evidence adduced during these proceedings, the Commission believes that both Parties had a commitment to the most fundamental principles bearing on prisoners of war. Both parties conducted organized, official training programs to instruct their troops on procedures to be followed when POWs are taken. In contrast to many other contemporary armed conflicts, both Eritrea and Ethiopia regularly and consistently took POWs. Enemy personnel who were *hors de combat* were moved away from the battlefield to conditions of greater safety. Further, although these cases involve two of the poorest countries in the world, both made significant efforts to provide for the sustenance and care of the POWs in their custody.

13. There were deficiencies of performance on both sides, sometimes significant occasionally grave. Nevertheless, the evidence in these cases shows that both Eritrea and Ethiopia endeavored to observe their fundamental humanitarian obligations to collect and protect enemy soldiers unable to resist on the battlefield.

6.3.1.5 Eritrea–Ethiopia Claims Commission, *Partial Award: Prisoners of War – Eritrea's Claim 17* (2003) 26 (2) RIAA 23

Note: *The facts of this matter are as set out in Section 6.3.1.4. In the parallel award in relation to Eritrea's claim, the Commission said:*

58. A State's obligation to ensure humane treatment of enemy soldiers can be severely tested in the heated and confused moments immediately following capture or surrender and during evacuation from the battlefront to the rear. Nevertheless, customary international law as reflected in Geneva Conventions I and III absolutely prohibits the killing of POWs, requires the wounded and sick to be collected and cared for, and demands prompt and humane evacuation.

59. The forty-eight Eritrean POW declarations recount a few disquieting instances of Ethiopian soldiers deliberately killing POWs following capture. Three declarants gave eyewitness accounts alleging that wounded comrades were shot and abandoned to speed up evacuation.

60. The Commission received no evidence that Ethiopian authorities conducted inquiries into any such battlefield events or pursued discipline as required under Article 121 of Geneva Convention III. However, several Eritrean POW declarants described occasions when Ethiopian soldiers threatened to kill Eritrean POWs at the front or during evacuation, but either restrained themselves or were stopped by their comrades. Ethiopia presented substantial evidence regarding the international humanitarian law training given to its troops. The accounts of capture and its immediate aftermath presented to the Commission in this Claim suggest that this training generally was effective in preventing unlawful killing, even "in the heat of the moment" after capture and surrender. . . .

62. In contrast, Eritrea did present clear and convincing evidence, in the form of cumulative and reinforcing accounts in the Eritrean POW declarations, of frequent physical abuse of Eritrean POWs by their captors both at the front and during evacuation. A significant number of the declarants reported that Ethiopian troops threatened and beat Eritrean prisoners, sometimes brutally and sometimes inflicting blows directly to wounds. In some cases, Ethiopian soldiers deliberately subjected Eritrean POWs to verbal and physical abuse, including beating and stoning from civilian crowds in the course of transit.

63. This evidence of frequent beatings and other unlawful physical abuse of Eritrean POWs at capture or shortly after capture is clear, convincing and essentially unrebutted. Although the Commission has no evidence that Ethiopia encouraged its soldiers to abuse POWs at capture, the conclusion is unavoidable that, at a minimum, Ethiopia failed to take effective measures, as required by international law, to prevent such abuse. . . .

64. The Commission turns next to Eritrea's allegations that Ethiopia failed to provide necessary medical attention to Eritrean POWs after capture and during evacuation, as required under customary international law as reflected in Geneva Conventions I (Article 12) and III (Articles 20 and 15).

65. The Commission believes that the requirement to provide POWs with medical care during the initial period after capture must be assessed in light of the harsh conditions on the battlefield and the limited extent of medical training and equipment available to front line troops. On balance, and recognizing the logistical and resource limitations on the medical care Ethiopia could provide at the front, the evidence indicates that, on the whole, Ethiopian forces gave wounded Eritrean soldiers basic first aid treatment upon capture. . . .

66. Eritrea also alleges that, in addition to poor medical care, Ethiopia failed to ensure humane evacuation conditions. As reflected in Articles 19 and 20 of Geneva Convention III, the Detaining Power is obliged to evacuate prisoners humanely, safely and as soon as possible from combat zones; only if there is a greater risk in evacuation may the wounded or sick be temporarily kept in the combat zone, and they must not be unnecessarily exposed to danger. The measure of a humane evacuation is that, as set out in Article 20, POWs should be evacuated "in conditions similar to those for the forces of the Detaining Power." ...

68. On balance, and with one exception, the Commission finds that Ethiopian troops satisfied the legal requirements for evacuations from the battlefield under the harsh geographic, military and logistical circumstances. The exception is the frequent, but not invariable, Ethiopian practice of seizing footwear, testified to by several declarants. Although the harshness of the terrain and weather on the marches to the camps may have been out of Ethiopia's control, to force the POWs to walk barefoot in such conditions unnecessarily compounded their misery. ... The Commission finds Ethiopia liable for inhumane treatment during evacuations from the battlefield as a result of its forcing Eritrean POWs to go without footwear during evacuation marches.

6.3.1.6 Eritrea–Ethiopia Claims Commission, *Partial Award: Prisoners of War – Ethiopia's Claim 4* (2003) 26 (3) RIAA 73
Note: *The facts of this case are set out in Section 6.3.1.4. As to the treatment of POW, the Commission found*:

82. The testimony at the hearing of a former POW and the declarations of the other POWs are consistent and persuasive that the Eritrean guards at the various POW camps relied often upon brutal force for the enforcement of rules and as means of punishment. ... Beatings with wooden sticks were common and, on occasion, resulted in broken bones and lack of consciousness. There were multiple, consistent accounts that, at Digdigta, several POWs who had attempted to escape were beaten senseless, with one losing an eye, prior to their disappearance. Being forced to hold heavy objects over one's head for long periods of time, being punched or kicked, being required to roll on stony or thorny ground, to look at the sun, and to undergo periods of confinement in hot metal containers were notable among the other abuses, all of which violated customary international law, as exemplified by Articles 13, 42, 87 and 89 of Geneva Convention III. Regrettably, the evidence also indicates that the camp commanders did little to restrain these abuses and, in some cases, even threatened POWs by telling them that, as there was (prior to the first ICRC visits in August 2000) no list of prisoners, they could do anything they wanted to the POWs and could not be held accountable.

6.3.1.7 Human Rights Watch, *Up in Flames: Humanitarian Law Violations and Civilian Victims in the Conflict over South Ossetia* (2009)
4.5 Execution, Torture, and Other Degrading Treatment of Georgian Prisoners of War by Ossetian Forces, at times with Russian Forces

Georgian soldiers reported that they had been subjected to severe torture and ill-treatment throughout their detention by Ossetian forces. Human Rights Watch documented the execution of three Georgian servicemen while in the custody of Ossetian forces. ...

Russian forces had or ought to have had full knowledge that Ossetians detained Georgian servicemen. They apparently participated in the execution of two Georgian soldiers, as well as in interrogations of Georgian POWs in Ossetian custody. Furthermore, the Georgian soldiers were held in Tskhinvali, over which Russia exercised effective control from August 9, and therefore are to be regarded as having fallen into Russia's power. Russia was therefore obligated to afford them POW status and to treat them in conformity with the protections of the Third Geneva Convention, which include absolute prohibitions on ill-treatment and require POWs to be treated humanely and kept in good health. The execution, torture, and ill-treatment of prisoners of war are grave breaches of the Third Geneva Convention and constitute war crimes. The ICCPR and ECHR also provide an absolute prohibition on torture and other degrading or inhuman treatment and an obligation to protect the right to life of those in detention.

6.3.1.8 US, Department of Defense, *Law of War Manual*, Office of General Counsel (June 2015, Updated 2016)

9.5 HUMANE TREATMENT AND BASIC PROTECTIONS FOR POWS

POWs must at all times be humanely treated. POWs are entitled in all circumstances to respect for their persons and their honor. Likewise, POWs must at all times be protected, particularly against acts of violence or intimidation and against insults and public curiosity.

Any unlawful act or omission by the Detaining Power causing death or seriously endangering the health of a POW in its custody is prohibited, and will be regarded as a serious breach of the GPW.

9.5.1 Respect for Their Persons and Honor. POWs are entitled in all circumstances to respect for their persons and their honor. For example, the rape or other indecent assault of POWs is forbidden.

9.5.2 Protection Against Acts of Violence or Intimidation. POWs must at all times be protected, particularly against acts of violence or intimidation. For example, the murder of POWs is forbidden.

6.3.2 Treatment of Vulnerable Groups

6.3.2.1 Protection of Women

6.3.2.1.1 Canada, *Law of Armed Conflict at the Operational and Tactical Levels*, Office of the Judge Advocate General (2001)

1017. Treatment Of Female PW

1. Female PWs must be treated with due regard to their gender and must in no case be treated less favourably than male PWs. Their gender must also be taken into account in the allocation of labour and in the provision of sleeping and sanitary facilities. They must also be specially protected against rape and other sexual assaults.

6.3.2.2 Protection of Children

6.3.2.2.1 **US**, Department of Defense, *Law of War Manual*, Office of General Counsel (June 2015, Updated 2016)

4.20.5.3 Treatment of Child Soldiers.

In general, children receive the rights, duties, and liabilities of combatant status on the same basis as other persons. For example, there is no age requirement for someone to receive POW status. ... Children who have participated in hostilities or been associated with an armed force who are detained might require additional consideration because of their age. For example, rules for the additional provision for their education might be applicable.

6.3.3 Interrogation

6.3.3.1 **Eritrea–Ethiopia Claims Commission**, *Partial Award: Prisoners of War – Ethiopia's Claim 4* (2003) 26 (3) RIAA 73

Note: *The facts of this matter are set out in Section 6.3.1.4. On the limits on the methods and means of interrogation of POW, the Commission found*:

75. ... International law does not prohibit the interrogation of POWs, but it does restrict the information they are obliged to reveal and prohibits torture or other measures of coercion, including threats and "unpleasant or disadvantageous treatment of any kind."

76. Ethiopia presented clear and convincing evidence, unrebutted by Eritrea, that Eritrean interrogators frequently threatened or beat POWs during interrogation, particularly when they were dissatisfied with the prisoner's answers. The Commission must conclude that Eritrea either failed to train its interrogators in the relevant legal restraints or to make it clear that they are imperative. Consequently, Eritrea is liable for permitting such coercive interrogation.

6.3.3.2 **UK**, British Ministry of Defence, *The Joint Service Manual of the Law of Armed Conflict*, (Joint Service Publication 383, 2004 Edition)

8.34 The capturing power may ask ... questions to obtain tactical or strategic information but the prisoner of war cannot be forced to disclose any such information. Questioning should be done in a language that the prisoner of war understands. No physical or mental torture or any other form of coercion may be used to obtain information. Nor may those who refuse to answer be threatened, insulted, or exposed to any unpleasant or disadvantageous treatment of any kind.

8.34.1 Wounded and sick prisoners of war may be interrogated, but not if it would seriously endanger their health, so medical advice should be taken in case of doubt.

8.34.2 Blindfolding and segregation may be necessary in the interests of security, the physical restraint of prisoners of war, or to prevent collaboration prior to interrogation, but these discomforts must be truly justified and be for as short a period as possible.

6.4 INTERNMENT IN POW CAMPS

6.4.1 General

6.4.1.1 **Canada**, *Law of Armed Conflict at the Operational and Tactical Levels*, Office of the Judge Advocate General (2001)

1024. PW CAMPS

1. PWs may only be interned on land. Centres of internment must be established in healthy areas, with PWs having facilities guaranteeing hygiene and healthfulness. They must not be detained in penitentiaries.

2. While officers should be housed separately, PWs should be gathered in camps according to nationality, language and customs, but should not without their consent be separated from others belonging to the forces with which they were serving at the time of capture.

3. A captor may restrict the movement of PWs to a fenced area. If they are not so confined, the captor may order them to remain within a defined area. The PWs may not, however, be held in close confinement, other than by way of penal or disciplinary measures in accordance with GIII, or because such confinement is necessary for their health or safety.

6.4.1.2 **Eritrea–Ethiopia Claims Commission**, *Partial Award: Prisoners of War – Eritrea's Claim 17* (2003) 26 (2) RIAA 23

Note: *The facts of this case are set out in Section 6.3.1.4. As to the treatment of POW while interned, the Commission said:*

87. A fundamental principle of Geneva Convention III is that detention of POWs must not seriously endanger the health of those POWs. This principle, which is also a principle of customary international law, is implemented by rules that mandate camp locations where the climate is not injurious; shelter that is adequate, with conditions as favorable as those for the forces of the Detaining Power who are billeted in the area, including protection from dampness and adequate heat and light, bedding and blankets; and sanitary facilities which are hygienic and are properly maintained. Food must be provided in a quantity and quality adequate to keep POWs in good health, and safe drinking water must be adequate. Soap and water must also be sufficient for the personal toilet and laundry of the POWs.

88. Geneva Convention III declares the principle that any "unlawful act or omission by the Detaining Power ... seriously endangering the health of a prisoner ... will be regarded as a serious breach of the present Convention." The Commission believes this principle should guide its determination of the liability of the Parties for alleged violations of any of the obligations noted above. ...

89. ... Neither Party has sought to avoid liability by arguing that its limited resources and the difficult environmental and logistical conditions confronting those charged with establishing and administering POW camps could justify any condition within them that did in fact endanger the health of prisoners. Rather, in defense against claims of serious violations, each Party has relied primarily on the declarations of officers charged with the administration of each of its camps. All of these officers have indicated their full awareness

of the basic standards of Geneva Convention III for camp conditions, have described the steps taken to meet them, and have denied that any conditions existed that seriously endangered the health of the POWs.

Standard of Medical Care

115. A Detaining Power has the obligation to provide in its POW camps the medical assistance on which the POWs depend to heal their battle wounds and to prevent further damage to their health. This duty is particularly crucial in camps with a large population and a greater risk of transmission of contagious diseases.

116. The protections provided by Articles 15, 20, 29, 30, 31, 109 and 110 of Geneva Convention III are unconditional. These rules, which are based on similar rules in Articles 4, 13, 14, 15 and 68 of the Geneva Convention Relative to the Treatment of Prisoners of War of July 27, 1929, are part of customary international law.

117. Many of these rules are broadly phrased and do not characterize precisely the quality or extent of medical care necessary for POWs. . . . The lack of definition regarding the quality or extent of care "required" led to difficulties in assessing this claim. Indeed, standards of medical practice vary around the world, and there may be room for varying assessments of what is required in a specific situation. Moreover, the Commission is mindful that it is dealing here with two countries with very limited resources.

118. Nevertheless, the Commission believes certain principles can be applied in assessing the medical care provided to POWs. The Commission began by considering Article 15's concept of the maintenance of POWs, which it understands to mean that a Detaining Power must do those things required to prevent significant deterioration of a prisoner's health. Next, the Commission paid particular attention to measures that are specifically required by Geneva Convention III such as the requirements for segregation of prisoners with infectious diseases and for regular physical examinations.

6.4.1.3 UK, British Ministry of Defence, *The Joint Service Manual of the Law of Armed Conflict*, (Joint Service Publication 383, 2004 Edition)

8.44 Every prisoner of war camp must be under the immediate authority of a responsible commissioned officer of the regular forces of the detaining power. This prohibits camps from being commanded by members of paramilitary or even non-military organizations. The camp commander must keep a copy of the Convention in his possession and ensure that the camp staff and guards know its provisions. He is responsible, under the direction of his government, for the application of the Convention and has disciplinary powers over prisoners of war.

6.4.2 Segregation of POW

6.4.2.1 Eritrea–Ethiopia Claims Commission, *Partial Award: Prisoners of War – Eritrea's Claim 17* (2003) 26 (2) RIAA 23

Note: *The details of this case are outlined in Section 6.3.1.4. As to the use of segregation during the detention of POW, the Commission said as follows:*

84. … Ethiopia admits that its camps were organized in a manner that resulted in the segregation of various groups of POWs from each other. … Such segregation is contrary to Article 22 of Geneva Convention III, which states that "prisoners shall not be separated from prisoners of war belonging to the armed forces with which they were serving at the time of their capture, except with their consent." Ethiopia argues that this segregation was done to reduce hostility between the groups, but the Commission finds that argument unpersuasive. It seems far more likely that these actions were taken to promote defections of POWs and to break down any sense of internal discipline and cohesion among the POWs.

85. In that connection, the Commission notes that Ethiopia conducted extensive indoctrination programs … and encouraged the discussion among groups of POWs of questions raised in these programs. … While Ethiopia asserts that attendance at these indoctrination and discussion sessions was not compulsory there is considerable evidence that, except for sick or wounded POWs, attendance was effectively made compulsory by Ethiopia, contrary to Article 38 of Geneva Convention III. Moreover, there is substantial evidence that POWs were sometimes put under considerable pressure to engage in self-criticism during the discussion sessions. While there are some allegations that those POWs who made statements that appealed to the Ethiopian authorities were subsequently accorded more favorable treatment than those who refused to make such statements, the Commission does not find sufficient evidence to prove such a violation of the fundamental requirement of Article 16 of Geneva Convention III that all POWs must be treated alike, "without any adverse distinction based on race, nationality, religious belief or political opinions, or any other distinction founded on similar criteria." Nevertheless, the Commission notes with concern the evidence of mental and emotional distress felt by many Eritrean POWs and concludes that such distress was caused in substantial part by these actions by Ethiopia in violation of Articles 22 and 38 of the Convention.

6.4.3 Labour of POW

6.4.3.1 **ICTY**, *Prosecutor* v. *M. Naletilić and V. Martinović*, (Judgment), Case No IT-98-34-T, Trial Chamber (31 March 2003)

Note: *The facts of this case are set out in Chapter 1, Section 1.7.1. On the use of POW for labour, the Trial Chamber said:*

252. … As a preliminary remark, it is apparent that not all labour is prohibited during times of armed conflict, but that specific provisions must be respected. Furthermore, forced labour does not always amount to unlawful labour. Article 49 of Geneva Convention III establishes a principle of compulsory labour for prisoners of war. The basic principle stated in Paragraph 1 of this provision "is the right of the Detaining Power to require prisoners of war to work". Nevertheless, this principle is subject to two fundamental conditions, the first one relating to the prisoner himself, and the second one to the nature of the work required. …

254. Thus, prisoners of war may be required to work provided that this is done in their own interest, and those considerations relating to their age and sex, physical aptitude and rank are taken into account. In this respect, it is also noteworthy that according to Article 51 of

Geneva Convention III, prisoners of war must work under "suitable working conditions, especially as regards to accommodation, food" and "climatic conditions."

255. Articles 50 and 52 of Geneva Convention III define which type of labour might be required and which might not. . . .

256. . . . First, Article 50 of Geneva Convention III grants a general authorisation for any work "connected with camp administration, installation or maintenance", bearing in mind that this type of work "is done by prisoners of war in their own interest". Secondly, prisoners of war may always be compelled to perform work in relation to agriculture, commercial business, arts and crafts, and domestic services, regardless of whether the "produce of their labour is intended for soldiers in the frontline or for the civilian population of the country". Thirdly, prisoners of war may be compelled to perform work in industries other than metallurgical, machinery and chemical industries, public works and building operations, transport and handling of stores and public utility services, provided that those forms of labour have no military character or purpose. While the condition that the work has no military character or purpose is of delicate interpretation, the Commentary provides some guidance. It states that:

> "Everything which is commanded and regulated by the military authority is of military character, in contrast to what is commanded and regulated by the civil authorities."

The Commentary further suggests a flexible interpretation of the concept of "military purpose":

> "Prisoners of war may therefore be employed on all work which in the categories under consideration normally serves to maintain civilian life, even if the military authorities incidentally benefit by it. The participation of prisoners of war in such work is prohibited, however, whenever it is done for the sole or principal benefit of the military, to the exclusion of civilians."

257. However, other classes of labour may not be imposed on prisoners of war. As just discussed, they first include work in industries, public works and building operations, transport and handling of stores and public utility services where it has a military character or purpose. Secondly, Article 50 of Geneva Convention III expressly prohibits the forced employment of prisoners of war in the metallurgical, machinery and chemical industries. The Commentary emphasises the importance of this prohibition, "for in the event of a general war, these industries will always be turned over to armaments production". Thirdly, Article 52 of Geneva Convention III prohibits the use of prisoners of war to perform unhealthy or dangerous work unless the prisoners volunteer to undertake such work. While this provision expressly only refers to mine-lifting as constituting dangerous labour, the Commentary provides further guidance by distinguishing three situations: (1) work which is not dangerous in itself but which may be dangerous by reason of the general conditions in which it is carried out: this situation is intended to cover particularly work done "in the vicinity either of key military objectives (ports, barracks, airfields, munition dumps, factories), or of the battlefield", (2) work which by its very nature is dangerous or unhealthy, and (3) work which is not in itself dangerous but which may be or may become so if it is done in inadequate technical conditions. An essential aspect of this protection afforded to prisoners of war is the responsibility that rests on the detaining authorities to ensure that the work is

performed with maximum safety. Finally, Article 52 of Geneva Convention III prohibits the assignment of prisoners of war to labour, which would be deemed humiliating for a member of the detaining forces.

258. The Chamber notes that those forms of labour may only be lawful where the prisoner of war volunteers or consents to the work. While the possibility for prisoners to consent is expressly formulated in Article 52 of Geneva Convention III, there is no clear provision on the possibility for prisoners of war to consent to perform military related work under Article 50. In this context, the Chamber interprets this Article and the related Commentary so as to aim at regulating only the forced utilisation of prisoners' labour. Article 50 of Geneva Convention III provides that prisoners of war may be compelled to perform certain forms of work. Accordingly, the prohibited act is that of compelling a prisoner of war against his or her will. . . . Such interpretation is also in accordance with Article 52 of Geneva Convention III, which allows prisoners to consent to perform dangerous or unhealthy labour.

6.5 PUNISHMENT OF POW

6.5.1 Geneva Convention III Relative to the Treatment of Prisoners of War (Adopted 12 August 1949, Entered into Force 21 October 1950)

On signing the Convention relative to the Treatment of Prisoners of War, the Government of the Union of Soviet Socialist Republics makes the following reservations . . .

Article 85: "The Union of Soviet Socialist Republics does not consider itself bound by the obligation, which follows from Article 85, to extend the application of the Convention to prisoners of war who have been convicted under the law of the Detaining Power, in accordance with the principles of the Nuremberg trial, for war crimes and crimes against humanity, it being understood that persons convicted of such crimes must be subject to the conditions obtaining in the country in question for those who undergo their punishment."

6.5.2 South Africa, *The State* v. *Sagarius and Others* [Original Source South West Africa Law Reports 1983 Vol. I pp. 833–8][2]

Note: *The accused were part of a group of twenty-two members of SWAPO (South West African People's Organisation), which infiltrated South West African territory in possession of firearms and explosives. The accused were taken prisoner while retreating towards the northern frontier of South West Africa. On the issue of punishment of POW, the Court said:*

. . . I have already expressed the view that in my judgment a South African Court has no option but to exercise criminal jurisdiction over SWAPO; that a Court cannot simply direct that members of SWAPO be treated as prisoners of war. Nevertheless, it is my view, having regard to new developments in international humanitarian law as reflected in Protocol 1 of the 1977 Geneva Convention and having regard to the special status of a Namibian, that

---

[2]   https://casebook.icrc.org/topics/punishmentprosecution-pows.

such factors should be taken into account when it comes to the imposition of a sentence and, in particular, it is my view that a Court might have regard to these developments when it comes to the question of the death penalty because the Convention on Prisoners of War of 1949 makes it clear that a prisoner of war may not be executed by the detaining power for military activities prior to his arrest unless they amounted to war crimes.

6.5.3 US, *United States of America* v. *Noriega et al.*, 746 F. Supp. 1506 (S. D. Fla. 1990)

Note: The case concerns the indictment of General Manuel Antonio Noriega according to which he was alleged to have exploited his positions as head of the intelligence arm of the Panamanian National Guard and Commander-in-Chief of the Panamanian Defence Forces to assist and protect international drug traffickers. On 15 December 1989 Noriega declared that a 'state of war' existed with the United States. President Bush subsequently ordered troops into Panama. On 3 January 1990 Noriega surrendered to US military officials. Noriega subsequently argued he was a prisoner of war pursuant to the GCs. The US District Court for Florida said:

Defendants Noriega and Del Cid contend that they are prisoners of war ("POW") within the meaning of the Geneva Convention Relative to the Treatment of Prisoners of War, (Geneva III), a status, Defendants maintain, which divests this Court of jurisdiction to proceed with this case. For the purposes of the motion at bar, the Government does not maintain that Defendants are not prisoners of war, but rather argues that even were Defendants POWs, the Geneva Convention would not divest this Court of jurisdiction. Thus, the Court is not presented with the task of determining whether or not Defendants are POWs under Geneva III, but proceeds with the motion at bar as if Defendants were entitled to the full protection afforded by the Convention. Defendants' arguments under the Geneva Convention are grounded in Articles 82, 84, 85, 87, and 99, and 22, ... each of which is examined, in turn, below.

As is evident from its face, Article 82 pertains to disciplinary and penal procedures against POWs for offenses committed after becoming POWs, allowing for prosecutions against POWs only for acts which would be prosecutable against a member of the detaining forces. Thus, Article 82 is clearly inapplicable to the instant case because Noriega and Del Cid are being prosecuted not for offenses committed after their capture but for offenses committed well before they became prisoners of war. ...

Under 18 U.S.C. at 3231, federal district courts have concurrent jurisdiction with military courts over all violations of the laws of the United States committed by military personnel. The indictment charges Defendants with various violations of federal law, including narcotics trafficking. ... These are allegations of criminal misconduct for which any member of the United States Armed Forces could be prosecuted. Consequently, the prohibition embodied in Article 84, paragraph 1 does not divest this Court of jurisdiction. It has not been argued by Defense Counsel that the district court does not offer the essential guarantees of independence and impartiality "as generally recognized. ... ." Neither do Defendants contend that they will not be afforded the full measure of rights provided for in Article 105. Those rights include representation of counsel and prior notification of charges. . . . Indeed, Defendants will enjoy the benefit of all constitutional guarantees afforded any person accused of a federal crime. . . .

Rather than supporting Defendants' overall position pressed under the Geneva Convention, this Article [Art. 85] appears to recognize the right to prosecute asserted by the Government. The Article refers to "prisoners . . . prosecuted under the laws of the Detaining Power" (i.e., the United States) and for acts "committed prior to capture." Further, the benefits of the Convention shall be afforded the POW "even if convicted." The indictment charges the Defendants with violations of the laws of the United States allegedly committed between December 1982 and March 1986 – well before the military action and apprehension by surrender. . . .

Article 82 reflects the principle of "equivalency" embodied in other Articles of the Convention. That principle provides that, in general, prisoners of war may be prosecuted for criminal violations only if a member of the armed forces of the detaining country would be subject to like prosecution for the same conduct. The specific application of the 'equivalency principle' in Article 87 prevents prisoners of war from being subject to penalties not imposed on the detaining power's soldiers for the same acts. Assuming Defendants are convicted of one or more of the crimes with which they are charged, they face criminal sentences no greater nor less than would apply to an American soldier convicted of the same crime. The instant prosecution is therefore consistent with the provisions of Article 87. . . .

Article 99 proscribes the prosecution of prisoners of war under ex post facto laws, and prohibits coerced confessions. This Article further codifies other fundamental rights secured to any criminal defendant under the Constitution of the United States of America. All accused defendants, "prisoner of war" status notwithstanding, are guaranteed these basic protections.

The Defense has not contended, and of course cannot contend, that the narcotics offenses with which Defendants are charged were permitted under U.S. law at the time the acts were allegedly committed. Neither has there been any assertion that Defendants were coerced into admitting guilt or that any effort was made in that direction. Defendants are represented by competent counsel and are being afforded all rights to which they are entitled under the law. Article 99 thus does not operate to divest the Court of jurisdiction.

6.6 TERMINATION OF CAPTIVITY AND REPATRIATION

6.6.1 ICRC, Memorandum from the International Committee of the Red Cross to the States Parties to the Geneva Conventions of August 12 1949 Concerning the Conflict Between Islamic Republic of Iran and Republic of Iraq (Geneva, 7 May 1983)

Repatriation

Severely injured and sick prisoners of war

The Third Geneva Convention states that "parties to the conflict are bound to send back to their own country, regardless of numbers or rank, seriously wounded and seriously sick prisoners of war, after having cared for them until they are fit to travel …". Although there have been four repatriation operations – on 16 June, 25 August and 15 December 1981 and on 1 May 1983 – and despite the constitution of a mixed medical commission, most of the severely wounded and sick prisoners of war have not been repatriated, as required by the Convention.

6.6.2 Report of the Mission dispatched by the [UN] Secretary-General on the Situation of Prisoners of War in the Islamic Republic of Iran and Iraq, UN Doc. S/20147, 24 August 1988

131. In both countries the outlook for repatriation in the context of the Islamic Republic of Iran's recent acceptance of Security Council resolution 598 (1987) was raised by the authorities.

132. The Third Geneva Convention, article 118, paragraph 1, provides that "prisoners of war shall be released and repatriated without delay after the cessation of active hostilities".

133. This principle puts an obligation on the detaining Power subject to no other condition than the cessation of active hostilities. The obligation is total, and not based on reciprocity. The timing and procedure are only partly regulated by articles 118 and 119 of the Convention.

134. Unlike the provisions governing repatriation during hostilities (arts. 109 – 117), which prohibit forcible repatriation for certain categories (art. 109, para. 3), the subjective will of the prisoner is not explicitly mentioned as a condition for repatriation of all prisoners after the cessation of hostilities. An interpretation which would entirely disregard this element and stress the right of the Power of origin to have their nationals forcibly returned, however, would not be correct. The Convention is an instrument protecting the prisoners in their own interest.

135. Limitations on the duty to repatriate have been recognised in practice, in particular after the Korean War. Also, the ICRC Commentary to the Third Geneva Convention (pp. 546 – 549) endorses the same idea. Today the limitations of a State party's duty under article 118 to repatriate POWs can also be based on overriding concepts of international refugee law and human rights. We have in mind the principles of the Refugee Convention of 1951 (which is, as such, binding only on the Islamic Republic of Iran), the Universal Declaration of Human Rights of 1948 and the two Covenants of 1966 (to which the Islamic Republic of Iran and Iraq are parties) as well as other instruments and practices. These elements lend support to the view that nobody can be returned to an area where he may be prosecuted. This principle of non-refoulement is sometimes described as ius cogens. The protection against deprivation of life or ill-treatment under non-derogable human-rights provisions also may be seen to bind the State considering repatriation, if that would carry with it a serious risk of such violations.

136. The duty of the detaining Power under article 118 depends on the terms "without delay" and "cessation of active hostilities". In the present case, however, the acceptance of Security Council resolution 598 (1987) including its paragraph 3 makes the duty effective upon the cease-fire which came into effect on 20 August 1988.

137. As in past wars, there will be a need in practice for some repatriation machinery as well as some co-ordination between the Islamic Republic of Iran and Iraq. Having accepted the Convention and the Security Council's resolution, the two States are, we think, under a duty to co-operate about all the issues which may arise concerning repatriation. Besides, and failing agreement, each of them "shall establish and execute without delay a plan of repatriation" (Third Convention, art. 118, para. 2)

6.6.3 US, US Department of Defense, *Final Report to Congress: Conduct of the Persian Gulf War – The Role of the Law of War* (1992) 31 ILM 615, 630

No EPW was forcibly repatriated. Coalition forces identified to the ICRC those Iraqi EPWs not desiring repatriation. Once an Iraqi EPW scheduled for repatriation reached the repatriation site, the ICRC reconfirmed his willingness to be repatriated. Those who indicated they no longer desired to return to Iraq were returned to the custody of the detaining power. . . .

On 5 August 1991, Iraqi EPWs still refusing repatriation were reclassified as refugees by the United States (in coordination with Saudi Arabia and the ICRC), concluding application of the GPW. . . .

6.7 INTERNMENT IN NIAC

6.7.1 PKK, Statement to the United Nations (Geneva, 24 January 1995)[3]

. . . We call on Turkey to comply with international laws and to cease its attacks on civilians. The PKK, as a party in this conflict, has always observed the conventions on war. The relevant application denoting such acceptance was submitted to the ICRC and other concerned bodies on January 23, 1995 on behalf of PKK General Secretary Abdullah Ocalan.

The declaration, moreover, also contains the following points:

1. In its conflict with the Turkish state forces, the PKK undertakes to respect the Geneva Conventions of 1949 and the First Protocol of 1977 regarding the conduct of hostilities and the protection of the victims of war and to treat those obligations as having the force of law within its own forces and the areas within its control.
2. To end any doubt, the PKK regards the following groups as part of the Turkish security forces and, therefore, as legitimate targets of attack:
   - a - members of the Turkish armed forces;
   - b - members of the Turkish contra-guerrilla forces;
   - c - members of the Turkish Intelligence Service (MIT);
   - d - members of the Turkish gendarmerie;
   - e - village guards. . . .
3. The PKK will treat captured members of the Turkish security forces as prisoners of war.

---

[3] www.hartford-hwp.com/archives/51/009.html.

4. The PKK will disseminate this statement and the rules of the Geneva Convention of 1949 and First Protocol of 1977 to its forces and asks for the assistance of the ICRC. It has adopted a system of discipline to ensure respect for these rules and the punishment of those who break them. It accepts the principle of command responsibility.

The PKK would accept an offer of services from the ICRC.

5. The PKK calls upon the Turkish government to give the same undertakings and to accept an offer for services from the ICRC.

Finally, the PKK calls upon all parties to the Geneva Convention, the UN, the OSCE, the Council of Europe, and the ICRC to take the necessary steps to end the war or ensure that the Turkish state and the PKK respect their obligations under international law.

On behalf of PKK General Secretary Abdullah Ocalan. January 24, 1995

6.7.2 UK, British Ministry of Defence, *The Joint Service Manual of the Law of Armed Conflict* (Joint Service Publication 383, 2004 Edition)

15.30.3 Prisoner of war status does not arise in internal armed conflicts unless the parties to the conflict agree, or decide unilaterally as a matter of policy to accord this status to detainees. Otherwise the treatment of detainees is governed by the domestic law of the country concerned, any human rights treaties binding on that state in time of armed conflict and the basic humanitarian principles mentioned in paragraph 15.30. It is recommended that while detained in military custody, persons who have taken a direct part in hostilities should be given the same treatment as if they were prisoners of war.

COMMENTARY

1. The existence of an IAC is necessary in order for captured combatants and certain specified categories of civilians to be entitled to POW status. As noted in Chapter 1, the changing nature of modern armed conflict and the range of actors participating in contemporary conflicts gives rise to issues regarding the classification of a conflict which inevitably affect the determination of POW status. Furthermore, existing definitions of IAC do not resolve the question of the threshold for the existence of such a conflict,[4] which again affects the determination of POW status and the status of captured persons in a situation falling below that threshold, although in the latter case IHRL would apply.

2. POW status has traditionally been described as of particular importance for an individual captured in the course of an IAC. Detention as a POW is not punitive but serves a military purpose of preventing combatants from taking part in the hostilities. For this reason, combatancy and POW status are closely linked, although certain categories of civilians authorised to accompany the armed forces such as war correspondents are also entitled to POW status.[5] A POW enjoys protections under GCIII, which also regulates the

---

[4] See Chapter 1 Section 1.2.1 and Commentary.
[5] See Art. 4(A)(4) GCIII. Medical and religious personnel are entitled to equivalent treatment. See Art. 33(1), GCIII.

conditions of detention, treatment and repatriation at the end of the armed conflict. POW should be subject to the same penal and disciplinary legislation as the members of the armed forces of the detaining State (principle of assimilation)[6] and should not be tried for participating in the armed conflict. Their POW status does not, however, make them immune from prosecution for war crimes or other international crimes.

3. In order to be entitled to POW status, a captured person must fall within one of the combatancy categories discussed in Chapter 4. As was noted in that chapter, the application of the criteria of Art. 4 GCIII was critical in the determination of the status of Taliban and Al-Qaeda fighters. Controversy over their status as combatants led to controversy over their entitlement to POW status. In order to reiterate what was said in Chapter 4, Art. 4 GCIII needs to be read in conjunction with Art. 43 API, which streamlines the definition of combatants as well as in line with Art. 44 API.

4. In cases of doubt as to whether a person is entitled to POW status, his/her status is determined by a competent tribunal according to Art. 5(2) GIII.[7] In *Public Prosecutor* v. *Koi*, the Privy Council required a claim to entitlement to POW status to have been made by the accused. This and the question of whether doubt arises now need to be considered in the light of Art. 45(1) API, which establishes a presumption of POW status and seems to reverse the burden of proof from the Claimant to the Tribunal. Article 5 tribunals do not necessarily need to be judicial but administrative bodies such as Commissions or Boards of Inquiry also suffice. What is required, however, is adherence to due process guarantees. That said, if the captured person is to be tried, his/her status should be determined by a judicial tribunal.[8]

5. Are captured persons who do not possess the status of POW unprotected by IHL? This relates to the treatment of so-called 'unlawful combatants', a term that does not exist in IHL, which recognises only two categories – combatants and civilians – but it has been used to describe captured persons who do not fulfil the combatancy criteria of Art. 4 GCIII.[9] These persons are thus civilians who participate unlawfully in an armed conflict and they are entitled to the protections of GCIV, whose scope of application is general and covers all persons who find themselves in the hands of a party to the conflict provided that they fulfil the nationality criteria of Art. 4 GCIV. If GCIV is not applicable, those persons are protected by Art. 75 API,[10] which applies to persons in the power of a party to the conflict who do not enjoy more favourable treatment under the GCs and API. Article 75 API contains certain fundamental guarantees and constitutes customary law. As a last resort, captured persons are protected by Common Article 3, which is considered to be a 'mini' convention applicable to all conflicts. That notwithstanding, they can be tried for unlawfully participating in an armed conflict and for war crimes or any other international crime they may have committed.

6. Whether POW status should be denied to captured combatants who had committed war crimes prior to capture was controversial with certain States denying them such status.

---

[6]   Art. 82, GCIII.
[7]   Art. 5(2), GCIII and Art. 45(1), API.
[8]   Art. 45(2), API.
[9]   See also Chapter 4 Section 4.3.
[10]   In relation with Art. 45(3), API.

States are now accepting the retention of POW under Art. 85 GCIII as the *Noriega* case shows.

7. The status of POW does not exist in NIACs. Detention in NIACs is examined in Chapter 10[11] but, in summary, it is regulated by Common Article 3, APII, domestic law and IHRL. That said, POW status may arise in the event of a declaration of belligerency, as in the case of the Biafran War, or by agreement between the government and insurgents. Whether POW status should be awarded to members of the military wing of an armed group, party to an armed conflict, is controversial. As was seen in Chapter 4 and will be further considered in Chapter 10,[12] their status is equivalent to combatants. In view of the fact that armed groups are expected to observe IHL and also in view of the fact that their commanders can be charged for violations of IHL, there are arguably sound policy reasons for the granting of POW status to those individuals.

8. The entitlement to POW status of specific categories of civilians such as war correspondents represents an anomaly in the structure of protection afforded to civilians in the hands of a party to the conflict contained in GCIV and API. Whereas internment of civilians is based on an identified and continuing security need coupled with a system of review,[13] for those civilians granted POW status under Art. 4 GCIII, detention is status based as in the case of combatants. They are detained as POW because their activities are important to the army. The issue of the entitlement of embedded journalists to POW status has given rise to debate.[14] The crucial issue is accreditation. Embedded as well as freelance journalists are not entitled in our view to POW status but can be detained for security reasons as provided in IAC and NIAC. In relation to civilians entitled to POW status, does their DPH prior to capture result in their loss of POW status? It is submitted that they lose such status and they can be detained for security reasons. They would also be liable to prosecution on the basis of such direct participation.

9. The question of detention of UN peacekeepers poses particular issues that relate to the status of the force as a party to an IAC or a NIAC as well as the status of its members as combatants or civilians.[15] In light of what was said previously, namely that members of the military contingent of a UN force that participate in an armed conflict become combatants for the duration of the armed conflict, it can be contended that they can also be detained for the duration of the armed conflict. It should, however, be noted that this view is contested by the UN and it may not be acceptable to TCC. Moreover, neither the 1999 Secretary-General's Bulletin nor the 1994 Convention on the Safety of United Nations and Associated Personnel are clear in this respect.[16] It should be recalled, however, that both documents adopt a very restricted view of combatancy. Applying the principles and spirit of the GCs, as Art. 8 of the 1994 Safety Convention requires, does not remove detained UN personnel from the purview of GCIII, even if they are not formally awarded POW status. This view is also in

---

[11] Chapter 10 Section 10.6.
[12] Chapter 4 Section 4.2; Chapter 10 Section 10.5.
[13] See Chapter 5.
[14] For the status of journalists, see Chapter 4.
[15] See Chapter 1, Section 1.8.1 and commentary. Also Chapter 5 Section 5.11 and commentary.
[16] See Art. 8 of the Convention on the Safety of United Nations and Associated Personnel (adopted 9 December 1994, entered into force 15 January 1999) 2051 UNTS 363.

sync with the principle of equality that underpins IHL. In NIACs, since POW status does not exist and the distinction between combatants and civilians is not formally recognised, detention of UN personnel will be regulated by Common Article 3, APII where applicable and customary IHL.[17]

10. Responsibility for POW lies with the State whose troops captured them. In the case of persons captured by UN forces in the course of an IAC, they will be treated in accordance with GCIII.[18] The issue of the allocation of responsibility for such prisoners between the UN and TCCs whose troops carried out the original capture is complicated.

11. The humane treatment of POW is central to the regime established under GCIII. This is reflected in Art. 13 of the Convention, providing for the protection of POW against violence, intimidation, insults and public curiosity. This long-standing principle, as embodied in the 1929 Prisoners of War Convention, was the basis of the prosecution and conviction of Lt Gen. Maelzer for his failure to protect the prisoners under his control. The prohibition of adverse discrimination introduced as a result of the experiences of POW in the Second World War at the hands of their captors has proved to be of continuing importance in a range of modern conflicts, from the conflicts following the break-up of the former Yugoslavia to the Iran–Iraq War, when ethnic and religious divisions have heightened the risk of ill-treatment. In the case of such conflicts, indoctrination of POW and discrimination on the basis of religion may be driven by State policy.

12. The protection of vulnerable groups such as women and children represents a significant aspect of the protection afforded under the POW regime. The treatment of women POW reflects to a considerable extent the protections afforded to civilian internees. The treatment of child soldiers has caused considerable debate. Increasingly, the emphasis in both IHL and IHRL has been on the illegality of the employment of child soldiers. Nonetheless, they continue to appear on the battlefield and the question arises as to whether they are entitled to POW status. It is submitted that to the extent that child soldiers satisfy the criteria of combatancy, they are entitled to POW status if captured. They should also be treated in accordance with relevant provisions contained in GCIII, GCIV, API as well as in accordance with IHRL and in particular the Convention on the Rights of the Child and its Optional Protocol on the Involvement of Children in Armed Conflict. The prosecution of children for war crimes or for other international crimes raises questions concerning the minimum age of criminal responsibility and, more critically, whether children should be prosecuted at all since international law seems to treat them merely as victims. The detention of children in NIAC is dealt with in Chapter 10.[19]

13. Internment of POW in camps has a long-standing history extending back to the early nineteenth century. A central feature of the organisation of such camps is the requirement that they be commanded by an officer of the regular forces of the detaining power. The officer is responsible on the basis of command responsibility doctrine for the care of the prisoners under his command as an agent of the State.[20] The need for the comprehensive

---

[17] See also Chapter 10.
[18] See Art. 8 of Secretary-General's Bulletin, *Observance by United Nations Forces of International Humanitarian Law* (6 August 1999) UN Doc. ST/SGB/1999/13.
[19] Chapter 10 Section 10.6.
[20] For command responsibility, see Chapter 12.

structure of detention of POW has been emphasised in GCIII. The ICTY Trial Chamber judgment in *Prosecutor* v. *Popović et al.* provides a graphic illustration of the justification for this element of the Convention. Again, reflecting the situation when an IAC is driven by ideological difference, segregation of prisoners has proved to be a significant issue in certain modern conflicts, as addressed in the UN Report on Prisoners of War in the Islamic Republic of Iran and Iraq in 1988.

14. Protections also exist with regard to physical transfer from one internment camp to another while remaining in the control of the detaining power and to transfers by the detaining power to another State. In the latter case, the transferring State must ensure that the other State is able and prepared to observe the provisions of the Convention. The ICTY jurisprudence as in *Prosecutor* v. *Mrkšić and Šljvančanin* illustrates this point.

15. Detention of POW normally lasts until the end of active hostilities. In the case of certain recent international armed conflicts, POW languished in detention for extended periods with reported consequential psychological trauma. While the POW regime reflects a necessary balance between the detaining State, the State of origin and the POW concerned, it is debatable whether in these particular instances appropriate regard was had to the interests of the POW. The associated issue of repatriation has continued to give rise to controversy from the end of the Second World War onwards. In the event that a POW refuses repatriation, it is questionable whether they retain that status or whether the status becomes that of an interned civilian.

7

Means and Methods of Warfare and the Law of Targeting

INTRODUCTION

IHL imposes restrictions on the means and methods of warfare as well as on their use. More specifically, IHL prohibits means and methods of warfare that are indiscriminate, cause superfluous injury or unnecessary suffering, or cause long-term and severe damage to the environment.[1] 'Means' refers to weapons and weapons launch and delivery systems whereas 'methods' refers to particular tactics in warfare. How weapons are used for attacks and what can be attacked are regulated by the law of targeting, which is premised on the distinction between civilians and combatants and between civilian objects and military objectives, justifying attacks only on the latter.[2] Military objectives are objects that (i) make an effective contribution to military action by virtue of their nature, location, use or purpose and (ii) their destruction, capture or neutralisation offers a definite military advantage.[3] Incidental harm to civilians or civilian objects is permitted only if it is proportionate.[4] If civilians or civilian objects are to be affected by the attack, precautionary measures must be taken.[5] IHL norms on means and methods of warfare and on targeting apply also to NIACs.[6] That said, how these norms regulate the use of certain weapons or warfare methods gives rise to many questions, which will be examined in further detail herein. What will also be examined is how IHL regulates the procurement and acquisition of weapons. With regard to targeting, the definition of military objectives, the factors that are taken into consideration when assessing proportionality, and what precautions are needed are issues that have triggered many debates and will also be considered. To what extent new-technology weapons such as cyber weapons or autonomous and automated weapons comply with the relevant IHL rules is nowadays critical and will be examined in this chapter.

Resources: Arts 35–42, 43–58, API

---

[1] Arts 35, 51 and 55, API.
[2] Arts 48, 51 and 52, API. See also Chapter 4 and Chapter 2 Section 2.4.
[3] Art. 52(2), API.
[4] Art. 57(2)(b), API.
[5] Art. 57(2)(a)(i) and Art. 58, API.
[6] This becomes evident by the criminalisation of violations of such norms in NIACs. See Art. 8(2)(3), ICC St.

Cases and Materials

7.1 REGULATION OF MEANS AND METHODS OF WARFARE

7.1.1 General

7.1.1.1 Georgia, *Independent International Fact-Finding Mission on the Conflict in Georgia*, Report, Volume II (September 2009)

338. (i) The types of weapons used and the ways in which they were used

IHL governing the use of weapons is articulated in general principles prohibiting the use of means or methods of warfare that provoke superfluous injury or unnecessary suffering or indiscriminate effects, and specific rules banning or limiting the use of particular weapons. None of the weapons used in the context of this conflict is covered by a specific ban, whether be it conventional or customary. Nevertheless, while none of the weapons used during the August 2008 conflict could be regarded as unlawful *per se* under the general principles of IHL, the way in which these weapons were used raises serious concern in terms of legality. This is significant considering that the weapons in question were used mostly in populated areas. The two types of controversial weapon are the GRAD rockets and cluster bombs.

7.1.2 Prohibition of Weapons Causing Superfluous Injury or Unnecessary Suffering

7.1.2.1 **ICJ**, *Legality of the Threat or Use of Nuclear Weapons* (Advisory Opinion) [1996] I.C.J. Rep. 226

Note: *The background to this case is outlined in Chapter 2, Section 2.4.2. Having regard to the consequence of the use of weapons, in this case nuclear weapons, the ICJ reinforced that the use of weapons must conform to IHL norms in the following terms:*

78. ... According to the second principle, it is prohibited to cause unnecessary suffering to combatants: it is accordingly prohibited to use weapons causing them such harm or uselessly aggravating their suffering. In application of that second principle, States do not have unlimited freedom of choice of means in the weapons they use. ...

In conformity with the aforementioned principles, humanitarian law, at a very early stage, prohibited certain types of weapons either because of their indiscriminate effect on combatants and civilians or because of the unnecessary suffering caused to combatants, that is to say, a harm greater than that unavoidable to achieve legitimate military objectives. If an envisaged use of weapons would not meet the requirements of humanitarian law, a threat to engage in such use would also be contrary to that law.

7.1.3 Prohibition of Indiscriminate Weapons[7]

7.1.3.1 **ICTY**, *Prosecutor* v. *Kupreškić et al.*, (Judgment), Case No. IT-95-16-T, Trial Chamber (14 January 2000)

Note: *The facts of this case are outlined in Chapter 2, Section 2.1.3. Addressing the use of indiscriminate attacks, the ICTY said as follows:*

524 ... In addition, attacks, even when they are directed against legitimate military targets, are unlawful if conducted using indiscriminate means or methods of warfare, or in such a way as to cause indiscriminate damage to civilians. These principles have to some extent been spelled out in Articles 57 and 58 of the First Additional Protocol of 1977. Such provisions, it would seem, are now part of customary international law

7.1.3.2 UK, British Ministry of Defence, *The Joint Service Manual of the Law of Armed Conflict*, (Joint Service Publication 383, 2004 Edition)

6.4 It is prohibited to employ weapons which cannot be directed at a specific military objective or the effects of which cannot be limited as required by Additional Protocol I and consequently are of a nature to strike military objectives and civilians or civilian objects without distinction.

6.4.1 This provision operates as an effective prohibition on the use of weapons that are so inaccurate that they cannot be directed at a military target. The V1 flying bomb used in the

---

[7]   For indiscriminate attacks, see Chapter 4.

Second World War and the Scud rocket used during the Gulf conflict of 1990–91 are examples of weapons likely to be caught by this provision.

7.1.3.3 Human Rights Council, *Report of the United Nations Fact-Finding Mission on the Gaza Conflict* (25 September 2009), 12th Session, UN Doc. A/HRC/12/48

903. Flechettes are used in an anti-personnel role and are discharged in such quantities that they cover an area forward of the canister shell. As an area weapon, on impact the darts will hit whatever is within a certain zone. They are incapable of discriminating between objectives after detonation. They are, therefore, particularly unsuitable for use in urban settings where there is reason to believe civilians may be present.

7.1.3.4 Georgia, *Independent International Fact-Finding Mission on the Conflict in Georgia*, Report, Volume II (September 2009)

340 ... Much of the destruction in Tskhinvali was caused by GRADLAR MLRS (GRAD) launched rockets, which are known to be difficult to direct with any great precision." ...

The Fact-Finding Mission concludes that during the offensive on Tskhinvali the shelling in general, and the use of GRAD MLRS as an area weapon in particular, amount to indiscriminate attacks by Georgian forces, owing to the characteristics of the weaponry and its use in a populated area.

7.1.3.5 ICTY, *Prosecutor* v. *Gotovina et al.*, (Judgment), Case IT-06-90-A, Appeals Chamber (16 November 2012)

Note: *The facts of this case are set out in Chapter 1, Section 1.4.5. On appeal, the ICTY overturned the Trial Chamber's finding that artillery attacks impacting beyond a 200-metre radius were indiscriminate.*

64. ... In each of the Four Towns, the Trial Chamber found at least one target which the HV [Croatian Army] could have believed possessed military advantage. With no exceptions, it concluded that impact sites within 200 metres of such targets were evidence of a lawful attack, and impact sites beyond 200 metres from such targets were evidence of an indiscriminate attack. The Appeals Chamber recalls that it has found that the Trial Chamber failed to provide a reasoned opinion in deriving the 200 Metre Standard ...

7.1.3.6 US, Department of Defense, *Law of War Manual*, Office of General Counsel (June 2015, Updated 2016)

6.7 INHERENTLY INDISCRIMINATE WEAPONS

Inherently indiscriminate weapons, *i.e.*, weapons that are incapable of being used in accordance with the principles of distinction and proportionality, are prohibited. Such weapons include weapons that are specifically designed to conduct attacks against the civilian population as well as weapons that, when used, would necessarily cause incidental harm that is excessive compared the [*sic*] military advantage expected to be gained from their use.

7.1.4 Prohibition of Weapons Harming the Environment

7.1.4.1 UK, British Ministry of Defence, *The Joint Service Manual of the Law of Armed Conflict* (Joint Service Publication 383, 2004 Edition)

5.29.1 ... Article 35 [API] deals with direct protection of the environment whereas Article 55 tends more towards protecting the environment from the incidental effects of warfare, especially if it prejudices the health or survival of the civilian population. The only difference of substance is that while Article 35 relates to all methods of warfare whether on land, sea, or in the air wherever in the world they are utilized, Article 55 only relates to environmental damage on the territory or in the territorial sea of a state party to the conflict.

5.29.2 Additional Protocol I relates to widespread, long-term, and severe damage. The terms are not defined. Those who negotiated the Protocol understood 'long-term' as relating to a period of decades. ... Unfortunately, there was no such understanding as to the meaning of 'severe' or 'widespread'.

7.2 REGULATION OF CERTAIN WEAPONS

7.2.1 Nuclear Weapons

7.2.1.1 ICJ, *Legality of the Threat or Use of Nuclear Weapons*, Advisory Opinion, 8 July 1996, ICJ Reports 1996
Note: *The facts of this case are set out in Chapter 2, Section 2.4.2. The ICJ rendered its opinion on the use of nuclear weapons in the following terms:*

95. ... Thus, methods and means of warfare, which would preclude any distinction between civilian and military targets, or which would result in unnecessary suffering to combatants, are prohibited. In view of the unique characteristics of nuclear weapons, to which the Court has referred above, the use of such weapons in fact seems scarcely reconcilable with respect for such requirements. Nevertheless, the Court considers that it does not have sufficient elements to enable it to conclude with certainty that the use of nuclear weapons would necessarily be at variance with the principles and rules of law applicable in armed conflict in any circumstance.

7.2.1.2 UK, British Ministry of Defence, *The Joint Service Manual of the Law of Armed Conflict*, (Joint Service Publication 383, 2004 Edition)

6.17 There is no specific rule of international law, express or implied, which prohibits the use of nuclear weapons. The legality of their use depends upon the application of the general rules of international law, including those regulating the use of force and the conduct of hostilities. ... However, the rules introduced by Additional Protocol I 'apply exclusively to conventional weapons without prejudice to any other rules of international law applicable to other types of weapons. In particular, the rules so introduced do not have any effect on and do not regulate or prohibit the use of nuclear weapons'.

7.2.2 Cluster Munitions

7.2.2.1 ICTY, *Prosecutor* v. *Milan Martić*, (Judgment), Case No. IT-95-11-T, Trial Chamber I (12 June 2007)

Note: *The facts of this case are set out in Chapter 2, Section 2.2.7. In addition to being indicted for crimes against humanity and violations of the laws and customs of war, Milan Martić was also charged with the shelling of Zagreb on 2 and 3 May 1995 using M-87 Orkan rockets. The ICTY addressed the use of cluster munitions as follows:*

462. The M-87 Orkan is a non-guided projectile, the primary military use of which is to target soldiers and armoured vehicles. Each rocket may contain either a cluster warhead with 288 so called bomblets or 24 anti-tank shells ...

463. ... Moreover, the Trial Chamber notes the characteristics of the weapon, it being a non-guided high dispersion weapon. The Trial Chamber therefore concludes that the M-87 Orkan, by virtue of its characteristics and the firing range in this specific instance, was incapable of hitting specific targets. For these reasons, the Trial Chamber also finds that the M-87 Orkan is an indiscriminate weapon, the use of which in densely populated civilian areas, such as Zagreb, will result in the infliction of severe casualties.

7.2.2.2 US, Department of Defense, *Law of War Manual*, Office of General Counsel (June 2015, Updated 2016)

6.13 CLUSTER MUNITIONS

Cluster munitions are not specifically prohibited or restricted by the law of war. DoD has policies on cluster munitions. The use of cluster munitions, in certain circumstances, is likely to reduce the risk of incidental harm as compared to other weapons.

7.2.3 Unmanned Aerial Vehicles (UAVs)

7.2.3.1 Human Rights Council, *Report of the Special Rapporteur on Extrajudicial, Summary or Arbitrary Executions*, Philip Alston (Addendum, Study on Targeted Killings) (28 May 2010), 14th Session, UN Doc. A/HRC/14/24/Add.6

79. ... It is true that IHL places limits on the weapons States may use, and weapons that are, for example, inherently indiscriminate (such as biological weapons) are prohibited. However, a missile fired from a drone is no different from any other commonly used weapon, including a gun fired by a soldier or a helicopter or gunship that fires missiles. The critical legal question is the same for each weapon: whether its specific use complies with IHL.

7.2.3.2 US, Department of Defense, *Law of War Manual*, Office of General Counsel (June 2015, Updated 2016)

6.5.8 Remotely Piloted Aircraft. There is no prohibition in the law of war on the use of remotely piloted aircraft (also called "unmanned aerial vehicles"). Such weapons may offer certain advantages over other weapons systems.

7.2.3.3 US, Report on Process for Determining Targets of Lethal or Capture Operations *(U) An explanation of the legal and policy considerations and approval processes used in determining whether an individual or group of individuals could be the target of a lethal or capture operation conducted by the Armed Forces of the United States outside the United States and outside of Afghanistan (U)*, Submitted in response to the reporting requirement contained in section 1043 of the National Defense Authorization Act for Fiscal Year 2014 (Public Law 113-66), pp.2–3.[8]

(U) These well-established rules [military necessity, humanity, distinction, proportionality] that govern the use of force in armed conflict apply regardless of the type of weapon system used. From a legal standpoint, the use of remotely piloted aircraft for lethal operations against identified individuals presents the same issues as similar operations using manned aircraft. However, advanced precision technology gives us a greater ability to observe and wait until the enemy is away from innocent civilians before launching a strike, and thus to minimize the risk to innocent civilians.

7.2.4 Autonomous and Automated Weapons Systems

7.2.4.1 US, Department of Defense, *Directive 3000.09, Autonomy in Weapons Systems* (21 November 2012)[9]

4. POLICY. It is DoD policy that:

a. Autonomous and semi-autonomous weapon systems shall be designed to allow commanders and operators to exercise appropriate levels of human judgment over the use of force.
   (1) ... These measures will ensure that autonomous and semi-autonomous weapon systems:
      (a) Function as anticipated in realistic operational environments against adaptive adversaries.
      (b) Complete engagements in a timeframe consistent with commander and operator intentions and, if unable to do so, terminate engagements or seek additional human operator input before continuing the engagement.
      (c) Are sufficiently robust to minimize failures that could lead to unintended engagements or to loss of control of the system to unauthorized parties.
b. Persons who authorize the use of, direct the use of, or operate autonomous and semi-autonomous weapon systems must do so with appropriate care and in accordance with the law of war, applicable treaties, weapon system safety rules, and applicable rules of engagement (ROE).

---

[8] www.aclu.org/sites/default/files/field_document/8.5.16_report_on_process_of_determining_targets_of_lethal_or_capture_operations.pdf.
[9] www.dtic.mil/whs/directives/corres/pdf/300009p.pdf.

7.3 REGULATION OF CERTAIN METHODS OF WARFARE

7.3.1 Perfidy and Ruses of War

7.3.1.1 US, Department of Defense, *Final Report to Congress: Conduct of the Persian Gulf War – The Role of the Law of War* (1992) 31 ILM 612 at pp. 631–2

In contrast, perfidy is prohibited by the law of war . . .

Perfidious acts include the feigning of an intent to surrender or negotiate under a flag of truce, or the feigning of protected status through improper use of the Red Cross or Red Crescent distinctive emblem.

Perfidious acts are prohibited on the basis that perfidy may damage mutual respect for the law of war, may lead to unnecessary escalation of the conflict, may result in the injury or death of enemy forces legitimately attempting to surrender or discharging their humanitarian duties, or may impede the restoration of peace.

There were few examples of perfidious practices during the Persian Gulf War. The most publicized were those associated with the battle of Ras Al-Khafji, which began on 29 January. As that battle began, Iraqi tanks entered Ras Al-Khafji with their turrets reversed, turning their guns forward only at the moment action began between Iraqi and Coalition forces. While there was some media speculation that this was an act of perfidy, it was not; a reversed turret is not a recognized indication of surrender *per se*. Some tactical confusion may have occurred, since Coalition ground forces were operating under a defensive posture at that time, and were to engage Iraqi forces only upon clear indication of hostile intent, or some hostile act.

However, individual acts of perfidy did occur. On one occasion, Iraqi soldiers waved a white flag and laid down their weapons. When a Saudi Arabian patrol advanced to accept their surrender, it was fired upon by Iraqi forces hidden in buildings on either side of the street. During the same battle, an Iraqi officer approached Coalition forces with his hands in the air, indicating his intention to surrender. When near his would-be captors, he drew a concealed pistol from his boot, fired, and was killed during the combat that followed.

7.3.1.2 UK, British Ministry of Defence, *The Joint Service Manual of the Law of Armed Conflict*, (Joint Service Publication 383, 2004 Edition)

5.9 It is prohibited to kill, injure or capture an adversary by resort to perfidy.

5.9.1 Perfidy is defined as 'acts inviting the confidence of an adversary to lead him to believe that he is entitled to, or is obliged to accord, protection under the rules of international law applicable in armed conflict, with intent to betray that confidence'.

7.3.1.3 US, Department of Defense, *Law of War Manual*, Office of General Counsel (June 2015, Updated 2016)

5.25 RUSES OF WAR AND OTHER LAWFUL DECEPTIONS

Ruses of war are considered permissible. In general, a belligerent may resort to those measures for mystifying or misleading the enemy against which the enemy ought to take measures to protect itself. . . .

5.25.1 *Definition of Ruses of War.* Ruses of war are acts that are intended to mislead an adversary or to induce him to act recklessly, but that do not infringe upon any rule of international law applicable in armed conflict and that are not perfidious because they do not invite the confidence of an adversary with respect to protection under that law. Ruses of war are methods, resources, and techniques that can be used either to convey false information or deny information to opposing forces. They can include physical, technical, or administrative means, such as electronic warfare measures, flares, smoke, chaff, aerosol material, or dissemination devices.

7.3.2 Pillage

7.3.2.1 **UK, British Ministry of Defence,** *The Joint Service Manual of the Law of Armed Conflict,* (Joint Service Publication 383, 2004 Edition)

15.23 Pillaging a town or place, even when taken by assault, is forbidden.

15.23.1 Pillage, also known as plunder or looting, is the same as stealing, which is an offence in peace or war. It must be distinguished from the lawful requisitioning of property for military, rather than private, purposes.

7.3.2.2 **ICTY,** *Prosecutor* v. *Blaškić,* (Judgment), Case No. IT-95-14-T, Trial Chamber (3 March 2000)

Note: *The facts of this case are outlined in Chapter 1, Section 1.2.2.1. Blaškić's crimes included destruction and plunder of property. On the issue of plunder in armed conflict, the ICTY said as follows:*

184. The prohibition on the wanton appropriation of enemy public or private property extends to both isolated acts of plunder for private interest and to the "organized seizure of property undertaken within the framework of a systematic economic exploitation of occupied territory". Plunder "should be understood to embrace all forms of unlawful appropriation of property in armed conflict for which individual criminal responsibility attaches under international law, including those acts traditionally described as 'pillage'."

7.3.2.3 **ICC,** *The Prosecutor* v. *Germain Katanga,* (Judgment Pursuant to Article 74 of the Statute), Case No. ICC-01/04-01/07 Trial Chamber II (7 March 2014)

Note: *The facts of this case are set out in Chapter 2, Section 2.2.10. On the crime of pillaging, the ICC concluded:*

950. The Chamber considers that Bogoro was extensively pillaged during the 24 February 2003 attack. ...

951. The property was stolen for essentially personal reasons by combatants. ... The Chamber notes in this respect that the Accused himself testified that as the combatants had no salary, pillaging was a form of remuneration.

952. Having regard to the evidence put before it, the Chamber also finds that the acts of appropriation of property in which the Ngiti combatants engaged were intentional and that they acted out of private or personal gain. In the view of the Chamber, even where food

alone was involved, the pillaging was therefore not perpetrated out of military necessity, as the Defence alleged, but out of personal gain. ....

957. In the light of the body of evidence and the findings ensuing from its examination of the contextual elements of the war crimes, the Chamber finds beyond reasonable doubt that during the 24 February 2003 attack on Bogoro, Ngiti combatants pillaged houses, livestock and houseware, thereby committing pillaging constituting a war crime under article 8(2)(e)(v) of the Statute.

7.3.2.4 US, Department of Defense, *Law of War Manual*, Office of General Counsel (June 2015, Updated 2016)

5.17.4 *Pillage Prohibited.* Pillage is prohibited, both in general and specifically with respect to:

- the wounded, sick, shipwrecked, and dead;
- POWs;
- protected persons under the GC;
- persons in occupied territory and in areas of non-international armed conflict.

7.3.3 Espionage

7.3.3.1 UK, British Ministry of Defence, *The Joint Service Manual of the Law of Armed Conflict*, (Joint Service Publication 383, 2004 Edition)

8.13 Spies
A person who falls into the hands of an adverse party while engaging in espionage, does not have the right to the status of prisoner of war, although it may be given at the discretion of the detaining power. Even without the status of prisoner of war, a spy may only be subjected to punishment after trial by a court applying the prescribed safeguards. Captured spies remain entitled to the basic humanitarian guarantees provided by Additional Protocol I.

7.3.3.2 US, Department of Defense, *Law of War Manual*, Office of General Counsel (June 2015, Updated 2016)

4.17 SPIES, SABOTEURS, AND OTHER PERSONS ENGAGING IN SIMILAR ACTS BEHIND ENEMY LINES
Spying, sabotage, and similar acts behind enemy lines have a dual character under the law of war; States are permitted to employ persons who engage in these activities, but these activities are punishable by the enemy State.

Belligerents may employ spies and saboteurs consistent with the law of war. However, any person (including individuals who would otherwise receive the privileges of lawful combatants) engaging in spying, sabotage, or similar acts behind enemy lines, is regarded as an unprivileged belligerent while doing so. These persons forfeit entitlement to the privileges of combatant status and may be punished after a fair trial if captured.

4.17.2 *Spies.* A person may only be considered a spy when acting clandestinely or under false pretenses, (2) in the zone of operations of a belligerent, (3) he or she obtains, or endeavors to obtain, information, (4) with the intention of communicating it to the hostile party. During war, any person—military or civilian—whose actions meet all of these elements may be considered a spy under the law of war

7.4 WEAPONS REVIEW[10]

7.4.1 UK, British Ministry of Defence, *The Joint Service Manual of the Law of Armed Conflict*, (Joint Service Publication 383, 2004 Edition)

6.20.1 This obligation [to review] is imposed on all states party, not only those that produce weapons. To this end each state is required to have effective review procedures operating in accordance with the rules of international law but there is no requirement that the findings from these proceedings should be published. In the UK the weapons review process is conducted by the Ministry of Defence in a progressive manner as concepts for new means and methods of warfare are developed and as the conceptual process moves towards procurement. Qualified legal staff contribute to the weapon development process. The review process takes account not only of the law as it stands at the time of the review but also attempts to take account of likely future developments in the law of armed conflict.

7.4.2 ICRC, *A Guide to the Legal Review of New Weapons, Means and Methods of Warfare: Measures to Implement Article 36 of Additional Protocol I of 1977* (Geneva, January 2006)[11]

1. Material scope of application of the review mechanism
   1.1 ... The material scope of the Article 36 legal review is therefore very broad. It would cover:

- weapons of all types - be they anti-personnel or anti-materiel, "lethal", "non-lethal" or "less lethal" - and weapons systems;
- the ways in which these weapons are to be used pursuant to military doctrine, tactics, rules of engagement, operating procedures and counter-measures;
- all weapons to be acquired, be they procured further to research and development on the basis of military specifications, or purchased "off-the-shelf";
- a weapon which the State is intending to acquire for the first time, without necessarily being "new" in a technical sense;
- an existing weapon that is modified in a way that alters its function, or a weapon that has already passed a legal review but that is subsequently modified;
- an existing weapon where a State has joined a new international treaty which may affect the legality of the weapon.

---

[10]   Art. 36, API.
[11]   www.icrc.org/eng/assets/files/other/irrc_864_icrc_geneva.pdf.

7.4.3 US, Air Force Instruction 51–402, Legal Reviews of Weapons and Cyber Capabilities (27 July 2011)[12]

1.1. The Judge Advocate General (AF/JA) will:

1.1.1. Ensure all weapons being developed, bought, built, modified or otherwise being acquired by the Air Force that are not within a Special Access Program are reviewed for legality under LOAC, domestic law and international law prior to their possible acquisition for use in a conflict or other military operation. . . .

2.1. Upon cognizant legal authority's request, Air Force personnel will provide the following information, so that a judge advocate, or General Counsel in the instance of a special access program, may complete the reviews required by this Instruction: . . .

2.1.1. A general description of the weapon or cyber capability submitted for legal review. . . .

2.1.2. Statements of intended use (such as types of targets) or concept of operations. . . .

2.1.3. The reasonably anticipated effects of employment, to include all tests, computer modelling, laboratory studies, and other technical analysis and results that contribute to the assessment of reasonably anticipated effects.

3. Contents of the Legal Review of Weapons and Cyber Capabilities.

3.1. A legal review conducted under this Instruction will include, at a minimum:

3.1.1. Whether there is a specific rule of law, whether by treaty obligation of the United States or accepted by the United States as customary international law, prohibiting or restricting the use of the weapon or cyber capability in question.

3.1.2. If there is no express prohibition, the following questions are considered:

3.1.2.1. Whether the weapon or cyber capability is calculated to cause superfluous injury, in violation of Article 23(e) of the Annex to Hague Convention IV; and

3.1.2.2. Whether the weapon or cyber capability is capable of being directed against a specific military objective and, if not, is of a nature to cause an effect on military objectives and civilians or civilian objects without distinction.

3.2. The fact that another Service or the forces of another country have adopted the weapon or cyber capability may be considered in determining the legality of such weapon or cyber capability, but such fact shall not be binding for purposes of any legal review conducted under this Instruction.

7.4.4 UK, Ministry of Defence, Development, Concepts and Doctrine Centre, *UK Weapon Reviews* (2016)[13]

UK legal reviews take place at key milestones in the procurement process of a piece of equipment. Broadly, these are at:

---

[12] http://nsarchive.gwu.edu/NSAEBB/NSAEBB424/docs/Cyber-053.pdf. For autonomous or semi-autonomous weapons see Department of Defense, Directive 3000.09, Autonomy in Weapons Systems (21 November 2012) www.dtic.mil/whs/directives/corres/pdf/300009p.pdf.

[13] www.gov.uk/government/uploads/system/uploads/attachment_data/file/507319/20160308-UK_weapon_reviews.pdf.

- MOD's decision to commit funds to developing a specific capability (known as 'Initial Gate');
- MOD's decision to commit fully to the procurement of a particular piece of equipment or weapon (known as 'Main Gate'); and
- at the date the finalised equipment enters service. ...

DCDC [Development Concepts and Doctrine Centre] nominates one lawyer to monitor development and then be the lead reviewer for a new technology. Once the nominated lawyer has completed a draft review, that review is sent to the procurement team for them to consider: most importantly, to confirm that the reviewing lawyer's technical understanding of the system is correct and complete. No piece of equipment is reviewed in isolation and the legal team peer-review each other's work. This has recently been formalised such that every weapon review advice is now signed and approved by two lawyers: the lead reviewer, and a second reviewer.

7.5 TARGETING

7.5.1 General

7.5.1.1 *Final Report to the Prosecutor by the Committee Established to Review the NATO Bombing Campaign Against the Federal Republic of Yugoslavia* (1999)[14]

28. In brief, in combat military commanders are required: a) to direct their operations against military objectives, and b) when directing their operations against military objectives, to ensure that the losses to the civilian population and the damage to civilian property are not disproportionate to the concrete and direct military advantage anticipated. ... it should be borne in mind that commanders deciding on an attack have duties:

a) to do everything practicable to verify that the objectives to be attacked are military objectives,
b) to take all practicable precautions in the choice of methods and means of warfare with a view to avoiding or, in any event to minimizing incidental civilian casualties or civilian property damage, and
c) to refrain from launching attacks which may be expected to cause disproportionate civilian casualties or civilian property damage.

7.5.1.2 **ICTY**, *Prosecutor* v. *Galić*, (Judgment), Case No. IT-98-29-T, Trial Chamber (5 December 2003)

Note: *The facts of this case are set out in Chapter 2, Section 2.4.3. Considering the rules on targeting in light of the principles of distinction and protection of civilians, the ICTY said as follows:*

51. As mentioned above, in accordance with the principles of distinction and protection of the civilian population, only military objectives may be lawfully attacked. ... In case of doubt as to whether an object which is normally dedicated to civilian purposes is being used

---

14   www.icty.org/x/file/Press/nato061300.pdf.

to make an effective contribution to military action, it shall be presumed not to be so used. The Trial Chamber understands that such an object shall not be attacked when it is not reasonable to believe, in the circumstances of the person contemplating the attack, including the information available to the latter, that the object is being used to make an effective contribution to military action.

52. "Attack" is defined in Article 49 of Additional Protocol I as "acts of violence against the adversary, whether in offence or in defence." The Commentary makes the point that "attack" is a technical term relating to a specific military operation limited in time and place, and covers attacks carried out both in offence and in defence. The jurisprudence of the Tribunal has defined "attack" as a course of conduct involving the commission of acts of violence.

7.5.1.3 US, Joint Publication 3-60, *Joint Targeting* (31 January 2013)[15]

I-1

a. A target is an entity (person, place, or thing) considered for possible engagement or action to alter or neutralize the function it performs for the adversary. A target's importance derives from its potential contribution to achieving a commander's objective(s) or otherwise accomplishing assigned tasks. These objectives must be consistent with national strategic direction and selected to accomplish the assigned missions and tasks. Targets nominated for attack may include the following:

(1) Facility: a geographically located, defined physical structure, group of structures, or area that provides a function that contributes to a target system's capability.
(2) Individual(s): a person or persons who provide a function that contributes to a target system's capability.
(3) Virtual: an entity in cyberspace that provides a function that contributes to a target system's capability.
(4) Equipment: a device that provides a function that contributes to a target system's capability ...

I-6 ...

c. The purpose of targeting is to integrate and synchronize fires into joint operations by utilizing available capabilities to generate a specific lethal or nonlethal effect on a target. The joint targeting cycle provides an iterative, logical methodology for the development, planning, execution, and assessment of targeting, weapons, and capabilities effectiveness. ....

II-3

a. The joint targeting cycle is a six phase iterative process ...

(1) End state and commander's objectives.
(2) Target development and prioritization.
(3) Capabilities analysis.
(4) Commander's decision and force assignment.
(5) Mission planning and force execution.
(6) Assessment.

---

[15]   www.dtic.mil/doctrine/new_pubs/jointpub_operations.htm.

7.5.2 Military Objectives

7.5.2.1 *Final Report to the Prosecutor by the Committee Established to Review the NATO Bombing Campaign Against the Federal Republic of Yugoslavia (1999)*[16]

35. The most widely accepted definition of "military objective" is that in Article 52 of Additional Protocol I . . .

36. Where objects are concerned, the definition has two elements: (a) their nature, location, purpose or use must make an effective contribution to military action, and (b) their total or partial destruction, capture or neutralization must offer a definite military advantage in the circumstances ruling at the time. Although this definition does not refer to persons, in general, members of the armed forces are considered combatants, who have the right to participate directly in hostilities, and as a corollary, may also be attacked. . . .

55. The choice of targets by NATO includes some loosely defined categories such as military-industrial infrastructure and government ministries and some potential problem categories such as media and refineries. All targets must meet the criteria for military objectives. If they do not do so, they are unlawful. A general label is insufficient. The targeted components of the military industrial infrastructure and of government ministries must make an effective contribution to military action and their total or partial destruction must offer a definite military advantage in the circumstances ruling at the time. Refineries are certainly traditional military objectives but tradition is not enough and due regard must be paid to environmental damage if they are attacked. The media as such is not a traditional target category. To the extent particular media components are part of the C3 (command, control and communications) network they are military objectives. If media components are not part of the C3 network then they may become military objectives depending upon their use. . . . The media does have an effect on civilian morale. If that effect is merely to foster support for the war effort, the media is not a legitimate military objective. If the media is used to incite crimes, as in Rwanda, it can become a legitimate military objective. If the media is the nerve system that keeps a war-monger in power and thus perpetuates the war effort, it may fall within the definition of a legitimate military objective. . . .

72. The bombing of the TV studio was part of a planned attack aimed at disrupting and degrading the C3 (Command, Control and Communications) network. . . . Accordingly, NATO stressed the dual-use to which such communications systems were put, describing civilian television as "heavily dependent on the military command and control system and military traffic is also routed through the civilian system". . . .

75. . . . Insofar as the attack actually was aimed at disrupting the communications network, it was legally acceptable.

76. If, however, the attack was made because equal time was not provided for Western news broadcasts, that is, because the station was part of the propaganda machinery, the legal

---

[16]   www.icty.org/x/file/Press/nato061300.pdf.

basis was more debatable. Disrupting government propaganda may help to undermine the morale of the population and the armed forces, but justifying an attack on a civilian facility on such grounds alone may not meet the "effective contribution to military action" and "definite military advantage" criteria required by the Additional Protocols.

7.5.2.2 UK, British Ministry of Defence, *The Joint Service Manual of the Law of Armed Conflict* (Joint Service Publication 383, 2004 Edition)

5.4.4 The definition of military objectives contains various elements that require explanation ...

c. 'Nature' refers to the type of object, for example, military transports, command and control centres, or communications stations.

d. 'Location' includes areas which are militarily important because they must be captured or denied to the enemy or because the enemy must be made to retreat from them. An area of land can, thus, be a military objective.

e. 'Purpose' means the future intended use of an object while 'use' means its present function.

f. The words 'nature, location, purpose or use' seem at first sight to allow a wide discretion, but they are subject to the qualifications later in the definition of 'effective contribution to military action' and the offering of 'a definite military advantage'. There does not have to be geographical proximity between 'effective contribution' and 'military advantage'. ...

g. 'Military action' means military action generally, not a limited or specific military operation.

h. The words 'in the circumstances ruling at the time' are important. If, for example, the enemy moved a divisional headquarters into a disused textile factory, an attack on that headquarters would be permissible (even though the factory might be destroyed in the process) because of the prevailing circumstances. Once the enemy moved their headquarters away, the circumstances would change again and the immunity of the factory would be restored.

i. 'Definite' means a concrete and perceptible military advantage rather than a hypothetical and speculative one.

j. 'Military advantage'. The military advantage anticipated from an attack refers to the advantage anticipated from the attack considered as a whole and not only from isolated or particular parts of the attack. The advantage need not be immediate.

7.5.2.3 Eritrea-Ethiopia Claims Commission, *Partial Award: Western Front, Aerial Bombardment and Related Claims-Eritrea's Claims 1, 3, 5, 9–13, 14, 21, 25 and 26 between The State of Eritrea and the Federal Republic of Ethiopia* (2005) 26 (8) RIAA 291

Note: *The facts of this matter are outlined in Chapter 6, Section 6.3.1.4. As to the issue of legitimacy of military objectives, the Commission commented in the following terms:*

113. .... The Commission is of the view that the term "military advantage" can only properly be understood in the context of the military operations between the Parties taken as a

whole, not simply in the context of a specific attack. Thus, with respect to the present claim, whether the attack on the power station offered a definite military advantage must be considered in the context of its relation to the armed conflict as a whole at the time of the attack. . . .

117. As a first step, the Commission must decide whether the power plant was an object that by its nature, location, purpose or use made an effective contribution to military action at the time it was attacked. The Commission agrees with Ethiopia that electric power stations are generally recognized to be of sufficient importance to a State's capacity to meet its wartime needs of communication, transport and industry so as usually to qualify as military objectives during armed conflicts. The Commission also recognizes that not all such power stations would qualify as military objectives, for example, power stations that are known, or should be known, to be segregated from a general power grid and are limited to supplying power for humanitarian purposes, such as medical facilities, or other uses that could have no effect on the State's ability to wage war. . . .

121. The remaining question is whether the Hirgigo power plant's "total or partial destruction . . . in the circumstances ruling" in late May 2000 "offer[ed] a definite military advantage." In general, a large power plant being constructed to provide power for an area including a major port and naval facility certainly would seem to be an object the destruction of which would offer a distinct military advantage. Moreover, the fact that the power station was of economic importance to Eritrea is evidence that damage to it, in the circumstances prevailing in late May 2000 when Ethiopia was trying to force Eritrea to agree to end the war, offered a definite advantage. "The purpose of any military action must always be to influence the political will of the adversary." . . . The infliction of economic losses from attacks against military objectives is a lawful means of achieving a definite military advantage, and there can be few military advantages more evident than effective pressure to end an armed conflict that, each day, added to the number of both civilian and military casualties on both sides of the war. For these reasons, the Commission, by a majority, finds that, in the circumstances prevailing on May 28, 2000, the Hirgigo power station was a military objective, as defined in Article 52, paragraph 2, of Geneva Protocol I and that Ethiopia's aerial bombardment of it was not unlawful. Consequently, this Claim is dismissed on the merits.

7.5.2.4 ICTY, *Prosecutor* v. *Gotovina et al.*, (Judgment), Case No. IT-06-90-T, Trial Chamber I (15 April 2011)

Note: *The facts of this case are outlined in Chapter 1, Section 1.4.5. The ICTY determined targetable military objectives as follows:*

1899. . . . The Trial Chamber is satisfied that the SVK headquarters, the Northern barracks, and the Senjak barracks constituted military targets. Further, given Martić's position within the RSK and SVK, the Trial Chamber is satisfied that firing at his residence could disrupt his ability to move, communicate, and command and so offered a definite military advantage, such that his residence constituted a military target. . . .

1900. On 4 and 5 August 1995, the HV [Croatian Army] fired artillery projectiles which impacted within a 200-metre radius of the intersection in the centre of Knin. . . . Thus, . . .

disrupting or denying the SVK's ability to make use of this intersection and move through Knin could offer a definite military advantage. . . .

1902. On 4 August 1995 the HV also fired artillery projectiles which impacted within a 200-metre radius of the TVIK factory. . . . The Trial Chamber recalls that the evidence before it indicates that the SVK planned to produce weapons-related products at the TVIK factory, although it does not establish whether and if so to what extent these plans were in operation by early August 1995. Under these circumstances, the Trial Chamber considers that the evidence allows for the reasonable interpretation that the HV may have determined in good faith that firing at the TVIK factory would have offered a definite military advantage.

1903. The Trial Chamber will now address its findings concerning artillery impacts on 4 and 5 August 1995 on areas which are further removed (beyond 200 metres) from the objects the HV identified as military targets and reported firing on. . . .

1907. There is no evidence indicating any fixed SVK or police presence in or near the aforementioned areas, nor evidence otherwise indicating that firing at these areas would offer a definite military advantage. . . .

1908. However, even if the HV had had artillery observers with a view of Knin on 4 and 5 August 1995, the Trial Chamber has received evidence of only very few occasions on which SVK or police trucks, tanks or units were observed moving through Knin, . . . For the foregoing reasons, the Trial Chamber does not consider it a reasonable interpretation of the evidence that the HV could have determined in good faith that targeting these areas would have offered a definite military advantage.

7.5.2.5 US, Department of Defense, *Law of War Manual*, Office of General Counsel (June 2015, Updated 2016)

5.7 MILITARY OBJECTIVES

Military objectives refers to persons and objects that may be made the object of attack. . . .

    5.7.1.2 *Dual-Use Objects*. . . . from the legal perspective, such objects are either military objectives or they are not; there is no intermediate legal category. If an object is a military objective, it is not a civilian object and may be made the object of attack. However, it will be appropriate to consider in a proportionality analysis the harm to the civilian population resulting from the destruction of such a military objective.

5.7.4 <u>Objects Categorically Recognized as Military Objectives</u>. Two types of objects are categorically recognized as military objectives. . . .

    5.7.4.1 *Military Equipment and Bases*. . . .

    5.7.4.2 *Objects Containing Military Objectives*. . . .

5.7.6 *Contribution to military action*. The first part of the test is whether the object, by its nature, location, purpose, or use makes an effective contribution to the enemy's military action. . . .

    5.7.6.2 *Make an Effective Contribution to Military Action*. The object must make or be intended to make an effective contribution to military action; however, this contribution need not be "direct" or "proximate." For example, an object might make an effective, but remote, contribution to the enemy's military action and nonetheless meet this aspect of the definition. Similarly, an object might be geographically distant from most of the fighting and nonetheless satisfy this element.

Military action has a broad meaning and is understood to mean the general prosecution of the war. It is not necessary that the object provide immediate tactical or operational gains or that the object make an effective contribution to a specific military operation. Rather, the object's effective contribution to the war-fighting or war-sustaining capability of an opposing force is sufficient. Although terms such as "war-fighting," "war-supporting," and "war-sustaining" are not explicitly reflected in the treaty definitions of military objective, the United States has interpreted the military objective definition to include these concepts. . . .

5.7.7.1 *Capture or Neutralization.* . . . Capture refers to the possibility of seizure (rather than destruction), which would confer a military advantage. . . .

Neutralization refers to a military action that denies an object to the enemy without capturing or destroying it. . . .

5.7.7.3 *Definite Military Advantage.* "Definite" means a concrete and perceptible military advantage, rather than one that is merely hypothetical or speculative. The advantage need not be immediate. . . .

"Military advantage" refers to the advantage anticipated from an attack when considered as a whole, and not only from its isolated or particular parts. Similarly, "military advantage" is not restricted to immediate tactical gains, but may be assessed in the full context of the war strategy.

The definite military advantage offered by damaging, destroying, or neutralizing the object may result from denying the enemy the ability to use this object in its military operations (*i.e.*, to benefit from the object's effective contribution to the military action). . . .

The military advantage from an attack is broader than only denying the enemy the benefit of that object's contribution to its military action. . . . The military advantage from an attack may involve a variety of other considerations, including improving the security of the attacking force. The military advantage from an attack may result from harm to the morale of enemy forces. Diminishing the morale of the civilian population and their support for the war effort does not provide a definite military advantage. However, attacks that are otherwise lawful are not rendered unlawful if they happen to result in diminished civilian morale. . . .

5.7.8.1 *Examples of Military Objectives – Leadership Facilities.* . . .

5.7.8.2 *Examples of Military Objectives – Communications Objects.* . . .

5.7.8.5 *Examples of Military Objectives – Economic Objects Associated With Military Operations.* Economic objects associated with military operations or with war-supporting or war-sustaining industries have been regarded as military objectives. Electric power stations are generally recognized to be of sufficient importance to a State's capacity to meet its wartime needs of communication, transport, and industry so as usually to qualify as military objectives during armed conflicts. Oil refining and distribution facilities and objects associated with petroleum, oil, and lubricant products (including production, transportation, storage, and distribution facilities) have also been regarded as military objectives

7.5.3 Proportionality in Attack

7.5.3.1 *Final Report to the Prosecutor by the Committee Established to Review the NATO Bombing Campaign Against the Federal Republic of Yugoslavia (1999)*[17]

49. The questions which remain unresolved once one decides to apply the principle of proportionality include the following:

a) What are the relative values to be assigned to the military advantage gained and the injury to non-combatants and or the damage to civilian objects?
b) What do you include or exclude in totaling your sums?
c) What is the standard of measurement in time or space? and
d) To what extent is a military commander obligated to expose his own forces to danger in order to limit civilian casualties or damage to civilian objects? ...

52. ... The committee understands the above formulation, instead, to refer to an overall assessment of the totality of civilian victims as against the goals of the military campaign. ...

77. Assuming the station [RTS] was a legitimate objective, the civilian casualties were unfortunately high but do not appear to be clearly disproportionate. ...

78. ... The proportionality or otherwise of an attack should not necessarily focus exclusively on a specific incident. ... The attack on the RTS building must therefore be seen as forming part of an integrated attack against numerous objects, including transmission towers and control buildings of the Yugoslav radio relay network which were "essential to Milosevic's ability to direct and control the repressive activities of his army and special police forces in Kosovo" and which comprised "a key element in the Yugoslav air defence network".

7.5.3.2 ICTY, *Prosecutor* v. *Galić*, (Judgment), Case No. IT-98-29-T, Trial Chamber (5 December 2003)

Note: *The facts of this case are outlined in Chapter 2, Section 2.4.3. On the issue of proportionality of an attack, the ICTY commented as follows:*

58. ... In determining whether an attack was proportionate it is necessary to examine whether a reasonably well-informed person in the circumstances of the actual perpetrator, making reasonable use of the information available to him or her, could have expected excessive civilian casualties to result from the attack.

7.5.3.3 Human Rights Council, *Report of the United Nations Fact-Finding Mission on the Gaza Conflict* (25 September 2009), 12th Session, UN Doc. A/HRC/12/48

593. Even if the Israeli Government's position regarding the position of Palestinian armed groups is taken at face value, the Mission concludes that, given the evident threat of substantial damage to several hundred civilian lives and to civilian property in using white

---

[17]   www.icty.org/x/file/Press/nato061300.pdf.

phosphorous in that particular line of fire, the advantage gained from using white phosphorous to screen Israeli armed forces' tanks from anti-tank fire from armed opposition groups could not be deemed proportionate. ...

703. Whatever the truth, the Mission is of the view that the deployment of at least four mortarshells to attempt to kill a small number of specified individuals in a setting where large numbers of civilians were going about their daily business and 1,368 people were sheltering nearby cannot meet the test of what a reasonable commander would have determined to be an acceptable loss of civilian life for the military advantage sought.

7.5.3.4 ICTY, *Prosecutor* v. *Gotovina et al.*, (Judgment), Case No. IT-06-90-T, Trial Chamber I (15 April 2011)

Note: *The facts of this case are outlined in Chapter 1, Section 1.4.5. On the issue of proportionality in respect of the targeting of Martić, a legitimate military objective, the ICTY commented in the following terms:*

1910. ... The Trial Chamber has found above that firing at Martić's apartment could disrupt his ability to move, communicate, and command and so offered a definite military advantage. ... The Trial Chamber considers that Martić's apartment was located in an otherwise civilian apartment building and that both the apartment and the area ... were in otherwise predominantly civilian residential areas. ... At the times of firing, namely between 7:30 and 8 a.m. and in the evening on 4 August 1995, civilians could have reasonably been expected to be present on the streets of Knin near Martić's apartment and in the area marked R on P2337. Firing twelve shells of 130 millimetres at Martić's apartment and an unknown number of shells of the same calibre at the area marked R on P2337, from a distance of approximately 25 kilometres, created a significant risk of a high number of civilian casualties and injuries, as well as of damage to civilian objects. The Trial Chamber considers that this risk was excessive in relation to the anticipated military advantage of firing at the two locations where the HV believed Martić to have been present. This disproportionate attack shows that the HV paid little or no regard to the risk of civilian casualties and injuries and damage to civilian objects when firing artillery at a military target on at least three occasions on 4 August 1995.

7.5.3.5 US, Department of Defense, *Law of War Manual*, Office of General Counsel (June 2015, Updated 2016)

5.12.3 *Harm to Certain Categories of Persons and Objects That is Understood Not to Prohibit Attacks Under the Proportionality Rule.* Harm to the following categories of persons and objects would be understood not to prohibit attacks under the proportionality rule: (1) military objectives; (2) certain categories of individuals who may be employed in or on military objectives; and (3) human shields.

5.12.4 *"Excessive".* Under the proportionality rule, the potential attack against the military objective is prohibited only when the expected incidental harm is excessive compared to the military advantage to be gained. The weighing or comparison between the expected incidental harm and the expected military advantage does not necessarily lend itself to empirical analyses. ... In less clear-cut cases, the question of whether the expected incidental harm is excessive may be a highly open-ended legal inquiry, and the answer may be subjective and imprecise.

5.12.5 *"Concrete and Direct Military Advantage Expected to Be Gained"*. The expected military advantage gained from attacking a particular military objective must be "concrete and direct." ...

Military advantage may involve a variety of considerations, including: (1) denying the enemy the ability to benefit from the object's effective contribution to its military action (*e.g.*, using this object in its military operations); (2) improving the security of the attacking force; and (3) diverting the enemy's resources and attention.

7.5.4 Precautions

7.5.4.1 ICRC, *Draft Rules for the Limitation of the Dangers Incurred by the Civilian Population in Time of War* (1956)[18]

Art. 9. All possible precautions shall be taken, both in the choice of the weapons and methods to be used, and in the carrying out of an attack, to ensure that no losses or damage are caused to the civilian population in the vicinity of the objective, or to its dwellings, or that such losses or damage are at least reduced to a minimum. In particular, in towns and other places with a large civilian population, which are not in the vicinity of military or naval operations, the attack shall be conducted with the greatest degree of precision. It must not cause losses or destruction beyond the immediate surroundings of the objective attacked. The person responsible for carrying out the attack must abandon or break off the operation if he perceives that the conditions set forth above cannot be respected.

7.5.4.2 *Final Report to the Prosecutor by the Committee Established to Review the NATO Bombing Campaign Against the Federal Republic of Yugoslavia* (1999)[19]

77. ... Although NATO alleged that it made "every possible effort to avoid civilian casualties and collateral damage" ..., some doubts have been expressed as to the specificity of the warning given to civilians by NATO of its intended strike, and whether the notice would have constituted "effective warning ... of attacks which may affect the civilian population, unless circumstances do not permit" as required by Article 57(2) of Additional Protocol I. ... Although knowledge on the part of Yugoslav officials of the impending attack would not divest NATO of its obligation to forewarn civilians under Article 57(2), it may nevertheless imply that the Yugoslav authorities may be partially responsible for the civilian casualties resulting from the attack and may suggest that the advance notice given by NATO may have in fact been sufficient under the circumstances.

---

[18] https://ihl-databases.icrc.org/ihl/INTRO/420?OpenDocument.
[19] www.icty.org/x/file/Press/nato061300.pdf.

7.5.4.3 UK, British Ministry of Defence, *The Joint Service Manual of the Law of Armed Conflict*, (Joint Service Publication 383, 2004 Edition)

Target identification

5.32.2 There is a legal obligation to do everything feasible to verify that the proposed target is not protected from attack and that it is a military objective. . . . Any commander selecting a target will have to pay regard to some or all of the following factors before he makes up his mind to attack it:

a. whether he can personally verify the target;
b. instructions from higher authority about objects which are not to be targeted;
c. intelligence reports, aerial or satellite reconnaissance pictures, and any other information in his possession about the nature of the proposed target;
d. any rules of engagement imposed by higher authority under which he is required to operate;
e. the risks to his own forces necessitated by target verification.

Target lists

5.32.3 It is important that target lists are constantly reviewed in the light of fresh information and changing circumstances. . . .

5.32.5 *Factors to be considered*

In considering the means or methods of attack to be used, a commander should have regard to the following factors:

a. the importance of the target and the urgency of the situation;
b. intelligence about the proposed target—what it is being, or will be, used for and when;
c. the characteristics of the target itself, for example, whether it houses dangerous forces;
d. what weapons are available, their range, accuracy, and radius of effect;
e. conditions affecting the accuracy of targeting, such as terrain, weather, and time of day;
f. factors affecting incidental loss or damage, such as the proximity of civilians or civilian objects in the vicinity of the target or other protected objects or zones and whether they are inhabited, or the possible release of hazardous substances as a result of the attack;
g. the risks to his own troops of the various options open to him.

Timing

5.32.6 The timing of an attack can be important. If it is known, for example, that a bridge is heavily used by civilians during the day but hardly at all at night, a night-time attack would reduce the risk of civilian casualties.

Cancelling, suspending, or re-planning attacks

5.32.7 There is the duty to cancel or suspend attacks if the incidental damage may be expected to be disproportionate to the military advantage anticipated. . . .

Warnings

5.32.8 There is a duty to give advance warning of an attack that 'may' affect the civilian population, unless circumstances do not permit. . . . The object of warnings is to enable civilians to take shelter or leave the area and to enable the civil defence authorities to take appropriate measures. To be effective the warning must be in time and sufficiently specific and comprehensible to enable them to do this. Warnings can be given by radio and television broadcasts as well as by dropping or distributing leaflets. They can also be given by word of mouth in the case, for example, of resistance forces operating in territory which is controlled by enemy troops. Warnings are not required if circumstances do not permit.

7.5.4.4 Israel, *The Operation in Gaza 27 December 2008–18 January 2009: Factual and Legal Aspects* (July 2009)[20]

138. During the Gaza Operation, the IDF took precautions that were consistent with the safeguards required by law or suggested by the practice of other countries. ..., the IDF not only implemented a range of precautions related to targeting and munitions, but also used an extensive system of graduated warnings to civilians, including both general advance warnings through media broadcasts and widespread leafleting, regional warnings to alert civilians to leave specific areas before IDF operations commenced, and specific warnings to civilians in or near military targets, through telephone calls and warning shots with light weapons. ...

139. The parties in control of the territory where the hostilities take place also have obligations under the Law of Armed Conflict to minimise civilian harm, including with regard to their own population. ... This means they should "*avoid locating* military objectives within or near densely populated areas" and in anticipation of hostilities, they must "*endeavour to remove* the civilian population, individual civilians and civilian objects under their control from the vicinity of military objectives". To do the opposite – to place weapons systems in or near apartment buildings, schools, mosques or medical facilities, or to encourage civilians to gather in areas that are likely military targets – violates the Law of Armed Conflict, because such tactics inevitably increase civilian casualties beyond what otherwise might occur in connection with an attack on a legitimate military target.

7.5.4.5 Human Rights Council, *Report of the United Nations Fact-Finding Mission on the Gaza Conflict* (25 September 2009), 12th Session, UN Doc. A/HRC/12/48

530. Article 57 (2) (c) requires the warning to be effective. The Mission understands by this that it must reach those who are likely to be in danger from the planned attack, it must give them sufficient time to react to the warning, it must clearly explain what they should do to avoid harm and it must be a credible warning. The warning also has to be clear so that the civilians are not in doubt that it is indeed addressed to them. As far as possible, warnings should state the location to be affected and where the civilians should seek safety. A credible warning means that civilians should be in no doubt that it is intended to be acted upon, as a false alarm of hoax may undermine future warnings, putting civilians at risk. ...

594. Having been fully alerted not to the risks but to the actual consequences of the course of action, Israeli armed forces continued with precisely the same conduct as a result of which further shells hit the compound. ...

---

[20] www.mfa.gov.il/mfa/foreignpolicy/terrorism/palestinian/pages/operation_in_gaza-factual_and_legal_aspects.aspx.

595. The Mission, therefore, concludes on the basis of the information it received and in the absence of any credible refuting evidence that Israeli armed forces violated the customary international law requirement to take all feasible precautions in the choice of means and method of attack with a view to avoiding and in any event minimizing incidental loss of civilian life, injury to civilians and damage to civilian objects as reflected in article 57 (2) (a) (ii) of Additional Protocol I to the Geneva Conventions.

7.5.4.6 Georgia, *Independent International Fact-Finding Mission on the Conflict in Georgia* Report Volume II (September 2009) pp. 347–50

While the identification of legitimate military targets and the efforts made by the Georgian forces to minimise those located in the city or near populated areas seem to meet the requirements of IHL, some issues remain: one concerns the choice of artillery for conducting the attacks; another concerns the list of targets "identified during the hostilities," for example during the ground offensive. Most important are the issue of the intelligence used to select targets and the question of the presence of the civilian population in Tskhinvali at the time of the offensive. . . .

Russia described as follows the precautions its forces took in the course of the conflict:

"*. . . During the active phase of the operation the Russian command undertook a number of effective measures aimed at minimising the damage for the civilian population and to the property of local citizens. Artillery fire and air strikes were planned and carried out in areas situated at a considerable distance from local communities against clearly identified targets only. Key artillery fire missions were completed against well-observed targets – in the process, commanders of combined arms units adjusted artillery fire through spotters and artillery reconnaissance units. Local communities and civilian facilities were not fired upon. All fire would cease once Georgian units withdrew from their positions. The Russian air component acting in support of the army units on the ground delivered a number of strikes against pockets of Georgian forces, firing emplacements and columns of military equipment en route. The Russian air component did not fly any missions in areas adjacent to or bordering on residential communities. All kill fire was monitored. As a result of these measures civilian casualties were minimised.*"

While the above description shows efforts to minimise civilian casualties and damage to civilian objects, it also presents the Russian forces as having systematically proceeded with the appropriate precautions. The evidenced use in populated areas by Russia of cluster munitions, a weapon which, by virtue of its wide area coverage and its unexploded duds, demonstrates that the obligation to take all feasible precautions in the choice of means of warfare was not systematically respected. . . .

During the offensive on Tskhinvali and other villages in South Ossetia, Georgian forces failed to take the precautions required under IHL. In several cases the Russian forces also failed to comply with their obligations under IHL with regard to precautions before attacks.[21]

---

[21] Bold in original.

7.5.4.7 Germany, Federal Ministry of Defence, *Law of Armed Conflict – Manual – Joint Service Regulation (ZDv) 15/2* (May 2013)

416. With respect to attacks, every responsible military commander must take the following **precautions in attack** prior to engaging an objective:

- do everything feasible to verify on the basis of all information available at the time that the objective to be attacked is a military objective and that the attack is not prohibited by international law;
- choose the means and methods of attack with a view to avoiding, and in any event minimising, civilian collateral damage;
- refrain from launching an attack that may be expected to cause civilian collateral damage that would be excessive in relation to the concrete and direct military advantage anticipated;
- give the civilian population advance **warning** of attacks that may affect it, unless circumstances do not permit;
- when a choice is possible between several military objectives of equal importance, engage the objective an attack on which may be expected to cause the least collateral damage).

7.5.4.8 US, Department of Defense, *Law of War Manual*, Office of General Counsel (June 2015, Updated 2016)

5.11 FEASIBLE PRECAUTIONS IN CONDUCTING ATTACKS TO REDUCE THE RISK OF HARM TO PROTECTED PERSONS AND OBJECTS

Combatants must take feasible precautions in conducting attacks to reduce the risk of harm to civilians and other protected persons and objects. . . . Feasible precautions in conducting attacks may include the following:

5.11.1 *Effective Advance Warning Before an Attack That May Affect the Civilian Population.*

> 5.11.1.1 *Effective Advance Warning.* There is no set form for warnings. Warnings may be general, communicated to the national leadership of the enemy State, or delivered to the civilian population through military information support operations (such as broadcast or leaflets) advising the civilian population of risk of injury if they remain near military objectives. Giving the specific time and place of an attack is not required. . . .

> 5.11.1.3 *Unless Circumstances Do Not Permit.* These circumstances include legitimate military reasons, such as exploiting the element of surprise in order to provide for mission accomplishment and preserving the security of the attacking force.

5.11.2 *Adjusting the Timing of the Attack.* Adjusting the timing of an attack may reduce the risk of incidental harm. . . .

5.11.3 *Selecting Weapons (Weaponeering).* Depending on the circumstances, the use of certain weapons rather than others may lower the risk of incidental harm, while offering the same or superior military advantage in neutralizing or destroying a military objective.

5.11.4 *Identifying Zones in Which Military Objectives Are More Likely to Be Present or Civilians Are Likely to Be Absent.*

7.6 CYBER WARFARE

7.6.1 M.N. Schmitt (ed.), *Tallinn Manual on the International Law Applicable to Cyber Warfare* (CUP 2013), pp. 108, 124, 125, 127, 134 and 159

RULE 30 – Definition of cyber attack

A cyber attack is a cyber operation, whether offensive or defensive, that is reasonably expected to cause injury or death to persons or damage or destruction to objects.

...

10. Within the International Group of Experts, there was extensive discussion about whether interference by cyber means with the functionality of an object constitutes damage or destruction for the purposes of this Rule. Although some Experts were of the opinion that it does not, the majority of them are of the view that interference with functionality qualifies as damage if restoration of functionality requires replacement of physical components. ...

RULE 37 – Prohibition on Attacking Civilian Objects

Civilian objects shall not be made the object of cyber attacks. Computers, computer networks, and cyber infrastructure may be made the object of attack if they are military objectives

...

RULE 38 – Civilian Objects and Military Objectives

...

5. The majority of the International Group of Experts agreed that the law of armed conflict notion of object should not be interpreted as including data. Data is intangible and therefore neither falls within the "ordinary meaning" of the term object ...

RULE 39 – Objects Used for Civilian and Military Purposes

An object used for both civilian and military purposes—including computers, computer networks, and cyber infrastructure—is a military objective.

RULE 51 – Proportionality

A cyber attack that may be expected to cause incidental loss of civilian life, injury to civilians, damage to civilian objects, or a combination thereof, which would be excessive in relation to the concrete and direct military advantage anticipated is prohibited.

COMMENTARY

1. IHL rules on means and methods of warfare derive from the principles of humanity and military necessity and the associated principle of distinction.[22] With regard to weapons, it is

---

[22]   See also Chapters 2 and 4.

either their inherent characteristics or their use that may fall foul of these rules. In this respect, it should be noted that there are a number of treaties that either ban certain weapons or restrict their use.[23]

2. Weapons are prohibited if they cause superfluous injury or unnecessary suffering, that is, injury or suffering that serves no military purpose or is excessive compared to the military advantage sought.[24] That said, how to quantify the suffering or injury against the military advantage is a difficult exercise because of the dissimilar values they represent. Other suggested factors to be taken into account include mortality rates, the type of wounds, whether the weapon makes death inevitable or whether it inflicts serious or permanent disability.

3. A weapon is inherently indiscriminate if (i) it cannot be directed against a specific target and (ii) its effects cannot be controlled. Conversely, a discriminate weapon may be used for an indiscriminate attack. Such use is equally prohibited because it falls foul of the principle of distinction.[25] In the *Gotovina* case, the Trial Chamber's finding that artillery weapons with a 200-metre margin of error were discriminate whereas those beyond a 200-metre radius were indiscriminate was overturned by the Appeal Chamber as not sufficiently reasoned. The decision attracted strong criticisms.[26]

4. Cluster munitions are considered to be inherently indiscriminate. According to the Convention on Cluster Munitions, States parties should not use cluster munitions; develop, produce, otherwise acquire, stockpile, retain or transfer to anyone, directly or indirectly, cluster munitions; or assist, encourage or induce anyone to engage in any activity prohibited under the Convention.[27] A number of important States are not parties to the Convention and consider cluster munitions to be lawful if kept within the bounds of IHL.

5. Nuclear weapons are not prohibited per se. A number of States parties to API declared that the Protocol does not apply to nuclear weapons. That does not mean, however, that IHL principles and related customary norms do not apply either. Whether nuclear weapons are indiscriminate depends on whether their effects can be controlled, which is a contextual question. Also, whether the incidental effects of the use of nuclear weapons on civilians and civilian objects are proportionate varies and depends on the circumstances. That said, the use of nuclear weapons might cause superfluous injury and unnecessary suffering and long-term harm to the environment.

6. Legal review of means and methods of warfare is another way of ensuring their compliance with IHL. Regarding weapons, reviews cover the study, development,

---

[23] See, for example, the Convention on the Prohibition of the Development, Production and Stockpiling of Bacteriological (Biological) and Toxin Weapons and on their Destruction (adopted 10 April 1972, entered into force 26 March 1975) 1015 UNTS 163; Convention on Prohibitions or Restrictions on the Use of Certain Conventional Weapons which may be deemed to be Excessively Injurious or to have Indiscriminate Effects (with Protocols I, II, III, IV, and V) (adopted 10 October 1980, entered into force 2 December 1983) 1342 UNTS 137; Convention on the prohibition of the development, production, stockpiling and use of chemical weapons and on their destruction (adopted 3 September 1992, entered into force 29 April 1997) 1974 UNTS 45; Convention on the Prohibition of the Use, Stockpiling, Production and Transfer of Anti-Personnel Mines and on their Destruction (adopted 18 September 1997, entered into force 1 March 1999) 2056 UNTS 211.

[24] Per ICJ, *Legality of the Threat or Use of Nuclear Weapons* (Advisory Opinion) [1996] I.C.J. Rep. 226.

[25] For indiscriminate attacks on civilians see Chapter 5 Section 5.1.2.

[26] Dissenting Opinion of Judge Fausto Pocar, *Prosecutor v. Gotovina et al.*, (Judgment), ICTY Case No. T-06-90.

[27] Art. 1(1) Convention on Cluster Munitions (adopted 30 May 2008, entered into force 1 August 2010) 2688 UNTS 39.

acquisition or adoption of weapons. Reviews take into consideration the characteristics of the weapon, its actual or expected use as well as its foreseeable effects on combatants and civilians. The aim of the review is to determine the accuracy and reliability of the weapon, whether its effects can be controlled and whether its use can be controlled in time and space. Legal reviews are conducted against existing treaty law, customary international law, and international law in general, including IHRL and the IHL principles on means and methods of warfare. Legal reviews are conducted at the national level but not all States have established formal procedures to perform such reviews. That said, in principle, all States need to conduct reviews when they are producing, buying or modifying weapons but certain States conduct reviews only when there is doubt.

7. Legal reviews give rise to questions concerning the definition of 'weapon' for review purposes; whether the review is conducted against existing law or also against soft law; the type of evidence and expertise (military, technical, health, environmental) that need to be taken into consideration; the implications of new evidence on reviews; whether information can be shared;[28] whether the conclusions should be made public; the binding or non-binding character of findings and recommendations; the implications of divergent findings by different stakeholders (for example by the manufacturing and purchasing States). The underlying question is of course how law can keep pace with evolving technologies.

8. Related to legal review is the review of weapons for law enforcement purposes to the extent that the military may be engaged in law enforcement operations and, conversely, law enforcement agents may use force during hostilities.[29] IHRL is critical in this context and, in particular, the right to life, the freedom from torture, inhumane and degrading treatment, the right to health, the right to assembly, and the freedom of expression. However, the different legal frameworks that apply may lead to different conclusions. For instance, whereas the use of riot-control agents in law enforcement operations is not prohibited, their use as a method of warfare is prohibited because of their indiscriminate effects.[30] The blurring between peace and war may exacerbate these problems.

9. Automated and autonomous weapons systems describe systems that possess different degrees of autonomy: the former are pre-programmed to respond to certain conditions whereas the latter can select and engage targets independently. Automated and autonomous weapons systems give rise to many difficult legal and ethical questions. For example, to what extent can they process information in order to comply with the IHL principles of distinction, proportionality and precautions? Can they suspend or abort an attack if new information comes to light? Other questions relate to the expertise needed to review and

---

[28] See Art. 84, API.
[29] See Chapter 3. See Basic Principles on the Use of Force and Firearms by Law Enforcement Officials UN Doc. A/CONF.144/28/Rev.1 (1990) Principle 3: 'The development and deployment of non-lethal incapacitating weapons should be carefully evaluated in order to minimize the risk of endangering uninvolved persons, and the use of such weapons should be carefully controlled.' Also see *Study on the situation of trade in and production of equipment which is specifically designed to inflict torture or other cruel, inhuman or degrading treatment, its origin, destination and forms*, submitted by Theo van Boven, Special Rapporteur on torture, pursuant to resolution 2002/38 of the Commission on Human Rights, UN Doc. E/CN.4/2003/69, 13 January 2003 and UN General Assembly Resolution 66/150 (19 December 2011) A/RES/66/150 (1990).
[30] *Contra* UK *Law of War Manual* (June 2015, Updated 2016), para. 6.8.3.

handle such weapons systems and whether the review should be performed during the development of such a system or after its production. If review should take place during development, can their capabilities and performance be fully assessed *a priori*? In any case, to the extent that such weapons systems are based on technology, a critical question is how accurately their capabilities can be assessed in light of new technological developments that may affect their reliability and predictability. It should be noted, however, that evolving technology might also make automated or autonomous weapons systems IHL compliant. Other questions concern the propriety of delegating decision making to non-humans, and who bears responsibility if violations of IHL are committed.

10. The law of targeting contains rules on who or what can be attacked in order to attain the military objectives set out by a party to the armed conflict. The targeting process involves the selection of targets and their prioritisation as well as the planning and execution of the operation. Planning and execution involve decisions on weapons, methods, proportionality, precautions and post-attack assessment.[31] It is evident that targeting involves legal, strategic, operational and tactical considerations and is intelligence dependent. When targeting is planned in advance, it is called deliberate targeting. When targeting is a reaction to an immediate need or to a target that is on the move, it is called dynamic targeting.

11. According to Art. 52(2) API, attacks are limited to military objectives. An object becomes a military objective if it (i) makes an effective contribution to military action by nature, location, use or purpose and (ii) its destruction, capture or neutralisation offers a definite military advantage. Both tests need to be satisfied, but there are questions as to whether they should be satisfied simultaneously. This is particularly critical in the context of cyber attacks where the military advantage may appear later. If the two tests do not need to be satisfied simultaneously, the meaning of military objectives expands. That said, there are certain objects that are specifically protected such as cultural objects and property[32] or medical facilities.[33] Although the law speaks of objects, persons, such as combatants (armed forces or forces of armed groups) as well as civilians directly participating in hostilities, are also lawful targets.[34]

12. With regard to the first prong of the test, US doctrine includes war-fighting as well as war-sustaining capabilities, thus justifying attacks on economic or political targets. A similar view was held by the Ethiopia-Eritrea Claims Commission (EECC)[35] and coincides with the effects-based operations doctrine. This approach expands the definition of military

---

[31] 'Applying the Law of Targeting to the Modern Battlefield' As Prepared, Jennifer M. O'Connor, New York University School of Law, New York, Nov. 28, 2016 www.defense.gov/Portals/1/Documents/pubs/Applying-the-Law-of-Targeting-to-the-Modern-Battlefield.pdf. See Nicholas Tsagourias, 'Targeting in International Humanitarian Law' Oxford Bibliographies Online www.oxfordbibliographies.com/view/document/obo-9780199796953/obo-9780199796953-0142.xml.

[32] Art. 53, API, Convention for the Protection of Cultural Property in the Event of Armed Conflict and its First Protocol, 1954 and Second Protocol for the Protection of Cultural Property in the Event of Armed Conflict, 1999. www.unesco.org/new/en/culture/themes/armed-conflict-and-heritage/the-hague-convention/text-of-the-convention-and-its-1st-protocol/#hague.

[33] Arts 33 and 34, GCI.

[34] See Chapters 4 and 10.

[35] Ethiopia-Eritrea Claims Commission, Western Front, Chapter 7, Case 7.5.2.3, para. 113, but also see Dissenting Opinion Houtte, paras 8, 10.

objectives and seems not to be in sync with accepted interpretations of what is 'military action', in particular when the contribution of such objects to military action is only indirect. As to whether the contribution is effective, this is an objective rather than a subjective test, but a direct link between the object and the military action should be established. With regard to the second prong of the test, the military advantage should be definite, thus excluding speculative or hypothetical advantages, but it is a subjective rather than an objective test. Moreover, the anticipated military advantage is assessed against the attack as a whole and not against individual acts which are part of an attack. Whether the military advantage should be interpreted in accordance with the interpretation of military action and include political or economic determinants as the EECC opined, is debated. Finally, to the extent that the military advantage is assessed in the circumstances prevailing at the time, its definition is quite flexible.

13. Cyber war poses particular challenges to targeting. Are cyber attacks that cause loss of system functionality without causing external physical effects attacks for targeting purposes? Is replacement of parts necessary in order to characterise them as attacks?[36] In our view, loss of functionality can be an attack similar to 'neutralisation'.

14. The determination of whether cyber objects are military objectives by nature, location, use or purpose can cause certain difficulties. Although military cyber infrastructure can be a military objective because of its nature, is the Internet a military objective? If the answer is in the affirmative, is it because of location and, if it is, does this require some geographical or other connection to the military action? Is the Internet a military objective because of use? Are data military objectives because of their location or use? This leads to another question which is whether data as such are objects and whether virtual attacks on data, which destroy, capture or neutralise them are attacks. If objects are tangible things[37] that is, material ones, then data are not objects[38] but if an object is defined by the way it can be attacked in the sense of being destroyed, captured or neutralised as Art. 52(2), API requires, then data constitute objects. If data are not objects and consequently military objectives, one may consider as military objectives those objects or persons that are actually affected by the interference with data. This leads to another question, namely whether it is the direct or also the indirect effects of a cyber attack that should be taken into account and, in the latter case, whether intention and causation play any role.

15. The assessment of the proportionality of any incidental injury or collateral damage is a rather difficult exercise.[39] First, the law speaks of 'expected' harm, which is 'excessive' in relation to 'anticipated' military advantage. One approach applies a completely subjective test based on the good-faith assessment of the commander; another approach adopts an objective test of 'a reasonable commander'; whereas a third employs a combination of the two.[40] In any case, assessments of proportionality are prospective and depend on

---

[36]   See M.N. Schmitt (ed.), *Tallinn Manual on the International Law Applicable to Cyber Warfare* (CUP, 2013), Rule 30 and its commentary.
[37]   Y. Sandoz, C. Swinarski and B. Zimmermann (eds), *Commentary on the Additional Protocols of 8 June 1977 to the Geneva Conventions of 12 August 1949* (Martinus Nijhoff, 1987) pp. 633–34.
[38]   See Tallinn Manual Rule 38 and its Commentary.
[39]   See also Chapter 2.
[40]   I. Henderson, *The Contemporary Law of Targeting: Military Objectives, Proportionality and Precautions in Attack under Additional Protocol I* (Martinus Nijhoff, 2009), p. 223.

information and intelligence at the time the decision is made. Second, the comparison is between the harm to civilians and the anticipated concrete and direct military advantage which are dissimilar values. Third, is the anticipated concrete and direct advantage the reasonably foreseeable advantage that is closely linked to the attack? If that is the case, it will be difficult to apply this formulation to cyber attacks where the effects may appear in the distant future or when their effects are secondary or tertiary.[41] Fourth, is the protection of the attacking force included in the assessment of direct and concrete advantage as indeed certain States such as the United States claim? If that is the case, cyber attacks satisfy this requirement easily. Fifth, if cyber weapons may legitimise attacks on targets, which, if carried out by kinetic weapons, would be excessive, does this expand the scope of military objectives in cyber war? Sixth, since cyber attacks are technologically dependent, what technical knowledge and information should the person that makes the decision possess?

16. The obligation to take precautions in attack as well as against the effects of an attack[42] is an obligation of conduct and not of result. Whether precautions after the attack are also needed, as the EECC opined, is debated. With regard to warnings prior to an attack, it all depends on feasibility and functionality. The protection of the attacking force is a relevant consideration.

17. Precautions in cyber war give rise to questions concerning the extent and level of technical expertise of those making decisions; the scope of military–civilian cooperation and the obligations of the private sector to the extent that large portions of the cyber infrastructure are privately owned or controlled. Whether military cyber infrastructure can be segregated from civilian infrastructure is another critical issue.

18. The treatment of dual-use objects, that is, objects used or potentially used for civilian and military purposes, is critical for targeting purposes. Dual-use objects are, for example, bridges or communications systems whereas most cyber infrastructure such as networks is dual use. Being dual use does not make such objects immune from attack if the requirements of Art. 52(2) API are satisfied, with incidental effects being taken into account in the proportionality calculus. This would make, for example, the Internet as the network of networks a military objective but whether its destruction or neutralisation will offer any military advantage can be debated if, for example, traffic can be automatically diverted or when recovery from the attack is swift. Whether the proportionality assessment should also take into consideration the long-term effects of destroying a dual-use object is debated.

19. As was commented in Chapters 2 and 4, modern types of warfare such as asymmetric war or hybrid warfare pose challenges to existing IHL principles and rules. Hybrid warfare, as was explained in Chapter 2, refers to the integrated use of military and non-military means and methods in an overt or covert manner to achieve certain strategic aims.[43] It thus blurs the distinction between the law of peace and the law of war and exploits legal thresholds, gaps or normative disagreements. A tool of hybrid war is lawfare. Lawfare

---

[41]   M.N. Schmitt (ed.), *Tallinn Manual on the International Law Applicable to Cyber Warfare* (CUP, 2013), Rule 51.
[42]   Arts 57 and 58, API.
[43]   F.G. Hoffman, 'Hybrid Warfare and Challenges' (2009) 52 *Joint Forces Quarterly* 97.

can be described as the strategy of using – or misusing – law to achieve an objective[44] by exploiting any legal gaps and ambiguities that exist or by deliberately inducing violations of IHL. It has been claimed that hybrid war is not a new phenomenon and that IHL norms and principles can regulate hybrid wars. However, it must be recognised that hybrid war exploits not only the lack of rules, but also bright-line rules and impinges on the political neutrality of the law, which is important for its effectiveness. As was said in Chapter 2, the blurring of the physical and normative distinctions upon which IHL is based and the loss of neutrality of the law inevitably affect the application and effectiveness of IHL and give rise to calls for its adaptation to the new environment.

[44] Charles J. Dunlap Jr, 'Lawfare Today: A Perspective' (Winter 2008) *Yale J. I. Affairs* 146; O. Kittrie, *Lawfare: Law as a Weapon of War* (OUP, 2015).

8

Law of Neutrality

INTRODUCTION

In IHL, neutrality describes the position taken by States to abstain from participating in an armed conflict. Neutrality entails certain duties: the duty not to participate in an armed conflict; the duty of impartiality vis-à-vis belligerents; and the duty to resist violations of neutrality (in sum: the duties of abstention, impartiality and prevention). Neutrality also gives rise to rights, with the main one being the inviolability of the neutral's territory. If troops belonging to the belligerents are found on the territory of a neutral State they should be interned. If a neutral State breaches one of its duties it forfeits its rights as neutral and the belligerents may take measures against that State. Which acts cause the loss of neutrality and whether the State in this case becomes a belligerent are subject to debate. The changing nature of armed conflict, in particular cyber war, challenges the traditional concept of neutrality as does the UN collective security system and diverse military alliances.

Resources: Arts 1–17, HCV; Arts 6–24, Hague Convention XIII (HCXIII); Arts 4, 19, 22, 23, 47, GCI; Art. 5, GCII; Arts 4, 109–111, GCIII; Art. 4, GCIV; Arts 2, 19, 47, API; Arts 2(5), 39–42, 103, UN Charter

Cases and Materials

8.1 Definition of Neutrality; Rights and Duties of Neutrals
8.2 Neutrality and Sea Warfare
8.3 Neutrality and Air Warfare
8.4 Neutrality and Cyber Warfare
Commentary

8.1 DEFINITION OF NEUTRALITY; RIGHTS AND DUTIES OF NEUTRALS

8.1.1 US Supreme Court, *The Santissima Trinidad*, 20 U.S. 283 (1822), pp. 337–8

Note: *The case arises in the context of the civil war between Spain and her colonies. The United States recognised them as belligerents. The Neutrality Act of 1794 provided for the nation's*

impartiality and prohibited its citizens from assisting the belligerents but US citizens violated the
Act. In 1817, the Consul of Spain filed a libel claim in the District Court of Virginia in relation to
the seizure of goods from the ship The Santissima Trinidad. *As to the principle of neutrality and*
the duties incumbent on a neutral State, the US Supreme Court said as follows:

The government of the United States has recognized the existence of a civil war between
Spain and her colonies, and has avowed a determination to remain neutral between the
parties, and to allow to each the same rights of asylum and hospitality and intercourse.
Each party is therefore deemed by us a belligerent nation, having, so far as concerns us, the
sovereign rights of war, and entitled to be respected in the exercise of those rights. We
cannot interfere to the prejudice of either belligerent without making ourselves a party to
the contest, and departing from the posture of neutrality. All captures made by each must
be considered as having the same validity, and all the immunities which may be claimed
by public ships in our ports under the law of nations must be considered as equally the
right of each, and as such must be recognized by our courts of justice, until Congress shall
prescribe a different rule. This is the doctrine heretofore asserted by this Court, and we see
no reason to depart from it.

8.1.2 US Supreme Court, *Prize Cases*, 67 U.S. 635 (1862), pp. 669–70

Note: *The* Prize Cases *arose in the context of the American Civil War when President Abraham*
Lincoln, in order to avoid a formal declaration of war against the Confederate States, which he
thought would be tantamount to recognising the legitimacy of the Confederacy as a nation,
ordered the blockade of southern ports and the seizure of many ships. Affirming the prerequisites
for a declaration of neutrality, the US Supreme Court said:

It is not necessary that the independence of the revolted province or State be acknowledged
in order to constitute it a party belligerent in a war according to the law of nations. Foreign
nations acknowledge it as war by a declaration of neutrality. The condition of neutrality
cannot exist unless there be two belligerent parties. ...

As soon as the news of the attack on Fort Sumter, ... the Queen of England issued her
proclamation of neutrality, "recognizing hostilities as existing between the Government of
the United States of American and certain States styling themselves the Confederate States
of America."

This was immediately followed by similar declarations or silent acquiescence by other
nations.

After such an official recognition by the sovereign, a citizen of a foreign State is estopped
to deny the existence of a war with all its consequences as regards neutrals.

8.1.3 *Alabama Claims of the United States of America Against Great*
Britain: Award Rendered on 14 September 1872 by the Tribunal
of Arbitration Established by Article I of the Treaty of Washington
of 8 May 1871, (1871) XXIX RIAA 125–34, 130

Note: *The* Alabama Claims *were a series of demands for damages brought against the United*
Kingdom by the United States as a result of events during the American Civil War when ships

including the Confederate cruiser Alabama, *which was built in England, was used to capture and sink Union ships. Britain was accused of violating neutrality. As to the duties of neutral States, the Arbitration Tribunal said:*

And whereas, with respect to the vessel called the Alabama, it clearly results from all the facts relative to the construction of the ship at first designated by the number "290" in the port of Liverpool, and its equipment and armament ..., that the British government failed to use due diligence in the performance of its neutral obligations; and especially that it omitted, notwithstanding the warnings and official representations made by the diplomatic agents of the United States during the construction of the said number "290," to take in due time any effective measures of prevention, and that those orders which it did give at last, for the detention of the vessel, were issued so late that their execution was not practicable ...

8.1.4 The Netherlands, *Bouman* v. *The State of the Netherlands*, District Court of The Hague, First Chamber (1921) 1 ILR 489

Note: *The case concerned the sequestration of a vessel by the Dutch authorities on crossing the frontier with the Netherlands on suspicion that it was acquired as a consequence of an act of war.*

489 ... The status of neutrality obliges a Government strictly to abstain from any act favouring either of the belligerents.

8.1.5 International Military Tribunal, *The Trial of German Major War Criminals, Proceedings of the International Military Tribunal Sitting at Nuremberg, Germany* (Part 22, Judgment of 1 October 1946), p. 434

Note: *The background to the Nuremberg Trials is well known and concerns the trial of major civilian and military leaders of the Nazi regime. The accused were indicted with war crimes and crimes against humanity. The trials of individual military leaders are considered in Chapter 2, Sections 2.2.3 and 2.2.4. On the issue of the reciprocal obligations of the law of neutrality, the Tribunal referred to the following example:*

On 2nd September, 1939, after the outbreak of war with Poland, Germany sent a solemn assurance to Norway in these terms:

"The German Reich Government is determined, in view of the friendly relations which exist between Norway and Germany, under no circumstance to prejudice the inviolability and integrity of Norway, and to respect the territory of the Norwegian State. In making this declaration the Reich Government naturally expects, on its side, that Norway will observe an unimpeachable neutrality towards the Reich and will not tolerate any breaches of Norwegian neutrality by any third party which might occur. Should the attitude of the Royal Norwegian Government differ from this so that any such breach of neutrality by a third party occurs, the Reich Government would then obviously be compelled to safeguard the interests of the Reich in such a way as the resulting situation might dictate."

8.1.6 Egypt, *The Fjeld*, Prize Court of Alexandria (1950) 17 ILR 345, 349

Note: *The case concerned the seizure of cargo from a ship chartered by a Greek company, the legality of which depended on whether a state of war existed between Egypt and Israel in 1948.*

... It is established that the Palestinian conflict constitutes from the legal point of view, a true war with international aspects. This imposes upon neutrals the duties resulting from neutrality and requires them to submit to the rights of the belligerents, whether or not such neutrals have officially proclaimed their neutrality, for neutrality is only one of the consequences of a state of war, and subjects neutrals, by reason only of their knowledge of such a state, to the action of the belligerents.

8.1.7 US, *Amerada Hess Shipping Corp.* v. *Argentine Republic*, 830 F.2d 421 (2d Cir., 1987)

Note: *In May 1982 a US oil tanker ship* Hercules *travelled near the South Atlantic where an armed conflict had broken out between the United Kingdom and Argentina: the Falklands War. In order to protect US-interest ships, the US Maritime Administration telexed the United Kingdom and Argentina a list of US vessels that would be crossing the South Atlantic so as to ensure neutral ships were not attacked. On 8 June,* Hercules, *which was nearly 500 miles from the Falkland Islands and in international waters, was attacked by Argentine aircraft. As to the rights of neutral ships on the high seas, the US Court of Appeals, Second Circuit, found as follows:*

12 In short, it is beyond controversy that attacking a neutral ship in international waters, without proper cause for suspicion or investigation, violates international law. Indeed, the relative paucity of cases litigating this customary rule of international law underscores the longstanding nature of this aspect of freedom of the high seas. Where the attacker has refused to compensate the neutral, such action is analogous to piracy, one of the earliest recognized violations of international law. ... Accordingly, we turn to the jurisdictional ramifications of our holding that appellants have stated a claim of a violation of international law.

8.1.8 US, Department of Defense, *Final Report to Congress: Conduct of the Persian Gulf War – The Role of the Law of War* (1992) 31 ILM 615, 626–9

CONDUCT OF NEUTRAL NATIONS

Neutrality normally is based on a nation's proclamation of neutrality or assumption of a neutral posture with respect to a particular conflict. Iran and Jordan each issued proclamations of neutrality during the Persian Gulf crisis and, ... refrained from active participation in the war. Other nations, such as Austria and Switzerland, enjoy relative degrees of international guarantees of their neutrality.

Neutrality in the Persian Gulf War was controlled in part by the 1907 Hague V Convention; but traditional concepts of neutral rights and duties are substantially modified when, as in this case, the United Nations authorizes collective action against an aggressor nation.

It was the US position during the Persian Gulf crisis that, regardless of assertions of neutrality, all nations were obligated to avoid hindrance of Coalition operations undertaken pursuant to, or in conjunction with, UNSC decisions, and to provide whatever assistance possible.

. . .

The declarations of "neutrality" by Jordan and Iran were subordinate to their obligation as UN members to comply with UNSC resolutions. Although Jordan's attitude toward Iraq and the Coalition appeared inconsistent with its UN obligations, mere sympathy for one belligerent does not constitute a violation of traditional neutral duties, nor even a rejection of the obligations imposed by the UNSC resolutions cited. Conduct is the issue.

There were reports that Jordan supplied materials (including munitions) to Iraq during Operations Desert Shield and Desert Storm. Furnishing supplies and munitions to a belligerent traditionally has been regarded as a violation of a neutral's obligations. In this case, it would have been an even more palpable contravention of Jordan's obligations – both because of the request of UNSC Resolution 678 . . . and because [of] the sanctions Resolution 661 . . . .

As the US became aware of specific allegations of Jordanian failure to comply with UNSC sanctions, they were raised with the Government of Jordan. . . . the Government of Jordan acted to stop the actions and reassured the United States those instances had been the result of individual initiative rather than as a result of government policy. Such logistical assistance as Jordan may have provided Iraq did not substantially improve Iraq's ability to conduct operations, nor did it have an appreciable effect on Coalition forces' operational capabilities. . . .

Iran's conduct during Operations Desert Shield and Desert Storm essentially was consistent with that expected of a neutral under traditional principles of international law, including Hague V. Immediately after the Operation Desert Storm air campaign began, many Iraqi civil and military aircraft began fleeing to Iran, presumably to avoid damage or destruction by Coalition air forces. Under Article 11 of Hague V and traditional law of war principles regarding neutral rights and obligations, when belligerent military aircraft land in a nation not party to a conflict, the neutral must intern the aircraft, aircrew, and accompanying military personnel for the duration of the war. . . . With respect to tactical aircraft, however, it appears Iran complied with the traditional obligations of a neutral. . . .

Although military aircraft must gain permission to enter another State's airspace (except in distress), both Switzerland and Austria routinely granted such clearance for US military transport aircraft prior to the Iraqi invasion of Kuwait. . . . Despite initial misgivings, based upon their traditional neutrality, each nation assented. That there was a reluctance to grant permission early in the crisis – that is, when the United States was not involved in the hostilities, and thus not legally a belligerent – demonstrates that the view by these two States of neutrality may be more expansive than the traditional understanding of the role of neutrality in the law of war. . . .

Given their reluctance to permit pre-hostilities overflights, it was natural to expect that Switzerland and Austria would weigh very carefully any requests for overflights once offensive actions began, which each did. In light of the UNSC request that all States support the efforts of those acting to uphold and implement UNSC resolutions, each government decided that overflights by US military transport aircraft would not be inconsistent with its neutral obligations. Accordingly, permission for overflights was granted, easing logistical support for combat operations. ...

On 25 August, the Security Council adopted Resolution 665, which called upon UN members to enforce sanctions by means of a maritime interception operation. This contemplated intercepting so-called "neutral" shipping as well as that of non-neutral nations. These resolutions modified the obligation of neutral powers to remain impartial with regard to Coalition UN members.

The law of war regarding neutrality traditionally permits neutral nations to engage in non-war-related commerce with belligerent nations. During the Persian Gulf crisis, however, the Coalition Maritime Interception Force (MIF) was directed to prevent all goods (except medical supplies and humanitarian foodstuffs expressly authorized for Iraqi import by the UNSC Sanctions Committee) from leaving or entering Iraqi-controlled ports or Iraq, consistent with the relevant UNSC resolutions. The claim of neutral status by Iran and Jordan, or any of the traditional neutral nations, did not adversely affect the conduct of the Coalition's ability to carry out military operations against Iraq.

8.1.9 ICJ, *Legality of the Threat or Use of Nuclear Weapons* (Advisory Opinion) [1996] I.C.J. Rep. 226

Note: *The facts of this case are set out in Chapter 2, Section 2.4.2. Defining the scope of the principle of neutrality, the ICJ said as follows:*

89. The Court finds that as in the case of the principles of humanitarian law applicable in armed conflict, international law leaves no doubt that the principle of neutrality, whatever its content, which is of a fundamental character similar to that of the humanitarian principles and rules, is applicable (subject to the relevant provisions of the United Nations Charter), to all international armed conflict, whatever type of weapons might be used.

8.1.10 Canada, *The Law of Armed Conflict at the Operational and Tactical Levels*, Office of the Judge Advocate General (Joint Doctrine Manual, 13 August 2001)

1303. COMMENCEMENT OF NEUTRAL STATUS

1. Apart from those States, which apply permanently the Law of Neutrality, the neutrality of a nonparticipating state commences with the outbreak of an armed conflict between other States.

2. A neutral state does not need to declare its status formally ...

3. Neutrality can result from the factual behaviour of a state.

SECTION 2 – RIGHTS AND DUTIES ON AND OVER NEUTRAL LAND AND WATER TERRITORY

1304. GENERAL DUTY OF NEUTRAL STATES

1. In general, the territory of a neutral State, including its airspace and territorial waters, are inviolate and must be respected. Belligerents are forbidden from violating or carrying on hostilities in or across this territory.

2. A neutral State may not support any of the parties to the conflict.

3. A neutral state is permitted to resist any attempted violation of its borders by force and such resistance does not make the neutral a party to the conflict. If enemy forces enter neutral such territory and the neutral state is unwilling or unable to intern or expel them, the opposing party is entitled to attack them there, or to demand compensation from the neutral for this breach of neutrality.

1307. TREATMENT OF MEMBERS OF BELLIGERENT ARMED FORCES

1. It is not a violation of neutrality for a neutral state to allow belligerent troops to take refuge in its territory. However, these troops must be interned and prevented from taking any further part in the hostilities. Whether or not the neutral power is a party to the Geneva Convention Relative to the Treatment of Prisoners of War (GIII), it must afford such internees treatment at least up to the standard required by that Convention.

2. Escaped POWs and prisoners brought by forces seeking refuge in neutral territory are to retain their liberty, although the neutral power may assign them a place of residence.

. . .

1309. OBLIGATION TO ACCEPT EXERCISE OF BELLIGERENT RIGHTS

1. It is the duty of a belligerent to respect neutral territory, including its territorial sea and airspace, and its right to continue intercourse with other states, even including the enemy. However, the belligerent has the right to demand that the neutral shall, in addition to its duty to behave with impartiality, recognize the validity of a blockade of the enemy country and to observe any rules relating to contraband which may have been proclaimed.

1313. NATIONALS OF NEUTRAL STATES IN BELLIGERENT TERRITORY

1. Neutrals present in belligerent territory, other than on a temporary or transient basis, may be treated by the adverse party as enemies and be subject to the same restrictions as are enemy nationals. Companies owned by Nationals of neutral states in or operating from enemy territory may be considered as enemies for the purposes of Trading with Enemy legislation restricting trade with enemy states.

2. Nationals of neutral states who remain in the territory of a belligerent are only entitled to treatment as protected persons under the GIV if they are nationals of a state, which is a party to that Convention, so long as that state does not maintain normal diplomatic representation in the territory in question.

. . .

8.1.11 Ireland, *Edward Horgan* v. *An Taoiseach, the Minister for Foreign Affairs, the Minister for Transportation, the Government of Ireland, Ireland and the Attorney General,* (Judgment), Case No. 3739P, High Court (28 April 2003), pp. 52–4

Note: *The Plaintiff sought a declaration that the decision of the Irish government to allow US military and civilian aircraft engaged in the prosecution of the 2003 Iraq war to overfly Ireland, to land and refuel at Shannon airport and to allow US troops transit through Ireland en route to the war in Iraq breached Ireland's duty as a neutral State. The High Court said:*

... 1907 Hague Convention V is asserted to be declaratory of customary international law. The various texts relied upon by the plaintiff certainly tend to support such an interpretation. The defendants have argued that a more qualified or nuanced form of neutrality also exists, being one which has been practised by this State for many years, and indeed throughout the Second World War. However, it does not appear to me that even that form of neutrality is to be seen as including the notion that the granting of passage over its territory by a neutral State for large numbers of troops and munitions from one belligerent State only en route to a theatre of war with another is compatible with the status of neutrality in international law. No authority has been offered to the court by the defendants to support such a view. Nor can it be an answer to say that a small number of other states have done the same thing in recent times. Different questions and considerations may well arise where measures of collective security are carried out or led by the UN in conformity with the Charter: Article 2 (5) of the Charter obliges *all* members to assist the UN in any action it takes in accordance with the Charter.

The court is prepared to hold therefore that there is an identifiable rule of customary law in relation to the status of neutrality whereunder a neutral state may not permit the movement of large numbers of troops or munitions of one belligerent State through its territory en route to a theatre of war with another.

8.1.12 UK, British Ministry of Defence, *The Joint Service Manual of the Law of Armed Conflict* (Joint Service Publication 383, 2004 Edition)

1.43 Certain fundamental principles of neutrality law remain applicable:

a. Neutral states must refrain from allowing their territory to be used by belligerent states for the purposes of military operations. If a neutral state is unable or unwilling to prevent the use of its territory for the purposes of such military operations, a belligerent state may become entitled to use force in self-defence against enemy forces operating from the territory of that neutral state. Whether or not they are so entitled will depend on the ordinary rules of the *jus ad bellum.*

b. Given the duties of neutral states, targets in neutral territory cannot be legitimate military objectives and they must not be attacked by belligerent states.

8.1.13 UN High Commissioner for Refugees, Stéphane Jaquemet, *Under What Circumstances Can a Person Who Has Taken an Active Part in the Hostilities of an International or a Non-International Armed Conflict Become an Asylum Seeker?* PPLA/2004/01 (June 2004)

. . .

3. The formal non-applicability of the law of neutrality

... It is therefore reasonable to conclude that Article 11 of the 5th Hague Convention belongs to these core norms applicable to all armed conflicts, including internal ones. ICRC agrees that the provisions of the 5th Hague Convention "can be considered to have attained customary status" and that it is "ICRC's view that it can also be applied by analogy in situations of non-international conflicts, in which combatants either from the government side or from armed opposition groups have fled into a neutral state."

8.1.14 Germany, Bundesverwaltungsgericht – BVerwG – German Federal Administrative Court (Supreme Court) of 21 June 2005 – BVerwG 2 WD 12.04

Note: *In 2003, a German major refused to carry out two orders of his superior to collaborate on the development of a military software program. The major justified his refusal on the grounds such acts would support the 2003 Iraq war. Furthermore, the major argued that his superior had not been able to expressly rule out that working on the project would support the participation of the Bundeswehr in the war in Iraq, which the major saw as contrary to international law. As to Germany's neutrality, the German Federal Administrative Court said:*

1.1.4.12 ... A state that is not involved in an armed conflict between other states has the status of a "neutral state". .... Apart from the rules that in the case of legally established "constant neutrality" (e.g. Switzerland and Austria) already apply in peacetime, the obligation of a state that is not involved in an armed conflict between other states ("neutral state") to be neutral within the meaning of the 5th H.C. begins with the outbreak of the armed conflict. The consequences of the neutral status are mutual rights and obligations between the neutral state on the one hand and the parties to the conflict on the other. According to art.1 5th H.C. the territory of a "neutral" state, i.e. one not involved in the armed conflict, is "inviolable"; any act of war on it is forbidden, especially "leading troops or munitions or supply columns through the territory of a neutral power" (art. 2 of 5th H.C.). A "neutral state" – hence therefore in respect of the war waged against Iraq solely by the USA and its allies since March 20, 2003 also the Federal Republic of Germany – may not support "any of the parties to the conflict" on its territory, and in particular may not "tolerate any of the acts described in articles 2 to 4" (art. 5 of 5th H.C.). This applies both to moving troops, munitions or supply columns through the territory (art. 5 para. 1 in conjunction with art. 2 of 5th H.C.) and to setting up or using a radiotelegraphic (*"radiotélégraphique"*) station or any other system that is intended to facilitate communication with the warring land or sea forces" (art. 5 para. 1 in conjunction with art. 3 letters a) and b) 5th H.C.).

Furthermore, the parties to the conflict are "forbidden to penetrate into neutral airspace with military aircraft, rockets or other flying objects". . . . Relative to a party to a conflict who contravenes the prohibitions of arts. 1 to 4 of the 5th H.C., and thus within the meaning of the 5th H.C. uses the territory of a neutral state as the basis for military operations in the broadest sense, the "neutral state" has an obligation to take action and hence to intervene in order to end the violation of neutrality. . . . The "neutral state" is required under international law to "reject any violation of its neutrality, if necessary by force", although this obligation is admittedly restricted by the prohibition of the use of force under international law. The armed forces of a party to a conflict that are located in the territory of the "neutral state" are to be prevented from taking part in the fighting; troops of parties to a conflict that "enter" the neutral territory, i.e. who arrive in the neutral territory after the armed conflict has begun, are "to be interned". . . . Only officers who give their word of honor not to leave the neutral territory without permission may be freed (art. 11 para. 3 of 5th H.C). . . . The obligation of internment results from the sense and purpose of neutrality law, since only in this way is it possible to prevent fighting being supported from within the neutral territory and as a result an escalation of the armed conflict involving the neutral state . . . .

4.1.4.1.3 In the case of the war which was begun on March 20, 2003, against which there are serious concerns under international law, the Federal Republic of Germany is not exempted from the above obligations under international law by virtue of being (then and now) a member of NATO, of which the war-waging USA and UK (and other members of the war coalition) are also members.

. . . However, neither the NATO Treaty of April 4, 1949 . . . nor the NATO Status of Forces Agreement (SOFA) of June 19, 1951 provide for an obligation on the part of the Federal Republic of Germany, contrary to the UN Charter and applicable international law to support acts – in contravention of international law – by NATO partners.

. . . This means at the same time that a war that is not justified by art. 51 UN Charter also cannot constitute or justify a "NATO alliance case" per art. 5 NATO Treaty . . .

Art. 5 NATO Treaty standardizes a duty of assistance under international law for each party to the treaty "only" in the case of an armed attack "against one or more of them in Europe or North America". At the same time the scope of this duty of assistance is expressly left open. . . .

In the case of the war that was begun on March 20, 2003 against Iraq, the NATO Council did not decide on such an "alliance case". Independently of the fact that a "preventive war" that is not justified by art. 51 UN Charter cannot constitute or justify a "NATO alliance case" per art. 5 NATO Treaty, therefore already for this reason no NATO state was obligated under the NATO Treaty to assist NATO partners with military means in the Iraq war. A war that is not justified per art. 51 UN Charter already per arts. 1, 5 and 6 NATO Treaty does not establish obligations of assistance. Rather it precisely conflicts with these – as in particular the provision of art. 1 NATO Treaty makes clear.

The NATO Treaty in addition to this contains an express legal reservation according to which no party to the Treaty can be forced by the NATO Treaty or by later decisions in the implementation of the treaty (e.g. resolutions in the NATO committees) to violate its own constitution (called the "protective clause"). … In the event of a conflict the provision under the constitutional law of each respective partner to the alliance and the treaty take precedence over the provision in the NATO Treaty …

4.1.4.1.4 Assessment of the military acts of assistance under international law

As results from the explanations above, serious concerns in relation to international law exist about the Federal Republic of Germany's assistance in favor of the USA and UK in connection with the war against Iraq which began on March 20, 2003, … .. This applies at any rate for the granting of overflight rights for military aircraft of the USA and UK, which in connection with the Iraq war flew across the federal territory into the war zone in the Gulf region or came back from there. This also applies for the approval to send troops, transport weapons and military supplies and materials from German soil into the war zone and for all operations that could result in the territory of Germany serving as a starting point or "hub" for military operations directed against Iraq. For the objective sense and purpose of these actions was to facilitate or even support the military proceedings of the US and UK. Owing to these objectives, there are serious concerns in respect of international law about the actions of the Federal Government in this connection with regard to the prohibition of the use of force under international law and the listed provisions of the 5th H.C. …

Whether these serious concerns under international law also apply to the involvement of *Bundeswehr* soldiers in deployments of AWACS flights over Turkey and their use to monitor barracks and military and civil facilities of US armed forces in Germany is not without doubt.

In the case of the AWACS flights the answer to the question depends substantially on whether the data gained from these missions was significant for the acts of war in Iraq and whether the armed forces of the USA and UK *de facto* had access to this data. The compatibility with applicable international law of the protection and guarding of facilities of the US forces situated in Germany by the *Bundeswehr* depended on whether as a result corresponding tasks of the units relocated to the war zone were performed as it were on their behalf and compensatorily in order to enable or facilitate the US to move corresponding troops into the war zone. If this had been the case, serious concerns under international law would exist on account of this violation against the prohibition standardized in art. 5 para. 1 in conjunction with art. 2 of the 5th H.C. "not to support any of the parties in the conflict".

8.1.15 US, *Ghaleb Nassar Al Bihani* v. *Barack Obama, President of the United States, et al.,* Case No. 09-5051, 590 F.3d 866, 26 (D.C. Cir. 2010)

Note: *Al-Bihani served in the 55th Arab Brigade, a paramilitary group allied with the Taliban. The Brigade included Al-Qaeda members in its command structure. Al-Bihani served as a cook and carried a Brigade-issued weapon, but never fired it in combat. Al-Bihani was captured and eventually detained at Guantanamo Bay in 2002. As to the Brigade's neutrality towards the United States, the US Court of Appeals said:*

Al-Bihani … points to the international laws of co-belligerency to demonstrate that the brigade should have been allowed the opportunity to remain neutral upon notice of a conflict between the United States and the Taliban. … But even if Al-Bihani's argument were relevant to his detention and putting aside all the questions that applying such elaborate rules to this situation would raise, the laws of co-belligerency affording notice of war and the choice to remain neutral have only applied to nation states.

8.1.16 Germany, Federal Ministry of Defence, *Law of Armed Conflict – Manual – Joint Service Regulation (ZDv) 15/2* (May 2013)

1201. **Neutrality in an international armed conflict** is defined in international law as the **status** of a State that is not participating in an armed conflict between other States. … A neutral status entails mutual rights and duties for the neutral State and the Parties to the conflict. … The law of neutrality aims to protect neutral States and their citizens, avoid an escalation of the conflict, and also to protect the Parties to a conflict and their citizens.

1202. The neutrality of a State in an international armed conflict **begins** with the outbreak of an international armed conflict between other States which is of such **duration or intensity** that it requires the application of the law of neutrality. The law of neutrality thus has a smaller scope of application than the rest of the law applicable in international armed conflicts. The neutral status **ceases** with the end of the international armed conflict or if the hitherto neutral State becomes a Party to the conflict. However, neither limited measures aimed at an armed defence of neutrality nor breaches of particular neutrality obligations mean that this State is considered to be a Party to the conflict.

1203. Neutrality in an armed conflict is to be distinguished from **permanent neutrality**. …

1204. Based on the **Charter of the United Nations** and particularly the prohibition of the use of force, peculiarities may arise in certain situations. The Charter of the United Nations does not generally supersede the law of neutrality. Within the framework of international law, every State may make a sovereign decision on whether or not it will participate in a conflict on the side of the victim (what is known as collective self-defence), provided that the victim accepts the assistance. If the United Nations Security Council has made a binding decision according to Chapter VII of the Charter of the United Nations, no State may invoke the law of neutrality in order to justify behaviour that is inconsistent with its obligations under the Charter (24, 25, 39 and 103).

8.1.17 US, Department of Defense, *Law of War Manual*, Office of General Counsel (June 2015, Updated 2016)

15.3.2 Neutral Duties – Abstention From Participation Hostilities and Impartial Conduct Toward Contending Parties. The principal duties of a neutral State are to abstain from any participation in the conflict and to be impartial in conduct towards contending parties. …

The duties of a neutral State may also be classified in terms of: (1) abstention (obligations to refrain from taking certain actions); (2) prevention (obligations to take certain actions); and (3) acquiescence (obligations to accept certain actions by belligerents).

15.4.2. Belligerent Use of Self-Help When Neutral States Are Unable or Unwilling to Prevent Violations of Neutrality. Should the neutral State be unable, or fail for any reason, to prevent violations of its neutrality by the forces of one belligerent entering or passing through its territory (including its lands, waters, and airspace), the other belligerent State may be justified in attacking the enemy forces on the neutral State's territory. This view has been reflected in the military manuals of other States. For example, consistent with the *jus ad bellum* requirements for self-defense, belligerent forces may act in self-defense when attacked or threatened with attack from enemy forces unlawfully present in neutral territory, including by taking appropriate action to counter the use of neutral territory as a base of enemy operations when the neutral State is unwilling or unable to prevent such violations.

8.2 NEUTRALITY AND SEA WARFARE

8.2.1 *Declaration Respecting Maritime Law ('Paris Declaration')* (16 April 1856, entered into force 16 April 1856) 46 BFSP (1855–1856) 26

. . .

1. Privateering is, and remains, abolished;
2. The neutral flag covers enemy's goods, with the exception of contraband of war;
3. Neutral goods, with the exception of contraband of war, are not liable to capture under enemy's flag;
4. Blockades, in order to be binding, must be effective, that is to say, maintained by a force sufficient really to prevent access to the coast of the enemy.

8.2.2 Canada, Joint Doctrine Manual, *The Law of Armed Conflict at the Operational and Tactical Levels*, Office of the Judge Advocate General (13 August 2001)

809. ACTIONS PERMITTED IN NEUTRAL WATERS

1. A neutral state has a duty of impartiality. However, a neutral state may, without jeopardizing its neutrality, permit the following acts within its neutral waters:

a. innocent passage through its territorial sea or its archipelagic waters by warships, auxiliary vessels and prizes of belligerent states;
b. replenishment by a belligerent warship or auxiliary vessel of its food, water and fuel sufficient to reach a port in its own territory; and
c. repairs of belligerent warships or auxiliary vessels found necessary by the neutral state to make them seaworthy, but such repairs may not restore or increase their fighting strength.

811. DUTY OF STATE TO PREVENT VIOLATIONS OF NEUTRALITY

1. A neutral state is under an obligation to take the measures necessary to terminate a violation of its neutrality by a belligerent.

2. If the neutral state fails to terminate the violation of its neutral waters by a belligerent, the opposing belligerent must notify the neutral state and give it a reasonable time to terminate the violation. The belligerent may, in the absence of any feasible and timely alternative, use such force as is strictly necessary to respond to the threat posed by the violation

8.2.3 International Institute of Humanitarian Law, *San Remo Manual on International Law Applicable to Armed Conflicts at Sea* (12 June 1994)

14. Neutral waters consist of the internal waters, territorial sea, and, where applicable, the archipelagic waters, of neutral States. Neutral airspace consists of the airspace over neutral waters and the land territory of neutral States.

15. Within and over neutral waters, including neutral waters comprising an international strait and waters in which the right of archipelagic sea lanes passage may be exercised, hostile actions by belligerent forces are forbidden. A neutral State must take such measures as are consistent with Section II of this Part, including the exercise of surveillance, as the means at its disposal allow, to prevent the violation of its neutrality by belligerent forces. . . .

17. Belligerent forces may not use neutral waters as a sanctuary. . . .

18. Belligerent military and auxiliary aircraft may not enter neutral airspace . . .

19. . . ., a neutral State may, on a non-discriminatory basis, condition, restrict or prohibit the entrance to or passage through its neutral waters by belligerent warships and auxiliary vessels. . . .

20. Subject to the duty of impartiality, . . ., a neutral State may, without jeopardizing its neutrality, permit the following acts within its neutral waters:

(a) passage through its territorial sea, and where applicable its archipelagic waters, by warships, auxiliary vessels and prizes of belligerent States; warships, auxiliary vessels and prizes may employ pilots of the neutral State during passage;

   . . .

22. Should a belligerent State be in violation of the regime of neutral waters, as set out in this document, the neutral State is under an obligation to take the measures necessary to terminate the violation. . . .

26. Neutral warships, auxiliary vessels, and military and auxiliary aircraft may exercise the rights of passage provided by general international law through, under and over belligerent international straits and archipelagic waters. The neutral State should, as a precautionary measure, give timely notice of its exercise of the rights of passage to the belligerent State. . . .

67. Merchant vessels flying the flag of neutral States may not be attacked unless they:

(a) are believed on reasonable grounds to be carrying contraband or breaching a blockade, and after prior warning they intentionally and clearly refuse to stop, or intentionally and clearly resist visit, search or capture;
(b) engage in belligerent acts on behalf of the enemy;
(c) act as auxiliaries to the enemy's armed forces;
(d) are incorporated into or assist the enemy's intelligence system;
(e) sail under convoy of enemy warships or military aircraft; or
(f) otherwise make an effective contribution to the enemy's military action . . .

166. Nationals of a neutral State:

(a) who are passengers on board enemy or neutral vessels or aircraft are to be released and may not be made prisoners of war unless they are members of the enemy's armed forces or have personally committed acts of hostility against the captor;
(b) who are members of the crew of enemy warships or auxiliary vessels or military aircraft or auxiliary aircraft are entitled to prisoner-of-war status and may be made prisoners of war;

8.3 NEUTRALITY AND AIR WARFARE

8.3.1 HPCR, *Manual on International Law Applicable to Air and Missile Warfare* (Bern, 15 May 2009)

166. Hostilities between Belligerent Parties must not be conducted within neutral territory.

167. (a) Belligerent Parties are prohibited in neutral territory to conduct any hostile actions, establish bases of operations or use such territory as a sanctuary. Furthermore, neutral territory must not be used by Belligerent Parties for the movement of troops or supplies, including overflights by military aircraft or missiles, or for operation of military communication systems.

(b) However, when Belligerent Parties use for military purposes a public, internationally and openly accessible network such as the Internet, the fact that part of this infrastructure is situated within the jurisdiction of a Neutral does not constitute a violation of neutrality.

168. (a) A Neutral must not allow any of the acts referred to in Rule 167 (a) to occur within its territory and must use all the means available to it to prevent or terminate them.

(b) If the use of the neutral territory or airspace by a Belligerent Party constitutes a serious violation, the opposing Belligerent Party may, in the absence of any feasible and timely alternative, use such force as is necessary to terminate the violation of neutrality.

169. The fact that a Neutral resists, even by force, attempts to violate its neutrality cannot be regarded as a hostile act. However, the use of force by the Neutral must not exceed the degree required to repel the incursion and maintain its neutrality.

170. (a) Any incursion or transit by a belligerent military aircraft (including a UAV/UCAV) or missile into or through neutral airspace is prohibited. This is without prejudice to the

right of transit passage through straits used for international navigation or archipelagic sea lanes passage.

(b) A Neutral must exercise surveillance, to the extent that the means at its disposal allow, to enable it to prevent the violation of its neutrality by belligerent forces.

(c) In the event a belligerent military aircraft enters neutral airspace (other than straits used for international navigation or archipelagic sea lanes), the Neutral must use all the means at its disposal to prevent or terminate that violation. If captured, the aircraft and their crews must be interned for the duration of the armed conflict.

171. Belligerent Parties must not commit any of the following acts:

(a) Attack on or capture of persons or objects located in neutral airspace.
(b) Use of neutral territory or airspace as a base of operations – for attack, targeting, or intelligence purposes – against enemy targets in the air, on land or on water outside that territory.
(c) Conducting interception, inspection, diversion or capture of vessels or aircraft in neutral territory.
(d) Any other activity involving the use of military force or contributing to the war-fighting effort, including transmission of data or combat search-and-rescue operations in neutral territory.

172. (a) Belligerent military aircraft may not enter the airspace of Neutrals, except that:

(i) Belligerent military aircraft in distress may be permitted to enter neutral airspace and to land in neutral territory under such safeguards as the Neutral may wish to impose. The Neutral is obligated to require such aircraft to land and to intern the aircraft and their crews.
(ii) The airspace above neutral international straits and archipelagic sea lanes remains open at all times to belligerent aircraft, including armed military aircraft engaged in transit or archipelagic sea lanes passage.
(iii) The Neutral may permit belligerent military aircraft to enter for purposes of capitulation.

(b) Neutrals must use the means at their disposal to require capitulating belligerent military aircraft to land within their territory, and must intern the aircraft and their crews for the duration of the international armed conflict. Should such an aircraft commit hostile acts, or should it fail to follow the instructions to land, it may be attacked without further notice.

173. A Neutral is not bound to prevent the private export or transit on behalf of a Belligerent Party of aircraft, parts of aircraft, or material, supplies or munitions for aircraft. However, a Neutral is bound to use the means at its disposal:

(a) To prevent the departure from its jurisdiction of an aircraft in a condition to make a hostile attack against a Belligerent Party, if there is reason to believe that such aircraft is destined for such use.
(b) To prevent the departure from its jurisdiction of the crews of military aircraft, as well as passengers and crews of civilian aircraft, who are members of the armed forces of a Belligerent Party.

174. ..., the following activities may render a neutral civilian aircraft a military objective:

(a) It is believed on reasonable grounds to be carrying contraband, and, after prior warning or interception, it intentionally and clearly refuses to divert from its destination, or intentionally and clearly refuses to proceed for inspection to a belligerent airfield that is safe for the type of aircraft involved and reasonably accessible.
(b) Engaging in hostile actions in support of the enemy, ...
(c) Facilitating the military actions of the enemy's armed forces, e.g. transporting troops, carrying military materials, or refuelling military aircraft.
(d) Being incorporated into or assisting the enemy's intelligence gathering system, ...
(e) Refusing to comply with the orders of military authorities, including instructions for landing, inspection and possible capture, or it clearly resists interception.
(f) Otherwise making an effective contribution to military action.

175. The fact that a civilian aircraft bears the marks of a Neutral is *prima facie* evidence of its neutral Character

8.4 NEUTRALITY AND CYBER WARFARE

8.4.1 M.N. Schmitt (ed.), *Tallinn Manual on the International Law Applicable to Cyber Warfare* (CUP, 2013), pp. 251, 252 and 254

Rule 92
The exercise of belligerent rights by cyber means in neutral territory is prohibited

Rule 93
A neutral State may not knowingly allow the exercise of belligerent rights by the parties to the conflict from cyber infrastructure located in its territory or under its exclusive control.

Rule 94
If a neutral State fails to terminate the exercise of belligerent rights on its territory, the aggrieved party to the conflict may take such steps, including by cyber operations, as are necessary to counter that conduct.

8.4.2 US, Department of Defense, *Law of War Manual*, Office of General Counsel (June 2015, Updated 2016)

16.4 CYBER OPERATIONS AND THE LAW OF NEUTRALITY

The law of neutrality may be important in certain cyber operations. For example, under the law of neutrality, belligerent States are bound to respect the sovereign rights of neutral States. Because of the interconnected nature of cyberspace, cyber operations targeting networked information infrastructures in one State may create effects in another State that is not a party to the armed conflict.

16.4.1. Cyber Operations That Use Communications Infrastructure in Neutral States. ... The use of communications infrastructure in neutral States may be implicated under the general rule that neutral territory may not serve as a base of operations for one belligerent against another. In particular, belligerent States are prohibited from erecting on the territory of a neutral State any apparatus for the purpose of communicating with belligerent forces on land or sea, or from using any installation of this kind established by them before the armed conflict on the territory of a neutral State for purely military purposes, and which has not been opened for the service of public messages.

However, merely relaying information through neutral communications infrastructure (provided that the facilities are made available impartially) generally would not constitute a violation of the law of neutrality that belligerent States would have an obligation to refrain from and that a neutral State would have an obligation to prevent. This rule was developed because it was viewed as impractical for neutral States to censor or screen their publicly available communications infrastructure for belligerent traffic. Thus, for example, it would not be prohibited for a belligerent State to route information through cyber infrastructure in a neutral State that is open for the service of public messages, and that neutral State would have no obligation to forbid such traffic. This rule would appear to be applicable even if the information that is being routed through neutral communications infrastructure may be characterized as a cyber weapon or otherwise could cause destructive effects in a belligerent State (but no destructive effects within the neutral State or States).

COMMENTARY

1. The law of neutrality applies as soon as an IAC breaks out. It follows that any uncertainty surrounding the outbreak, cessation or character of an armed conflict affects the application of the law of neutrality. Another contentious issue is whether a higher threshold of intensity is needed to trigger the law of neutrality. Due to its serious legal implications, a high threshold may be more appropriate. If the law of neutrality is not applicable, the relations between belligerents and third States are regulated by other rules of IHL or other bodies of international law.

2. The application of the law of neutrality to NIACs is also contentious. The view that the law of neutrality does not apply to NIACs is broadly held unless the conflict is internationalised due to external intervention or recognition of belligerency. Interference by third States in a NIAC is instead regulated by the *jus ad bellum*. That said, States may adopt a policy of neutrality in relation to NIACs.

3. A neutral State should not provide assistance to belligerents in the form of war materials, aid or services that can influence the outcome of the conflict.[1] The provision of weapons or other materials by private parties does not violate neutral duties[2] unless permission by the government is needed or involves industries or individuals under State control.

---

[1] Art. 5, HCV.
[2] Art. 7, HCV.

4. If the neutrality of a State is violated by belligerents, the neutral State has an obligation to react in order to maintain its neutrality.[3] If a neutral State violates the law of neutrality, aggrieved belligerents can react. Such reactions, which may also include the use of force, should be compatible with the *jus ad bellum* and *jus in bello*.

5. Do neutral States that violate their neutral duties become belligerents? For example, did those European States that provided assistance to the 2003 Coalition action against Iraq become belligerents? Did the United States become belligerent by supporting the United Kingdom before its formal entry to the Second World War?[4] This state of affairs invokes the policy of 'non-belligerency' according to which States can provide assistance to belligerents – short of actively participating in hostilities – without becoming a party to the conflict.[5] It is submitted that the status of 'non-belligerency' in international law is ambivalent and that it most probably violates the law of neutrality. However, it currently provides some relief to States that host foreign military bases or troops on their territories.

6. Whether neutrality in IHL or the political status of permanent neutrality have been qualified by the UN Charter needs to be considered in light of Articles 2(5) and 25 of the UN Charter, the collective security provisions in Chapter VII and Article 103 of the UN Charter according to which the UN Charter obligations supersede contrary obligations. These rules impact on the neutral duties of abstention, impartiality and prevention and on the means used by parties to enforce neutrality.[6] Neutrality has been modified in cases where the SC determines the existence of an aggressor and mandates States to use military force against the aggressor. The same applies to cases where the SC authorises the use of force, but in such cases neutrality remains a possibility for States that do not act upon the SC authorisation.[7] A critical question is what happens if, in the absence of SC authorisation but after a SC determination of the existence of a breach of the peace or of an act of aggression, States decide to unilaterally or collectively use force.[8] Finally, neutrality is not violated when the SC imposes or authorises non-forcible sanctions against an aggressor.

7. Permanent neutrality is also challenged when neutral States become members of international organisations such as NATO or the EU which provide for common defence or, in the case of the EU, where Member States have a duty of solidarity.[9] In response to this, certain neutral EU Member States changed their position as far as neutrality is concerned.

8. Does a State that assists a belligerent State as part of the right to collective self-defence[10] violate its neutrality? That State's use of force may be legal under the *jus ad bellum* but, in view of the separation of *jus ad bellum* and *jus in bello*, it violates its neutral duties unless the collective self-defence action has been authorised by the SC as in SC Res

---

[3]   Art. 10, HCV.
[4]   Neutrality Act of 1939 in (1940) 34 AJIL 44ff.
[5]   On qualified neutrality see US, Department of Defense, *Law of War Manual*, Office of General Counsel (June 2015, Updated 2016), 15.2.2.
[6]   See GA Res 50/80 on Permanent Neutrality of Turkmenistan (12 December 1995) 90th Plenary Meeting, UN Doc. A/RES/50/80 (1995).
[7]   Art. 103 of UN Charter (adopted 26 June 1945, entered into force 24 October 1945) 892 UNTS 119 also covers authorisations to use force.
[8]   In relation to the 2003 action against Iraq, the critical question is whether it was legally justified. See ibid 2005 Federal Administrative Tribunal, Judgment.
[9]   Consolidated Version of the Treaty on European Union [2008] OJ C115/13 ('TEU'), Art. 42.
[10]   See Art. 51 UN Charter, (adopted 26 June 1945, entered into force 24 October 1945) 892 UNTS 119.

678 (1990) with regard to Iraq. However, even in the absence of authorisation, the violation of the law of neutrality can be excused by self-defence as a circumstance precluding wrongfulness provided that this provision also covers violations of obligations towards third States.[11]

9. Cyber war poses many challenges to the law of neutrality because of the interconnected nature of cyberspace. Neutrals have an obligation not to allow belligerents to use their cyber infrastructure for military operations. Neutrals should thus take appropriate measures to terminate such activities when they acquire knowledge thereof.[12] This is a duty of conduct and not of result. Does this obligation also require that neutrals build their capacity in order to be able to suppress such activities? Do neutrals need to acquire knowledge of such activities and prevent their occurrence? In this case, human rights questions regarding the scope of the neutral's monitoring power are raised.

10. Other issues concern the effects on the law of neutrality of the use of zombie computers or of spoofed computers from neutral territory. This may constitute an act of perfidy by a belligerent or violate the duty not to recruit or form groups of combatants on neutral territory.[13] The question of how the affected belligerent should react remains open and relates to issues of attribution. Does the routing of cyber operations through a neutral's infrastructure violate the law of neutrality? In this regard, a lot depends on how data are characterised. If data are not weapons, their routing through neutral infrastructure does not raise any legal issues under the law of neutrality. If data are weapons, travelling through neutral infrastructure would violate the neutral State's duties and trigger its obligation to suppress such operations. However, States cannot always control how data travel, neither is the offensive nature of data evident. It thus transpires that such an obligation would put a disproportionate burden on neutral States. A related question is whether the hosting of governmental services on a neutral's networks violates the law of neutrality. It will not violate the law of neutrality if it is not for military purposes.[14]

11. In light of all the changes that have occurred since the codification of the law of neutrality in 1907, is a new codification of the law necessary? For example, should the application of the law of neutrality be defined against the concept of armed conflict rather than the traditional concept of war? Should the way the law of neutrality applies in the context of the UN collective security system be clarified? Should the mandatory or optional application of the law of neutrality be clarified?

---

[11]   Art. 21 Articles on Responsibility of States for Internationally Wrongful Acts (2001). See also N. Tsagourias, 'Self-Defence against Non-State Actors: The Interaction between Self-Defence as a Primary Rule and Self-Defence as a Secondary Rule' (2016) 29 *Leiden JIL* 801, 819–24.
[12]   See M.N. Schmitt (ed.), *Tallinn Manual on the International Law Applicable to Cyber Warfare* (CUP, 2013) Rule 93.
[13]   Art. 4, HCV and Art. 6, HCXIII.
[14]   Art. 3, HCV.

9

Law of Occupation

INTRODUCTION

Occupation has a lengthy history and the law of belligerent occupation is comprehensive; however, its application continues to be the subject of vigorous debate.

The provisions in the 1907 Hague Regulations Concerning the Laws and Customs of War on Land (HCIV) regarding belligerent occupation, although limited in scope, established the fundamental structure of what is now the customary international law of occupation.

Historically, the law of belligerent occupation was primarily concerned with the preservation of the interests of the sovereign State concerned and the security of the occupying power. The nature of early twentieth-century society, with emphasis being placed on protection of private property and minimal State interference in everyday life, led to an assumption of correspondingly limited responsibilities on the part of an occupying power. Additionally, the emphasis placed on State sovereignty in international law militated against the adoption of an interventionist approach.

This position changed following the Second World War, with the emphasis in the law of occupation shifting from the interests of the State to the protection of the civilian population in occupied territory. The 1949 Geneva Convention IV, and to a lesser extent the 1977 Additional Protocol I, built on the structure of the occupation regime established under the Hague Regulations. In recent years, IHRL has also played an increasing part in the international legal regime governing occupation, lending additional emphasis to the protection of the rights of the civilian population.

Changes in the nature of modern armed conflict have continued to impact on the law of occupation, as illustrated in the transformative concept of occupation adopted in Iraq and the prolonged Israeli occupation of the Palestinian territories. Such modern examples of belligerent occupation have thrown up a range of challenges regarding such fundamental aspects of the law of occupation as its definition, commencement and termination, the rights and duties of occupying powers, the extent to which transformation is compatible with occupation law or must rest on another legal foundation and the impact of prolonged occupation on the law.

Resources: Arts 42–56, HCIV; Arts 27–34, 47–78, 79–143, GCIV; Arts 54, 63, 69, 73, AP1

Cases and Materials

9.1 DEFINITION OF OCCUPATION

9.1.1 ICTY, *Prosecutor* v. *M. Naletilić and V. Martinović*, (Judgment), Case No. IT-98-34-T, Trial Chamber (31 March 2003)

Note: *The facts of this case are outlined in Chapter 1, Section 1.7.1. On the definition of occupation, the ICTY said:*

214. . . . Occupation is defined as a transitional period following invasion and preceding the agreement on the cessation of the hostilities. This distinction imposes more onerous duties on an occupying power than on a party to an international armed conflict.

215. . . . The Chamber is of the view that while Geneva Convention IV constitutes a further codification of the rights and duties of the occupying power, it has not abrogated the Hague Regulations on the matter. Thus, in the absence of a definition of "occupation" in the Geneva Conventions, the Chamber refers to the Hague Regulations and the definition provided therein, bearing in mind the customary nature of the Regulations.

216. Article 42 of the Hague Regulations provides the following definition of occupation: Territory is considered occupied when it is actually placed under the authority of the hostile army. The occupation extends only to the territory where such authority has been established and can be exercised. The Chamber endorses this definition.

217. To determine whether the authority of the occupying power has been actually established, the following guidelines provide some assistance:

– the occupying power must be in a position to substitute its own authority for that of the occupied authorities, which must have been rendered incapable of functioning publicly;
– the enemy's forces have surrendered, been defeated or withdrawn. In this respect, battle areas may not be considered as occupied territory. However, sporadic local resistance, even successful, does not affect the reality of occupation;
– the occupying power has a sufficient force present, or the capacity to send troops within a reasonable time to make the authority of the occupying power felt;
– a temporary administration has been established over the territory;
– the occupying power has issued and enforced directions to the civilian population;

218. The law of occupation only applies to those areas actually controlled by the occupying power and ceases to apply where the occupying power no longer exercises an actual authority over the occupied area. As a result, the Chamber finds that it must determine on a case by case basis whether this degree of control was established at the relevant times and in the relevant places. There is no requirement that an entire territory be occupied, provided that the isolated areas in which the authority of the occupied power is still functioning "are effectively cut off from the rest of the occupied territory".

9.1.2 ICJ, *Legal Consequences of the Construction of a Wall in the Occupied Palestinian Territory* (Advisory Opinion) [2004] I.C.J. Rep. 136

Note: *The facts of this case are set out in Chapter 2, Section 2.2.6. Refining the definition of 'occupation', the ICJ commented in the following terms:*

78. The Court would observe that, under customary international law as reflected ... in Article 42 of the Regulations Respecting the Laws and Customs of War on Land annexed to the Fourth Hague Convention of 18 October 1907 (hereinafter "the Hague Regulations of 1907"), territory is considered occupied when it is actually placed under the authority of the hostile army, and the occupation extends only to the territory where such authority has been established and can be exercised.

9.2 BEGINNING OF OCCUPATION

9.2.1 ICTY, *Prosecutor* v. *Tadić,* (Opinion and Judgment), Case No. IT-94-1-T, Trial Chamber (7 May 1997)

Note: *The facts of this case are set out in Chapter 1, Section 1.1.1. As to the interaction of the protection under Art. 4, GCIV and occupation, the ICTY said as follows:*

579. ... the expression "in the hands of" is not restricted to situations in which the individual civilian is physically in the hands of a Party or Occupying Power. ...

Consequently, those persons who found themselves in territory effectively occupied by a party to the conflict can be considered to have been in the hands of that party. . . .

580. . . . Whether or not the victims were "protected persons" depends on when it was that they fell into the hands of the occupying forces. The exact moment when a person or area falls into the hands of a party to a conflict depends on whether that party has effective control over an area.

9.2.2 Eritrea–Ethiopia Claims Commission, *Partial Award: Central Front, Eritrea's Claims 2, 4, 6, 7, 8 & 22* (2004) 26(4) RIAA 115

Note: *The State of Eritrea brought claims against the Federal Democratic Republic of Ethiopia for a finding of liability for losses and damage suffered by Eritrea's nationals, persons of national origin and agents as a result of infractions of international law on the Central Front during the IAC between the two States between 1998 and 2000. As to the nexus between combat, control and occupation, the Commission said:*

57. On the one hand, clearly an area where combat is ongoing and the attacking forces have not yet established control cannot normally be considered occupied within the meaning of the Geneva Conventions of 1949. On the other hand, where combat is not occurring in an area controlled even for just a few days by the armed forces of a hostile Power, the Commission believes that the legal rules applicable to occupied territory should apply.

9.2.3 UK, British Ministry of Defence, *The Joint Service Manual of the Law of Armed Conflict* (Joint Service Publication 383, 2004 Edition)

11.3 To determine whether a state of occupation exists, it is necessary to look at the area concerned and determine whether two conditions are satisfied: first, that the former government has been rendered incapable of publicly exercising its authority in that area; and, secondly, that the occupying power is in a position to substitute its own authority for that of the former government.

11.3.2 Patrols, commando, and similar units, which move on or withdraw after carrying out their mission, do not normally occupy territory since they are not there long enough to set up an administration. The use of airborne forces and of mechanized warfare may make it difficult to determine whether occupation exists. When hostilities continue in enemy territory, occupation only arises in areas coming under the control of the adverse party, even if that control is only temporary, provided that measures are taken to administer the areas in question. Occupation does not take effect merely because the main forces of the country have been defeated but depends on whether authority is actually being exercised over the civilian population. However, for occupation of an area it is not necessary to keep troops permanently stationed throughout that area. It is sufficient that the national forces have withdrawn, that the inhabitants have been disarmed, that measures have been taken to protect life and property and to secure order, and that troops are available, if necessary to enforce authority in the area.

9.2.4 Eritrea–Ethiopia Claims Commission, *Partial Award: Western Front, Aerial Bombardment and Related Claims – Eritrea's Claims 1, 3, 5, 9–13, 14, 21, 25 & 26 between The State of Eritrea and the Federal Republic of Ethiopia* (2005) 26 (8) RIAA 291

Note: *The claim was brought by the State of Eritrea against the Federal Democratic Republic of Ethiopia for loss, damage and injury suffered by Eritrean nationals and persons of Eritrean national origin and agents during the 1998–2000 conflict between the parties. The complaint alleged illegal conduct of military operations on the Western Front of the conflict, illegal aerial bombardment of Eritrea and illegal displacement of Eritrean nationals.*

27. The Commission ... recognizes that not all of the obligations of Section III of Part III of Geneva Convention IV (the section that deals with occupied territories) can reasonably be applied to an armed force anticipating combat and present in an area for only a few days.

9.2.5 ICJ, *Case Concerning Armed Activities on the Territory of the Congo (Democratic Republic of the Congo* v. *Uganda)* (Judgment) [2005] I.C.J. Rep. 168

Note: *The facts of this case are set out in Chapter 1, Section 1.7.2. As to the test for establishing whether a State is an 'occupying Power', the ICJ said:*

173. In order to reach a conclusion as to whether a State, the military forces of which are present on the territory of another State as a result of an intervention, is an "occupying Power" in the meaning of the term as understood in the jus in bello, the Court must examine whether there is sufficient evidence to demonstrate that the said authority was in fact established and exercised by the intervening State in the areas in question.

9.3 END OF OCCUPATION

9.3.1 SC, *Security Council Resolution 1546 on Formation of a Sovereign Interim Government of Iraq* (8 June 2004) 4987th Meeting, UN Doc. S/RES/1546 (2004)

The Security Council,

Welcoming the beginning of a new phase in Iraq's transition to a democratically elected government, and looking forward to the end of the occupation and the assumption of full responsibility and authority by a fully sovereign and independent Interim Government of Iraq by 30 June 2004 ...

Recognizing the request conveyed in the letter of 5 June 2004 from the Prime Minister of the Interim Government of Iraq to the President of the Council, which is annexed to this resolution, to retain the presence of the multinational force;

Recognizing also the importance of the consent of the sovereign Government of Iraq for the presence of the multinational force and of close coordination between the multinational force and that government ...

9.3.2 Israel, *Jaber Al-Bassiouni Ahmed et al.* v. *Prime Minister et al.*, (Judgment), Case No. HCJ 9132/07, Israeli Supreme Court sitting as the High Court of Justice (30 January 2008)

Note: *The case concerned events in the Gaza Strip and the decision of the Israeli government, in response to ongoing acts of terrorism directed against civilians and IDF soldiers, to limit the supply of fuel and electricity to the Gaza Strip. On the obligations of a State when occupation is at an end, the Israeli High Court of Justice said:*

12. ... We should point out in this context that since September 2005 Israel no longer has effective control over what happens in the Gaza Strip. Military rule that applied in the past in this territory came to an end by a decision of the government, and Israeli soldiers are no longer stationed in the territory on a permanent basis, nor are they in charge of what happens there. In these circumstances, the State of Israel does not have a general duty to ensure the welfare of the residents of the Gaza Strip or to maintain public order in the Gaza Strip according to the laws of belligerent occupation in international law. Neither does Israel have any effective capability, in its present position, of enforcing order and managing civilian life in the Gaza Strip. In the prevailing circumstances, the main obligations of the State of Israel relating to the residents of the Gaza Strip derive from the state of armed conflict that exists between it and the Hamas organization that controls the Gaza Strip; these obligations also derive from the degree of control exercised by the State of Israel over the border crossings between it and the Gaza Strip, as well as from the relationship that was created between Israel and the territory of the Gaza Strip after the years of Israeli military rule in the territory, as a result of which the Gaza Strip is currently almost completely dependent upon the supply of electricity from Israel.

9.3.3 UN Human Rights Council, *Human Rights in Palestine and Other Occupied Arab Territories, Report of the United Nations Fact-Finding Mission on the Gaza Conflict ('The Goldstone Report')* (25 September 2009), 12th Session, UN Doc. A/HRC/12/48

278. Given the specific geopolitical configuration of the Gaza Strip, the powers that Israel exercises from the borders enable it to determine the conditions of life within the Gaza Strip. ...

279. The ultimate authority over the Occupied Palestinian Territory still lies with Israel. Under the law and practice of occupation, the establishment by the occupying Power of a temporary administration over an occupied territory is not an essential requirement for occupation, although it could be one element among others that indicates the existence of such occupation. In fact, ... the occupier can leave in place an existing local administration or allow a new one to be installed for as long as it preserves for itself the ultimate authority ... When Israel unilaterally evacuated troops and settlements from the Gaza Strip, it left in place a Palestinian local administration. There is no local governing body to which full authority has been transferred.

9.3.4 ECtHR, *Sargsyan* v. *Azerbaijan* [GC], (App No. 40167/06) (Judgment (Merits), 16 June 2015)

Note: *The case was lodged by Minas Sargsyan, an Armenian national, against the State of Azerbaijan, which he alleged had violated the ECHR by denying him his rights to return to his home in the village of Gulistan, to have access to his property, or to be compensated for its loss, and to visit the graves of his relatives in Gulistan. Affirming the requirement of actual authority over territory in order to establish occupation, the ECtHR said*:

144. The Court notes that under international law (in particular Article 42 of the 1907 Hague Regulations) a territory is considered occupied when it is actually placed under the authority of a hostile army, "actual authority" being widely considered as translating to effective control and requiring such elements as presence of foreign troops, which are in a position to exercise effective control without the consent of the sovereign. . . . On the basis of all the material before it and having regard to the above establishment of facts, the Court finds that Gulistan is not occupied by or under the effective control of foreign forces as this would require a presence of foreign troops in Gulistan.

9.3.5 ICRC, *Report on International Humanitarian Law and the Challenges of Contemporary Armed Conflict*, 32nd International Conference, EN 32IC/15/11 (Geneva, 31 October 2015), p.12

In principle, the effective-control test is equally applicable when establishing the end of occupation, meaning that the criteria to be met should generally mirror those used to determine the beginning of occupation, only in reverse. . . .

The ICRC considers, however, that in some specific and rather exceptional cases – in particular when foreign forces withdraw from occupied territory (or parts thereof) but retain key elements of authority or other important governmental functions usually performed by an occupying power – the law of occupation may continue to apply within the territorial and functional limits of such competences. Indeed, despite the lack of the physical presence of foreign forces in the territory concerned, the retained authority may amount to effective control for the purposes of the law of occupation and entail the continued application of the relevant provisions of this body of norms. This is referred to as the "functional approach" to the application of occupation law. This test will apply to the extent that the foreign forces still exercise, within all or part of the territory, governmental functions acquired when the occupation was undoubtedly established and ongoing.

. . .

It may be argued that technological and military developments have made it possible to assert effective control over a foreign territory (or parts thereof) without a continuous foreign military presence in the concerned area. In such situations, it is important to take into account the extent of authority retained by the foreign forces rather than to focus exclusively on the means by which it is actually exercised. It should also be recognized that, in these circumstances, the geographical contiguity between belligerent States could facilitate the remote exercise of effective control. . . . The continued application of the relevant provisions of the law of occupation is all the more important in this scenario as these were specifically designed to regulate the sharing of authority – and the resulting assignment of responsibilities – between the belligerent States concerned.

9.4 RIGHTS AND DUTIES OF THE OCCUPYING POWER

9.4.1 Hague Convention IV 1907 as Customary Law

9.4.1.1 **ICJ,** *Legal Consequences of the Construction of a Wall in the Occupied Palestinian Territory* (Advisory Opinion) [2004] I.C.J. Rep. 136
Note: *The facts of this case are detailed in Chapter 2, Section 2.2.6. Reinforcing that the Hague Regulations are part of customary international law, the ICJ said:*

89. . . . . The Court considers that the provisions of the Hague Regulations have become part of customary law, as is in fact recognized by all the participants in the proceedings before the Court. The Court also observes that, pursuant to Article 154 of the Fourth Geneva Convention, that Convention is supplementary to Sections II and III of the Hague Regulations. Section III of those Regulations, which concerns "Military authority over the territory of the hostile State", is particularly pertinent in the present case.

9.4.2 Public Order and Safety

9.4.2.1 **Israel,** *Jam'iat Iscan Al-Ma'almoun* v. *IDF Commander in the Judea and Samaria Area,* (Judgment), Case No. HCJ 393/82, Israeli Supreme Court sitting as the High Court of Justice (28 December 1983)
Note: *The case concerned the requisition, by Israel, of land belonging to the Petitioners for the purposes of constructing service roads from the West Bank to Israel. Affirming the requirement that an occupying power should balance its interests against those of the occupied State, the Israeli High Court of Justice said:*

13. . . . A territory held under belligerent occupation is not an open field for economic or other exploitation. . . . Therefore, the military government may not plan and implement a road system in an Area held under belligerent occupation if the purpose of this planning and implementation are simply to constitute a "service road" for its own state. . . . As we shall see, the planning and implementation of a road system may be carried out for reasons relating to the best interest of the local population. This planning and implementation may not be carried out simply to serve the holding state. . . .

18. The first clause of Regulation 43 of the Hague Regulations vests in the military government the power and imposes upon it the duty to restore and ensure public order and safety. This authority is twofold: first, restoring public order and safety in places where they had previously been interrupted; second, ensuring the continued existence of public order and safety. The Regulation does not limit itself to a certain aspect of public order and safety. It spans all aspects of public order and safety. . . .

19. The key question – which lies at the foundation of the legal dispute between the parties is the one related to the scope of the power of the military government to ensure public

order and safety. Does the military government have the same powers as an ordinary government, or rather does its nature as a military government limit its possibilities and if so, under what circumstances? . . .

20. It seems to me that the scope of the power of the military government – alongside security and military considerations – is delimited by two major parameters: the first concerns the duty of the military government to act as a proper government which sees to the needs of the local population in all areas of life; the second concerns the limits of a military government which is not a permanent government but a temporary one that is not a sovereign but rather a ruler pursuant to the laws of war.

21. . . . This court acts in accordance with the Hague Regulations as long as they have not been changed by new customs or an international treaty which is applicable in Israel. However, in the framework of the Regulations themselves, there is room to address the powers and functions of a proper government, and this not according to social views which were prevalent more than a hundred years ago, but according to what is accepted and practiced among civilized peoples in our day and age.

9.4.2.2 Amnesty International, *Iraq: Looting, Lawlessness and Humanitarian Consequences* (11 April 2003) MDE14/085/2003[1]

Recommendations to the occupying powers

Amnesty International urges the US/UK forces to live up to their responsibilities under international humanitarian law as occupying powers. These include the duty to restore and maintain public order and safety (Article 43 of the Hague Regulations). Any use of force that may be required should comply with international human rights and humanitarian law, including the Basic Principles on the Use of Force and Firearms by Law Enforcement Officials. In areas under their control, the occupying forces should urgently take measures to enforce law and order, specifically by preventing acts of looting and pillage, including of official Iraqi government documents, destruction and violence towards people. While recognizing that the UK/US military forces are not a policing force, Amnesty International urges them to do everything in their power to maintain law and order within the requirements of international human rights and humanitarian laws. Troops with the appropriate training and in adequate numbers must be deployed as a matter of urgency to ensure such functions. Amnesty International reminds the occupying powers that they are obliged to ensure, if necessary, the provision of food and medical supplies to the inhabitants of the occupied territories (Article 55 of the Fourth Geneva Convention). The Fourth Geneva Convention further states that the occupying power has the duty "of ensuring and maintaining, with the cooperation of national and local authorities, the medical and hospital establishments and services, public health and hygiene in the occupied territories". The occupying powers should also ensure the availability of necessary supplies so that hospitals and medical services can work properly.

---

[1]   www.refworld.org/docid/3f1306084.html.

9.4.2.3 **South Ossetia,** Human Rights Watch, *Up in Flames: Humanitarian Law Violations and Civilian Victims in the Conflict over South Ossetia* (2009), p.123

3.7 Russia's Responsibility as Occupying Power

When Russian forces entered Georgia, including South Ossetia and Abkhazia, which are de jure parts of Georgia, they did so without the consent or agreement of Georgia. International humanitarian law on occupation therefore applied to Russia as an occupying power as it gained effective control over areas of Georgian territory ...

... overall, Russian authorities did not take measures to stop the widespread campaign of destruction and violence against civilians in villages in South Ossetia ... and in the buffer zone in undisputed Georgian territory. .... This deliberate violence against civilians started in the immediate aftermath of Georgian forces' withdrawal from South Ossetia and continued in waves in the weeks that followed; concomitantly, Russian forces' failure to ensure protection of civilians in territories under their control was persistent. Russian forces therefore violated their obligation as an occupying power to "ensure public order and safety" and to provide security to the civilian population in the territory under its control. This is a serious violation of international humanitarian law.

9.4.3 Security Needs of Occupying Power

9.4.3.1 **Israel,** *Ayub et al.* v. *Minister of Defence et al.,* (Judgment), Case No. HCJ 606/78, Israeli Supreme Court sitting as the High Court of Justice (15 March 1979)

Note: *The Petitioners were landowners in the occupied region of Judea and Samaria. The case concerned complaints that the Respondents had confiscated the Petitioners' land, denied their rights to enter and use their land, and allowed Jewish settlements on the confiscated land. The Respondents argued the confiscation order was required for 'exigent military needs'. On the issue of the security needs of occupying powers, the Court said:*

... the thing which motivated the petitioners to turn to us at this late stage was the fact that their lands were now used for the purpose of erecting civil settlements for Jewish communities. Said use – they argue – completely contradicts respondents' argument that said areas are required for military and security purposes. This is, in fact, their main complaint. .... But the main thing is that as far as the pure security consideration is concerned there is no doubt that the fact that settlements – even "civilian" settlements – of citizens of the occupying power, are located in the territories, makes a significant contribution to the security of that area and helps the military to fulfil its duties. It is not necessary to be an expert on military and security matters to understand that it is easier for terrorist elements to act against the enemy in an area inhabited only by indifferent or supportive population, as opposed to an area which is also inhabited by people who may follow them and inform the authorities of any suspicious act. They will not provide perpetrators refuge, assistance and equipment. This is clear and there is no need to elaborate. It should only be reminded that according to respondents' affidavits, the settlers are subordinated to the military authority, either formally or due to the circumstances. Their presence over there is made possible and facilitated by the military. Therefore I still hold the opinion, ... that Jewish settlement in an occupied territory – for as long as there is a belligerent situation – serves genuine military needs.

9.4.3.2 Israel, *Beit Sourik Village Council* v. *The Government of Israel and Commander of the IDF Forces in the West Bank*, (Judgment) Case No. HCJ 2056/04, Israeli Supreme Court Sitting as the High Court of Justice (2 May 2004)

Note: *The case concerned the legality of a 'separation fence' being built by the Israeli government in the occupied territories in the West Bank. As to whether the 'separation fence' could be justified on grounds related to the security needs of the occupying powers, the Israeli High Court of Justice said*:

23. The general point of departure of all parties – which is also our point of departure – is that Israel holds the area in belligerent occupation (occupatio bellica). ... In the areas relevant to this petition, military administration, headed by the military commander, continues to apply. ... The authority of the military commander flows from the provisions of public international law regarding belligerent occupation. ...

36. The problem of balancing between security and liberty is not specific to the discretion of a military commander of an area under belligerent occupation. It is a general problem in the law, both domestic and international. Its solution is universal. It is found deep in the general principles of law, including reasonableness and good faith. One of those foundational principles which balance between the legitimate objective and the means of achieving it is the principle of proportionality. According to it, the liberty of the individual can be limited (in this case, the liberty of the local inhabitants under belligerent occupation), on the condition that the restriction is proportionate. ...

44. The principle of proportionality applies to our examination of the legality of the separation fence. ... Indeed, our point of departure is that the separation fence is intended to realize a security objective which the military commander is authorized to achieve. The key question regarding the route of the fence is: is the route of the separation fence proportionate? The proportionality of the separation fence must be decided by the three following questions, which reflect the three subtests of proportionality. First, does the route pass the appropriate means test (or the rational means test)? The question is whether there is a rational connection between the route of the fence and the goal of the construction of the separation fence. Second, does it pass the test of the least injurious means? The question is whether, among the various routes which would achieve the objective of the separation fence, is the chosen one the least injurious. Third, does it pass the test of proportionality in the narrow sense? The question is whether the separation fence route, as set out by the military commander, injures the local inhabitants to the extent that there is no proper proportion between this injury and the security benefit of the fence. According to the relative examination of this test, the separation fence will be found disproportionate if an alternate route for the fence is suggested that has a smaller security advantage than the route chosen by respondent, but which will cause significantly less damage than that original route. ...

84. The injury caused by the separation fence is not restricted to the lands of the inhabitants and to their access to these lands. The injury is of far wider a scope. It strikes across the fabric of life of the entire population. In many locations, the separation fence passes right by their homes. In certain places (like Beit Sourik), the separation fence surrounds the village from the west, the south and the east. The fence directly affects the links between the local inhabitants and the urban centers (Bir Nabbala and Ramallah). This link is difficult even without the separation fence. This difficulty is multiplied sevenfold by the construction of the fence.

85. The task of the military commander is not easy. He must delicately balance between security needs and the needs of the local inhabitants. We were impressed by the sincere desire of the military commander to find this balance, and his willingness to change the original plan in order to reach a more proportionate solution. . . . Despite all this, we are of the opinion that the balance determined by the military commander is not proportionate. There is no escaping, therefore, a renewed examination of the route of the fence, according to the standards of proportionality that we have set out.

9.4.4 Amendment of Domestic Laws of Occupied Territory

9.4.4.1 UK, British Ministry of Defence, *The Joint Service Manual of the Law of Armed Conflict* (Joint Service Publication 383, 2004 Edition)

11.11 Legislative measures may be taken for the security of the occupying forces, the maintenance of order, the proper administration of the territory, and to enable the occupying power to carry out its obligations under the Convention for the welfare of the inhabitants. The occupying power may, however, repeal or amend laws that are contrary to international law and is also entitled to make changes mandated or encouraged by the UN Security Council. . . .

11.25 There is an obligation during the occupation to respect the laws in force in the occupied territory unless absolutely prevented. An occupying power would be prevented from respecting the laws in force if they conflicted with its obligations under international law, especially Geneva Convention IV 1949. The occupying power is not obliged to use the full powers available under the laws in force in occupied territory. It may suspend any of those laws that affect its own security, for example, those concerning conscription, electoral enfranchisement, rights of public assembly, the bearing of arms, and the freedom of the press. The right of the inhabitants to take legal action in the local courts must not be affected. The occupying power may amend the existing law of the occupied territory or promulgate new law if this is necessitated by the exigencies of armed conflict, the maintenance of order, or the welfare of the population. The domestic law of the occupying power (apart from that affecting its own armed forces) does not extend to occupied territory. Since the occupying power has a duty to look after the welfare of the inhabitants, regulations, for example, fixing prices and securing the equitable distribution of food and other commodities, are permissible. The occupying power should make no more changes to the law than are absolutely necessary, particularly where the occupied territory already has an adequate legal system. . . .

11.56 During the occupation, the existing criminal law of the occupied territory remains in force. It may be amended, suspended, or repealed by the occupying power only if it constitutes a threat to security or impedes compliance with international law. To the same extent, the courts of occupied territory may continue to administer the criminal law.

11.57 The occupying power may introduce new criminal laws as necessary to enable it to fulfil its international obligations, maintain orderly government, and ensure the security of the occupying power, its forces, administration, establishments, and lines of communication.

9.4.5 Prolonged Occupation of Territory

9.4.5.1 Israel, *Jam'iat Iscan Al-Ma'almoun* v. *IDF Commander in the Judea and Samaria Area*, (Judgment), Case No. HCJ 393/82, Israeli Supreme Court sitting as the High Court of Justice (28 December 1983)

Note: *The facts of this case are set out in Section 9.4.2.1. Emphasising the difference in the short- and long-term occupation and the parallel effect this has on an occupying power's obligations under the international law regime, the High Court of Justice of Israel said:*

22. In establishing the scope of the powers of the military government according to the formula regarding "public order and safety," it is appropriate to take into consideration the distinction between short term military government and long term military government. This distinction runs through the legal literature regarding the laws of belligerent occupation. ... The Hague Regulations themselves were developed and formulated against the background of short term military occupation. ... This distinction between a short term military government and a long term military government has significant influence over the content which is to be infused into securing "public order and safety." ... It is only natural that in short term military occupation, military-security needs reign supreme. However, in long term military occupation, the needs of the local population receive extra validity ... The fact that the Hague Regulations were enacted against the backdrop of short term belligerent occupation may cause the situation whereby there is no appropriate answer in the Regulations to many of the questions which arise in the daily life of a long term military occupation. Here too, we cannot change the Hague Regulations. We must implement them, since they form part of our law. However, this distinction between the types of military government according to the time element may serve as a consideration for policy in all those cases where there is room to develop such policy within the framework of the Regulations themselves. A clear example of this is Regulation 43. Public order and safety require consideration of the time element and the very fact that the Regulations in their entirety were formulated against the backdrop of a short term military government does not prevent the development of rules regarding the scope of authority in a long term military government within the broad and flexible framework created by Regulation 43 of the Hague Regulations. ...

23. The second parameter affecting the framework of the authorities of the military government is related to the character of the military regime, a regime which does not imbibe life from election by locals, which is not a sovereign by its own right and which

receives its power from the laws of war itself. It is, of its essence, a temporary regime even if this temporariness is of long duration. Therefore, the conclusion that some powers which are vested in the ordinary sovereign are not vested in a military government follows from the very essence of the military government. ...The conclusion that follows is that a military government is not permitted to make substantive changes of a permanent character to the political, administrative or judicial institutions in an area which is under belligerent occupation other than in extraordinary cases such as where existing institutions contravene, in content, the principles of basic justice and morality. ... Thus, for example, this parameter necessarily leads to the conclusion that a military government may not sell government real estate and its legal status in this real estate is that of usufructory only.

24. The two aforesaid parameters – good governance on one hand and the temporary lack of sovereignty on the other – outline the framework inside which the military government's authority exists. ...

9.4.5.2 Israel, 'Yesh Din'-Volunteers for Human Rights v. The Commander of the IDF Forces in the West Bank et al., (Judgment), Case No. HCJ 2164/09, Israeli Supreme Court Sitting as the High Court of Justice (26 December 2011)

Note: *The case concerned an application by the 'Yesh Din' Association for an order that the Respondent should cease quarrying activity in Israeli-owned quarries within Area C of the occupied territory of Judea and Samaria. As to whether such an order would comply with international law, the High Court of Israel said:*

10. ... Following our review of the parties' stances in that context, we came to the conclusion that considering the factual basis presented to us by the State, and while considering the unique circumstances of the Area, the State's interpretation of the manner in which it exercises its powers in accordance with Article 55 [HCIV] is reasonable, and thus it requires the adjustment of the laws of occupation to the reality of prolonged occupation.

11. Accordingly, we shall first examine the extent of the quarrying and its effect on the Area's resources pool. The data presented by the State in this context shows that the usage of the minerals of the Area is indeed relatively limited, and could be deemed as usage by usufructuary, which does not constitute a depletion of the capital. Therefore, it seems that the quarrying activity, in its current extent of operation, does not contradict the provisions of Article 55.

12. It should be stated further, as aforementioned, that the State announced that the recommendations submitted to the political echelon had stated, inter alia, that no new quarries, which are primarily aimed at producing quarrying materials for the sale thereof to Israel, shall be established in the Area. ... The state of affairs is somewhat different regarding the activities of currently active quarries, most of which, if not all of which, seem to be the outcome of the development momentum the industry gained during the mid-1970s, following the beginning of the belligerent occupation era. ... As inferred from the material brought before us by both parties, even those scholars who hold the opinion that there is no prohibition on making beneficial use of the minerals of a territory held in belligerent occupation under Article 55, do acknowledge the existence of a dispute regarding whether one may also consider new quarrying sources that had not existed in the era preceding the occupation, as resting within the limits of legitimate use set by Article 55.

An answer to this issue, under the circumstances of this case, is directly connected to the question regarding the compliance of the Quarries' activities with Article 43 of the Hague Regulations.

13. ... When considering the interpretation of international law governing the Area, as it has been held in the course of our rulings, one may fear that adopting the Petitioner's strict view might result in the failure of the military commander to perform his duties pursuant to international law. For instance, adopting the stance, according to which under the current circumstances the military commander must cease the operations of the Quarries, might cause harm to existing infrastructures and a shut-down of the industry, which might consequently harm, of all things, the wellbeing of the local population.

9.4.6 Transformative Occupation

9.4.6.1 Iraq, Iraq Coalition Provisional Authority, CPA Order No 39 (as amended) (20 December 2003)

Pursuant to my authority as Administrator of the Coalition Provisional Authority (CPA) and the laws and usages of war, and consistent with relevant UN Security Council resolutions, including Resolution 1483 (2003), ...

Noting that facilitating foreign investment will help to develop infrastructure, foster the growth of Iraqi business, create jobs, raise capital, result in the introduction of new technology into Iraq and promote the transfer of knowledge and skills to Iraqis

Recognizing the problems arising from Iraq's legal framework regulating commercial activity and the way in which it was implemented by the former regime. ...

Recognizing the CPA's obligation to provide for the effective administration of Iraq, to ensure the well being of the Iraqi people and to enable the social functions and normal transactions of every day life,

Acting in a manner consistent with the Report of the Secretary General to the Security Council of July 17, 2003, concerning the need for the development of Iraq and its transition from a non-transparent centrally planned economy to a market economy characterized by sustainable economic growth through the establishment of a dynamic private sector, and the need to enact institutional and legal reforms to give it effect,

Having coordinated with the international financial institutions, as referenced in paragraph 8(e) of the U.N. Security Council Resolution 1483, ...

9.5 USE OF LETHAL FORCE IN OCCUPIED TERRITORY

9.5.1 Israel, *The Public Committee against Torture in Israel et al.* v. *The Government of Israel et al. ('Targeted Killing Case'),* (Judgment), Case No. HCJ 769/02, Israeli Supreme Court Sitting as the High Court of Justice (11 December 2005)

Note: *The facts of this case are outlined in Chapter 1, Section 1.6.1. On the use of force in conditions of belligerent occupation, the Israeli High Court of Justice said:*

40. . . . Second, a civilian taking a direct part in hostilities cannot be attacked at such time as he is doing so, if a less harmful means can be employed. In our domestic law, that rule is called for by the principle of proportionality. Indeed, among the military means, one must choose the means whose harm to the human rights of the harmed person is smallest. Thus, if a terrorist taking a direct part in hostilities can be arrested, interrogated, and tried, those are the means which should be employed. . . . Trial is preferable to use of force. A rule-of-law state employs, to the extent possible, procedures of law and not procedures of force. . . . Arrest, investigation, and trial are not means which can always be used. At times the possibility does not exist whatsoever; at times it involves a risk so great to the lives of the soldiers, that it is not required. . . . However, it is a possibility which should always be considered. It might actually be particularly practical under the conditions of belligerent occupation, in which the army controls the area in which the operation takes place, and in which arrest, investigation, and trial are at times realizable possibilities. Of course, given the circumstances of a certain case, that possibility might not exist. At times, its harm to nearby innocent civilians might be greater than that caused by refraining from it. In that state of affairs, it should not be used. . . .

9.6 FORCED LABOUR

9.6.1 South Ossetia, **Human Rights Watch,** *Up in Flames: Humanitarian Law Violations and Civilian Victims in the Conflict over South Ossetia* (2009), pp. 178–9

Ossetian forces forced many of the male detainees to work, which included recovering decomposing bodies from the streets of Tskhinvali, digging graves, and burying bodies, as well as clearing the streets of building debris from the hostilities. . . . None of the workers received any compensation for this work. Under the Fourth Geneva Convention, adults (individuals age 18 or older) may be required to work as is necessary to maintain public utilities, and to meet needs of the army and humanitarian needs, such as activities related to feeding, sheltering, clothing, and health care of the civilian population. People must be appropriately compensated for their work, and there can be no obligation to work based on any form of discrimination. Unpaid or abusive forced labor, or work that amounts to partaking in military operations, is strictly prohibited.

9.7 TRANSFER OF OCCUPYING POWER'S POPULATION INTO OCCUPIED TERRITORY

9.7.1 ICJ, *Legal Consequences of the Construction of a Wall in the Occupied Palestinian Territory* (Advisory Opinion) [2004] I.C.J. Rep. 136

Note: *The facts of this case are set out in Chapter 2, Section 2.2.6. On the issue of an occupying power transferring its population into an occupied territory, the ICJ said:*

120. As regards these settlements, the Court notes that Article 49, paragraph 6, of the Fourth Geneva Convention provides: "The Occupying Power shall not deport or transfer parts of its own civilian population into the territory it occupies." That provision prohibits ... any measures taken by an occupying Power in order to organize or encourage transfers of parts of its own population into the occupied territory. In this respect, the information provided to the Court shows that, since 1977, Israel has conducted a policy and developed practices involving the establishment of Settlements in the Occupied Palestinian Territory, contrary to the terms of Article 49, paragraph 6, just cited. The Security Council has thus taken the view that such policy and practices "have no legal validity". It has also called upon "Israel, as the occupying Power, to abide scrupulously" by the Fourth Geneva Convention and: "to rescind its previous measures and to desist from taking any action which would result in changing the legal status and geographical nature and materially affecting the demographic composition of the Arab territories occupied since 1967, including Jerusalem and, in particular, not to transfer parts of its own civilian population into the occupied Arab territories" (resolution 446 (1979) of 22 March 1979). The Council reaffirmed its position in resolutions 452 (1979) of 20 July 1979 and 465 (1980) of 1 March 1980. ... The Court concludes that the Israeli settlements in the Occupied Palestinian Territory (including East Jerusalem) have been established in breach of international law.

9.7.2 ECtHR, *Demopoulos* v. *Turkey (Decision as to Admissibility)* [GC], (App Nos 46113/99, 3843/02, 13751/02, 13466/03, 10200/04, 14163/04, 19993/04, 21819/04) (ECHR, 1 March 2010)

Note: *The case arises out of the Turkish military operations in Northern Cyprus in July and August 1974 and the continued division of the territory thereafter. All the parties in the case claimed ownership of fixed or moveable property in the northern part of Cyprus under the control of the Turkish Republic of Northern Cyprus (TRNC). The Applicants claimed this violated their property rights. The ECtHR found in the following terms:*

85. Thus, the Court finds itself faced with cases burdened with a political, historical and factual complexity flowing from a problem that should have been resolved by all parties assuming full responsibility for finding a solution on a political level. This reality, as well as the passage of time and the continuing evolution of the broader political dispute must inform the Court's interpretation and application of the Convention which cannot, if it is to be coherent and meaningful, be either static or blind to concrete factual circumstances ...

116. The Court must also remark that some thirty-five years after the applicants, or their predecessors in title, left their property, it would risk being arbitrary and injudicious for it to attempt to impose an obligation on the respondent State to effect restitution in all cases, or even in all cases save those in which there is material impossibility, a suggested condition put forward by the applicants and intervening Government which discounts all legal and practical difficulties barring the permanent loss or destruction of the property. It cannot agree that the respondent State should be prohibited from taking into account other considerations, in particular the position of third parties. It cannot be within this Court's task in interpreting and applying the provisions of the Convention to impose an

unconditional obligation on a Government to embark on the forcible eviction and rehous-
ing of potentially large numbers of men, women and children even with the aim of
vindicating the rights of victims of violations of the Convention.

9.8 DEPORTATION

9.8.1 Israel, *Affo et al.* v. *Commander of IDF Forces in the West Bank*, (Judgment), Case No. HCJ 785/87, Israeli Supreme Court Sitting as the High Court of Justice (10 April 1988)

Note: *The Petitioners were deported from various occupied territories on the grounds they were conducting hostile activities towards the State of Israel 'so as to endanger the state and public peace'. On the issue whether the deportation of the Petitioners violated their rights under Article 49, Fourth Hague Convention, the Israeli HCJ said:*

3h. . . . What concerned the draftsmen of the Convention were the mass deportations for
purposes of extermination, mass population transfers for political or ethnic reasons or for
forced labour. This concern is the "legislative purpose" and this is the material context. It is
reasonable to conclude that the reference to mass and individual deportations in the text of
the Article was inserted in reaction also to the Nazi methods of operation used in World
War II, in which mass transfers were conducted, sometimes on the basis of common ethnic
identity, or by rounding up people in Ghettos, in streets or houses, at times on the basis of
individual summonses through lists of names. Summons by name was done for the purpose
of sending a person to death, to internment in a concentration camp, or for recruitment for
slave labour in the factories of the occupier or in agriculture. Moreover, it seems that the
summons to slave labour was always on an individual basis.

(i) The gist of the Petitioners' argument is that the first paragraph prohibits any transfer
of a person from the territory against his will. . . . The implications of this thesis are that
Article 49 does not refer only to deportations, evacuations and transfers of civilian
populations, as they were commonly defined in the period of the last war, but also to the
removal of any person from the territory under any circumstances, whether after a legitimate judicial proceeding (e.g. an extradition request), or after proving that the residence was
unlawful and without permission . . ., or for any other legal reason, based upon the internal
law of the occupied territory. According to the said argument, from the commencement of
military rule over the territory there is a total freeze on the removal of persons, and
whosoever is found in a territory under military rule cannot be removed for any reason
whatsoever, as long as the military rule continues.

9.8.2 ICTY, *Prosecutor* v. *Stakić*, (Appeal Judgment), Case No. IT-97-24-A, Appeal Chamber (22 March 2006)

Note: *The case concerns Stakić's involvement in events in the Municipality of Prijedor between April and September 1992. Stakić was indicted with complicity in genocide, extermination,* *crimes against humanity, persecutions, other inhuman acts and deportation. On the issue of deportation, the ICTY said*:

300. In the view of the Appeals Chamber, the crime of deportation requires the displacement of individuals across a border. The default principle under customary international law with respect to the nature of the border is that there must be expulsion across a de jure border to another country, as illustrated in Article 49 of Geneva Convention IV and the other references set out above. Customary international law also recognises that displacement from 'occupied territory', as expressly set out in Article 49 of Geneva Convention IV and as recognised by numerous Security Council Resolutions, is also sufficient to amount to deportation.

9.9 DETENTION[2]

9.9.1 ECtHR, *Al-Jedda* v. *The United Kingdom* [GC], (App No. 27021/08) (Judgment, 7 July 2011)

Note: *On 10 October 2004, US soldiers, acting on UK intelligence, arrested the applicant and conveyed him to Basra where he was detained by British forces at the Sha'aibah Divisional Temporary Detention Facility. The Applicant was interned until December 2007. The Applicant subsequently claimed his internment violated his rights under Article 5 ECHR (right to liberty and security). As to the use of detention by an occupying power, the ECtHR held as follows*:

108. ... Article 43 of the Hague Regulations requires an Occupying Power to take "all the measures in his power to restore, and ensure, as far as possible, public order and safety, while respecting, unless absolutely prevented, the laws in force in the country". While the International Court of Justice in its judgment *Armed Activities on the Territory of the Congo* interpreted this obligation to include the duty to protect the inhabitants of the occupied territory from violence, including violence by third parties, it did not rule that this placed an obligation on the Occupying Power to use internment; indeed, it also found that Uganda, as an Occupying Power, was under a duty to secure respect for the applicable rules of international human rights law, including the provisions of the International Covenant for the Protection of Civil and Political Rights, to which it was a signatory. In the Court's view it would appear from the provisions of the Fourth Geneva Convention that under international humanitarian law internment is to be viewed not as an obligation on the Occupying Power but as a measure of last resort. ...

109. In conclusion, therefore, the Court considers that United Nations Security Council Resolution 1546, in paragraph 10, authorised the United Kingdom to take measures to contribute to the maintenance of security and stability in Iraq. However, neither Resolution 1546 nor any other United Nations Security Council Resolution explicitly or implicitly required the United Kingdom to place an individual whom its authorities considered to constitute a risk to the security of Iraq into indefinite detention without charge. In these

---

[2]   See Chapter 3 Section 3.6.

circumstances, in the absence of a binding obligation to use internment, there was no conflict between the United Kingdom's obligations under the Charter of the United Nations and its obligations under Article 5 § 1 of the Convention.

110. In these circumstances, where the provisions of Article 5 § 1 were not displaced and none of the grounds for detention set out in sub-paragraphs (a) to (f) applied, the Court finds that the applicant's detention constituted a violation of Article 5 § 1.

9.9.2 Israel, *Marab et al.* v. *IDF Commander in the West Bank et al.*, (Judgment), Case No. HCJ 3239/02, Israeli Supreme Court Sitting as the High Court of Justice (28 July 2002)

Note: *A petition was issued challenging the legality of a special order authorising the detention of thousands of people in the occupied territories of Judea and Samaria as part of the IDF 'Operation Defensive Shield', which aimed to destroy Palestinian terrorist infrastructures in the region. The High Court of Justice said as follows:*

19. Detention for the purpose of investigation infringes the liberty of the detainee. Occasionally, in order to prevent the disruption of investigatory proceedings or to ensure public peace and safety, such detention is unavoidable. A delicate balance must be struck between the liberty of the individual, who enjoys the presumption of innocence, and between public peace and safety. Such is the case with regard to the internal balance within the state—between the citizen and his state—and such is the case with regard to the external balance outside the state—between a state that is engaged in war, and between persons detained during that war. . . .

The prohibition is not against detention, but rather against arbitrary detention. The various laws which apply to this matter, whether they concern times of peace or times of war, are intended to establish the proper balance by which the detention will no longer be arbitrary. . . .

21. . . . On the one hand, the liberty of each resident of occupied territory is, of course, recognized. On the other hand, international law also recognizes the duty and power of the occupying state, acting through the military commander, to preserve public peace and safety; see Article 43 of the Annex to the Hague Convention Regulations Respecting The Laws and Customs of War on Land-1907 [hereinafter Hague Regulations]. In this framework, the military commander has the authority to promulgate security legislation intended to allow the occupying state to fulfil its function of preserving the peace, protecting the security of the occupying state, and the security of its soldiers. See Article 64 of the Geneva Convention Relative to the Protection of Civilian Persons in Time of War-1949 [hereinafter the Fourth Geneva Convention]. Consequently, the military commander has the authority to detain any person suspect of committing criminal offences, and any person he considers harmful to the security of the area. He may also set regulations concerning detention for investigative purposes—as in the matter at hand—or administrative detention—which is not our interest in this petition. . . . True, the Fourth Geneva Convention contains no specific article regarding the authority of the commander to order detentions for investigative purposes. However, this authority can be derived from the law

in the area and is included in the general authority of the commander of the area to preserve peace and security. This law may be changed by security legislation under certain circumstances. Such legislation must reflect the necessary balance between security needs and the liberty of the individual in the territory. An expression of this delicate balance may be found in Article 27 of the Fourth Geneva Convention. . . . Moreover, Article 78 of the Fourth Geneva Convention provides that residents of the area may, at most, be subjected to interment or assigned residence. This appears to allow for the possibility of detention for the purpose of investigating an offence against security legislation. We would reach this same conclusion if we were to examine this from the perspective of international human rights law. International law, of course, recognizes the authority to detain for investigative purposes, and demands that this authority be balanced properly against the liberty of the individual. Thus, regular criminal detention is acceptable, while arbitrary detention is unacceptable.

9.10 DESTRUCTION OF PROPERTY

9.10.1 Eritrea-Ethiopia Claims Commission, *Partial Award: Central Front, Eritrea's Claims 2, 4, 6, 7, 8 & 22* (2004) 26(4) RIAA 115

Note: *The facts of this case are set out in Section 9.2.2. As to the destruction of property during belligerent occupation, the Commission said:*

c. Infrastructure Destruction

85. The principal damage claim by Eritrea relating to Senafe Town is for the deliberate, unlawful destruction of infrastructure, in particular of a number of substantial buildings. The Commission received evidence from multiple sources showing that a significant number of local government and other important buildings in Senafe had been destroyed by the time Eritrea resumed administration of the town in June 2001. Most of these buildings had been demolished by military explosives, including anti-tank mines of types found in the weapons inventories of both Parties. . . .

87. Ethiopia . . . asserts that, even if it had destroyed some of the buildings in question, such destruction would have been lawful. The Commission cannot agree with that assertion. The relevant rule of law is found in Article 53 of Geneva Convention IV, which states: Any destruction by the Occupying Power of real or personal property belonging individually or collectively to private persons, or to the State, or to other public authorities, or to social or cooperative organizations, is prohibited, except where such destruction is rendered absolutely necessary by military operations.

88. Ethiopia has not suggested any reason why the destruction of any of the properties in question could have been rendered "absolutely necessary" by military operations other than simply to prevent their reuse by Eritrea if and when it should regain control of Senafe Town. The Commission does not agree that denial of potential future use of properties like these, which are not directly usable for military operations as are, for example, bridges or railways, could ever be justified under Article 53.

9.11 APPLICATION OF IHRL IN MILITARY OCCUPATION[3]

9.11.1 ECtHR, *Loizidou* v. *Turkey (Preliminary Objections)*, (App No. 55721/07) (ECHR, 13 March 1995)

Note: *The Applicant, a Cypriot national, claimed that Turkish forces were preventing her from peacefully enjoying her property in the occupied part of Cyprus, thereby violating her property rights contrary to Article 1 of Protocol No. 1 ECHR. Turkey claimed the ECtHR was not competent to adjudge the claim as the alleged violations did not fall under Turkey's jurisdiction, but rather that of the TRNC. Affirming that an occupying power should secure compliance with Convention rights, the ECtHR said as follows:*

62. . . . Bearing in mind the object and purpose of the Convention, the responsibility of a Contracting Party may also arise when as a consequence of military action - whether lawful or unlawful - it exercises effective control of an area outside its national territory. The obligation to secure, in such an area, the rights and freedoms set out in the Convention derives from the fact of such control whether it be exercised directly, through its armed forces, or through a subordinate local administration.

9.11.2 ICJ, *Case Concerning Armed Activities on the Territory of the Congo (Democratic Republic of the Congo* v. *Uganda)* (Judgment) [2005] I.C.J. Rep. 168

216. The Court first recalls that it had occasion to address the issues of the relationship between international humanitarian law and international human rights law and of the applicability of international human rights law instruments outside national territory in its Advisory Opinion of 9 July 2004 on the Legal Consequences of the Construction of a Wall in the Occupied Palestinian Territory. . . . It thus concluded that both branches of international law, namely international human rights law and international humanitarian law, would have to be taken into consideration. The Court further concluded that international human rights instruments are applicable "in respect of acts done by a State in the exercise of its jurisdiction outside its own territory", particularly in occupied territories.

220. The Court thus concludes that Uganda is internationally responsible for violations of international human rights law and international humanitarian law committed by the UPDF and by its members in the territory of the DRC and for failing to comply with its obligations as an occupying Power in Ituri in respect of violations of international human rights law and international humanitarian law in the occupied territory.

9.11.3 ECtHR, *Cyprus* v. *Turkey (Just Satisfaction)*, (App No. 25781/94) (Judgment, ECHR 12 May 2014)

Note: *The case arose out of the earlier judgment of the ECtHR in 2001 in which it found numerous violations of the Convention by Turkey in the context of its military operations in*

---

[3]   See Chapter 3 Section 3.3.

Northern Cyprus. Addressing the question of Turkey's IHRL obligations as an occupying power, the ECtHR said:

77. ... Having effective overall control over northern Cyprus, its [Turkey's] responsibility cannot be confined to the acts of its own soldiers or officials in northern Cyprus but must also be engaged by virtue of the acts of the local administration which survives by virtue of Turkish military and other support. It follows that, in terms of Article 1 of the Convention, Turkey's "jurisdiction" must be considered to extend to securing the entire range of substantive rights set out in the Convention and those additional Protocols which she has ratified, and that violations of those rights are imputable to Turkey.

9.11.4 ECtHR, *Jaloud* v. *The Netherlands,* (App No. 47708/08) (Judgment, 20 November 2014)

Note: *The Applicant was the father of the late Azhar Jaloud, an Iraqi national, killed by Netherlands soldiers at a vehicle checkpoint north of Ar Rumaytah in South-Eastern Iraq. The Applicant alleged the Netherlands had breached Article 2 of the Convention by failing to investigate his son's death. Affirming 'authority and control' as relevant criteria for determining the application of IHRL in the context of belligerent occupation, the ECtHR said:*

152. ... The checkpoint had been set up in the execution of SFIR's mission, under United Nations Security Council Resolution 1483 ... to restore conditions of stability and security conducive to the creation of an effective administration in the country. The Court is satisfied that the respondent Party exercised its "jurisdiction" within the limits of its SFIR mission and for the purpose of asserting authority and control over persons passing through the checkpoint. That being the case, the Court finds that the death of Mr Azhar Sabah Jaloud occurred within the "jurisdiction" of the Netherlands, as that expression is to be construed within the meaning of Article 1 of the Convention.

9.12 UN ADMINISTRATION OF TERRITORY

9.12.1 SC, *Security Council Resolution 1244 on the Situation in Kosovo* (10 June 1999), 4011th Meeting, UN Doc. S/RES/1244 (1999)

... 9. Decides that the responsibilities of the international security presence to be deployed and acting in Kosovo will include:

a. Deterring renewed hostilities, maintaining and where necessary enforcing a ceasefire, and ensuring the withdrawal and preventing the return into Kosovo of Federal and Republic military, police and paramilitary forces, except as provided in point 6 of annex 2;
b. Demilitarizing the Kosovo Liberation Army (KLA) and other armed Kosovo Albanian groups as required in paragraph 15 below;
c. Establishing a secure environment in which refugees and displaced persons can return home in safety, the international civil presence can operate, a transitional administration can be established, and humanitarian aid can be delivered;

d. Ensuring public safety and order until the international civil presence can take responsibility for this task;

e. Supervising demining until the international civil presence can, as appropriate, take over responsibility for this task;

f. Supporting, as appropriate, and coordinating closely with the work of the international civil presence;

g. Conducting border monitoring duties as required;

h. Ensuring the protection and freedom of movement of itself, the international civil presence, and other international organizations;

11. Decides that the main responsibilities of the international civil presence will include:

a. Promoting the establishment, pending a final settlement, of substantial autonomy and self-government in Kosovo, taking full account of annex 2 and of the Rambouillet accords (S/1999/648);

b. Performing basic civilian administrative functions where and as long as required;

c. Organizing and overseeing the development of provisional institutions for democratic and autonomous self-government pending a political settlement, including the holding of elections;

d. Transferring, as these institutions are established, its administrative responsibilities while overseeing and supporting the consolidation of Kosovo's local provisional institutions and other peace-building activities;

e. Facilitating a political process designed to determine Kosovo's future status, taking into account the Rambouillet accords (S/1999/648);

f. In a final stage, overseeing the transfer of authority from Kosovo's provisional institutions to institutions established under a political settlement;

g. Supporting the reconstruction of key infrastructure and other economic reconstruction;

h. Supporting, in coordination with international humanitarian organizations, humanitarian and disaster relief aid;

i. Maintaining civil law and order, including establishing local police forces and meanwhile through the deployment of international police personnel to serve in Kosovo;

j. Protecting and promoting human rights;

k. Assuring the safe and unimpeded return of all refugees and displaced persons to their homes in Kosovo.

COMMENTARY

1. Modern-day occupations continue to give rise to significant challenges. These have arisen not only with respect to the application of the law of belligerent occupation, but also with regard to the wider issue of its ability to regulate modern forms of occupation. An already challenging situation is made more complex by the reluctance of some States to accept their status as occupying powers with the resultant obligations.

2. The definition of belligerent occupation in Article 42 HCIV is generally regarded as representing the customary international law definition of a state of occupation. It has,

however, been criticised as creating a gap in the protection afforded to the civilian population during an invasion and before the establishment of an occupation. In consequence, a separate and distinct functional definition based on Geneva Convention IV has been proposed by some commentators, under which an occupation exists when civilians fall into the hands of the enemy in the course of an invasion and was arguably adopted in the ICTY *Naletilić* Trial Judgment. It is submitted, however, that absent a further definition of occupation in the Convention and in view of the relationship between the Hague Regulations and the Convention established under Article 154 of the Convention, the customary international law definition must be regarded as representing the only applicable definition of occupation.[4]

3. An occupation is established when the occupying power establishes effective control over the occupied territory. Although there is consensus that an occupation may be limited in area, the issue of how long effective control must be established is debated. The EECC proposed a matter of days was enough, although it is difficult to regard even a temporary occupation as being established in these circumstances in any meaningful sense unless a functional definition of occupation is adopted. The presence of enemy troops on the ground is regarded as essential for the establishment of an occupation but it is not enough in itself, there must be more. In addition to the requirement for ground forces, the ICRC has identified two further elements: that the former government is incapable of exercising its authority over the area as a result of their presence and that the enemy forces are able to exercise authority in place of that government. Should this last requirement be read narrowly, as in the *Armed Activities in the Republic of the Congo* case, in which the ICJ required that the authority of the occupying force had been 'in fact established and exercised ... in the areas in question', or is it to be interpreted more broadly in terms of an ability to exercise control? Under one view, which has support from the ICRC, the latter interpretation is justified in order to prevent an occupying power from seeking to deny the existence of occupation and avoid its resultant obligations. The relevant text in both the UK and US manuals of the law of armed conflict, however, indicates a similar position to that adopted by the ICJ, namely the requirement for actual rather than potential control.[5]

4. A functional approach has been proposed by the ICRC with support among academic commentators and the EECC under which some of the occupation provisions under Geneva Convention IV are applicable prior to the establishment of occupation but, in contrast to the

---

[4]   See discussion in M. Zwanenburg, M. Bothe and M. Sassoli, 'Is the Law of Occupation Applicable to the Invasion Phase?' (2012) 94(885) *International Review of the Red Cross* 29–50. Despite its basis in Pictet's Commentary this interpretation is not accepted by the ICRC, see T. Ferraro, 'Determining the Beginning and End of an Occupation under International Humanitarian Law' (2012) 94(885) *International Review of the Red Cross* 137, fn.14. The *Naletilić* Trial Chamber accepted this relationship at paras 215–16 before going on to adopt Pictet's interpretation of a different concept of occupation with respect to civilians following invasion.
[5]   See also *United States* v. *Wilhelm List et al.,* Case No. 47 ('The Hostages Case') (Nuremberg, 19 February 1948) Law Reports of Trials of War Criminals, Vol. VIII (1949), p. 1243. Rather than referring to potential control the reference to the ability to exercise control is construed more narrowly. See note 4 above and UK British Ministry of Defence, *Manual of the Law of Armed Conflict* (Joint Service Publication 383, 2004 edition), para. 11.3.2, '... for occupation of an area it is not necessary to keep troops permanently stationed throughout that area. It is sufficient that ... troops are available, if necessary, to enforce authority in the area'.

Naletilić judgment without proposing a different model of occupation under GCIV.[6] Without formally accepting the functional approach, States may apply the law of occupation on a *de facto* basis prior to the establishment of effective occupation.[7] This has been criticised as giving rise to indeterminacy as to the application of the protective elements of the regime; however, this appears an equally valid criticism of the functional approach.[8]

5. The consensus is that absence of consent to the presence of the occupying force is a central element for the existence of belligerent occupation. The existence of valid consent falls to be determined in accordance with public international law with particular reference to treaty law. However, the possible existence of coerced consent will not necessarily give rise to the existence of an occupation, as illustrated by the situation in Kosovo, if the basis for action is in accordance with the UN Charter and the consent was validated by subsequent UN Security Council approval.

6. If the definition of the beginning of occupation has caused debate, it is fair to say that assessing the end of occupation has given rise to controversy, related mainly to the Coalition occupation of Iraq and the Israeli occupation of the Gaza Strip.[9] It is suggested that care must be exercised, as in other areas of occupation law, in developing a general principle on the basis of a single factual situation.

7. In the majority of cases it appears that the tests for the end of occupation are accepted as mirroring those for its establishment, namely the withdrawal of enemy ground forces, the ending of the suspension of the territorial State's authority and the substitution of the occupying power's authority in its stead, and the consent of the national government to the presence of the former occupation forces.

8. The ICRC has proposed, however, that exceptionally, despite the physical withdrawal of the occupying forces, if governmental functions which were exercised in the course of the occupation continue to be retained when the occupying forces withdraw, under a functional approach, this may amount to the retention of effective control justifying the occupation being regarded as continuing.[10] The continued existence of occupation establishes the continued existence of positive obligations on the part of the occupying power with respect to the territory's civilian population, as opposed to the negative obligations applicable in blockade, the primary alternative characterisation of the situation. This does not, however, appear to have significant support in either State practice, or indeed international jurisprudence. As the ECtHR concluded in *Sargsyan*, the physical presence of an occupying force forms an essential element of occupation. It has been proposed by the Supreme Court of Israel in the *Bassiouni* judgment that the continuing existence of

---

[6] Eritrea–Ethiopia Claims Commission, *Partial Award: Western Front, Aerial Bombardment and Related Claims – Eritrea's Claims 1, 3, 5, 9–13, 14, 21, 25 & 26 between The State of Eritrea and The Federal Republic of Ethiopia*, (2005) 26 (8) RIAA 291, para. 27. This approach is supported by Y. Dinstein, *The International Law of Belligerent Occupation* (CUP, 2009), p. 40.

[7] See US, Department of Defense, *Law of War Manual*, Office of General Counsel (June 2015, updated 2016), para. 11.1.3.1.

[8] See ICRC Report: *Expert Meeting: Occupation and Other Forms of Administration of Foreign Territory* (Geneva, 2012), p. 25.

[9] A situation which indeed applies to other areas of occupation law, such as the situation regarding prolonged occupation and transfer of population.

[10] ICRC, *Report on International Humanitarian Law and the Challenges of Contemporary Armed Conflicts*, 32nd International Conference, EN 32IC/15/11 (Geneva, 31 October 2015).

responsibilities on the part of Israel in the Gaza Strip lies rather in residual responsibilities arising from the previous prolonged occupation of that territory. The basis in law for their finding is difficult to determine. Under one analysis this is to be found in IHRL, although it may be arguable that it can be found in the general principles of IHL.[11]

9. The end of occupation on the basis of the consent of the national government to the continued presence of the former occupying forces, as was the case in Iraq, can give rise to controversy. It is, however, generally agreed that consent forms a valid basis to the end of occupation, for absence of consent is necessary for its existence, provided that the national government possesses real authority. In the case of Iraq, this was supported by the situation on the ground and the position of the UN Security Council that the occupation had ended at that point.

10. Under customary international law, the rights and duties of the occupier derive from the existence of occupation, accordingly Articles 42 and 43 HCIV are closely linked, with the latter establishing the core structure of duties imposed on the occupying power, supplemented by Article 64 of Geneva Convention IV. In contrast to the earlier restricted view of the freedom afforded to occupying powers to intervene in the administration of occupied territory, this is now generally accepted as enabling greater attention to be paid to the interests of the civil population of the occupied territory in line with the general shift in focus initiated by the Convention.

11. The concept of necessity under the law of occupation based on the second element of the text of Article 43 has been proposed to include three elements: military, relating to the security of the occupying power; legal, relating to the change in the legislative structure of the occupied territory; and, finally, material, the measures necessary to ensure that the requirements for the operation of modern civil society are satisfied. It has been proposed that particular weight requires to be given to the last element in prolonged occupation.

12. The occupying power may take necessary measures to protect the security of the occupying forces as well as being responsible for the maintenance of public order and safety. Restrictions are imposed on the ability of the occupying power to amend the legal system generally and the criminal law in particular. The Supreme Court of Israel has adopted an unusual position in the *Beth El* case in that the establishment of Israeli settlements in the occupied Palestinian territories has been justified on the basis that they support military needs, which are regarded as equating to security needs, notwithstanding their different focuses.

13. In contrast to the security detention of POW, where such prisoners as a class are regarded as posing a security threat justifying their detention until the conclusion of hostilities, the security detention of civilians must be justified on an individual basis with the initial decision to detain and the continuation of it the subject of review. Notwithstanding the basis of the prohibition on deportation originating in the mass deportations carried out by the Nazi regimes in occupied territory and contrary again to

---

[11]   See Y. Shany, *The Law Applicable to Non-Occupied Gaza: A Comment on Bassiouni* v. *Prime Minster of Israel (February 27, 2009)*. Hebrew University International Law Research Paper No. 13-09. Available at SSRN: https://ssrn.com/abstract=1350307.

Israeli domestic jurisprudence, the deportation of individual members of the civilian population is prohibited under Geneva Convention IV.

14. The use of force by the occupying power gives rise to difficult issues in view of the range of challenges that may be faced by the occupying power with uncertainty as to the applicable legal regime. Two models exist in practice; that of law enforcement within the structure of Article 43 HCIV, which assumes a relatively stable security situation, and that of the conduct of hostilities based on either the continuation of hostilities in the original IAC or their resumption. Both models imply significant differences regarding the use of force. The issue of whether one model applies to the occupied territory or whether both may arise simultaneously is debated. Does the requirement for the existence of effective control in the establishment or maintenance of occupation affect the analysis? Practice indicates that in view of the complex nature of modern occupation both may be simultaneously applicable. This does not render the decision as to which is applicable in response to a particular situation any easier and again practice indicates that their use will be dependent either on a situation-specific assessment or a sliding-scale assessment. In the case of the latter, there is support for the conduct-of-hostilities model to be applied on a comparable basis to its application in NIACs.[12]

15. The Supreme Court of Israel in reviewing the use of lethal force against civilians directly participating in hostilities has proposed that, in a limited category of cases, particularly in the case of occupation, there may be an expectation that the State will apply the law enforcement paradigm and seek to arrest the suspect. This analysis has received support in the *ICRC Interpretive Guidance*.[13] The majority view, however, is that it does not represent the position in the conduct of hostilities generally, although the law enforcement paradigm may apply in certain circumstances in occupation.

16. Although there is broad consensus as to the application of IHRL in the context of military occupation, supported by the international jurisprudence in both the *Wall* and the *DRC* v. *Uganda* cases, this is still contested by some States and commentators.[14] The developing ECtHR jurisprudence concerning the extraterritorial application of the Convention supports the application of either effective control or State agent authority.[15] The ECtHR *Hassan* judgment shows Article 5 ECHR being interpreted in the light of IHL on the basis of complementarity. While the ECHR is of course a regional human rights treaty, both the ICCPR and ICESCR have universal application. In view of the nature of the obligations under the latter, arguably a higher level of control is required to be exercised by the occupying power, with the ICESCR provisions assuming greater prominence in the case

---

[12]   See ICRC, *Expert Meeting Occupation and Other Forms of Administration of Foreign Territory*, Expert Meeting Occupation and Other Forms of Administration of Foreign Territory Report prepared and edited by T. Ferraro, ICRC, Geneva, April 2012, pp. 109ff.

[13]   See *Interpretive Guidance on the Notion of Direct Participation in Hostilities Under International Law* (Geneva, May 2009), with specific reference to section IX.

[14]   As A. Roberts notes in 'Transformative Military Occupation: Applying the Laws of War and Human Rights' (2006) 100 *American Journal of International Law* 580, 597, the underlying analysis regarding the extraterritorial application of the ICCPR in the *Wall* case is open to serious criticism which affects the value of the authority beyond its basic application. See discussion in Chapter 3.

[15]   See Chapter 3 Section 3.3.

of prolonged occupation. Can there be said, however, to be a central core of social and economic rights, which will impact on all cases of occupation?

17. The occupation of Iraq from 2003 to 2004 is an illustration of a transformative occupation. How far can this be regarded as having been governed by the law of occupation and to what extent was it rather authorised by the UN Security Council Mandate? CPA Order No 39 in setting out the basis for the transformation of the economic structures and the legal system referred both to IHL and UNSCR 1483. The current emphasis on the welfare of the population of the occupied territory is regarded as justifying a more permissive approach than had historically been the case. This may permit some transformative action being taken in the course of an occupation, for example in connection with the application of IHRL, although how far change is permitted on this basis is debated. The conservationist principle of the law of occupation still precludes a transformative occupation in the full sense.

18. Turning from transformative to long-term occupation, a central question again is the extent to which the occupying power can move beyond the conservationist approach under the law of occupation to meet the changing requirements of the civilian population of the occupied territory. The Supreme Court of Israel, sitting as the High Court of Justice, concluded that there is indeed a relevant distinction between short- and long-term occupation, with the needs of the civilian population of the occupied territories having to be given proper consideration and Article 43 HCIV being assessed against the requirements for public order and safety in a 'modern civilized country at the end of the twentieth century'.[16] There is general agreement that this domestic decision reflects the position under the current interpretation of the law of occupation.

19. The transfer of an occupying power's population into an occupied territory, that is, settlement within an occupied territory by members of the occupying power's population, is prohibited under Article 49(6) of Geneva Convention IV. This has been a particularly controversial issue with respect to the Israeli occupation of the Palestinian occupied territories, but it is one that arises in the context of other occupations such as in Northern Cyprus or the Western Sahara although less prominently.[17] What impact does the prolonged existence of such settlement have both *de facto* and *de jure*? The impact of large-scale population transfers such as that in both the latter occupations is readily apparent. The ECtHR *Demopoulos* decision highlights the need to have regard to the rights of settlers as well as the original population when considering the issue of restitution of property as opposed to compensation. This ruling, within the human rights model, may suggest a significant shift in the weighing of the balance of interests in such cases, with regard being had to the rights of established settlers as opposed to the original and still legal owners.

20. Finally, related to the definition of belligerent occupation is the question of the application of the law of occupation to UN operations. The issue here does not concern military occupations in the course of a Chapter VII authorised operation that have been

---

[16] *Jam'iat Iscan Al-Ma'almoun v. IDF Commander in the Judea and Samaria Area* (Judgment), Case No. HCJ 393/82, Israeli Supreme Court sitting as The High Court of Justice (28 December 1983), para. 21.

[17] See E. Kontorovich, 'Unsettled: A Global Study of Settlements in Occupied Territories', North Western University School of Law Public Law and Legal Theory Series, No 16-20 (2016).

preceded by invasion, which are regarded as being governed by IHL. The question relates rather to UN operations in recent years in which the UN was concerned with the transitional administration of territory such as Kosovo and East Timor following what some commentators described as coerced consent. The absence of consent is the principal difference between belligerent occupation and UN operations despite common elements. Notwithstanding the question of the validity of consent, it may nonetheless be regarded as valid, in view of Article 52 of the Vienna Convention, if the operation is in furtherance of the aims of the UN Charter and if the UN Security Council subsequently validates the consent. Although the law of occupation may not apply *de jure* in such cases, it has been proposed that the *de facto* application of occupation law by analogy to such UN-administered territory may assist in providing answers to the situations confronting such administrations. There is, however, resistance to this position, with some commentators taking the view that the appropriate model is the accepted IHRL paradigm and that the *de facto* application of the law of occupation in such circumstances would be of little benefit and would potentially carry considerable risk in view of the lack of certainty and the absence of the protections afforded by the *de jure* application of occupation law. Opposing this position are those who consider that the law of occupation provides a more appropriate model for the conduct of such an administration, which is likely to confront similar issues with respect to public order and security to those found in a military occupation.

10

The Law of Non-International Armed Conflict

INTRODUCTION

Non-international armed conflicts (NIACs) are nowadays the prevalent type of armed conflict; however, their legal regulation remains rudimentary, partly due to the State-centred nature of international law and partly due to States' interests in protecting their sovereignty. Common Article 3 forms the basis of the legal regulation of NIACs and has acquired customary law status. APII, which specifically regulates NIACs, applies only to States that have ratified the Protocol although some of its provisions have customary law character. Common Article 3 and APII have different thresholds of application: Common Article 3 requires a minimum level of organisation of armed groups and a minimum level of intensity; whereas APII requires a higher level of organisation, protracted violence and control of territory by armed groups.[1] Moreover, APII does not apply to hostilities between armed groups. Inevitably, NIACs give rise to many questions relating to, among others, the applicable IHL and IHRL rules, their geographic and temporal scope, the legal basis upon which armed groups are bound by IHL and IHRL, the application of the principle of distinction to the targeting of individuals[2] and the regulation of detention in NIACs.

Resources: Common Article 3; Arts 1–6, 13–18 APII

Cases and Materials

---

[1] See Chapter 1, Sections 1.2.4–1.2.6 for the definition of a NIAC and of its conditions.
[2] See also Chapter 4.

10.1 APPLICABLE LAW

10.1.1 ICJ, *Case Concerning Military and Paramilitary Activities in and Against Nicaragua (Nicaragua v. United States of America) (Merits, Judgment)* [1986] I.C.J. Rep. 14

Note: *The facts of this case are outlined in Chapter 1, Section 1.2.3.1. On the law applicable to NIACs the ICJ said as follows:*

218. ... Article 3 which is common to all four Geneva Conventions of 12 August 1949 defines certain rules to be applied in the armed conflicts of a non-international character. There is no doubt that, in the event of international armed conflicts, these rules also constitute a minimum yardstick, in addition to the more elaborate rules which are also to apply to international conflicts; and they are rules which, in the Court's opinion, reflect what the Court in 1949 called "elementary considerations of humanity".

10.1.2 ICTY, *Prosecutor* v. *Tadić*, (Decision on the Defence Motion for Interlocutory Appeal on Jurisdiction), Case No. IT-94-1, Appeals Chamber (2 October 1995)

Note: *The facts of this case are outlined in Chapter 1, Section 1.1.1. On the application of IHL to NIAC, the ICTY said the following:*

97. Since the 1930s, however, the aforementioned distinction [between international and non-international armed conflict] has gradually become more and more blurred, and international legal rules have increasingly emerged or have been agreed upon to regulate internal armed conflict. There exist various reasons for this development. ... Fourthly, the impetuous development and propagation in the international community of human rights doctrines, particularly after the adoption of the Universal Declaration of Human Rights in 1948, has brought about significant changes in international law, notably in the approach to problems besetting the world community. A State-sovereignty-oriented approach has been gradually supplanted by a human-being-oriented approach. ... It follows that in the area of armed conflict the distinction between interstate wars and civil wars is losing its

value as far as human beings are concerned. . . . If international law, while of course duly safeguarding the legitimate interests of States, must gradually turn to the protection of human beings, it is only natural that the aforementioned dichotomy should gradually lose its weight.

10.1.3 ICTY, *Prosecutor* v. *Delalić et al., ('Celebici Case')* (Judgment), Case No. IT-96-21-A, Appeals Chamber (20 November 2001)

Note: *The facts of this case are outlined in Chapter 5, Section 5.4.4.1. Confirming the status of Common Article 3 as the 'minimum yardstick' applicable to both IAC and NIAC, the ICTY said the following:*

143. It is indisputable that common Article 3, which sets forth a minimum core of mandatory rules, reflects the fundamental humanitarian principles which underlie international humanitarian law as a whole, and upon which the Geneva Conventions in their entirety are based. These principles, the object of which is the respect for the dignity of the human person, developed as a result of centuries of warfare and had already become customary law at the time of the adoption of the Geneva Conventions because they reflect the most universally recognised humanitarian principles. These principles were codified in common Article 3 to constitute the minimum core applicable to internal conflicts, but are so fundamental that they are regarded as governing both internal and international conflicts. . . .

147. Common Article 3 may thus be considered as the "minimum yardstick" of rules of international humanitarian law of similar substance applicable to both internal and international conflicts. It should be noted that the rules applicable to international conflicts are not limited to the minimum rules set out in common Article 3, as international conflicts are governed by more detailed rules.

10.1.4 ICRC, *Increasing Respect for International Humanitarian Law in Non-International Armed Conflicts* (February 2008),[3] p. 7

The rules of IHL applicable in situations of non-international armed conflict are found in both treaty and customary law. . . .

   Although the existence of so many provisions and treaties may appear to be sufficient, the treaty rules applicable in non-international armed conflicts are, in fact, rudimentary compared to those applicable in international armed conflicts. . . .

   The rules of customary international humanitarian law, however, fill some important gaps in the regulation of non-international armed conflicts. First, many of the provisions of Additional Protocol II are now considered to be part of customary international law and, thus, binding on all parties to non-international armed conflicts. These rules include the prohibition of attacks on civilians, the obligation to respect and protect medical and religious personnel, medical units and transports, the prohibition of starvation, the

---

[3] www.icrc.org/sites/default/files/topic/file_plus_list/0923-increasing_respect_for_international_humanitar
ian_law_in_non-international_armed_conflicts.pdf.

prohibition of attacks on objects indispensable to the survival of the civilian population, the obligation to respect the fundamental guarantees of persons who are not taking a direct part, or who have ceased to take a direct part, in hostilities, the obligation to search for and respect and protect the wounded, sick and shipwrecked, the obligation to search for and collect the dead, the obligation to protect persons deprived of their liberty, the prohibition of the forced movement of civilians, and specific protection for women and children.

Customary international humanitarian law also goes beyond the rudimentary provisions of common Article 3 and Additional Protocol II. Practice has created a substantial number of additional customary rules relating to the conduct of hostilities (e.g. the distinction between civilian objects and military objectives, the prohibition of indiscriminate attacks and attacks in violation of the principle of proportionality), rules on specifically protected persons and objects (e.g. humanitarian relief personnel and objects, journalists, and protected zones), and rules on specific methods of warfare (e.g. prohibitions of denial of quarter and perfidy).

However, IHL is not the only body of law that guarantees protection for persons in situations of non-international armed conflict. The provisions of international human rights law – particularly, non-derogable human rights – are complementary to IHL and also protect those who are vulnerable in such situations. Moreover, domestic law – in the State in which a conflict is taking place – often provides additional protections and limits on behaviour, and may provide a framework of safeguards that have to be respected in situations of non-international armed conflict.

10.2 ARMED GROUPS AND IHL

10.2.1 Philippines, *Comprehensive Agreement on Respect for Human Rights and International Humanitarian Law between the Government of the Republic of the Philippines and the National Democratic Front of the Philippines* (16 March 1998)[4]

Article 1. In the exercise of their inherent rights, the Parties to the armed conflict shall adhere to and be bound by the generally accepted principles and standards of international humanitarian law

10.2.2 SCSL, *Prosecutor* v. *Kallon & Kamara* (Decision on Challenge to Jurisdiction: Lomé Accord Amnesty) Case No. SCSL-2004-15-AR72 (E), SCSL-04-15-PT-060-I, ICL 24 (SCSL 2004), Appeals Chamber (13 March 2004)

Note: *The case arises out of the armed conflict in Sierra Leone between March 1991 and July 1999. The conflict was initiated by the Revolutionary United Front (RUF), an armed group,*

---

[4]   www.incore.ulst.ac.uk/services/cds/agreements/pdf/phil8.pdf.

seeking to overthrow the one-party rule of the All Peoples Congress. The accused were members of the RUF and they were charged with crimes against humanity, serious violations of IHL including conscription of children and violations of Common Article 3 GCs.

45. Notwithstanding the absence of unanimity among international lawyers as to the basis of the obligation of insurgents to observe the provisions of Common Article 3 to the Geneva Conventions, there is now no doubt that this article is binding on States and insurgents alike and that insurgents are subject to international humanitarian law. That fact, however, does not by itself invest the RUF with international personality under international law. . . .

47. It suffices to say, for the purpose of the present case, that no one has suggested that insurgents are bound because they have been vested with personality in international law of such a nature as to make it possible for them to be a party to the Geneva Conventions. Rather, a convincing theory is that they are bound as a matter of international customary law to observe the obligations declared by Common Article 3 which is aimed at the protection of humanity.

10.2.3 UN, *Report of the International Commission of Inquiry on Darfur to the United Nations Secretary-General Pursuant to Security Council Resolution 1564 of 18 September 2004* (Geneva, 25 January 2005)

172. The SLM/A and JEM, like all insurgents that have reached a certain threshold of organization, stability and effective control of territory, possess international legal personality and are therefore bound by the relevant rules of customary international law on internal armed conflicts referred to above. The same is probably true also for the NMRD.

10.2.4 ICRC, *Increasing Respect for International Humanitarian Law in Non-International Armed Conflicts* (February 2008),[5] p. 10

Who is bound by humanitarian law in non-international armed conflicts?

All parties to non-international armed conflicts – whether State actors or armed groups – are bound by the relevant rules of IHL.

. . .

Although only States may formally ratify or become party to the various international treaties, armed groups party to a non-international armed conflict also must comply with common Article 3, customary IHL, and, where applicable, Additional Protocol II. The extensive practice of international courts and tribunals and other international bodies affirms this obligation.

---

[5] www.icrc.org/sites/default/files/topic/file_plus_list/0923-increasing_respect_for_international_humanitar ian_law_in_non-international_armed_conflicts.pdf.

10.2.5 Sudan, *Agreement between the Government of the Republic of Sudan and the Sudan People's Liberation Movement to Protect Non-Combatant Civilians and Civilian Facilities from Military Attack* (31 March 2002)[6]

Article 1 Basic Undertakings

1. The Government of the Republic of Sudan (GOS) and the Sudan People's Liberation Movement (SPLM) (hereafter referred to as the "Parties") reconfirm their obligations under international law, including common Article 3 of the 1949 Geneva Conventions, to take constant care to protect the civilian population, civilians and civilian objects against the dangers arising from military operations.

10.2.6 Philippines, *Agreement on the Civilian Protection Component of the International Monitoring Team Bangerter Internal Control (IMT)* [Government of the Republic of the Philippines and Moro Islamic Liberation Front] (27 October 2009)[7]

The Parties reconfirm their obligations under humanitarian law and human rights law to take constant care to protect the civilian population and civilian properties against the dangers arising in armed conflict situations. In this context, the Parties commit themselves to:

a. Refrain from intentionally targeting or attacking non-combatants, prevent suffering of the civilian population and avoid acts that would cause collateral damage to civilians;
b. Refrain from targeting or intentionally attacking civilian properties or facilities such as schools, hospitals, religious premises, health and food distribution centres, or relief operations, or objects or facilities indispensable to the survival of the civilian population and of a civilian nature; . . .
d. Take all precautions feasible to avoid incidental loss of civilian life, injury to civilians, and danger to civilian objects;

10.2.7 Myanmar, Appel de Genève (Geneva Call), *Deed of Commitment Under Geneva Call for the Protection of Children from the Effects of Armed Conflict 17 November 2014*

We, the Pa-Oh National Liberation Organisation/Pa-Oh National Liberation Army (PNLO/PNLA), through our duly authorized representative(s) . . .

HEREBY solemnly commit ourselves to the following terms:

1. TO ADHERE to a total ban to the use of children in hostilities
2. TO ENSURE that children are not recruited into our armed forces, voluntarily or involuntarily. Children will not be allowed to join or remain in our armed forces . . .

---

[6] http://peacemaker.un.org/sites/peacemaker.un.org/files/SD_020331_Agreement%20to%20Protect%20Non-Combatant%20Civilians%20from%20Military%20Attack.pdf.
[7] http://peacemaker.un.org/sites/peacemaker.un.org/files/PH_091027_Agreement%20on%20Civilian%20Protection%20Component.pdf.

10.3 HUMAN RIGHTS IN NIACS[8]

10.3.1 General

10.3.1.1 IACtHR, *Case of the Serrano-Cruz Sisters* v. *El Salvador* (Judgment, Preliminary Objections), Inter-Am. Ct. H.R., Series C, No. 118 (23 November 2004)

Note: *This case involved the 'capture, abduction and forced disappearance' of the Serrano-Cruz sisters by soldiers from the Atlacati Battalion of the Salvadorian Army during a military operation in San Antonio de la Cruz on or about 2 June 1982. Reinforcing the complementary relationship of IHL and IHRL in NIACs and acknowledging the convergence of the norms, the IACtHR said the following:*

115. Likewise, in Article 3 common to all the Geneva Conventions of 12 August 1949, international humanitarian law establishes the complementarity of its norms with international human rights law, when it establishes, inter alia, the obligation of the State in the case of armed conflict not of an international nature to provide humane treatment, without any adverse distinction to persons taking no active part in the hostilities, including members of armed forces who have laid down their arms and those placed hors de combat by any cause. In particular, international humanitarian law prohibits, at any time or in any place, violence to the life, integrity and dignity with regard to the above-mentioned persons.

116. Moreover, the Additional Protocol to the Geneva Conventions of 12 August 1949, relating to the protection of victims of non international armed conflicts (Protocol II), acknowledges in its preamble the complementarity or convergence of the norms of international humanitarian law and those of international human rights law, ... And, Article 75 of Protocol I to these Conventions, on the protection of victims of international armed conflicts (when referring to fundamental guarantees for all persons who are in the power of a Party to the conflict and who do not benefit from more favorable treatment under the said Conventions or under that Protocol), and Article 4 of Protocol II (when referring to the fundamental guarantees of all persons who do not take a direct part or who have ceased to take part in hostilities, whether or not their liberty has been restricted), indicate that such persons are entitled to such guarantees, thus embodying the complementarity of international human rights law and international humanitarian law. ...

118. Based on the above, the Court observes that the State cannot question the full applicability of the human rights embodied in the American Convention, based on the existence of a non international armed conflict. The Court considers that it is necessary to reiterate that the existence of a non international armed conflict does not exempt the State from fulfilling its obligations to respect and guarantee the rights embodied in the American Convention to all persons subject to its jurisdiction, or to suspend their application.

---

[8]   See also, Chapter 3 Section 3.1.

10.3.2 Derogations[9]

10.3.2.1 ECtHR, *Aksoy* v. *Turkey*, (App No 21987/93) (Judgment, 18 December 1996)

Note: *The Applicant was arrested by Turkish police on the grounds he had been identified as a member of the Workers' Party of Kurdistan (PKK). The Applicant was taken into custody for a period of fourteen days wherein he was subjected to a form of torture known as 'Palestinian hanging' and was also electrocuted and beaten. The Applicant alleged violations of his Article 3, 5, 6 and 13 rights under the ECHR. On the issue of derogation from IHRL norms in states of public emergency, the ECtHR held as follows:*

68. The Court recalls that it falls to each Contracting State, with its responsibility for "the life of [its] nation", to determine whether that life is threatened by a "public emergency" and, if so, how far it is necessary to go in attempting to overcome the emergency. By reason of their direct and continuous contact with the pressing needs of the moment, the national authorities are in principle better placed than the international judge to decide both on the presence of such an emergency and on the nature and scope of the derogations necessary to avert it. Accordingly, in this matter a wide margin of appreciation should be left to the national authorities.

Nonetheless, Contracting Parties do not enjoy an unlimited discretion. It is for the Court to rule whether, inter alia, the States have gone beyond the "extent strictly required by the exigencies" of the crisis. The domestic margin of appreciation is thus accompanied by a European supervision. . . .

70. The Court considers, in the light of all the material before it, that the particular extent and impact of PKK terrorist activity in South East Turkey has undoubtedly created, in the region concerned, a "public emergency threatening the life of the nation" . . .

84. The Court has taken account of the unquestionably serious problem of terrorism in South East Turkey and the difficulties faced by the State in taking effective measures against it. However, it is not persuaded that the exigencies of the situation necessitated the holding of the applicant on suspicion of involvement in terrorist offences for fourteen days or more in incommunicado detention without access to a judge or other judicial officer. . . .

87. In conclusion, the Court finds that there has been a violation of Article 5 (3) of the Convention.

10.3.3 Human Rights Obligations of Armed Groups

10.3.3.1 El Salvador, *Human Rights Agreement between El Salvador and the Frente Farabundo Marti para la Liberación Nacional* (FMLN)[10] (26 July 1990)

The Government of El Salvador and the Frente Farabundo Marti para la Liberación Nacional (hereinafter referred to as "the Parties"),

Bearing in mind that the legal system of El Salvador provides for the recognition of human rights and the duty of the State to respect and guarantee such rights;

---

[9]   See also Chapter 3 Section 3.2, in particular, Human Rights Committee, General Comment 29: Article 4: Derogation during a State of Emergency (31 August 2001), 72nd Session, UN Doc. CCPR/C/21/Rev.1/Add.11.
[10]   http://theirwords.org/media/transfer/doc/sv_fmln_1990_01-2842601fe245f1d0622515dc9f668b92.pdf.

Considering also that the State has assumed obligations of this nature under many international conventions to which it is party;

Bearing in mind that the Frente Farabundo Marti para la Liberación Nacional has the capacity and the will and assumes the commitment to respect the inherent attributes of the human person;

Reiterating the common purpose, expressed in the Geneva Agreement, to guarantee unrestricted respect for human rights in El Salvador;

. . .

On the understanding that for the purposes of the present political agreement, "human rights" shall mean those recognized by the Salvadorian legal system, including treaties to which El Salvador is a party, and by the declarations and principles on human rights and humanitarian law adopted by the United Nations and the Organization of American States;

Have concluded the following agreement in pursuance of the initial objective of the Geneva Agreements

1. All necessary steps and measures shall be taken immediately to avoid any act or practice which constitutes an attempt upon the life, integrity, security or freedom of the individual.
2. Similarly, all necessary steps and measures shall be taken to eliminate any practice involving enforced disappearances and abductions. Priority shall be given to the investigation of any cases of this kind which may arise and to the identification and punishment of the persons found guilty.

10.3.3.2 Human Rights Council, *Report of the International Commission of Inquiry to Investigate All Alleged Violations of International Human Rights Law in the Libyan Arab Jamahiriya* (1 June 2011) 17th Session, UN Doc. A/HRC/17/44

72. Non-state actors in Libya, in particular the authorities and forces of the National Transitional Council cannot formally become parties to the international human rights treaties and are thus not formally given obligations under the treaties. Although the extent to which international human rights law binds non-state actors remains contested (. . .), it is increasingly accepted that where non-state groups exercise de facto control over territory, they must respect fundamental human rights of persons in that territory. The Commission has taken the approach that since the NTC has been exercising de facto control over territory akin to that of a Governmental authority, it will examine also allegations of human rights violations committed by the its forces. The Commission notes that the NTC has made a public undertaking in which it committed to "build a constitutional democratic civil state based on the rule of law, respect for human rights and the guarantee of equal rights and opportunities for all its citizens including full political participations by all citizens and equal opportunities between men and women and the promotion of women empowerment."

10.3.3.3 Human Rights Council, *Report of the Independent International Commission of Inquiry on the Syrian Arab Republic* (22 February 2012), 19th Session, UN Doc. A/HRC/19/69

106. The commission carefully reviewed the information gathered on the operations and activities to date of FSA groups. In this regard, the commission notes that, at a minimum,

human rights obligations constituting peremptory international law (ius cogens) bind States, individuals and non-State collective entities, including armed groups. Acts violating ius cogens – for instance, torture or enforced disappearances – can never be justified ...

133. The commission renews its recommendation that all armed groups ensure respect for and act in accordance with international human rights law. Armed groups, in particular the FSA and its local groups, should:

(a) Adopt and publicly announce rules of conduct that are in accordance with international human rights law and other applicable international standards, including those reflected in the Declaration of Minimum Humanitarian Standards;
(b) Publicly pledge not to torture or execute captured soldiers, Shabbiha members or civilians, not to target people who take no part in the clashes, and not to take hostages, whether civilian or military;
(c) Instruct FSA members to abide by these commitments and hold perpetrators of abuses within their ranks accountable;
(d) Take care to minimize the risk of civilians coming under Government fire or facing reprisals as a result of the deployment of FSA members in specific places;
(e) Provide relevant humanitarian and human rights institutions with all available information on the fate of persons it has captured, and give such actors full and unimpeded access to detainees.

10.4 GEOGRAPHIC AND TEMPORAL SCOPE OF NIACS[11]

10.4.1 ICTY, *Prosecutor* v. *Ramush Haradinaj*, (Judgment), Case No. IT-04-84-T, Trial Chamber I (3 April 2008)

Note: *The facts of this case are outlined in Chapter 1, Section 1.2.5.2. Reinforcing the earlier decision in* Tadić, *as to the temporal scope of NIACs, the ICTY said:*

100. ... However, since according to the *Tadić* test an internal armed conflict continues until a peaceful settlement is achieved, and since there is no evidence of such a settlement during the indictment period, there is no need for the Trial Chamber to explore the oscillating intensity of the armed conflict in the remainder of the indictment period.

10.4.2 Germany, *Aerial Drone Deployment on 4 October 2010 in Mir/Ali Pakistan ('Targeted Killing in Pakistan Case')*, Decision to Terminate Proceedings, Federal Prosecutor General, Case No 3 BJs 7/12-4 (23 July 2013), 157 ILR 722, pp. 744–6

Note: *The facts of this case are set out in Chapter 1, Section 1.2.4.6. As to the geographic scope of the NIAC in Afghanistan, the Court said:*

---

[11] See also Chapter 1 Section 1.4.

(d) *Territorial limitation of the conflict*

A determination that an armed conflict exists will be valid only where it is made with respect to a specific territorial extent and duration of time. Thus, the present analysis is limited exclusively to the situation given in the Pakistani FATA region during the years 2009 and 2010; ... Based on international law as it currently stands, the application of the international laws of war, with their special prohibitions and empowerments, continue to be limited in territorial scope to actual theatres of war only.

2. *Connection to the armed conflict*

The military deployment of the aerial drone in question served the targeted suppression of members of insurgent groups that had taken root in North Waziristan and thus did not occur merely on the occasion of combat. Given this functional context, the military operation in question occurred in connection with the identified armed conflict.

10.5 THE PRINCIPLE OF DISTINCTION IN NIACS[12]

10.5.1 ICTY, *Prosecutor* v. *Tadić*, (Decision on the Defence Motion for Interlocutory Appeal on Jurisdiction), Case No. IT-94-1, Appeals Chamber (2 October 1995)

Note: *The facts of this case are set out in Chapter 1, Section 1.1.1. On the issue of protection of civilians from hostilities, the ICTY commented:*

127. Notwithstanding these limitations, it cannot be denied that customary rules have developed to govern internal strife. These rules, as specifically identified in the preceding discussion, cover such areas as protection of civilians from hostilities, in particular from indiscriminate attacks, protection of civilian objects, in particular cultural property, protection of all those who do not (or no longer) take active part in hostilities, as well as prohibition of means of warfare proscribed in international armed conflicts and ban of certain methods of conducting hostilities.

10.5.2 IACHR, *Juan Carlos Abella* v. *Argentina*, Case 11.137, Report No. 55/97, Inter-Am. C.H.R., OEA/Ser.L/V/II.95, Doc 7 rev. (18 November 1997)

Note: *The factual background to this case is discussed at Chapter 1, Section 1.2.5.1. Having determined the existence of a NIAC and addressing the effect of DPH on the principle of distinction, the IACHR said as follows:*

178. When civilians, such as those who attacked the Tablada base, assume the role of combatants by directly taking part in fighting, whether singly or as a member of a group, they thereby become legitimate military targets. As such, they are subject to direct individualized attack to the same extent as combatants. Thus, by virtue of their hostile acts, the Tablada

---

[12]   See also Chapter 4 Section 4.2 and Chapter 2 Section 2.4.

attackers lost the benefits of the above mentioned precautions in attack and against the effects of indiscriminate or disproportionate attacks pertaining to peaceable civilians. In contrast, these humanitarian law rules continued to apply in full force with respect to those peaceable civilians present or living in the vicinity of the La Tablada base at the time of the hostilities.

10.5.3 ICTR, *The Prosecutor* v. *Rutaganda*, (Judgment and Sentence), Case No. ICTR-96-3-T, Trial Chamber I (6 December 1999)

Note: *The facts of this case are set out in Chapter 1, Section 1.1.3. On the issue of DPH, the ICTR commented in the following terms:*

100. . . . There is no concise definition of "civilian" in the Protocols. As such, a definition has evolved through a process of elimination, whereby the civilian population is made up of persons who are not combatants or persons placed hors de combat, in other words, who are not members of the armed forces. Pursuant to Article 13(2) of the Additional Protocol II, the civilian population, as well as individual civilians, shall not be the object of attack. However, if civilians take a direct part in the hostilities, they then lose their right to protection as civilians *per se* and could fall within the class of combatant. To take a "direct" part in the hostilities means acts of war which by their nature or purpose are likely to cause actual harm to the personnel and equipment of the enemy armed forces.

10.5.4 International Institute of Humanitarian Law, *Manual on the Law of Non-International Armed Conflicts with Commentary* (San Remo, 2006)

1.1.2 Fighters
a. For the purposes of this Manual, fighters are members of armed forces and dissident armed forces or other organized armed groups, or taking an active (direct) part in hostilities. . . .

1. . . . The term "fighters" has been employed in lieu of "combatants" in order to avoid any confusion with the meaning of the latter term in the context of the international law of armed conflict.

2. The phrases "active participation" and "direct participation" in hostilities are often used interchangeably. . . . There is no substantive distinction between the two terms in this context. What is required is "a sufficient causal relationship between the active participation and its immediate consequences."

3. It is important to distinguish active (direct) participation in hostilities from participation in the war effort. The former term is much more restrictive. Examples of active (direct) participation in hostilities include such activities as attacking the enemy, his materiel or facilities; sabotaging enemy installations; acting as members of a gun crew or artillery spotters; delivering ammunition; or gathering military intelligence in the area of hostilities. It would not include, however, general contributions to the war effort, such as working in a munitions factory.

4. Under Article 13.3 of Additional Protocol II, the loss of protection exists only "for such time as [civilians] take a direct part in hostilities." However, this limitation is not confirmed by customary international law. Such an approach would create an imbalance between the government's armed forces on the one hand and members of armed groups on the other, inasmuch as the former remain legitimate targets (under international law) throughout the conflict. Moreover, the proposition is impractical to implement on the ground.

Ordinary soldiers would be required to make complex and immediate assessments as to whether an individual's participation in hostilities is ongoing, at a time when the facts available are incomplete or unclear

1.1.3 Civilians
Civilians are all those who are not fighters.

For the purposes of this Manual, civilians who actively (directly) participate in hostilities are treated as "fighters".

10.5.5 ICRC, *Interpretive Guidance on the Notion of Direct Participation in Hostilities Under International Law* (Geneva, May 2009)[13]

II. THE CONCEPT OF CIVILIAN IN NON-INTERNATIONAL ARMED CONFLICT

For the purposes of the principle of distinction in non-international armed conflict, all persons who are not members of State armed forces or organized armed groups of a party to the conflict are civilians and, therefore, entitled to protection against direct attack unless and for such time as they take a direct part in hostilities. In non international armed conflict, organized armed groups constitute the armed forces of a non-State party to the conflict and consist only of individuals whose continuous function it is to take a direct part in hostilities ("continuous combat function").

10.5.6 ICC, *The Prosecutor* v. *Bahar Idriss Abu Garda*, (Decision on the Confirmation of Charges), Case No. ICC-02/05-02/09, Pre-Trial Chamber I (8 February 2010)

Note: *The facts of this case are outlined in Chapter 4, Section 4.4.3. Addressing the principle of distinction in the context of peacekeeping missions involved in a NIAC, the ICC said as follows:*

89. ... the Majority concludes that installations, material, units or vehicles involved in a peacekeeping mission in the context of an armed conflict not of an international character shall not be considered military objectives, and thus shall be entitled to the protection given to civilian objects, unless and for such time as their nature, location, purpose or use make an effective contribution to the military action of a party to a conflict and insofar as their total or partial destruction, capture or neutralization, in the circumstances ruling at the time, offers a definite military advantage.

---

[13] www.icrc.org/eng/assets/files/other/icrc-002-0990.pdf.

10.6 DETENTION[14]

10.6.1 General

10.6.1.1 ECtHR, *Case of Al-Jedda* v. *the United Kingdom* [GC], (App No. 27021/08) (Judgment, 7 July 2011)

Note: *On 10 October 2004, US soldiers, acting on UK intelligence, arrested the Applicant and conveyed him to Basra where he was detained by British forces at the Sha'aibah Divisional Temporary Detention Facility. The Applicant was interned until December 2007. The Applicant subsequently claimed his internment violated his rights under Article 5 ECHR (right to liberty and security). Addressing the authority to detain in post-occupation Iraq and the balance to be struck between the United Kingdom's obligations under the UN Charter and the ECHR, the ECtHR said as follows:*

107. The Court has considered whether, in the absence of express provision in Resolution 1546, there was any other legal basis for the applicant's detention which could operate to disapply the requirements of Article 5 § 1 of the Convention. ...

108. A further legal basis might be provided by the agreement, set out in the letters annexed to Resolution 1546, between the Iraqi government and the United States government, on behalf of the other States contributing troops to the Multinational Force, including the United Kingdom, that the Multinational Force would continue to carry out internment in Iraq where the Multinational Force considered this necessary for imperative reasons of security. However, such an agreement could not override the binding obligations under the Convention. ...

109. In conclusion, therefore, the Court considers that United Nations Security Council Resolution 1546, in paragraph 10, authorised the United Kingdom to take measures to contribute to the maintenance of security and stability in Iraq. However, neither Resolution 1546 nor any other United Nations Security Council resolution explicitly or implicitly required the United Kingdom to place an individual whom its authorities considered to constitute a risk to the security of Iraq in indefinite detention without charge. In these circumstances, in the absence of a binding obligation to use internment, there was no conflict between the United Kingdom's obligations under the Charter of the United Nations and its obligations under Article 5 § 1 of the Convention.

10.6.1.2 *Copenhagen Process on the Handling of Detainees in International Military Operations* (19 October 2012)

IX. *The Copenhagen Process Principles and Guidelines* are intended to apply to international military operations in the context of non-international armed conflicts and peace operations; they are not intended to address international armed conflicts.

10.6.1.3 ICRC, *Opinion Paper, Internment in Armed Conflict: Basic Rules and Challenges* (November 2014)[15]

... Detention is thus explicitly mentioned as one of the "causes" that will give rise to the application of the protections of Common Article 3. These protections are meant to apply to

---

[14]   See also Chapter 3 Section 3.6 and Chapter 5 Section 5.4.
[15]   www.icrc.org/en/document/internment-armed-conflict-basic-rules-and-challenges.

any form of detention related to the armed conflict, and will therefore also apply to detention for serious security reasons, i.e. internment. Additional Protocol II to the Geneva Conventions, adopted in 1977 - most provisions of which are widely considered to also reflect customary IHL - likewise governs deprivation of liberty in NIAC. ...

As is evident, Common Article 3 is silent on the grounds or procedural safeguards for persons interned in NIAC, even though internment is practiced by both States and non-State armed groups. Additional Protocol II explicitly mentions internment, thus confirming that it is a form of deprivation of liberty inherent to NIAC, but likewise does not refer to the grounds for internment or the procedural rights. ... In addition to the paucity of IHL, there are also unresolved issues related to the application of human rights law, some of which are mentioned below. It is thus submitted that the legal framework governing internment in NIAC should be determined on a case-by-case basis, i.e. taking into account the relevant legal obligations in each context.

In a "traditional" NIAC occurring in the territory of a State between government armed forces and one or more non-State armed groups, domestic law, informed by the State's human rights obligations, and IHL, constitutes the legal framework for the possible intern-ment by States of persons whose activity is deemed to pose a serious security threat. ...

Identifying the legal framework governing internment becomes particularly complicated in NIACs with an extraterritorial element, i.e. those in which the armed forces of one or more State, or of an international or regional organization, fight alongside the armed forces of a host State, in its territory, against one or more organized non-State armed groups.

... One view is that a legal basis for internment would have to be explicit, as it is in the Fourth Geneva Convention; in the absence of such a rule, IHL cannot provide it implicitly. Another view, shared by the ICRC, is that both customary and treaty IHL contain an inherent power to intern and may in this respect be said to provide a legal basis for internment in NIAC. ...

Whichever view one adopts, it is submitted that in the absence of specific provisions in common Article 3 or Additional Protocol II, additional authority related to the grounds for internment and the process to be followed needs to be obtained, in keeping with the principle of legality. Thus, an international agreement between an international force(s) and a host State should be concluded to this end. Alternatively, domestic law should be adopted, specifying the grounds and process for internment. In the latter case the domestic law basis should be provided by the host State or, in exceptional circumstances, by the State(s) to which the international force(s) belong. Grounds and process for internment may also be provided for in the Standard Operating Procedures of the international force(s), or other equivalent document binding on the force(s).

In this context it should be recalled that a UN Security Council resolution adopted under Chapter VII of the UN Charter would also provide a legal basis for internment in an extraterritorial NIAC. Legal experts differ as to whether such a resolution must expressly authorize internment or whether the standard formula of authorization to use "all necessary means" (to accomplish a mission) is sufficient. It is submitted that specificity as to the authorization for internment is preferable. The grounds and process for internment would then still need to be identified by reference to one of the sources mentioned above.

In addition to the challenges that have already been briefly noted, others arise, related to the application of human rights law in situations of NIAC with an extraterritorial element: State(s) composing the relevant international force(s) may not all be bound by the same human rights treaties; the extent of the extraterritorial reach of human rights law obligations is evolving (and remains disputed by some States), and the question of whether the assisting States must derogate from their human rights obligations in order to intern persons abroad with or without judicial review is unresolved in practice (no State has done so to date).

10.6.1.4 UK, *Serdar Mohammed* v. *Ministry of Defence* [2014] EWHC 1369 (QB)

Note: *The facts of this case are outlined in Chapter 4, Section 4.1.1.4. Reviewing the legal framework surrounding the Claimant's detention, the UK High Court said as follows:*

241. I am unable to accept the argument that CA3 and/or AP2 provide a legal power to detain, for five reasons.

242. First, I think it reasonable to assume that if CA3 and/or AP2 had been intended to provide a power to detain they would have done so expressly – in the same way as, for example, Article 21 of the Third Geneva Convention provides a power to intern prisoners of war. . . .

243. Second, all that seems to me to be contemplated or implicit in CA3 and AP2 is that during non-international armed conflicts people will in fact be detained. Such detention may be lawful under the law of the state on whose territory the armed conflict is taking place, or under some other applicable law; or it may be entirely unlawful. There is nothing in the language of CA3 or AP2 to suggest that those provisions are intended to authorise or themselves confer legality on any such detentions. . . .

244. Third, . . . the aim of both CA3 and Article 5 of AP2 is to guarantee certain basic minimum standards of treatment to all individuals who are deprived of their liberty for reasons relating to the armed conflict. The need to observe such minimum standards is equally relevant to all people who are in fact detained, and does not depend on whether or not their detention is legally justified.

245. Fourth, there are cogent reasons, mentioned earlier, which explain why states subscribing to the Geneva Conventions and Additional Protocols would not have agreed to establish by treaty a power to detain in the circumstances of a non-international armed conflict. In particular, given that CA3 applies to "each Party to the conflict" and AP2 applies to organised armed groups who are able to implement it, providing a power to detain would have meant authorising detention by dissident and rebel armed groups. That would be anathema to most states which face a non-international armed conflict on their territory and do not wish to confer any legitimacy on rebels and insurgents or accept that such groups have any right to exercise a function which is a core aspect of state sovereignty.

246. Fifth, I do not see how CA3 or AP2 could possibly have been intended to provide a power to detain, nor how they could reasonably be interpreted as doing so, unless it was possible to identify the scope of the power. However, neither CA3 nor AP2 specifies who may be detained, on what grounds, in accordance with what procedures, or for how long.

247. In the context of non-international armed conflicts, defining these matters poses intractable problems. The rules applicable to international armed conflicts are based on the assumption that there is a reasonably clear distinction between combatants and civilians. ... In non-international armed conflicts such as that taking place in Afghanistan the distinction between combatants and civilians may often be elusive. ...

248. Another feature of non-international armed conflicts is that they may be of long and uncertain duration, as illustrated by the fact that such a conflict has now been continuing in Afghanistan for nearly 12 years. There may also be no clearly identifiable point at which it can be said that the hostilities have come to an end. In such circumstances a power to detain until the end of hostilities would be particularly problematic.

249. A solution to some of these difficulties advocated by the ICRC is to advocate a power of detention which depends, not on the status of the detainee, but on a determination that detention of the individual is justified by "imperative reasons of security" ... On this approach detention is justified as long as such "imperative reasons of security" continue to exist. Even if this approach were to become generally accepted, it would still be necessary to identify procedures by which such determinations are to be made.

250. None of these matters, however, is addressed by CA3 or AP2. This confirms that it is not the purpose of these provisions to establish a legal basis for detention.

251. All these reasons lead, in my view, to the clear conclusion that CA3 and AP2 are not intended to, and do not, provide a legal basis for detention. Rather, their purpose is simply to guarantee a minimum level of humanitarian treatment for people who are in fact detained during a non-international armed conflict.

10.6.1.5 UK, Ministry of Defence, *Joint Doctrine Publication 1-10 Captured Persons* (January 2015, Third Edition)

146. During non-international armed conflict, the law governing the treatment of CPERS [captured persons] detained by our Armed Forces differs markedly from that described above. The situation will be governed by a combination of:

- the Law of Armed Conflict;
- the law of the nation in which hostilities are taking place;
- applicable international human rights treaties to which the UK is a party, for example, the European Convention of Human Rights and other international laws; and
- any international mandate for the operation, for example a UNSCR.

10.6.1.6 US, Department of Defense, *Law of War Manual*, Office of General Counsel (June 2015, Updated 2016)

17.17 DETENTION IN NIAC

17.17.1 State Authority to Detain. Law of war treaties have not limited the scope of whom a State may detain for reasons related to a non-international armed conflict, but have prescribed humane treatment for such persons. A State's authority to conduct detention operations has often been understood as incident to the legal basis of the State to engage in operations against the non-State armed group.

The precise legal requirements for a detention regime established by a State in non international armed conflict would likely depend a great deal on its domestic law.

17.17.1.1 *Non-Punitive Detention in Non-International Armed Conflict.* Non-punitive detention may be conducted on a variety of legal theories under international law. For example, although enemy non-State armed groups would not be entitled to POW status, a State may detain persons belonging to enemy armed groups, by analogy to the detention of POWs in international armed conflict. Similarly, although persons would not be protected persons under the GC, a State may detain persons for security reasons, by analogy to the detention of protected persons in international armed conflict or occupation. Other legal rationales for the detention of persons in non-international armed conflict also may be available.

17.17.1.2 *Punitive Detention in Non-International Armed Conflict.* During non-international armed conflict, a State could also detain persons pursuant to its criminal law. . . .

17.17.2 *Detention by Non-State Armed Groups.* Non-State armed groups typically would lack domestic legal authority to conduct detention operations. Their actions may be subject to prosecution under domestic statutes making punishable kidnapping, hostage taking, false imprisonment, interference with State officials, etc. Nonetheless, detention during non international armed conflict by non-State armed groups is not prohibited by international law. In any case, non-State armed groups that conduct detention operations must provide humane treatment to detainees.

17.17.3 Humane Treatment and Other Applicable Requirements. All persons (including those belonging to the State or those belonging to non-State armed groups) who are detained by the adverse party are entitled to the protections of Common Article 3 of the 1949 Geneva Conventions, including humane treatment. Although detainees are afforded humane treatment, they do not receive POW status.

10.6.1.7 International Commission of Jurists, *Legal Commentary on Elements of the Basic Principles and Guidelines Pertaining to Detention in Armed Conflict* (September 2015)[16]

Consistent with the view of many experts, this Commentary ... takes the view that Common Article 3 and Protocol II do not provide a legal authority to deprive a person of liberty in NIAC. The ICJ considers that these provisions simply guarantee a minimum level of humanitarian treatment for people who are in fact detained during a NIAC.

1. *If the Geneva Conventions and their Additional Protocols had intended to provide a power to detain in a NIAC, such authority would have been expressly provided ...*
2. *It is highly likely that the negotiating States to the Geneva Convention did not want to authorize grounds for detention in NIACs*
3. *If Common Article 3 and Articles 5 and 6 of Protocol II were to be interpreted as implying an authority to detain in NIACs, it would be necessary (but it is not possible) to identify the scope of such an implied power*

---

[16]   www.icj.org/icj-legal-commentary-on-the-right-to-challenge-the-lawfulness-of-detention-in-armed-conflict/.

4. *Because the scope of any implied power to intern in NIACs is not discernible, such internment would be arbitrary*

5. *IHL contemplates internment as a form of deprivation of liberty in NIACs, but only as a matter of fact, not as a matter of law*

6. *The purpose of Common Article 3 and Articles 5 and 6 of Protocol II is simply to guarantee a minimum level of humanitarian treatment*

7. *Customary international humanitarian law does not, as an alternative, authorize detention in NIACs*

Because IHL does not imply any authority to detain persons in a NIAC, the practical consequences of this are that any detention or internment in a NIAC must either: be fully compliant with the prohibition against arbitrary and unlawful detention under Article 9(1) of the ICCPR, without an accompanying derogation from the right to liberty; or be subject to a lawful derogation under Article 4 of the ICCPR.

10.6.1.8 **Human Rights Council,** *Investigation by the Office of the United Nations High Commissioner for Human Rights on Libya: Detailed Findings* (15 February 2016), 31st Session, UN Doc. A/HRC/31/CRP.3[17]

(b) Legal framework

128. Although international treaty law applicable to non-international armed conflict does not deal explicitly with the topic, the requirement that civilians and other protected persons be treated humanely is understood to require protection from arbitrary deprivation of liberty. Under customary international law, any security related detention must be justified by the existence of a present, direct and imperative threat by the individual concerned, and is subject to strict procedural requirements including that the person may effectively challenge the lawfulness of the detention, that the detention does not last any longer than absolutely necessary, and that there be initial and periodic reviews by an independent body possessing the same attributes of independence and impartiality as the judiciary.

10.6.1.9 UK, *Abd Ali Hameed Al-Waheed* v. *Ministry of Defence; Serdar Mohammed* v. *Ministry of Defence* [2017] UKSC 2

Note: *The facts of this case are set out in Chapter 5, Section 5.4.2.2. The Supreme Court held the power to detain in NIAC was conferred by the relevant UNSCR:*

44. International humanitarian law does not specifically authorise detention in a non-international armed conflict. But, as I have explained, the relevant Security Council Resolutions did authorise detention, and international humanitarian law regulates its consequences on the assumption that it is an inevitable feature of state practice. In that respect, the Resolutions served the same function in a non-international armed conflict as the authority to detain under article 21 of the Third Geneva Convention does in an international armed conflict. It conferred an authority in international law to detain in circumstances where this was necessary for imperative reasons of security.

---

[17] www.ohchr.org/Documents/Countries/LY/A_HRC_31_CRP_3.pdf.

10.6.2 Guarantees

10.6.2.1 The Islamic Emirate of Afghanistan, *The Layha [Code of Conduct] For Mujahideen: An Analysis of the Code of Conduct for the Taliban Fighters Under Islamic Law* 93 (881) IRRC (March 2011) 81

. . .

Chapter 2 – About prisoners

9. When an enemy, regardless of whether they are a local or a foreigner is captured, he will be handed over immediately to the person responsible in the province. After the handover it is at the discretion of the person responsible for the province whether to keep him [captive] with the particular Mujahids [those who captured him] or to hand him over to others.

10. If a local soldier, policeman, an official or other responsible person with affiliations to the slave administration has been captured, it is at the discretion of the governor to release them in the case of prisoners exchange, as part of a goodwill gesture or in exchange of solid guaranties. Receiving money for the prisoner's release is forbidden. Only Imam, Najib Imam and the provincial judge have the authority to execute or to punish. Nobody else has this authority. If a judge has not been appointed yet in a province it is up to the person responsible in the province to decide the fate [of a prisoner] with regard to their execution or punishment.

. . .

12. If a military infidel has been captured, his execution, release through prisoner exchange, intentional release or release upon payment in case the Muslims need money, is at the discretion of the Imam and Najib Imam. No one else has of the authority to make this decision. If the captive becomes Muslim, the Imam or Najib Imam has the authority to release him in a prisoner exchange, provided that there will be no danger of his becoming an infidel again.

13. If the Mujahids capture prisoners and, during transportation to their [Mujahids'] military centres, encounter a threat and are unable to take the captives to a safe place, and if the captives are people of the opposite side who have been captured during the war or who are officials of the opposite side, then the Mujahids present can kill them [the captives]. However, if they do not belong to these groups of people and there are doubts about the prisoners' status and they have not been identified yet or have been captured in relation to juridical [legal] issues, then the Mujahids are not authorized to kill them even if there is no option but to leave the captives at the scene.

14. If a policeman or soldier will surrender to the Mujahids and repent, the Mujahids are not allowed to kill him. If the policeman or soldier has a weapon with him, or if he had accomplished any great deeds, the Mujahids should express endearment towards him.

15. Mujahids should not expose those detained by them to starvation, thirst, cold or heat even if they deserve death. The Mujahids should punish the detained persons in accordance with the decision provided by Sharia concerning them, whether that would entail execution or any other type of punishment.

10.6.2.2 UK, British Ministry of Defence, *The Joint Service Manual of the Law of Armed Conflict*, (Joint Service Publication 383, 2004 Edition)

Treatment of persons in the hands of a party to the conflict

15.30 Humane treatment

Persons in the hands of a party to the conflict, whether the government side, dissident armed forces, or other armed groups, are entitled to humane treatment at all times. They must not be discriminated against on grounds of race, colour, religion or faith, sex, birth, or wealth, or similar criteria. The following acts are always prohibited with respect to these persons:

a. violence to life and person, in particular murder of all kinds, mutilation, cruel treatment, and torture;
b. taking of hostages;
c. 'rape, sexual slavery, enforced prostitution, forced pregnancy, forced sterilization, and any other form of sexual violence also constituting a serious violation of' Common Article 3;
d. other outrages upon personal dignity, in particular humiliating and degrading treatment;
e. 'physical mutilation or medical or scientific experiments of a kind which are neither justified by medical, dental or hospital treatment of the person concerned nor carried out in his or her interest, and which causes death to or seriously endangers the health of' that person;
f. the passing of sentences and the carrying out of executions without previous judgment pronounced by a regularly constituted court, affording all the judicial guarantees which are recognized as indispensable by civilized peoples.

15.30.3 Prisoner of war status does not arise in internal armed conflicts unless the parties to the conflict agree, or decide unilaterally as a matter of policy, to accord this status to detainees. Otherwise, the treatment of detainees is governed by the domestic law of the country concerned, any human rights treaties binding on that state in time of armed conflict and the basic humanitarian principles mentioned in paragraph 15.30. It is recommended that while detained in military custody, persons who have taken a direct part in hostilities should be given the same treatment as if they were prisoners of war. . . .

15.30.5 Indispensable judicial guarantees include as a minimum:

a. individual criminal responsibility (so that collective punishments would be unlawful);
b. the right of the accused not to be compelled to testify against himself;
c. the presumption of innocence until proved guilty;
d. notification to the accused of the charges against him;
e. adequate time and opportunity for the accused to prepare his defence;
f. the attendance of both prosecution and defence witnesses and, if necessary, an interpreter;
g. trial in person and public judgment.

15.30.6 Death penalties must not be pronounced or carried out.

10.6.2.3 ICRC, *Procedural Principles and Safeguards for Internment/Administrative Detention in Armed Conflict and Other Situations of Violence*, 87 (858) IRRC (June 2005) 375

Internment/administrative detention is an exceptional measure

Internment/administrative detention is not an alternative to criminal proceedings

Internment/administrative detention can only be ordered on an individual case-by-case basis, without discrimination of any kind

Internment/administrative detention must cease as soon as the reasons for it cease to exist

Internment/administrative detention must conform to the principle of legality

Right to information about the reasons for internment/administrative Detention

Right to be registered and held in a recognized place of internment/administrative detention

A person subject to internment/administrative detention has the right to challenge, with the least possible delay, the lawfulness of his or her detention

Review of the lawfulness of internment/administrative detention must be carried out by an independent and impartial body

An internee/administrative detainee should be allowed to have legal assistance

An internee/administrative detainee has the right to periodical review of the lawfulness of continued detention

An internee/administrative detainee and his or her legal representative should be able to attend the proceedings in person

An internee/administrative detainee must be allowed to have contacts with – to correspond with and be visited by – members of his or her family

An internee/administrative detainee has the right to the medical care and attention required by his or her condition

Access to persons interned/administratively detained

10.6.2.4 Libya, *Codes of Conduct National Transitional Council* 2011, 93 (882) IRRC (June 2011) 483, pp. 497, 499

. . .

Rules on the treatment of detainees

Detainees must receive humane treatment AT ALL TIMES, from the moment of capture. DO respect detainees and protect them from harm

Humane Treatment:

   DO NOT use any form of physical, sexual or mental violence against any detainee. No form of torture or intimidation is allowed.

   DO NOT subject detainees to humiliating or degrading treatment such as displaying them in a publicly humiliating fashion.

   DO NOT take revenge on detainees.

   DO NOT hold individuals answerable for acts for which they are not personally responsible.

DO NOT remove personal property from the detainees unless this is for security reasons. If any property is removed, a receipt must be provided to the detainee.

DO NOT obey an order to carry out any of these prohibited acts. That order is unlawful.

REPORT ANY INCIDENTS OF INHUMANE TREATMENT TO A SUPERIOR OFFICER

10.6.2.5 OHCHR, *United Nations Basic Principles and Guidelines on Remedies and Procedures on the Right of Anyone Deprived of their Liberty to Bring Proceedings Before a Court*, Report of the Working Group on Arbitrary Detention, (July 2015), UN Doc. A/HRC/30/376

Principle 16 . . .

31. Administrative detention or internment in the context of a non-international armed conflict may only be permitted in times of public emergency threatening the life of the nation and the existence of which is officially proclaimed. Any consequent deviation from procedural elements of the right to bring proceedings before a court to challenge the arbitrariness and lawfulness of the deprivation of liberty and to receive without delay appropriate and accessible remedies must be in conformity with the present Basic Principles and Guidelines, including on the principles of non-derogability, the right to be informed and the court as reviewing body, and the guidelines on equality of arms and burden of proof.

10.6.2.6 UK, Ministry of Defence, *Joint Doctrine Publication 1-10 Captured Persons* (January 2015, Third Edition)

1–8. Section 4 – Basic principles

120. Personal responsibility. . . .

121. Humane treatment. . . .

122. Sound administration. . . .

123. Legitimacy and campaign planning. **Abuse or mistreatment of any CPERS is illegal and is therefore a criminal offence.**[18] . . .

124. Reporting and accountability. . . .

125. Thorough training. . . .

126. Using subject matter experts. . . .

2–8. Section 2 – Prohibited acts

CPERS must not be subjected to torture, cruel, inhuman or degrading treatment, or violence to life in any form.

The threshold of cruel, inhuman and degrading treatment may also be reached from an aggregation of conditions which, if taken in isolation, may individually appear to be acceptable.

2–9. It is forbidden to take or distribute photographs, or otherwise make images, of CPERS (dead or alive) for personal reasons.

---

[18]   Bold in the original.

2-13. The five techniques [stress positions, hooding, subjection to noise, deprivation of sleep and rest, deprivation of food and water] must never be used as an aid to tactical questioning or interrogation, as a form of punishment, discriminatory conduct, intimidation, coercion or as deliberate mistreatment

HOODING IS PROHIBITED IN ALL CIRCUMSTANCES[19]

10.6.3 Transfer of Detainees[20]

10.6.3.1 Canada, *Amnesty International Canada and BCCLA* v. *Chief of the Defence Staff for the Canadian Forces and Attorney General of Canada* (2008 FCA 401), A-149-08 (Can)

Note: *In 2007 it emerged that some thirty Afghan prisoners who were captured by Canadian forces had been tortured by the Afghan National Directorate of Security (NDS) after having been transferred from Canadian custody to the NDS. The Federal Court of Appeal dismissed the application for judicial review in the following terms:*

[53] As part of Canada's military operations in Afghanistan, Canadian Forces are from time to time required to capture and detain insurgents, or those assisting the insurgents, who may pose a threat to the safety of Afghan nationals, as well as to members of the Canadian military and allied forces. . . .

[63] The Canadian Forces have the sole discretion to determine whether a detainee "shall be retained in custody, transferred to [the Afghan National Security Forces] or released." These determinations are made on a case-by-case basis by the Canadian Commander of Task Force Afghanistan at regular review meetings.

[64] Before transferring a detainee into Afghan custody, General Laroche must be satisfied that there are no substantial grounds for believing that there exists a real risk that the detainee would be in danger of being subjected to torture or other forms of mistreatment at the hands of Afghan authorities. . . .

[346] For the foregoing reasons, the questions posed by this motion should be answered as follows:

1. Does the *Canadian Charter of Rights and Freedoms* apply during the armed conflict in Afghanistan to the detention of non-Canadians by the Canadian Forces or their transfer to Afghan authorities to be dealt with by those authorities?
   NO
2. If the answer to the above question is "no" then would the Charter nonetheless apply if the applicants were ultimately able to establish that the transfer of the detainees in question would expose them to a substantial risk of torture?
   NO

---

[19]   Capitals in the original.
[20]   See also Chapter 3 Section 3.7, in particular the Agreements between the UK and Canadian governments and Afghanistan.

10.6.3.2 UK, *R (On the Application of Evans)* v. *Secretary of State for Defence* [2010] EWHC 1445 (Admin)

Note: *The case concerned the UK policy and practice, in the course of operations in Afghanistan, of transferring suspected insurgents detained by UK armed forces to the Afghan authorities. It was alleged such detainees would be at real risk of torture or serious mistreatment if transferred. On the issue of the transfer of detainees into the custody of the NDS, the High Court held the following conditions should be observed in order to safeguard the transferred detainees against risk of torture or mistreatment:*

293. At the centre of the case are the UK-Afghanistan MoU and the related EoL [Exchange of Letters]. Those documents contain what are on the face of it important assurances given by the Government of Afghanistan concerning the treatment of detainees, together with provisions for access to detainees for the purpose of verifying that the commitments entered into have been honoured in practice. … In a case such as this, where the assurances are backed up by provisions for monitoring and where the practical operation of the system can be assessed over a period of several years, we think it wrong to start with a dismissive attitude towards them. The position has to be looked at in the round. …

320. We have concluded, after some hesitation, that UK-captured detainees could now be transferred to NDS Kandahar without a real risk of their being subjected to torture or serious mistreatment at the hands of the NDS, *provided that* the existing safeguards are strengthened by observance of the following conditions: (i) all transfers must be made on the express basis (spelling out the requirements of the MoU and EoL) that the UK monitoring team is to be given access to each transferee on a regular basis, with the opportunity for a private interview on each occasion; (ii) each transferee must in practice be visited and interviewed in private on a regular basis; and (iii) the UK must consider the immediate suspension of further transfers if full access is denied at any point without an obviously good reason (we have in mind circumstances such as a security alert) or if a transferee makes allegations of torture or serious mistreatment by NDS staff which cannot reasonably and rapidly be dismissed as unfounded. We have expressed the third condition in terms of an obligation to consider immediate suspension of transfers rather than an automatic requirement to suspend transfers, because in relation to a matter as important as suspension it would be wrong to preclude an exercise of judgment based on the particular circumstances that have arisen; but the decision should in our view be conditioned by the same precautionary approach as led to the moratorium on transfers to NDS Kandahar in mid-2009. …

323. We have reached our conclusions in relation to NDS Kandahar and NDS Lashkar Gah with hesitation because, on the evidence taken as a whole, there is plainly a *possibility* of torture or serious mistreatment of UK transferees at those facilities. In our judgment, however, the operation of the monitoring system (reinforced by observance of the conditions we have set out), within the framework of the MoU and EoL, is sufficient to guard against the occurrence of abuse at those facilities on such a scale as to give rise to a *real risk* of torture or serious mistreatment in accordance with the principles considered earlier in this judgment. Isolated examples of abuse may occur, but we are not satisfied that a consistent pattern of abuse is reasonably likely, such as to expose all UK transferees to a real risk of ill-treatment.

324. We repeat that in reaching our conclusions we have taken into account the possibility of onward transfer of a detainee from NDS Kandahar or NDS Lashkar Gah to NDS Kabul, where we are not satisfied that the system provides sufficient safeguards for the protection of UK transferees. The practical limitations on onward transfer to NDS Kabul mean that the possibility is insufficiently large to give rise to a real risk of torture or serious mistreatment. We would have preferred to see the imposition of a condition that detainees transferred by the UK to NDS Kandahar or NDS Lashkar Gah are not to be transferred on to NDS Kabul, but we doubt whether such a condition would be realistic and we do not think that its absence should preclude transfers to NDS Kandahar or NDS Lashkar Gah.

325. On the basis indicated above, we conclude on the existing evidence that UK transfers to NDS Kandahar and NDS Lashkar Gah can proceed without breach of the Secretary of State's policy but that it would be a breach of that policy and therefore unlawful for UK transfers to be made to NDS Kabul.

326. The conclusion we have reached in this open judgment is in our view consistent with the contents of the closed judgment.

10.6.3.3 *Copenhagen Process on the Handling of Detainees in International Military Operations* (19 October 2012)

2. All persons detained or whose liberty is being restricted will in all circumstances be treated humanely and with respect for their dignity without any adverse distinction founded on race, colour, religion or faith, political or other opinion, national or social origin, sex, birth, wealth or other similar status. Torture, and other cruel, inhuman, or degrading treatment or punishment is prohibited. . . .

4. Detention of persons must be conducted in accordance with applicable international law. . . .

6. Physical force is not to be used against a detained person except in circumstances where such force is necessary and proportionate.

7. Persons detained are to be promptly informed of the reasons for their detention in a language that they understand. . . .

9. Detaining authorities are responsible for providing detainees with adequate conditions of detention . . .

11. In non-international armed conflict and where warranted in other situations, the detaining authority is to notify the ICRC or other impartial humanitarian organisation of the deprivation of liberty, release or transfer of a detainee. . . .

Detaining authorities are to provide the ICRC or other relevant impartial international or national organisations with access to detainees.

12. A detainee whose liberty has been deprived for security reasons is to, in addition to a prompt initial review, have the decision to detain reconsidered periodically by an impartial and objective authority that is authorised to determine the lawfulness and appropriateness of continued detention. . . .

15. A State or international organisation is to only transfer a detainee to another State or authority in compliance with the transferring State's or international organisation's international law obligations.

10.6.4 Detention by Armed Groups

10.6.4.1 IACHR, *Third Report on the Situation of Human Rights in Colombia* (1999), Chapter IV

131. The Commission deems it necessary to clarify why it does not condemn, as violative of international law, the acts of armed dissident groups in capturing members of the Army and security forces where the captives are not converted into hostages. . . .

132. As noted above, international humanitarian law prohibits the taking of hostages and the detention or internment of civilians other than for imperative reasons of security. International humanitarian law does not prohibit the capture of combatants. It simply treats such captures as a situation of deprivation of liberty which may, in practice, occur in armed conflict. International humanitarian law then proceeds to impose obligations on the captors to treat captives humanely, with respect and dignity. Violence to the life, health and physical or mental well-being of the captives is expressly and absolutely prohibited. Humanitarian law does not prevent the State from prosecuting and sanctioning under domestic law the individuals responsible for the capture and detention of its troops.

10.6.4.2 Kosovo, *Prosecutor* v. *Latif Gashi, Nazif Mehmeti, Naim Kadriu, Rrustem Mustafa,* (Verdict), Case No. 425/2001, District Court of Pristina (16 July 2003), pp. 16 and 21[21]

Note: *The accused were indicted in respect of their conduct between August 1998 and June 1999 in relation to detainees at five detention centres located at Bajgora, Llapashtica, Majac, Potok and Kolec in Kosovo. The allegations included murder. Reviewing the circumstances and legality of detention, the District Court of Pristina held as follows:*

Conclusion: the evidence showed that the vast majority of persons detained by the KLA Llap zone were detained for reasons that cannot fairly be said to be sufficient to justify detention. Further, and no matter what the merits of imposing detention upon them, it follows that once detention was imposed upon them the victims were at all material times thereafter persons who were taking no active part in hostilities and who thus enjoyed the protection of the rights granted under Common Article 3 and Article 4 of Additional Protocol II.

. . . However, "Illegal detention," as such is neither mentioned in Common Article 3 nor in Additional Protocol II. Nonetheless, the ICC Statute makes provision for the offence of war crime in the event that proper judicial process is denied for protected persons in international armed conflict, and similar provisions apply for those taking no active part in hostilities in internal armed conflict.

---

[21] www.legal-tools.org/en/browse/record/966720/.

In the vast majority of cases, persons were detained for reasons that the trial panel found were insufficient, sometimes grossly so, even for the preliminary step of arrest to be justified. In those cases, detention was arbitrary from the moment of arrest. In cases where the trial panel found that the reasons could justify arrest it was clear that no independent process of review, nor any subsequent judicial process was established by which a detainee could challenge the order for his or her detention. In all cases, the intention to prosecute detainees for their alleged offences or other violations according to the KLA, was pursued in breach of the requirements of Common Article 3 and Protocol II.

The evidence in the case indicates that whether or not a detainee was released from detention depended on the view of the senior KLA commanders and no one else. . . . It was clear from the evidence of the defendants that the detention of the detainees was effected with a view to some form of summary trial process being carried out. The fact that such trial proceedings as took place lacked basic judicial guarantees, and yet the detention of many persons was maintained, leads inevitably to the conclusion that the detention of those persons was a blatant breach of Article 9 of the ICCPR, Common Article 3 and Article 6 of Protocol II. The absence of any clear legal directives by the KLA governing detention and trial in areas of Kosovo under KLA control only serves to aggravate this situation.

10.6.4.3 Syria, *Code of Conduct of the Free Syrian Army* (2014)[22]
Article III

Any person who takes up arms in the name of the regime, regardless of their rank, should be arrested and remain in the custody of the Free Syrian Army. In the event that an individual is arrested, and it is determined that the individual was working for the regime, voluntarily or for payment, to supply information about revolutionary activists, that individual shall be considered a prisoner and treated in accordance with laws governing prisoners of war.

10.6.5 Detention by UN Peacekeeping and Authorised Forces[23]

10.6.5.1 SC, *Security Council Resolution 169 on The Congo Question* (24 November 1961), UN Doc. S/RES/169 (1961)

4. *Authorizes* the Secretary-General to take vigorous action, including the use of the requisite measure of force, if necessary, for the immediate apprehension, detention pending legal action and/or deportation of all foreign military and paramilitary personnel and political advisers not under the United Nations Command, and mercenaries, as laid down in paragraph 2 of Security Council resolution 161 A (1961) of 21 February 1961

10.6.5.2 UN, Secretary-General's Bulletin, *Observance by United Nations Forces of International Humanitarian Law* (6 August 1999) UN Doc. ST/SGB/1999/13
Section 8

Treatment of detained persons

---

22   https://casebook.icrc.org/case-study/syria-code-conduct-free-syrian-army.
23   See also Chapter 5 Section 5.4.3.

The United Nations force shall treat with humanity and respect for their dignity detained members of the armed forces and other persons who no longer take part in military operations by reason of detention. Without prejudice to their legal status, they shall be treated in accordance with the relevant provisions of the Third Geneva Convention of 1949, as may be applicable to them mutatis mutandis. In particular:

(a) Their capture and detention shall be notified without delay to the party on which they depend and to the Central Tracing Agency of the International Committee of the Red Cross (ICRC), in particular in order to inform their families;
(b) They shall be held in secure and safe premises which provide all possible safeguards of hygiene and health, and shall not be detained in areas exposed to the dangers of the combat zone;
(c) They shall be entitled to receive food and clothing, hygiene and medical attention;
(d) They shall under no circumstances be subjected to any form of torture or ill-treatment;
(e) Women whose liberty has been restricted shall be held in quarters separated from men's quarters, and shall be under the immediate supervision of women;
(f) In cases where children who have not attained the age of sixteen years take a direct part in hostilities and are arrested, detained or interned by the United Nations force, they shall continue to benefit from special protection. In particular, they shall be held in quarters separate from the quarters of adults, except when accommodated with their families;
(g) ICRC's right to visit prisoners and detained Section 10 persons shall be respected and guaranteed.

10.6.5.3 SC, *Security Council Resolution 1638* on the Situation in Liberia
(11 November 2005), 5304th Meeting, UN Doc. S/RES/1638 (2005)

Acting under Chapter VII of the Charter of the United Nations,

1. Decides that the mandate of the United Nations Mission in Liberia (UNMIL) shall include the following additional element: to apprehend and detain former President Charles Taylor in the event of a return to Liberia and to transfer him or facilitate his transfer to Sierra Leone for prosecution before the Special Court for Sierra Leone and to keep the Liberian Government, the Sierra Leonean Government and the Council fully informed.

10.6.5.4 UN, Patricia O'Brien, 'Respecting IHL: Challenges and Responses'
(Statement made at 36th Roundtable on Current Issues of International Humanitarian Law, San Remo, Italy, 5 September 2013)[24]

Besides the conduct of military operations, another immediate concern for my Office is the situation where members of armed groups are captured by the Intervention Brigade.

The Secretary-General's Bulletin and the Interim Standard Operating Procedures on Detention by United Nations peacekeeping operations provide minimum rules on the humane treatment of captured persons and humane material conditions of any facility in

---

[24] http://legal.un.org/ola/media/info_from_lc/POB-San-Remo-36th-Roundtable-5-September-2013.pdf.

which captured persons are to be held. However, the Bulletin merely lays down some basic principles; while the Interim SOP on Detention was not crafted with the situation in mind in which a United Nations peacekeeping operation captures persons in the course of an armed conflict.

COMMENTARY

1. Non-international armed conflicts are the most prevalent type of conflict today, but their regulation remains rudimentary. For this reason, there is a tendency, exhibited in particular by the ICTY, to apply to NIACs rules pertinent to IACs, leading to the construction of a common body of rules that are applicable to all armed conflicts.[25] Whereas this approach fills gaps, provides more protections and fulfils the humanitarian aims of IHL, questions remain as to whether armed groups have the capacity and resources to respect these rules and, above all, whether the distinctions upon which these rules are founded apply to NIACs.[26]

2. Critical to the application of IHL is the determination of when a NIAC comes into existence and when it ends. As was noted in the introduction and in Chapter 1, different instruments apply different thresholds and criteria[27] and in the absence of a central authority to make such a determination, the interpretation of facts by the parties is critical. Concerning the termination of a NIAC, one could say that if a party to the conflict ceases to exist or when hostilities fade away, with or without any peace agreement, the conflict comes to an end, but what is critical is the existence of a continuous and stable condition of non-conflict.

3. The geographic scope of NIACs is another contested issue with important legal consequences.[28] Whereas IHL applies in principle to the whole territory of the State concerned, questions may be asked as to whether it also regulates activities in areas where no hostilities take place. Does it only regulate acts connected to the armed conflict whereas all other acts are regulated by domestic law, including IHRL? Does the application of IHL depend on the intensity of the armed conflict, with low-intensity ones being regulated mainly by IHRL as the ECtHR often does in its jurisprudence?[29]

4. The application of IHL to extraterritorial NIACs is equally important in view of contemporary armed conflicts involving terrorists. Whereas the application of APII is

---

[25]   *Prosecutor* v. *Tadić*, (Decision on the Defence Motion for Interlocutory Appeal on Jurisdiction), Case No. IT-94-1, Appeals Chamber (2 October 1995), paras 97, 119. To this one should add certain Conventions concerning weapons that apply equally to IACs and NIACs such as the 1997 Ottawa Convention on Anti-Personnel Landmines.

[26]   See Commentary in Chapter 1.

[27]   For example, compare Common Article 3, Art. 1(1) APII, the *Tadić* definition and Art. 8(2)(f) of the Rome Statute of the International Criminal Court.

[28]   See Chapter 1 Section 1.4.

[29]   See Chapter 3 and relevant case law. Also see *Isayeva, Yusupova and Bazayeva* v. *Russia* (App Nos 57947/00, 57948/00, 57949/00) (Judgment, ECtHR, 24 February 2005); *Finogenov and Others* v. *Russia* (App Nos 18299/03, 27311/03) (Judgment, ECtHR, 10 December 2011); *Khamzayev* v. *Russia* (App No. 1503/02) (Judgment, ECtHR, 3 May 2011).

geographically contained, Common Article 3 has been applied to NIACs between a State and an armed group that spills over to neighbouring States or takes place on the territory of a third State if there is a functional or *rationae personae* link to an existing NIAC. Does this make NIACs global in nature? If that is the case, a related question is whether the law applicable to NIACs applies to the whole territory of the neighbouring State or of the third State or only to those parts of their territory where hostilities take place. How this question is answered is important because it can justify harm to persons or objects on their territory. If the neighbouring State or third State oppose the action, does an IAC arise?[30] Similar questions are asked in relation to States that assist the government of another State to fight armed groups. Does the law of NIAC apply to the territory of the assisting State thus justifying action against that State by the targeted armed groups? If IHL applies in the above scenarios, is it moulded by IHRL? If it does not apply, is the use of lethal force or any other act of violence regulated by IHRL or domestic law? It should be noted that because of the complexity of the issues, such extraterritorial uses of lethal force are often justified according to the *jus ad bellum* right to self-defence.

5. Although no combatant status exists in NIAC, the distinction between civilians and those civilians taking direct part in hostilities is critical in order to protect persons from the consequences of the armed conflict.[31] The ICRC's *Interpretive Guidance* introduced three criteria to determine civilian DPH: (i) threshold of harm; (ii) direct causation; and (iii) belligerent nexus.[32] That said, their interpretation and application to specific situations are not free from difficulties. Civilians who directly participate in hostilities forfeit their protection from attack, but the *Interpretive Guidance* goes on to say that, depending on the circumstances, they should be captured rather than attacked. This creates disparity between IACs and NIACs regarding the treatment of those taking part in hostilities. The *Interpretive Guidance* also introduced the concept of 'continuous combatant function' for members of an organised armed group; they lose their IHL protections for the duration of their continuous combatant function and regain it when they affirmatively disengage therefrom.[33] Establishing continuous combat function depends on evidence, which is difficult to collect and, moreover, creates an imbalance between State armies and armed groups since the scope of DPH is limited. For these reasons, it is submitted that membership of the military wing of an armed group that is party to an armed conflict should be sufficient to remove the civilian protection and not the individual's continuous function of directly participating in hostilities.[34] In other words, it is membership rather than function that matters. In this way, members of the military wings of armed groups will be treated in the same way as members of a State's armed forces and be targetable at all times. That said, other questions arise.

---

[30] See Commentary in Chapter 1.
[31] See also Chapter 4 Section 4.2.
[32] ICRC, *Interpretive Guidance on the Notion of Direct Participation in Hostilities Under International Law* (Geneva, May 2009), pp. 46–54.
[33] ICRC, *Interpretive Guidance on the Notion of Direct Participation in Hostilities Under International Law* (Geneva, May 2009), pp. 32–35. See also Nils Melzer, 'Keeping the Balance between Military Necessity and Humanity: A Response to Four Critiques of the ICRC's Interpretive Guidance on the Notion of Direct Participation in Hostilities' (2010) 42 *N.Y.U. J. Int'l L. & Pol.* 831ff.
[34] For critiques of the ICRC Interpretive Guidance see M.N. Schmitt, 'The Interpretive Guidance on the Notion of Direct Participation in Hostilities: A Critical Analysis' (2010) 1 *Harvard National Security Journal* 5.

Conceptually, does it implicitly introduce the notion of combatancy in NIAC, a category not formally recognised in NIACs? Furthermore, how can one distinguish the military from the political wing of an armed group? Does this depend on the level of organisation of the armed group? Even if such distinctions can be made, should the political leadership of the group which provides overall direction to the military activities of the group lose its protection? It should be noted that these questions are also pertinent to the functional approach adopted by the ICRC.

6. It is broadly accepted that armed groups are bound by IHL but the basis upon which they are so bound is not clear. As will be explained in the next paragraph dealing with their IHRL obligations, arguments vary but it should be noted that without their active participation the binding force of the law is weakened. For this reason, armed groups often affirm and specify their IHL obligations through other means such as agreements with the opposing government, unilateral declarations, codes of conduct, oaths and standing or operational orders. However, the degree of respect for and compliance with IHL varies.[35] Whether a model code of conduct laying out their IHL or their other obligations will be effective in ensuring respect for IHL is debated, but at least it can provide some ground rules for behaviour.

7. The question of whether armed groups have IHRL obligations and, if they do, what their specific obligations are is also of critical importance. Armed groups are not directly bound by IHRL yet it has been claimed that they are bound by IHRL on the basis of the doctrine of legislative jurisdiction or, in the alternative, because of their limited legal personality when they exercise effective control over territories and people. Yet, none of these approaches view them as participants in the creation of IHRL. Often armed groups assume IHRL obligations by signing agreements with the opposing government or through unilateral declarations. As to which human rights bind armed groups, they are primarily bound by those human rights to which they have agreed and/or by customary human rights. Regarding the latter, questions arise as to whether they are bound by all customary human rights rules or only by those related to their function or those rules that they have the capacity and resources to comply with. In any case, what is evident is that their obligations are partial and questions of implementation and enforcement are raised.[36]

8. The law that applies to NIACs does not contain detailed rules regarding the authority to detain or the grounds for detention by States or indeed by armed groups.[37] There are instead rules concerning the treatment of detainees, the conditions of confinement as well as certain procedural rules. These are found in Common Article 3, APII and in customary humanitarian law supplemented by IHRL. Regarding the authority of States to detain, arguments range from implicit authority, customary law, domestic law or SC authorisations, but in view of the ECtHR's *Al-Jedda* judgment, SC authorisations need to specifically authorise detention.

---

[35]   See Chapter 11.
[36]   See Chapter 11.
[37]   See Common Article 3 and Arts 4–6, APII. See also Chapter 5 Section 5.4.

9. Detention is widely practised by armed groups and the question of its lawfulness is critical in order to shield armed groups or their members from criminal prosecution. Concerning their legal authority to detain, the IHL of NIAC does not explicitly empower armed groups to detain, but such a right may be inherent or implicit or derived from the principle of equality of belligerents. Still, the question is how such power to detain can be reconciled with domestic law, which usually criminalises detention by private actors.

10. In order to be lawful, detention should not be arbitrary, but when is detention by armed groups non-arbitrary? Common Article 3, APII and customary law lay down a number of guarantees but if detention should be prescribed by law, is this the law promulgated by the armed group?

11. Another question concerns the grounds for detention by armed groups. 'Imperative reasons of security' has been accepted as a valid ground for detention by both States and armed groups in NIACs, but what are the security imperatives of armed groups vis-à-vis the State or other armed groups? Is it only individuals taking direct part in hostilities that meet this requirement or also those taking an indirect part in hostilities, for example by providing indirect support to the fighting? Should rules on targeting be conflated with the grounds for detention? Can regular forces be detained? Can groups that do not satisfy the criteria to become party to an armed conflict detain? Which legal framework applies to detention by such groups?

12. Another set of questions concerns the procedural guarantees that apply to detention by armed groups. Who can decide on the lawfulness of detention and who can perform regular reviews? Is it the courts of the armed groups? For how long can persons be detained? Should the conditions of detention be comparable to those of the local population[38] or instead satisfy certain minimum standards? Can armed groups satisfy these minimum standards? How is the transfer of detainees by armed groups regulated?

13. In view of the above, it may be the case that a specific legal regime needs to be developed with regard to detention in NIACs.[39] The Copenhagen Principles provide a common denominator but they are not binding, they do not explicitly endorse human rights and they do not apply to armed groups. Moreover, it is not clear whether they apply to situations below the NIAC threshold although an affirmative answer can be implied.

14. Detention of children engaged in armed conflict is practised by both States and armed groups. Children are even more vulnerable in situations of armed conflict as they have specific needs and detention may have lasting effects on them. Questions are raised concerning the age under which a child can be detained, the grounds for detention as well as how procedural guarantees and safeguards can apply to detained children.[40]

---

[38]   Art. 59(2), APII.
[39]   JB Bellinger III and VM Padmanabhan, 'Detention Operations in Contemporary Conflicts: Four Challenges for the Geneva Conventions and Other Existing Law' (2011) 105 *American Journal of International Law* 201.
[40]   See United Nations Standard Minimum Rules for the Administration of Juvenile Justice (The 'Beijing' Rules) UNGA Res 40/33 (1985); Principles and Guidelines On Children Associated with Armed Forces or Armed Groups (The Paris Principles) (UNICEF, 2007); Annual Report of the Special Representative of the Secretary-General for Children and Armed Conflict (22 December 2016), UN Doc. A/HRC/34/44.

Another question is whether children recruited by armed groups should be treated as victims instead of being detained.

15. UN peacekeeping forces can detain on the basis of a SC or General Assembly (GA) authorisation. As was noted, an immediate question is whether the authorisation to detain should be explicit or implicit under the mantra 'all necessary means'.[41] In our view, such authorisations grant States discretionary power to determine what means are necessary and, therefore, no explicit authorisation is required. Another question is whether SC authorisations supersede other standards applicable to detention in light of Article 103 UN Charter.[42] According to the ECtHR jurisprudence, an affirmative answer depends on whether detention is explicitly authorised but, on our view, the superseding effects of Article 103 are not thus limited. In the absence of authorisation, the legal basis for detention by UN peacekeeping forces becomes complicated. In such cases, the authority to detain, but also the legal framework regulating detention, can be found in IHL, IHRL, domestic law, the law of the troop-contributing countries, the Status of Forces Agreement, and UN law. The UN has adopted Interim Standard Operating Procedures on Detention in United Nations Peace Operations (2010),[43] which do not apply when the force has become party to the conflict and IHL applies, in which case detention is regulated by the 1999 Secretary-General's Bulletin and the relevant law.

16. The 1999 Secretary-General's Bulletin gives rise to questions concerning the requirements of detention, the conditions of detention, the treatment in detention, the length of detention as well as the release or transfer of detainees. Regarding transfer of detainees, the principal concerns relate to UN obligations during and after the transfer but also to the handling of transfers in the absence of functioning local authorities. If detention is contracted out, then questions of oversight and responsibility arise. In addition to these legal issues, one should also note the operational difficulties UN forces encounter. These relate to the screening and assessment of persons on the basis of information and intelligence. Broader questions relate to the reputation and legitimacy of the UN in cases of wrongful detention or if the UN fails to detain persons who eventually pose a security threat.

17. How IHL and IHRL interact in NIACs is central to their concurrent application. Applying the *lex specialis* principle in NIACs poses some difficulties because there may be no IHL rules to apply as, for example, with regard to certain aspects of detention and, equally, there may be no specific IHRL, for example with regard to armed groups. Moreover, there may be gaps in both IHL and IHRL, for example with regard to the return of detainees handed over to the host State in case of maltreatment. Furthermore, IHRL may not be entirely appropriate to fill gaps or even to act as a complementary source because its rationale is different from IHL as, for example, with regard to the grounds for detention. Yet, courts such as the ECtHR often apply IHRL to NIACs, even if they use language that is

---

[41] In the *Al-Jedda* case, whereas the House of Lords grounded the authority to detain on the authorising SC resolution, the ECtHR opined that the SC resolution should explicitly provide such authority. See ECtHR, *Al-Jedda* v. *The United Kingdom* [GC] (App No. 27021/08) (Judgment, ECtHR, 7 July 2011), paras 100, 107 109.
[42] See also Chapter 3 Section 3.9.
[43] They remain confidential.

reminiscent of IHL. They rely on the fact that the State has made no derogation from human rights treaties[44] but their jurisprudence is subject to criticism.

18. In view of the above, and to the extent that most armed conflicts nowadays are NIACs and are fought with extreme cruelty, it is important that a full set of rules apply thereto and, for this reason, revisiting the law of NIAC is imperative.

---

[44]   See Chapter 3 Section 3.2. Also see *Isayeva, Yusupova and Bazayeva* v. *Russia* (App Nos 57947/00, 57948/00, and 57949/00) (Judgment, ECHR, 19 December 2002); *Khatsiyeva and Others* v. *Russia* (App No. 5108/02) (Judgment, ECHR, 17 January 2008); *Esmukhambetov and Others* v. *Russia* (App No. 23445/0329) (Judgment, ECHR, 29 March 2011); *Georgia* v. *Russia* (App No. 38263/08) (Judgment, ECHR, 13 December 2011).

11

Enforcement of International Humanitarian Law

INTRODUCTION

Enforcement of IHL is achieved through various legal and non-legal mechanisms. They include the institution of Protecting Powers, Fact-Finding Commissions, belligerent reprisals, national and international judicial (civil or criminal) processes, and action by human rights bodies or by the UN. A central feature of IHL enforcement is that it is State oriented. States have an obligation to respect and ensure respect for IHL[1] and this obligation entails action prior, during or after the end of an armed conflict with the aim of preventing, suppressing and repressing violations. More specifically, States should enact legislation, disseminate the GCs, provide training and education, monitor compliance, and investigate, prosecute or extradite those responsible for violations of IHL. A State may be held responsible for violations of IHL pursuant to Article 3 Hague Convention IV and Article 91 API or according to the law of State responsibility if the attribution tests are satisfied but it should be noted that State responsibility is not criminal responsibility. Individuals may be held criminally responsible for violations of IHL at the national or at the international level before specifically established tribunals or before the International Criminal Court. Proceedings before international criminal courts and tribunals are often complementary to national proceedings. Judicial enforcement at the national level is hampered by the fact that States or foreign officials enjoy immunity but immunities do not apply before international courts. Although the ICRC is guarantor of the GCs, it is not an enforcer. This notwithstanding, its role in the implementation and enforcement of IHL is critical.

This chapter will thus present and assess the scope and effectiveness of the available enforcement mechanisms and remedies in relation to States, individuals, armed groups and international organisations.

Resources: Article 3 HCIV; Arts II, V, VIII Convention on the Privileges and Immunities of the United Nations; Common Article 1 GCs; Arts 8, 49–54 GCI; Arts 8, 50–53 GCII; Arts 8, 129–132 GCIII; Arts 9, 146–149 GCIV; Arts 5, 51, 52, 83–91 API; Art. 19 APII; Arts 8, 13 ICC St.

---

[1] Common Article 1, GCs.

Cases and Materials

11.1 PROTECTING POWERS

11.1.1 US Military Tribunal Nuremberg, *The United States of America* v. *Ernst von Weizsäcker et al.*, (Judgment of 11 April 1949) *Trials of War Criminals Before the Nuremberg Military Tribunals*, Vol. XIV, p. 460

Note: *The indictment charged the Defendants with crimes against peace, war crimes, crimes against humanity and with having participated in a common plan and conspiracy to commit crimes against peace. On the role and importance of Protecting Powers, the Tribunal at Nuremberg affirmed as follows:*

However, under the Geneva Convention and Hague Regulation ... Germany was under the duty of truthfully reporting to the Protecting Power, the facts surrounding the treatment of prisoners of war, and of the circumstances relating to the deaths of such prisoners. To make a false report was a breach of its international agreement, and a breach of international law. ...

If a belligerent ... can, with impunity, give false information to the Protecting Power, the restraining influence which Protecting Powers can exercise in the interests of helpless unfortunates would be wholly eliminated. Thus, the duty to give honest and truthful reports in answer to inquiries such as were addressed by the Swiss Government is implicit.

11.2 INTERNATIONAL HUMANITARIAN FACT-FINDING COMMISSION

11.2.1 IHFFC, *What Is the International Humanitarian Fact Finding Commission and What Is Its Role in Armed Conflict Situations?*[2] pp. 6–7

Competence of the Commission

The raison d'être of the Commission is to assist in the protection of victims of armed conflicts by enabling States to uphold the principles and rules of international humanitarian law.

For this purpose, the Commission has been provided with the following competences:

(i) to enquire into any facts alleged to be a grave breach as defined in the 1949 Geneva Conventions and the First Additional Protocol or any other serious violations of the Conventions or the Protocol . . .

(ii) to carry out good offices in order to facilitate the restoration of an attitude of respect for the Conventions and the Protocol . . .

(iii) to contribute, in general, to the better implementation of international humanitarian law.

For the fulfilment of its fact-finding and good offices competences, the Commission needs the consent of the States concerned. In the case of those States that have already accepted the competence of the Commission by means of the appropriate declaration, such consent is deemed in relation to allegations made by any other such State (Article 90(2)(a)). However, in addition, Article 90(2)(d) provides a further possibility in that, even where a party has not accepted the competence of the Commission, the Commission may still act where it has the consent of all parties concerned. . . .

The Commission is an investigative body and not a court or other judicial body; it does not hand down judgments.

11.3 HUMAN RIGHTS BODIES

11.3.1 Human Rights Commission, *Report on the Situation of Human Rights in Occupied Kuwait, prepared by Mr. Walter Kälin, Special Rapporteur of the United Nations Human Rights Commission* (16 January 1992), E/CN/1992/26

B. Responsibility and compensation

1. State responsibility

. . .

252. The Special Rapporteur concludes, on the basis of the information available to him, that Iraq is internationally responsible for the violations of human rights described in this report. . . .

---

[2] www.ihffc.org/Files/ihffc_brochure_2015_final_thilo.cha.pdf.

2. Individual Responsibility

254. Individual responsibility for the most serious violations of human rights and humanitarian norms is generally recognized, at least for times of armed conflict. . . .

257. . . . Therefore, the Special Rapporteur, . . . recommends proceedings against individuals responsible for grave breaches of violations of humanitarian norms on the basis of articles 129 of the Third and Article 146 of the Fourth Geneva Convention. . . .

. . .

C. Recommendations

262. The Special Rapporteur recommends that the competent organs of the United Nations:

. . .

(e) Invite all States concerned to proceed against individuals responsible for grave breaches by the Iraqi occupying forces of humanitarian norms, on the basis of article 129 of the Third and article 146 of the Fourth Geneva Convention;

(f) Provide for compensation, through the compensation fund established in accordance with Security Council Resolution 687 (1991), for victims of human rights violations and grave breaches of humanitarian norms committed by the Iraqi occupying forces, regardless of their nationality and present status.

11.3.2 IACHR, *Avilán* v. *Colombia*, Case 11.142, Report No. 26/97 (30 September 1997)

Note: *The case concerns the death of Arturo Ribón Avilán as a result of an armed clash between members of the army and the dissident group M-19 in Colombia. On the competence of human rights bodies to hold a State responsible for violations of IHL and IHRL, the Inter-American Commission on Human Rights said as follows:*

34. Once the members of the M-19 were hors de combat and in the custody of the Colombian authorities, the Colombian State had no right to attack them or kill them. These combatants who were wounded or defenseless, like any wounded civilian, had the absolute right to the guarantees of humane treatment provided for in the non-derogable guarantees of Common Article 3 of the Geneva Conventions and of the American Convention. The evidence submitted in this case supports the petitioners' claim that the victims were executed extrajudicially by state agents in a clear violation of Common Article 3 of the Geneva Conventions as well as the American Convention. . . .

148. The various cases herein described and proven entail the international responsibility of the Colombian State and constitute grave violations of human rights and humanitarian law. . . .

170. The State, however, argues . . . that the Commission is not competent to apply humanitarian law in individual cases, . . . The Commission rejects the State's argument and affirms that, in the processing and consideration of certain individual cases, it is competent to apply directly provisions of international humanitarian law or to refer to

these norms to inform its interpretations of relevant provisions of the American Convention. . . .

174. . . . Both Common Article 3 of the Geneva Conventions and the American Convention guarantee these rights and prohibit extrajudicial execution, and the Commission should apply both bodies of law.

175. Apart from these considerations, the Commission's competence to apply the provisions of humanitarian law is based on the text of the Convention and the jurisprudence of the Court. . . .

177. The right to the protection of humanitarian law is recognized in the Colombian legal regime. . . .

178. Therefore, given that Colombian domestic law provides for the application of humanitarian law, the Convention itself authorizes the Commission to analyze humanitarian law in cases such as this one,

11.3.3 IACHR, *Third Report on the Human Rights Situation in Colombia*, OEA/Ser.L/V/II.102, Doc. 9 rev. 1 (26 February 1999)

Chapter IV

. . .

I. RECOMMENDATIONS

Based on the foregoing, the Commission makes the following recommendations:

1. All parties to the internal armed conflict in Colombia should, through their command and control structures, respect, implement and enforce the rules governing hostilities set forth in international humanitarian law, with particular emphasis on those norms providing for the protection of civilians.
2. The Colombian State should intensify training in human rights and international humanitarian law directed towards State agents, particularly members of the State's security forces.
3. The Colombian State should take additional measures to disseminate, to State agents and to the population in general, information and materials relating to human rights and international humanitarian law.
4. The Colombian State should take immediate energetic measures to prevent violations of human rights and international humanitarian law by State agents. These measures should include serious, impartial and effective criminal investigations into all cases involving alleged human rights and humanitarian law violations, as a priority and as an especially crucial element of prevention. In particular, the State should seek out, apprehend and prosecute all persons who planned, ordered and/or perpetrated serious violations of human rights and international humanitarian law.
5. The Colombian State should remove from service those members of the security forces who have been identified as having taken part in human rights violations while awaiting a final decision in any disciplinary or criminal proceedings which might have been initiated.

6. The Colombian State should take immediate and energetic measures to combat, dismantle and disarm all paramilitary and other proscribed self-defense groups operating in
Colombia. These measures should include the prosecution and sanction of the members,
supporters and leaders of those groups in conformity with the law.

11.3.4 African Commission on Human and Peoples' Rights, *D. R. Congo* *v. Burundi, Rwanda and Uganda*, Communication No. 227/99 (33rd Ordinary Session, May 2003)

Note: *The Democratic Republic of Congo brought a complaint alleging violations of the African Charter as well as GCs, APs, UN Charter and UN Declaration on Friendly Relations. The DRC alleged the Respondent States, Burundi, Rwanda and Uganda, had been occupying the border provinces on the eastern edges of the DRC and committing mass violations of IHRL and IHL. The African Commission found as follows:*

69. The Complainant State alleges grave and massive violations of human and peoples'
rights committed by the armed forces of the Respondent States in its eastern provinces. . . .
As noted earlier on, the series of violations alleged to have been committed by the armed
forces of the Respondent States fall within the province of humanitarian law, and
therefore rightly covered by the Four Geneva Conventions and the Protocols additional
to them. . . .

70. . . . By virtue of Articles 60 and 61, [of the African Charter] the [African] Commission
holds that the Four Geneva Conventions and the two Additional Protocols covering armed
conflicts constitute part of the general principles of law recognised by African States. . . .

79. The [African] Commission finds the killings, massacres, rapes, mutilations and other
grave human rights abuses committed while the Respondent States' armed forces were still
in effective occupation of the eastern provinces of the Complainant State reprehensible and
also inconsistent with their obligations under Part III of the *Geneva Convention Relative to
the Protection of Civilian Persons in Time of War* of 1949 and *Protocol 1 of the Geneva
Convention.*

80. They also constitute flagrant violations of Article 2 of the African Charter, such acts
being directed against the victims by virtue of their national origin; and Article 4, which
guarantees respect for life and the integrity of one's person and prohibits the arbitrary
deprivation [of] rights. . . .

84. The besieg[ing] of the hydroelectric dam may also be brought within the prohibition
contained in *The Hague Convention (II) with Respect to the Laws and Customs of War on
Land* . . .

86. The raping of women and girls, as alleged and not refuted by the Respondent States, is
prohibited under Article 76 of the *First Protocol Additional to the Geneva Conventions of
1949,*. . . It also offends both the African Charter and the *Convention on the Elimination of
All Forms of Discrimination against Women*; and on the basis of Articles 60 and 61 of the
African Charter find the Respondent States in violation of the Charter.

. . .

For the above reasons, the [African] Commission, Finds the Respondent States in violation of ... the African Charter; Urges the Respondent States to abide by their obligations under the Charters of the UN, the OAU, the African Charter.

11.3.5 Human Rights Council, *Report of the Independent International Commission of Inquiry on the Syrian Arab Republic* (12 February 2014), 25th Session, UN Doc. A/HRC/25/65

157. The Commission of inquiry recommends that all parties:

(a) Ensure the protection of civilians, guaranteeing their safety and security effectively;

(b) ...

(c) Distinguish military from civilian objectives, refraining from all indiscriminate and disproportionate attacks;

(d) Not submit anyone, civilian or combatant, to torture or other cruel, inhuman or degrading treatment, including sexual violence;

(e) Adhere to the ban on the recruitment and use of children in hostilities;

(f) Treat all persons in detention humanely and provide an impartial, neutral and independent organization with regular access to persons in detention;

(g) Protect aid workers and facilitate the rapid and unimpeded passage of relief supplies;

(h) Respect and protect schools and hospitals, and maintain their civilian character;

(i) Ensure safe passage and protection for medical personnel, hospitals and ambulances;

(j) Commit to ensuring the preservation of the material evidence of violations and international crimes to protect the right to truth of the Syrian people. ...

158. The Commission recommends that the Government of the Syrian Arab Republic:

(a) Cease using illegal weaponry, such as incendiary weapons and other weapons such as barrel bombs, that are unguided or poorly guided, on civilian areas

159. The Commission recommends that non-State armed groups:

(a) Allow access for an independent humanitarian assessment of needs in Nubul and Zahra;

(b) Detach themselves from extreme elements that fail to comply with international law.

160. The commission recommends that countries with influence over the warring parties, in particular the permanent members of the Security Council work in concert to put pressure on the parties to end the violence and to initiate all-inclusive negotiations for a sustainable political transition process in the country.

163. The Commission recommends that the Security Council:

...

(c) Enhance the enforcement and implementation of international human rights and humanitarian law through the range of powers and measures at its disposal as part of the imperative of accountability, pertaining to all actors.

11.4 STATE RESPONSIBILITY AND IMMUNITIES

11.4.1 State Responsibility

11.4.1.1 ICJ, *Case Concerning Military and Paramilitary Activities in and Against Nicaragua (Nicaragua* v. *United States of America)* (Merits, Judgment) [1986] I.C.J. Rep. 14

Note: *The facts of this case are outlined in Chapter 1, Section 1.2.3.1. On the issue of the United States' responsibility for violations of IHL by the contras in Nicaragua, the ICJ said as follows:*

115. . . . All the forms of United States participation mentioned above, and even the general control by the respondent State over a force with a high degree of dependency on it, would not in themselves mean, without further evidence, that the United States directed or enforced the perpetration of the acts contrary to human rights and humanitarian law alleged by the applicant State. Such acts could well be committed by members of the *contras* without the control of the United States. For this conduct to give rise to legal responsibility of the United States, it would in principle have to be proved that that State had effective control of the military or paramilitary operations in the course of which the alleged violations were committed. . . .

220. The Court considers that there is an obligation on the United States Government, in the terms of Article 1 of the Geneva Conventions, to "respect" the Conventions and even "to ensure respect" for them "in all circumstances", since such an obligation does not derive only from the Conventions themselves, but from the general principles of humanitarian law to which the Conventions merely give specific expression. The United States is thus under an obligation not to encourage persons or groups engaged in the conflict in Nicaragua to act in violation of the provisions of Article 3 common to the four 1949 Geneva Conventions.

11.4.1.2 ICJ, *Case Concerning Armed Activities on the Territory of the Congo (Democratic Republic of the Congo* v. *Uganda)* (Judgment) [2005] I.C.J. Rep. 168

Note: *The facts of this case are outlined in Chapter 1, Section 1.7.2. Reinforcing the responsibility of States for the acts of its armed forces in a conflict, the ICJ said the following:*

214. . . . According to a well-established rule of a customary nature, as reflected in Article 3 of the Fourth Hague Convention respecting the Laws and Customs of War on Land of 1907 as well as in Article 91 of Protocol I additional to the Geneva Conventions of 1949, a party to an armed conflict shall be responsible for all acts by persons forming part of its armed forces.

11.4.2 State Immunity

11.4.2.1 Greece, *Prefecture of Voiotia* v. *Federal Republic of Germany ('Distomo Massacre Case')*, Case No. 11/2000, Court of Cassation *(Areios Pagos)* (4 May 2000) 129 ILR 513, pp. 519–21

Note: *The case concerns events of June 1944 when German forces occupying Greece massacred over 300 inhabitants of the village of Distomo. In 1995 proceedings were brought in the Greek* *courts by the relatives of the victims of the massacre. The Court of First Instance of Livadia awarded compensation to relatives of the victims of the Nazi massacre in Distomo. Germany appealed on the basis they were immune from the Court's jurisdiction. On the issue of State immunity, the Court of Cassation held:*

[The majority of the Court considers] that State immunity cannot be dispensed with in relation to claims for damages arising [from military action] in situations of armed conflict, which generally involve conflict between States where harm to civilians necessarily results and where resultant claims are normally dealt with through inter-State agreements after the war has ended. But the exception to the immunity rule should apply where the offences for which compensation is sought (especially crimes against humanity) did not target civilians generally, but specific individuals in a given place who were neither directly nor indirectly connected with the military operations. . . .

[The majority of this Court considers that] these cruel murders were objectively in any case not necessary for the conservation of the military occupation or to reduce the resistance action and were carried out on the territory of the State of the forum, by organs of the Third Reich, in excess of their sovereign powers. Because organs of the defendant State were involved in the commission of these crimes, the relevant claims for damages and pecuniary compensation fall within the international jurisdiction of the trial court, as exceptions to the prerogative of immunity in accordance with the norm of customary international law which, as concluded above, has acquired the force of law.

Consequently, the trial court was entitled to rule that it had international jurisdiction over the relevant claims for damages and pecuniary satisfaction brought by the plaintiffs, albeit on the different ground that the defendant State could not invoke its right of immunity, which it had tacitly waived since the acts for which it was being sued were carried out by its organs in contravention of the rules of *jus cogens* (Article 46 of the Regulations on the Laws and Customs of War Annexed to the Fourth Hague Convention of 1907) and did not have the character of acts of sovereign power. The trial court therefore correctly concluded, as to the result in relation to the question of the existence of its international jurisdiction, that the plea of lack of international jurisdiction was inadmissible.

11.4.2.2 ICJ, *Case Concerning the Arrest Warrant of 11 April 2000 (Democratic Republic of the Congo* v. *Belgium)* (Judgment) [2002] I.C.J. Rep. 3

Note: *On 11 April 2000 a judge of the Brussels tribunal de première instance issued an international arrest warrant against Abdulaye Ndombasi, the Minister for Foreign Affairs of the Congo, charging him with offences in breach of the GCs and the APs. The DRC alleged, inter alia, that Belgium had violated the diplomatic immunity of the Minister for Foreign Affairs of a sovereign State. Addressing State immunity, the ICJ said the following:*

58. The Court has carefully examined State practice, including national legislation and those few decisions of national higher courts, such as the House of Lords or the French Court of Cassation. It has been unable to deduce from this practice that there exists under customary international law any form of exception to the rule according immunity from criminal jurisdiction and inviolability to incumbent Ministers for Foreign Affairs, where they are suspected of having committed war crimes or crimes against humanity. . . .

60. The Court emphasizes, however, that the *immunity* from jurisdiction enjoyed by incumbent Ministers for Foreign Affairs does not mean that they enjoy *impunity* in respect of any crimes they might have committed, irrespective of their gravity. Immunity from criminal jurisdiction and individual criminal responsibility are quite separate concepts. While jurisdictional immunity is procedural in nature, criminal responsibility is a question of substantive law. Jurisdictional immunity may well bar prosecution for a certain period or for certain offences; it cannot exonerate the person to whom it applies from all criminal responsibility.

11.4.2.3 ECtHR, *Kalogeropoulou and others* v. *Greece and Germany* (App No. 5902/00) (Decision, ECHR, 12 December 2002) pp. 8–9

Note: *This case arises out of the earlier decision of the Court of Cassation in* Prefecture of Voiotia v. Germany, *which upheld the award of damages against Germany. Germany failed to comply with the decision. The Plaintiffs sought to enforce the decision against German property in Greece. To do so, i.e., to enforce a decision against a foreign State, permission of the Greek Minister of Justice was required. The Minister of Justice did not give permission. The Court of Appeal of Athens subsequently upheld an objection to enforcement of the decision by Germany. The Plaintiffs complained to the ECtHR that both Greek and German authorities had violated their rights under Article 6 ECHR. The ECtHR held as follows:*

In the instant case the applicants were found to be entitled to compensation from the German State, but were unable to obtain payment of the amounts in question on account of the Greek State's refusal to allow them to bring enforcement proceedings against Germany. That refusal was confirmed by the Greek courts. ...

The Court must first determine whether the restriction pursued a legitimate aim. It notes in this connection that sovereign immunity of States is a concept of international law, developed out of the principle *par in parem non habet imperium*, by virtue of which one State shall not be subject to the jurisdiction of another State. The Court considers that the grant of sovereign immunity to a State in civil proceedings pursues the legitimate aim of complying with international law to promote comity and good relations between States.

The Court must next assess whether the restriction was proportionate to the aim pursued. ...

It follows that measures taken by a High Contracting Party which reflect generally recognised rules of public international law on State immunity cannot generally be regarded as imposing a disproportionate restriction on the right of access to a court as embodied in Article 6 § 1. Just as the right of access to a court is an inherent part of the fair trial guarantee in that Article, so some restrictions on access must likewise be regarded as inherent, an example being those limitations generally accepted by the community of nations as part of the doctrine of State immunity.

In the light of the foregoing considerations, the Court considers that although the Greek courts ordered the German State to pay damages to the applicants, this did not necessarily oblige the Greek State to ensure that the applicants could recover their debt through enforcement proceedings in Greece. Referring to judgment no. 11/2000 of the Court of Cassation, the applicants appeared to be asserting that international law on crimes against humanity was so fundamental that it amounted to a rule of *jus cogens* that took precedence over all other principles of international law, including the principle of sovereign immunity. The Court does not find it established, however, that there is yet acceptance in international law of the proposition that States are not entitled to immunity in respect of civil claims for damages brought against them in another State for crimes against humanity.

11.4.2.4 Italy, *Ferrini* v. *Germany*, (Appeal Decision), Case No. 5044/4; ILDC 19 (IT 2004) (11 March 2004)

Note: *Ferrini brought proceedings against Germany for damages arising out of his physical and psychological injury as a result of his capture and deportation to a German forced labour/ extermination camp in 1944. Considering Germany's defence of jurisdictional immunity from suit, the Italian Court of Cassation held as follows:*

H4 There was no controversy over the fact that Germany's actions on which Ferrini's claim is based had been an expression of its sovereign power, as they took place in the course of an armed conflict. The different question in the present case was whether immunity should be upheld even when specific behaviours within such conflict constituted international crimes and violations of fundamental norms of international law. . . .

H5 According to international treaty law and international judicial practice on the subject, deportation and forced labour constitute international crimes. . . .

H6 . . . Granting immunity to states responsible for such crimes runs into clear contradiction with these developments. That contradiction could only be resolved by acknowledging the superiority of higher norms, and by rejecting the argument that a state can invoke immunity from jurisdiction in such cases. . . .

H11 Functional immunity of state officials of the foreign state could no longer be invoked in cases of international crimes. Treaty law and ample international judicial practice were unequivocal on this matter. There was then no reason why, in the same way, state immunity–of which functional immunity is only one aspect–should subsist for behaviours that can be defined as international crimes.

H12 The Court's discussion was based on facts having taken place, in part, in Italy. However, as they amounted to international crimes, the principle of universal jurisdiction would, in any event, apply.

11.4.2.5 ICJ, *Jurisdictional Immunities of the State (Germany* v. *Italy: Greece intervening)*, (Judgment) [2012] I.C.J. Rep. 99

Note: *Germany instituted proceedings against Italy for failing to recognise the jurisdictional immunity enjoyed by Germany under international law. It was Germany's case that since Italy had allowed civil claims to be brought against Germany for compensation arising out the actions of the German Reich in the Second World War it had violated Germany's immunity from suit. The ICJ said as follows:*

91. The Court concludes that, under customary international law as it presently stands, a State is not deprived of immunity by reason of the fact that it is accused of serious violations of international human rights law or the international law of armed conflict. In reaching that conclusion, the Court must emphasize that it is addressing only the

immunity of the State itself from the jurisdiction of the courts of other States; the question of whether, and if so to what extent, immunity might apply in criminal proceedings against an official of the State is not in issue in the present case. . . .

93. This argument therefore depends upon the existence of a conflict between a rule, or rules, of *jus cogens*, and the rule of customary law which requires one State to accord immunity to another. In the opinion of the Court, however, no such conflict exists. . . . The two sets of rules address different matters. The rules of State immunity are procedural in character and are confined to determining whether or not the courts of one State may exercise jurisdiction in respect of another State. They do not bear upon the question whether or not the conduct in respect of which the proceedings are brought was lawful or unlawful. . . .

97. Accordingly, the Court concludes that even on the assumption that the proceedings in the Italian courts involved violations of *jus cogens* rules, the applicability of the customary international law on State immunity was not affected.

11.4.2.6 Italy, *The Constitutional Court*, Judgment No. 238 (2014)[3]

Note: *The Tribunal of Florence questioned the constitutionality of Italian law, which incorporated international custom as found in the decision of the ICJ in* Germany v. Italy *2012 insofar as it denied jurisdiction of Italian courts to hear civil claims for damages in respect of war crimes committed by the Third Reich. The Constitutional Court said as follows:*

3.4 . . . In the present case, the customary international norm of immunity of foreign States, defined in its scope by the ICJ, entails the absolute sacrifice of the right to judicial protection, insofar as it denies the jurisdiction of [domestic] courts to adjudicate the action for damages put forward by victims of crimes against humanity and gross violations of fundamental human rights. . . .

Immunity from jurisdiction of other States can be considered tenable from a legal standpoint, and even more so from a logical standpoint, and thus can justify on the constitutional plane the sacrifice of the principle of judicial protection of inviolable rights guaranteed by the Constitution, only when it is connected – substantially and not just formally – to the sovereign functions of the foreign State, i.e. with the exercise of its governmental powers.

Respect for fundamental principles and inviolable human rights, identifying elements of the constitutional order, is the limit that indicates . . . the receptiveness of the Italian legal order to the international and supranational order. . . . This in itself rules out that acts such as deportation, slave labor, and massacres, recognized to be crimes against humanity, can justify the absolute sacrifice in the domestic legal order of the judicial protection of inviolable rights of the victims of those crimes.

Therefore, in an institutional context characterized by the centrality of human rights, emphasized by the receptiveness of the constitutional order to external sources . . . the denial of judicial protection of fundamental rights of the victims of the crimes at issue (now dating back in time), determines the completely disproportionate sacrifice of two supreme

---

3   www.cortecostituzionale.it/documenti/download/doc/recent_judgments/S238_2013_en.pdf.

principles of the Constitution. They are indeed sacrificed in order to pursue the goal of not interfering with the exercise of the governmental powers of the State even when, as in the present case, state actions can be considered war crimes and crimes against humanity, in breach of inviolable human rights, and as such are excluded from the lawful exercise of governmental powers.

11.5 ARBITRATION

11.5.1 Eritrea–Ethiopia Claims Commission, *Partial Award – Central Front: Eritrea's Claims 2, 4, 6, 7, 8 & 22* (2004) 26(4) RIAA 115[4]

Note: *The facts of this matter are set out in Chapter 9, Section 9.2.2. The Commission found:*

D. Findings of Liability for Violation of International Law

The Respondent is liable to the Claimant for the following violations of international law committed by its military personnel or by other officials of the State of Ethiopia:

1. For permitting the looting and stripping of buildings in Tserona Town while it occupied the town from late May 2000 until late February 2001, it is liable for 75% (seventy-five percent) of the total damage caused by looting and stripping in the town;
2. For permitting the looting and stripping of the adjacent Tserona Patriots Cemetery, it is liable for 75% (seventy-five percent) of the total damage caused by looting and stripping of the cemetery;
3. For the destruction of the Sub-Zoba Administrative Building, the Sub-Zoba Health Center, and the Warsai Hotel in Tserona Town;
4. For inflicting damage on the infrastructure of the village of Serha during its occupation of that village, it is liable for 70% (seventy percent) of the total damage inflicted on Serha from May 1998 through February 2001;
5. For failure to take effective measures to prevent rape of women by its soldiers during its occupation of Senafe Town;
6. For permitting looting and stripping in Senafe Town during its occupation, it is liable for 75% (seventy-five percent) of the total damage from looting and stripping suffered in the town between May 26, 2000 and June 2001;
7. For the unlawful destruction of or severe damage to the following thirteen major structures in Senafe Town during the Ethiopian occupation of the town:

   a. The Electrical Authority (two buildings);
   b. The Ministry of Agriculture (two buildings);
   c. The New Town Administrative Headquarters;
   d. The Old Town Administrative Headquarters and Offices West;
   e. The Old Town Administrative Headquarters and Offices East;
   f. Senafe Secondary School;
   g. Senafe Hospital;

---

[4]   For Ethiopia's similar claim see *Partial Award: Central Front: Ethiopia's Claim 2* (2004) 26(5) *RIAA* 155.

h. Sub-Zoba Administrative and Residential (three buildings); and

i. Telecommunications Building.

The liability is for 100% (one hundred percent) of the damage to each of these structures, except for the hospital, where the liability is 90% (ninety percent); and

8. For permitting, while occupying the area, deliberate damage by explosion to the Stela of Matara, an ancient monument in the Senafe Sub-Zoba.

11.6 INDIVIDUAL CRIMINAL RESPONSIBILITY

11.6.1 *Agreement for the Prosecution and Punishment of the Major War Criminals of the European Axis, and Charter of the International Military Tribunal* (adopted 8 August 1945, entered into force 8 August 1945) 82 UNTS 280

Article 6.

The Tribunal established by the Agreement referred to in Article 1 hereof ... shall have the power to try and punish persons who, acting in the interests of the European Axis countries, whether as individuals or as members of organizations, committed any of the following crimes.

. . .

(b) War Crimes: namely, violations of the laws or customs of war. Such violations shall include, but not be limited to, murder, ill-treatment or deportation to slave labor or for any other purpose of civilian population of or in occupied territory, murder or ill-treatment of prisoners of war or persons on the seas, killing of hostages, plunder of public or private property, wanton destruction of cities, towns or villages, or devastation not justified by military necessity.

11.6.2 International Military Tribunal, *The Trial of German Major War Criminals, proceedings of the International Military Tribunal sitting at Nuremberg, Germany* (Part 22, Judgment of 1 October 1946), pp. 446–7

Note: *The facts attendant to the Trials at Nuremberg are discussed in Chapter 8, Section 8.1.5. Addressing the criminal responsibility of individuals for breaches of international law, the Tribunal said as follows:*

It was submitted that International Law is concerned with the actions of sovereign States and provides no punishment for individuals; and further, that where the act in question is an act of State, those who carry it out are not personally responsible, but are protected by the doctrine of the sovereignty of the State. In the opinion of the Tribunal, both these submissions must be rejected. That International Law imposes duties and liabilities upon individuals as well as upon States has long been recognized.. . .

… Crimes against International Law are committed by men, not by abstract entities, and only by punishing individuals who commit such crimes can the provisions of International Law be enforced.

The principle of International Law, which under certain circumstances protects the representatives of a State, cannot be applied to acts which are condemned as criminal by International Law. The authors of these acts cannot shelter themselves behind their official position in order to be freed from punishment in appropriate proceedings.

11.6.3 ICTY, *Prosecutor* v. *Tadić*, (Decision on the Defence Motion for Interlocutory Appeal on Jurisdiction), Case No. IT-94-1, Appeals Chamber (2 October 1995)

Note: *The facts of this case are outlined in Chapter 1, Section 1.1.1. Affirming the position that the conduct of individuals in both NIAC and IAC can result in a finding of individual criminal responsibility, the ICTY commented as follows:*

134. All of these factors confirm that customary international law imposes criminal liability for serious violations of common Article 3, as supplemented by other general principles and rules on the protection of victims of internal armed conflict, and for breaching certain fundamental principles and rules regarding means and methods of combat in civil strife.

11.7 REPARATIONS

11.7.1 State Reparations

11.7.1.1 *Treaty of Peace with Japan* (adopted, 8 September 1951, entered into force 28 April 1952) 1832 UNTS 46
Article 14
(a) It is recognized that Japan should pay reparations to the Allied Powers for the damage and suffering caused by it during the war. Nevertheless it is also recognized that the resources of Japan are not presently sufficient, if it is to maintain a viable economy, to make complete reparation for all such damage and suffering and at the same time meet its other obligations.

11.7.1.2 **Japan,** *Ryuichi Shimoda et al.* v. *The State*, District Court of Tokyo (7 December 1963) 32 ILR 626, pp. 635–6
Note: *The facts of this case are dealt with in Chapter 2, Section 2.3.1. Addressing the issue of State liability to make reparations for damage caused during hostilities, the District Court of Tokyo said as follows:*

It is an established principle of international law that a belligerent who causes damage to the other belligerent by acts of hostilities contrary to international law is under an obligation to make compensation to the latter for the damage.

Since it is not disputed that the act of atomic bombing on Hiroshima and Nagasaki was a regular act of hostilities performed by an aircraft of the United States Army Air Force, and that Japan suffered damage from this bombing, it goes without saying that Japan has a claim for damages against the United States in international law. ...

It has now become clear from what has been said above that there is in general no way open to an individual who suffers injuries from an act of hostilities contrary to international law to claim damages on the level of international law, ... Accordingly, the question left to the individual is whether he can ask for redress before a municipal court of one or both of the belligerent States. However, redress before a Japanese court is impossible, because the position of an individual who brings an action before a Japanese court against the State in question as defendant, in this case the United States, is subjected to an established principle of international law that a sovereign State is not subject to the jurisdiction of the civil courts of other States, a principle which is recognized in Japan.

11.7.1.3 ICJ, *Case Concerning Armed Activities on the Territory of the Congo (Democratic Republic of the Congo v. Uganda)* (Judgment) [2005] I.C.J. Rep. 168

Note: *The facts of this case are dealt with in Chapter 1, Section 1.7.2. Confirming the obligation to make reparations for damage caused by 'internationally wrongful acts', the ICJ said as follows:*

259. The Court observes that it is well established in general international law that a State which bears responsibility for an internationally wrongful act is under an obligation to make full reparation for the injury caused by that act ... Upon examination of the case file ..., the Court considers that those acts resulted in injury to the DRC and to persons on its territory. Having satisfied itself that this injury was caused to the DRC by Uganda, the Court finds that Uganda has an obligation to make reparation accordingly.

260. The Court further considers appropriate the request of the DRC for the nature, form and amount of the reparation due to it to be determined by the Court, failing agreement between the Parties, in a subsequent phase of the proceedings. The DRC would thus be given the opportunity to demonstrate and prove the exact injury that was suffered as a result of specific actions of Uganda constituting internationally wrongful acts for which it is responsible. It goes without saying, however, as the Court has had the opportunity to state in the past, "that in the phase of the proceedings devoted to reparation, neither Party may call in question such findings in the present Judgment as have become *res judicata*".

11.7.1.4 Eritrea-Ethiopia Claims Commission, *Final Award: Ethiopia's Damages Claims:* (2009) 26 (18) RIAA 631[5]

Note: *The facts attendant to the Eritrea–Ethiopian Arbitral Awards can be found in Chapters 5, Section 5.2.2 and Chapter 9, Sections 9.2.2 and 9.2.4. As to the assessment of reparations, the Commission said as follows:*

---

[5] For Eritrea's similar claim see Eritrea-Ethiopia Claims Commission, *Final Award: Eritrea's Damages Claims:* (2009) 26 (17) *RIAA* 505.

18. In assessing both Parties' damages claims, the Commission has been mindful of the harsh fact that these countries are among the poorest on earth. In both rounds of damages proceedings, both Parties sought amounts that were huge, both absolutely and in relation to the economic capacity of the country against which they were directed. . . .

22. . . . Accordingly, the Commission could not disregard the possibility that large damages awards might exceed the capacity of the responsible State to pay or result in serious injury to its population if such damages were paid. It thus considered whether it was necessary to limit its compensation awards in some manner to ensure that the ultimate financial burden imposed on a Party would not be so excessive, given its economic condition and its capacity to pay, as to compromise its ability to meet its people's basic needs. . . .

61. The Commission has great reservations regarding Ethiopia's moral damages claims. . . .

103. Given the manner in which Ethiopia presented its claims, the Commission has had to make its best estimates of the gravity and extent of Eritrea's *jus in bello* violations on the three fronts involving death, physical injury, disappearance, forced labor and conscription of civilians based on the evidence previously in the record. In doing so, it has given important weight to the seriousness of the offenses against life and human dignity proved at the liability phase. . . .

110. Accordingly, the Commission awards Ethiopia (as it does Eritrea in its parallel Award) US$2,000,000 in damages for failing to prevent the rape of known and unknown victims in Irob, Dalul and Elidar Weredas. In so doing, the Commission expresses the hope that Ethiopia (and Eritrea) will use the funds awarded to develop and support health programs for women and girls in the affected areas. . . .

135. The extensive gaps and ambiguities in the record, and the limited geographic scope of the Commission's liability findings, compel the Commission to estimate the extent of damage to housing for purposes of Ethiopia's *jus in bello* claim. In doing so, the Commission has given considerable weight to international agencies' estimates of the number of damaged or destroyed houses prepared during and after the war. It has also given weight to evidence indicating that shelling was a major cause of damage to housing. Such damage from shelling can only be considered in connection with Ethiopia's *jus ad bellum* housing claim. The Commission accordingly awards Ethiopia the sum of US$1,900,000 for the *jus in bello* component of its claims for damage to housing. . . .

209. The claims before the Commission are the claims of the Parties, not the claims of individual victims. . . . While the Commission encourages the Parties to compensate appropriately the individual victims of warfare, it calculates the damages owed by one Party to the other, including for mistreatment of POWs, on the basis of its evaluation of the evidence with respect to the seriousness of the unlawful acts or omissions, the total numbers of probable victims of those unlawful acts or omissions.

11.7.2 Individual Reparations

11.7.2.1 Human Rights Commission, *Report on the Situation of Human Rights in Occupied Kuwait, Prepared by Mr. Walter Kälin, Special Rapporteur of the United Nations Human Rights Commission* (16 January 1992) E/CN/1992/26

3. Compensation

258. In paragraph 18 of its resolution 687 (1991) the Security Council decided to create "a fund to pay compensation for claims that fall within paragraph 16" . . .

259. The establishment of the fund ensures that compensation will be paid for material damage caused to public and private property in Kuwait. This means that there will be compensation for important aspects of the violation of economic, social and cultural rights and the corresponding guarantees of international humanitarian law, namely the dismantling, pillaging and destruction of health-care, educational, research and cultural institutions and facilities.

260. The Special Rapporteur recommends that victims of other types of human rights violations and grave breaches of humanitarian norms should also be compensated for their injuries, including non-material damage. . . .

261. Compensation should be granted to victims of human rights violations regardless of their nationality and their present status in Kuwait in order to make sure that victims of human rights violations committed by Iraq who have left Kuwait since 26 February 1991 and who are stateless are also justly compensated.

11.7.2.2 Germany, *German Federal Supreme Court: The Distomo Massacre Case (Greek Citizens* v. *Federal Republic of Germany)* [2003] 42 ILM 1030, pp. 1037–8

Note: *The background to this case is outlined in Section 11.4.2.1. As to the right of individuals to claim reparations for violations of international law, the German Federal Supreme Court said as follows:*

The Court of Appeals found that plaintiffs are not entitled to claim damages or compensation for a violation of international law. It reasoned that the acts constitute war crimes but that according to generally accepted principles of international law, not the injured individual had a cause of action but only his state of nationality. . . . If an individual was treated by a foreign state in a way that violated international law, only his state of nationality had a cause of action. The state, by resorting to diplomatic action, asserts its own right, namely the right to ensure in the person of its nationals respect for the rules of international law. . . . In addition, an individual had neither in international nor in national laws an enforceable right that his state of nationality resorts to diplomatic action. This is in accordance with Article 2 of the Hague Convention Respecting the Laws and Customs of War on Land of October 18, 1907 (Hague Convention - HCWL) pursuant to which the Convention provisions "do not apply except between Contracting Powers" and with Article 3 pursuant to which "a belligerent party" (in relation to another belligerent party) is liable to pay compensation.

11.7.2.3 ICJ, *Legal Consequences of the Construction of a Wall in the Occupied Palestinian Territory* (Advisory Opinion) [2004] I.C.J. Rep. 136

Note: *For the background of this case see Chapter 2, Section 2.2.6. As to Israel's obligation to make reparations to individuals affected by construction of the wall in Palestinian territory, the ICJ affirmed as follows:*

153. Israel is accordingly under an obligation to return the land, orchards, olive groves and other immovable property seized from any natural or legal person for purposes of construction of the wall in the Occupied Palestinian Territory. In the event that such restitution should prove to be materially impossible, Israel has an obligation to compensate the persons in question for the damage suffered. The Court considers that Israel also has an obligation to compensate, in accordance with the applicable rules of international law, all natural or legal persons having suffered any form of material damage as a result of the wall's construction.

11.7.2.4 GA, *Basic Principles and Guidelines on the Right to a Remedy and Reparation for Victims of Gross Violations of International Human Rights Law and Serious Violations of International Humanitarian Law* (16 December 2005), UN Doc. A/RES/60/147

3. The obligation to respect, ensure respect for and implement international human rights law and international humanitarian law as provided for under the respective bodies of law, includes, inter alia, the duty to:

. . .

(c) Provide those who claim to be victims of a human rights or humanitarian law violation with equal and effective access to justice, as described below, irrespective of who may ultimately be the bearer of responsibility for the violation; and

(d) Provide effective remedies to victims, including reparation, as described below.

8. For purposes of the present document, victims are persons who individually or collectively suffered harm, including physical or mental injury, emotional suffering, economic loss or substantial impairment of their fundamental rights, through acts or omissions that constitute gross violations of international human rights law, or serious violations of international humanitarian law. . . .

11. Remedies for gross violations of international human rights law and serious violations of international humanitarian law include the victim's right to the following as provided for under international law:

(a) Equal and effective access to justice;

(b) Adequate, effective and prompt reparation for harm suffered;

(c) Access to relevant information concerning violations and reparation mechanisms . . .

18. In accordance with domestic law and international law, and taking account of individual circumstances, victims of gross violations of international human rights law and serious violations of international humanitarian law should, as appropriate and proportional to the gravity of the violation and the circumstances of each case, be provided with full and effective reparation, ..., which include the following forms: restitution, compensation, rehabilitation, satisfaction and guarantees of non-repetition.

11.7.2.5 **ILA,** *Reparation for Victims of Armed Conflict, Declaration of International Law Principles on Reparation for Victims of Armed Conflict (Substantive Issues),* Resolution No. 2/2010, (74th Conference, The Hague, 2010)[6]

ARTICLE 1

Reparation

1. For the purposes of the present Declaration, the term "reparation" is meant to cover measures that seek to eliminate all the harmful consequences of a violation of rules of international law applicable in armed conflict and to re-establish the situation that would have existed if the violation had not occurred.

2. Reparation shall take the form of restitution, compensation, satisfaction and guarantees and assurances of non-repetition, either singly or in combination.

11.7.2.6 **Germany,** Abstract of the German Federal Constitutional Court's Order of 13 August 2013, 2 BvR 2660/06, 2 BvR 487/07, [GER-2013-2-019] (Varvarin Case)[7]

Note: *The Plaintiffs brought a case claiming financial compensation for loss caused by NATO's action in Kosovo.*

. . .

Undoubtedly, there is no general provision of international law that gives individuals a direct claim to compensation against the responsible state in the case of breaches of international humanitarian law.

11.7.2.7 **ICC,** *Prosecutor* v. *Thomas Lubanga Dyilo,* (Judgment on the Appeals Against the 'Decision Establishing the Principles and Procedures to be Applied to Reparations' of 7 August 2012 with AMENDED order for reparations (Annex A) and public annexes 1 and 2), Case No. ICC-01/04-01/06 A A 2 A 3, Appeals Chamber (3 March 2015)

Note: *The facts of the* Lubanga *case are dealt with in Chapter 1, Section 1.2.1.1. As to the requirements for making an award of reparations against an individual, the ICC said as follows:*

1. An order for reparations under article 75 of the [ICC] Statute must contain, at a minimum, five essential elements: 1) it must be directed against the convicted person; 2) it must

---

[6] See also ILA, *Reparation for Victims of Armed Conflict, Procedural Principles for Reparation Mechanisms,* Resolution No. 1/2014 (76th Conference, Washington D.C., 2014).

[7] www.bundesverfassungsgericht.de/SharedDocs/Entscheidungen/EN/2013/08/rk20130813_2bvr266006en.html?nn=5404872.

establish and inform the convicted person of his or her liability with respect to the reparations awarded in the order; 3) it must specify, and provide reasons for, the type of reparations ordered, either collective, individual or both, . . .; 4) it must define the harm caused to direct and indirect victims as a result of the crimes for which the person was convicted, as well as identify the modalities of reparations that the Trial Chamber considers appropriate based on the circumstances of the specific case before it; and 5) it must identify the victims eligible to benefit from the awards for reparations or set out the criteria of eligibility based on the link between the harm suffered by the victims and the crimes for which the person was convicted . . .

6. A convicted person's liability for reparations must be proportionate to the harm caused and, inter alia, his or her participation in the commission of the crimes for which he or she was found guilty, in the specific circumstances of the case. . . .

212. The Appeals Chamber notes that certain crimes may have an effect on a community as a whole. The Appeals Chamber considers that, if there is a sufficient causal link between the harm suffered by members of that community and the crimes of which Mr Lubanga was found guilty, it is appropriate to award collective reparations to that community, understood as a group of victims. Therefore, an award of collective reparations to a community is not necessarily an error. However, the Appeals Chamber considers that the scope of the convicted person's liability for reparations in respect of a community must be specified. . . .

214. . . . the Trial Chamber granted an award for reparations to communities without setting out any criteria for distinction between those members of the communities who meet the above-mentioned eligibility criteria and other members of the communities. As a result, such an award of reparations may lead to imposing liability on Mr Lubanga for reparations with respect to persons who, despite being members of the communities identified by the Trial Chamber, suffered harm that did not result from the crimes for which Mr Lubanga was found guilty, . . .

11.7.3 Reparations by Armed Groups

11.7.3.1 Uganda, Juba Peace Agreement on Accountability and Reconciliation (29 June 2007)[8]

This agreement, between the Government of the Republic of Uganda and the Lord's Resistance Army/Movement (LRA/M) (herein referred to as the Parties), witnesseth that:

. . .

Reparations

9.1. Reparations may include a range of measures such as: rehabilitation; restitution; compensation; guarantees of non-recurrence and other symbolic measures such as apologies, memorials and commemorations. Priority shall be given to members of vulnerable groups.

9.2. The Parties agree that collective as well as individual reparations should be made to victims through mechanisms to be adopted by the Parties upon further consultation.

---

[8]   See also Uganda, Annexure to the Agreement on Accountability and Reconciliation (19 February 2008).

9.3. Reparations, which may be ordered to be paid to a victim as part of penalties and sanctions in accountability proceedings, may be paid out of resources identified for that purpose.

11.7.3.2 UN, Secretary-General (UNSG), *Report of the Secretary-General's Panel of Experts on Accountability in Sri Lanka* (31 March 2011)

419. ... In addition, funds acquired by the LTTE from the diaspora and elsewhere, and which still exist, should be secured for the purpose of making reparations to those in the Sri Lankan Tamil community who were victims in the conflict.

11.8 UNITED NATIONS

11.8.1 Immunity

11.8.1.1 The Netherlands, *Mothers of Srebrenica et al.* v. *State of the Netherlands and the United Nations*, (Judgment), Case No. 10/04437, Supreme Court of the Netherlands (13 April 2012)

Note: *In July 1995 the safe haven of Srebrenica in Bosnia-Herzegovina was attacked and overrun by Bosnian Serb forces. The attack resulted in the deaths of 8,000 to 10,000 individuals. A claim was filed before the District Court of The Hague by the mothers of those who died in the genocide alleging liability on the part of the UN and the Netherlands for not preventing the genocide. The Supreme Court of the Netherlands said as follows:*

4.1.1 ... The immunity granted to the UN is directly connected to the general interest served by the maintenance of peace and security in the world. That is why it is essential for the immunity enjoyed by the UN to be as unconditional as possible and for it to be subject to as little debate as possible. Accordingly, only compelling reasons can lead to the conclusion that UN immunity is not proportional to the purpose it is intended to serve.

...

4.3.5 The interim conclusion must be that the appeal court erred in examining, ..., whether the right of access to the courts as referred to in article 6 ECHR prevailed over the immunity invoked on behalf of the UN.

4.3.6 That immunity is absolute. Moreover, respecting it is among the obligations on UN member states which, as the ECtHR took into consideration in Behrami, Behrami and Saramati, under article 103 of the UN Charter, prevail over conflicting obligations from another international treaty.

4.3.7 However, this does not answer the question of whether ... the right of access to the courts should prevail in the present case over UN immunity because the claims are based on the accusation of involvement in – notably in the form of failing to prevent – genocide and other grave breaches of fundamental human rights (torture, murder and rape). ...

4.3.14 Although UN immunity should be distinguished from State immunity, the difference is not such as to justify ruling on the relationship between the former and the right of access to the courts in a way that differs from the ICJ's decision on the relationship between State immunity and the right of access to the courts. The UN is entitled to immunity regardless of the extreme seriousness of the accusations on which the Association et al. base their claims.

11.8.1.2 US, *Georges v. United Nations*, No. 15-455 (2d Cir. 2016)

Note: *The Plaintiffs in this case were US and Haitian citizens who brought a punitive class action for damages as a result of a cholera epidemic that broke out in Haiti in October 2010. The Plaintiffs alleged the UN was responsible for the outbreak and the subsequent injury to the Plaintiffs as it deployed personnel from Nepal where cholera was endemic and where a surge in infection had been reported prior to deployment. On the issue of UN immunity from suit, the Second Circuit of the US Court of Appeals held:*

The principal question presented by this appeal is whether the fulfilment by the United Nations ("UN") of its obligation under Section 29 of the Convention on Privileges and Immunities of the United Nations (the "CPIUN"), ... to "make provisions for appropriate modes of settlement of" certain disputes is a condition precedent to its immunity under Section 2 of the CPIUN, which provides that the UN "shall enjoy immunity from every form of legal process except insofar as in any particular case it has expressly waived its immunity," such that the UN's alleged disregard of its Section 29 obligation "compel[s] the conclusion that the UN's immunity does not exist."

We hold that the UN's fulfilment of its Section 29 obligation is not a condition precedent to its Section 2 immunity. For this reason ... we ... dismiss plaintiffs' action against defendants the UN, the UN Stabilization Mission in Haiti ("MINUSTAH"), UN Secretary-General Ban Ki-moon ("Ban"), and former MINUSTAH Under-Secretary-General Edmond Mulet ("Mulet") for lack of subject matter jurisdiction.

11.8.2 Enforcement and Responsibility in Peacekeeping Operations

11.8.2.1 GA, *Comprehensive Review of the Whole Question of Peacekeeping Operations in All Their Aspects, Model Status-of-Forces Agreement for Peacekeeping Operations, Report of the Secretary-General* (9 October 1990), UN Doc. A/45/594

Jurisdiction

46. All members of the United Nations peace-keeping operation including locally recruited personnel shall be immune from legal process in respect of words spoken or written and all acts performed by them in their official capacity. Such immunity shall continue even after they cease to be members of or employed by the United Nations peace-keeping operation and after the expiration of the other provisions of the present Agreement. ...

48. The Secretary-General of the United Nations will obtain assurances from Governments of participating States that they will be prepared to exercise jurisdiction with respect to crimes or offences that may be committed by members of their national contingents serving with the peace-keeping operation.

11.8.2.2 GA, *Financing of the United Nations Protection Force, the United Nations Confidence Restoration Operation in Croatia, the United Nations Preventive Deployment Force and the United Nations Peace Forces Headquarters; Administrative and Budgetary Aspects of the Financing of the United Nations Peacekeeping Operations: Financing of the United Nations Peacekeeping Operations*, Report of the Secretary-General (20 September 1996), UN Doc. A/51/389

6. The international responsibility of the United Nations for the activities of United Nations forces is an attribute of its international legal personality and its capacity to bear international rights and obligations. . . .

16. The applicability of international humanitarian law to United Nations forces when they are engaged as combatants in situations of armed conflict entails the international responsibility of the Organization and its liability in compensation for violations of international humanitarian law committed by members of United Nations forces. . . .

17. The international responsibility of the United Nations for combat-related activities of United Nations forces is premised on the assumption that the operation in question is under the exclusive command and control of the United Nations. Where a Chapter VII-authorized operation is conducted under national command and control, international responsibility for the activities of the force is vested in the State or States conducting the operation. . . .

18. In joint operations, international responsibility for the conduct of the troops lies where operational command and control is vested according to the arrangements establishing the modalities of cooperation between the State or States providing the troops and the United Nations. In the absence of formal arrangements between the United Nations and the State or States providing troops, responsibility would be determined in each and every case according to the degree of effective control exercised by either party in the conduct of the operation. . . .

42. In the relationship between the United Nations and the host State, the Organization is internationally responsible for the activities of United Nations forces. However, in the relationship between the Organization and the States contributing contingents, the Organization may seek recovery from the State of nationality if the damage was caused as a result of gross negligence or wilful misconduct of a member of its national contingent, or has entailed his international criminal responsibility.

11.8.2.3 ECtHR, *Agim Behrami and Bekir Behrami* v. *France* [GC] (App No. 71412/01) and *Ruzhdi Saramati* v. *France, Germany and Norway* [GC] (App No. 78166/01), (Decision as to Admissibility) (2 May 2007)

Note: *The facts of this case are outlined in Chapter 3, Section 3.10.2. On the issue of judicial scrutiny of UN-authorised peacekeeping missions, the ECtHR held as follows:*

133. The Court considers that the key question is whether the UNSC retained ultimate authority and control so that operational command only was delegated. . . ..

139. The Court is not persuaded that TCN involvement, either actual or structural, was incompatible with the effectiveness (including the unity) of NATO's operational command. ...

140. Accordingly, ... the Court finds that the UNSC retained ultimate authority and control and that effective command of the relevant operational matters was retained by NATO.

141. In such circumstances, the Court observes that KFOR was exercising lawfully delegated Chapter VII powers of the UNSC so that the impugned action was, in principle, "attributable" to the UN ...

143. ... the Court notes that UNMIK was a subsidiary organ of the UN created under Chapter VII of the Charter so that the impugned inaction was, in principle, "attributable" to the UN in the same sense. ...

146. The question arises in the present case whether the Court is competent *ratione personae* to review the acts of the respondent States carried out on behalf of the UN and, more generally, as to the relationship between the Convention and the UN acting under Chapter VII of its Charter.

149. ... Since operations established by UNSC Resolutions under Chapter VII of the UN Charter are fundamental to the mission of the UN to secure international peace and security and since they rely for their effectiveness on support from member states, the Convention cannot be interpreted in a manner which would subject the acts and omissions of Contracting Parties which are covered by UNSC Resolutions and occur prior to or in the course of such missions, to the scrutiny of the Court. To do so would be to interfere with the fulfilment of the UN's key mission in this field including, as argued by certain parties, with the effective conduct of its operations. It would also be tantamount to imposing conditions on the implementation of a UNSC Resolution which were not provided for in the text of the Resolution itself. ...

151. ... In the present cases, the impugned acts and omissions of KFOR and UNMIK cannot be attributed to the respondent States and, moreover, did not take place on the territory of those States or by virtue of a decision of their authorities. ...

152. In these circumstances, the Court concludes that the applicants' complaints must be declared incompatible *ratione personae* with the provisions of the Convention.

11.8.2.4 UN, *Memorandum of Understanding Between the United Nations and the Government of ... Contributing Resources to [the United Nations Peacekeeping Operation] in* Manual on Policies and Procedures Concerning the Reimbursement and Control of Contingent-Owned Equipment of Troop/ Police Contributors Participating in Peacekeeping Missions (COE Manual) (20 January 2015), 50th Session, UN Doc. A/C.5/69/18

Article 7 bis

United Nations standards of conduct

7.2. The Government shall ensure that all members of the Government's national contingent are required to comply with the United Nations standards of conduct ...

Article 7 quinquiens

Exercise of jurisdiction by the Government

7.22 Military members and any civilian members subject to national military law of the national contingent provided by the Government are subject to the Government's exclusive jurisdiction in respect of any crimes or offences that might be committed by them while they are assigned to the military component of [United Nations peacekeeping operation]. The Government assures the United Nations that it shall exercise such jurisdiction with respect to such crimes or offences.

. . .

Article 7 sexiens

Accountability

7.24. If either a United Nations investigation or an investigation conducted by the competent authorities of the Government concludes that suspicions of misconduct by any member of the Government's national contingent are well founded, the Government shall ensure that the case is forwarded to its appropriate authorities for due action. . . . The Government agrees to notify the Secretary-General of progress on a regular basis, including the outcome of the case.

11.8.3 Liability and Reparations in Peacekeeping Operations

11.8.3.1 GA, *Comprehensive Review of the Whole Question of Peacekeeping Operations in all their Aspects, Model Status-of-Forces Agreement for Peacekeeping Operations, Report of the Secretary-General* (9 October 1990), UN Doc. A/45/594

51. . . ., any dispute or claim of a private law character to which the United Nations peacekeeping operation or any member thereof is a party and over which the courts of [host country/territory] do not have jurisdiction because of any provision of the present Agreement, shall be settled by a standing claims commission to be established for that purpose. One member of the commission shall be appointed by the Secretary-General of the United Nations, one member by the Government and a chairman jointly by the Secretary-General and the Government . . .. The awards of the commission shall be final and binding, unless the Secretary-General of the United Nations and the Government permit an appeal to a tribunal established in accordance with paragraph 53.

11.8.3.2 GA, *Third-Party Liability: Temporal and Financial Limitations* (17 July 1998), UN Doc. A/RES/52/247

6. *Endorses* the view of the Secretary-General that liability is not engaged in relation to third-party claims resulting from or attributable to the activities of members of peacekeeping operations arising from "operational necessity" . . .;

9. *Decides also*, in respect of third-party claims against the Organization for personal injury, illness or death resulting from peacekeeping operations, that:

(a) Compensable types of injury or loss shall be limited to economic loss, such as medical and rehabilitation expenses, loss of earnings, loss of financial support, transportation expenses associated with the injury, illness or medical care, legal and burial expenses;

(b) No compensation shall be payable by the United Nations for non-economic loss, such as pain and suffering or moral anguish, as well as punitive or moral damages;

(c) No compensation shall be payable by the United Nations for homemaker services and other such damages that, in the sole opinion of the Secretary-General, are impossible to verify or are not directly related to the injury or loss itself;

(d) The amount of compensation payable for injury, illness or death of any individual, including for the types of loss and expenses described in subparagraph (a) above, shall not exceed a maximum of 50,000 United States dollars, provided, however, that within such limitation the actual amount is to be determined by reference to local compensation standards;

(e) In exceptional circumstances, the Secretary-General may recommend to the General Assembly, for its approval, that the limitation of 50,000 dollars provided for in subparagraph (d) above be exceeded in a particular case if the Secretary-General, after carrying out the required investigation, finds that there are compelling reasons for exceeding the limitation;

11.8.3.3 UNMISS, *The Status of Forces Agreement Between the United Nations and the Government of the Republic of South Sudan Concerning the United Nations Mission in South Sudan ('SOFA')* (2011)

55. ..., any dispute or claim of a private law character, not resulting from the operational necessity of UNMISS, to which UNMISS or any member thereof is a party, and over which the courts of South Sudan do not have jurisdiction because of any provision of the present Agreement shall be settled by a standing claims commission to be established for that purpose. One member of the commission shall be appointed by the Secretary-General of the United Nations, one member by the Government and one member jointly by the Secretary-General and the Government. ... The awards of the commission shall be final.

11.8.3.4 GA, *Memorandum of Understanding Between the United Nations and the Government of ... Contributing Resources to [the United Nations Peacekeeping Operation] in* Manual on Policies and Procedures Concerning the Reimbursement and Control of Contingent-Owned Equipment of Troop/Police Contributors Participating in Peacekeeping Missions (COE Manual) (20 January 2015), 50th Session, UN Doc. A/C.5/69/18

Article 9 Claims by third parties

9. The United Nations will be responsible for dealing with any claims by third parties where the loss of or damage to their property, or death or personal injury, was caused by the personnel or equipment provided by the Government in the performance of services or any other activity or operation under this MOU. However, if the loss, damage, death or injury arose from gross negligence or wilful misconduct of the personnel provided by the Government, the Government will be liable for such claims.

11.8.3.5 UN, *Letter from Pedro Medrano, Assistant UN Secretary-General, Senior Coordinator for Cholera Response, to Ms. Farha, Mr. Gallon, Mr. Pura and Ms. De Albuquerque* (25 November 2014)[9]

. . .

88. Claims under Section 29(a) [Convention on the Privileges and Immunities] are distinct from public law claims, which are understood as claims that would arise between an individual and a public authority, such as a State. On the international level, these claims may be addressed in various ways, such as through political, diplomatic or other means, including a body established for that specific purpose.

89. As the Secretary-General has explained, claims "based on political or policy-related grievances," such as those "related to actions or decisions taken by the Security Council or the General Assembly," are excluded from the scope of any obligation to provide an appropriate mode of settlement. That is, in contrast to claims arising from circumstances in which the United Nations is acting like a private person, claims attacking the political or policymaking functions of the Organization are not private law in character. In this context, an assertion that the United Nations has not adopted or implemented certain policies or practices does not generate a dispute of a private law character.

90. When assessing a claim under Section 29(a), the Organization does not rely solely on the allegations of the claim itself, but also assesses the character of the claim in the context of all its circumstances. The mere allegation of tortious conduct does not make a claim one of a private law character. The nature of the duty allegedly owed by the Organization, the nature of the conduct or activity at issue, and other relevant circumstances are all pertinent to determining whether the claim involves a dispute of a private law character.

11.8.3.6 **Kosovo**, *N.M. and Others* v. *UNMIK*, Case No. 26/08 (The Human Rights Advisory Panel) (26 February 2016), 77–78[10]

Note: *From 1999, members of the Roma, Ashkali and Egyptian communities of Kosovo occupied various camps for internally displaced persons in North Mitrovicë/Mitrovic. The complaints alleged lead poisoning and other health problems owing to soil contamination in the camps due to the proximity of the Trepca smelter and mining complex as well as the poor hygiene and living conditions in the camp generally. The complaint was brought against UNMIK, the UN peacekeeping operation in Kosovo, which established the IDP (internally displaced persons) camps. The Advisory Panel found that Arts 2, 3, 8, 11 and 14 ECHR had been violated and recommended as follows:*

RECOMMENDS THAT UNMIK:

a. PUBLICLY ACKNOWLEDGES, INCLUDING THROUGH THE MEDIA, UNMIK'S FAILURE TO COMPLY WITH APPLICABLE HUMAN RIGHTS STANDARDS IN RESPONSE TO THE

---

[9] Accessed at www.scribd.com/doc/261396640/Secretary-General-s-response. See also UN, *Letter from Patricia O'Brien, Under Secretary-General for Legal Affairs, to Brian Concannon, Director, Institute for Justice and Democracy in Haiti* (5 July 2013) www.ijdh.org/wp-content/uploads/2013/07/20130705164515.pdf.

[10] www.unmikonline.org/hrap/Eng/Cases%20Eng/26-8%20NM%20etal%20Opinion%20FINAL%2026feb16 .pdf. Capitals in the original.

ADVERSE HEALTH CONDITION CAUSED BY LEAD CONTAMINATION IN THE IDP CAMPS AND THE CONSEQUENT HARMS SUFFERED BY THE COMPLAINANTS, AND MAKES A PUBLIC APOLOGY TO THEM AND THEIR FAMILIES;

b. TAKES APPROPRIATE STEPS TOWARDS PAYMENT OF ADEQUATE COMPENSATION TO THE COMPLAINANTS FOR MATERIAL DAMAGE IN RELATION TO THE FINDING OF VIOLATIONS OF THE HUMAN RIGHTS PROVISIONS LISTED ABOVE;

c. TAKES APPROPRIATE STEPS TOWARDS PAYMENT OF ADEQUATE COMPENSATION TO THE COMPLAINANTS FOR MORAL DAMAGE IN RELATION TO THE FINDING OF VIOLATIONS OF THE HUMAN RIGHTS PROVISIONS LISTED ABOVE;

d. TAKES APPROPRIATE STEPS TOWARDS REIMBURSEMENT OF ALL FEES AND EXPENSES INCURRED BY THE COMPLAINANTS IN RELATION WITH THE PROCEED-INGS BEFORE THE PANEL;

e. TAKES APPROPRIATE STEPS TO ENSURE THAT UN BODIES WORKING WITH REFU-GEES AND IDPS PROMOTE AND ENSURE RESPECT FOR INTERNATIONAL HUMAN RIGHTS STANDARDS AND THAT THE FINDINGS AND RECOMMENDATIONS OF THE PANEL IN THIS CASE ARE SHARED WITH THESE BODIES, AS A GUARANTEE OF NON-REPETITION;

11.8.4 Criminal Responsibility in Peacekeeping Operations

11.8.4.1 GA, *Report of the Group of Legal Experts on Ensuring the Accountability of United Nations Staff and Experts on Mission with Respect to Criminal Acts Committed in Peacekeeping Operations* (16 August 2006), UN Doc. A/60/980, Annex III[11]

Draft convention on the criminal accountability of United Nations officials and experts on mission

Article 2 Scope of application

1. This Convention applies to United Nations officials and experts on mission. . . .

3. This Convention does not apply to a United Nations operation authorized by the Security Council as an enforcement action under Chapter VII of the Charter of the United Nations, in which a United Nations official or expert on mission is engaged as a combatant against organized armed forces and to which the law of international armed conflict applies.

4. This Convention does not affect the immunity from legal process of any person pursuant to the General Convention or to the terms of the status-of-forces agreement between the United Nations and the host State, or the waiver of such immunity by the competent organ of the United Nations.

---

[11] See also GA, *Criminal Accountability of United Nations Officials and Experts on Mission* (8 January 2008), UN Doc. A/RES/62/63.

Article 3 Crimes committed during United Nations peacekeeping operations

. . .

2. The serious crimes referred to in paragraph 1 of the present article are, for each State party establishing and exercising jurisdiction pursuant to this Convention, those which, under the national law of that State party, correspond to:

(a) Murder;
(b) Wilfully causing serious injury to body or health;
(c) Rape and acts of sexual violence;
(d) Sexual offences involving children;
(e) An attempt to commit any crime set out in subparagraphs (a) to (d); and
(f) Participation in any capacity, such as an accomplice, assistant or instigator in any crime set out in subparagraphs (a) to (e)

Article 4 Establishment of jurisdiction

1. Each State party shall take such measures as may be necessary to establish its jurisdiction over the crimes set out in article 3 when:

(a) The crime is committed in the territory of that State; or
(b) The crime is committed by a national of that State.

2. A State party may also establish its jurisdiction over any of the crimes set out in article 3 when:

(a) The crime is committed against a national of that State; or
(b) The crime is committed by a stateless person who has his or her habitual residence in the territory of that State.

11.9 BELLIGERENT REPRISALS

11.9.1 US, *General Orders No. 100: Instructions for the Government of Armies of the United States in the Field* (Lieber Code) (adopted 24 April 1863)

Article 27: The law of war can no more wholly dispense with retaliation than can the law of nations, of which it is a branch. Yet civilized nations acknowledge retaliation as the sternest feature of war. A reckless enemy often leaves to his opponent no other means of securing himself against the repetition of barbarous outrage

Article 28: Retaliation will, therefore, never be resorted to as a measure of mere revenge, but only as a means of protective retribution, and moreover, cautiously and unavoidably; that is to say, retaliation shall only be resorted to after careful inquiry into the real occurrence, and the character of the misdeeds that may demand retribution.

Unjust or inconsiderate retaliation removes the belligerents farther and farther from the mitigating rules of regular war, and by rapid steps leads them nearer to the internecine wars of savages.

11.9.2 US Military Tribunal, Nuremberg, *United States of America* v. *Otto Ohlendorf et al., (Judgment, 8–9 April 1948) Trials of War Criminals before the Nuremberg Military Tribunals, Vol. IV* (1949), pp. 492–4

Note: *The facts of the Nuremberg Trials are outlined in Chapter 8, Section 8.1.5. On the issue of the remedy of reprisals, the Tribunal said as follows:*

From time to time the word "reprisals" has appeared in the Einsatzgruppen reports. Reprisals in war are the commission of acts which, although illegal in themselves, may, under the specific circumstances of the given case, become justified because the guilty adversary has himself behaved illegally, and the action is taken in the last resort, in order to prevent the adversary from behaving illegally in the future. Thus, the first prerequisite to the introduction of this most extraordinary remedy is proof that the enemy has behaved illegally. While generally the persons who become victims of the reprisals are admittedly innocent of the acts against which the reprisal is to retaliate, there must at least be such close connection between these persons and these acts as to constitute a joint responsibility.

. . .

Thus when, as one report says, 859 out of 2,100 Jews shot in alleged reprisal for the killing of 21 German soldiers near Topola were taken from concentration camps in Yugoslavia, hundreds of miles away, it is obvious that a flagrant violation of international law occurred and outright murder resulted. . . . Reprisals, if allowed, may not be disproportionate to the wrong for which they are to retaliate.

11.9.3 French Permanent Military Tribunal at Dijon, *Trial of Franz Holstein and Two Others* (Judgment of 3 February 1947) Trials of War Criminals Selected and Prepared by the United Nations War Crimes Commission, Vol. VIII (1949), pp. 27–8

Note: *The accused were members of the German army, the Gestapo and Security Police who committed crimes against the people of Dijon in 1944. Crimes included the murder of civilians, which the court characterised as 'reprisals', destruction of property by means of arson, pillage and ill-treatment of civilians. On the issue of reprisals, the Tribunal said:*

. . . The subject of "reprisals" is one of difficulty in International Law. Its limitations are still not well defined, and regarding the rules guiding it one has chiefly to rely on the opinion of learned publicists and on judicial precedents of a differing nature. This gap is particularly felt within the sphere of the laws and customs of war. . . .

It was admitted that "reprisals between belligerents cannot be dispensed with, for the effect of their use and of the fear of their being used cannot be denied."

It would thus appear that, in the present stage of its growth, International Law still recognises reprisals, admittedly within certain conditions and limitations. . . .

In conditions created by a state at war, the question of reprisals arises when one belligerent violates the rules of warfare and the other belligerent retaliates in order to bring about a cessation of such violations. The problem then consists in determining the scope and nature of acts which the retaliating party is deemed entitled to undertake.

11.9.4 ICTY, *Prosecutor* v. *Kupreškić et al.*, (Judgment), Case No. IT-95-16-T, Trial Chamber (14 January 2000)

Note: *The background to this case is dealt with in Chapter 2, Section 2.1.3. Outlining the law as it relates to reprisals against civilians, the ICTY commented as follows:*

528. The question of reprisals against civilians is a case in point. It cannot be denied that reprisals against civilians are inherently a barbarous means of seeking compliance with international law. The most blatant reason for the universal revulsion that usually accompanies reprisals is that they may not only be arbitrary but are also not directed specifically at the individual authors of the initial violation. . . .

529. In addition, the reprisal killing of innocent persons, more or less chosen at random, without any requirement of guilt or any form of trial, can safely be characterized as a blatant infringement of the most fundamental principles of human rights. . . .

530. It should be added that while reprisals could have had a modicum of justification in the past, when they constituted practically the only effective means of compelling the enemy to abandon unlawful acts of warfare and to comply in future with international law, at present they can no longer be justified in this manner. A means of inducing compliance with international law is at present more widely available and, more importantly, is beginning to prove fairly efficacious: the prosecution and punishment of war crimes and crimes against humanity by national or international courts. . . .

532. . . . The aforementioned elements seem to support the contention that the demands of humanity and the dictates of public conscience, as manifested in *opinio necessitatis*, have by now brought about the formation of a customary rule also binding upon those few States that at some stage did not intend to exclude the abstract legal possibility of resorting to the reprisals under discussion. . . .

535. It should also be pointed out that at any rate, even when considered lawful, reprisals are restricted by; (a) the principle whereby they must be a last resort in attempts to impose compliance by the adversary with legal standards (which entails, amongst other things, that they may be exercised only after a prior warning has been given which has failed to bring about the discontinuance of the adversary's crimes); (b) the obligation to take special precautions before implementing them (they may be taken only after a decision to this effect has been made at the highest political or military level; in other words they may not be decided by local commanders); (c) the principle of proportionality (which entails not only that the reprisals must not be excessive compared to the precedent unlawful act of warfare, but also that they must stop as soon as that unlawful act has been discontinued) and; (d) 'elementary considerations of humanity' (as mentioned above).

11.10 ARMED GROUPS AND ENFORCEMENT OF IHL

11.10.1 Philippines, *Comprehensive Agreement on Respect for Human Rights and International Humanitarian Law between the Government of the Republic of the Philippines and the National Democratic Front of the Philippines* (16 March 1998)

Article 6. The persons liable for violations of the principles of international humanitarian law shall be subject to investigation and, if evidence warrants, to prosecution and trial. The victims or their survivors shall be indemnified. All necessary measures shall be undertaken to remove the conditions for such violations and to render justice to and indemnify the victims.

11.10.2 The Islamic Emirate of Afghanistan, *The Layha [Code of Conduct] For Mujahideen* Annex (881) IRRC (March 2011) 103

... After the publication of the second edition, every person in charge and every Mujahid of the Islamic Emirate has a responsibility and duty in terms of obeying [the rules of] this Laiha and its implementation.

All military and administrative authorities as well as ordinary Mujahids of the Islamic Emirate in matters of Jihad affairs are bound to all principles of This Laiha and obliged to organise their daily Jihad activities in the light of the regulations of this Code of Conduct. ...

40. It is compulsory for the Mujahids to obey their [military] squad leader; for the squad leader to obey the district leader; for the district leader to obey the provincial leader; for the provincial leader to obey the organizing director and for the organizing director to obey the Imam and Najib Imam as long as it is rightful under the Sharia.

41. Anyone who is appointed as a person with responsibility must have the following characteristics: Inventiveness, piety, courage, compassion, and generosity. If none [of the candidates] have all these characteristics, then at least inventiveness and piety are required. ...

56. Those valiant warrior Mujahids who are entering the enemy centre in order to conduct a group armed attack should consider the following points:

1. These valiant warrior Mujahids should receive a good training and each of them should be given particular tasks.
2. These valiant warrior Mujahids should be very well supplied and equipped in order to be able to resist for a long time and inflict a lot of damage on the enemy.
3. The Mujahids and their leaders should receive in advance full information and understanding about the area they are going to attack.

57. Regarding martyrdom attacks, the four following points should be considered:

FIRST: A martyr Mujahid should be well-trained prior to the attack.
SECOND: A martyrdom attack should be used for important and high-value targets. The self-sacrificing heroes of the Islamic Ummah must not be used for low and worthless targets.

THIRD: In martyrdom attacks, much more care should be taken to prevent the deaths and injuries of common people.

FOURTH: Apart from those Mujahids who received an individual programme and permission from the Leadership, all other Mujahids must receive permission and instructions from the person responsible in the province before carrying out martyrdom attacks.

11.10.3 Sudan, *Agreement between the Government of the Republic of Sudan and the Sudan People's Liberation Movement to Protect Non-Combatant Civilians and Civilian Facilities from Military Attack* (31 March 2002)[12]

2. In order to lessen the suffering of non-combatant civilians, the Parties shall:

a) Issue or re-issue orders to all their military units (including associated militias) to conduct their operations consistent with their obligations and commitments described in paragraph 1.
b) Agree to the establishment of a Verification Mission to investigate, evaluate and report on alleged incidents involving serious violations of their obligations or commitments described in paragraph 1.

11.10.4 UN, *Report of the International Commission of Inquiry on Darfur to the United Nations Secretary-General* (Geneva, 25 January 2005)

600. It is in light of this international legal regulation that the obligation of the Sudan to pay compensation for all the crimes perpetrated in Darfur by its agents and officials or de facto organs must be seen. A similar obligation is incumbent upon rebels for all crimes they may have committed, whether or not the perpetrators are identified and punished.

11.10.5 Human Rights Council, *Report of the United Nations Fact-Finding Mission on the Gaza Conflict* (25 September 2009), 12th Session, UN Doc. A/HRC/12/48

1836. The Gaza authorities are responsible for ensuring that effective measures for accountability for violations of IHRL and IHL committed by armed groups acting in or from the Gaza Strip are established. The Mission points out that such responsibility would continue to rest on any authority exercising government-like functions in the Gaza Strip. ....

1843. The Palestinian Authority has a duty to respect and ensure respect for human rights and humanitarian law in the areas under its authority and control. The duty to investigate and, if appropriate, prosecute alleged perpetrators of serious crimes is also incumbent upon it. It has a general duty to provide an effective remedy to those who allege that their rights have been infringed.

---

[12] http://peacemaker.un.org/sites/peacemaker.un.org/files/SD_020331_Agreement%20to%20Protect%20Non-Combatant%20Civilians%20from%20Military%20Attack.pdf.

11.10.6 Northern Ireland, *Mark Christopher Breslin & Ors* v. *Seamus McKenna & Ors* [2009] NIQB 50

Note: *The Plaintiffs issued a claim against the Defendants, members of the Real Irish Republican Army (IRA), for damages caused by personal injuries arising out of an incident on 15 August 1998 when a bomb exploded in Omagh town centre. Claims were also brought by the estates of some family members who died in the explosion. One of the issues in this case was whether a claim against the Real IRA, an unincorporated association, could be maintained. The High Court of Justice in Northern Ireland said as follows:*

[83] The real issue in connection with this defendant is whether as a matter of law it is possible to maintain an action against it [Real IRA]. In legal terms the Real IRA is an unincorporated association. Such an association cannot be made a defendant in its own right to action ... The issue is whether this Rule provides a mechanism whereby the plaintiffs are entitled to maintain this action against the Real IRA.

[84] [...] In addition to that it is necessary to recognise that the nature of a claim for damages is a personal action against the wrongdoer and liability, if established, is not, therefore, limited to the common fund but extends to the entire assets of the person represented for his individual wrongdoing. That may bear upon the issue of whether there is a common interest in defending the claim.

[85] These are formidable arguments. If correct they would inhibit the plaintiffs from securing any judgment against the organisation's common funds which the plaintiffs could not attribute to individual defendants against whom liability had been established. ... In those circumstances the law in relation to representative proceedings should not prevent the plaintiffs from recovering against the members of this organisation who have consistently and relentlessly pursued the terrorist campaign identified in the evidence before me.

11.10.7 Philippines, *Agreement on the Civilian Protection Component of the International Monitoring Team Bangerter Internal Control (IMT) [Government of the Republic of the Philippines and Moro Islamic Liberation Front]* (27 October 2009)[13]

Article 2 Civilian Protection Component
The Parties hereby agree to expand the mandate of the IMT to include civilian protection. The IMT shall monitor, verify and report non-compliance by the Parties to their basic undertaking to protect civilians and civilian communities. ...

The Parties shall designate humanitarian organizations and non-governmental organizations, both international and national, with proven track record for impartiality, neutrality and independence, to carry out the civilian protection functions.

---

[13]   http://peacemaker.un.org/sites/peacemaker.un.org/files/PH_091027_Agreement%20on%20Civilian%20Protection%20Component.pdf.

11.10.8 Human Rights Council, *Report of the International Commission of Inquiry to Investigate All Alleged Violations of International Human Rights Law in the Libyan Arab Jamahiriya* (1 June 2011), 17th Session, UN Doc. A/HRC/17/44

269. The Commission calls on the National Transitional Council:

- To ensure immediately the implementation of applicable international humanitarian law and international human rights law;
- To conduct exhaustive, impartial and public investigations into all allegations of international human rights law and international humanitarian law violations, and in particular to investigate with a view to prosecuting cases of extrajudicial, summary or arbitrary executions and torture with full respect of judicial guarantees;
- To grant adequate reparations to the victims or their families and take all appropriate measures to prevent the recurrence of such violations;
- To undertake further efforts to ensure strict control over weapons in possession of individual;
- To ensure free, full and unrestricted access to all places of detention for humanitarian and human rights organizations, . . .

270. With respect to the humanitarian situation, the Commission calls on the Government of Libya and the National Transitional Council:

- To fulfil their respective obligations under international humanitarian law, particularly those regarding the protection of civilians, including the facilitation of immediate, free and unimpeded access for humanitarian personnel to all persons in need of assistance.

11.11 UNITED NATIONS ACTION

11.11.1 SC, *Security Council Resolution 670 on Iraq–Kuwait* (25 September 1990), UN Doc. S/RES/670 (1990)

13. Reaffirms that the Fourth Geneva Convention applies to Kuwait and that as a High Contracting Party to the Convention Iraq is bound to comply fully with all its terms and, in particular, is liable under the Convention in respect of the grave breaches committed by it, as are individuals who commit or order the commission of grave breaches.

11.11.2 SC, *Security Council Resolution 692 on UN Compensation Commission for Iraq* (20 May 1991) UN Doc. S/RES/692 (1991)

Acting under Chapter VII of the Charter of the United Nations,

3. Decides to establish the Fund and Commission referred to in paragraph 18 of resolution 687 (1991) in accordance with Part I of the Secretary-General's report, and that the Governing Council will be located at the Offices of the United Nations at Geneva and that

the Governing Council may decide whether some of the activities of the Commission should be carried out elsewhere

11.11.3 SC, *Security Council Resolution 827 on former Yugoslavia, ICTY* (25 May 1993) UN Doc. S/RES/827 (1993)

Acting under Chapter VII of the Charter of the United Nations,

2. Decides hereby to establish an international tribunal for the sole purpose of prosecuting persons responsible for serious violations of international humanitarian law committed in the territory of the former Yugoslavia between 1 January 1991 and a date to be determined by the Security Council upon the restoration of peace and to this end to adopt the Statute of the International Tribunal annexed to the above-mentioned report.

11.11.4 SC, *Security Council Resolution 955 on Rwanda* (8 November 1994) UN Doc. S/RES/955 (1994)

Acting under Chapter VII of the Charter of the United Nations,

1. *Decides* hereby, having received the request of the Government of Rwanda (S/1994/1115), to establish an international tribunal for the sole purpose of prosecuting persons responsible for genocide and other serious violations of international humanitarian law committed in the territory of Rwanda and Rwandan citizens responsible for genocide and other such violations committed in the territory of neighbouring States, between 1 January 1994 and 31 December 1994 and to this end to adopt the Statute of the International Criminal Tribunal for Rwanda annexed hereto.

11.11.5 SC, *Security Council Resolution 1564 on Darfur,* (18 September 2004) UN Doc. S/RES/ 1564 (2004)

12. *Requests* that the Secretary-General rapidly establish an international commission of inquiry in order immediately to investigate reports of violations of international humanitarian law and human rights law in Darfur by all parties, to determine also whether or not acts of genocide have occurred, and to identify the perpetrators of such violations with a view to ensuring that those responsible are held accountable, *calls on* all parties to cooperate fully with such a commission, and *further requests* the Secretary-General, in conjunction with the Office of the High Commissioner for Human Rights, to take appropriate steps to increase the number of human rights monitors deployed to Darfur.

11.11.6 SC, *Security Council Resolution 1593 Darfur, Referral to ICC* (31 March 2005), UN Doc. S/RES/1593 (2005)

Acting under Chapter VII of the Charter of the United Nations,

1. *Decides* to refer the situation in Darfur since 1 July 2002 to the Prosecutor of the International Criminal Court;

2. *Decides* that the Government of Sudan and all other parties to the conflict in Darfur shall cooperate fully with and provide any necessary assistance to the Court and the Prosecutor ...

6. *Decides* that nationals, current or former officials or personnel from a contributing State outside Sudan which is not a party to the Rome Statute of the International Criminal Court shall be subject to the exclusive jurisdiction of that contributing State for all alleged acts or omissions arising out of or related to operations in Sudan established or authorized by the Council or the African Union, unless such exclusive jurisdiction has been expressly waived by that contributing State;

11.11.7 SC, *Security Council Resolution 1265 on Protection of Civilians in Armed Conflict*, UN Doc. S/RES/1265 (2006)[14]

4. Urges all parties concerned to comply strictly with their obligations under international humanitarian, human rights and refugee law, in particular those contained in the Hague Conventions of 1899 and 1907 and in the Geneva Conventions of 1949 and their Additional Protocols of 1977, as well as with the decisions of the Security Council.

11.11.8 SC, *Security Council Resolution 1970 Libya Referral to ICC* (26 February 2011), UN Doc. S/RES/1970 (2011)

Acting under Chapter VII of the Charter of the United Nations, and taking measures under its Article 41

4. *Decides* to refer the situation in the Libyan Arab Jamahiriya since 15 February 2011 to the Prosecutor of the International Criminal Court;

5. *Decides* that the Libyan authorities shall cooperate fully with and provide any necessary assistance to the Court and the Prosecutor ...;

6. *Decides* that nationals, current or former officials or personnel from a State outside the Libyan Arab Jamahiriya which is not a party to the Rome Statute of the International Criminal Court shall be subject to the exclusive jurisdiction of that State for all alleged acts or omissions arising out of or related to operations in the Libyan Arab Jamahiriya established or authorized by the Council, unless such exclusive jurisdiction has been expressly waived by the State.

11.11.9 SC, *Security Council Resolution 2139 on Syria* (22 February 2014), UN Doc. S/RES/2139 (2014)

3. Demands that all parties immediately cease all attacks against civilians, as well as the indiscriminate employment of weapons in populated areas, including shelling and aerial bombardment, such as the use of barrel bombs, and methods of warfare which are of a nature to cause superfluous injury or unnecessary suffering, and *recalls* in this regard the

---

[14] See also the relevant reports by the Secretary-General with recommendations such as *Report of the Secretary-General on the Protection of Civilians in Armed Conflict* (29 May 2009) UN Doc. S/2009/277.

obligation to respect and ensure respect for international humanitarian law in all circumstances, and further recalls, in particular, the obligation to distinguish between civilian populations and combatants, and the prohibition against indiscriminate attacks, and attacks against civilians and civilian objects as such.

COMMENTARY

1. Violations of IHL are pervasive and often very serious. The ICRC study *Roots of Behaviour in War: Understanding and Preventing IHL Violations* identified five main causes that could explain violations of IHL by individuals: (1) the encouragement to crime that is part of the nature of war, (2) the definition of war aims, (3) reasons of opportunity, (4) psycho-sociological reasons and (5) reasons connected with the individual.[15] To these, ideological, political, economic or other causes at the State or armed group level should be added.

2. IHL does not possess superseding monitoring and enforcement mechanisms. Its mechanisms are decentralised and State centred, something that affects the consistency and effectiveness of its enforcement. The complexity of modern conflicts and the involvement of non-State actors are additional factors that challenge the effectiveness of existing enforcement mechanisms. However, a number of factors induce enforcement such as the need to maintain discipline, public opinion and the reciprocal interest of adversaries to comply with IHL.

3. State responsibility and individual criminal responsibility for violations of IHL are distinct forms of responsibility. Only individuals can incur criminal responsibility.[16] In the *Bosnia Genocide* case the ICJ aligned certain modes of State responsibility with similar modes of individual criminal responsibility (for example complicity with aiding and abetting) and attributed the *mens rea* and *actus reus* of certain individuals to a State in order to establish State responsibility.[17] However, although it accepted that individuals committed genocide, Serbia was not responsible for committing genocide because the responsible individuals were not acting under the instructions, direction or control of Serbia and were not completely dependent on it.[18]

4. Criminal prosecution at the national level is central to enforcing IHL but its scope is limited by the jurisdictional immunities enjoyed by foreign State officials. Jurisdictional immunities do not apply before international courts but this rule operates only among States parties to the relevant treaties.

---

[15]   Daniel Muñoz-Rojas and Jean-Jacques Frésard, *Roots of Behaviour in War: Understanding and Preventing IHL Violations* (ICRC, 2004) 2 available at www.icrc.org/eng/assets/files/other/icrc_002_0853.pdf.
[16]   ICJ, *Case Concerning Application of the Convention on the Prevention and Punishment of the Crime of Genocide (Bosnia and Herzegovina v. Serbia and Montenegro)* (Judgment) [2007] I.C.J. Rep. 43, paras 170–173.
[17]   A. Cassese, 'On the Use of Criminal Law Notions in Determining State Responsibility for Genocide' (2007) 5 *JICJ* 875.
[18]   ICJ, *Case Concerning Application of the Convention on the Prevention and Punishment of the Crime of Genocide (Bosnia and Herzegovina v. Serbia and Montenegro)* (Judgment) [2007] I.C.J. Rep. 43, paras 392, 404.

5. States may use international mechanisms to enforce IHL against other States. These may include judicial mechanisms such as the ICJ,[19] arbitration, negotiation or other dispute settlement mechanisms. As far as courts are concerned, their jurisdiction may be *rationae materiae* and *rationae personae* limited, standards of evidence and proof may be high, violations by individuals or armed groups need to be attributed to a State which is quite an onerous exercise, proceedings may be slow and compliance with judgments may be haphazard. Arbitration may be more effective if, of course, States comply with the award.

6. The enforcement of IHL by armed groups can take many different strands. It includes dissemination, teaching and raising awareness of IHL among members of the armed group, internal regulations and codes of conduct, special agreements[20] to bring into force the GCs, unilateral declarations,[21] written or oral, formal or informal commitments to respect IHL, deeds of commitment,[22] training and assistance in IHL by external actors, self-reporting to IHRL bodies, monitoring of their activities by such bodies and sanctions for violations of IHL. That said, there are important practical and legal challenges. These relate to the clandestine nature of many armed groups, the lack of human resources, inadequate education and training, weak or informal organisation and control over members, lack of permanence, lack of ownership of IHL rules and the fact that armed groups often pursue diverse political objectives which are not always in sync with the rule of law.

7. Armed groups often establish their own courts to enforce IHL.[23] This seems to be in sync with their obligation not to pass sentences and carry out executions without previous judgment pronounced by a regularly constituted court[24] and their general obligation to respect and ensure respect of IHL.[25] Yet questions arise regarding the legitimacy, independence, impartiality and fairness of the proceedings before such courts. As a matter of fact, failings in this regard may constitute a war crime.[26] Another set of questions concerns the law that such courts should apply: should they apply national law, customary international law or the law promulgated by the armed group? Applying national law offers continuity and stability but if the armed group challenges the government, it would be unreasonable to expect it to apply national law. Even if these courts are to apply national law, it does not necessarily mean that national law is always compliant with IHRL or IHL. Moreover, armed groups may still be able to change national law for security reasons or in order to be able to comply with their IHL obligations. If armed groups are to apply their own law, what should be the required checks and balances in the promulgation of that law in order for it to be valid? Another set of questions concerns the crimes that can be prosecuted by armed groups' courts and, more specifically, whether they can prosecute ordinary crimes or also

---

[19] See ICJ, *Case Concerning Military and Paramilitary Activities in and Against Nicaragua (Nicaragua v. United States of America)* (Merits, Judgment) [1986] I.C.J. Rep. 14.
[20] Common Article 3.
[21] Art. 96(3), API; Art. 7(4) of the Convention on Conventional Weapons 1980 (CCW).
[22] There are three types of such deeds: deeds banning the use of antipersonnel mines; deeds protecting children from the effects of armed conflict; deeds prohibiting sexual violence. Geneva Call, 'Deed of Commitment' www.genevacall.org/how-we-work/deed-ofcommitment.
[23] Commom Article 3, GCs and Art. 6, APII.
[24] Common Article 3, GCs.
[25] Commom Article 1, GCs.
[26] Art. 8(2)(c)(iv), ICC St.

war crimes committed by members of the armed group as well as by non-members. Finally, questions remain as to the application of the *res judicata, ne bis in idem* and complementarity principles in relation to trials by armed groups.

8. Holding armed groups as such responsible for IHL violations is impossible. There is no regime of criminal or civil responsibility applicable to armed groups but it is only their members that can incur criminal responsibility for violations of IHL. There are many reasons for this state of affairs with the most obvious being the fact that the content and scope of their IHL and IHRL, treaty or customary law obligations, is not clear. Other reasons are the fact that they lack *locus standi* before courts and tribunals and that, generally, they are not recognised as full legal subjects.

9. The obligation incumbent on States to make reparations for violations of IHL is contained in Article 3 of the 1907 Hague Convention IV and in Article 91 API and has customary law status, being thus applicable to both IACs and NIACs. The question is whether this is exclusively an inter-State obligation or whether individuals can also pursue claims for reparation.[27] As the *Varvarin* and other similar cases indicate, no individual right to reparation is recognised. As the EECC process also shows, it is States that act on behalf of their nationals in seeking reparations. It should be noted that even if a direct individual claim to reparation is recognised, its implementation will encounter many difficulties. First, IHL does not provide processes to entertain such claims. Secondly, States will invoke immunity from jurisdiction or invoke the Act of State doctrine. Thirdly, damages may be regulated by a peace treaty, thus overriding individual claims. With regard to the question of whether such an individual right can be exercised against armed groups, there are many difficulties which relate to the *locus standi* of armed groups and to their ability to offer reparations or pay compensation.

10. Due to the inter-State nature of the right to remedy in IHL, individuals often use human rights mechanisms (judicial or quasi-judicial), relying on the human right to an effective remedy.[28] However, as explained in Chapter 3, questions concerning the jurisdictional competence and expertise of human rights mechanisms to entertain such cases can be asked and as was also noted there, they often subordinate IHL to IHRL. Another problem with human rights courts entertaining IHL is that they may reverse the IHL principle of equality of parties because they only hear cases involving States since armed groups have no *locus standi*. Furthermore, their jurisdiction is limited to States parties only, thus ignoring the possible responsibility of non–State parties. For this reason, non–judicial human rights bodies, in particular UN bodies, can play an important role in enforcing IHL because of their quasi-universal membership. However, similar questions concerning their competence as those mentioned above are raised. Moreover, since their decisions are not binding, a lot depends on how their reports are received by the parties. Other limitations constitute the periodic nature of their reports and that they lack competence over armed groups. Finally, due to the diversity of human rights bodies, questions of consistency and

---

[27]   See *Basic Principles and Guidelines on the Right to a Remedy and Reparation for Victims of Gross Violations of International Human Rights Law and Serious Violations of International Humanitarian Law* (21 March 2006), 60th Session, UN Doc. A/RES/60/147.
[28]   See Chapters 3 and 10.

uniformity in their interpretation of IHL arise whereas their intervention may dilute IHL rules and set untenable standards of behaviour.

11. There are no criteria as to how reparations for violations of IHL are to be determined. For this reason, general international law can be of assistance. In general, reparations require that a range of measures be taken that are relevant to the particular context in order to ensure that the victims' rights are acknowledged and are given effect. In some situations, such measures will include monetary or other forms of compensation to redress the direct harm done to the victim while healthcare and other services can assist the victim's rehabilitation.[29] At the same time, the State may also take symbolic action to acknowledge the injustice and harm done to victims – for example by issuing a formal apology – and to initiate legal and institutional reforms, disarm and demobilize former combatants and strengthen the rule of law in order to eliminate the causes of conflict and prevent its recurrence. However, there are certain problems with reparations in view also of the scale of crimes committed in an armed conflict, with questions raised as to who should receive reparation and what type of reparation is adequate. Another set of problems concerns the definition of 'victim', the identification of victims and of the harm they have suffered, the identification of the type of reparation that is appropriate for victims and whether individual or collective reparations are appropriate. Due to limited funds, prioritising certain groups of victims may be necessary, but questions are asked about the relevant criteria. As to whether the reparations regime is effective, a lot depends on the political will to provide reparations and to make the necessary institutional changes as well as on the availability of financial resources.

12. Calculating compensation for violations of IHL is complicated and difficult. It is not easy, for instance, to measure moral or material harm. Issues of evidence are also critical. Whereas the ICJ required 'fully conclusive' evidence in the *Bosnia Genocide* case,[30] the EECC required clear and convincing evidence.[31] Claims may also be numerous and funds limited. For this reason, the resources of the parties need to be taken into account as the EECC did in its calculation of compensation. The United Nations Compensation Commission was more successful in this respect but this was due to the fact that it was able to deduct a percentage from the exports of Iraqi oil. Another problem with compensation is that it may not reach the victims.[32]

13. Armed groups can definitely comply with certain forms of reparation and as a matter of fact they have agreed to provide reparations in certain situations. However, questions arise as to whether they can provide collective reparations or monetary reparations.

14. In international criminal proceedings, reparations are awarded to the victims. They are measures of accountability against the convicted person and can be awarded individually and/or collectively. Standards of evidence and causality are critical as well as the apportionment of reparations among multiple perpetrators or in relation to multiple crimes. Other questions concern the form of reparations for different crimes and for different

---

[29] See, for example, Executive Order 13732 of 1 July 2016, https://fas.org/irp/offdocs/eo/eo-13732.htm.
[30] *Case Concerning Application of the Convention on the Prevention and Punishment of the Crime of Genocide (Bosnia and Herzegovina v. Serbia and Montenegro)* (Judgment) [2007] I.C.J. Rep. 43, paras 209–210.
[31] See this chapter, Section 11.5.1.
[32] See www.unog.ch/uncc/.

groups of victims by also taking into account gender and culture. That said, identifying and seizing the assets of the convicted person is not always easy and often requires international cooperation.

15. The enforcement of IHL against international organisations encounters many difficulties. First, the scope and content of their IHL obligations is not settled. Second, their IHL obligations may differ from those of TCCs. Third, attribution in multinational operations is complex. For instance, whereas the UN holds itself responsible for wrongful conduct committed in the course of military operations under its command and control, the Draft Articles on the Responsibility of International Organizations (2011) require effective control over the wrongful conduct.[33] Fourth, international organisations such as the UN and their officials enjoy absolute or functional immunity before national courts.[34] Fifth, international organisations lack *locus standi* before national or international courts.[35] For these reasons, claimants often bring suits against participating States in view of the fact that they retain full command and criminal jurisdiction over their troops as the *Srebrenica* cases before the Dutch courts demonstrate. Establishing their responsibility for the specific act is difficult, however, and could potentially disrupt the unity of command in military operations led by international organisations.

16. The UN is currently dealing with third-party claims arising from its operations by using review boards although the Model SOFA requires standing claims commissions.[36] Review boards do not, however, deal with claims relating to violations of IHL, but with personal injury, property loss or damage attributed to the activities of the operation other than those arising from operational necessity.[37] Monetary claims are subject to limitations. As the claims arising from the cholera outbreak in Haiti show, the UN takes a very narrow view of what constitutes a private claim. For this reason, more clarity is needed as to what constitutes a private or a public law claim.

17. The problems identified above regarding the enforcement of IHL against international organisations indicate that the UN or international organisations in general need to address this issue. Although immunity is an important attribute that facilitates the operation of the UN and other international organisations, it should not lead to impunity. The establishment of permanent or *ad hoc*, general or specific mechanisms of oversight in the form of tribunals, ombudspersons or claims commissions may be a way forward that can also circumvent the immunity barrier. Another issue that requires attention is that of sufficient financial resources to settle claims. Claims can be small but there can also be large claims involving class-action lawsuits. The UN currently makes compensation payments from its budget but claims may cripple the UN or any other organisation. For this reason, having a

---

[33] Arts 6–9, DARIO.

[34] In a recent case arising from the outbreak of cholera in Haiti, the plaintiffs claimed that the UN had waived its immunity by passing Resolution 52/247 of 1998 on third-party liability. The case is pending. *LaVenture et al v. United Nations*, Case No. 1:14-cv-01611-SLT-RLM, filed 06/23/17, United States District Court of Eastern District of New York.

[35] See, for example, *Behrami* v. *France* and *Saramati* v. *France, Germany and Norway* [GC] (App Nos 71412/01 and 78166/01) (Judgment, ECHR, 2 May 2007).

[36] See sections 51 and 53 Model SOFA.

[37] With regard to UNMIK, the Ombudsperson Institution had the competence to deal with claims involving human rights (UNMIK/REG/2006/6).

contingency plan or third-party insurance may be advisable. In this way, States may also be protected from lawsuits.[38]

18. The UN has been quite active in enforcing IHL. It often reminds parties of their IHL obligations, condemns violations of IHL, establishes commissions of inquiry, characterises violations of IHL as a 'threat to the peace', imposes sanctions on States and non-State actors for violations of IHL, establishes criminal tribunals and refers cases to the ICC.[39] United Nations peacekeeping operations are also mandated to protect civilians. However, the protection of civilians as a peacekeeping task should be differentiated from the protection of civilians in IHL. First, whereas in IHL the protection of civilians covers all civilians, in peacekeeping such protection is often limited to groups of civilians or to those facing imminent threat of violence.[40] Secondly, whereas in peacekeeping such protection may be geographically and temporally limited and is applicable during armed conflict as well as during peacetime, in IHL the protection applies during and for the duration of an armed conflict and covers all civilians. The UN has also created 'safe areas', which resemble the safety zones in IHL,[41] but in contrast to the latter, which are established with the consent of the parties to the conflict, the safe areas were were imposed on them and required UN peacekeepers to defend them.

19. Belligerent reprisals provide immediate and direct means of enforcing IHL in view of the ineffectiveness of the available enforcement mechanisms. Although the ICTY has emphatically opined in *Kupreškić* that belligerent reprisals are unlawful, the better view is that contemporary IHL does not prohibit belligerent reprisals provided that they meet certain conditions. This view is supported by relevant provisions found in API, State practice and *opinio juris*.[42] That said, there remain a number of questions regarding, first, the aim of belligerent reprisals and more specifically whether they are punitive or correct-ive; second, whether they are available in NIACs and whether non-State actors can resort to belligerent reprisals; third, whether IHRL has any impact on belligerent reprisals in view of the fact that there is no law of belligerent reprisals in NIAC whereas in IAC the law is not sufficiently specific for the *lex specialis* rule to apply; and, finally, how the principle of proportionality applies to belligerent reprisals.

20. Third States are also implicated in the enforcement of IHL. They have a duty under Common Article 1 to ensure respect for IHL by States involved in an armed conflict. Often this may take the form of action through the UN,[43] with individual action being quite rare.

21. In view of the problems identified above regarding the scope and effectiveness of current enforcement mechanisms, a legitimate question is whether new mechanisms should be introduced. The establishment of an IHL Commission has been suggested.[44] Questions

---

[38]   See Report of the Special Rapporteur on Extreme Poverty and Human Rights (26 August 2016), UN Doc. A/71/40823, 26 August 2016.

[39]   See Art. 13, ICC St.

[40]   For example, compare SC Res 1990 (2011) (UNISFA); SC Res 1990 (2011) (UNISFA) and SC Res 1856 (2008) (MONUC).

[41]   Art. 23, GCI; Art. 14, GCIV.

[42]   See, for example, US, Department of Defense, *Law of War Manual*, Office of General Counsel (June 2015, Updated 2016), paras 18.18ff.

[43]   See Art. 89, API.

[44]   Improving Compliance with International Humanitarian Law, ICRC Expert Seminars, Report prepared by the International Committee of the Red Cross Geneva, October 2003 www.icrc.org/eng/assets/files/other/improv ing_compliance_with_international_report_eng_2003.pdf.

that may be asked in this regard concern its status; whether it will apply treaty law or also customary IHL; the scope of its mandate and in particular whether its mandate will extend to NIACs and to international organisations; *locus standi* questions and in particular whether only States or also armed groups, individuals as well as international organisations can petition the Commission; the type of monitoring and enforcement mechanisms it will avail itself of and whether they are binding or not. The establishment of such a Commission, but also its successful operation, depends on the willingness of States and of other actors to cooperate. Other proposals include periodic reporting, regular meetings of the States parties to the GCs and thematic discussions. Currently, a Swiss-ICRC initiative to enhance the effectiveness of compliance with IHL is under way.[45]

---

[45]   www.icrc.org/en/document/strengthening-compliance-international-humanitarian-law-ihl-work-icrc-and-swiss-government.

12

Command Responsibility

INTRODUCTION

The doctrine of command responsibility was first utilised in war crimes prosecutions following the end of the Second World War. It has its roots in the IHL principle of responsible command, under which commanders have a duty to ensure that their subordinates respect IHL. Failure on the part of a commander to prevent or punish the commission of offences by his subordinates gives rise to criminal liability under command responsibility.[1] Command responsibility is thus a powerful tool for enforcing compliance with IHL. The *ad hoc* tribunals have played a significant role in the development of the customary form of the doctrine, applying interpretations that have ensured its continuing relevance to modern armed conflict. Despite the differences between the customary international law form of the doctrine and its conventional form under Article 28 ICC Statute, their jurisprudence is of significant precedential value. The customary form of the doctrine also retains direct relevance with respect to those States that are not parties to the ICC Statute.

The elements of command responsibility as developed in jurisprudence are (i) the existence of superior–subordinate relationships characterised by effective control over subordinates; (ii) knowledge or constructive knowledge by the superior that his subordinates are about to commit or have committed genocide, crimes against humanity or war crimes; and (iii) failure to adopt reasonable and necessary measures to prevent, punish or report the offences. Command responsibility doctrine is a complex form of criminal responsibility and this chapter addresses its nature, its objective and subjective elements, the issue of successor command responsibility, and the question of causation. It should be noted at the outset that although the doctrine is currently known as superior responsibility by also extending to civilian superiors, the chapter will only deal with the responsibility of military or military-like commanders.

Resources: Common Article 3 GCs; Arts 86(2), 87(3) API; Art. 6(3) ICTR Statute; Art. 7(3) ICTY Statute; Art. 29 Extraordinary Chambers in the Courts of Cambodia (ECCC); Art. 28 ICC St.

---

[1]   We use 'his' as a generic term; it also includes female commanders.

Cases and Materials

12.1 CONCEPT OF RESPONSIBLE COMMAND

12.1.1 ICTY, *Prosecutor* v. *Hadzihasanovic et al.*, (Decision on Interlocutory Appeal Challenging Jurisdiction in Relation to Command Responsibility), Case No. IT-01-47-AR72, Appeals Chamber (16 July 2003)

Note: *The indicted were military commanders in the Army of Bosnia and Herzegovina (ABiH) accused of violations of the laws or customs of war arising out of their acts and omissions between January 1993 and March 1994 in the territory of Bosnia-Herzegovina. It was alleged the accused were criminally responsible for failing in their duties as superiors to prevent or punish the murder and cruel treatment of Bosnian Croats and Bosnian Serbs by their subordinates. On the nature of command responsibility, the Tribunal said:*

22. The Appeals Chamber recognizes that there is a difference between the concepts of responsible command and command responsibility. The difference is due to the fact that the concept of responsible command looks to the duties comprised in the idea of command, whereas that of command responsibility looks at liability flowing from breach of those duties.

12.1.2 ICTY, *Prosecutor* v. *Halilović*, (Judgment), Case No. IT-01-48-T, Trial Chamber (16 November 2005)

Note: *The accused was the commander of troops responsible for the murder of Bosnian Croats in the villages of Grabovica and Uzdol in the Jablanica and Prozor areas in Herzegovina during 'Operation Neretva' in September 1993. On the concept of responsible command, the Tribunal said:*

40. The concept of responsible command can be seen in the earliest modern codifications of the laws of war. It was incorporated in the 1899 Hague Convention with Respect to the Laws and Customs of War on Land. It was also reproduced in Article 1 of the Regulations Respecting the Laws and Customs of War on Land annexed to the Fourth Hague Convention of 1907 which states: The laws, rights and duties of war apply not only to armies, but also to militia and volunteer corps fulfilling the following criteria: To be commanded by a person responsible for his subordinates . . .

12.2 SCOPE OF APPLICATION OF DOCTRINE OF COMMAND RESPONSIBILITY

12.2.1 ICTY, *Prosecutor* v. *Delalić et al.*, *('Celebici Case')*, (Judgment), Case No. IT-96-21-T, Trial Chamber (16 November 1998)

Note: *The facts of this case are set out in Chapter 5, Section 5.4.1.1. Affirming the existence of a duty, in international law, on superiors to control the acts of their subordinates, the Tribunal said:*

340. Nonetheless, there can be no doubt that the concept of the individual criminal responsibility of superiors for failure to act is today firmly placed within the corpus of international humanitarian law. Through the adoption of Additional Protocol I, the principle has now been codified and given a clear expression in international conventional law. Thus, article 87 of the Protocol gives expression to the duty of commanders to control the acts of their subordinates and to prevent or, where necessary, to repress violations of the Geneva Conventions or the Protocol. The concomitant principle under which a superior may be held criminally responsible for the crimes committed by his subordinates where the superior has failed to properly exercise this duty is formulated in article 86 of the Protocol.

12.2.2 ICTY, *Prosecutor* v. *Hadzihasanovic et al.*, (Decision on Interlocutory Appeal Challenging Jurisdiction in Relation to Command Responsibility), Case No. IT-01-47-AR72, Appeals Chamber (16 July 2003)

Note: *The facts of this case are dealt with at page 338. On the scope of the doctrine of command responsibility, the Tribunal held:*

15. The position is no different as regards internal armed conflicts. Responsible command was an integral notion of the prohibition imposed by Article 3 common to the

1949 Geneva Conventions against the doing of certain things in the course of an internal armed conflict. ....

16. ... It is evident that there cannot be an organized military force save on the basis of responsible command. It is also reasonable to hold that it is responsible command which leads to command responsibility. Command responsibility is the most effective method by which international criminal law can enforce responsible command.

17. It is true that, domestically, most States have not legislated for command responsibility to be the counterpart of responsible command in internal conflict. This, however, does not affect the fact that, at the international level, they have accepted that, as a matter of customary international law, relevant aspects of international law (including the concept of command responsibility) govern the conduct of an internal armed conflict, though of course not all aspects of international law apply. The relevant aspects of international law unquestionably regard a military force engaged in an internal armed conflict as organized and therefore as being under responsible command. In the absence of anything to the contrary, it is the task of a court to interpret the underlying State practice and *opinio juris* (relating to the requirement that such a military force be organized) as bearing its normal meaning that military organization implies responsible command and that responsible command in turn implies command responsibility.

18. In short, wherever customary international law recognizes that a war crime can be committed by a member of an organised military force, it also recognizes that a commander can be penally sanctioned if he knew or had reason to know that his subordinate was about to commit a prohibited act or had done so and the commander failed to take the necessary and reasonable measures to prevent such an act or to punish the subordinate.

12.3 ELEMENTS OF THE DOCTRINE OF COMMAND RESPONSIBILITY

12.3.1 ICTY, *Prosecutor* v. *Delalić et al. ('Celebici Case')*, (Judgment), Case No. IT-96-21-T, Trial Chamber (16 November 1998)

Note: *The facts of this case are set out in Chapter 5, Section 5.4.4.1. Identifying the requisite elements required to demonstrate superior responsibility, the Tribunal stated:*

346. While it is evident that the commission of one or more of the crimes under Articles 2 to 5 of the Statute is a necessary prerequisite for the application of Article 7(3), the Trial Chamber agrees with the Prosecution's proposition that the principle of superior responsibility properly is analysed as containing three constitutive parts. From the text of Article 7(3) it is thus possible to identify the essential elements of command responsibility for failure to act as follows:

  (i) the existence of a superior-subordinate relationship;

  (ii) the superior knew or had reason to know that the criminal act was about to be or had been committed; and

  (iii) the superior failed to take the necessary and reasonable measures to prevent the criminal act or punish the perpetrator thereof.

12.3.2 ICC, *The Prosecutor* v. *Jean-Pierre Bemba Gombo*, (Judgment Pursuant to Article 74 of the Statute), Case No. ICC–01/05–01/08 66/364, Trial Chamber III (21 March 2016)

Note: *The facts of this case are set out in Chapter 1, Section 1.2.3.5. Identifying the elements that must be proved to establish liability under Article 28(a), the ICC stated:*

170. Article 28(a) codifies the responsibility of military commanders and persons effectively acting as military commanders. The Chamber finds that, for an accused to be found guilty and convicted as a military commander or person effectively acting as a military commander under Article 28(a), the following elements must be fulfilled:

a. crimes within the jurisdiction of the Court must have been committed by forces;
b. the accused must have been either a military commander or a person effectively acting as a military commander;
c. the accused must have had effective command and control, or effective authority and control, over the forces that committed the crimes;
d. the accused either knew or, owing to the circumstances at the time, should have known that the forces were committing or about to commit such crimes;
e. the accused must have failed to take all necessary and reasonable measures within his power to prevent or repress the commission of such crimes or to submit the matter to the competent authorities for investigation and prosecution; and
f. the crimes committed by the forces must have been a result of the failure of the accused to exercise control properly over them.

12.4 THE UNDERLYING OFFENCE

12.4.1 The Commission of an Offence

12.4.1.1 ICTY, *Prosecutor* v. *Delalić et al.*, *('Celebici Case')*, (Judgment), Case No. IT–96–21–T, Trial Chamber (16 November 1998)

Note: *The facts of this case are set out in Chapter 5, Section 5.4.4.1. Affirming the requirement that an offence be committed in order to engage the superior responsibility doctrine, the Tribunal said:*

346. .... [I]t is evident that the commission of one or more of the crimes under Articles 2 to 5 of the Statute is a necessary prerequisite for the application of Article 7(3).

12.4.1.2 ICTY, *Prosecutor* v. *Blagojević and Jokić*, (Judgment), Case No. IT–02–60–A, Appeals Chamber (9 May 2007)

Note: *The accused were the Commander and Chief of Engineering in the Bratunac and Zvornik Brigades respectively, charged individually with complicity in genocide, extermination, crimes against humanity, murder and violations of the laws or customs of war in relation to the killing of Bosnian Muslims following the fall of the Srebrenica enclave in July 1995. Clarifying the interpretation of 'commit' as used in Article 7(3) of the Statute, the Tribunal held:*

281. The Appeals Chamber has previously determined that criminal responsibility under Article 7(3) is based primarily on Article 86(2) of Protocol I. Accordingly, the meaning of "commit", as used in Article 7(3) of the Statute, necessarily tracks the term's broader and more ordinary meaning, as employed in Protocol I. . . .

282. In this context, the Appeals Chamber cannot accept that the drafters of Protocol I and the Statute intended to limit a superior's obligation to prevent or punish violations of international humanitarian law to only those individuals physically committing the material elements of a crime and to somehow exclude subordinates who as accomplices substantially contributed to the completion of the crime. Accordingly, "commit" as used in Article 7(3) of the Statute must be understood as it is in Protocol I, in its ordinary and broad sense.

12.4.1.3 ICTR, *Prosecutor* v. *Nahimana et al.*, (Judgment), Case No. ICTR-99-52-A, Appeals Chamber (28 November 2007)

Note: *The accused were charged with conspiracy to commit genocide, direct and public incitement to commit genocide, complicity in genocide and crimes against humanity as well as violations of the GCs in respect of their involvement in the 'true hate media' in the form of Radio Télévision Libre des Mille Collines (RTLM) and the Kangura newspaper, which were intended to ensure 'widespread dissemination of the calls to ethnic violence'. Such calls targeted Tutsis and political opponents who were identified by name and threatened by the media. As to the commission of the underlying crime, the Tribunal held:*

486. The Appeals Chamber endorses this reasoning and holds that an accused may be held responsible as a superior under Article 6(3) of the Statute where a subordinate "planned, instigated, ordered, committed or otherwise aided and abetted in the planning, preparation or execution of a crime referred to in Articles 2 to 4 of the present Statute", provided, of course, that all the other elements of such responsibility have been established

12.4.1.4 ICC, *The Prosecutor* v. *Jean-Pierre Bemba Gombo*, (Judgment Pursuant to Article 74 of the Statute), Case No. ICC-01/05-01/08 66/364, Trial Chamber III (21 March 2016)

Note: *The facts of this case are outlined in Chapter 1, Section 1.2.3.5. The ICC confirmed the requirement that crimes are committed in order to engage liability under the doctrine:*

175. As noted above, it is required that crimes within the jurisdiction of the Court have been actually committed by the relevant forces.

12.4.2 Knowledge of the Identity of the Responsible Subordinate

12.4.2.1 ICTY, *Prosecutor* v. *Orić*, (Judgment), Case No. IT-03-68-T, Trial Chamber (30 June 2006)

Note: *The accused was charged with individual criminal responsibility for the murder and cruel treatment of prisoners in Srebrenica in 1992 and 1993. The Tribunal affirmed that superior responsibility includes conduct of subordinates via all modes of participation. Reinforcing that the direct perpetrators need not be identical to the subordinates of the superior, the Tribunal found:*

478. Before examining the Defence submission that murder and cruel treatment were committed by persons entering the detention facilities from the outside, the Trial Chamber refers to its earlier finding regarding the law on superior criminal responsibility, which does not presuppose that the direct perpetrators of a crime punishable under the Statute be identical to the subordinates of a superior. It is only required that the relevant subordinates, by their own acts or omissions, be criminally responsible for the acts and omissions of the direct perpetrators.

12.4.2.2 ICTY, *Prosecutor* v. *Hadzihasanovic et al.*, (Judgment), Case No. IT-01-47-T, Trial Chamber (15 March 2006)

Note: *The facts of this case are outlined in Section 12.1.1. Affirming that an accused commander need only exercise control over an identified group of perpetrators, the Tribunal said:*

90. ... The Chamber recalls the observation made by the Chamber in Krnojelac: "if the Prosecution is unable to identify those directly participating in such events by name, it will be sufficient for it to identify them at least by reference to their 'category' (or their official position) as a group". Accordingly, to establish the existence of a superior-subordinate relationship, the Chamber finds it sufficient to specify to which group the perpetrators belonged and to show that the Accused exercised effective control over that group.

12.4.2.3 ICC, *The Prosecutor* v. *Jean-Pierre Bemba Gombo*, (Judgment Pursuant to Article 74 of the Statute), Case No. ICC-01/05-01/08 66/364, Trial Chamber III (21 March 2016)

Note: *The facts of this case are detailed in Chapter 1, Section 1.2.3.5. The ICC outlined the limits of liability under Article 28 in the following terms:*

194. Article 28 does not require that the commander knew the identities of the specific individuals who committed the crimes. In addition, it is unnecessary to establish that the accused mastered every detail of each crime committed by the forces, an issue that becomes increasingly difficult as one goes up the military hierarchy.

12.5 THE EXISTENCE OF A SUPERIOR–SUBORDINATE RELATIONSHIP

12.5.1 The Superior–Subordinate Relationship

12.5.1.1 ICTY, *Prosecutor* v. *Popović et al.*, (Judgment) Case No IT-05-88-T, Trial Chamber II (10 June 2010)

Note: *The case concerned the detention and summary execution of thousands of Bosnian Muslim males over the course of a few days in July 1995 after the fall of Srebrenica. In parallel to these executions, Bosnian Muslim women, children and the elderly were transferred out of this area of Eastern Bosnia. At paragraph 2021 of the judgment, the Tribunal emphasised the importance of the existence of a superior–subordinate command relationship when determining liability:*

2021. For Pandurevic to be held individually responsible pursuant to Article 7(3) of the Statute, it must first be established that a superior-subordinate relationship existed at the time between Pandurevic and the perpetrators.

12.5.1.2 Cambodia, *Kaing Guek Eav alias Duch*, (Judgment), Case File/Dossier No. 001/18-07-2007/ECCC/TC, Extraordinary Chambers in the Courts of Cambodia (26 July 2010)

Note: *The facts of this case are set out in Chapter 1, Section 1.2.1.2. As to the nature of superior-subordinate responsibility and the facts that may demonstrate the exercise of effective control over a subordinate, the ECCC said:*

540. Formal designation as a commander or a superior is not required in order to trigger superior responsibility: such responsibility can arise by virtue of a superior's power, whether in law or in fact, over those who committed the crime. In order to demonstrate the existence of a superior-subordinate relationship, it must be established that the accused exercised effective control over the subordinate. In other words, the accused must have had the material ability to prevent or punish the subordinate's commission of the crime.

541. Factors that would demonstrate that an accused exercised effective control over a subordinate include: the nature of the accused's position, including his or her position within the military or political structure; the procedure for appointment and the actual tasks performed; the accused's capacity to issue orders and whether or not such orders are actually executed; the fact that subordinates show greater discipline in the presence of the accused; the authority to invoke disciplinary measures; and the authority to release or transfer prisoners.

542. Further, superior responsibility may ensue on the basis of both direct and indirect relationships of subordination. Every person in the chain of command who exercises effective control over subordinates is responsible for the crimes of those subordinates, provided that the other requirements of superior responsibility are met.

12.5.2 *De Jure* and *De Facto* Relationships

12.5.2.1 ICTY, *Prosecutor* v. *Delalić et al.*, *('Celebici Case')*, (Judgment), Case No. IT-96-21-A, Appeals Chamber (20 February 2001)

Note: *The facts of this case are outlined in Chapter 5, Section 5.4.4.1. On the relationship between* de jure *and* de facto *authority and command structures, the Tribunal stated:*

193. In many contemporary conflicts, there may be only de facto, self-proclaimed governments and therefore de facto armies and paramilitary groups subordinate thereto. Command structure, organised hastily, may well be in disorder and primitive. To enforce the law in these circumstances requires a determination of accountability not only of individual offenders but of their commanders or other superiors who were, based on evidence, in control of them without, however, a formal commission or appointment. A tribunal could find itself powerless to enforce humanitarian law against de facto superiors if it only accepted as proof of command authority a formal letter of authority, despite the fact that the superiors acted at the relevant time with all the powers that would attach to an officially appointed superior or commander.

12.5.2.2 **ICTY,** *Prosecutor* v. *Orić,* (Judgment), Case No. IT-03-68-A, Appeals
Chamber (3 July 2008)

Note: *The facts are outlined in Section 12.4.2.1. The Tribunal confirmed in the following terms that* de jure *power does not always presuppose effective control:*

91. Whereas the possession of de jure powers may certainly suggest a material ability to prevent or punish criminal acts of subordinates, it may be neither necessary nor sufficient to prove such ability. If de jure power always results in a presumption of effective control, then the Prosecution would be exempted from its burden to prove effective control beyond reasonable doubt.

12.5.2.3 **ICC,** *The Prosecutor* v. *Jean-Pierre Bemba Gombo,* (Judgment Pursuant to
Article 74 of the Statute), Case No. ICC-01/05-01/08 66/364, Trial Chamber
III (21 March 2016)

Note: *The facts of this case are outlined in Chapter 1, Section 1.2.3.5. Identifying the scope of command, the ICC said as follows:*

177. Article 28(a) not only provides for the liability of military commanders, but also extends to "person[s] effectively acting as military commander[s]" ... These individuals are not formally or legally appointed as military commanders, but they will effectively act as commanders over the forces that committed the crimes. In addition, the phrase "military commander or person effectively acting as a military commander" includes individuals who do not perform exclusively military functions.

12.5.3 Existence of a Chain of Command

12.5.3.1 **ICTY,** *Prosecutor* v. *Delalić et al., ('Celebici Case'),* (Judgment), Case No.
IT-96-21-T, Trial Chamber (16 November 1998)

Note: *The facts of this case are set out in Chapter 5, Section 5.4.4.1. The case concerned events in a prison camp in the village of Celibeci, in the Konjic municipality in Bosnia-Herzegovina. The camp commandant, deputy commandant and a guard were convicted of war crimes and crimes against humanity, as direct participants and as superiors as a result of their treatment of the camp inmates. The case concerned the first convictions on the basis of superior responsibility since the Second World War. The Tribunal analysed the effect of informal command structures in the following terms:*

354. The requirement of the existence of a "superior-subordinate" relationship which, in the words of the Commentary to Additional Protocol I, should be seen "in terms of a hierarchy encompassing the concept of control", is particularly problematic in situations such as that of the former Yugoslavia during the period relevant to the present case - situations where previously existing formal structures have broken down and where, during an interim period, the new, possibly improvised, control and command structures, may be ambiguous and ill-defined. It is the Trial Chamber's conclusion, the reasons for which are set out below, that persons effectively in command of such more informal structures, with power to

prevent and punish the crimes of persons who are in fact under their control, may under certain circumstances be held responsible for their failure to do so.

12.5.3.2 ICTY, *Prosecutor* v. *Orić*, (Judgment), Case No. IT-03-68-T, Trial Chamber (30 June 2006)

Note: *The facts are set out in Section 12.4.2.1. On the required nexus between the superior and subordinate, the Trial Chamber said as follows:*

310. . . . Thus, regardless of which chain of command or position of authority the superior-subordinate relationship may be based [*sic*], it is immaterial whether the subordination of the perpetrator to the accused as superior is direct or indirect, and formal or factual. In the same vein, the mere ad hoc or temporary nature of a military unit or an armed group does not per se exclude a relationship of subordination between the member of the unit or group and its commander or leader.

12.6 EFFECTIVE CONTROL

12.6.1 ICTY, *Prosecutor* v. *Halilović*, (Judgment), Case No. IT-01-48-T, Trial Chamber (16 November 2005)

Note: *The facts of this case are set out in Section 12.1.2. Clarifying the nature and limits of the 'effective control' criterion, the Tribunal said:*

311. . . . [P]roof of a superior-subordinate relationship ultimately depends on the existence of effective control which requires that the superior must have had the material ability to prevent or punish the commission of the principal crimes. On the one hand, this needs more than merely having 'general influence' on the behaviour of others. Likewise, merely being tasked with coordination does not necessarily mean to have command and control. On the other hand, effective control does not presuppose formal authority to issue binding orders or disciplinary sanctions, as the relevant threshold rather depends on the factual situation, i.e., the ability to maintain or enforce compliance of others with certain rules and orders. Whether this sort of control is directly exerted upon a subordinate or mediated by other sub superiors or subordinates is immaterial, as long as the responsible superior would have means to prevent the relevant crimes from being committed or to take efficient measures for having them sanctioned.

12.6.2 ICTY, *Prosecutor* v. *Halilović*, (Judgment), Case No. IT-01-48-A, Appeals Chamber (16 October 2007)

Note: *The facts are set out in Section 12.1.2. Regarding the relationship between 'effective control' and subordination, the Appeal Chamber said as follows:*

59. . . . the accused has to be, by virtue of his position, senior in some sort of formal or informal hierarchy to the perpetrator. The ability to exercise effective control in the sense of a material power to prevent or punish, which the Appeals Chamber considers to be a

minimum requirement for the recognition of a superior-subordinate relationship for the purpose of superior responsibility, will almost invariably not be satisfied unless such a relationship of subordination exists.

12.6.3 ICC, *The Prosecutor* v. *Jean-Pierre Bemba Gombo*, (Judgment Pursuant to Article 74 of the Statute), Case No. ICC-01/05-01/08 66/364, Trial Chamber III (21 March 2016)

Note: *The facts are set out in Chapter 1, Section 1.2.3.5. On the degree of control over subordinates for Article 28(a) purposes, the ICC said:*

181. The Chamber concurs with the Pre-Trial Chamber that the terms "command" and "authority" have "no substantial effect on the required level or standard of 'control'", but rather denote the modalities, manner, or nature in which a military commander or person acting as such exercises control over his or her forces. Regardless of whether an accused is a military commander or a person effectively acting as such, and regardless of whether he exercises "effective command" or "effective authority", the required level of control remains the same. . . .

183. For the purpose of Article 28(a), following consistent international criminal jurisprudence, the Chamber finds that "effective control" requires that the commander have the material ability to prevent or repress the commission of the crimes or to submit the matter to the competent authorities. Any lower degree of control, such as the ability to exercise influence – even substantial influence – over the forces who committed the crimes, would be insufficient to establish command responsibility. . . .

185. The Chamber notes the Defence's allegation that MLC troops were resubordinated to the CAR authorities, and therefore, it cannot be concluded that Mr Bemba had effective control over those forces. The Chamber finds, however, that Article 28 contains no requirement that a commander have sole or exclusive authority and control over the forces who committed the crimes. Further, the effective control of one commander does not necessarily exclude effective control being exercised by another commander. A fact-specific analysis is required in each case to determine whether or not the accused commander did in fact have effective control at the relevant time. Similarly, international criminal jurisprudence supports the possibility that multiple superiors can be held concurrently responsible for actions of their subordinates. . . .

188. The Chamber considers that the question of whether a commander had effective control over particular forces is case specific. There are a number of factors that may *indicate* the existence of "effective control", which requires the material ability to prevent or repress the commission of crimes or to submit the matter to the competent authorities; these have been properly considered as "more a matter of evidence than of substantive law". These factors may include: (i) the official position of the commander within the military structure and the actual tasks that he carried out; (ii) his power to issue orders, including his capacity to order forces or units under his command, whether under his immediate command or at lower levels, to engage in hostilities; (iii) his

capacity to ensure compliance with orders including consideration of whether the orders were actually followed; (iv) his capacity to re-subordinate units or make changes to command structure; (v) his power to promote, replace, remove, or discipline any member of the forces, and to initiate investigations; (vi) his authority to send forces to locations where hostilities take place and withdraw them at any given moment; (vii) his independent access to, and control over, the means to wage war, such as communication equipment and weapons; (viii) his control over finances; (ix) the capacity to represent the forces in negotiations or interact with external bodies or individuals on behalf of the group; and (x) whether he represents the ideology of the movement to which the subordinates adhere and has a certain level of profile, manifested through public appearances and statements. . . .

190. Conversely, some factors may indicate a *lack* of effective control over forces, such as (i) the existence of a different exclusive authority over the forces in question; (ii) disregard or non-compliance with orders or instructions of the accused; or (iii) a weak or malfunctioning chain of command.

12.7 THE *MENS REA* REQUIREMENT

12.7.1 Actual Knowledge

12.7.1.1 ICTY, *Prosecutor* v. *Delalić et al.*, *('Celebici Case')*, (Judgment), Case No. IT-96-21-T, Trial Chamber (16 November 1998)

Note: *The facts of this case are set out in Chapter 5, Section 5.4.4.1. For circumstantial knowledge, the Tribunal said:*

386. It is, accordingly, the Trial Chamber's view that, in the absence of direct evidence of the superior's knowledge of the offences committed by his subordinates, such knowledge cannot be presumed, but must be established by way of circumstantial evidence. In determining whether a superior, despite pleas to the contrary, in fact must have possessed the requisite knowledge, the Trial Chamber may consider, *inter alia*, the following indicia, listed by the Commission of Experts in its Final Report:

(a) The number of illegal acts;
(b) The type of illegal acts;
(c) The scope of illegal acts;
(d) The time during which the illegal acts occurred;
(e) The number and type of troops involved;
(f) The logistics involved, if any;
(g) The geographical location of the acts;
(h) The widespread occurrence of the acts;
(i) The tactical tempo of operations;
(j) The modus operandi of similar illegal acts;
(k) The officers and staff involved;
(l) The location of the commander at the time.

12.7.1.2 ICTY, *Prosecutor* v. *Aleksovski*, (Judgment), Case No. IT-95-14/1-T, Trial Chamber (25 June 1999)

Note: *The accused, who was a warden at the Kaonik prison in the Lašva Valley in the area of Busovača, central Bosnia, was indicted for inhuman treatment, outrages upon personal dignity and wilfully causing great suffering or serious injury to the body or health of Muslim prisoners. As to the circumstances relevant to the assessment of mens rea, the Tribunal said as follows:*

80. The Trial Chamber deems however that an individual's superior position *per se* is a significant indicium that he had knowledge of the crimes committed by his subordinates. The weight to be given to that indicium however depends *inter alia* on the geographical and temporal circumstances.

12.7.1.3 ICTY, *Prosecutor* v. *Blaškić*, (Judgment), Case No. IT-95-14-T, Trial Chamber (3 March 2000)

Note: *The facts of this case are set out in Chapter 1, Section 1.2.2.1. Setting out the criteria that may be relevant in determining whether a superior had the requisite degree of knowledge, the Tribunal concluded:*

307. Knowledge may not be presumed. However, the Trial Chamber agrees that "knowledge" may be proved through either direct or circumstantial evidence. With regard to circumstantial evidence, the Trial Chamber concurs with the view expressed by the Trial Chamber in the *Celebici* case. . . .

308. These indicia must be considered in light of the accused's position of command, if established. Indeed, as was held by the *Aleksovski* Trial Chamber, an individual's command position *per se* is a significant indicium that he knew about the crimes committed by his subordinates.

12.7.1.4 ICTY, *Prosecutor* v. *Orić*, (Judgment), Case No. IT-03-68-T, Trial Chamber (30 June 2006)

Note: *The facts are outlined in Section 12.4.2.1. As to the level of knowledge required by the superior commander for the purposes of determining the existence of mens rea, the Tribunal said:*

320. Although the required knowledge is in principle the same both for military and civil superiors, the various indications must be assessed in light of the accused's position of command. This may, in particular, imply that the threshold required to prove knowledge of a superior exercising more informal types of authority is higher than for those operating within a highly disciplined and formalised chain of command with established reporting and monitoring systems.

12.7.1.5 SCSL, *Prosecutor* v. *Taylor*, (Judgment), Case No. SCSL-03-01-T, Trial Chamber II (18 May 2012)

Note: *The accused was indicted with war crimes and crimes against humanity during the civil war in Sierra Leone between November 1996 and January 2002, which he was alleged to have committed while holding a position of superior responsibility over subordinate members of the National Patriotic Front of Liberia (NPFL), Armed Forces Revolutionary Council (AFRC),*

AFRC/Revolutionary United Front Junta or alliance and/or Liberian fighters. Addressing the definition of actual knowledge, the Trial Chamber said:

497. Actual knowledge may be defined as the awareness that the relevant crimes were committed or about to be committed. There is no presumption of such knowledge but, in the absence of direct evidence, it may be established through circumstantial evidence. Factors indicative of actual knowledge include, first of all, an individual's superior position and the superior's geographical and temporal proximity to the crimes; also, the type and scope of crimes, the time during which they occurred, the number and type of troops and logistics involved, the widespread occurrence of crimes, the tactical tempo of operations, the *modus operandi* of similar illegal acts and the officers and staff involved.

12.7.1.6 ICC, *The Prosecutor* v. *Jean-Pierre Bemba Gombo*, (Judgment Pursuant to Article 74 of the Statute), Case No. ICC-01/05-01/08 66/364, Trial Chamber III (21 March 2016)

Note: *The facts of this case are set out in Chapter 1, Section 1.2.3.5. Examining the knowledge element, the ICC said:*

191. The Chamber considers that actual knowledge on the part of a commander cannot be presumed. Rather, it must be established either by direct or indirect (circumstantial) evidence. Examples of direct evidence include the accused's admission of knowledge or statements he may have made about the crimes.

192. When the Chamber accepts proof of an accused's state of mind by inference, that inference must be the only reasonable conclusion available based on the evidence. Such inference, moreover, must relate directly to the accused; what needs to be inferred is the *accused's* knowledge, not that of the general public or others in the organization to which the accused belongs.

193. Relevant factors that may indicate knowledge include any orders to commit crimes, or the fact that the accused was informed personally that his forces were involved in criminal activity. Other indicia include the number, nature, scope, location, and timing of the illegal acts, and other prevailing circumstances; the type and number of forces involved; the means of available communication; the *modus operandi* of similar acts; the scope and nature of the commander's position and responsibility in the hierarchical structure; the location of the command at the time; and the notoriety of illegal acts, such as whether they were reported in media coverage of which the accused was aware. Such awareness may be established by evidence suggesting that, as a result of these reports, the commander took some kind of action.

12.7.2 Constructive Knowledge

12.7.2.1 ICTY, *Prosecutor* v. *Delalić et al.*, *('Celebici Case')*, (Judgment), Case No. IT-96-21-T, Trial Chamber (16 November 1998)

Note: *The facts of this case are detailed in Chapter 5, Section 5.4.1.1. Considering the role of constructive knowledge as a factor relevant to the assessment of the* mens rea *standard, the Tribunal said:*

387. ... There can be no doubt that a superior who simply ignores information within his actual possession compelling the conclusion that criminal offences are being committed, or are about to be committed, by his subordinates commits a most serious dereliction of duty for which he may be held criminally responsible under the doctrine of superior responsibility. Instead, uncertainty arises in relation to situations where the superior lacks such information by virtue of his failure to properly supervise his subordinates.

388. In this respect, it is to be noted that the jurisprudence from the period immediately following the Second World War affirmed the existence of a duty of commanders to remain informed about the activities of their subordinates ...

390. While this body of precedent accordingly may be thought to support the position advocated by the Prosecution, the Trial Chamber is bound to apply customary law as it existed at the time of the commission of the alleged offences. Accordingly, the Trial Chamber must, in its construction of Article 7(3), give full consideration to the standard established by article 86 of Additional Protocol I, in addition to these precedents. ...

393 ... [A] superior can be held criminally responsible only if some specific information was in fact available to him which would provide notice of offences committed by his subordinates. This information need not be such that it by itself was sufficient to compel the conclusion of the existence of such crimes. It is sufficient that the superior was put on further inquiry by the information, or, in other words, that it indicated the need for additional investigation in order to ascertain whether offences were being committed or about to be committed by his subordinates. This standard, which must be considered to reflect the position of customary law at the time of the offences alleged in the Indictment, is accordingly controlling for the construction of the *mens rea* standard established in Article 7(3).

12.7.2.2 ICTY, *Prosecutor* v. *Blaškić*, (Judgment), Case No. IT-95-14-T, Trial Chamber (3 March 2000)

Note: *The facts of this case are outlined in Chapter 1, Section 1.2.2.1. Addressing the issue of constructive knowledge and whether ignorance can be a defence, the Tribunal said as follows:*

324. The Trial Chamber now turns to codification at the international level, namely the adoption of Additional Protocol I in 1977. The pertinent question is this: was customary international law altered with the adoption of Additional Protocol I, in the sense that a commander can be held accountable for failure to act in response to crimes by his subordinates only if some specific information was in fact available to him which would provide notice of such offences? ... [T]he Trial Chamber is of the view that this is not so. ...

332. In conclusion, the Trial Chamber finds that if a commander has exercised due diligence in the fulfilment of his duties yet lacks knowledge that crimes are about to be or have been committed, such lack of knowledge cannot be held against him. However, taking into account his particular position of command and the circumstances prevailing at the time, such ignorance cannot be a defence where the absence of knowledge is the result of negligence in the discharge of his duties: this commander had reason to know within the meaning of the Statute.

12.7.2.3 ICTY, *Prosecutor* v. *Delalić et al.*, (*'Celebici Case'*), (Judgment), Case No. IT-96-21-A, Appeals Chamber (20 February 2001)

Note: *The facts of this case are set out in Chapter 5, Section 5.4.1.1. Further clarifying the role of constructive knowledge in the assessment of* mens rea *for the purposes of command responsibility, the Appeals Chamber said*:

235. The consistency in the language used by Article 86(2) of Additional Protocol I, and the ILC Report and the attendant commentary, is evidence of a consensus as to the standard of the *mens rea* of command responsibility. If "had reason to know" is interpreted to mean that a commander has a duty to inquire further, on the basis of information of a general nature he has in hand, there is no material difference between the standard of Article 86(2) of Additional Protocol I and the standard of "should have known" as upheld by certain cases decided after the Second World War. . . .

238. A showing that a superior had some general information in his possession, which would put him on notice of possible unlawful acts by his subordinates would be sufficient to prove that he "had reason to know". . . . As to the form of the information available to him, it may be written or oral, and does not need to have the form of specific reports submitted pursuant to a monitoring system. This information does not need to provide specific information about unlawful acts committed or about to be committed. . . .

239. Finally, the relevant information only needs to have been provided or available to the superior, or in the Trial Chamber's words, "in the possession of". It is not required that he actually acquainted himself with the information.

12.7.2.4 SCSL, *Prosecutor* v. *Taylor*, (Judgment), Case No. SCSL-03-01-T, Trial Chamber II (18 May 2012)

Note: *The facts are set out in Section 12.7.1.5. On the issue of constructive knowledge as to the commission of crimes by subordinates, the Trial Chamber said*:

498. In determining whether a superior "had reason to know", or imputed knowledge, that his or her subordinates were committing or about to commit a crime, it must be shown that specific information was available which would have put the superior on notice of crimes committed or about to be committed. The superior may not be held liable for failing to acquire such information in the first place. However, it suffices for the superior to be in possession of sufficient information, even general in nature, written or oral, of the likelihood of illegal acts by subordinates. The superior need only have notice of a risk that crimes might be carried out and there is no requirement that this be a strong risk or a substantial likelihood.

499. . . . What is required is the superior's awareness of information which should have prompted him or her to acquire further knowledge. Responsibility pursuant to Article 6(3) of the Statute will attach when the superior remains wilfully blind to the information that is available to him.

12.7.2.5 ICC, *Prosecutor* v. *Jean-Pierre Bemba Gombo*, (Decision Pursuant to
         Article 61(7)(a) and (b) of the Rome Statute on the Charges),
         Case No. ICC-01/05-01/08-424, Pre-Trial Chamber II (15 July 2009)

Note: *The facts of this case are set out in Chapter 1, Section 1.2.3.5. Examining the 'should have known' standard and comparing it with the 'had reason to know' standard, the ICC said:*

432. The "should have known" standard requires the superior to "ha[ve] merely been negligent in failing to acquire knowledge" of his subordinates' illegal conduct. . . .

433. Thus, it is the Chamber's view that the "should have known" standard requires more of an active duty on the part of the superior to take the necessary measures to secure knowledge of the conduct of his troops and to inquire, regardless of the availability of information at the time on the commission of the crime. The drafting history of this provision reveals that it was the intent of the drafters to take a more stringent approach towards commanders and military-like commanders compared to other superiors that fall within the parameters of article 28(b) of the Statute. This is justified by the nature and type of responsibility assigned to this category of superiors.

434. The Chamber is mindful of the fact that the "had reason to know" criterion embodied in the statutes of the ICTR, ICTY and SCSL sets a different standard to the "should have known" standard under article 28 (a) of the Statute. However, despite such a difference, which the Chamber does not deem necessary to address in the present decision, the criteria or indicia developed by the ad hoc tribunals to meet the standard of "had reason to know" may also be useful when applying the "should have known" requirement.

12.8 FAILURE TO ADOPT NECESSARY AND REASONABLE MEASURES

12.8.1 The Duty to Prevent and the Duty to Punish

12.8.1.1 **ICTY,** *Prosecutor* v. *Blaškić*, (Judgment), Case No. IT-95-14-T, Trial
         Chamber (3 March 2000)

Note: *The facts are set out in Chapter 1, Section 1.2.2.1. Affirming the interrelationship between the duty to prevent and the duty to punish, the Tribunal said:*

336. Lastly, the Trial Chamber stresses that the obligation to "prevent or punish" does not provide the accused with two alternative and equally satisfying options. Obviously, where the accused knew or had reason to know that subordinates were about to commit crimes and failed to prevent them, he cannot make up for the failure to act by punishing the subordinates afterwards.

12.8.1.2 **ICTY,** *Prosecutor* v. *Blaškić*, (Judgment), Case No. IT-95-14-A, Appeals
         Chamber (29 July 2004)

Note: *Considering the issue of the relationship between the duties to prevent and punish further, the Appeal Chamber in Blaškić said:*

83. . . . Article 87(3) of Additional Protocol I reads: The High Contracting Parties and Parties to the conflict shall require any commander who is aware that subordinates or other persons

under his control are going to commit or have committed a breach of the Conventions or of this Protocol, to initiate such steps as are necessary to prevent such violations of the Conventions or this Protocol, and, where appropriate, to initiate disciplinary or penal action against violators thereof. Disciplinary or penal action can only be initiated *after* a violation is discovered, and a violator is one who has already violated a rule of law. Further, it is illogical to argue both that "a superior's responsibility for the failure to punish is construed as a sub-category of his liability for failing to prevent the commission of unlawful acts," and that "failure to punish only led to the imposition of criminal responsibility if it resulted in a failure to prevent the commission of future crimes." The failure to punish and failure to prevent involve different crimes committed at different times: the failure to punish concerns past crimes committed by subordinates, whereas the failure to prevent concerns future crimes of subordinates.

12.8.2 Material Ability to Prevent and Punish

12.8.2.1 ICTY, *Prosecutor* v. *Krnojelac* (15 March 2002), Case No. IT-97-25-T, Trial Chamber (15 March 2002)

Note: *The accused, who was commander of the Foca Kazneo-Popravni Dom, one of the largest prisons in the former Yugoslavia, was charged with individual criminal responsibility for crimes against humanity committed against the detainees at the prison. Outlining the obligations on the superior in discharging his duty to prevent and punish, the Tribunal said:*

95. It must be shown that the superior failed to take the necessary and reasonable measures to prevent or punish the crimes of his subordinates. The measures required of the superior are limited to those which are feasible in all the circumstances and are "within his power". A superior is not obliged to perform the impossible. However, the superior has a duty to exercise the powers he has within the confines of those limitations.

12.8.2.2 ICTY, *Prosecutor* v. *Blaškić*, (Judgment), Case No. IT-95-14-A, Appeals Chamber (29 July 2004)

Note: *The facts of this case are set out in Chapter 1, Section 1.2.2.1. On the issue of a commander's ability to prevent and punish, the Appeal Chamber said:*

72. ... necessary and reasonable measures are such that can be taken within the competence of a commander as evidenced by the degree of effective control he wielded over his subordinates. The measure of submitting reports is again an example, applicable "under some circumstances." The Appeals Chamber considers that it was open to the Trial Chamber not to list measures that might vary from case to case, since it had made it clear that such measures should be necessary and reasonable to prevent subordinates' crimes or punish subordinates who had committed crimes. What constitutes such measures is not a matter of substantive law but of evidence, whereas the effect of such measures can be defined by law, as has been so defined by the Trial Chamber in this case. The appeal in this regard is rejected.

12.8.2.3 **ICTY,** *Prosecutor* v. *Halilović,* (Judgment), Case No. IT-01-48-A, Appeals Chamber (16 October 2007)

Note: *The facts of this case are set out in Section 12.1.2. On the meaning of 'necessary and reasonable' in the context of a commander's duty to prevent and punish, the Tribunal said:*

63. The general duty of commanders to take the necessary and reasonable measures is well rooted in customary international law and stems from their position of authority. The Appeals Chamber stresses that "necessary" measures are the measures appropriate for the superior to discharge his obligation (showing that he genuinely tried to prevent or punish) and "reasonable" measures are those reasonably falling within the material powers of the superior. What constitutes "necessary and reasonable" measures to fulfil a commander's duty is not a matter of substantive law but of evidence.

12.8.2.4 **ICC,** *The Prosecutor* v. *Jean-Pierre Bemba Gombo,* (Judgment Pursuant to Article 74 of the Statute), Case No. ICC-01/05-01/08 66/364, Trial Chamber III (21 March 2016)

Note: *The facts of this case are set out in Chapter 1, Section 1.2.3.5. Examining the duties to prevent and punish in the context of Article 28(a), the ICC said:*

201. Under Article 28(a)(ii), three distinct duties are imposed upon commanders: (i) preventing the commission of crimes; (ii) repressing the commission of crimes; or (iii) submitting the matter to the competent authorities for investigation and prosecution. Although the Statute uses alternative language ("or") it is clear that failure to discharge any of these duties may attract criminal liability. For example, a failure to prevent the crimes, when the commander was under a duty to do so, cannot be remedied by subsequently punishing the perpetrators.

202. The ordinary meaning of *prevent* is to "keep from happening", "keep someone from doing something", or "hinder or impede". The Chamber considers that a commander violates his duty to prevent when he fails to take measures to stop crimes that are about to be committed or crimes that are being committed. The duty to prevent arises before the commission of the crimes, and it includes crimes in progress and crimes which involve on-going elements.

203. The scope of the duty to prevent depends on the material power of the commander to intervene in a specific situation. This is dependent on the circumstances at the relevant time. The Pre-Trial Chamber identified relevant measures which include: (i) ensuring that the forces are adequately trained in international humanitarian law; (ii) securing reports that military actions were carried out in accordance with international law; (iii) issuing orders aiming at bringing the relevant practices into accord with the rules of war; and (iv) taking disciplinary measures to prevent the commission of atrocities by the forces under the commander's command.

204. Additional measures which should be taken under Article 28(a)(ii) may include: (i) issuing orders specifically meant to prevent the crimes, as opposed to merely issuing routine orders; (ii) protesting against or criticising criminal conduct; (iii) insisting before a superior authority that immediate action be taken; (iv) postponing military operations;

(v) suspending, excluding, or redeploying violent subordinates; and (vi) conducting military operations in such a way as to lower the risk of specific crimes or to remove opportunities for their commission.

205. Article 28(a)(ii) also criminalises the failure of the commander to "repress" the crimes. The word "repress" means to "put down", "subdue", "restrain", and "keep or hold back". The notion of "repression" therefore overlaps to a certain degree with "prevention", particularly in terms of a duty to prevent crimes in progress and crimes which involve on-going elements being committed over an extended period.

206. The Chamber concurs with the Pre-Trial Chamber that the duty to repress also encompasses an obligation to punish forces after the commission of crimes. . . .

207. A commander's lack of formal competence to take certain measures does not relieve the commander of the duty to take all necessary and reasonable measures within his power to repress the crimes. In the event the commander holds disciplinary power, he is required to exercise it, within the limits of his competence. If he does not hold disciplinary power, measures which may, depending upon the circumstances, satisfy the commander's duties include proposing a sanction to a superior who has disciplinary power or remitting the case to the judicial authority with such factual evidence as it was possible to find. The *ad hoc* tribunals have established what has been termed a "minimum standard" for measures that may fulfil the duty to punish, directing that a Trial Chamber "must look at what steps were taken to secure an adequate investigation capable of leading to the criminal prosecution of the perpetrators". The duty to punish includes, at least, the obligation to investigate possible crimes in order to establish the facts. The commander is required to take an "important step in the disciplinary process".

208. If the commander has no power to sanction those who committed the crimes, he has an obligation to submit the matter to the competent authorities. This obligation to submit the matter also arises where the commander has the ability to take certain measures, but such measures would be inadequate.

12.8.3 Successor Command Responsibility

12.8.3.1 ICTY, *Prosecutor* v. *Hadzihasanovic et al.*, (Decision on Interlocutory Appeal Challenging Jurisdiction in Relation to Command Responsibility), Case No. IT-01-47-AR72, Appeals Chamber (16 July 2003)

Note: *The facts are set out in Section 12.1.1. Discussing whether a commander can be liable for the acts of his subordinates prior to his assumption of command, the Tribunal said as follows:*

44. In considering the issue of whether command responsibility exists in relation to crimes committed by a subordinate prior to an accused's assumption of command over that subordinate, the Appeals Chamber observes that it has always been the approach of this Tribunal not to rely merely on a construction of the Statute to establish the applicable law on criminal responsibility, but to ascertain the state of customary law in force at the time the crimes were committed.

45. In this particular case, no practice can be found, nor is there any evidence of *opinio juris* that would sustain the proposition that a commander can be held responsible for crimes committed by a subordinate prior to the commander's assumption of command over that subordinate.

46. In fact, there are indications that militate against the existence of a customary rule establishing such criminal responsibility. . . .

51. . . . the Appeals Chamber holds that an accused cannot be charged under Article 7(3) of the Statute for crimes committed by a subordinate before the said accused assumed command over that subordinate. The Appeals Chamber is aware that views on this issue may differ. However, the Appeals Chamber holds the view that this Tribunal can impose criminal responsibility only if the crime charged was clearly established under customary law at the time the events in issue occurred. In case of doubt, criminal responsibility cannot be found to exist, thereby preserving full respect for the principle of legality.

12.8.3.2 ICTY, *Prosecutor* v. *Hadzihasanovic et al.*, (Decision on Interlocutory Appeal Challenging Jurisdiction in Relation to Command Responsibility, *Separate and Partially Dissenting Opinion of Judge David Hunt*), Case No. IT-01-47-AR2, Appeals Chamber (16 July 2003)

Note: *In his partially dissenting opinion, Judge David Hunt said as follows:*

8. . . . Customary international law recognises that a commander is criminally responsible if he knew or had reason to know that the subordinate was about to commit acts amounting to a war crime or had done so and if he failed to take the necessary and reasonable measures to prevent such acts or to punish the subordinate. That principle may be applied to whatever situation reasonably falls within the application of the principle. In my opinion, the situation of a superior who (after assuming command) knows or has reason to know that a person who has become his subordinate had committed a crime before he became that person's superior falls reasonably within that principle.

12.8.3.3 ICTY, *Prosecutor* v. *Orić*, (Judgment), Case No. IT-03-68-T, Trial Chamber (30 June 2006)

Note: *The facts are detailed in Section 12.4.2.1. As to the level of control the superior must have held over the subordinates at the material time, the Tribunal said as follows:*

335. Similar considerations of a coherent system of prevention and punishment could also provide guidance as to what position the superior must have held while the crime of a subordinate was committed and as to when it was to be punished. The superior must certainly have effective control of the relevant subordinates at the time when measures of investigation and punishment are to be taken against them. Such a link, however, appears less essential, if necessary at all, with regard to the time at which the crime was committed. The duty to prevent calls for action by the superior prior to the commission of the crime, and thus presupposes his power to control the conduct of his subordinates. The duty to punish, by contrast, follows the commission of a crime of which the superior need

not have been aware, and thus at the moment of commission was in fact out of his or her control to prevent. Since a superior in such circumstances is obliged to take punitive measures notwithstanding his or her inability to prevent the crime due to his or her lack of awareness and control, it seems only logical that such an obligation would also extend to the situation wherein there has been a change of command following the commission of a crime by a subordinate. The new commander in such a case, now exercising power over his or her subordinates and being made aware of their crimes committed prior to the change of command, for the sake of coherent prevention and control, should not let them go unpunished. This is best understood by realising that a superior's duty to punish is not derived from a failure to prevent the crime, but rather is a subsidiary duty of its own. The cohesive interlinking of preventing and punishing would be disrupted if the latter were made dependent on the superior's control at the time of commission of the crimes. Consequently, for a superior's duty to punish, it should be immaterial whether he or she had assumed control over the relevant subordinates prior to their committing the crime. Since the Appeals Chamber, however, has taken a different view for reasons which will not be questioned here, the Trial Chamber finds itself bound to require that with regard to the duty to punish, the superior must have had control over the perpetrators of a relevant crime both at the time of its commission and at the time that measures to punish were to be taken.

12.8.3.4 ICC, *Prosecutor* v. *Jean-Pierre Bemba Gombo*, (Decision Pursuant to Article 61(7)(a) and (b) of the Rome Statute on the Charges), Case No. ICC-01/05-01/08-424, Pre-Trial Chamber II (15 July 2009)

Note: *The facts are detailed at Chapter 1, Section 1.2.3.5. Discussing the requirement of control in determining liability, the ICC said as follows:*

419. ... [T]he Chamber is of the view that according to article 28(a) of the Statute, the suspect must have had effective control at least when the crimes were about to be committed. This finding is supported by the language of the chapeau of article 28(a) of the Statute, which states in the relevant part that a military commander or a person effectively acting as such shall be criminally responsible for the crimes committed by forces under his effective control "as a result of his or her failure to exercise control properly over such forces ...". The reference to the phrase "failure to exercise control properly" suggests that the superior was already in control over the forces before the crimes were committed.

12.8.4 Causation

12.8.4.1 ICTY, *Prosecutor* v. *Delalić et al.*, *('Celebici Case')*, (Judgment), Case No. IT-96-21-T, Trial Chamber (16 November 1998)

Note: *The facts of this case are outlined in Chapter 5, Section 5.4.4.1. Assessing the role of causation in determining the liability of superiors for the acts of their subordinates, the Tribunal said the following:*

398. Notwithstanding the central place assumed by the principle of causation in criminal law, causation has not traditionally been postulated as a *conditio sine qua non* for the imposition of criminal liability on superiors for their failure to prevent or punish offences committed by their subordinates. Accordingly, the Trial Chamber has found no support for the existence of a requirement of proof of causation as a separate element of superior responsibility, either in the existing body of case law, the formulation of the principle in existing treaty law, or, with one exception, in the abundant literature on this subject.

399. This is not to say that, conceptually, the principle of causality is without application to the doctrine of command responsibility insofar as it relates to the responsibility of superiors for their failure to prevent the crimes of their subordinates. In fact, a recognition of a necessary causal nexus may be considered to be inherent in the requirement of crimes committed by subordinates and the superior's failure to take the measures within his powers to prevent them. In this situation, the superior may be considered to be causally linked to the offences, in that, but for his failure to fulfil his duty to act, the acts of his subordinates would not have been committed.

12.8.4.2 ICC, *The Prosecutor* v. *Jean-Pierre Bemba Gombo*, (Judgment Pursuant to Article 74 of the Statute), Case No. ICC-01/05-01/08 66/364, Trial Chamber III (21 March 2016)

Note: *The facts are dealt with in Chapter 1, Section 1.2.3.5. On the importance of causation and the existence of a nexus between the commander and the crimes of his subordinates, the ICC said as follows:*

210. The Chamber recalls that Article 28(a) stipulates that a military commander, or person effectively acting as such, shall: ... be criminally responsible for crimes ... committed by forces under his or her effective command and control, or effective authority and control as the case may be, *as a result of his or her failure to exercise control properly over such forces* ...

211. It is a core principle of criminal law that a person should not be found individually criminally responsible for a crime in the absence of some form of personal nexus to it. The Chamber concurs with the Pre-Trial Chamber that the portion of text emphasised above does not require the establishment of "but for" causation between the commander's omission and the crimes committed.

212. The Chamber has had regard to the particular nature of superior responsibility, as considered above. Additionally, practical and legal considerations militate against imposing a standard which would be incapable of consistent and objective application, bearing in mind the hypothetical assessment required in cases of omission.

213. A nexus requirement would clearly be satisfied when it is established that the crimes would not have been committed, in the circumstances in which they were, had the commander exercised control properly, or the commander exercising control properly would have prevented the crimes. Noting the foregoing analysis, the Chamber emphasises that such a standard is, however, higher than that required by law. Nonetheless, in light of the factual findings below, the Chamber does not consider it necessary to further elaborate on this element.

12.9 THE NATURE OF COMMAND RESPONSIBILITY

12.9.1 ICTY, *Prosecutor* v. *Halilović*, (Judgment), Case No. IT–01–48–T, Trial Chamber (16 November 2005)

Note: *The facts are set out in Section 12.1.2. On the nature of command responsibility, the Tribunal said as follows:*

53. While the post-World War II case law was divergent as to the question of the exact nature of command responsibility, and Article 86(2) of Additional Protocol I and Article 7(3) are silent as to the nature of the responsibility of commanders, whether command responsibility is a mode of liability for the crimes of subordinates or responsibility of a commander for dereliction of duty has not been considered at length in the jurisprudence of the Tribunal. However, the consistent jurisprudence of the Tribunal has found that a commander is responsible for the crimes of his subordinates under Article 7(3). . . .

54. The Trial Chamber finds that under Article 7(3) command responsibility is responsibility for an omission. The commander is responsible for the failure to perform an act required by international law. This omission is culpable because international law imposes an affirmative duty on superiors to prevent and punish crimes committed by their subordinates. Thus "for the acts of his subordinates" as generally referred to in the jurisprudence of the Tribunal does not mean that the commander shares the same responsibility as the subordinates who committed the crimes, but rather that because of the crimes committed by his subordinates, the commander should bear responsibility for his failure to act. The imposition of responsibility upon a commander for breach of his duty is to be weighed against the crimes of his subordinates; a commander is responsible not as though he had committed the crime himself, but his responsibility is considered in proportion to the gravity of the offences committed.

12.9.2 ICTY, *Prosecutor* v. *Hadzihasanovic et al.*, (Judgment), Case No. IT–01–47–T, Trial Chamber (15 March 2006)

Note: *The facts are outlined in Section 12.1.1. Clarifying the nature of liability under the doctrine of command responsibility, the Tribunal said as follows:*

2075. The Chamber would note that this Judgement is the first in the history of the Tribunal to convict Accused persons solely on the basis of Article 7(3) of the Statute and recalls that command responsibility must be conceived as a type of personal responsibility for failure to act. The Accused will not be convicted for crimes committed by his subordinates but for failing in his obligation to prevent the crimes or punish the perpetrators.

2076. When a person is found responsible solely on the basis of Article 7(1) of the Statute, or cumulatively in conjunction with Article 7(3), the gravity of the offence is evaluated in view of two elements: the inherent gravity of the acts committed and the form and degree of the Accused's participation in the crimes in question. The concept of command responsibility in this regard is exceptional in law in that it allows for a superior to be found guilty of a crime even if he had no part whatsoever in its commission (absence of an *actus reus*), and even if he never intended to commit the crime (absence of *mens rea*). Accordingly, the Chamber finds that the *sui generis* nature of command responsibility under Article 7(3) of the Statute may justify the fact that the sentencing scale applied to those Accused convicted solely on the basis of Article 7(1) of the Statute, or cumulatively under Articles 7(1) and 7(3), is not applied to those convicted solely under Article 7(3), in cases where nothing would allow that responsibility to be assimilated or linked to individual responsibility under Article 7(1).

12.9.3 ICTY, *Prosecutor* v. *Orić*, (Judgment), Case No. IT-03-68-T, Trial Chamber (30 June 2006)

Note: *The facts are detailed in Section 12.4.2.1. Clarifying the basis of the superior's responsibility for the acts of his subordinate, the Tribunal said as follows:*

293. [I]t is not uncommon to find the superior described as responsible "for the acts of his subordinates". This does not mean, however, that the superior shares the same responsibility as the subordinate who commits the crime in terms of Article 7(1) of the Statute, but that the superior bears responsibility for his own omission in failing to act. In this sense, the superior cannot be considered as if he had committed the crime himself, but merely for his neglect of duty with regard to crimes committed by subordinates. By this essential element being distinct from the subordinate's responsibility under Article 7(1) of the Statute, the superior's responsibility under 7(3) of the Statute can indeed be called a responsibility *sui generis*.

12.9.4 ICC, *The Prosecutor* v. *Jean-Pierre Bemba Gombo*, (Judgment Pursuant to Article 74 of the Statute), Case No. ICC-01/05-01/08 66/364, Trial Chamber III (21 March 2016)

Note: *The facts are set out in Chapter 1, Section 1.2.3.5. Discussing the nature of command responsibility, the ICC said as follows:*

171. Before analysing each of these elements, the Chamber considers it appropriate to briefly address the nature of liability under Article 28. While there has been considerable debate regarding the precise nature of superior responsibility, the Chamber concurs with the Pre-Trial Chamber that Article 28 provides for a mode of liability, through which superiors may be held criminally responsible for crimes within the jurisdiction of the Court committed by his or her subordinates.

172. The Chamber considers that Article 28 is designed to reflect the responsibility of superiors by virtue of the powers of control they exercise over their subordinates. These responsibilities of control aim, *inter alia*, at ensuring the effective enforcement of fundamental principles of international humanitarian law, including the protection of protected persons and objects during armed conflict.

173 ... In this regard, it is, however, important to recognise that the responsibility of a commander under Article 28 is different from that of a person who "commits" a crime

within the jurisdiction of the Court. This is supported by the language of Article 28 itself: the crimes for which the commander is held responsible are "committed" by forces, or subordinates, under his or her effective command and control, or effective authority and control, rather than by the commander directly.

174. Consequently, Article 28 must be viewed as a form of *sui generis* liability. The Chamber recognises that, in certain circumstances, a commander's conduct may be capable of satisfying a material element of one or more modes of liability.

COMMENTARY

1. As noted in Chapter 11, violations of IHL are both pervasive and serious. The complexity of modern armed conflicts poses additional challenges to enforcing compliance with IHL. Among such challenges is the issue of system criminality concerning both direct and indirect perpetrators in the commission of IHL violations. Command responsibility addresses the responsibility of the indirect perpetrator in a command position for failure to prevent, punish or report the crimes of his subordinates. It thus acts as a deterrent to the commission of war crimes by preventing their commission or by punishing the perpetrators. Put differently, the commander acts as the 'guarantor' of IHL, and command responsibility is part of a system of overlapping obligations and responsibilities to guarantee compliance with IHL.

2. The doctrine of command responsibility in the ICTY and ICTR Statutes and jurisprudence is founded on the customary law form of the doctrine, having its foundations in the post–Second World War jurisprudence and in the partial codification of the doctrine in Articles 86(2) and 86(3) API. The development of the doctrine by the jurisprudence of these tribunals as, for example, in relation to the concept of the *de facto* commander, successor command responsibility or in relation to the nature of the doctrine has been accomplished in different stages,[2] in contrast to the formulation of the doctrine in the ICC Statute, which is the product of detailed negotiation.

3. The elements of the doctrine in the jurisprudence of the *ad hoc* tribunals were established in the *Celebici* case. They include the existence of an effective superior-subordinate relationship; knowledge, either actual or constructive; and failure by the superior to take necessary and reasonable measures to prevent or punish the commission of the underlying crime.[3] These elements reflect the structure of the customary form of the doctrine.

4. Article 28 ICC St. adopted a more elaborate structure. The requirement for the commission of an underlying crime becomes an additional element of the doctrine, whereas in the jurisprudence of the *ad hoc* tribunals it was treated as a requirement for the application of the doctrine.[4] Also, in contrast to the jurisprudence of the *ad hoc* tribunals,

---

[2] Elies van Sleidregt, 'Command Responsibility at the ICTY' in B. Swart, A. Zahar and G. Sluiter (eds), *The Legacy of the International Criminal Tribunal for the Former Yugoslavia* (OUP, 2011), p. 380.
[3] *Prosecutor* v. *Delalić et al. ('Celebici case')*, (Judgment), Case No. IT-96-21-T, Trial Chamber (16 November 1998), para. 346.
[4] *Prosecutor* v. *Orić*, (Judgment), ICTY Case No. IT-03-68-T, Trial Chamber (30 June 2006), para. 294.

the causal link between the superior's omission and the underlying crime has been included as an element of the doctrine in Art. 28 ICC St.

5. The *ad hoc* tribunals have adopted a purposive approach to the doctrine, leading to a broad reading of the term 'commission', which covers all modes of direct participation under their respective Statutes.[5] This has been vigorously challenged as being contrary to the post-war precedents and to the nature and purpose of the doctrine. It has also been claimed that it represents an undesirable loosening of the link between superiors and the underlying offence. The *ad hoc* tribunals' approach can be explained by the fact that, whereas their early jurisprudence, as illustrated by the *Celebici* case,[6] concerned low-ranking superiors who were closely linked to the subordinates who committed the underlying crime, later jurisprudence concerned more senior superiors with a more remote connection to the subordinates. Whether the requirement in Art. 28 ICC St. of the 'commission of a crime within the jurisdiction of the Court' will be interpreted in light of Art. 25 ICC St., which defines the different modes of criminal responsibility, remains to be seen.[7] In the *Bemba Gombo* trial judgment, the relevant underlying offences were committed in all their elements by the subordinates and therefore the Chamber did not deal with this issue.[8]

6. A related question is whether it is also necessary to establish the criminal responsibility of an identifiable subordinate. The *ad hoc* tribunals have held it is sufficient that subordinates can be identified through membership of an identifiable group over which the superior exercised effective control individually.[9]

7. A superior–subordinate relationship is one of the essential elements of command responsibility. Such a relationship may be based either on *de jure* or *de facto* authority, the latter based on the existence of effective powers of control. The development of the latter concept has been described as one of the most significant advances in the *ad hoc* tribunals' jurisprudence, enabling the customary form of the doctrine to deal with those effectively acting as commanders in response to the changing nature of modern armed conflict. In contrast to the *de jure* commander, formally appointed to a position of command, the *de facto* equivalent exercises similar authority on the basis of the ability to exercise effective control over subordinates.

8. The absence of a *de jure* appointment creates difficulties with regard to the existence of a pre-existing obligation to act in the context of the superior–subordinate relationship. It has been proposed that the existence of an expectation of obedience and subordination establishes the necessary duty with regard to such commanders. This appears to offer a partial but not a complete answer. Arguably, the answer can be found in the proposition

---

[5] Art. 7(1), ICTY Statute; Art. 6(1), ICTR Statute. See *Prosecutor* v. *Orić*, (Judgment), ICTY Case No. IT-03-68-T, Trial Chamber (30 June 2006), para. 299, affirmed *Prosecutor* v. *Blagojevic and Jokic*, (Judgment), ICTY Case No. IT-02-60-A, Appeals Chamber (28 November 2007), para. 281.

[6] *Prosecutor* v. *Delalić et al ('Celebici case')*, (Judgment), Case No. IT-96-21-T, Trial Chamber (16 November 1998).

[7] See Art. 25, ICC St.

[8] *Prosecutor* v. *Jean-Pierre Bemba Gombo*, (Judgment), ICC Case No. ICC-01/05–01/08 66/364, Trial Chamber III (21 March 2016), para. 175 and related footnotes.

[9] *Prosecutor* v. *Hadzihasanovic and Kubura*, (Judgment), ICTY Case No. IT-01047-T, Trial Chamber (15 March 2006), para. 90 and also *Prosecutor* v. *Orić*, (Judgment), ICTY Case No. IT-03-68A, Appeals Chamber (3 July 2008), para. 35.

that commanders are entrusted with the role of guarantors of IHL and that this position generates a responsibility for failure to act.[10]

9. In both the *ad hoc* tribunals and the ICC, the superior–subordinate relationship must exist at the time that the underlying crime has been committed. In the case of the ICC, there has been little debate regarding this issue as the structure of Article 28, incorporating the phrase 'failure to exercise control properly', clearly indicates that the accused must have had effective control prior to the commission of the underlying crime.[11] In the case of the *ad hoc* tribunals the issue has contrastingly been the subject of considerable judicial controversy. The debate is closely linked to the question of whether the doctrine is to be regarded as a mode of liability, or as a separate offence of negligent performance of a duty.

10. Despite the finding of the majority in the *Hadzihasanovic* Appeals Chamber that there was no basis to establish successor command (superior) responsibility for crimes committed prior to the commander's assumption of command, thus reversing the Trial Chamber's findings,[12] the minority vigorously dissented, arguing that successor command responsibility fell within command (superior) responsibility doctrine. The minority judges linked their interpretation to their analysis that superior responsibility is to be regarded as a separate neglect-of-duty offence, rather than as a form of liability.[13] The issue emerged again in the *Orić* Appeals Chamber judgment when the majority declined to address the issue.

11. Actual or constructive knowledge is required in order for a commander to incur command responsibility. The question of the possession of actual knowledge is not problematic in principle. Knowledge may be established directly or indirectly through circumstantial evidence. In the determination of whether the superior possessed actual knowledge the *ad hoc* tribunals made use of the indicia listed by the UN Commission of Experts Final Report.[14] This position was also adopted in the *Bemba Gombo* Trial Chamber judgment, where the ICC noted these indicia as relevant.[15]

12. The issue of constructive knowledge is the subject of judicial and academic debate. The *Celebici* and *Blaškić* Trial Chambers arrived at differing analyses of the requirement. The *Celebici* Trial Chamber found that Additional Protocol I had set a new and different standard for constructive knowledge, finding in consequence that there must be some information available to put superiors on notice of the need for investigation regarding their subordinates' activities.[16] The *Blaškić* Trial Chamber interpreted Additional Protocol I

---

[10]   *Prosecutor* v. *Halilović*, (Judgment), ICTY Case No. IT-01-48-T, Trial Chamber (16 November 2005), Trial Chamber, para. 81. See G. Mettraux, *The Law of Command Responsibility* (Oxford University Press, 2010), pp. 105–10.

[11]   See *Prosecutor* v. *Jean-Pierre Bemba Gombo* (Decision on the Confirmation of Charges), Ibid, Pre-Trial Chamber II (15 June 2009), para. 208.

[12]   See *Prosecutor* v. *Hadzihasanovic and Kubura*, (Decision on Joint Challenge to Jurisdiction), ICTY Case No. IT-01-47-AR72, Appeals Chamber (16 July 2003).

[13]   See ibid, Partial Dissenting Opinion of Judge Shahabuddeen and Separate and Partially Dissenting Opinion of Judge Hunt.

[14]   See *Final Report of the Commission of Experts Established Pursuant to Security Council Resolution 780 (1992)* (27 May 1994), UN Doc. S/1994/674 at p. 7.

[15]   *Prosecutor* v. *Jean-Pierre Bemba Gombo*, (Judgment), ICC Case No. ICC-01/05–01/08 66/364, Trial Chamber III (21 March 2016), para. 193.

[16]   *Prosecutor* v. *Delalić et al.* ('Celebici case'), (Judgment), Trial Chamber, Ibid, para. 393.

differently, affirming the continued existence of an affirmative duty of knowledge on the part of commanders.[17] The issue was settled by the *Celebici* Appeals Chamber affirmation of the *Celebici* Trial Chamber's interpretation of the requirement.[18]

13. The constructive knowledge requirement under Article 28 ICC St. differs significantly from the 'had reason to know' standard applied under the *ad hoc* tribunals' jurisprudence. More specifically, Article 28(a) ICC St. provides that a commander incurs responsibility when 'owing to the circumstances at the time' he 'should have known' that the forces under his command and control were committing or were about to commit crimes. In the *Bemba Gombo* Trial Chamber judgment the accused was convicted on the basis of his actual knowledge of his subordinates' crimes and for this reason the Chamber did not find it necessary to consider the constructive knowledge standard. This aspect was, however, considered by the Pre-Trial Chamber in the Decision on the Confirmation of charges in the case.[19] Following the analysis adopted in the *Blaškić* case, the Pre-Trial Chamber concluded that the standard imposed an active duty on the superior to obtain knowledge regarding his troops' behaviour, regardless of the information in his possession at the time regarding the commission of the underlying crime.

14. It remains unclear, however, how the 'owing to the circumstances at the time' proviso qualifies the standard of constructive knowledge. It has been claimed that, taking this broad qualification into account, the standard moves towards that established under the *ad hoc* tribunals' jurisprudence. That said, the standard applied to commanders appears to give rise to the same issue identified in the *ad hoc* tribunals' jurisprudence of a mismatch between a negligent omission on the part of the commander and an underlying-intent crime. Further clarification must await when the constructive knowledge standard is applied to a military commander in the ICC.

15. The third element in the customary form of the doctrine concerns the superiors' failure to take necessary and reasonable measures in order to prevent or punish the underlying crimes committed by his subordinates. The duty to prevent and the duty to punish have been established as distinct and autonomous forms of responsibility. It is generally agreed that the obligation to punish is secondary to the obligation to prevent, which represents the primary obligation of the superior under the doctrine in view of its relationship with the principle of responsible command. However, the duty to prevent does not require that a commander discover crimes or, in general, police his subordinates but he must act with due diligence. The autonomous character of the duty to punish only arises when a superior either lacked actual or constructive knowledge of the subordinates' crimes prior to their commission, or did not have the material ability to prevent them.

16. Article 28 ICC St. includes a duty to repress the commission of crimes. The *Bemba Gombo* Trial Chamber affirmed the Pre-Trial Chamber's analysis that the term overlaps with

---

[17]   *Prosecutor* v. *Blaškić*, (Judgment), ICTY Case No. IT-96–21-T, Trial Chamber (16 November 1998), para. 332.
[18]   *Prosecutor* v. *Delalić et al.* ('*Celebici case*'), (Judgment), Ibid, Appeal Chamber, para. 232.
[19]   *See Prosecutor* v. *Jean-Pierre Bemba Gombo*, (Decision on the Confirmation of Charges), ICC Case No. ICC-01/05-01/08-424, Pre-Trial Chamber II (15 June 2009), paras 432–434.

the duty to prevent and to punish in the sense that 'to repress' means to stop ongoing crimes as well as punishing the offenders.[20] The duty to submit the matter to the competent authorities is an innovation of Art. 28 ICC St. and arises when the commander does not have the power to perform his other duties.

17. Command responsibility does not represent a strict form of liability and, accordingly, it is necessary to establish that an accused failed in his duty to take the necessary and reasonable measures to prevent or to punish. A commander can only be expected to take feasible measures that are within his formal or material capabilities. The jurisprudence distinguishes between necessary and reasonable measures; the former are those measures which derive from his legal duty to act and are within his formal competence, while reasonable measures are those falling within his material powers. For example, a commander will not be held responsible under command responsibility if he failed to take administrative measures to prevent the commission of crimes if administrative matters did not fall within his competences or if he had no such control over subordinates to allow him to take administrative action.

18. The jurisprudence has made it clear that there is no objective standard as to what measures a superior can take. The commander has discretion as to the measures which he considers it appropriate to adopt in the particular circumstances of the case and it is then for the tribunal to assess whether the steps he took were regarded as necessary and reasonable.[21] It is not for the court to seek to substitute its judgment for that of the commander. It must, however, be recognised that in view of the nature of the crimes under discussion, matters will normally require to be reported by a superior with a view to investigation and possible prosecution by the appropriate authorities.

19. The requirement for a causal link is a generally accepted requirement of criminal law. The established position in the *ad hoc* tribunals' jurisprudence is, however, that command responsibility does not require the establishment of a causal link between the conduct of a commander and the underlying crimes committed by his subordinates. This is particularly so in relation to the duty to punish where no causal link can be established between the omission of the commander and the crime. The relevant reasoning of the *ad hoc* tribunals is, however, complex. Also in the case of failure to prevent, it has been contended that causality is not a requirement.[22]

20. The position under Art. 28 ICC St. is different, with the requirement for a causal link becoming an element of command responsibility. The reference to the failure to exercise control properly over the subordinates is not to be viewed as an example of a 'but for' causal standard but what the causality threshold should be is difficult to fathom. The *Bemba*

---

[20] *Prosecutor* v. *Jean-Pierre Bemba Gombo*, (Judgment), ICC Case No. ICC-01/05–01/08 66/364, Trial Chamber III (21 March 2016), para. 206.

[21] See *Prosecutor* v. *Halilović*, (Judgment), ICTY Case No. IT-01-48-T, Trial Chamber (16 November 2005), para. 74 and also *Prosecutor* v. *Strugar*, (Judgment), ICTY Case No. IT-01-42-T, Trial Chamber (31 January 2005), para. 378.

[22] *Prosecutor* v. *Delalić et al*, ('*Celebici case*'), (Judgment), ICTY Case No. IT-96-21-T, Trial Chamber (16 November 1998), paras 398 to 400; ICTY, *Prosecutor* v. *Blaškić*, (Judgment), Case No. IT-95-14-A, Appeals Chamber (29 July 2004), para. 77; ICTY, *Prosecutor* v. *Halilović*, (Judgment), Case No. IT-01-48-T, Trial Chamber (16 November 2005), para. 78.

Gombo Trial Chamber analysis of the causal standard is difficult to follow and in fact led to two dissenting opinions regarding the threshold to be established.[23]

21. Concerning the nature of command responsibility in the *ad hoc* tribunals' jurisprudence, the early jurisprudence treated command responsibility as a mode of liability for the offences committed by the superior's subordinates. However, this analysis was challenged in the later cases, concerning more senior superiors, in which the Trial Chambers developed a new analysis of the nature of the doctrine as a separate neglect-of-duty offence based on the omission of the commander to exercise effective control over his subordinates. This has attracted considerable support among jurists and commentators as better according with the principle of culpability than the mode-of-liability analysis. It is, however, open to criticism – specifically that it does not have support in customary international law.

22. The position adopted by the ICC in their first command responsibility judgment differs from that adopted by the *ad hoc* international tribunals. Both Trial and Pre-Trial Chambers are in agreement that Article 28 provides for a mode of liability, through which commanders may be held criminally responsible for crimes within the jurisdiction of the Court committed by subordinates. The conclusion is unsurprising in view of the wording adopted in Art. 28 ICC St.

23. Jurisprudence on command responsibility has demonstrated the difficulties in seeking to define a complex form of criminal responsibility incorporating differing forms of criminal responsibility within a unitary form. For this reason and contrary to statements that command responsibility and other forms of responsibility are not mutually exclusive,[24] the *ad hoc* tribunals have often rejected the cumulative application of individual and command responsibility or dealt with the responsibility of commanders under the doctrine of joint criminal enterprise or under other forms of liability such as complicity.[25] It remains to be seen whether, or to what extent, the ICC will pursue its own course on this matter.

---

[23]   ICC-01/05-01/08-3343-AnxI, *Separate Opinion of Judge Steiner* and ICC-01/05-01/08-3343-AnxII, *Separate Opinion of Judge Ozaki.*

[24]   ICTR, *Kayishema et al.*, (Judgment), Case No. ICTR-95-1-T, Trial Chamber II (21 May 1999), para. 210.

[25]   ICTY, *Krnojelac*, (Judgment), Case No. IT-97-25-T, Trial Chamber II (15 March 2002), para. 173; ICTY, *Prosecutor v. Stakić*, (Trial Judgment), Case No. IT-97-24-T, Trial Chamber II (31 July 2003), paras 463–464; ICTY, *Prosecutor v. Đorđević*, (Judgment), Case No. IT-05-87/1-T, Trial Chamber II, (23 February 2011), para. 1891; ICTR, *The Nyiramasuhuko et al.*, (Judgment and Sentence), Case No. ICTR-98-42-T, Trial Chamber II (24 June 2011), para. 5652; ICTR, *Karemera et al.*, (Judgment and Sentence), Case No. ICTR-98-44-T, Trial Chamber III (2 February 2012), paras 1502–1503. See also ECCC, *Kaing Guek Eav alias Duch*, (Judgment), Case No. 0001/18-07-2007/ECCC/TC, Trial Chamber (26 July 2010), para. 539.

Index